# Transitions

· · · · · · · · · · · · · · · · · · · · · · ·

*Lives in America*

# Transitions

## *Lives in America*

Irina L. Raicu · Gregory Grewell

SAN JOSE STATE UNIVERSITY

Mayfield Publishing Company

MOUNTAIN VIEW, CALIFORNIA

LONDON · TORONTO

Library of Congress Cataloging-in-Publication Data

Transitions : lives in America / [edited by] Irina Raicu, Gregory
    Grewell.
         p.   cm.
       Includes index.
       ISBN 1-55934-958-1
        1. Readers—Social sciences.   2. United States—Social life and
    customs—Problems, exercises, etc.   3. Report writing—Problems,
    exercises, etc.   4. English language—Rhetoric.   5. Readers—United
    States.   6. College readers.   I. Raicu, Irina.   II. Grewell, Gregory.
    PE1127.S6T73   1997
    808'.0427—dc21                            97-12825
                                                        CIP

Manufactured in the United States of America
10  9  8  7  6  5  4  3  2

Mayfield Publishing Company
1280 Villa Street
Mountain View, California 94041

*Sponsoring editor,* Thomas V. Broadbent; *production editor,* Carla L. White; *text and cover designer,* Laurie Anderson; *cover art,* "Imagination" © John Martin/ The Image Bank; *art and design manager,* Susan Breitbard; *photo researcher,* Brian Pecko; *manufacturing manager,* Randy Hurst. The text was set in 11/12.5 Minion by TBH Typecast, Inc. and printed on 45# Glatfelter Restorecote by Malloy Lithography Inc.

*To the memory of Eugen Raicu,*
*and to Yagil, who helped so much*

*To Gabriele Rico and John Engell,*
*for their unequivocal support in*
*this and other endeavors, and*
*to Linda Dawn Carlson*

# TO THE INSTRUCTOR

. . . . . . . . . . . . . . . . .

Our main goal in creating *Transitions: Lives in America* is to provide instructors with a reader that will offer accessible, thought-provoking selections while creating a flow, a continuum, in the term-long interaction that a composition course represents. Because we are asking the students to write essays that weave various points together into a unified whole, we feel that a composition textbook should model this skill.

To this end, we have paid particular attention to the organization of the text. The themes of the first five sections ("Growing Up," "Entering the Gender Arena," "Love and Other Metaphors," "Work Is a Four-Letter Word," and "The Evolving Environment") appear in the order in which those issues tend to become prominent in most of our lives. Within each chapter, the readings generally follow a chronological order—not necessarily based on the time when the selections were written but on the development of ideas related to the chapter's theme.

In addition, special selections appear between chapters: Each one of these is itself a transition, dealing both with the theme of the preceding chapter and with the theme developed in the chapter that follows. However, since all of the themes are deeply interconnected, an instructor could choose to present the chapters in a different order yet still find readings that can act as transitions between themes; the Instructor's Manual that accompanies this text includes our suggestions for such alternate transitions. The effect created by the use of transitional selections is one of a unified exploration rather than one of a disconnected, haphazard leap from one subject to another.

Throughout the text, we offer selections that will enlarge the students' field of vision while encouraging critical thinking, and we include sections of brief but thorough advice on writing that the students can turn to outside of class.

## The Readings

- *Transitions: Lives in America* contains more than eighty readings grouped thematically into six sections: "Growing Up," "Entering the Gender Arena," "The Metaphor of Love," "Work Is a Four-Letter Word,"

"The Evolving Environment," and "Issues in American Culture." Each section contains nine to eleven readings that provide a broad range of perspectives on each theme (the last section, with twenty-three selections, is the exception). At the same time, the book includes an alternate table of contents that lists the readings by their primary rhetorical mode.

- **The selections exemplify a variety of genres:** Although most of the readings are essays, some are poems, short stories, and newspaper articles; the book also includes several brief selections from the Bible, as well as an interview, a fable, and a letter.

- **The writers included represent diverse ethnic and cultural backgrounds:** Included are such frequently anthologized authors as Martin Luther King, Jr., Maxine Hong Kingston, and Gloria Naylor, as well as powerful voices that don't often appear in composition textbooks: Martin Espada, Arturo Islas, Becky Birtha, Robert F. Jones. The readings also reflect a balance of both male and female authors.

- **The selections reflect the approaches of a variety of disciplines:** Among the authors are professors of political science, history, and religious studies, as well as psychologists and biologists.

- **Each section in the reader includes at least one student essay (the last chapter includes two):** Among them are Pei Kwan's "Chink-Minded" (Section 1), Kristina Milam's "Do I?" (Section 3), and Darron Reese's "Get Off My Jock: A Definition of What It Means to Be a Student Athlete" (Section 6).

- **Although most of the selections included are contemporary, several of the readings in each section provide historical perspective on the theme discussed:** Examples include a selection from the Song of Songs, a letter expressing some of Benjamin Franklin's views on immigration, and an 1852 editorial about the Woman's Rights Convention.

- **Each section contains both short and long readings,** allowing the instructor the flexibility to assign several of them together or to work with the brief ones exclusively in class (using them, for example, as prompts for in-class essays). Aside from the poems, a number of the prose selections included are only one to two pages long.

- **Several humorous selections lighten the tone while still encouraging critical thinking:** Some examples are Dave Barry's piece about men and relationships and P. J. O'Rourke's article taking issue with environmentalism.

## The Pedagogy

- **Thorough advice on writing essays:** Each section ends with a brief yet thorough discussion of either a particular stage of the writing process or a particular type of essay. These discussions build on each other—from advice on choosing a topic and prewriting to coverage of drafting, revising, and incorporating outside sources. The last segment discusses the writing of research papers, in the context of the section's broader coverage of argumentative essays.

- **Focus on specific language issues:** Each section begins with a brief segment that looks at issues such as descriptive language, loaded words, clichés, and figures of speech.
- **Questions that help the students understand and challenge both content and rhetorical devices:** Each reading is followed by five to twelve questions (depending on the length and complexity of the piece) that invite the students to focus on key issues raised by the text.
- **"Connections" questions that can also function as writing assignments:** Each selection is followed by one to four broad questions or assignments that further encourage critical thinking by asking the students to draw connections between various readings from this text, comparing and contrasting both content and writing techniques.
- **Topics for writing:** Each section is followed by ten to twelve suggestions for writing, related either to the section's theme or to the essay-writing advice presented in that section (Section 6, which is about twice as long as the other sections, is followed by twenty writing topics).
- **Biographical headnotes:** Each reading is preceded by a brief biographical note about its author, offering the students a contextual sketch for the text.
- **"Warm-up" sections:** Each selection is introduced by a question or assignment designed to engage the students' preexisting knowledge and opinions about the topic of the selection they are about to read.

## The Illustrations

- **Section-opening photographs or graphs** visually comment on the sections' themes, allowing students to hone an additional type of literacy.

## The Instructor's Manual

The Instructor's Manual offers **brief overviews** that answer the questions posed in each selection, advice about some of the issues that the students are likely to be grappling with after reading the text, and suggestions for **collaborative projects** that will encourage cooperation and enhance the students' involvement with the material discussed.

The Instructor's Manual also includes **suggestions for alternative ways of grouping the readings,** including alternative transitional selections (for instructors who would like to approach the sections in a different order than the one presented in the text or who will need to skip some sections altogether). In addition, the manual contains a list of **suggested movies** that relate to topics raised by the reading selections; instructors can choose to show some of these videos in the classroom or encourage the students to watch them on their own.

## Acknowledgments

The production and design teams at Mayfield Publishing Company have put a lot of care and effort into the development of *Transitions.* Our editor, Tom Broadbent, added his perceptive comments to the encouragement and critique offered by our reviewers, whose input made this a stronger text: Valerie M. Balester, Texas A & M University; Michael Delahoyde, Washington State University; Dr. Gary R. Hafer, Lycoming College; Jennifer Hicks, Massachusetts Bay Community College; Laura L. Hope, Chaffey Community College; Susan C. Imbarrato, Scripps College; Patricia W. Julius, Michigan State University; K. Peter McLean, Cabrillo College; and Donna Mintie, California State University, Fullerton. Finally, our gratitude to Randall Adams, without whose support this text wouldn't have made the transition from idea to bound book.

# TO THE STUDENT

As you are reading this, you are a person in transition. We all are, always—although we often aren't aware of it. You might have just made the transition from being a high school student to being a college student; from being an adolescent to being, legally, an adult; or, as so many of us do today, from being a full-time mother or member of the workforce to being a student again, sharpening your skills for a new job.

This book aims to help you make another transition: from whatever level of writing skill you have today to a level where you are more aware, more confident, and more effective as a writer.

To this end, we've included in the text advice about various aspects of writing, as well as a collection of essays, short stories, and poems, written by both professional and nonprofessional authors, including students. The readings are meant to serve both as models and as sources for ideas for your own writing; while all of them possess some qualities worth emulating, they are also all meant to be targets for your critique, in terms of both content and style.

We have titled this text *Transitions* in part to draw your attention to one of the most important elements of good writing (and the one most overlooked by beginning writers): the words, phrases, sentences, or paragraphs that serve as bridges, explaining the connection between a point discussed and the point that follows it. Without transitions, a composition reads like a list of points; with them, it flows as a whole.

Because this flow, this feeling of dealing with a unified whole, is generally preferable to disjointedness, we've also tried to organize the readings in this text along a clear continuum. The themes of the first five sections ("Growing Up," "Entering the Gender Area," "Love and Other Metaphors," "Work Is a Four-Letter Word," and "The Evolving Environment") appear in the order in which those issues tend to become prominent in our lives. Within each section, the readings generally follow a chronological order—not necessarily based on the time when the selections were written but on the development of ideas related to the section's theme.

Special selections appear between sections: Each one of these is itself a transition, dealing both with the theme on the preceding section and with the theme developed in the section that follows. Since all of the themes are deeply interconnected, however, your instructor may choose to present the sections in a different order and find other selections that can act as transitions between themes. In addition, some of the questions that follow each reading encourage you to consider the connections between it and other pieces included in the book. The effect created is that of a unified exploration—rather than disconnected, haphazard leaps from one subject to another.

Finally, the last section of the text brings together various issues that have shaped and continue to shape the identity of our particular society. Aside from its Native American population, whose members have been forced to go through drastic but unique transitions, the American people is comprised of those or the descendants of those who made a great (voluntary or involuntary) transition from one country and culture to another. Like any one of us, American society is always in transition. Through its history, it has so far become more socially egalitarian, more multiracial, more wealthy as a whole; some would also argue that it has become more materialistic, more unequal in economic terms, more splintered into special-interest groups, more crime-ridden.

It's important to remember that we as individuals are not just strands in our society's fabric but also active participants in some or all of its changes. As we evolve from one stage of our lives into another, we can also make the transition from being what the outside world tells us we *should* be to being the people who we *want* to be; from being powerless to being—in part through our ability to express ourselves in writing—powerful.

# CONTENTS

. . . . . . . . . . .

## Section 1  *Growing Up*  1

## Section 4 *Work Is a Four-Letter Word*     241

# RHETORICAL
# TABLE OF CONTENTS

· · · · · · · · · · · · · · ·

## Description

## Narration

## Classification

## Comparison and Contrast

## Cause-Effect Analysis

## Argument and Persuasion

## Fiction

## Poetry

# Transitions

· · · · · · · · · · · · · · · · · · · ·

*Lives in America*

SECTION *1*

. . . . . . . . . . . . . . . . . . . . . .

# Growing Up

# Words as Tools—or, Singing through a Microphone instead of a Tin Can

If you've ever cooked or built something, you know how important raw materials are: You need fresh carrots for a good stew, smooth wood for a good desk, or a certain kind of sand for a really good castle. Few people, however, stop to think that words are ingredients, too—that spiced (or glued) with some punctuation marks, they make up the substance of writing. Because we talk so much, many of us see the use of words as a reflex, like breathing. In writing, however, awareness of the effect of words gets rewarded.

Told in bland or inaccurate words, even the most exciting story or the most passionate plea can sound boring or garbled by the time it reaches its readers. Once, for example, after a heated class discussion about the role of religion and spirituality in our lives today, a student came to my office. He was visibly moved and troubled. For most of the following hour, however, about half of his statements consisted of the phrases "oh, man," "and, you know," and "I was, like . . ." Still, I wasn't bored, because he was there in front of me and his body language filled in a lot of the gaps; had the conversation been transcribed and read, however, the student would have sounded merely like background noise.

A less drastic example might illustrate what happens when a writer suffers from a "lazy vocabulary." If you hold up and then release a feather and a brick, they can both be described as "falling"—but they do very different things. The feather glides or floats; the brick plummets, slams, crashes. To call the action of one or the other "falling" would not be inaccurate—but it would be flat and bland.

Aside from being more accurate or descriptive than others, some words also carry certain overtones or implications (we will discuss this further in Section 6, in the section on "loaded" language). Calling a female human being a "woman" is different from calling her "chick," "womyn," or "lady." When choosing words, you must be sensitive to context as well as accuracy. This does not mean that "nice" words are always appropriate; rather, accurate, specific words are. If you were writing a story about a man who demeans women, for example, you might want to convey his attitude by having him call a woman a "bitch" or something similar.

Along somewhat similar lines, don't assume that "bigger" words are better. A person who writes that his grandfather "expressed" to him that he is now a big boy or that a friend at school "queried" him about where he was going would be better off writing "he told me I was now a big boy" and "she asked me where I was going." In both of these situations, you should choose language that fits the context; because these are informal situations, the language you use to describe them should also be informal. Simple, natural language is most effective and makes it less likely that you'll use a word without being completely sure what it means; the point is to use descriptive words to convey meaning precisely, not complicated words to confuse meaning.

Sometimes, as you write, you will feel that the "right" word escapes you. The good news is that it's fairly easy to find the right word—the microphone that will amplify your ideas instead of garbling them. You just need to turn to a dictionary, a thesaurus, or another person. If you start questioning your word choices and spotting areas that can be improved, you might find a better word in a drawer of your brain that just hadn't been open during your first-draft attempt.

So be aware of the words that you use when you write, and, just as importantly, try to be aware of the words you read in this book. On the first reading of a text, you're looking mostly for the ideas and the story line, but on the second reading (even if you're just skimming), you should try to find out how the author "built" his or her piece, and out of what. This advice applies not only to unfamiliar words that you may encounter—like the ones you'll find glossed in the readings the first time they are used in this book—but also to all the words that you think are well chosen in a specific text.

## ~ Eleven

*Sandra Cisneros*

Sandra Cisneros was born in Chicago in 1954 to a Mexican father and a
Mexican American mother. She has been a teacher for high-school dropouts,
a poet, a college recruiter, and a visiting writer at various universities. She is
the author of two books of poetry (*My Wicked Wicked Ways* [1987] and
*Loose Woman*, which was published in 1994) and two collections of short
stories: *The House on Mango Street* (1991) and *Woman Hollering Creek*
(1993), where the following story appears.

**WARM-UP:** In a few paragraphs, describe an incident that happened
to you in grade school.

What they don't understand about birthdays and what they never tell you
is that when you're eleven, you're also ten, and nine, and eight, and
seven, and six, and five, and four, and three, and two, and one. And when you
wake up on your eleventh birthday you expect to feel eleven, but you don't.
You open your eyes and everything's just like yesterday, only it's today. And
you don't feel eleven at all. You feel like you're still ten. And you are—underneath the year that makes you eleven.

Like some days you might say something stupid, and that's the part of you
that's still ten. Or maybe some days you might need to sit on your mama's lap
because you're scared, and that's the part of you that's five. And maybe one day
when you're all grown up maybe you will need to cry like if you're three, and
that's okay. That's what I tell Mama when she's sad and needs to cry. Maybe
she's feeling three.

Because the way you grow old is kind of like an onion or like the rings
inside a tree trunk or like my little wooden dolls that fit one inside the other,
each year inside the next one. That's how being eleven years old is.

You don't feel eleven. Not right away. It takes a few days, weeks even,
sometimes even months before you say Eleven when they ask you. And you
don't feel smart eleven, not until you're almost twelve. That's the way it is.

Only today I wish I didn't have only eleven years rattling inside me like
pennies in a tin Band-Aid box. Today I wish I was one hundred and two
instead of eleven because if I was one hundred and two I'd have known what
to say when Mrs. Price put the red sweater on my desk. I would've known how
to tell her it wasn't mine instead of just sitting there with that look on my face
and nothing coming out of my mouth.

1

5

"Whose is this?" Mrs. Price says, and she holds the red sweater up in the air for all the class to see. "Whose? It's been sitting in the coatroom for a month."

"Not mine," says everybody. "Not me."

"It has to belong to somebody," Mrs. Price keeps saying, but nobody can remember. it's an ugly sweater with red plastic buttons and a collar and sleeves all stretched out like you could use it for a jump rope. It's maybe a thousand years old and even if it belonged to me I wouldn't say so.

Maybe because I'm skinny, maybe because she doesn't like me, that stupid Sylvia Saldívar says, "I think it belongs to Rachel." An ugly sweater like that, all raggedy and old, but Mrs. Price believes her. Mrs. Price takes the sweater and puts it right on my desk, but when I open my mouth nothing comes out.

"That's not, I don't, you're not . . . Not mine," I finally say in a little voice that was maybe me when I was four.

"Of course it's yours," Mrs. Price says. "I remember you wearing it once." Because she's older and the teacher, she's right and I'm not.

Not mine, not mine, not mine, but Mrs. Price is already turning to page thirty-two, and math problem number four. I don't know why but all of a sudden I'm feeling sick inside, like the part of me that's three wants to come out of my eyes, only I squeeze them shut tight and bite down on my teeth real hard and try to remember today I am eleven, eleven. Mama is making a cake for me for tonight, and when Papa comes home everybody will sing Happy birthday, happy birthday to you.

But when the sick feeling goes away and I open my eyes, the red sweater's still sitting there like a big red mountain. I move the red sweater to the corner of my desk with my ruler. I move my pencil and books and eraser as far from it as possible. I even move my chair a little to the right. Not mine, not mine, not mine.

In my head I'm thinking how long till lunchtime, how long till I can take the red sweater and throw it over the schoolyard fence, or leave it hanging on a parking meter, or bunch it up into a little ball and toss it in the alley. Except when math period ends Mrs. Price says loud and in front of everybody, "Now, Rachel, that's enough," because she sees I've shoved the red sweater to the tippy-tip corner of my desk and it's hanging all over the edge like a waterfall, but I don't care.

"Rachel," Mrs. Price says. She says it like she's getting mad. "You put that sweater on right now and no more nonsense."

"But it's not—"

"Now!" Mrs. Price says.

This is when I wish I wasn't eleven, because all the years inside of me—ten, nine, eight, seven, six, five, four, three, two, and one—are pushing at the back of my eyes when I put one arm through one sleeve of the sweater that smells like cottage cheese, and then the other arm through the other and stand there with my arms apart like if the sweater hurts me and it does, all itchy and full of germs that aren't even mine.

That's when everything I've been holding in since this morning, since when Mrs. Price put the sweater on my desk, finally lets go, and all of a sudden I'm crying in front of everybody. I wish I was invisible but I'm not. I'm eleven and it's my birthday today and I'm crying like I'm three in front of everybody. I put my head down on the desk and bury my face in my stupid clown-sweater arms. My face all hot and spit coming out of my mouth because I can't stop the little animal noises from coming out of me, until there aren't any more tears left in my eyes, and it's just my body shaking like when you have the hiccups, and my whole head hurts like when you drink milk too fast.

But the worst part is right before the bell rings for lunch. That stupid Phyllis Lopez, who is even dumber than Sylvia Saldívar, says she remembers the red sweater is hers! I take it off right away and give it to her, only Mrs. Price pretends like everything's okay. 20

Today I'm eleven. There's a cake Mama's making for tonight, and when Papa comes home from work we'll eat it. There'll be candles and presents and everybody will sing Happy birthday, happy birthday to you, Rachel, only it's too late.

I'm eleven today. I'm eleven, ten, nine, eight, seven, six, five, four, three, two, and one, but I wish I was one hundred and two. I wish I was anything but eleven, because I want today to be far away already, far away like a runaway balloon, like a tiny *o* in the sky, so tiny-tiny you have to close your eyes to see it.

## QUESTIONS

1. What would you say is the overall feeling (emotion) that this story conveys?
2. List various messages about childhood implied by the story.
3. Explain your understanding of what the first line of the story means.
4. Note a few points where the writer uses descriptive words. What is she describing? Why do you think she offers so many details? What is their effect?
5. Point to various passages or expressions that would have made you believe that this narrator is a child, even if you hadn't been told so outright.
6. Describe Rachel. What kind of person is she? Point to elements from the story that support your description.
7. Identify the reasons Rachel provides to explain why Mrs. Price is "right."

8. Rachel knows only the years up to eleven. What would you tell her about what it's like to be fourteen? seventeen? or your age today?

**CONNECTIONS**

Compare and contrast Cisneros's writing style in this story with the writing style of any other author you've read (be it Shakespeare or Stephen King, Alice Walker or Martin Luther King, Jr.).

# ∼ The Childhood Origins of Natural Writing

## Gabriele Lusser Rico

Having emigrated from Germany to the United States at the age of eleven, Gabriele Rico taught high school English before earning her Ph.D. from Stanford University and becoming a professor of English and creative arts at San Jose State University. She has studied extensively the implications of brain research on writing, the creative process, and clustering (a prewriting technique that we'll discuss later in this section). She has also led numerous writing workshops across the United States. The following selection is a chapter from her first book, *Writing the Natural Way* (1983); her most recent book is entitled *Pain and Possibility* (1991).

**WARM-UP:** Write down either "I love writing because . . ." or "I hate writing because . . ." and finish that thought in one or two paragraphs.

The playfulness, the willingness to take risks, the spontaneity that are char- 1 acteristic of creative behavior in general and natural writing in particular depend on two fundamental acts you engaged in from the moment you began to talk: wonder and storying. "Whazzat, Daddy? Whazzat, Mommy?" was your insistent cry. You wondered about everything because everything was new to you. "Twinkle, twinkle, little star/How I wonder what you are" captures the curiosity and the sense of delight that seem to be the rule of childhood existence. Wonder is so crucial to creative behavior that D. H. Lawrence elevated it to the status of a sixth sense.

## Wonder and Storying

Theologian/philosopher Sam Keen has written about the importance of wonder in our lives in *Apology for Wonder:* "To wonder is to live in the world of novelty rather than law (or habit), of delight rather than obligation, and of the present rather than the future." Wonder, Keen continues, requires a relaxed attitude, receptivity, an intuitive sense, a delight in juxtaposing° and savoring particulars, sensuousness, openness, and participation. . . .

Children make sense of their world by wondering, and as a result create their own realities in answer to that wonder. The Russian linguistic scholar Kornei Chukovsky writes that the child from two to five is the most inquisitive

---

*juxtaposing:* Placing side by side in unexpected combinations.

creature on earth in the service of comprehending its world. In his book *From Two to Five* he cites the example of five-year-old Volik:

> After swallowing each bit, Volik would stop and listen to what was happening inside of him. Then he would smile gaily and say: "It just ran down the little ladder to the stomach."
>
> "What do you mean—down the little ladder?"
>
> "I have a little ladder there (and he pointed from the neck to the stomach); everything I eat runs down this ladder . . . and then there are other little ladders in my arms and legs . . . all over what I eat runs down little ladders to my body. . . ."
>
> "Did someone tell you all this?"
>
> "No, I saw it myself."
>
> "Where?"
>
> "Oh, when I was in your tummy, I saw the kind of ladders you had there . . . and that means that I, too, have the same kind. . . ."

Wondering, as you can see from Volik's virtuoso performance, leads naturally to the second fundamental act of early childhood: "storying."

5     Storying is a term created by psychologist Renée Fuller, who maintains that this act is so fundamental to intellectual development that we underestimate its importance. The child's ability to create wholeness out of his or her manifold experience, in the form of stories, occurs at the most formative stage of intellectual development according to Fuller, and it occurs in all cultures. As soon as children learn to talk, words and ideas tumble forth in an uninhibited flow, limited only by the boundaries of their vocabulary. Storying expresses an innate human need to make mental connections, to perceive patterns, to create relationships among people, things, feelings, and events—and to express these perceived connections to others.

In fact, storying seems to evolve as naturally as a child's language acquisition itself, long before the imposition of formal learning of rules. According to linguist Noam Chomsky, our predisposition for language is innate—that is, built into our brain. Because no one as yet knows exactly how language is learned, let's say children learn language simply by using it. No one, least of all the average mother, knows how to *teach* it to them. Children's innate capacity naturally shapes them to pay attention to it, and then—at a learning rate that is breathtaking—to tumble forth experiences and perceptions of the world in increasingly sophisticated ways.

Kornei Chukovsky calls every two-year-old a "linguistic genius":

> Beginning with the age of two, every child becomes for a short period of time a linguistic genius. . . . There is no trace left in the eight-year-old of this creativity with words, since the need for it has passed; by this age the

child already has fully mastered the basic principles of his native language. If his former talent for word invention and construction had not abandoned him, he would, even by the age of ten, eclipse any of us with his suppleness and brilliance of speech.

As children, every time we told an experience or tried to express our feelings about something, we were storying, and through storying we built our sense of who we were and what was significant for our gradually expanding world view. Our mothers patiently reinforced our utterances, correcting us only when we called a pony, which we were seeing for the first time, a doggie —after all, both are four-legged, both have ears, tail, eyes, and so forth. Soon enough we learned to beg to ride that horsie, and when we were lucky enough to get permission, we uninhibitedly and excitedly told our father or sister what we had done, how we felt, and what the horsie looked like. Thus, through storying, an essential and natural expressive mode, our horizon and delight in words continually expanded, augmented by the wonder and joy in stories our parents read us out of books.

The same fascination these stories held for us as children played a significant role in our growing desire to get our own stories on paper: the wonder and surprise of holding the fleeting images of our mind fast on the page and the satisfaction in creating coherence out of the world at large.

## The Magic of the Written Word

When at some point in our development—as early as age two and certainly by four—we realized that those black squiggly lines on pages in books made up the stories we loved to hear, it seemed so magical to us that many of us attempted to duplicate the feat by making our own squiggly lines and then "reading" the resulting "story" to our parents. Then, once we learned to identify letters, connect those letters with sounds, and combine letters to make words, a whole new world opened up to us. Gradually we gained the power to put stubby pencil to paper to hold fast our storying efforts—both real and imagined. Our story on the page became a silent testimonial of our mind's pictures.

In his autobiography, *The Words,* Jean-Paul Sartre recalled what drew his childhood self to writing—he felt the irresistible need to make the pictures in his head somehow real: "I'm playing moving-pictures" (I would answer). Indeed, I was trying to pluck the pictures from my head and *realize* them outside of me." Writing was so central to his life, he continues, that "when I began writing, I began my birth over again."

At the beginning, this desire to express the pictures in our heads through storying was as natural as our delight in making drawings or chanting jump-rope rhymes. There was no anxiety associated with it; we were compelled to

10

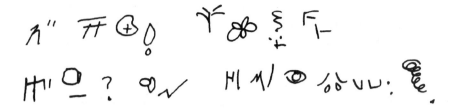

communicate our thoughts. Rarely stumped or inhibited by what they don't know, children actually seem to thrive on novelty, which they appropriate to create their own meaning: elbow macaroni is transformed into a necklace; a box of plain wooden blocks becomes a thriving city; nonsense figures become a story. Given the nonsense markings shown above, a first-grader detailed the following story.

> *The Street Accident*
> A point is going into the street. Two cars crash in each other. Had to get to the hospital. Water came up. Saw a butterfly. They saw the terrible lights that they bumped into. Then they saw a full accident on the street. The whole world was bunked into the street of cars. Then they had to stay there in the one little box. Then they thought a little bit. Then a firefly came by the street. His name was Helper. He rescued them. Then they are free again on the street and could go anywhere. Then an eye appeared on the street. It was coming closer and closer until everyone rushed away. The End!
>
> TRACY OWEN, 6

No matter how crude their work appears to sometimes critical parents, it brings these small storytellers themselves profound feelings of satisfaction, just as their artful scribbles do.

The sense of wholeness and the sense of pleasure in storying are two important qualities you will learn to recapture in your own natural writing. They are the basis of aesthetic activity: consciousness of a unified whole and consciousness of intense pleasure. They are the result of having discovered or fashioned a form out of the chaos of one's experience. Aesthetic activity is not only a central feature of a child's development—for young children seem to be guided by aesthetic criteria rather than logical criteria much of the time—but a necessary ingredient of all creative activity.

## Stages of Creative Development

15      In an article titled "Impression and Expression in Artistic Development," art educator Harry Broudy has classified three stages of aesthetic/creative

development that are not only highly useful to an understanding of natural writing but correspond remarkably to the stages of brain development. . . . He refers to them as the stage of the "innocent eye, ear, and hand," the stage of the "conventional eye, ear, and hand," and the stage of the "cultivated eye, ear, and hand."

### The Innocent Eye, Ear, and Hand

This stage of innocent creative expression lasts from about age two to age seven. It is characterized by innocence of perception—that is, children have few preconceived notions about what the world *ought* to be like, about how they *should* feel, about what they *must* do according to certain prescribed formulas. The world is sheer possibility and, as discussed, a child's characteristic stance toward it is wonder. Each day is filled with the delight of new discoveries rather than the dead weight of obligations; each minute, each activity is experienced as "now" rather than as a worried look into the future. Wondering is openness to the unknown; in fact, wondering makes it quite acceptable *not* to know, precisely because it sets the stage for spontaneous discoveries.

Writing in this stage is characterized, as we have already discussed, by wholeness at the expense of logic, by vivid images like Volik's ladders, by accidental metaphors° ("Can't you see I'm barefoot all over?"), by sensitivity to language rhythms, by frequent recurrence of key words, and by a juxtaposition of logically incommensurate° elements. This early stage clearly encompasses the most salient° features of natural writing. A poignant° example is the recently republished turn-of-the-century diary of a six-year-old girl, Opal Whitely, entitled *Opal*. An orphan, she lived in a mining camp with foster parents. Her original parents were well educated and had taught her to read and write. To make sense of her existence, and also to make it more bearable, Opal storied with ferocious intensity, using whatever scraps of paper she could garner, often writing under the bed where she was sent as punishment. Her writing attests to the power of the imagination and reflects the wondering receptivity of a child to all the world about her.

> Today the grandpa dug potatoes in the field
> I followed along after.
> I picked them up and piled them in piles.
> Some of them were very plump.
> And all the time I was picking up potatoes
> I did have conversations with them.
> To some potatoes I did tell about

---

*metaphor:* A figure of speech that compares two things by saying not that one is *like* the other but that one *is* the other.   *incommensurate:* Disproportionate, inadequate.   *salient:* Notable, striking. *poignant:* Moving, touching, heartfelt.

my hospital in the near woods
and all the little folk in it
and how much prayers and songs
and mentholatum helps them to have well feels.

To other potatoes I did talk about my friends—
how the crow, Lars Porsena,
does have a fondness for collecting things,
how Aphrodite, the mother pig, has a fondness
for chocolate creams,
how my dear pig, Peter Paul Rubens, wears a
little bell coming to my cathedral service.

Potatoes are very interesting folks.
I think they must see a lot
of what is going on in the earth.
They have so many eyes.
Too, I did have thinks
of all their growing days
there in the ground,
and all the things they did hear.

And after, I did count the eyes
that every potatoe did have,
and their numbers were in blessings.

I have thinks these potatoes growing here
did have knowings of star songs.
I have kept watch in the field at night
and I have seen the stars
look kindness down upon them.
And I have walked between the rows of potatoes
and I have watched
the star gleams on their leaves.

There you have it: the intense openness to experience, the unclouded power of observation, the vivid images, the charming childish terminology— "well feels," "did have thinks." But what is most striking in this excerpt of a child's writing is its sense of wholeness, its completeness as a vignette. It is achieved through the unwavering focus on potatoes, almost as if Opal had clustered.° The opening line explains that "the grandpa dug potatoes in the field," followed by Opal's "conversations with them," followed by her near

---

*clustering:* A technique that helps authors to gather material for their writing (see pp. 84–85).

identification with their "feelings," recognizing how much they "see and hear," followed by a profound (for a six-year-old) musing on the unity of the universe: "potatoes . . . /have knowings of star songs"; "the stars/look kindness down upon them"; "I have watched/the star gleams on their leaves." This, from a six-year-old, is in amazing example of natural writing.

Unfortunately, in the course of a child's writing development, wonder is eclipsed by the complacency inherent in valuing and writing about the conventional, the widely accepted, the correctness-dampened—hence the stage of the conventional eye, ear, and hand.

### The Conventional Eye, Ear, and Hand

From about age eight through sixteen, our manual dexterity° is considerably strengthened through continually improving eye-hand coordination. Consequently, there is considerable improvement in handwriting skills, and we gain mastery over the mechanics of language because of the heavy emphasis on these left-brain skills in school. We also gradually eliminate the logical gaps in our stories—characteristic of our earlier stage of perception—as intense preoccupation with the whole vision gives way to preoccupation with appropriateness of detail. As a result, our writing and oral storying become increasingly conventional and literal, with a concomitant loss of the spontaneity and originality of our earlier efforts.

The writing of my fourteen-year-old daughter Stephanie can be used to illustrate many of the characteristics of writing in the conventional stage. Rhyme tends to subtract instead of adding to the effect, and the content is unimaginative.

*Everyday Things*
My Birkenstocks
Are the neatest shoes
Without socks
I really groove
With those socks
My feet are warm
In my Birkenstocks—
They're such a charm!
    *Stephanie Rico*

During these years of conventional perception and expression, we are well entrenched in a school curriculum that emphasizes logical/linear, rule-governed learnings taught piece by piece, and usually in the absence of a larger

---

*dexterity:* Ability, skill, aptitude.

context that would allow us to hook these bits and pieces of learning to a larger picture. Education is compartmentalized as we begin to move from a class in English to a class in science to a class in mathematics, and so forth.

At this stage our vocabulary is firmly enough established so that we feel little need to invent metaphors in an effort to communicate meaning. By now we know that a star is, by definition, a "hot gaseous mass floating in space," in contrast to our innocent stage, when, looking out at the star-filled sky, we pointed to the largest one and excitedly exclaimed, "That star is a flower without a stem!"

Yet, at this stage it is reassuring to "know" the same things our classmates know; it feels good to have familiar labels to classify the world around us; it feels good to be comfortably grounded in a consensual reality. (I know, for as an eleven-year-old German stranger in a land whose language was Greek to me, it was painful not to be part of the consensual° reality my peers drew on as naturally as breath.) Children at this stage usually aspire to an exaggerated conformity.

25    Understandably, with such an imposition of rules and criticism about "the right way" and "the wrong way" to accomplish learning, our writing becomes more anxious, less spontaneous, far less daring and grandiose in conception. Imagine for a moment how young children would fare if they had to learn to speak by a process equivalent to the way they now are taught to write. We learn to speak largely in a yes-world, but learning to write tends to become a no-world of rules, corrections, and often artificial—and thus hard to follow—prescriptions that have little to do with natural expressiveness.

Yet the other side of the coin is that our increasing store of new words grounds us in the security of clear and unambiguous references. We happily begin to participate in certain uniformities of perception; for example, how we love to identify the different breeds of dogs or makes of automobiles at this stage. We also participate in uniformities of expression to a degree that adults often cringe at, slaves to the currently popular slang terms dictated by the generation that spawns them.

Our writing at this stage displays two distinct characteristics. First, it tends to be insistently literal, as this adolescent's typical note demonstrates:

Thursday

Stephers:
Hola! Heh! I am in a good mood. I am glad I went to third—otherwise Mr. P would have been ticked. I can't wait til Friday. It's gonna be so fun!

---

*consensual:* Mutually agreed upon.

Stephie, now I am getting tired. This class is too boring (for me, at least). We are doing stupid grammar stuff. Hey, 17 days til my birthday EEEEE!!! Oh well,

Gotta go,
Love
Chris

Second, it tends to be highly clichéd—that is, riddled with overused and trite° language or observations. My other daughter Simone's poem at age eleven will illustrate.

*I Wish*
I wish I could soar with the birds in the sky
I wish I could run with a horse,
I wish I could swim with the fish in the sea,
I wish I could burrow with the ground squirrel on his underground
     course.
I wish everybody could forgive and forget,
I wish everybody could love,
I wish everybody could live in peace,
Under the sign of the dove.

Most of us at this stage gradually slide into a negative attitude about writing, with the result that we write only when it is required of us: book reports, perfunctory° thank-you notes, and tests, endless tests. Writing becomes synonymous in our minds with the hard labor of following impossible injunctions and, all too often, punishment. Thus, writing becomes tedious, anxiety-provoking, and pleasureless. . . . Perceived as a necessary evil, our once free-wheeling expressive powers that were grounded in an openness to wonder and an innate love of storying become mired in the ruts of convention.

And that's where most of us have stayed. Wonder was gradually replaced by the complacency of knowing what everyone else knew, of seeing what everyone else saw, and of writing what everyone else wrote. And our world began to narrow, our potential to constrict, and our erstwhile° trust in ourselves to ebb away into the river of the commonplace.                              30

Fortunately, the human brain is constituted to grow and learn and change as it comes across alternative ways of seeing and doing. When this happens, no matter what our age, we open ourselves to possibility and, consequently, to moving into a stage of creative expressive power, a childlike "innocence of

---

*trite:* Stale, worn out.   *perfunctory:* Mechanical, routine.   *erstwhile:* Former, previous.

eye" that Dorothea Brande calls the hallmark of the "author of genius." This is the stage of the cultivated eye, ear, and hand.

### The Cultivated Eye, Ear, and Hand

In this stage, we recover the characteristics of the innocent eye, ear, and hand, beginning with wonder, and cultivating it for a mature expression of our innate storying impulses.

It is a paradox of creativity that the very way to move beyond the conventional stage is not to try harder, but to take a seeming step backward: to reawaken and cultivate in ourselves some of the ways we had of perceiving and expressing when we were children. Physician/writer Richard Moss, in *The I That Is We,* calls this step "a fundamental return to beginner's mind, to the child state, to Beingness prior to conditioned and memorized ideas about life."

**QUESTIONS**

1.  Briefly summarize what Rico means by "wonder" and "storying."
2.  What are the three stages of creative development as defined by Harry Broudy? Describe the main characteristics of each stage.
3.  What does Rico see as the main difference between the way children learn to speak and the way they learn to write?
4.  According to Rico, why do children take pleasure in telling and writing stories?
5.  According to Rico, why do most people become afraid of and turned off by writing?
6.  Does your experience support Rico's claim that, as we grow up, "we gain mastery over the mechanics of language" because "we are well entrenched in a school curriculum that emphasizes logical/linear, rule-governed learnings taught piece by piece"?

**CONNECTIONS**

1.  Which stage of creative development would you say that Rachel, the character from the story "Eleven," is in? Explain the reasons for your response.
2.  Find Rico's description of the characteristics of the use of language exhibited by a child in the stage you chose in the preceding Connections question. Then find examples of those characteristics in Rachel's use of language.

# ∽ The Enchanted Bluff

*Willa Cather*

Pulitzer Prize-winning writer Willa Cather was born in 1873 in Virginia, spent most of her childhood in Nebraska, and found her spiritual home in the Southwest. She worked as a journalist and as a teacher before becoming the author of twelve novels including *My Antonia,* published in 1918, and *Death Comes for the Archbishop* (1927), as well as poems, short stories, and essays. The following story first appeared in *Harper's Magazine* in April 1909. Cather received honorary degrees from Columbia University, the University of California, and Princeton University; in 1944, she received the National Institute for Arts and Letters gold medal for fiction. She died in 1947.

**WARM-UP:** Was there a place where you spent a lot of time during your childhood? What did that place offer you? What drew you there?

W e had our swim before sundown, and while we were cooking our supper     1
the oblique rays of light made a dazzling glare on the white sand about us. The translucent red ball itself sank behind the brown stretches of corn field as we sat down to eat, and the warm layer of air that had rested over the water and our clean sand-bar grew fresher and smelled of the rank ironweed and sunflowers growing on the flatter shore. The river was brown and sluggish, like any other of the half-dozen streams that water the Nebraska corn lands. On one shore was an irregular line of bald clay bluffs where a few scrub-oaks with thick trunks and flat, twisted tops threw light shadows on the long grass. The western shore was low and level, with corn fields that stretched to the sky-line, and all along the water's edge were little sandy coves and beaches where slim cottonwoods and willow saplings flickered.

The turbulence of the river in springtime discouraged milling, and, beyond keeping the old red bridge in repair, the busy farmers did not concern themselves with the stream; so the Sandtown boys were left in undisputed possession. In the autumn we hunted quail through the miles of stubble and fodder land along the flat shore, and, after the winter skating season was over and the ice had gone out, the spring freshets° and flooded bottoms gave us our great excitement of the year. The channel was never the same for two successive

---

*freshets:* Streams created by the overflow caused by heavy rains or melted snow.

seasons. Every spring the swollen stream undermined a bluff to the east, or bit out a few acres of corn field to the west and whirled the soil away to deposit it in spumy° mud banks somewhere else. When the water fell low in midsummer, new sand-bars were thus exposed to dry and whiten in the August sun. Sometimes these were banked so firmly that the fury of the next freshet failed to unseat them; the little willow seedlings emerged triumphantly from the yellow froth, broke into spring leaf, shot up into summer growth, and with their mesh of roots bound together the moist sand beneath them against the batterings of another April. Here and there a cottonwood soon glittered among them, quivering in the low current of air that, even on breathless days when the dust hung like smoke above the wagon road, trembled along the face of the water.

It was on such an island, in the third summer of its yellow green, that we built our watch-fire; not in the thicket of dancing willow wands, but on the level terrace of fine sand which had been added that spring; a little new bit of world, beautifully ridged with ripple marks, and strewn with the tiny skeletons of turtles and fish, all as white and dry as if they had been expertly cured. We had been careful not to mar the freshness of the place, although we often swam to it on summer evenings and lay on the sand to rest.

This was our last watch-fire of the year, and there were reasons why I should remember it better than any of the others. Next week the other boys were to file back to their old places in the Sandtown High School, but I was to go up to the Divide to teach my first country school in the Norwegian district. I was already homesick at the thought of quitting the boys with whom I had always played; of leaving the river, and going up into a windy plain that was all windmills and corn fields and big pastures; where there was nothing wilful or unmanageable in the landscape, no new islands, and no chance of unfamiliar birds—such as often followed the watercourses.

5       Other boys came and went and used the river for fishing or skating, but we six were sworn to the spirit of the stream, and we were friends mainly because of the river. There were the two Hassler boys, Fritz and Otto, sons of the little German tailor. They were the youngest of us; ragged boys of ten and twelve, with sunburned hair, weather-stained faces, and pale blue eyes. Otto, the elder, was the best mathematician in school, and clever at his books, but he always dropped out in the spring term as if the river could not get on without him. He and Fritz caught the fat, horned catfish and sold them about the town, and they lived so much in the water that they were as brown and sandy as the river itself.

There was Percy Pound, a fat, freckled boy with chubby cheeks, who took half a dozen boys' story-papers and was always being kept in for reading detective stories behind his desk. There was Tip Smith, destined by his freckles

_spumy:_ Foamy, frothy.

and red hair to be the buffoon in all our games, though he walked like a timid little old man and had a funny, cracked laugh. Tip worked hard in his father's grocery store every afternoon, and swept it out before school in the morning. Even his recreations were laborious. He collected cigarette cards and tin tobacco-tags indefatigably,° and would sit for hours humped up over a snarling little scroll-saw which he kept in his attic. His dearest possessions were some little pill-bottles that purported to contain grains of wheat from the Holy Land, water from the Jordan and the Dead Sea, and earth from the Mount of Olives. His father had bought these dull things from a Baptist missionary who peddled them, and Tip seemed to derive great satisfaction from their remote origin.

The tall boy was Arthur Adams. He had fine hazel eyes that were almost too reflective and sympathetic for a boy, and such a pleasant voice that we all loved to hear him read aloud. Even when he had to read poetry aloud at school, no one ever thought of laughing. To be sure, he was not at school very much of the time. He was seventeen and should have finished the High School the year before, but he was always off somewhere with his gun. Arthur's mother was dead, and his father, who was feverishly absorbed in promoting schemes, wanted to send the boy away to school and get him off his hands; but Arthur always begged off for another year and promised to study. I remember him as a tall, brown boy with an intelligent face, always lounging among a lot of us little fellows, laughing at us oftener than with us, but such a soft, satisfied laugh that we felt rather flattered when we provoked it. In after-years people said that Arthur had been given to evil ways even as a lad, and it is true that we often saw him with the gambler's sons and with old Spanish Fanny's boy, but if he learned anything ugly in their company he never betrayed it to us. We would have followed Arthur anywhere, and I am bound to say that he led us into no worse places than the cat-tail marshes and the stubble fields. These, then, were the boys who camped with me that summer night upon the sand-bar.

After we finished our supper we beat the willow thicket for driftwood. By the time we had collected enough, night had fallen, and the pungent, weedy smell from the shore increased with the coolness. We threw ourselves down about the fire and made another futile effort to show Percy Pound the Little Dipper. We had tried it often before, but he could never be got past the big one.

"You see those three big stars just below the handle, with the bright one in the middle?" said Otto Hassler; "that's Orion's belt, and the bright one is the clasp." I crawled behind Otto's shoulder and sighted up his arm to the star that

---

*indefatigably:* Untiringly.

seemed perched upon the tip of his steady forefinger. The Hassler boys did seine°-fishing at night, and they knew a good many stars.

10    Percy gave up the Little Dipper and lay back on the sand, his hands clasped under his head. "I can see the North Star," he announced, contentedly, pointing toward it with his big toe. "Anyone might get lost and need to know that."

We all looked up at it.

"How do you suppose Columbus felt when his compass didn't point north any more?" Tip asked.

Otto shook his head. "My father says that there was another North Star once, and that maybe this one won't last always. I wonder what would happen to us down here if anything went wrong with it?"

Arthur chuckled. "I wouldn't worry, Ott. Nothing's apt to happen to it in your time. Look at the Milky Way! There must be lots of good dead Indians°."

15    We lay back and looked, meditating, at the dark cover of the world. The gurgle of the water had become heavier. We had often noticed a mutinous, complaining note in it at night, quite different from its cheerful daytime chuckle, and seeming like the voice of a much deeper and more powerful stream. Our water had always these two moods: the one of sunny complaisance,° the other of inconsolable, passionate regret.

"Queer how the stars are all in sort of diagrams," remarked Otto. "You could do most any proposition in geometry with 'em. They always look as if they meant something. Some folks say everybody's fortune is all written out in the stars, don't they?"

"They believe so in the old country," Fritz affirmed.

But Arthur only laughed at him. "You're thinking of Napoleon, Fritzey. He had a star that went out when he began to lose battles. I guess the stars don't keep any close tally on Sandtown folks."

We were speculating on how many times we could count a hundred before the evening star went down behind the corn fields, when someone cried, "There comes the moon, and it's as big as a cart wheel!"

20    We all jumped up to greet it as it swam over the bluffs behind us. It came up like a galleon° in full sail; an enormous, barbaric thing, red as an angry heathen god.

"When the moon came up red like that, the Aztecs used to sacrifice their prisoners on the temple top," Percy announced.

"Go on, Perce. You got that out of *Golden Days.* Do you believe that, Arthur?" I appealed.

---

*seine:* Mesh or lure.    *"Look at the Milky Way! There must be lots of good dead Indians.":* According to legend, the spirits of brave Native Americans formed the Milky Way.   *complaisance:* Obligingness (sometimes used to mean excessive willingness to comply).   *galleon:* A heavy sailing ship used centuries ago.

Arthur answered, quite seriously: "Like as not. The moon was one of their gods. When my father was in Mexico City he saw the stone where they used to sacrifice their prisoners."

As we dropped down by the fire again some one asked whether the Mound-Builders were older than the Aztecs. When we once got upon the Mound-Builders we never willingly got away from them, and we were still conjecturing when we heard a loud splash in the water.

"Must have been a big cat jumping," said Fritz. "They do sometimes. They must see bugs in the dark. Look what a track the moon makes!" 25

There was a long, silvery streak on the water, and where the current fretted over a big log it boiled up like gold pieces.

"Suppose there ever *was* any gold hid away in this old river?" Fritz asked. He lay like a little brown Indian, close to the fire, his chin on his hand and his bare feet in the air. His brother laughed at him, but Arthur took his suggestion seriously.

"Some of the Spaniards thought there was gold up here somewhere. Seven cities chuck full of gold, they had it, and Coronado and his men came up to hunt it. The Spaniards were all over this country once."

Percy looked interested. "Was that before the Mormons went through?" We all laughed at this. 30

"Long enough before. Before the Pilgrim Fathers, Perce. Maybe they came along this very river. They always followed the watercourses."

"I wonder where this river really does begin?" Tip mused. That was an old and a favorite mystery which the map did not clearly explain. On the map the little black line stopped somewhere in western Kansas; but since rivers generally rose in mountains, it was only reasonable to suppose that ours came from the Rockies. Its destination, we knew, was the Missouri, and the Hassler boys always maintained that we could embark at Sandtown in floodtime, follow our noses, and eventually arrive at New Orleans. Now they took up their old argument. "If us boys had grit enough to try it, it wouldn't take no time to get to Kansas City and St. Joe."

We began to talk about the places we wanted to go to. The Hassler boys wanted to see the stock-yards in Kansas City, and Percy wanted to see a big store in Chicago. Arthur was interlocutor° and did not betray himself.

"Now it's your turn, Tip."

Tip rolled over on his elbow and poked the fire, and his eyes looked shyly 35 out of his queer, tight little face. "My place is awful far away. My Uncle Bill told me about it."

Tip's Uncle Bill was a wanderer, bitten with mining fever, who had drifted into Sandtown with a broken arm, and when it was well had drifted out again.

---

*interlocutor:* Here meaning "questioner."

"Where is it?"

"Aw, it's down in New Mexico somewheres. There aren't no railroads or anything. You have to go on mules, and you run out of water before you get there and have to drink canned tomatoes."

"Well, go on, kid. What's it like when you do get there?"

Tip sat up and excitedly began his story.

"There's a big red rock there that goes right up out of the sand for about nine hundred feet. The country's flat all around it, and this here rock goes up all by itself, like a monument. They call it the Enchanted Bluff down there, because no white man has ever been on top of it. The sides are smooth rock, and straight up, like a wall. The Indians say that hundreds of years ago, before the Spaniards came, there was a village away up there in the air. The tribe that lived there had some sort of steps, made out of wood and bark, hung down over the face of the bluff, and the braves went down to hunt and carried water up in big jars swung on their backs. They kept a big supply of water and dried meat up there, and never went down except to hunt. They were a peaceful tribe that made cloth and pottery, and they went up there to get out of the wars. You see, they could pick off any war party that tried to get up their little steps. The Indians say they were a handsome people, and they had some sort of queer religion. Uncle Bill thinks they were Cliff-Dwellers who had got into trouble and left home. They weren't fighters, anyhow.

"One time the braves were down hunting and an awful storm came up— a kind of waterspout—and when they got back to their rock they found their little staircase had been all broken to pieces, and only a few steps were left hanging away up in the air. While they were camped at the foot of the rock, wondering what to do, a war party from the north came along and massacred 'em to a man, with all the old folks and women looking on from the rock. Then the war party went on south and left the village to get down the best way they could. Of course they never got down. They starved to death up there, and when the war party came back on their way north, they could hear the children crying from the edge of the bluff where they had crawled out, but they didn't see a sign of a grown Indian, and nobody has ever been up there since."

We exclaimed at this dolorous° legend and sat up.

"There couldn't have been many people up there," Percy demurred. "How big is the top, Tip?"

"Oh, pretty big. Big enough so that the rock doesn't look nearly as tall as it is. The top's bigger than the base. The bluff is sort of worn away for several hundred feet up. That's one reason it's so hard to climb."

---

*dolorous:* Full of misery or grief.

I asked how the Indians got up, in the first place.

"Nobody knows how they got up or when. A hunting party came along once and saw that there was a town up there, and that was all."

Otto rubbed his chin and looked thoughtful. "Of course there must be some way to get up there. Couldn't people get a rope over someway and pull a ladder up?"

Tip's little eyes were smiling with excitement. "I know a way. Me and Uncle Bill talked it all over. There's a kind of rocket that would take a rope over—life-savers use 'em—and then you could hoist a rope-ladder and peg it down at the bottom and make it tight with guy-ropes on the other side. I'm going to climb that there bluff, and I've got it all planned out."

Fritz asked what he expected to find when he got up there.                    50

"Bones, maybe, or the ruins of their town, or pottery, or some of their idols. There might be 'most anything up there. Anyhow, I want to see."

"Sure nobody else has been up there, Tip?" Arthur asked.

"Dead sure. Hardly anybody ever goes down there. Some hunters tried to cut steps in the rock once, but they didn't get higher than a man can reach. The Bluff's all red granite, and Uncle Bill thinks it's a boulder the glaciers left. It's a queer place, anyhow. Nothing but cactus and desert for hundreds of miles, and yet right under the Bluff there's good water and plenty of grass. That's why the bison used to go down there."

Suddenly we heard a scream above our fire, and jumped up to see a dark, slim bird floating southward far above us—a whooping-crane, we knew by her cry and her long neck. We ran to the edge of the island, hoping we might see her alight, but she wavered southward along the rivercourse until we lost her. The Hassler boys declared that by the look of the heavens it must be after midnight, so we threw more wood on our fire, put on our jackets, and curled down in the warm sand. Several of us pretended to doze, but I fancy we were really thinking about Tip's Bluff and the extinct people. Over in the wood the ring-doves were calling mournfully to one another, and once we heard a dog bark, far away. "Somebody getting into old Tommy's melon patch," Fritz murmured sleepily, but nobody answered him. By and by Percy spoke out of the shadows.

"Say, Tip, when you go down there will you take me with you?"            55

"Maybe."

"Suppose one of us beats you down there, Tip?"

"Whoever gets to the Bluff first has got to promise to tell the rest of us exactly what he finds," remarked one of the Hassler boys, and to this we all readily assented.

Somewhat reassured, I dropped off to sleep. I must have dreamed about a race for the Bluff, for I awoke in a kind of fear that other people were getting ahead of me and that I was losing my chance. I sat up in my damp clothes and looked at the other boys, who lay tumbled in uneasy attitudes about the dead fire. It was still dark, but the sky was blue with the last wonderful azure of night. The stars glistened like crystal globes, and trembled as if they shone through a depth of clear water. Even as I watched, they began to pale and the sky brightened. Day came suddenly, almost instantaneously. I turned for another look at the blue night, and it was gone. Everywhere the birds began to call, and all manner of little insects began to chirp and hop about in the willows. A breeze sprang up from the west and brought the heavy smell of ripened corn. The boys rolled over and shook themselves. We stripped and plunged into the river just as the sun came up over the windy bluffs.

60       When I came home to Sandtown at Christmas time, we skated out to our island and talked over the whole project of the Enchanted Bluff, renewing our resolution to find it.

Although that was twenty years ago, none of us have ever climbed the Enchanted Bluff. Percy Pound is a stockbroker in Kansas City and will go nowhere that his red touring-car cannot carry him. Otto Hassler went on the railroad and lost his foot braking; after which he and Fritz succeeded their father as the town tailors.

Arthur sat about the sleepy little town all his life—he died before he was twenty-five. The last time I saw him, when I was home on one of my college vacations, he was sitting in a steamer-chair under a cottonwood tree in the little yard behind one of the two Sandtown saloons. He was very untidy and his hand was not steady, but when he rose, unabashed, to greet me, his eyes were as clear and warm as ever. When I had talked with him for an hour and heard him laugh again, I wondered how it was that when Nature had taken such pains with a man, from his hands to the arch of his long foot, she had ever lost him in Sandtown. He joked about Tip Smith's Bluff, and declared he was going down there just as soon as the weather got cooler; he thought the Grand Canyon might be worth while, too.

I was perfectly sure when I left him that he would never get beyond the high plank fence and the comfortable shade of the cottonwood. And, indeed, it was under that very tree that he died one summer morning.

Tip Smith still talks about going to New Mexico. He married a slatternly, unthrifty country girl, has been much tied to a perambulator,° and has grown stooped and gray from irregular meals and broken sleep. But the worst of his difficulties are now over, and he has, as he says, come into easy water. When I was last in Sandtown I walked home with him late one moonlight night, after he had balanced his cash and shut up his store. We took the long way around

---

*perambulator:* Baby carriage.

and sat down on the schoolhouse steps, and between us we quite revived the romance of the lone red rock and the extinct people. Tip insists that he still means to go down there, but he thinks now he will wait until his boy Bert is old enough to go with him. Bert has been let into the story, and thinks of nothing but the Enchanted Bluff.

### QUESTIONS

1. What does Cather's story suggest about childhood?
2. What does the ending of this story suggest about adulthood?
3. Write a character description of the narrator, using as many details from the story as you can.
4. What role does Arthur play in the story? Why do you think Cather included him?
5. A symbol is an object that stands for or suggests something else—be it a different object or an idea. Reread the paragraph describing the enchanted bluff: What might the rock symbolize?
6. The river is described in great detail in the story. What might it symbolize? Again, before answering, reread the description of the river and its banks.
7. Can you remember a story or legend that fascinated you as you were growing up, the way that the legend of the bluff fascinates the boys in Cather's story? What was that story? What made it so powerful for you?

### CONNECTIONS

1. Which stage of creative development, as described by Gabriele Rico, would you say Cather was in when she wrote this story? Justify your response.
2. Compare and contrast the use of language in Cather's story with the use of language in Sandra Cisneros's "Eleven."
3. Which stage of creative development, as described by Rico, was each of the boys in by the story's conclusion?

## ～ Those Winter Sundays

*Robert Hayden*

Born in 1913 into an uneducated, working-class family, Robert Hayden
began writing poems during the Harlem Renaissance, an African American
cultural movement of the 1920s and '30s. Following that experience, he
attended Detroit City College (now Wayne State University), worked as a
part-time drama and music critic for a black Detroit newspaper, and later
earned a master's degree from the University of Michigan. Hayden then
taught at the University of Michigan and at Fisk University, compiled an
anthology entitled *Afro-American Literature* (1971), and published several
books of verse, including *How I Write* (1972), *Angle of Ascent* (1975), from
which the following poem comes, and *The Legend of John Brown* (1978). He
died in 1980.

**WARM-UP:** When you consider the way you acted toward your parents when you were younger, would you describe yourself as a *good* son
or daughter? Why or why not?

1    Sundays too my father got up early
and put his clothes on in the blueblack cold,
then with cracked hands that ached
from labor in the weekday weather made
5    banked° fires blaze. No one ever thanked him.

I'd wake and hear the cold splintering, breaking.
When the rooms were warm, he'd call,
and slowly I would rise and dress,
fearing the chronic angers of that house,

10   Speaking indifferently to him,
who had driven out the cold
and polished my good shoes as well.
What did I know, what did I know
of love's austere° and lonely offices°?

---

5 *banked:* Here meaning "covered with fresh fuel and adjusted."   14 *austere:* Stern, simple, severe.
*offices:* Here meaning "duties."

**QUESTIONS**

1. Was the father described in "Those Winter Sundays" a good parent? Why or why not?
2. Was the child described a good son or daughter? Support your answer with evidence from the poem.
3. What economic class does the family discussed in the poem belong to? Offer evidence from the poem to support your answer.
4. Explain your understanding of the line "I would rise and dress / fearing the chronic angers of that house."
5. What feeling does the speaker express in the last two lines of the poem?
6. What are the "austere and lonely offices" of parental love?
7. Cluster around the word "poetry" or "poem"; then create a definition of poetry. (Clustering is explained on pages 84–85.) Does "Those Winter Sundays" meet your definition? Explain your response.

**CONNECTIONS**

1. Compare or contrast the speaker's feelings toward his father with Rachel's feelings toward her teacher in "Eleven."
2. Compare or contrast the image of adulthood presented in this poem to that presented at the end of "The Enchanted Bluff."

# ∼ It's Good to Know the Opposition

### *Michael Buenaflor*

> Michael Buenaflor is a family physician in Allentown, Pennsylvania and the father of three teenagers. His article appeared in November 1994 in *Newsweek* in the column entitled "My Turn." Both professional and amateur writers are invited to submit essays for this column, expressing their feelings, beliefs, and thoughts about any subject important to them.

> **WARM-UP:** Write a list of the most common complaints that parents have about their teenage children.

1    Finding myself on a recent winter's day with a broken shovel and more snow than I could handle, I didn't expect the teenage boys hanging out on the street to turn down the opportunity to earn some easy money. But they did. They said they were "saving" themselves.

The following spring, as a workman and his teenage assistant were building my porch, the young apprentice kept asking when they would be done because he, too, was . . . "saving" himself. Aside from saving their energy for channel-surfing, telephone tag and videogames, I'm convinced that teens' energies are used to skillfully manipulate us, the parents.

Others routinely criticize bad teens—the juvenile delinquents, the criminals and the all-round troublemakers. I choose to incriminate the majority— the typical, seemingly innocent American teenager—the "good kid" who is the best rested; best fed; best recreated, clothed, transported, and the most manipulative individual in the history of the world.

So many parents work extra hours or at two jobs to meet the demands of their teenage consumers. I see parents working the fast-food drive-throughs, in jobs too demeaning for their kids to have, in order to provide their children the good life. We have far less control over our teens' lives than they do of ours. This is because we haven't recognized their strategic maneuvers and formulated an organized parental response.

5    The "good" kids claim to be doing their best even when they're not. That's supposed to end the discussion because you can't do better than your best, right? Whether in schoolwork or chores, they figure you'll either blame someone else for their shortcomings or finish the job for them. If they do a bad enough job at some assigned task, chances are you won't ask them to do it again. They know if they hold back it always gives them the cushion needed to show improvement and maybe even be rewarded. I'm still trying to find out

when parents got sucked into the bad habit of bribing or rewarding kids for schoolwork or other duties they're supposed to do anyway.

Another teen ploy is to wait until the last minute to request something or ask for transportation: This creates a greater sense of urgency for you to act upon. Inaction brings the accusation that we just don't care enough about them.

Because of selective hearing, teens can detect us talking about them in another room yet block out what we tell them when they're right in front of us. They accuse us of not understanding them, which to them means that we must fully accept and condone their view in order to claim to be understanding.

Crying may work when used selectively, as well as reminders that we're not keeping up with the times. Some parents feel younger and more hip when they comply. Portraying some material desire as not just a casual wish but as something "really needed" imposes the fear of being negligent parents if we don't respond immediately. I often wonder why, if "everybody is going," no one else ever seems to have a ride until I am conveniently volunteered.

Then there's that barbaric invention, the sleep-over, often used as a means to be in a crowd for a whole night that might not even be desirable company during the day. It provides "sleepees" an alibi for two days to catch up on sleep, during which time it is "unfair" to ask anything of them.

How many parents don't have serious doubts about their mental compe- 10 tence when their children claim they got permission to do things during alleged conversations that the parents can't remember?

I'm still waiting for perpetrators to say that some wrong deed was actually their fault and not that of someone else—usually a convenient someone I don't know and can't question "because he doesn't live around here." Maybe he's the one who leaves lights on, doors open and empty dishes in the fridge.

Lies come easier since so many of the plots in the movies and TV shows involve successfully putting one over on dumb, unsuspecting parents. There's an assimilated herd mentality that says if it's OK for those cool television and movie teens, it's OK for them, too. After all, "everybody's doing it." Have you noticed how indignant they are, how offended they act, when squarely caught in a lie? But then they turn it around and accuse us of the crime of not trusting them!

It is easy for them to stretch a given permission to cover a later curfew than was granted or a different destination than was approved. When we later point out that they didn't keep their part of the deal, they quickly remind us that we came up with the deal but that they didn't agree to it. Parenting should invoke binding arbitration.

Then there's the trap of being the first parent to say yes—on which all their friends base their request for permission when approaching their own parents. Sometimes your name has already been offered as an endorsement before you've been asked.

15     When permission is denied and they proceed anyway, they are fearless of our meager punishments—few of us hold the line for the full term of our original grounding sentence. Besides, how austere can it be to spend time in a bedroom where there may be a television, stereo or VCR?

Playing one parent against the other is an essential and fundamental skill of adolescence. It may involve some truth-twisting, especially when teens are routinely told to go ask the other parent for a final ruling. In separate-parent households interparental disdain falls right into teens' manipulative little hands.

The reason we have trouble controlling teenagers is they're too busy controlling us. They have more time and energy to organize a battle plan. They so often position themselves in win-win situations. On the other hand, we seem to "win" cooperation or peace only if we give in. However, that might be less the case if we start regularly comparing notes with other parents. That always makes teens nervous.

It might just allow us to "save" ourselves.

## QUESTIONS

1. Do most of Buenaflor's accusations directed at teenagers sound accurate to you? Explain your response.
2. What audience does the writer envision for this essay? Explain and support your answer with evidence from the text.
3. What does the last line of the essay mean?
4. What do you think is the purpose of this essay? What is Buenaflor trying to achieve?
5. How would you describe Buenaflor's tone in this piece?
6. Do you find this essay effective? Why or why not?
7. Does the essay flow well? Are there points where you feel the author should have clarified the connection between various paragraphs (that is, added transitions)?

## CONNECTIONS

1. Compare and contrast the father described in "Those Winter Sundays" with Buenaflor as a father (judging by this essay).
2. Do Robert Hayden and Buenaflor convey similar messages about the relationship between parents and children? Explain your response.

# America Skips School

*Benjamin R. Barber*

Benjamin R. Barber was born in 1939 and is now a professor of political science and the director of the Whitman Center at Rutgers University in New
Jersey. Barber coedited *The Artist and Political Vision* (1982) and has published several books, including *The Conquest of Politics: Liberal Philosophy in
Democratic Times* (1988), *An Aristocracy of Everyone: The Politics of Education and the Future of America* (1992), and *Jihad and McWorld* (1995). The
following essay appeared in *Harper's Magazine* in November 1993.

**WARM-UP:** These days everyone seems to think that children in the
United States are receiving a poor education. Who do you think is at
fault: the students? the schools? other groups or institutions? Why?

On September 8, the day most of the nation's children were scheduled to     1
return to school, the Department of Education Statistics issued a report,
commissioned by Congress, on adult literacy and numeracy in the United
States. The results? More than 90 million adult Americans lacked simple literacy. Fewer than 20 percent of those surveyed could compare two metaphors in
a poem; not 4 percent could calculate the cost of carpeting at a given price for
a room of a given size, using a calculator. As the DOE report was being issued,
as if to echo its findings, two of the nation's largest school systems had delayed
their openings: in New York, to remove asbestos from aging buildings; in
Chicago, because of a battle over the budget.

Inspired by the report and the delays, pundits once again began chanting
the familiar litany of the education crisis. We've heard it all many times before:
130,000 children bring guns along with their pencils and books to school each
morning; juvenile arrests for murder increased by 85 percent from 1987 to
1991; more than 3,000 youngsters will drop out today and every day for the
rest of the school year, until about 600,000 are lost by June—in many urban
schools, perhaps half the enrollment. A lot of the dropouts will end up in
prison, which is a surer bet for young black males than college: one in four will
pass through the correctional system, and at least two out of three of those
will be dropouts.

In quiet counterpoint to those staggering facts is another set of statistics:
teachers make less than accountants, architects, doctors, lawyers, engineers,
judges, health professionals, auditors, and surveyors. They can earn higher
salaries teaching in Berlin, Tokyo, Ottawa, or Amsterdam than in New York or
Chicago. American children are in school only about 180 days a year, as against

240 days or more for children in Europe or Japan. The richest school districts (school financing is local, not federal) spend twice as much per student as poorer ones do. The poorer ones seem almost beyond help: children with venereal disease or AIDS (2.5 million adolescents annually contract a sexually transmitted disease), gangs in the schoolyard, drugs in the classroom, children doing babies instead of homework, playground firefights featuring Uzis and Glocks.°

Clearly, the social contract that obliges adults to pay taxes so that children can be educated is in imminent danger of collapse. Yet for all the astonishing statistics, more astonishing still is that no one seems to be listening. The education crisis is kind of like violence on television: the worse it gets the more inert we become, and the more of it we require to rekindle our attention. We've had a "crisis" every dozen years or so at least since the launch of *Sputnik*,° in 1957, when American schools were accused of falling behind the world standard in science education. Just ten years ago, the National Commission on Excellence in Education warned that America's pedagogical inattention was putting America "at risk." What the commission called "a rising tide of mediocrity" was imperiling "our very future as a Nation and a people." What was happening to education was an "act of war."

5      Since then, countless reports have been issued decrying the condition of our educational system, the DOE report being only the most recent. They have come from every side, Republican as well as Democrat, from the private sector as well as the public. Yet for all the talk, little happens. At times, the schools look more like they are being dismantled than rebuilt. How can this be? If Americans over a broad political spectrum regard education as vital, why has nothing been done?

I have spent thirty years as a scholar examining the nature of democracy, and even more as a citizen optimistically celebrating its possibilities, but today I am increasingly persuaded that the reason for the country's inaction is that Americans do not really care about education—the country has grown comfortable with the game of "let's pretend we care."

As America's educational system crumbles, the pundits, instead of looking for solutions, search busily for scapegoats. Some assail the teachers—those "Profscam" pedagogues° trained in the licentious° Sixties who, as aging hippies, are supposedly still subverting the schools—for producing a dire illiteracy. Others turn on the kids themselves, so that at the same moment as we are transferring our responsibilities to the shoulders of the next generation, we are blaming them for our own generation's most conspicuous failures. Allan

---

*Uzis and Glocks:* Types of automatic weapons.   *Sputnik:* The first satellite, launched in space by the Soviet Union in 1957.   *pedagogues:* Teachers or instructors.   *licentious:* Immoral, disregarding restraints.

Bloom was typical of the many recent critics who have condemned the young as vapid,° lazy, selfish, complacent, self-seeking, materialistic, small-minded, apathetic, greedy, and, of course, illiterate. E. D. Hirsch in his *Cultural Literacy* and Diane Ravitch and Chester E. Finn Jr. in their *What Do Our Seventeen-Year-Olds Know?* have lambasted° the schools, the teachers, and the children for betraying the adult generation from which they were to inherit, the critics seemed confident, a precious cultural legacy.

How this captious° literature reeks of hypocrisy! How sanctimonious° all the hand-wringing over still another "education crisis" seems. Are we ourselves really so literate? Are our kids stupid or smart for ignoring what we preach and copying what we practice? The young, with their keen noses for hypocrisy, are in fact adept readers—but not of books. They are society-smart rather than school-smart, and what they read so acutely are the social signals emanating from the world in which they will have to make a living. Their teachers in that world, the nation's true pedagogues, are television, advertising, movies, politics, and the celebrity domains they define. We prattle about deficient schools and the gullible youngsters they turn out, so vulnerable to the siren song of drugs, but think nothing of letting the advertisers into the classroom to fashion what an *Advertising Age* essay calls "brand and product loyalties through classroom-centered, peer-powered lifestyle patterning."

Our kids spend 900 hours a year in school (the ones who go to school) and from 1,200 to 1,800 hours a year in front of the television set. From which are they likely to learn more? Critics such as Hirsch and Ravitch want to find out what our seventeen-year-olds know, but it's really pretty simple: they know exactly what our forty-seven-year-olds know and teach them by example—on television, in the boardroom, around Washington, on Madison Avenue, in Hollywood. The very first lesson smart kids learn is that it is much more important to heed what society teaches implicitly by its deeds and reward structures than what school teaches explicitly in its lesson plans and civic sermons. Here is a test for adults that may help reveal what the kids see when they look at our world.

*Real-World Cultural Literacy*

1. According to television, having fun in America means
   a. going blond
   b. drinking Pepsi
   c. playing Nintendo
   d. wearing Air Jordans
   e. reading Mark Twain

---

*vapid:* Flat, uninteresting.   *lambasted:* Attacked violently (verbally).   *captious:* Critical, inclined to stress faults and raise objections.   *sanctimonious:* Insincere, hypocritical.

2. A good way to prepare for a high-income career and to acquire status in our society is to

   a. win a slam-dunk contest
   b. take over a company and sell off its assets
   c. start a successful rock band
   d. earn a professional degree
   e. become a kindergarten teacher

3. Book publishers are financially rewarded today for publishing

   a. mega-cookbooks
   b. mega–cat books
   c. megabooks by Michael Crichton
   d. megabooks by John Grisham
   e. mini-books by Voltaire

4. A major California bank that advertised "no previous credit history required" in inviting Berkeley students to apply for Visa cards nonetheless turned down one group of applicants because

   a. their parents had poor credit histories
   b. they had never held jobs
   c. they had outstanding student loans
   d. they were "humanities majors"

5. Colleges and universities are financially rewarded today for

   a. supporting bowl-quality football teams
   b. forging research relationships with large corporations
   c. sustaining professional programs in law and business
   d. stroking wealthy alumni
   e. fostering outstanding philosophy departments

6. Familiarity with *Henry IV, Part II* is likely to be of vital importance in

   a. planning a corporate takeover
   b. evaluating budget cuts in the Department of Education
   c. initiating a medical-malpractice lawsuit
   d. writing an impressive job résumé
   e. taking a test on what our seventeen-year-olds know

7. To help the young learn that "history is a living thing," Scholastic, Inc., a publisher of school magazines and paperbacks, recently distributed to 40,000 junior and senior high-school classrooms

   a. a complimentary video of the award-winning series *The Civil War*
   b. free copies of Plato's *Dialogues*
   c. an abridgment of Alexis de Tocqueville's *Democracy in America*

    d. a wall-size Periodic Table of the elements

    e. gratis copies of Billy Joel's hit single "We Didn't Start the Fire"
       (which recounts history via a vaguely chronological list of warbled
       celebrity names)

My sample of forty-seven-year-olds scored very well on the test. Not sur-    10
prisingly, so did their seventeen-year-old children. (For each question, either
the last entry is correct or all responses are correct *except* the last one.) The
results of the test reveal again the deep hypocrisy that runs through our
lamentations about education. The illiteracy of the young turns out to be our
own reflected back to us with embarrassing force. We honor ambition, we
reward greed, we celebrate materialism, we worship acquisitiveness,° we cherish success, and we commercialize the classroom—and then we bark at the
young about the gentle arts of the spirit. We recommend history to the kids
but rarely consult it ourselves. We make a fuss about ethics but are satisfied to
see it taught as an "add-on," as in "ethics in medicine" or "ethics in business"
—as if Sunday morning in church could compensate for uninterrupted sin-
ning from Monday to Saturday.

    The children are onto this game. They know that if we really valued
schooling, we'd pay teachers what we pay stockbrokers; if we valued books,
we'd spend a little something on the libraries so that adults could read, too; if
we valued citizenship, we'd give national service and civic education more
than pilot° status; if we valued children, we wouldn't let them be abused,
manipulated, impoverished, and killed in their beds by gang-war cross fire
and stray bullets. Schools can and should lead, but when they confront a society that in every instance tells a story exactly opposite to the one they are supposed to be teaching, their job becomes impossible. When the society undoes
each workday what the school tries to do each school day, schooling can't
make much of a difference.

    Inner-city children are not the only ones who are learning the wrong
lessons. TV sends the same messages to everyone, and the success of Donald
Trump, Pete Rose, Henry Kravis, or George Steinbrenner makes them potent
role models, whatever their values. Teen dropouts are not blind; teen drug sell-
ers are not deaf; teen college students who avoid the humanities in favor of
pre-business or pre-law are not stupid. Being apt pupils of reality, they learn
their lessons well. If they see a man with a rubber arm and an empty head who
can throw a ball at 95 miles per hour pulling down millions of dollars a year
while a dedicated primary-school teacher is getting crumbs, they will avoid
careers in teaching even if they can't make the major leagues. If they observe
their government spending up to $35,000 a year to keep a young black behind

---

*acquisitiveness:* Strong desire to possess.    *pilot:* Here meaning "on a trial basis."

bars but a fraction of that to keep him in school, they will write off school (and probably write off blacks as well).

Our children's illiteracy is merely our own, which they assume with commendable prowess. They know what we have taught them all too well: there is nothing in Homer or Virginia Woolf, in Shakespeare or Toni Morrison, that will advantage them in climbing to the top of the American heap. Academic credentials may still count, but schooling in and of itself is for losers. Bookworms. Nerds. Inner-city rappers and fraternity-house wise guys are in full agreement about that. The point is to start pulling down the big bucks. Some kids just go into business earlier than others. Dropping out is the national pastime, if by dropping out we mean giving up the precious things of the mind and the spirit in which America shows so little interest and for which it offers so little payback. While the professors argue about whether to teach the ancient history of a putatively° white Athens or the ancient history of a putatively black Egypt, the kids are watching televised political campaigns driven by mindless image-mongering and inflammatory polemics that ignore history altogether. Why, then, are we so surprised when our students dismiss the debate over the origins of civilization, whether Eurocentric or Afrocentric, and concentrate on cash-and-carry careers? Isn't the choice a tribute not to their ignorance but to their adaptive intelligence? Although we can hardly be proud of ourselves for what we are teaching them, we should at least be proud of them for how well they've learned our lessons.

Not all Americans have stopped caring about the schools, however. In the final irony of the educational endgame, cynical entrepreneurs like Chris Whittle are insinuating television into the classroom itself, bribing impoverished school boards by offering free TV sets on which they can show advertising for children—sold to sponsors at premium rates. Whittle, the mergers and acquisitions mogul of education, is trying to get rich off the poverty of public schools and the fears of parents. Can he really believe advertising in the schools enhances education? Or is he helping to corrupt public schools in ways that will make parents even more anxious to use vouchers for private schools—which might one day be run by Whittle's latest entrepreneurial venture, the Edison Project?

15      According to Lifetime Learning Systems, an educational-software company, "kids spend 40 percent of each day ... where traditional advertising can't reach them." Not to worry, says Lifetime Learning in an *Advertising Age* promo: "Now, you can enter the classroom through custom-made learning materials created with your specific marketing objectives in mind. Communicate with young spenders directly and, through them, their teachers and fami-

---

*putatively:* Speculatively.

lies as well." If we redefine young learners as "young spenders," are the young really to be blamed for acting like mindless consumers? Can they become young spenders and still become young critical thinkers, let alone informed citizens? If we are willing to give TV cartoons the government's imprimatur° as "educational television" (as we did a few years ago, until the FCC changed its mind), can we blame kids for educating themselves on television trash?

Everyone can agree that we should educate our children to be something more than young spenders molded by "lifestyle patterning." But what should the goals of the classroom be? In recent years it has been fashionable to define the educational crisis in terms of global competition and minimal competence, as if schools were no more than vocational institutions. Although it has talked sensibly about education, the Clinton Administration has leaned toward this approach, under the tutelage of Secretary of Labor Robert Reich.

The classroom, however, should not be merely a trade school. The fundamental task of education in a democracy is what Tocqueville once called the apprenticeship of liberty: learning to be free. I wonder whether Americans still believe liberty has to be learned and that its skills are worth learning. Or have they been deluded by two centuries of rhetoric into thinking that freedom is "natural" and can be taken for granted?

The claim that all men are born free, upon which America was founded, is at best a promising fiction. In real life, as every parent knows, children are born fragile, born needy, born ignorant, born unformed, born weak, born foolish, born dependent—born in chains. We acquire our freedom over time, if at all. Embedded in families, clans, communities, and nations, we must learn to be free. We may be natural consumers and born narcissists, but citizens have to be made. Liberal-arts education actually means education in the arts of liberty; the "servile arts" were the trades learned by unfree men in the Middle Ages, the vocational education of their day. Perhaps this is why Thomas Jefferson preferred to memorialize his founding of the University of Virginia on his tombstone rather than his two terms as president; it is certainly why he viewed his Bill for the More General Diffusion of Knowledge in Virginia as a centerpiece of his career (although it failed passage as legislation—times were perhaps not so different). John Adams, too, boasted regularly about Massachusetts's high literacy rates and publicly funded education.

Jefferson and Adams both understood that the Bill of Rights offered little protection in a nation without informed citizens. Once educated, however, a

---

*imprimatur:* Here meaning "approval."

people was safe from even the subtlest tyrannies. Jefferson's democratic pro-
clivities° rested on his conviction that education could turn a people into a
safe refuge—indeed "the only safe depository" for the ultimate powers of society. "Cherish therefore the spirit of our people," he wrote to Edward Carring-
ton in 1787, "and keep alive their attention. Do not be severe upon their
errors, but reclaim them by enlightening them. If once they become inattentive to public affairs, you and I and Congress and Assemblies, judges and governors, shall all become wolves."

20        The logic of democracy begins with public education, proceeds to informed citizenship, and comes to fruition in the securing of rights and liberties. We have been nominally democratic for so long that we presume it is our
natural condition rather than the product of persistent effort and tenacious
responsibility. We have decoupled rights from civic responsibilities and sev-
ered citizenship from education on the false assumption that citizens just happen. We have forgotten that the "public" in public schools means not just paid
for by the public but procreative of the very idea of a public. Public schools are
how a public—a citizenry—is forged and how young, selfish individuals turn
into conscientious, community-minded citizens.

Among the several literacies that have attracted the anxious attention of
commentators, civic literacy has been the least visible. Yet this is the fundamental literacy by which we live in a civil society. It encompasses the competence to participate in democratic communities, the ability to think critically
and act with deliberation in a pluralistic world, and the empathy to identify
sufficiently with others to live with them despite conflicts of interest and differences in character. At the most elementary level, what our children suffer
from most, whether they're hurling racial epithets° from fraternity porches or
shooting one another down in schoolyards, is the absence of civility. Security
guards and metal detectors are poor surrogates for civility, and they make our
schools look increasingly like prisons (though they may be less safe than prisons). Jefferson thought schools would produce free men: we prove him right
by putting dropouts in jail.

Civility is a work of the imagination, for it is through the imagination
that we render others sufficiently like ourselves for them to become subjects of
tolerance and respect, if not always affection. Democracy is anything but a
"natural" form of association. It is an extraordinary and rare contrivance° of
cultivated imagination. Give the uneducated the right to participate in making collective decisions, and what results is not democracy but, at best, mob
rule: the government of private prejudice once known as the tyranny of opin-

*proclivities:* Inclinations, tendencies toward something.    *epithets:* Disparaging or abusive words.
*contrivance:* Stratagem, scheme.

ion. For Jefferson, the difference between the democratic temperance he admired in agrarian America and the rule of the rabble° he condemned when viewing the social unrest of Europe's teeming cities was quite simply education. Madison had hoped to "filter" out popular passion through the device of representation. Jefferson saw in education a filter that could be installed within each individual, giving to each the capacity to rule prudently. Education creates a ruling aristocracy constrained by temperance and wisdom; when that education is public and universal, it is an aristocracy to which all can belong. At its best, the American dream of a free and equal society governed by judicious citizens has been this dream of an aristocracy of everyone.

To dream this dream of freedom is easy, but to secure it is difficult as well as expensive. Notwithstanding their lamentations, Americans do not appear ready to pay the price. There is no magic bullet for education. But I no longer can accept that the problem lies in the lack of consensus about remedies—in a dearth of solutions. There is no shortage of debate over how to repair our educational infrastructure. National standards or more local control? Vouchers or better public schools? More parental involvement or more teacher autonomy? A greater federal presence (only 5 or 6 percent of the nation's education budget is federally funded) or fairer local school taxes? More multicultural diversity or more emphasis on what Americans share in common? These are honest disputes. But I am convinced that the problem is simpler and more fundamental. Twenty years ago, writer and activist Frances Moore Lappé captured the essence of the world food crisis when she argued that starvation was caused not by a scarcity of food but by a global scarcity in democracy. The education crisis has the same genealogy. It stems from a dearth of democracy: an absence of democratic will and a consequent refusal to take our children, our schools, and our future seriously.

Most educators, even while they quarrel among themselves, will agree that a genuine commitment to any one of a number of different solutions could help enormously. Most agree that although money can't by itself solve problems, without money few problems can be solved. Money also can't win wars or put men in space, but it is the crucial facilitator. It is also how America has traditionally announced, We are serious about this!

If we were serious, we would raise teachers' salaries to levels that would attract the best young professionals in our society: starting lawyers get from $70,000 to $80,000—why don't starting kindergarten teachers get the same? Is their role in vouchsafing° our future less significant? And although there is evidence suggesting that an increase in general educational expenditures

25

---

*rabble:* Mob, riffraf.    *vouchsafing:* Permitting, granting.

doesn't translate automatically into better schools, there is also evidence that an increase aimed specifically at instructional services does. Can we really take in earnest the chattering devotion to excellence of a country so wedded in practice to mediocrity, a nation so ready to relegate teachers—conservators of our common future—to the professional backwaters?

If we were serious, we would upgrade physical facilities so that every school met the minimum standards of our better suburban institutions. Good buildings do not equal good education, but can any education at all take place in leaky, broken-down habitats of the kind described by Jonathan Kozol in his *Savage Inequalities*? If money is not a critical factor, why are our most successful suburban school districts funded at nearly twice the level of our inner-city schools? Being even at the starting line cannot guarantee that the runners will win or even finish the race, but not being even pretty much assures failure. We would rectify the balance not by penalizing wealthier communities but by bringing poorer communities up to standard, perhaps by finding other sources of funding for our schools besides property taxes.

If we were serious, we'd extend the school year by a month or two so that learning could take place throughout the year. We'd reduce class size (which means more teachers) and nurture more cooperative learning so that kids could become actively responsible for their own education and that of their classmates. Perhaps most important, we'd raise standards and make teachers and students responsible for them. There are two ways to breed success: to lower standards so that everybody "passes" in a way that loses all meaning in the real world; and to raise standards and then meet them, so that school success translates into success beyond the classroom. From Confucian China to Imperial England, great nations have built their success in the world upon an education of excellence. The challenge in a democracy is to find a way to maintain excellence while extending educational opportunity to everyone.

Finally, if we were serious, parents, teachers, and students would be the real players while administrators, politicians, and experts would be secondary, at best advisers whose chief skill ought to be knowing when and how to facilitate the work of teachers and then get out of the way. If the Democrats can clean up federal government bureaucracy (the Gore plan), perhaps we can do the same for educational bureaucracy. In New York up to half of the city's teachers occupy jobs outside the classroom. No other enterprise is run that way: Half the soldiers at company headquarters? Half the cops at stationhouse desks? Half the working force in the assistant manager's office? Once the teachers are back in the classroom, they will need to be given more autonomy, more professional responsibility for the success or failure of their students. And parents will have to be drawn in not just because they have rights or because they are politically potent but because they have responsibilities and their children are unlikely to learn without parental engagement. How to define the parental role in the classroom would become serious business for educators.

Some Americans will say this is unrealistic. Times are tough, money's short, and the public is fed up with almost all of its public institutions: the schools are just one more frustrating disappointment. With all the goodwill in the world, it is still hard to know how schools can cure the ills that stem from the failure of so many other institutions. Saying we want education to come first won't put it first.

America, however, has historically been able to accomplish what it sets its mind to. When we wish it and will it, what we wish and will has happened. Our successes are willed; our failures seem to happen when will is absent. There are, of course, those who benefit from the bankruptcy of public education and the failure of democracy. But their blame is no greater than our own: in a world where doing nothing has such dire consequences, complacency has become a greater sin than malevolence.°

In wartime, whenever we have known why we were fighting and believed in the cause, we have prevailed. Because we believe in profits, we are consummate° salespersons and efficacious entrepreneurs. Because we love sports, ours are the dream teams. Why can't a Chicago junior high school be as good as the Chicago Bulls? Because we cherish individuality and mobility, we have created a magnificent (if costly) car culture and the world's largest automotive consumer market. Even as our lower schools are among the worst in the Western world, our graduate institutions are among the very best—because professional training in medicine, law, and technology is vital to our ambitions and because corporate America backs up state and federal priorities in this crucial domain. Look at the things we do well and observe how very well we do them: those are the things that as a nation we have willed.

Then observe what we do badly and ask yourself, Is it because the challenge is too great? Or is it because, finally, we aren't really serious? Would we will an end to the carnage° and do whatever it took—more cops, state militias, federal marshals, the Marines?—if the dying children were white and middle class? Or is it a disdain° for the young—white, brown, and black—that inures° us to the pain? Why are we so sensitive to the retirees whose future (however foreshortened) we are quick to guarantee—don't worry, no reduced cost-of-living allowances, no taxes on social security except for the well-off—and so callous to the young? Have you noticed how health care is on every politician's agenda and education on no one's?

To me, the conclusion is inescapable: we are not serious. We have given up on the public schools because we have given up on the kids; and we have given

30

---

*malevolence:* Ill-will, spite, or hatred.  *consummate:* Skilled, accomplished.  *carnage:* Massacre, bloodbath.  *disdain:* Contempt, ridicule.  *inures:* Accustoms, familiarizes.

up on the kids because we have given up on the future—perhaps because it looks too multicolored or too dim or too hard. "Liberty," said Jean-Jacques Rousseau, "is a food easy to eat but hard to digest." America is suffering from a bad case of indigestion. Finally, in giving up on the future, we have given up on democracy. Certainly there will be no liberty, no equality, no social justice without democracy, and there will be no democracy without citizens and the schools that forge civic identity and democratic responsibility. If I am wrong (I'd like to be), my error will be easy to discern, for before the year is out we will put education first on the nation's agenda. We will put it ahead of the deficit, for if the future is finished before it starts, the deficit doesn't matter. Ahead of defense, for without democracy, what liberties will be left to defend? Ahead of all the other public issues and public goods, for without public education there can be no public and hence no truly public issues or public goods to advance. When the polemics° are spent and we are through hyperventilating about the crisis in education, there is only one question worth asking: are we serious? If we are, we can begin by honoring that old folk homily° and put our money where for much too long our common American mouth has been. Our kids, for once, might even be grateful.

### QUESTIONS

1. What does Barber consider the main reason that students in the United States are not as well educated as they used to be?
2. What do you feel is the most disturbing statistic he quotes? Why?
3. In a line or two, summarize Barber's main point.
4. Explain what Barber sees as the "deep hypocrisy that runs through our lamentations about education."
5. According to Barber, what does our society honor and reward instead of education? Do you agree with him? Explain your response.
6. Barber is angry at the marketing company that referred to students as "young spenders." Discuss the significance of the company's word choice.
7. According to Barber, what is the greatest danger posed to our country by the poor education of its citizens?
8. Explain what Barber means by "civic literacy."
9. What is Barber's tone in this essay? Is it consistent throughout the piece? If not, where does it change?
10. What solutions does Barber propose for the problems he describes? Do you agree with the solutions he offers?

*polemics:* Debates, controversies.    *homily:* Sermon, lecture.

11. Who do you imagine Barber envisions as his audience for this essay?
12. Is this a convincing essay? Why or why not?

## CONNECTIONS

Compare Barber's writing style with Michael Buenaflor's. Consider issues like word choice, sentence length, style of introduction and conclusion, types of evidence used to support the thesis, and use of description.

# The "Banking" Concept of Education

*Paolo Freire*

Paolo Freire was born in 1921 into a middle-class family in Recife, Brazil. He soon found the socioeconomic conditions changing around him; by the 1930s, his family was living in poverty. As a result, at age 11 he made a vow to himself to dedicate his life to the struggle against hunger. This led him into the field of education at the University of Recife, where he eventually became Professor of the History and Philosophy of Education. After a military coup in 1964, Freire was jailed for 70 days, then released and exiled to Chile, where he spent five years working with the United Nations Educational, Scientific and Cultural Organization (UNESCO) and the Chilean Institute for Agrarian Reform in programs of adult education. Later, in the United States, Freire became a consultant for Harvard University's School of Education. He has written several books and articles in both Portuguese and Spanish; among his books are *The Politics of Education: Culture, Power, and Liberation* (1985) and *Learning to Question* (1989). Freire presently serves as Special Consultant to the Office of Education of the World Council of Churches in Geneva; he travels around the United States and elsewhere, speaking at education conferences. The following excerpt is from his book *Pedagogy of the Oppressed* (1970).

**WARM-UP:** Describe a course you took—in junior high, high school, or college—that you feel was useless, that didn't really contribute to your education. What factor(s) accounted for your experience?

1    A careful analysis of the teacher-student relationship at any level, inside or outside the school, reveals its fundamentally *narrative* character. This relationship involves a narrating Subject (the teacher) and patient, listening objects (the students). The contents, whether values or empirical° dimensions of reality, tend in the process of being narrated to become lifeless and petrified. Education is suffering from narration sickness.

The teacher talks about reality as if it were motionless, static, compartmentalized, and predictable. Or else he expounds on a topic completely alien to the existential° experience of the students. His task is to "fill" the students with the contents of his narration—contents which are detached from reality, disconnected from the totality that engendered° them and could give them significance. Words are emptied of their concreteness and become a hollow, alienated, and alienating verbosity.

---

*empirical:* Based solely on observation or experience.    *existential:* Grounded in the experience of existence, of life.    *engendered:* Produced, originated.

The outstanding characteristic of this narrative education, then, is the sonority of words, not their transforming power. "Four times four is sixteen; the capital of Pará is Belém." The student records, memorizes, and repeats these phrases without perceiving what four times four really means, or realizing the true significance of "capital" in the affirmation "the capital of Pará is Belém," that is, what Belém means for Pará and what Pará means for Brazil.

Narration (with the teacher as narrator) leads the students to memorize mechanically the narrated content. Worse yet, it turns them into "containers," into "receptacles" to be "filled" by the teacher. The more completely she fills the receptacles, the better a teacher she is. The more meekly the receptacles permit themselves to be filled, the better students they are.

Education thus becomes an act of depositing, in which the students are the depositories and the teacher is the depositor. Instead of communicating, the teacher issues communiqués° and makes deposits which the students patiently receive, memorize, and repeat. This is the "banking" concept of education, in which the scope of action allowed to the students extends only as far as receiving, filing, and storing the deposits. They do, it is true, have the opportunity to become collectors or cataloguers of the things they store. But in the last analysis, it is the people themselves who are filed away through the lack of creativity, transformation, and knowledge in this (at best) misguided system. For apart from inquiry, apart from the praxis,° individuals cannot be truly human. Knowledge emerges only through invention and re-invention, through the restless, impatient, continuing, hopeful inquiry human beings pursue in the world, with the world, and with each other.

In the banking concept of education, knowledge is a gift bestowed by those who consider themselves knowledgeable upon those whom they consider to know nothing. Projecting an absolute ignorance onto others, a characteristic of the ideology of oppression, negates education and knowledge as processes of inquiry. The teacher presents himself to his students as their necessary opposite; by considering their ignorance absolute, he justifies his own existence. . . .

The *raison d'être* of libertarian° education, on the other hand, lies in its drive towards reconciliation. Education must begin with the solution of the teacher-student contradiction, by reconciling the poles of the contradiction so that both are simultaneously teachers *and* students.

This solution is not (nor can it be) found in the banking concept. On the contrary, banking education maintains and even stimulates the contradiction through the following attitudes and practices, which mirror oppressive society as a whole:

*communiqués:* Bulletins, messages.   *praxis:* Practice of an art, science, or skill.   *libertarian:* Upholding absolute and unrestricted freedom.

a. the teacher teaches and the students are taught;
b. the teacher knows everything and the students know nothing;
c. the teacher thinks and the students are thought about;
d. the teacher talks and the students listen—meekly;
e. the teacher disciplines and the students are disciplined;
f. the teacher chooses and enforces his choice, and the students comply;
g. the teacher acts and the students have the illusion of acting through the action of the teacher;
h. the teacher chooses the program content, and the students (who were not consulted) adapt to it;
i. the teacher confuses the authority of knowledge with his or her own professional authority, which she and he sets in opposition to the freedom of the students;
j. the teacher is the Subject of the learning process, while the pupils are mere objects.

It is not surprising that the banking concept of education regards men as adaptable, manageable beings. The more students work at storing the deposits entrusted to them, the less they develop the critical consciousness which would result from their intervention in the world as transformers of that world. The more completely they accept the passive role imposed on them, the more they tend simply to adapt to the world as it is and to the fragmented view of reality deposited in them.

10    The capability of banking education to minimize or annul the students' creative power and to stimulate their credulity° serves the interests of the oppressors, who care neither to have the world revealed nor to see it transformed. The oppressors use their "humanitarianism" to preserve a profitable situation. Thus they react almost instinctively against any experiment in education which stimulates the critical faculties and is not content with a partial view of reality but always seeks out the ties which link one point to another and one problem to another.

Indeed, the interests of the oppressors lie in "changing the consciousness of the oppressed, not the situation which oppresses them";[1] for the more the oppressed can be led to adapt to that situation, the more easily they can be dominated. To achieve this end, the oppressors use the banking concept of education in conjunction with a paternalistic social action apparatus, within which the oppressed receive the euphemistic title of "welfare recipients." They are treated as individual cases, as marginal persons who deviate from the general configuration of a "good, organized, and just" society. The oppressed are

---

*credulity:* Belief, faith (sometimes used to mean unjustified faith, too much trust).

regarded as the pathology of the healthy society, which must therefore adjust these "incompetent and lazy" folk to its own patterns by changing their mentality. These marginals need to be "integrated," "incorporated" into the healthy society that they have "forsaken."

The truth is, however, that the oppressed are not "marginals," are not people living "outside" society. They have always been "inside"—inside the structure which made them "beings for others." The solution is not to "integrate" them into the structure of oppression, but to transform that structure so that they can become "beings for themselves." Such transformation, of course, would undermine the oppressors' purposes; hence their utilization of the banking concept of education to avoid the threat of student *conscientização.*°

The banking approach to adult education, for example, will never propose to students that they critically consider reality. It will deal instead with such vital questions as whether Roger gave green grass to the goat, and insist upon the importance of learning that, on the contrary, *Roger gave green grass to the rabbit.* The "humanism" of the banking approach masks the effort to turn women and men into automatons—the very negation of their ontological° vocation to be more fully human.

Those who use the banking approach, knowingly or unknowingly (for there are innumerable well-intentioned bank-clerk teachers who do not realize that they are serving only to dehumanize), fail to perceive that the deposits themselves contain contradictions about reality. But sooner or later, these contradictions may lead formerly passive students to turn against their domestication and the attempt to domesticate reality. They may discover through existential experience that their present way of life is irreconcilable with their vocation to become fully human. They may perceive through their relations with reality that reality is really a *process,* undergoing constant transformation. If men and women are searchers and their ontological vocation is humanization, sooner or later they may perceive the contradiction in which banking education seeks to maintain them, and then engage themselves in the struggle for their liberation.

But the humanist, revolutionary educator cannot wait for this possibility    15
to materialize. From the outset, her efforts must coincide with those of the students to engage in critical thinking and the quest for mutual humanization. His efforts must be imbued with a profound trust in people and their creative power. To achieve this, they must be partners of the students in their relations with them.

---

*conscientização*: In Portuguese, meaning the process of becoming conscious of discrepancies in the social, political, and economic fields, and of moving to correct those discrepancies.    *ontological*: Relating to existence.

The banking concept does not admit to such partnership—and necessarily so. To resolve the teacher-student contradiction, to exchange the role of depositor, prescriber, domesticator, for the role of student among students would be to undermine the power of oppression and serve the cause of liberation.

Implicit in the banking concept is the assumption of a dichotomy° between human beings and the world: a person is merely *in* the world, not *with* the world or with others; the individual is spectator, not re-creator. In this view, the person is not a conscious being (*corpo consciente*); he or she is rather the possessor of *a* consciousness: an empty "mind" passively open to the reception of deposits of reality from the world outside. For example, my desk, my books, my coffee cup, all the objects before me—as bits of the world which surround me—would be "inside" me, exactly as I am inside my study right now. This view makes no distinction between being accessible to consciousness and entering consciousness. The distinction, however, is essential: the objects which surround me are simply accessible to my consciousness, not located within it. I am aware of them, but they are not inside me.

It follows logically from the banking notion of consciousness that the educator's role is to regulate the way the world "enters into" the students. The teacher's task is to organize a process which already occurs spontaneously, to "fill" the students by making deposits of information which he or she considers to constitute true knowledge.[2] And since people "receive" the world as passive entities, education should make them more passive still, and adapt them to the world. The educated individual is the adapted person, because she or he is better "fit" for the world. Translated into practice, this concept is well suited to the purposes of the oppressors, whose tranquility rests on how well people fit the world the oppressors have created, and how little they question it.

The more completely the majority adapt to the purposes which the dominant minority prescribe for them (thereby depriving them of the right to their own purposes), the more easily the minority can continue to prescribe. The theory and practice of banking education serve this end quite efficiently. Verbalistic° lessons, reading requirements,[3] the methods for evaluating "knowledge," the distance between the teacher and the taught, the criteria for promotion: everything in this ready-to-wear approach serves to obviate thinking.

20    The bank-clerk educator does not realize that there is no true security in his hypertrophied° role, that one must seek to live *with* others in solidarity. One cannot impose oneself, nor even merely co-exist with one's students. Solidarity requires true communication, and the concept by which such an educator is guided fears and proscribes° communication.

---

*dichotomy:* Division, separation into pairs.    *verbalistic:* Based on words, utterances.    *hypertrophied:* Excessively developed; overgrown.    *proscribes:* Prohibits, outlaws.

Yet only through communication can human life hold meaning. The teacher's thinking is authenticated only by the authenticity of the students' thinking. The teacher cannot think for her students, nor can she impose her thought on them. Authentic thinking, thinking that is concerned about *reality*, does not take place in ivory tower isolation, but only in communication. If it is true that thought has meaning only when generated by action upon the world, the subordination of students to teachers becomes impossible.

Because banking education begins with a false understanding of men and women as objects, it cannot promote the development of what Fromm calls "biophily," but instead produces its opposite: "necrophily."

> While life is characterized by growth in a structured, functional manner, the necrophilous person loves all that does not grow, all that is mechanical. The necrophilous person is driven by the desire to transform the organic into the inorganic, to approach life mechanically, as if all living persons were things. . . . Memory, rather than experience; having, rather than being, is what counts. The necrophilous person can relate to an object—a flower or a person—only if he possesses it; hence a threat to his possession is a threat to himself; if he loses possession he loses contact with the world. . . . He loves control, and in the act of controlling he kills life.[4]

Oppression—overwhelming control—is necrophilic; it is nourished by love of death, not life. The banking concept of education, which serves the interests of oppression, is also necrophilic. Based on a mechanistic, static, naturalistic, spatialized view of consciousness, it transforms students into receiving objects. It attempts to control thinking and action, leads women and men to adjust to the world, and inhibits their creative power.

When their efforts to act responsibly are frustrated, when they find themselves unable to use their faculties, people suffer. "This suffering due to impotence is rooted in the very fact that the human equilibrium has been disturbed."[5] But the inability to act which causes people's anguish also causes them to reject their impotence, by attempting

> . . . to restore [their] capacity to act. But can [they], and how? One way is to submit to and identify with a person or group having power. By this symbolic participation in another person's life, [men have] the illusion of acting, when in reality [they] only submit to and become a part of those who act.[6]

Populist manifestations perhaps best exemplify this type of behavior by the oppressed, who, by identifying with charismatic leaders, come to feel that they themselves are active and effective. The rebellion they express as they emerge in the historical process is motivated by that desire to act effectively.

25

The dominant elites consider the remedy to be more domination and repression, carried out in the name of freedom, order, and social peace (that is, the peace of the elites). Thus they can condemn—logically, from their point of view—"the violence of a strike by workers and [can] call upon the state in the same breath to use violence in putting down the strike."[7]

Education as the exercise of domination stimulates the credulity of students, with the ideological intent (often not perceived by educators) of indoctrinating them to adapt to the world of oppression. This accusation is not made in the naïve hope that the dominant elites will thereby simply abandon the practice. Its objective is to call the attention of true humanists to the fact that they cannot use banking educational methods in the pursuit of liberation, for they would only negate that very pursuit. Nor may a revolutionary society inherit these methods from an oppressor society. The revolutionary society which practices banking education is either misguided or mistrusting of people. In either event it is threatened by the specter of reaction.

Unfortunately, those who espouse the cause of liberation are themselves surrounded and influenced by the climate which generates the banking concept, and often do not perceive its true significance or its dehumanizing power. Paradoxically, then, they utilize this same instrument of alienation in what they consider an effort to liberate. Indeed, some "revolutionaries" brand as "innocents," "dreamers," or even "reactionaries" those who would challenge this educational practice. But one does not liberate people by alienating them. Authentic liberation—the process of humanization—is not another deposit to be made in men. Liberation is a praxis: the action and reflection of men and women upon their world in order to transform it. Those truly committed to the cause of liberation can accept neither the mechanistic concept of consciousness as an empty vessel to be filled, nor the use of banking methods of domination (propaganda, slogans—deposits) in the name of liberation.

Those truly committed to liberation must reject the banking concept in its entirety, adopting instead a concept of women and men as conscious beings, and consciousness as consciousness intent upon the world. They must abandon the educational goal of deposit-making and replace it with the posing of the problems of human beings in their relations with the world. "Problem-posing" education, responding to the essence of consciousness—*intentionality*—rejects communiqués and embodies communication. . . .

Liberating education consists in acts of cognition, not transferrals of information. It is a learning situation in which the cognizable° object (far from being the end of the cognitive act) intermediates the cognitive actors—teacher on the one hand and students on the other. Accordingly, the practice of problem-posing education entails at the outset that the teacher-student

*cognizable:* Capable of being known.

contradiction to be resolved. Dialogical relations—indispensable to the capacity of cognitive actors to cooperate in perceiving the same cognizable object—are otherwise impossible.

Indeed, problem-posing education, which breaks with the vertical patterns characteristic of banking education, can fulfill its function as the practice of freedom only if it can overcome the above contradiction. Through dialogue, the teacher-of-the-students and the students-of-the-teacher cease to exist and a new term emerges: teacher-student with students-teachers. The teacher is no longer merely the-one-who-teaches, but one who is himself taught in dialogue with the students, who in turn while being taught also teach. They become jointly responsible for a process in which all grow. In this process, arguments based on "authority" are no longer valid; in order to function, authority must be *on the side of* freedom, not *against* it. Here, no one teaches another, nor is anyone self-taught. People teach each other, mediated by the world, by the cognizable objects which in banking education are "owned" by the teacher.

The banking concept (with its tendency to dichotomize everything) distinguishes two stages in the action of the educator. During the first, he cognizes a cognizable object while he prepares his lessons in his study or his laboratory; during the second, he expounds to his students about that object. The students are not called upon to know, but to memorize the contents narrated by the teacher. Nor do the students practice any act of cognition, since the object towards which that act should be directed is the property of the teacher rather than a medium evoking the critical reflection of both teacher and students. Hence in the name of the "preservation of culture and knowledge" we have a system which achieves neither true knowledge nor true culture.

The problem-posing method does not dichotomize the activity of the teacher-student: she is not "cognitive" at one point and "narrative" at another. She is always "cognitive," whether preparing a project or engaging in dialogue with the students. He does not regard cognizable objects as his private property, but as the object of reflection by himself and the students. In this way, the problem-posing educator constantly re-forms his reflections in the reflection of the students. The students—no longer docile listeners—are now critical co-investigators in dialogue with the teacher. The teacher presents the material to the students for their consideration, and re-considers her earlier considerations as the students express their own. The role of the problem-posing educator is to create, together with the students, the conditions under which knowledge at the level of the *doxa*° is superseded by true knowledge, at the level of the *logos*.°

Whereas banking education anesthetizes and inhibits creative power, problem-posing education involves a constant unveiling of reality. The former

*doxa:* Greek, meaning "belief, opinion." *logos:* Greek, meaning "word" or "reason."

attempts to maintain the *submersion* of consciousness; the latter strives for the *emergence* of consciousness and *critical intervention* in reality.

Students, as they are increasingly posed with problems relating to themselves in the world and with the world, will feel increasingly challenged and obliged to respond to that challenge. Because they apprehend the challenge as interrelated to other problems within a total context, not as a theoretical question, the resulting comprehension tends to be increasingly critical and thus constantly less alienated. Their response to the challenge evokes new challenges, followed by new understandings; and gradually the students come to regard themselves as committed.

35      Education as the practice of freedom—as opposed to education as the practice of domination—denies that man is abstract, isolated, independent, and unattached to the world; it also denies that the world exists as a reality apart from people. Authentic reflection considers neither abstract man nor the world without people, but people in their relations with the world. In these relations consciousness and world are simultaneous: consciousness neither precedes the world nor follows it.

In problem-posing education, people develop their power to perceive critically *the way they exist* in the world *with which* and *in which* they find themselves; they come to see the world not as a static reality, but as a reality in process, in transformation. Although the dialectical° relations of women and men with the world exist independently of how these relations are perceived (or whether or not they are perceived at all), it is also true that the form of action they adopt is to a large extent a function of how they perceive themselves in the world. Hence, the teacher-student and the students-teachers reflect simultaneously on themselves and the world without dichotomizing this reflection from action, and thus establish an authentic form of thought and action.

Once again, the two educational concepts and practices under analysis come into conflict. Banking education (for obvious reasons) attempts, by mythicizing reality, to conceal certain facts which explain the way human beings exist in the world; problem-posing education sets itself the task of demythologizing. Banking education resists dialogue; problem-posing education regards dialogue as indispensable to the act of cognition which unveils reality. Banking education treats students as objects of assistance; problem-posing education makes them critical thinkers. Banking education inhibits creativity and domesticates (although it cannot completely destroy) the *intentionality* of consciousness by isolating consciousness from the world, thereby denying people their ontological and historical vocation of becoming more fully human. Problem-posing education bases itself on creativity and stimu-

---

*dialectical:* Argumentative, exploring different angles.

lates true reflection and action upon reality, thereby responding to the vocation of persons as beings who are authentic only when engaged in inquiry and
creative transformation. In sum: banking theory and practice, as immobiliz-
ing and fixating forces, fail to acknowledge men and women as historical
beings; problem-posing theory and practice take the people's historicity as
their starting point.

Problem-posing education affirms men and women as beings in the
process of *becoming*—as unfinished, uncompleted beings in and with a likewise unfinished reality. Indeed, in contrast to other animals who are unfinished, but not historical, people know themselves to be unfinished; they are
aware of their incompletion. In this incompletion and this awareness lie the
very roots of education as an exclusively human manifestation. The unfinished character of human beings and the transformational character of reality
necessitate that education be an ongoing activity.

Education is thus constantly remade in the praxis. In order to *be,* it must
*become.* . . . The banking method emphasizes permanence and becomes reactionary; problem-posing education—which accepts neither a "well-behaved"
present nor a predetermined future—roots itself in the dynamic present and
becomes revolutionary.

Problem-posing education is revolutionary futurity.° Hence it is     40
prophetic (and, as such, hopeful). Hence, it corresponds to the historical
nature of humankind. Hence, it affirms women and men as beings who transcend themselves, who move forward and look ahead, for whom immobility
represents a fatal threat, for whom looking at the past must only be a means of
understanding more clearly what and who they are so that they can more
wisely build the future. Hence, it identifies with the movement which engages
people as beings aware of their incompletion—an historical movement which
has its point of departure, its Subjects and its objective.

The point of departure of the movement lies in the people themselves.
But since people do not exist apart from the world, apart from reality, the
movement must begin with the human-world relationship. Accordingly, the
point of departure must always be with men and women in the "here and
now," which constitutes the situation within which they are submerged, from
which they emerge, and in which they intervene. Only by starting from this
situation—which determines their perception of it—can they begin to move.
To do this authentically they must perceive their state not as fated and unal-
terable, but merely as limiting—and therefore challenging.

Whereas the banking method directly or indirectly reinforces men's fatal-
istic perception of their situation, the problem-posing method presents this
very situation to them as a problem. As the situation becomes the object of

*futurity:* Future events or prospects.

their cognition, the naïve or magical perception which produced their fatalism gives way to perception which is able to perceive itself even as it perceives reality, and can thus be critically objective about that reality.

A deepened consciousness of their situation leads people to apprehend that situation as an historical reality susceptible of transformation. Resignation gives way to the drive for transformation and inquiry, over which men feel themselves to be in control. If people, as historical beings necessarily engaged with other people in a movement of inquiry, did not control that movement, it would be (and is) a violation of their humanity. Any situation in which some individuals prevent others from engaging in the process of inquiry is one of violence. The means used are not important; to alienate human beings from their own decision-making is to change them into objects.

This movement of inquiry must be directed towards humanization—the people's historical vocation. The pursuit of full humanity, however, cannot be carried out in isolation or individualism, but only in fellowship and solidarity; therefore it cannot unfold in the antagonistic relations between oppressors and oppressed. No one can be authentically human while he prevents others from being so. Attempting *to be more* human, individualistically, leads to *having more*, egotistically, a form of dehumanization. Not that it is not fundamental *to have* in order *to be* human. Precisely because it *is* necessary, some men's *having* must not be allowed to constitute an obstacle to others' *having*, must not consolidate the power of the former to crush the latter.

45     Problem-posing education, as a humanist and liberating praxis, posits as fundamental that the people subjected to domination must fight for their emancipation. To that end, it enables teachers and students to become Subjects of the educational process by overcoming authoritarianism and an alienating intellectualism; it also enables people to overcome their false perception of reality. The world—no longer something to be described with deceptive words—becomes the object of that transforming action by men and women which results in their humanization.

Problem-posing education does not and cannot serve the interests of the oppressor. No oppressive order could permit the oppressed to begin to question: Why? While only a revolutionary society can carry out this education in systematic terms, the revolutionary leaders need not take full power before they can employ the method. In the revolutionary process, the leaders cannot utilize the banking method as an interim measure, justified on grounds of expediency, with the intention of *later* behaving in a genuinely revolutionary fashion. They must be revolutionary—that is to say, dialogical—from the outset.

1. Simone de Beauvoir, *La Pensée de Droite, Aujord'hui* (Paris); ST, *El Pensamiento político de la Derecha* (Buenos Aires, 1963), p. 34.
2. This concept corresponds to what Sartre calls the "digestive" or "nutritive" concept of education, in which knowledge is "fed" by the teacher to the students to

"fill them out." See Jean-Paul Sartre, "Une idée fundamentale de la phénomenolo-gie de Husserl: L'intentionalité," *Situations I* (Paris, 1947).

3. For example, some professors specify in their reading lists that a book should be read from pages 10 to 15—and do this to "help" their students!
4. Fromm, *op. cit.*, p. 41.
5. *Ibid.*, p. 31.
6. *Ibid.*
7. Reinhold Niebuhr, *Moral Man and Immoral Society* (New York, 1960), p. 130.

## QUESTIONS

1. This selection was first published in 1970. Do you think that this description of education still applies, or is it outdated? Does it apply to some educational settings but not to others?
2. Explain Freire's view of the "'banking' concept of education." How is that kind of education like a bank? What is "deposited" where?
3. Freire writes that "knowledge emerges only through invention and reinvention, through the restless, impatient, continuing, hopeful inquiry [people] pursue in the world, with the world, and with each other." Explain whether or not you agree with this.
4. Would dialogical education work in all disciplines? Would it work better in some than in others? Explain your response.
5. What does Freire claim should be a student's main action in the classroom?
6. What does Freire mean by "problem-posing education"?
7. Find, quote, and explain Freire's definition of "authentic liberation."
8. In paragraph 44, Freire claims that "Attempting to be more human, individualistically, leads to *having more,* egotistically, a form of de-humanization." Find that statement and read it in the context of the paragraph. Do you agree with it? Why or why not?
9. Do you find Freire's writing style effective? Why or why not?

## CONNECTIONS

1. Compare and contrast Benjamin Barber's, Gabriele Rico's, and Paolo Freire's critiques of the current educational system.
2. Relate Freire's ideas about education to Thomas Jefferson's view that education turns people into "the only safe depository" of a society's powers (quoted in Barber's essay).

# ∽ Memory and Imagination

*Patricia Hampl*

Patricia Hampl was born, raised, and educated in Minnesota. She currently teaches at the University of Minnesota and writes poems, essays, and novels. Among her numerous publications are two books of poems, *Woman Before an Aquarium* (1978) and *Resort and Other Poems* (1983), and two works of fiction, *Spillville* (1987) and *Virgin Time* (1992).

**WARM-UP:** Choose an incident that you remember from your childhood and make a list of the things that you *don't* remember about it.

1    When I was seven, my father, who played the violin on Sundays with a nicely tortured flair which we considered artistic, led me by the hand down a long, unlit corridor in St. Luke's School basement, a sort of tunnel that ended in a room full of pianos. There many little girls and a single sad boy were playing truly tortured scales and arpeggios in a mash of troubled sound. My father gave me over to Sister Olive Marie, who did look remarkably like an olive.

Her oily face gleamed as if it had just been rolled out of a can and laid on the white plate of her broad, spotless wimple.° She was a small, plump woman; her body and the small window of her face seemed to interpret the entire alphabet of olive: her face was a sallow green olive placed upon the jumbo ripe olive of her black habit. I trusted her instantly and smiled, glad to have my hand placed in the hand of a woman who made sense, who provided the satisfaction of being what she was: an Olive who looked like an Olive.

My father left me to discover the piano with Sister Olive Marie so that one day I would join him in mutually tortured piano-violin duets for the edification of my mother and brother who sat at the table meditatively spooning in the last of their pineapple sherbet until their part was called for: they put down their spoons and clapped while we bowed, while the sweet ice in their bowls melted, while the music melted, and we all melted a little into each other for a moment.

But first Sister Olive must do her work. I was shown middle C, which Sister seemed to think terribly important. I stared at middle C and then glanced away for a second. When my eye returned, middle C was gone, its slim finger lost in the complicated grasp of the keyboard. Sister Olive struck it again, finding it with laughable ease. She emphasized the importance of middle C, its

---

*wimple:* A cloth covering worn by nuns over the head and around the neck.

central position, a sort of North Star of sound. I remember thinking, "Middle C is the belly button of the piano," an insight whose originality and accuracy stunned me with pride. For the first time in my life I was astonished by metaphor. I hesitated to tell the kindly Olive for some reason; apparently I understood a true metaphor is a risky business, revealing of the self. In fact, I have never, until this moment of writing it down, told my first metaphor to anyone.

Sunlight flooded the room; the pianos, all black, gleamed. Sister Olive, dressed in the colors of the keyboard, gleamed; middle C shimmered with meaning and I resolved never—never—to forget its location: it was the center of the world.

Then Sister Olive, who had had to show me middle C twice but who seemed to have drawn no bad conclusions about me anyway, got up and went to the windows on the opposite wall. She pulled the shades down, one after the other. The sun was too bright, she said. She sneezed as she stood at the windows with the sun shedding its glare over her. She sneezed and sneezed, crazy little convulsive sneezes, one after another, as helpless as if she had the hiccups.

"The sun makes me sneeze," she said when the fit was over and she was back at the piano. This was odd, too odd to grasp in the mind. I associated sneezing with colds, and colds with rain, fog, snow, and bad weather. The sun, however, had caused Sister Olive to sneeze in this wild way, Sister Olive who gleamed benignly and who was so certain of the location of the center of the world. The universe wobbled a bit and became unreliable. Things were not, after all, necessarily what they seemed. Appearance deceived: here was the sun acting totally out of character, hurling this woman into sneezes, a woman so mild that she was named, so it seemed, for a bland object on a relish tray.

I was given a red book, the first Thompson book, and told to play the first piece over and over at one of the black pianos where the other children were crashing away. This, I was told, was called practicing. It sounded alluringly adult, practicing. The piece itself consisted mainly of middle C, and I excelled, thrilled by my savvy at being able to locate that central note amidst the cunning camouflage of all the other white keys before me. Thrilled too by the shiny red book that gleamed, as the pianos did, as Sister Olive did, as my eager eyes probably did. I sat at the formidable machine of the piano and got to know middle C intimately, preparing to be as tortured as I could manage one day soon with my father's violin at my side.

But at the moment Mary Katherine Reilly was at my side, playing something at least two or three lessons more sophisticated than my piece. I believe she even struck a chord. I glanced at her from the peasantry of single notes, shy, ready to pay homage. She turned toward me, stopped playing, and sized me up.

10    Sized me up and found a person ready to be dominated. Without introduction she said, "My grandfather invented the collapsible opera hat."

I nodded, I acquiesced, I was hers. With that little stroke it was decided
between us—that she should be the leader, and I the side-kick. My job was
admiration. Even when she added, "But he didn't make a penny from it. He
didn't have a patent"—even then, I knew and she knew that this was not an
admission of powerlesssness, but the easy candor of a master, of one who can
afford a weakness or two.

With the clairvoyance of all fated relationships based on dominance and
submission, it was decided in advance: that when the time came for us to play
duets, I should always play second piano, that I should spend my allowance to
buy her the Twinkies she craved but was not allowed to have, that finally, I
should let her copy from my test paper, and when confronted by our teacher,
confess with convincing hysteria that it was I, I who had cheated, who had
reached above myself to steal what clearly belonged to the rightful heir of the
inventor of the collapsible opera hat. . . .

There must be a reason I remember that little story about my first piano lesson. In fact, it isn't a story, just a moment, the beginning of what could perhaps become a story. For the memoirist, more than for the fiction writer, the
story seems already *there*, already accomplished and fully achieved in history
("in reality," as we naively say). For the memoirist, the writing of the story is a
matter of transcription.

That, anyway, is the myth. But no memoirist writes for long without experiencing an unsettling disbelief about the reliability of memory, a hunch that
memory is not, after all, *just* memory. I don't know why I remembered this
fragment about my first piano lesson. I don't, for instance, have a single recollection of my first arithmetic lesson, the first time I studied Latin, the first
time my grandmother tried to teach me to knit. Yet these things occurred too,
and must have their stories.

15    It is the piano lesson that has trudged forward, clearing the haze of forget-
fulness, showing itself bright with detail more than thirty years after the event.
I did not choose to remember the piano lesson. It was simply there, like a book
that has always been on the shelf, whether I ever read it or not, the binding
and title showing as I skim across the contents of my life. On the day I wrote
this fragment I happened to take that memory, not some other, from the shelf
and paged through it. I found more detail, more event, perhaps a little more
entertainment than I had expected, but the memory itself was there from the
start. Waiting for me.

Or was it? When I reread what I had written just after I finished it, I realized that I had told a number of lies. I *think* it was my father who took me the
first time for my piano lesson—but maybe he only took me to meet my

teacher and there was no actual lesson that day. And did I even know then that he played the violin—didn't he take up his violin again much later, as a result of my piano playing, and not the reverse? And is it even remotely accurate to describe as "tortured" the musicianship of a man who began every day by belting out "Oh What a Beautiful Morning" as he shaved?

More: Sister Olive Marie did sneeze in the sun, but was her name Olive? As for her skin tone—I would have sworn it was olive-like; I would have been willing to spend the better part of an afternoon trying to write the exact description of imported Italian or Greek olive her face suggested: I wanted to get it right. But now, were I to write that passage over, it is her intense black eyebrows I would see, for suddenly they seem the central fact of that face, some indicative mark of her serious and patient nature. But the truth is, I don't remember the woman at all. She's a sneeze in the sun and a finger touching middle C. That, at least, is steady and clear.

Worse: I didn't have the Thompson book as my piano text. I'm sure of that because I remember envying children who did have this wonderful book with its pictures of children and animals printed on the pages of music.

As for Mary Katherine Reilly. She didn't even go to grade school with me (and her name isn't Mary Katherine Reilly—but I made that change on purpose). I met her in Girl Scouts and only went to school with her later, in high school. Our relationship was not really one of leader and follower; I played first piano most of the time in duets. She certainly never copied anything from a test paper of mine: she was a better student, and cheating just wasn't a possibility with her. Though her grandfather (or someone in her family) did invent the collapsible opera hat and I remember that she was proud of that fact, she didn't tell me this news as a deft move in a childish power play.

So, what was I doing in this brief memoir? Is it simply an example of the curious relation a fiction writer has to the material of her own life? Maybe. That may have some value in itself. But to tell the truth (if anyone still believes me capable of telling the truth), I wasn't writing fiction. I was writing memoir —or was trying to. My desire was to be accurate. I wished to embody the myth of memoir: to write as an act of dutiful transcription.

Yet clearly the work of writing narrative caused me to do something very different from transcription. I am forced to admit that memoir is not a matter of transcription, that memory itself is not a warehouse of finished stories, not a static gallery of framed pictures. I must admit that I invented. But why?

Two whys: why did I invent, and then, if a memoirist must inevitably invent rather than transcribe, why do I—why should anybody—write memoir at all?

I must respond to these impertinent questions because they, like the bumper sticker I saw the other day commanding all who read it to QUESTION AUTHORITY, challenge my authority as a memoirist and as a witness.

It still comes as a shock to realize that I don't write about what I know: I write in order to find out what I know. Is it possible to convey to a reader the enormous degree of blankness, confusion, hunch, and uncertainty lurking in the act of writing? When I am the reader, not the writer, I too fall into the lovely illusion that the words before me (in a story by Mavis Gallant, an essay by Carol Bly, a memoir by M. F. K. Fisher), which *read* so inevitably, must also have been *written* exactly as they appear, rhythm and cadence, language and syntax, the powerful waves of the sentences laying themselves on the smooth beach of the page one after another faultlessly.

25    But here I sit before a yellow legal pad, and the long page of the preceding two paragraphs is a jumble of crossed-out lines, false starts, confused order. A mess. The mess of my mind trying to find out what it wants to say. This is a writer's frantic, grabby mind, not the poised mind of a reader ready to be edified or entertained.

I sometimes think of the reader as a cat, endlessly fastidious, capable, by turns, of mordant° indifference and riveted attention, luxurious, recumbent, and ever poised. Whereas the writer is absolutely a dog, panting and moping, too eager for an affectionate scratch behind the ears, lunging frantically after any old stick thrown in the distance.

The blankness of a new page never fails to intrigue and terrify me. Sometimes, in fact, I think my habit of writing on long yellow sheets comes from an atavistic° fear of the writer's stereotypic "blank white page." At least when I begin writing, my page isn't utterly blank; at least it has a wash of color on it, even if the absence of words must finally be faced on a yellow sheet as truly as on a blank white one. Well, we all have our ways of whistling in the dark.

If I approach writing from memory with the assumption that I know what I wish to say, I assume that intentionality is running the show. Things are not that simple. Or perhaps writing is even more profoundly simple, more telegraphic and immediate in its choices than the grating wheels and chugging engine of logic and rational intention. The heart, the guardian of intuition with its secret, often fearful intentions, is the boss. Its commands are what a writer obeys—often without knowing it. Or, I do.

That's why I'm a strong adherent of the first draft. And why it's worth pausing for a moment to consider what first draft really is. By my lights, the piano lesson memoir is a first draft. That doesn't mean it exists here exactly as I first wrote it. I like to think I've cleaned it up from the first time I put it down on paper. I've cut some adjectives here, toned down the hyperbole there, smoothed a transition, cut a repetition—that sort of housekeeperly tidying-up. But the piece remains a first draft because I haven't yet gotten to know it,

---

*mordant:* Incisive, bitter.    *atavistic:* Related to the past.

haven't given it a chance to tell me anything. For me, writing a first draft is a little like meeting someone for the first time. I come away with a wary acquaintanceship, but the real friendship (if any) and genuine intimacy—that's all down the road. Intimacy with a piece of writing, as with a person, comes from paying attention to the revelations it is capable of giving, not by imposing my own preconceived notions, no matter how well-intentioned they might be.

I try to let pretty much anything happen in a first draft. A careful first       30
draft is a failed first draft. That may be why there are so many inaccuracies in the piano lesson memoir: I didn't censor, I didn't judge. I kept moving. But I would not publish this piece as a memoir on its own in its present state. It isn't the "lies" in the piece that give me pause, though a reader has a right to expect a memoir to be as accurate as the writer's memory can make it. No, it isn't the lies themselves that makes the piano lesson memoir a first draft and therefore "unpublishable."

The real trouble: the piece hasn't yet found its subject; it isn't yet about what it wants to be about. Note: what *it* wants, not what I want. The difference has to do with the relation a memoirist—any writer, in fact—has to unconscious or half-known intentions and impulses in composition.

Now that I have the fragment down on paper, I can read this little piece as a mystery which drops clues to the riddle of my feelings, like a culprit who wishes to be apprehended. My narrative self (the culprit who has invented) wishes to be discovered by my reflective self, the self who wants to understand and make sense of a half-remembered story about a nun sneezing in the sun. . . .

We only store in memory images of value. The value may be lost over the passage of time (I was baffled about why I remembered that sneezing nun, for example), but that's the implacable° judgment of feeling: *this,* we say somewhere deep within us, is something I'm hanging on to. And of course, often we cleave to things because they possess heavy negative charges. Pain likes to be vivid.

Over time, the value (the feeling) and the stored memory (the image) may become estranged. Memoir seeks a permanent home for feeling and image, a habitation where they can live together in harmony. Naturally, I've had a lot of experiences since I packed away that one from the basement of St. Luke's School; that piano lesson has been effaced by waves of feeling for other moments and episodes. I persist in believing the event has value—after all, I remember it—but in writing the memoir I did not simply relive the experience. Rather, I explored the mysterious relationship between all the images I

---

*implacable:* Unappeasable, relentless.

could round up and the even more impacted feelings that caused me to store the images safely away in memory. Stalking the relationship, seeking the congruence between stored image and hidden emotion—that's the real job of memoir.

35       By writing about the first piano lesson, I've come to know things I could not know otherwise. But I only know these things as a result of reading this first draft. While I was writing, I was following the images, letting the details fill the room of the page and use the furniture as they wished. I was their dutiful servant—or thought I was. In fact, I was the faithful retainer of my hidden feelings which were giving the commands.

I really did feel, for instance, that Mary Katherine Reilly was far superior to me. She was smarter, funnier, more wonderful in every way—that's how I saw it. Our friendship (or she herself) did not require that I become her vassal,° yet perhaps in my heart that was something I wanted; I wanted a way to express my feeling of admiration. I suppose I waited until this memoir to begin to find the way.

Just as, in the memoir, I finally possess that red Thompson book with the barking dogs and bleating lambs and winsome children. I couldn't (and still can't) remember what my own music book was, so I grabbed the name and image of the one book I could remember. It was only in reviewing the piece after writing it that I saw my inaccuracy. In pondering this "lie," I came to see what I was up to: I was getting what I wanted. At last.

The truth of many circumstances and episodes in the past emerges for the memoirist through details (the red music book, the fascination with a nun's name and gleaming face), but these details are not merely information, not flat facts. Such details are not allowed to lounge. They must work. Their work is the creation of symbol. But it's more accurate to call it *recognition* of symbol. For meaning is not "attached" to the detail by the memoirist; meaning is revealed. That's why a first draft is important. Just as the first meeting (good or bad) with someone who later becomes the beloved is important and is often reviewed for signals, meanings, omens and indications.

Now I can look at that music book and see it not only as "a detail," but for what it is, how it *acts*. See it as the small red door leading straight into the dark room of my childhood longing and disappointment. That red book *becomes* the palpable° evidence of that longing. In other words, it becomes symbol. There is no symbol, no life-of-the-spirit in the general or the abstract. Yet a writer wishes—indeed all of us wish—to speak about profound matters that are, like it or not, general and abstract. We wish to talk to each other about life and death, about love, despair, loss, and innocence. We sense that in order to

---

*vassal:* Servant.    *palpable:* Unmistakable, real.

live together we must learn to speak of peace, of history, of meaning and values. Those are a few.

    We seek a means of exchange, a language which will renew these ancient       40
concerns and make them wholly and pulsingly ours. Instinctively, we go to
our store of private images and associations for our authority to speak of
these weighty issues. We find, in our details and broken and obscured images,
the language of symbol. Here memory impulsively reaches out its arms and
embraces imagination. That is the resort to invention. It isn't a lie, but an act
of necessity, as the innate urge to locate personal truth always is.

All right. Invention is inevitable. But why write memoir? Why not call it fiction and be done with all the hashing about, wondering where memory stops
and imagination begins? And if memoir seeks to talk about "the big issues,"
about history and peace, death and love—why not leave these reflections to
those with expert and scholarly knowledge? Why let the common or garden
variety memoirist into the club? I'm thinking again of that bumper sticker:
why Question Authority?

    My answer, of course, is a memoirist's answer. Memoir must be written
because each of us must have a created version of the past. Created: that is,
real, tangible, made of the stuff of a life lived in place and in history. And the
down side of any created thing as well; we must live with a version that
attaches us to our limitations, to the inevitable subjectivity of our points of
view. We must acquiesce to our experience and our gift to transform experience into meaning and value. You tell me your story, I'll tell you my story.

    If we refuse to do the work of creating this personal version of the past,
someone else will do it for us. That is a scary political fact. "The struggle of
man against power," a character in Milan Kundera's novel *The Book of Laughter and Forgetting* says, "is the struggle of memory against forgetting." He
refers to willful political forgetting, the habit of nations and those in power
(Question Authority!) to deny the truth of memory in order to disarm moral
and ethical power. It's an efficient way of controlling masses of people. It
doesn't even require much bloodshed, as long as people are entirely willing to
give over their personal memories. Whole histories can be rewritten. As Czes-
law Milosz said in his 1980 Nobel Prize lecture, the number of books published that seek to deny the existence of the Nazi death camps now exceeds
one hundred.

    What is remembered is what *becomes* reality. If we "forget" Auschwitz, if
we "forget" My Lai,° what then do we remember? And what is the purpose of
our remembering? If we think of memory naively, as a simple story, logged

---

*My Lai:* A village whose inhabitants were massacred by U.S. troops during the Vietnam War.

like a documentary in the archive of the mind, we miss its beauty but also its function. The beauty of memory rests in its talent for rendering detail, for paying homage to the senses, its capacity to love the particles of life, the richness and idiosyncrasy of our existence. The function of memory, on the other hand, is intensely personal and surprisingly political.

45    Our capacity to move forward as developing beings rests on a healthy relation with the past. Psychotherapy, that widespread method of mental health, relies heavily on memory and on the ability to retrieve and organize images and events from the personal past. We carry our wounds and perhaps even worse, our capacity to wound, forward with us. If we learn not only to tell our stories but to listen to what our stories tell us—to write the first draft and then return for the second draft—we are doing the work of memoir.

Memoir is the intersection of narration and reflection, of story-telling and essay-writing. It can present its story *and* reflect and consider the meaning of the story. It is a peculiarly open form, inviting broken and incomplete images, half-recollected fragments, all the mass (and mess) of detail. It offers to shape this confusion—and in shaping, of course it necessarily creates a work of art, not a legal document. But then, even legal documents are only valiant attempts to consign the truth, the whole truth, and nothing but the truth to paper. Even they remain versions.

Locating touchstones—the red music book, the olive Olive, my father's violin playing—is deeply satisfying. Who knows why? Perhaps we all sense that we can't grasp the whole truth and nothing but the truth of our experience. Just can't be done. What can be achieved, however, is a version of its swirling, changing wholeness. A memoirist must acquiesce to selectivity, like any artist. The version we dare to write is the only truth, the only relationship we can have with the past. Refuse to write your life and you have no life. At least, that is the stern view of the memoirist.

Personal history, logged in memory, is a sort of slide projector flashing images on the wall of the mind. And there's precious little order to the slides in the rotating carousel. Beyond that confusion, who knows who is running the projector? A memoirist steps into this darkened room of flashing, unorganized images and stands blinking for a while. Maybe for a long while. But eventually, as with any attempt to tell a story, it is necessary to put something first, then something else. And so on, to the end. That's a first draft. Not necessarily the truth, not even *a* truth sometimes, but the first attempt to create a shape.

The first thing I usually notice at this stage of composition is the appalling inaccuracy of the piece. Witness my first piano lesson draft. Invention is screamingly evident in what I intended to be transcription. But here's the further truth: I feel no shame. In fact, it's only now that my interest in the piece truly quickens. For I can see what isn't there, what is shyly hugging the walls, hoping not to be seen. I see the filmy shape of the next draft. I see a more acute version of the episode or—this is more likely—an entirely new piece rising from the ashes of the first attempt.

The next draft of the piece would have to be a true re-vision, a new seeing of the materials of the first draft. Nothing merely cosmetic will do—no rough buffing up the opening sentence, no glossy adjective to lift a sagging line, nothing to attempt covering a patch of gray writing. None of that. I can't say for sure, but my hunch is the revision would lead me to more writing about my father (why was I so impressed by that ancestral inventor of the collapsible opera hat? Did I feel I had nothing as remarkable in my own background? Did this make me feel inadequate?). I begin to think perhaps Sister Olive is less central to this business than she is in this draft. She is meant to be a moment, not a character.

And so I might proceed, if I were to undertake a new draft of the memoir. I begin to feel a relationship developing between a former self and me.

And, even more compelling, a relationship between an old world and me. Some people think of autobiographical writing as the precious occupation of a particularly self-absorbed person. Maybe, but I don't buy that. True memoir is written in an attempt to find not only a self but a world.

The self-absorption that seems to be the impetus and embarrassment of autobiography turns into (or perhaps always was) a hunger for the world. Actually, it begins as hunger for *a* world, one gone or lost, effaced by time or a more sudden brutality. But in the act of remembering, the personal environment expands, resonates beyond itself, beyond its "subject," into the endless and tragic recollection that is history.

We look at old family photographs in which we stand next to black, boxy Fords and are wearing period costumes, and we do not gaze fascinated because there we are young again, or there we are standing, as we never will again in life, next to our mother. We stare and drift because there we are . . . historical. It is the dress, the black car that dazzle us now and draw us beyond our mother's bright arms which once caught us. We reach into the attractive impersonality of something more significant than ourselves. We write memoir, in other words. We accept the humble position of writing a version rather than "the whole truth."

I suppose I write memoir because of the radiance of the past—it draws me back and back to it. Not that the past is beautiful. In our commercial memoir, in history, the death camps *are* back there. In intimate life too, the record is usually pretty mixed. "I could tell you stories . . ." people say and drift off, meaning terrible things have happened to them.

But the past is radiant. It has the light of lived life. A memoirist wishes to touch it. No one owns the past, though typically the first act of new political regimes, whether of the left or the right, is to attempt to re-write history, to grab the past and make it over so the end comes out right. So their power looks inevitable.

No one owns the past, but it is a grave error (another age would have said a grave sin) not to inhabit memory. Sometimes I think it is all we really have. But that may be a trifle melodramatic. At any rate, memory possesses authority for the fearful self in a world where it is necessary to have authority in order to Question Authority.

There may be no more pressing intellectual need in our culture than for people to become sophisticated about the function of memory. The political implications of the loss of memory are obvious. The authority of memory is a personal confirmation of selfhood. To write one's life is to live it twice, and the second living is both spiritual and historical, for a memoir reaches deep within the personality as it seeks its narrative form and also grasps the life-of-the-times as no political treatise can.

Our most ancient metaphor says life is a journey. Memoir is travel writing, then, notes taken along the way, telling how things looked and what thoughts occurred. But I cannot think of the memoirist as a tourist. This is the traveller who goes on foot, living the journey, taking on mountains, enduring deserts, marveling at the lush green places. Moving through it all faithfully, not so much a survivor with a harrowing title to tell as a pilgrim, seeking, wondering.

## QUESTIONS

1. What do you think Hampl means when she says "a true metaphor is a risky business, revealing of the self" (paragraph 4)?
2. What does Hampl mean when she says that "the story seems already there"? Have you ever written an essay that seemed to be "already there"? Explain your response.
3. What, according to Hampl, is the difference between a writer's and a reader's mind? Explain whether your experience supports or contradicts Hampl's ideas.
4. What is Hampl's definition of "a first draft"?
5. Hampl observes, "It still comes as a shock to realize that I don't write about what I know; I write in order to find out what I know." Are your writing experiences similar? Explain your response.
6. According to Hampl, why should all of us write a memoir, some reminiscence of our lives?
7. How does memoir writing relate to politics and to history?
8. Summarize Hampl's advice about "re-vision."
9. Explain your understanding of the line "memory possesses authority for the fearful self" (paragraph 57). How does memory offer authority?

10. Have you ever reread your own nonscholastic writing, a diary entry, or a personal letter, long after you wrote it? What did you discover in doing so?
11. Do you find Hampl's essay interesting, well-written? Why or why not?

## CONNECTIONS

1. Both Gabriele Rico and Hampl write about writing; compare and contrast their two essays.
2. Compare and contrast Hampl's writing style with Paolo Freire's style in "The 'Banking' Concept of Education."

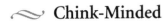

## ∽ Chink-Minded

*Pei Kuan*

> Born in Taiwan, Pei Kuan emigrated to the United States with her parents and older sister when she was six months old. After graduating from Logan High School in Union City, California, she enrolled at California State University–Hayward, intending to pursue a nursing major. Now, however, Kuan is "almost positive" that she may transfer to another university to major in engineering design. Kuan attends school full-time and works part-time (20 hour per week) as a teller at Fremont Bank.

> **WARM-UP:** Are there any words that you hate? Choose one and write a paragraph explaining why you hate it.

1    I was sitting on a bus the first time the word "Chink" was hurled at me. An old senile man passed by my seat mumbling, "You're nothing but a Chink." He then proceeded on his way to the back of the bus. I didn't think "Chink" was a bad word, but by the tone in the man's voice, I knew it couldn't be good. Automatically, I turned my face back to throw him a glare. I was so angry at the man for cursing me when he didn't even know me. Adrenaline rushed through the throbbing veins in my neck and up to my head, where all I could think of was, "Well, you're nothing but a sad, naive man."

I had heard of Chinese people being referred to as "Chinks" before, but never had anybody used the word directly at me. Up until that day, I had honestly thought that "Chink" was just an abbreviation for the word "Chinese." For this reason, I didn't understand why the man on the bus thought he was ridiculing me by abbreviating my nationality. Therefore, I knew that there must be a different meaning to the word "Chink." So I asked one of my Filipino friends if she knew what "Chink" meant. She replied, "Simple. I'm a Flip. You're a Chink." I wasn't mad at my friend when she called me that. Her tone of voice was much different than that of the man on the bus. Instead, I laughed to hear that my friend thought the same as I did—that "Chink" was just an abbreviation.

However, part of the reason why I was laughing was because I felt a little naive myself. Here we were, my friend and I, two high school graduates who didn't know the true context of a word. It's sad because all through our lives we take words for granted, listening to them come and go without stopping to understand what they mean or where they come from.

For this reason, I took it upon myself to look up the word "Chin dictionary. I thought the almighty dictionary that contains literally the usual of words must have the word "Chink." And sure enough, there it was on page 356 of *The World Book Dictionary*. Holding my breath, hoping not to read anything too humiliating about the word, I was surprised to read the first definition. "Chink" is defined as a "narrow opening; crack; slit." It was merely a noun, not at all an adjective pertaining to humans. But I could see or guess how and why people changed the noun to become a damaging adjective: possibly because of the stereotype that people may have of Chinese people having small eyes, the size of slits. I understood now why some people call Chinese people "Chinks." It infuriates me that people can be so narrow-minded as to group people and label them according to physical traits. Especially because physical traits touch upon the surface level and not the inner level.

As I was experiencing these emotions of hurt and anger, I stumbled upon the second meaning of the word. According to the dictionary, figuratively the word "Chink" also meant an area of weakness, a vulnerable place, and/or a weak side. I was surprised all the more to read this second definition because it totally pertained to what I was feeling toward the word: how this word "Chink" could be used to make fun of a group of people based on traits, and then expose the vulnerability or weakness that this mocking word can stir up.

Wanting to discover more about my newly learned word, I anxiously read the last definition. The last definition was the one that summed up the meanings of the previous two perfectly. Clearly, it stated, "n. U.S. slang; Unfriendly use. Chinese."

It's amazing how one single word can have the power to imply so much. I guess the reason why I can see the connection between the three definitions of the word "Chink" is because I'm Chinese. Maybe it takes a Chinese person to really understand the vulnerability and hurt that such an unfriendly descriptive word can stir up. All the more, it is the way one intends a word to mean that gives a word full impact. Perhaps the old man on the bus knew what he intended by calling me a Chink. Perhaps he didn't. But the next time someone calls me a Chink, I can say, "At least I'm not chink-minded."

## QUESTIONS

1. What prompted Pei Kuan to look up the word "Chink" in a dictionary? Have you ever looked up words because of the way they had been used around you, rather than because you found them in a textbook? If so, which words?
2. What conclusions does Kuan derive from her experience about the use of words?

3. Do you find Kuan's use of words effective? Support your answer with examples from the essay.
4. Do you find Kuan's introduction and conclusion effective? Why or why not?
5. Do you feel that the essay flows well? Why or why not?
6. If you could suggest to the author ways to improve her essay, what advice would you offer?

## CONNECTIONS

1. Is the experience described by Kuan an educational one? If so, compare and contrast it to the kinds of educational experiences that Paolo Freire describes.
2. Of the authors included in this chapter, neither Pei Kuan nor Michael Buenaflor are professional writers. Compare and contrast their essays. Which one do you like better? Why?

# ∽ The Quiet Girl

*Maxine Hong Kingston*

Maxine Hong Kingston was born and raised in Stockton, California. After she graduated from the University of California at Berkeley, she taught high-school and college English in California and in Hawaii; she currently teaches at the University of California, Berkeley. Her latest book is a novel entitled *Tripmaster Monkey: His Fake Book* (1987). The following is a selection from her best-known work, *The Woman Warrior: Memoirs of a Girlhood among Ghosts* (1975).

**WARM-UP:** Write a paragraph discussing a time in your childhood when you wished you were different than you were, and explain what caused you to feel that way.

Normal Chinese women's voices are strong and bossy. We American-Chinese girls had to whisper to make ourselves American-feminine. Apparently we whispered even more softly than the Americans. Once a year the teachers referred my sister and me to speech therapy, but our voices would straighten out, unpredictably normal, for the therapists. Some of us gave up, shook our heads, and said nothing, not one word. Some of us could not even shake our heads. At times shaking my head no is more self-assertion than I can manage. Most of us eventually found some voice, however faltering. We invented an American-feminine speaking personality, except for that one girl who could not speak up even in Chinese school.

She was a year older than I and was in my class for twelve years. During all those years she read aloud but would not talk. Her older sister was usually beside her; their parents kept the older daughter back to protect the younger one. They were six and seven years old when they began school. Although I had flunked kindergarten, I was the same age as most other students in our class; my parents had probably lied about my age, so I had had a head start and came out even. My younger sister was in the class below me; we were normal ages and normally separated. The parents of the quiet girl, on the other hand, protected both daughters. When it sprinkled, they kept them home from school. The girls did not work for a living the way we did. But in other ways we were the same.

We were similar in sports. We held the bat on our shoulders until we walked to first base. (You got a strike only when you actually struck at the ball.) Sometimes the pitcher wouldn't bother to throw to us. "Automatic walk," the other children would call, sending us on our way. By fourth or fifth grade, though, some of us would try to hit the ball. "Easy out," the other kids would say. I hit the ball a couple of times. Baseball was nice in that there was a definite spot to run to after hitting the ball. Basketball confused me because when I caught the ball I didn't know whom to throw it to. "Me. Me," the kids would be yelling. "Over here." Suddenly it would occur to me I hadn't memorized which ghosts were on my team and which were on the other. When the kids said, "Automatic walk," the girl who was quieter than I kneeled with one end of the bat in each hand and placed it carefully on the plate. Then she dusted her hands as she walked to first base, where she rubbed her hands softly, fingers spread. She always got tagged out before second base. She would whisper-read but not talk. Her whisper was as soft as if she had no muscles. She seemed to be breathing from a distance. I heard no anger or tension.

I joined in at lunchtime when the other students, the Chinese too, talked about whether or not she was mute, although obviously she was not if she could read aloud. People told how *they* had tried *their* best to be friendly. *They* said hello, but if she refused to answer, well, they didn't see why they had to say hello anymore. She had no friends of her own but followed her sister everywhere, although people and she herself probably thought I was her friend. I also followed her sister about, who was fairly normal. She was almost two years older and read more than anyone else.

5      I hated the younger sister, the quiet one. I hated her when she was the last chosen for her team and I, the last chosen for my team. I hated her for her China doll hair cut. I hated her at music time for the wheezes that came out of her plastic flute.

One afternoon in the sixth grade (that year I was arrogant with talk, not knowing there were going to be high school dances and college seminars to set me back), I and my little sister and the quiet girl and her big sister stayed late after school for some reason. The cement was cooling, and the tetherball poles made shadows across the gravel. The hooks at the rope ends were clinking against the poles. We shouldn't have been so late; there was laundry work to do and Chinese school to get to by 5:00. The last time we had stayed late, my mother had phoned the police and told them we had been kidnapped by bandits. The radio stations broadcast our descriptions. I had to get home before she did that again. But sometimes if you loitered long enough in the schoolyard, the other children would have gone home and you could play with the equipment before the office took it away. We were chasing one another through the playground and in and out of the basement, where the playroom and lavatory were. During air raid drills (it was during the Korean War, which you knew about because every day the front page of the newspaper printed a map of Korea with the top part red and going up and down like a window shade), we curled up in this basement. Now everyone was gone. The playroom was army green and had nothing in it but a long trough with drinking spigots in rows. Pipes across the ceiling led to the drinking fountains and to the toilets in the next room. When someone flushed you could hear the water and other matter, which the children named, running inside the big pipe above the drinking spigots. There was one playroom for girls next to the girls' lavatory and one playroom for boys next to the boys' lavatory. The stalls were open and the toilets had no lids, by which we knew that ghosts have no sense of shame or privacy.

Inside the playroom the lightbulbs in cages had already been turned off. Daylight came in x-patterns through the caging at the windows. I looked out and, seeing no one in the schoolyard, ran outside to climb the fire escape upside down, hanging on to the metal stairs with fingers and toes.

I did a flip off the fire escape and ran across the schoolyard. The day was a great eye, and it was not paying much attention to me now. I could disappear with the sun; I could turn quickly sideways and slip into a different world. It seemed I could run faster at this time, and by evening I would be able to fly. As the afternoon wore on we could run into the forbidden places—the boys' big yard, the boys' playroom. We could go into the boys' lavatory and look at the urinals. The only time during school hours I had crossed the boys' yard was when a flatbed truck with a giant thing covered with canvas and tied down with ropes had parked across the street. The children had told one another that it was a gorilla in captivity; we couldn't decide whether the sign said "Trail of the Gorilla" or "Trial of the Gorilla." The thing was as big as a house. The teachers couldn't stop us from hysterically rushing to the fence and clinging to the wire mesh. Now I ran across the boys' yard clear to the Cyclone fence and thought about the hair that I had seen sticking out of the canvas. It was going to be summer soon, so you could feel that freedom coming on too.

I ran back into the girls' yard, and there was the quiet sister all by herself. I ran past her, and she followed me into the girls' lavatory. My footsteps rang hard against cement and tile because of the taps I had nailed into my shoes. Her footsteps were soft, padding after me. There was no one in the lavatory but the two of us. I ran all around the rows of twenty-five open stalls to make sure of that. No sisters. I think we must have been playing hide-and-go-seek. She was not good at hiding by herself and usually followed her sister; they'd hide in the same place. They must have gotten separated. In this growing twilight, a child could hide and never be found.

I stopped abruptly in front of the sinks, and she came running toward me 10 before she could stop herself, so that she almost collided with me. I walked closer. She backed away, puzzlement, then alarm in her eyes.

"You're going to talk," I said, my voice steady and normal, as it is talking to the familiar, the weak, and the small. "I am going to make you talk, you sissy-girl." She stopped backing away and stood fixed.

I looked into her face so I could hate it close up. She wore black bangs, and her cheeks were pink and white. She was baby soft. I thought that I could put my thumb on her nose and push it bonelessly in, indent her face. I could poke dimples into her cheeks. I could work her face around like dough. She stood still, and I did not want to look at her face anymore; I hated fragility. I walked around her, looked her up and down the way the Mexican and Negro girls did when they fought, so tough. I hated her weak neck, the way it did not support her head but let it droop; her head would fall backward. I stared at the curve of her nape. I wished I was able to see what my own neck looked like from the back and sides. I hoped it did not look like hers; I wanted a stout neck. I grew my hair long to hide it in case it was a flower-stem neck. I walked around to the front of her to hate her face some more.

I reached up and took the fatty part of her cheek, not dough, but meat, between my thumb and finger. This close, and I saw no pores. "Talk," I said. "Are you going to talk?" Her skin was fleshy, like squid out of which the glassy blades of bones had been pulled. I wanted tough skin, hard brown skin. I had callused my hands; I had scratched dirt to blacken the nails, which I cut straight across to make stubby fingers. I gave her face a squeeze. "Talk." When I let go, the pink rushed back into my white thumbprint on her skin. I walked around to her side. "Talk!" I shouted into the side of her head. Her straight hair hung, the same all these years, no ringlets or braids or permanents. I squeezed her other cheek. "Are you? Huh? Are you going to talk?" She tried to shake her head, but I had hold of her face. She had no muscles to jerk away. Her skin seemed to stretch. I let go in horror. What if it came away in my hand? "No, huh?" I said, rubbing the touch of her off my fingers. "Say 'No,' then," I said. I gave her another pinch and a twist. "Say 'No.'" She shook her head, her straight hair turning with her head, not swinging side to side like the pretty girls'. She was so neat. Her neatness bothered me. I hated the way she folded the wax paper from her lunch; she did not wad her brown paper bag and her school papers. I hated her clothes—the blue pastel cardigan, the white blouse with the collar that lay flat over the cardigan, the homemade flat, cotton skirt she wore when everybody else was wearing flared skirts. I hated pastels; I would wear black always. I squeezed again, harder, even though her cheek had a weak rubbery feeling I did not like. I squeezed one cheek, then the other, back and forth until the tears ran out of her eyes as if I had pulled them out. "Stop crying," I said, but although she habitually followed me around, she did not obey. Her eyes dripped; her nose dripped. She wiped her eyes with her papery fingers. The skin on her hands and arms seemed powdery-dry, like tracing paper, onion skin. I hated her fingers. I could snap them like breadsticks. I pushed her hands down. "Say 'Hi,'" I said. "'Hi.' Like that. Say your name. Go ahead. Say it. Or are you stupid? You're so stupid, you don't know your own name, is that it? When I say, 'What's your name?' you just blurt it out, o.k.? What's your name?" Last year the whole class had laughed at a boy who couldn't fill out a form because he didn't know his father's name. The teacher sighed, exasperated, and was very sarcastic, "Don't you notice things? What does your mother call him?" she said. The class laughed at how dumb he was not to notice things. "She calls him father of me," he said. Even we laughed, although we knew that his mother did not call his father by name, and a son does not know his father's name. We laughed and were relieved that our parents had had the foresight to tell us some names we could give the teachers. "If you're not stupid," I said to the quiet girl, "what's your name?" She shook her head, and some hair caught in the tears; wet black hair stuck to the side of the pink and white face. I reached up (she was taller than I) and took a strand of hair. I pulled it. "Well, then, let's honk your hair," I said. "Honk. Honk." Then I pulled the other side—"ho-o-n-nk"— a long pull; "ho-o-n-n-nk"—a longer pull. I could see her little white ears, like white cutworms curled underneath the hair. "Talk!" I yelled into each cutworm.

I looked right at her. "I know you talk," I said. "I've heard you." Her eyebrows flew up. Something in those black eyes was startled, and I pursued it. "I was walking past your house when you didn't know I was there. I heard you yell in English and in Chinese. You weren't just talking. You were shouting. I heard you shout. You were saying, 'Where are you?' Say that again. Go ahead, just the way you did at home." I yanked harder on the hair, but steadily, not jerking. I did not want to pull it out. "Go ahead. Say, 'Where are you?' Say it loud enough for your sister to come. Call her. Make her come help you. Call her name. I'll stop if she comes. So call. Go ahead."

She shook her head, her mouth curved down, crying. I could see her tiny white teeth, baby teeth. I wanted to grow big strong yellow teeth. "You do have a tongue," I said. "So use it." I pulled the hair at her temples, pulled the tears out of her eyes. "Say, 'Ow,'" I said. "Just 'Ow.' Say, 'Let go.' Go ahead. Say it. I'll honk you again if you don't say, 'Let me alone.' Say, 'Leave me alone,' and I'll let you go. I will. I'll let go if you say it. You can stop this anytime you want to, you know. All you have to do is tell me to stop. Just say, 'Stop.' You're just asking for it, aren't you? You're just asking for another honk. Well then, I'll have to give you another honk. Say, 'Stop.'" But she didn't. I had to pull again and again.

Sounds did come out of her mouth, sobs, chokes, noises that were almost words. Snot ran out of her nose. She tried to wipe it on her hands, but there was too much of it. She used her sleeve. "You're disgusting," I told her. "Look at you, snot streaming down your nose, and you won't say a word to stop it. You're such a nothing." I moved behind her and pulled the hair growing out of her weak neck. I let go. I stood silent for a long time. Then I screamed, "Talk!" I would scare the words out of her. If she had had little bound feet,° the toes

15

---

bound feet: A traditional practice in China; Young girls were forced to have their feet tightly bound in order to keep them small. Prevented from growing normally, the feet became severely deformed and caused the women great pain.

twisted under the balls, I would have jumped up and landed on them—crunch!—stomped on them with my iron shoes. She cried hard, sobbing aloud. "Cry, 'Mama,'" I said. "Come on. Cry, 'Mama.' Say, 'Stop it.'"

I put my finger on her pointed chin. "I don't like you. I don't like the weak little toots you make on your flute. Wheeze. Wheeze. I don't like the way you don't swing at the ball. I don't like the way you're the last one chosen. I don't like the way you can't make a fist for tetherball. Why don't you make a fist? Come on. Get tough. Come on. Throw fists." I pushed at her long hands; they swung limply at her sides. Her fingers were so long, I thought maybe they had an extra joint. They couldn't possibly make fists like other people's. "Make a fist," I said. "Come on. Just fold those fingers up; fingers on the inside, thumbs on the outside. Say something. Honk me back. You're so tall, and you let me pick on you.

"Would you like a hanky? I can't get you one with embroidery on it or crocheting along the edges, but I'll get you some toilet paper if you tell me to. Go ahead. Ask me. I'll get it for you if you ask." She did not stop crying. "Why don't you scream, 'Help'?" I suggested. "Say, 'Help.' Go ahead." She cried on. "O.K. O.K. Don't talk. Just scream, and I'll let you go. Won't that feel good? Go ahead. Like this." I screamed, not too loudly. My voice hit the tile and rang it as if I had thrown a rock at it. The stalls opened wider and the toilets wider and darker. Shadows leaned at angles I had not seen before. It was very late. Maybe a janitor had locked me in with this girl for the night. Her black eyes blinked and stared, blinked and stared. I felt dizzy from hunger. We had been in this lavatory together forever. My mother would call the police again if I didn't bring my sister home soon. "I'll let you go if you say just one word," I said. "You can even say, 'a' or 'the,' and I'll let you go. Come on. Please." She didn't shake her head anymore, only cried steadily, so much water coming out of her. I could see the two duct holes where the tears welled out. Quarts of tears but no words. I grabbed her by the shoulder. I could feel bones. The light was coming in queerly through the frosted glass with the chicken wire embedded in it. Her crying was like an animal's—a seal's—and it echoed around the basement. "Do you want to stay here all night?" I asked. "Your mother is wondering what happened to her baby. You wouldn't want to have her mad at you. You'd better say something." I shook her shoulder. I pulled her hair again. I squeezed her face. "Come on! Talk! Talk! Talk!" She didn't seem to feel it anymore when I pulled her hair. "There's nobody here but you and me. This isn't a classroom or a playground or a crowd. I'm just one person. You can talk in front of one person. Don't make me pull harder and harder until you talk." But her hair seemed to stretch; she did not say a word. "I'm going to pull harder. Don't make me pull anymore, or your hair will come out and you're going to be bald. Do you want to be bald? You don't want to be bald, do you?"

Far away, coming from the edge of town, I heard whistles blow. The cannery was changing shifts, letting out the afternoon people, and still we were here at school. It was a sad sound—work done. The air was lonelier after the sound died.

"Why won't you talk?" I started to cry. What if I couldn't stop, and everyone would want to know what happened? "Now look what you've done," I scolded. "You're going to pay for this. I want to know why. And you're going to tell me why. You don't see I'm trying to help you out, do you? Do you want to be like this, dumb (do you know what dumb means?), your whole life? Don't you ever want to be a cheerleader? Or a pompon girl? What are you going to do for a living? Yeah, you're going to have to work because you can't be a housewife. Somebody has to marry you before you can be a housewife. And you, you are a plant. Do you know that? That's all you are if you don't talk. If you don't talk, you can't have a personality. You'll have no personality and no hair. You've got to let people know you have a personality and a brain. You think somebody is going to take care of you all your stupid life? You think you'll always have your big sister? You think somebody's going to marry you, is that it? Well, you're not the type that gets dates, let alone gets married. Nobody's going to notice you. And you have to talk for interviews, speak right up in front of the boss. Don't you know that? You're so dumb. Why do I waste my time on you?" Sniffling and snorting, I couldn't stop crying and talking at the same time. I kept wiping my nose on my arm, my sweater lost somewhere (probably not worn because my mother said to wear a sweater). It seemed as if I had spent my life in that basement, doing the worst thing I had yet done to another person. "I'm doing this for your own good," I said. "Don't you dare tell anyone I've been bad to you. Talk. Please talk."

I was getting dizzy from the air I was gulping. Her sobs and my sobs were bouncing wildly off the tile, sometimes together, sometimes alternating. "I don't understand why you won't say just one word," I cried, clenching my teeth. My knees were shaking, and I hung on to her hair to stand up. Another time I'd stayed too late, I had had to walk around two Negro kids who were bonking each other's head on the concrete. I went back later to see if the concrete had cracks in it. "Look. I'll give you something if you talk. I'll give you my pencil box. I'll buy you some candy. O.K.? What do you want? Tell me. Just say it, and I'll give it to you. Just say, 'yes,' or, 'O.K.,' or, 'Baby Ruth.'" But she didn't want anything.

I had stopped pinching her cheek because I did not like the feel of her skin. I would go crazy if it came away in my hands. "I skinned her," I would have to confess.

Suddenly I heard footsteps hurrying through the basement, and her sister ran into the lavatory calling her name. "Oh, there you are," I said. "We've been waiting for you. I was only trying to teach her to talk. She wouldn't cooperate, though." Her sister went into one of the stalls and got handfuls of toilet paper and wiped her off. Then we found my sister, and we walked home together.

"Your family really ought to force her to speak," I advised all the way home. "You mustn't pamper her."

The world is sometimes just, and I spent the next eighteen months sick in bed with a mysterious illness. There was no pain and no symptoms, though the middle line in my left palm broke in two. Instead of starting junior high school, I lived like the Victorian recluses° I read about. I had a rented hospital bed in the living room, where I watched soap operas on t.v., and my family cranked me up and down. I saw no one but my family, who took good care of me. I could have no visitors, no other relatives, no villagers. My bed was against the west window, and I watched the seasons change the peach tree. I had a bell to ring for help. I used a bedpan. It was the best year and a half of my life. Nothing happened.

25    But one day my mother, the doctor, said, "You're ready to get up today. It's time to get up and go to school." I walked about outside to get my legs working, leaning on a staff I cut from the peach tree. The sky and trees, the sun were immense—no longer framed by a window, no longer grayed with a fly screen. I sat down on the sidewalk in amazement—the night, the stars. But at school I had to figure out again how to talk. I met again the poor girl I had tormented. She had not changed. She wore the same clothes, hair cut, and manner as when we were in elementary school, no make-up on the pink and white face, while the other Asian girls were starting to tape their eyelids.° She continued to be able to read aloud. But there was hardly any reading aloud anymore, less and less as we got into high school.

I was wrong about nobody taking care of her. Her sister became a clerk-typist and stayed unmarried. They lived with their mother and father. She did not have to leave the house except to go to the movies. She was supported. She was protected by her family, as they would normally have done in China if they could have afforded it, not sent off to school with strangers, ghosts, boys.

## QUESTIONS

1. Make a list of all the characteristics (both physical and psychological) of the quiet girl that you can glean from the story. Then make a similar list of the narrator's characteristics.
2. Point out some examples of striking imagery and creative comparisons that you find effective in the story.

---

*recluses:* People who withdraw from society and live solitary lives.    *"Asian girls were starting to tape their eyelids":* To conform to Caucasian standards of beauty, some Asian women undergo operations to change the shape of their eyelids so that their eyes will look more round.

3. The narrator claims she hates the quiet girl. Do you believe her? Or might she actually hate someone or something else? Explain your response.

4. What reasons does the author give for torturing the quiet girl? Why do you think she does it?

5. Why is the narrator so adamant about making the quiet girl talk?

6. Is the setting of this story (at school, and mostly in the lavatory) significant? Does it add something to the meaning of the story? Would the story have been different if it were set in the Chinese school, or in one of the girls' homes?

7. Who are the "ghosts" that the narrator mentions?

8. Reread the description of the narrator's illness. Then explain why you think she claims, "It was the best year and a half of my life."

## CONNECTIONS

1. In what ways are the narrator of this selection and the narrator of "Eleven" similar?

2. "The Quiet Girl" is part of a memoir. In her essay "Memory and Imagination," Patricia Hampl offers various reasons why we should all write memoirs; does "The Quiet Girl" support Hampl's statements?

# Choosing a Topic and Prewriting:
# We Will Write No Draft Before Its Time

• • • • • • • • • • • • • • • • • • • • • • • • • •

Most of the essays that you write as a college student will be responses to assignments for various courses. Some assignments will be quite specific (for example, "discuss the circumstances that led to the Civil War"); however, instructors (especially English instructors) often ask open-ended questions, setting up some general topic parameters within which students can choose their own focus. Such assignments might ask you to evaluate the typical diet of a particular cultural group, to analyze a character from a novel you've read, or to compare and contrast two processes.

## Choosing a Topic

To write an effective essay, you need first to be excited about the project: You need to choose a topic that interests you, that perhaps you know something about or are curious to learn more about. While you should always consider the needs and expectations of your readers, keep in mind that an attempt to write about something that interests them but not you is likely to fail.

Once you've selected a general topic that interests you, the next step is to narrow it down so that you can really do it justice within the length limitations you have. If you choose an overly broad subject, you might discuss various parts of it and still find, many pages later, that other parts are left unaddressed (or else that you've been skimming the surface, without going into any real depth). In contrast, by focusing on a narrower topic, you give yourself room to explore it thoroughly, providing reasons and evidence to support your view and examples and details to grab your reader's attention.

For example, instead of choosing the impact of the automobile on U.S. society as your topic, you might want to write on the impact of cars on U.S. teenagers in particular—or on the role that cars play in the life of *one* U.S. citizen: you. Or instead of writing an essay about religion in general, you could focus on a particular denomination, or, zooming in even closer, on the stand that that particular denomination takes on a specific societal issue.

Think of a topic as an onion with many layers: Depending on the amount of time and the number of pages you can dedicate to its exploration, you need to choose one particular layer on which to focus your essay.

## Prewriting: Getting Started

To sit down with a piece of paper or a computer keyboard and expect to produce a complete essay, from introduction to conclusion, in one smooth line, is to set yourself up for a fall. That process works for very few people (or, for most of us, it works only when we're writing about something that we've thought about for so long that the essay needs only to be "transcribed" from the brain, not really created on the spot). For most people, this sort of an attempt will lead to writer's block, either before any ideas find their way to the paper or else after a couple of paragraphs.

So relax. Don't *do* the essay. Instead, try to think of writing as a process: The first step in that process is prewriting. Prewriting is a shaking up of the brain, an attempt to find responses that aren't on the surface. Prewriting happens once you've decided on a topic to write about: At that point, you need to jot down everything that you might have to say about the topic. The key here is to go for *quantity,* writing down anything that comes to you as you let your mind explore the subject. Write until you know you have too much material —until you feel satisfied that everything you think about the topic is mentioned in the notes in front of you, in words or symbols, anything you'd still be able to understand a day or two later. Nobody would expect all of your prewriting to find its way into the final draft of the essay; once you have a page (or pages) of notes, you can cut out anything that seems too tangential or otherwise ineffective. Then, you should reorder the material that you decide to keep, until you feel that you have the skeleton of a draft—its bones the ideas, joined together by transitions, so that, fleshed out, they'll become a lively whole.

The following are some of the techniques that writers use in prewriting.

*Freewriting*   Many people see brainstorming as a group activity: people sitting together and throwing out ideas related to a topic, playing off one another's comments. That's a good way to gather raw material for an essay; however, you won't always have the luxury of people off whom to bounce your ideas. You can brainstorm by yourself, though, by simply freewriting about your topic, trying to follow whatever leaps and connections your brain makes, without worrying about the order in which they come or about your grammar and spelling. At this point, you simply want to generate lots of ideas that you can develop and rearrange later.

*Listing*   Following the same logic that makes you write down, before going to the market, all the items you need to buy, this process entails listing all the ideas and associations you can think of that relate to your chosen topic. Listing is quick because you don't have to write more than one or two words per idea. This process will help you pin down the snippets of thought that tend to flash by and disappear as you are considering your topic. Be careful, though, to write down enough to ensure that, a day or two later, you'll still know what you meant by each entry in the list.

*Clustering*    To cluster, you need to pin down your topic in one word or brief phrase. Then, write down the word or phrase and draw a circle around it. As you think of ideas related to the topic, draw "rays" from the circle, each one ending with a new circle drawn around the associated idea. You can then draw new rays from those new circles as you add further associations and clarifying details. Here's an example of a cluster:

What a Word Can Mean

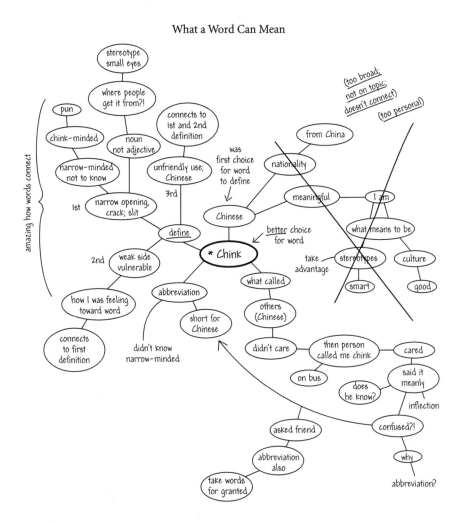

Clustering can have two advantages over brainstorming: First, because it's fragmented by design, clustering might prevent you from getting too involved (at this stage) in the shaping of sentences—keeping you focused on the search for content, ideas and descriptive details. Listing does the same thing, but the second advantage of clustering is that it might suggest a way to organize the information later: The items you have placed around the cluster's nucleus may become the main points of various paragraphs, and the items in the circles around those can flesh out the paragraphs. Of course, you may find that a topic in which you are more interested appears in one of the circles derived from the central one. In that event, that circle can become the center of a new cluster.

## Final Words

By the time they reach college, many students—even those who hate writing—have developed certain habits, certain rituals around the act of writing. Do you have some of these? Do you need a certain environment to write in or a certain instrument to write with? Do you always drink coffee or listen to music as you write?

Since you are now in a writing class, you are learning to stretch your writing abilities beyond their current limitations. To do so, you need to be willing to try new things. If you've never read an essay to try to understand how the writer achieved a particular effect, do it now. (This text will discuss various ways of achieving certain effects through the use of details, the repetition of key words, and other writing techniques.) If you've never used any form of prewriting, try one—or all—in the course of this term. Don't give up if the process doesn't make you an essay wizard right away—people are usually awkward when they first try something different. But if any of these new techniques and realizations makes writing easier and more fun for you, the effects will ripple throughout your education, during which you will write a lot, and also throughout the career you will enter after graduation.

Our modern society relies less and less on direct contact and more and more on the written word. In today's economy, most of us are destined to communicate our intentions to coworkers through memos, describe our products to our customers through users' manuals, and keep in touch with friends and relatives through e-mail and the Internet. Some people will know you only through your writing; you might as well improve it now.

---

**Prewriting:** gathering ideas in writing before drafting an essay.

- Freewriting
- Listing
- Clustering

## Topics for Writing about Growing Up

. . . . . . . . . . . . . . . . . . . . . . . . . .

1. Write an essay describing a childhood experience; try to make it sound (as Sandra Cisneros does) as if a child were narrating the story.

2. Write an essay responding, politely and seriously, to Michael Buenaflor's charges against teenagers.

3. Write an essay defining the word "teenager" for someone who has no idea what the term means.

4. Write an essay describing a place that you either loved or hated when you were a child. Without telling your audience outright, let your description show whether you loved or hated that place.

5. Write a history of your writing, from your first attempts at shaping the letters of the alphabet to the present. Try to remember and include in the essay specific writing-related incidents that happened along the way.

6. Find a sample of your early writing (from kindergarten to about sixth grade). Then analyze it from Gabriele Rico's perspective, writing an essay that explains what stage of creative development you were in at the time you wrote the sample. To support your thesis, quote specific uses of language from your early writing.

7. Write an essay explaining why you would (or wouldn't) want to be a child again.

8. Write a new version of the poem "Those Winter Sundays," this time from the father's point of view.

9. Write an essay explaining what you see as the main problem(s) of education in the United States today, and suggesting possible solutions.

10. Write an essay illustrating the ideas expressed by Paolo Freire: Create a few "problem-posing" practices, then describe how they might function in a classroom and what their goals would be.

11. Interview some young children about what they think of school, and present your findings in an essay. For this, you have to be very careful when phrasing your questions so that you don't unwittingly encourage the children to give any particular answer; ask questions that cannot be answered simply "yes" or "no" but that demand a more developed response.

12. Talk to an elderly person about his or her childhood and write an essay comparing and contrasting that childhood with your own.

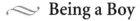 

## ∼ Being a Boy

*Julius Lester*

Julius Lester was born in 1939 in St. Louis into a religious family; his father was a minister. After graduating from Fisk University in Nashville, Lester worked as a folksinger, a radio talk show host, a teacher, and a writer. Lester has been a professor of African American studies and Near Eastern and Judaic studies at the University of Massachusetts since 1971. He has written several books and essays, including *The Long Journey Home: Stories from Black History* (1972), *Do Lord Remember Me* (1984), and *Lovesong: Becoming a Jew* (1988). The following essay was first published in *Ms.* magazine in 1973.

**WARM-UP:** Make a list of advice you've been given about how to "be a man" or "be a woman."

As boys go, I wasn't much. I mean, I tried to be a boy and spent many child- 1
hood hours pummeling° my hardly formed ego with failure at cowboys and Indians, baseball, football, lying, and sneaking out of the house. When our neighborhood gang raided a neighbor's pear tree, I was the only one who got sick from the purloined° fruit. I also failed at setting fire to our garage, an art at which any five-year-boy should be adept. I was, however, the neighborhood champion at getting beat up. "That Julius can take it, man," the boys used to say, almost in admiration, after I emerged from another battle, tears brimming in my eyes but refusing to fall.

My efforts at being a boy earned me a pair of scarred knees that are a record of a childhood spent falling from bicycles, trees, the tops of fences, and porch steps; of tripping as I ran (generally from a fight), walked, or simply tried to remain upright on windy days.

I tried to believe my parents when they told me I was a boy, but I could find no objective proof for such an assertion. Each morning during the summer, as I cuddled up in the quiet of a corner with a book, my mother would push me out the back door and into the yard. And throughout the day as my blood was let as if I were a patient of 17th-century medicine, I thought of the

---

*pummeling:* Pounding, beating.   *purloined:* Stolen.

girls sitting in the shade of porches, playing with their dolls, toy refrigerators and stoves.

There was the life, I thought! No constant pressure to prove oneself. No necessity always to be competing. While I humiliated myself on football and baseball fields, the girls stood on the sidelines laughing at me, because they didn't have to do anything except be girls. The rising of each sun brought me to the starting line of yet another day's Olympic decathlon, with no hope of ever winning even a bronze medal.

5    Through no fault of my own I reached adolescence. While the pressure to prove myself on the athletic field lessened, the overall situation got worse— because now I had to prove myself with girls. Just how I was supposed to go about doing this was beyond me, especially because, at the age of 14, I was four foot nine and weighed 78 pounds. (I think there may have been one 10-year-girl in the neighborhood smaller than I.) Nonetheless, duty called, and with my ninth-grade gym-class jockstrap flapping between my legs, off I went.

To get a girlfriend, though, a boy had to have some asset beyond the fact that he was alive. I wasn't handsome like Bill McCord, who had girls after him like a cop-killer has policemen. I wasn't ugly like Romeo Jones, but at least the girls noticed him: "That ol' ugly boy better stay 'way from me!" I was just there, like a vase your grandmother gives you at Christmas that you don't like or dislike, can't get rid of, and don't know what to do with. More than ever I wished I were a girl. Boys were the ones who had to take the initiative and all the responsibility. (I hate responsibility so much that if my heart didn't beat of itself, I would now be a dim memory.)

It was the boy who had to ask the girl for a date, a frightening enough prospect until it occurred to me that she might say no! That meant risking my ego, which was about as substantial as a toilet-paper raincoat in the African rainy season. But I had to thrust that ego forward to be judged, accepted, or rejected by some girl. It wasn't fair! Who was she to sit back like a queen with the power to create joy by her consent or destruction by her denial? It wasn't fair—but that's the way it was.

But if (God forbid!) she should say Yes, then my problem would begin in earnest, because I was the one who said where we would go (and waited in terror for her approval of my choice). I was the one who picked her up at her house where I was inspected by her parents as if I were a possible carrier of syphilis (which I didn't think one could get from masturbating, but then again, Jesus was born of a virgin, so what did I know?). Once we were on our way, it was I who had to pay the bus fare, the price of the movie tickets, and whatever she decided to stuff her stomach with afterward. (And the smallest girls are all stomach.) Finally, the girl was taken home where once again I was inspected (the father looking covertly at my fly and the mother examining the girl's hair). The evening was over and the girl had done nothing except honor me with her presence. All the work had been mine.

Imagining this procedure over and over was more than enough: I was a sophomore in college before I had my first date.

I wasn't a total failure in high school, though, for occasionally I would go to a party, determined to salvage my self-esteem. The parties usually took place in somebody's darkened basement. There was generally a surreptitious° wine bottle or two being passed furtively° among the boys, and a record player with an insatiable° appetite for Johnny Mathis records. Boys gathered on one side of the room and girls on the other. There were always a few boys and girls who'd come to the party for the sole purpose of grinding away their sexual frustrations to Johnny Mathis's falsetto,° and they would begin dancing to their own music before the record player was plugged in. It took a little longer for others to get started, but no one matched my talent for standing by the punch bowl. For hours, I would try to make my legs do what they had been doing without effort since I was nine months old, but for some reason they would show all the symptoms of paralysis on those evenings.

After several hours of wondering whether I was going to die ("Julius Lester, a sixteen-year-old, died at a party last night, a half-eaten Ritz cracker in one hand and a potato chip dipped in pimiento-cheese spread in the other. Cause of death: failure to be a boy"), I would push my way to the other side of the room where the girls sat like a hanging jury. I would pass by the girl I wanted to dance with. If I was going to be refused, let it be by someone I didn't particularly like. Unfortunately, there weren't many in that category. I had more crushes than I had pimples.

Finally, through what surely could only have been the direct intervention of the Almighty, I would find myself on the dance floor with a girl. And none of my prior agony could compare to the thought of actually dancing. But there I was and I had to dance with her. Social custom decreed° that I was supposed to lead, because I was the boy. Why? I'd wonder. Let her lead. Girls were better dancers anyway. It didn't matter. She stood there waiting for me to take charge. She wouldn't have been worse off if she'd waited for me to turn white.

But, reciting "Invictus" to myself, I placed my arms around her, being careful to keep my armpits closed because, somehow, I had managed to overwhelm a half jar of deodorant and a good-size bottle of cologne. With sweaty

*surreptitious:* Secret, clandestine.   *furtively:* Secretively.   *insatiable:* Incapable of being satisfied.
*falsetto:* An artificially high voice.   *decreed:* Dictated, commanded.

. . . . . . . . . . . . . . . . . . . . . . . . . . . . . . . . . . . . . . . .

armpits, "Invictus," and legs afflicted again with polio, I took her in my arms, careful not to hold her so far away that she would think I didn't like her, but equally careful not to hold her so close that she could feel the catastrophe which had befallen me the instant I touched her hand. My penis, totally disobeying the lecture I'd given it before we left home, was as rigid as Governor Wallace's jaw would be if I asked for his daughter's hand in marriage.

God, how I envied girls at that moment. Wherever *it* was on them, it didn't dangle between their legs like an elephant's trunk. No wonder boys talked about nothing but sex. That thing was always there. Every time we went to the john, there *it* was, twitching around like a fat little worm on a fishing hook. When we took baths, it floated in the water like a lazy fish and God forbid we should touch it! It sprang to life like lightning leaping from a cloud. I wished I could cut it off, or at least keep it tucked between my legs, as if it were a tail that had been mistakenly attached to the wrong end. But I was helpless. It was there, with a life and mind of its own, living no other function than to embarrass me.

15      Fortunately, the girls I danced with were discreet and pretended that they felt nothing unusual rubbing against them as we danced. But I was always convinced that the next day they were all calling up their friends to exclaim: "Guess what, girl? Julius Lester got one! I ain't lyin'!"

Now, of course, I know that it was as difficult being a girl as it was a boy, if not more so. While I stood paralyzed at one end of a dance floor trying to find the courage to ask a girl for a dance, most of the girls waited in terror at the other, afraid that no one, not even I, would ask them. And while I resented having to ask a girl for a date, wasn't it also horrible to be the one who waited for the phone to ring? And how many of those girls who laughed at me making a fool of myself on the baseball diamond would have gladly given up their places on the sidelines for mine on the field?

No, it wasn't easy for any of us, girls and boys, as we forced our beautiful, free-flowing child-selves into those narrow, constricting cubicles labeled *female* and *male*. I tried, but I wasn't good at being a boy. Now, I'm glad, knowing that a man is nothing but the figment° of a penis's imagination, and any man should want to be something more than that.

### QUESTIONS

1. Do you agree with Lester's experience? Is it difficult to be a boy?
2. As Lester describes it, who appears to hold more power in dating— males or females? Who do you believe holds the power?

*figment:* Something made up or contrived.

3. What evidence does Lester provide to support his claim that he was "a failure" as a boy?

4. Identify uses of transitional words or sentences throughout the essay.

5. Lester admits that he sometimes envied girls. What were those times? Why did he envy girls?

6. Identify places where Lester uses humor to emphasize an idea. Is his use of humor effective?

7. Summarize and explain in your own words the meaning of the final paragraph.

## CONNECTIONS

1. Compare and contrast the speaker in this essay with the narrator of "The Quiet Girl."

2. Patricia Hampl wrote that "metaphor is a risky business, revealing of the self." Identify several similes and metaphors in Lester's essay. What do these reveal about the author?

# Entering the Gender Arena

# Details: The Life of Language

. . . . . . . . . . . . . . . . . . . . . . . . . . .

I often play a game with my students; I call it "reducing levels of abstraction." I begin the game by telling my students, "I'm thinking of a specific type of food—what do you think it is?" They're puzzled, of course, but they begin guessing. One calls out, "pizza." Another, "potato chips." And another, "ice cream."

"Let me give you a hint," I say, intending to remain vague. "The type of food I'm thinking of has positive nutritional value." This moves them away from potato chips and ice cream. So now the students' guesses have some direction: "carrots," "oatmeal," "yogurt," "fruit." "Yes," I say, "it's a fruit—but which one?" Now the responses are quick, as we have moved from a very abstract level ("food") to a level still abstract but a little more defined ("food of positive nutritional value") to a specific category ("fruit").

Soon, someone calls out "apple." "Yes," I say, "that's it, almost—but what kind?" "Rome," one pipes. "Macintosh," yells another. "Nice tries," I say, "but this apple is green." Now, several call out "Granny Smith!"

Although I call this exercise a game, it would be more accurate to call it a demonstration with two purposes. One purpose is to show students how to narrow down a topic that was initially vague to a level of specificity that will make for a more effective essay. A second purpose is to help them realize that meaning is better communicated by detailed, specific language than by abstract generalizations. An abstraction or an abstract word can be difficult to understand, impersonal, and detached. The word "food," for example, is abstract not because it is difficult to understand but because it is somewhat detached from human experience: You don't eat "food"; you eat peanut butter and jelly sandwiches, red beans and rice, lemon grass chicken, chocolate chip cookies, bagels, oranges. If someone said to you, "I want some food," you would know that the person did not want either a bicycle or a tonsillectomy, but you wouldn't know precisely what the person wanted to eat.

Details are especially important in written communication, when we can't rely on voice inflection or body language—facial expressions, for example, and hand gestures—to convey meaning. The more detailed a piece of writing is, the more likely that readers will understand the exact shades of its meaning.

To help you realize the importance of detailed language, take a look at a recipe in a cookbook. You are not likely to find a recipe for chicken soup, for example, that reads "Throw a chicken and some other stuff into a pot and cook until ready." Rather, you will find the name and exact quantity of every ingredient, the exact length of the cooking time, the temperature required, and so forth.

For another example of the use of details, consider Patricia Hampl's description of Sister Olive Marie in the essay "Memory and Imagination." Hampl could have just written "Sister Olive was overweight." Instead, Hampl conveys parts of Sister Olive Marie's appearance precisely: "Her oily face gleamed. . . . She was a small, plump woman." By adding these details, Hampl helps you become not just a reader of words but a person sharing a common experience with another: in this case, the experience of observing the nun.

Detailed language has that power—the power of clarity, the power to move you. It has that power because it generally appeals to the senses—to sight, smell, hearing, taste, touch. Hampl, for instance, appeals to the senses of sight and touch with the words "oily," "small," and "plump." But let's look at several more examples. In "Eleven," Sandra Cisneros appeals to the senses of sight and smell when describing a sweater (and by using details, clarifies what she means by the abstract word "ugly"): "It's an ugly sweater with red plastic buttons and a collar and sleeves stretched out"; it "smells like cottage cheese." In the introduction to "The Enchanted Bluff," Willa Cather's description of the setting also includes appeals to the senses of sight, touch, and smell: "The translucent red ball itself sank behind the brown stretches of corn field as we sat down to eat, and the warm layer of air that had rested over the water and our clean sand-bar grew fresher and smelled of the rank ironweed and sunflowers growing on the flatter shore." In "The Quiet Girl," many of Maxine Hong Kingston's descriptions appeal to senses, as when she says that a girl's cheeks "had a weak rubbery feeling."

Student writer Megan Dietz included the following paragraph in an essay entitled "Tomboy," her response to Julius Lester's piece "Being a Boy" (which introduces this section):

> As newborns, baby girls are bundled in pink blankets and flower-patterned sleepers. As soon as we have enough hair to form a curl, a rose-colored plastic barrette is tenderly attached so people will know at first glance and correctly guess at our questionable gender. All too soon, we mature from infants to toddlers, and many a female child falls victim to frilly pink dresses and colorful ribbons tied in her curls. We become show pieces for our parents and are expected to smile sweetly and shyly at the admiration from their friends.

Like the professional authors previously quoted, Dietz offers details that illustrate and support the main point she wants to make in her essay.

Now, try your hand at using detailed language. Look at your shoes; then write down five details about them. Next time you are in a crowd, such as the one in your writing classroom, look around at other shoes in the room. If the five words describing your shoes also apply to many other shoes, then the details are not specific enough (or perhaps the other people in the room have similar taste in shoes). On the other foot, if the words describing your shoes describe only *your* shoes, you'll know that your description conveys meaning specifically.

If you've never thought about details before, make the search for them a conscious part of your reading and rewriting. When reading, notice what moves you about a piece of writing; it's likely to be the way an author uses details to make a description clear and powerful. Similarly, when you're drafting an essay, look for places where you could add some detail to emphasize the significance of an object or place and to make your ideas more accessible to your readers. After all, one of your main goals should be to make your writing not just acceptable but agreeable; the difference between these two should be as clear as that between a bicycle and a Granny Smith apple.

# The Woman's Rights Convention

## New York Herald *Editorial, September 12, 1852*

Following is an editorial response to the 1852 Seneca Falls convention, which is considered to be the starting point of the movement for women's suffrage in the United States. Organized by Lucretia Mott, Martha Wright, Mary Ann McClintock, and Elizabeth Cady Stanton (whose "Declaration of Sentiments," included in Section 6 of this text, was read at the convention), the gathering inspired the 1852 Woman's Rights Convention, which was attended by delegates from eight states and from Canada. The latter convention met "to discuss the social, civil and religious rights of women"; those who attended it worked to obtain equal rights for women. Susan B. Anthony was one of the convention's secretaries.

**WARM-UP:** Do you know people who don't believe that men and women should have equal rights? What reasons do they offer for their beliefs?

1    The farce at Syracuse has been played out. We publish to-day the last act, in which it will be seen that the authority of the Bible, as a perfect rule of faith and practice for human beings, was voted down, and what are called the laws of nature set up instead of the Christian code. We have also a practical exhibition of the consequences that flow from woman leaving her true sphere where she wields° all her influence, and coming into public to discuss questions of morals and politics with men. . . .

Who are these women? what do they want? what are the motives that impel° them to this course of action? The *dramatis personae*° of the farce enacted at Syracuse present a curious conglomeration° of both sexes. Some of them are old maids, whose personal charms were never very attractive, and who have been sadly slighted by the masculine gender in general; some of them women who have been badly mated, whose own temper, or their husbands', has made life anything but agreeable to them, and they are therefore down upon the whole of the opposite sex; some, having so much of the virago° in their disposition, that nature appears to have made a mistake in their gender—mannish women, like hens that crow; some of boundless vanity and egotism, who believe that they are superior in intellectual ability to

---

*wields:* Commands.   *impel:* Urge, force.   *dramatis personae:* The people involved in the drama or action.   *conglomeration:* Accumulation of elements of various kinds.   *virago:* A woman of great stature, strength, and courage; or a loud overbearing woman.

"all the world and the rest of mankind," and delight to see their speeches and addresses in print; and man shall be consigned° to his proper sphere—nursing the babies, washing the dishes, mending stockings, and sweeping the house. This is "the good time coming." Besides the classes we have enumerated,° there is a class of wild enthusiasts and visionaries—very sincere, but very mad—having the same vein as the fanatical Abolitionists, and the majority, if not all of them, being, in point of fact, deeply imbued with the anti-slavery sentiment. Of the male sex who attend these Conventions for the purpose of taking a part in them, the majority are hen-pecked husbands, and all of them ought to wear petticoats.

In point of ability, the majority of the women are flimsy, flippant, and superficial. Mrs. Rose alone indicates much argumentative power.

How did woman first become subject to man as she now is all over the world? By her nature, her sex, just as the negro is and always will be, to the end of time, inferior to the white race, and, therefore, doomed to subjection; but happier than she would be in any other condition, just because it is the law of her nature. The women themselves would not have this law reversed. It is a significant fact that even Mrs. Swisshelm, who formerly ran about to all such gatherings from her husband, is now "a keeper at home," and condemns these Conventions in her paper. How does this happen? Because, after weary years of unfruitfulness, she has at length got her rights in the shape of a baby. This is the best cure for the mania, and we would recommend a trial of it to all who are afflicted.

What do the leaders of the Woman's Rights Convention want? They want    5
to vote, and to hustle with the rowdies at the polls. They want to be members of Congress, and in the heat of debate to subject themselves to coarse jests and indecent language, like that of Rev. Mr. Hatch. They want to fill all other posts which men are ambitious to occupy—to be lawyers, doctors, captains of vessels, and generals in the field. How funny it would sound in the newspapers, that Lucy Stone, pleading a cause, took suddenly ill in the pains of parturition,° and perhaps gave birth to a fine bouncing boy in court! Or that Rev. Antoinette Brown was arrested in the middle of her sermon in the pulpit from the same cause, and presented a "pledge" to her husband and the congregation; or, that Dr. Harriot K. Hunt, while attending a gentleman patient for a fit of the gout or *fistula in ano°* found it necessary to send for a doctor, there and then, and to be delivered of a man or woman child—perhaps twins. A similar event might happen on the floor of Congress, in a storm at sea, or in the raging tempest of battle, and then what is to become of the woman legislator?

---

*consigned:* Given, transferred, or delivered.   *enumerated:* Listed.   *parturition:* The process of giving birth.   *fistula in ano:* Latin, meaning "anal ulcer".

**QUESTIONS**

1. How does this editorial characterize the women who attended the convention? How does it characterize the men who believe in equal rights for women? Does the author offer evidence for his claims regarding the convention's participants?
2. According to the author, what is "the best cure" for people who believe women should enjoy equal rights?
3. In pointing out what the women at the convention wanted, the author of the editorial indirectly suggests why they should not realize their goals. Since then, some of those goals *have* been met. How have the obstacles mentioned by the author been overcome?
4. Look up "feminism" in a dictionary; then explain what it means. Were the women who attended this convention feminists?
5. Why might some people who attended the convention be, according to the editorial, "deeply imbued with the anti-slavery sentiment"? What did the people at the convention and abolitionists have in common?
6. What is the author's tone in this editorial?

**CONNECTIONS**

In his essay, Julius Lester claims to envy girls for many reasons. How might the author of this editorial respond to that statement?

# ~ The Story of an Hour

## *Kate Chopin*

Kate O'Flaherty Chopin was born in St. Louis in 1851. In 1870, she married
Oscar Chopin, a Creole cotton broker and moved first to New Orleans, then
to a plantation elsewhere in Louisiana. After her husband died in 1882,
Chopin moved back to St. Louis with her six children. There she published
her first novel, *At Fault* (1890), when she was 40 years old; she also wrote
numerous short stories, including the selection reprinted here. Her novel
*The Awakening* (1899) is now considered her masterpiece; however, because
it depicts a woman trapped by society's conventions and does not condemn
adultery, the novel was once banned in St. Louis and elsewhere. Scorned by
critics and some acquaintances, Chopin wrote very little else. She died in
1904.

**WARM-UP:** Have you ever experienced the death of someone close to
you? How did you react to it?

Knowing that Mrs. Mallard was afflicted with a heart trouble, great care     1
was taken to break to her as gently as possible the news of her husband's
death.

It was her sister Josephine who told her, in broken sentences; veiled hints
that revealed in half concealing. Her husband's friend Richards was there, too,
near her. It was he who had been in the newspaper office when intelligence of
the railroad disaster was received, with Brently Mallard's name leading the list
of "killed." He had only taken the time to assure himself of its truth by a second telegram, and had hastened to forestall any less careful, less tender friend
in bearing the sad message.

She did not hear the story as many women have heard the same, with a
paralyzed inability to accept its significance. She wept at once, with sudden,
wild abandonment, in her sister's arms. When the storm of grief had spent
itself she went away to her room alone. She would have no one follow her.

There stood, facing the open window, a comfortable, roomy armchair.
Into this she sank, pressed down by a physical exhaustion that haunted her
body and seemed to reach into her soul.

She could see in the open square before her house the tops of trees that     5
were all aquiver with the new spring life. The delicious breath of rain was in
the air. In the street below a peddler was crying his wares. The notes of a distant song which some one was singing reached her faintly, and countless spar-
rows were twittering in the eaves.

There were patches of blue sky showing here and there through the clouds that had met and piled one above the other in the west facing her window.

She sat with her head thrown back upon the cushion of the chair, quite motionless, except when a sob came up into her throat and shook her, as a child who has cried itself to sleep continues to sob in its dreams.

She was young, with a fair, calm face, whose lines bespoke repression and even a certain strength. But now there was a dull stare in her eyes, whose gaze was fixed away off yonder on one of those patches of blue sky. It was not a glance of reflection, but rather indicated a suspension of intelligent thought.

There was something coming to her and she was waiting for it, fearfully. What was it? She did not know; it was too subtle and elusive to name. But she felt it, creeping out of the sky, reaching toward her through the sounds, the scents, the color that filled the air.

10  Now her bosom rose and fell tumultuously. She was beginning to recognize this thing that was approaching to possess her, and she was striving to beat it back with her will—as powerless as her two white slender hands would have been.

When she abandoned herself a little whispered word escaped her slightly parted lips. She said it over and over under her breath: "free, free, free!" The vacant stare and the look of terror that had followed it went from her eyes. They stayed keen and bright. Her pulses beat fast, and the coursing blood warmed and relaxed every inch of her body.

She did not stop to ask if it were or were not a monstrous joy that held her. A clear and exalted perception enabled her to dismiss the suggestion as trivial.

She knew that she would weep again when she saw the kind, tender hands folded in death; the face that had never looked save with love upon her, fixed and gray and dead. But she saw beyond that bitter moment a long procession of years to come that would belong to her absolutely. And she opened and spread her arms out to them in welcome.

There would be no one to live for her during those coming years; she would live for herself. There would be no powerful will bending hers in that blind persistence with which men and women believe they have a right to impose a private will upon a fellow-creature. A kind intention or a cruel intention made the act seem no less a crime as she looked upon it in that brief moment of illumination.

15  And yet she had loved him—sometimes. Often she had not. What did it matter! What could love, the unsolved mystery, count for in face of this possession of self-assertion which she suddenly recognized as the strongest impulse of her being!

"Free! Body and soul free!" she kept whispering.

Josephine was kneeling before the closed door with her lips to the keyhole, imploring for admission. "Louise, open the door! I beg; open the door—

you will make yourself ill. What are you doing, Louise? For heaven's sake open the door."

"Go away. I am not making myself ill." No; she was drinking in a very elixir of life through that open window.

Her fancy was running riot along those days ahead of her. Spring days, and summer days, and all sorts of days that would be her own. She breathed a quick prayer that life might be long. It was only yesterday she had thought with a shudder that life might be long.

She arose at length and opened the door to her sister's importunities.°    20 There was a feverish triumph in her eyes, and she carried herself unwittingly like a goddess of Victory. She clasped her sister's waist, and together they descended the stairs. Richards stood waiting for them at the bottom.

Some one was opening the front door with a latchkey. It was Brently Mallard who entered, a little travel-stained, composedly carrying his grip-sack and umbrella. He had been far from the scene of accident, and did not even know there had been one. He stood amazed at Josephine's piercing cry; at Richards' quick motion to screen him from the view of his wife.

But Richards was too late.

When the doctors came they said she had died of heart disease—of joy that kills.

### QUESTIONS

1. What does Mrs. Mallard notice when she sits in front of the window after hearing of her husband's death? What does the description suggest?
2. What is Mrs. Mallard trying "to beat back with her will"?
3. Based on what we know from the story, was Mr. Mallard a bad husband?
4. Does the story suggest that only women need to limit their assertion of self in a relationship?
5. Why do you think the author chose to refer to the main character as "Mrs. Mallard" throughout the story?
6. Is Mrs. Mallard a stereotypical woman? Explain your response.

### CONNECTIONS

1. Do you imagine that Louise Mallard would attend, oppose, or be indifferent to a woman's rights convention such as the one mentioned in the *New York Herald* editorial? Explain your response.

---

*importunities:* Requests, supplications.

2. Like Louise Mallard, the narrators of "Eleven" and "The Quiet Girl" both feel powerless. Consider the causes of that sense of powerlessness in each of these three cases.

# ∽ The Magnifying Mirror

*Virginia Woolf*

Novelist and essayist Virginia Woolf was born in London, England, in 1882 and is considered one of the great innovative novelists of the twentieth century. In 1905 she began writing as a critic for the *Times Literary Supplement,* and in 1915 she published her first novel, *The Voyage Out,* followed by several other novels, including *Mrs. Dalloway* (1925), *To the Lighthouse* (1927), *Orlando* (1928), and *The Waves* (1931). Woolf also championed women's rights by penning a classic of the feminist movement, *A Room of One's Own* (1929), from which the following selection is taken. Woolf drowned herself in the river Ouse in 1941.

**WARM-UP:** Do you believe that most men are more self-confident than most women? If so, why do you think that is? If you think that this used to be true in the past but not anymore, how do you account for the change?

The scene, if I may ask you to follow me, was now changed. The leaves were     1
still falling, but in London now, not Oxbridge; and I must ask you to imagine a room, like many thousands, with a window looking across people's hats and vans and motor-cars to other windows, and on the table inside the room a blank sheet of paper on which was written in large letters WOMEN AND FICTION, but no more. The inevitable sequel to lunching and dining at Oxbridge seemed, unfortunately, to be a visit to the British Museum. One must strain off what was personal and accidental in all these impressions and so reach the pure fluid, the essential oil of truth. For that visit to Oxbridge and the luncheon and the dinner had started a swarm of questions. Why did men drink wine and women water? Why was one sex so prosperous and the other so poor? What effect has poverty on fiction? What conditions are necessary for the creation of works of art?— a thousand questions at once suggested themselves. But one needed answers, not questions; and an answer was only to be had by consulting the learned and the unprejudiced, who have removed themselves above the strife of tongue and the confusion of body and issued the result of their reasoning and research in books which are to be found in the British Museum. If truth is not to be found on the shelves of the British Museum, where, I asked myself, picking up a notebook and a pencil, is truth?

Thus provided, thus confident and enquiring, I set out in the pursuit of truth. The day, though not actually wet, was dismal, and the streets in the neighbourhood of the Museum were full of open coal-holes, down which sacks were showering; four-wheeled cabs were drawing up and depositing on the pavement corded boxes containing, presumably, the entire wardrobe of some Swiss or Italian family seeking fortune or refuge or some other desirable commodity which is to be found in the boarding-houses of Bloomsbury in the winter. The usual hoarse-voiced men paraded the streets with plants on barrows. Some shouted; others sang. London was like a workshop. London was like a machine. We were all being shot backwards and forwards on this plain foundation to make some pattern. The British Museum was another department of the factory. The swing-doors swung open; and there one stood under the vast dome, as if one were a thought in the huge bald forehead which is so splendidly encircled by a band of famous names. One went to the counter; one took a slip of paper; one opened a volume of the catalogue, and . . . . . the five dots here indicate five separate minutes of stupefaction,° wonder and bewilderment. Have you any notion how many books are written about women in the course of one year? Have you any notion how many are written by men? Are you aware that you are, perhaps, the most discussed animal in the universe? Here had I come with a notebook and a pencil proposing to spend a morning reading, supposing that at the end of the morning I should have transferred the truth to my notebook. But I should need to be a herd of elephants, I thought, and a wilderness of spiders, desperately referring to the animals that are reputed longest lived and most multitudinously eyed, to cope with all this. I should need claws of steel and beak of brass even to penetrate the husk. How shall I ever find the grains of truth embedded in all this mass of paper? I asked myself, and in despair began running my eye up and down the long list of titles. Even the names of the books gave me food for thought. Sex and its nature might well attract doctors and biologists; but what was surprising and difficult of explanation was the fact that sex—woman, that is to say—also attracts agreeable essayists, light-fingered novelists, young men who have taken the M.A. degree; men who have taken no degree; men who have no apparent qualification save that they are not women. Some of these books were, on the face of it, frivolous and facetious; but many, on the other hand, were serious and prophetic, moral and hortatory.° Merely to read the titles suggested innumerable schoolmasters, innumerable clergymen mounting their platforms and pulpits and holding forth with a loquacity° which far exceeded the hour usually allotted to such discourse on this one subject. It was a most strange phenomenon; and apparently—here I consulted the letter M —one confined to the male sex. Women do not write books about men—a fact that I could not help welcoming with relief, for if I had first to read all that men have written about women, then all that women have written about men,

---

*stupefaction:* Astonishment.    *hortatory:* Giving advice.    *loquacity:* The quality of being very talkative.

the aloe that flowers once in a hundred years would flower twice before I could set pen to paper. So, making a perfectly arbitrary choice of a dozen volumes or so, I sent my slips of paper to lie in the wire tray, and waited in my stall, among the other seekers for the essential oil of truth.

What could be the reason, then, of this curious disparity, I wondered, drawing cart-wheels on the slips of paper provided by the British taxpayer for other purposes. Why are women, judging from this catalogue, so much more interesting to men than men are to women? A very curious fact it seemed, and my mind wandered to picture the lives of men who spend their time in writing books about women; whether they were old or young, married or unmarried, red-nosed or hump-backed—anyhow, it was flattering, vaguely, to feel oneself the object of such attention, provided that it was not entirely bestowed by the crippled and the infirm—so I pondered until all such frivolous thoughts were ended by an avalanche of books sliding down on to the desk in front of me. Now the trouble began. The student who has been trained in research at Oxbridge has no doubt some method of shepherding his question past all distractions till it runs into its answer as a sheep runs into its pen. The student by my side, for instance, who was copying assiduously° from a scientific manual was, I felt sure, extracting pure nuggets of the essential ore every ten minutes or so. His little grunts of satisfaction indicated so much. But if, unfortunately, one has had no training in a university, the question far from being shepherded to its pen flies like a frightened flock hither and thither, helter-skelter, pursued by a whole pack of hounds. Professors, schoolmasters, sociologists, clergymen, novelists, essayists, journalists, men who had no qualification save that they were not women, chased my simple and single question—Why are women poor?—until it became fifty questions; until the fifty questions leapt frantically into mid-stream and were carried away. Every page in my notebook was scribbled over with notes. To show the state of mind I was in, I will read you a few of them, explaining that the page was headed quite simply, WOMEN AND POVERTY, in block letters; but what followed was something like this:

Condition in Middle Ages of,
Habits in the Fiji Islands of,
Worshipped as goddesses by,
Weaker in moral sense than,
Idealism of,
Greater conscientiousness of,
South Sea Islanders, age of puberty among,
Attractiveness of,

*assiduously:* Carefully, persistently.

Offered as sacrifice to,
Small size of brain of,
Profounder sub-consciousness of,
Less hair on the body of,
Mental, moral and physical inferiority of,
Love of children of,
Greater length of life of,
Weaker muscles of,
Strength of affections of,
Vanity of,
Higher education of,
Shakespeare's opinion of,
Lord Birkenhead's opinion of,
Dean Inge's opinion of,
La Bruyère's opinion of,
Dr. Johnson's opinion of,
Mr. Oscar Browning's opinion of, . . .

Here I drew breath and added, indeed, in the margin, Why does Samuel Butler say, "Wise men never say what they think of women"? Wise men never say anything else apparently. But, I continued, leaning back in my chair and looking at the vast dome in which I was a single but by now somewhat harassed thought, what is so unfortunate is that wise men never think the same thing about women. Here is Pope:

Most women have no Character at all.

And here is La Bruyère:

Les femmes sont extrêmes; elles sont meillecures ou pires que les hommes—°

a direct contradiction by keen observers who were contemporary. Are they capable of education or incapable? Napoleon thought them incapable. Dr. Johnson thought the opposite.[1] Have they souls or have they not souls? Some savages say they have none. Others, on the contrary, maintain that women are half divine and worship them on that account.[2] Some sages hold that they are shallower in the brain; others that they are deeper in the consciousness. Goethe honoured them; Mussolini despises them. Wherever one looked men thought about women and thought differently. It was impossible to make head or tail of it all, I decided, glancing with envy at the reader next door who was making the neatest abstracts, headed often with an A or a B or a C, while

---

"Les femmes sont extremes; elles sont meilleures ou pires que les hommes": French, meaning "Women are extreme; they are either better or worse than men."

my own notebook rioted with the wildest scribble of contradictory jottings. It was distressing, it was bewildering, it was humiliating. Truth had run through my fingers. Every drop had escaped.

I could not possibly go home, I reflected, and add as a serious contribution to the study of women and fiction that women have less hair on their bodies than men, or that the age of puberty among the South Sea Islanders is nine—or is it ninety?—even the handwriting had become in its distraction indecipherable. It was disgraceful to have nothing more weighty or respectable to show after a whole morning's work. And if I could not grasp the truth about W. (as for brevity's sake I had come to call her) in the past, why bother about W. in the future? It seemed pure waste of time to consult all those gentlemen who specialise in woman and her effect on whatever it may be—politics, children, wages, morality—numerous and learned as they are. One might as well leave their books unopened.

But while I pondered I had unconsciously, in my listlessness,° in my desperation, been drawing a picture where I should, like my neighbour, have been writing a conclusion. I had been drawing a face, a figure. It was the face and the figure of Professor von X. engaged in writing his monumental work entitled *The Mental, Moral, and Physical Inferiority of the Female Sex.* He was not in my picture a man attractive to women. He was heavily built; he had a great jowl; to balance that he had very small eyes; he was very red in the face. His expression suggested that he was labouring under some emotion that made him jab his pen on the paper as if he were killing some noxious insect as he wrote, but even when he had killed it that did not satisfy him; he must go on killing it; and even so, some cause for anger and irritation remained. Could it be his wife, I asked, looking at my picture? Was she in love with a cavalry officer? Was the cavalry officer slim and elegant and dressed in astrachan?° Had he been laughed at, to adopt the Freudian theory, in his cradle by a pretty girl? For even in his cradle the professor, I thought, could not have been an attractive child. Whatever the reason, the professor was made to look very angry and very ugly in my sketch, as he wrote his great book upon the mental, moral and physical inferiority of women. Drawing pictures was an idle way of finishing an unprofitable morning's work. Yet it is in our idleness, in our dreams, that the submerged truth sometimes comes to the top. A very elementary exercise in psychology, not to be dignified by the name of psycho-analysis, showed me, on looking at my notebook, that the sketch of the angry professor had been made in anger. Anger had snatched my pencil while I dreamt. But what was anger doing there? Interest, confusion, amusement, boredom—all these emotions I could trace and name as they succeeded each other throughout the morning. Had anger, the black snake, been lurking among them? Yes,

5

---

*listlessness:* Indifference, apathy.    *astrachan:* A kind of cloth used chiefly as an edging or trimming for garments.

said the sketch, anger had. It referred me unmistakably to the one book, to the one phrase, which had roused the demon; it was the professor's statement about the mental, moral and physical inferiority of women. My heart had leapt. My checks had burnt. I had flushed with anger. There was nothing specially remarkable, however foolish, in that. One does not like to be told that one is naturally the inferior of a little man—I looked at the student next me— who breathes hard, wears a ready-made tie, and has not shaved this fortnight.° One has certain foolish vanities. It is only human nature, I reflected, and began drawing cartwheels and circles over the angry professor's face till he looked like a burning bush or a flaming comet—anyhow, an apparition without human semblance° or significance. The professor was nothing now but a faggot° burning on the top of Hampstead Heath. Soon my own anger was explained and done with; but curiosity remained. How explain the anger of the professors? Why were they angry? For when it came to analyzing the impression left by these books there was always an element of heat. This heat took many forms; it showed itself in satire, in sentiment, in curiosity, in reprobation.° But there was another element which was often present and could not immediately be identified. Anger, I called it. But it was anger that had gone underground and mixed itself with all kinds of other emotions. To judge from its odd effects, it was anger disguised and complex, not anger simple and open.

Whatever the reason, all these books, I thought, surveying the pile on the desk, are worthless for my purposes. They were worthless scientifically, that is to say, though humanly they were full of instruction, interest, boredom, and very queer facts about the habits of the Fiji Islanders. They had been written in the red light of emotion and not in the white light of truth. Therefore they must be returned to the central desk and restored each to his own cell in the enormous honeycomb. All that I had retrieved from that morning's work had been the one fact of anger. The professors—I lumped them together thus— were angry. But why, I asked myself, having returned the books, why, I repeated, standing under the colonnade° among the pigeons and the prehistoric canoes, why are they angry? And, asking myself this question, I strolled off to find a place for luncheon. What is the real nature of what I call for the moment their anger? I asked. Here was a puzzle that would last all the time that it takes to be served with food in a small restaurant somewhere near the British Museum. Some previous luncher had left the lunch edition of the evening paper on a chair, and, waiting to be served, I began idly reading the headlines. A ribbon of very large letters ran across the page. Somebody had made a big score in South Africa. Lesser ribbons announced that Sir Austen

---

*fortnight:* A two-week period.    *semblance:* Appearance.    *faggot:* Stick.    *reprobation:* Condemnation, rejection.    *colonnade:* A series of columns set at regular intervals and usually supporting the base of a roof structure.

Chamberlain was at Geneva. A meat axe with human hair on it had been found in a cellar. Mr. Justice —— commented in the Divorce Courts upon the Shamelessness of Women. Sprinkled about the paper were other pieces of news. A film actress had been lowered from a peak in California and hung suspended in mid-air. The weather was going to be foggy. The most transient visitor to this planet, I thought, who picked up this paper could not fail to be aware, even from this scattered testimony, that England is under the rule of a patriarchy.° Nobody in their senses could fail to detect the dominance of the professor. His was the power and the money and the influence. He was the proprietor of the paper and its editor and sub-editor. He was the Foreign Secretary and the Judge. He was the cricketer; he owned the racehorses and the yachts. He was the director of the company that pays two hundred per cent to its shareholders. He left millions to charities and colleges that were ruled by himself. He suspended the film actress in mid-air. He will decide if the hair on the meat axe is human; he it is who will acquit or convict the murderer, and hang him, or let him go free. With the exception of the fog he seemed to control everything. Yet he was angry. I knew that he was angry by this token. When I read what he wrote about women I thought, not of what he was saying, but of himself. When an arguer argues dispassionately he thinks only of the argument; and the reader cannot help thinking of the argument too. If he had written dispassionately about women, had used indisputable proofs to establish his argument and had shown no trace of wishing that the result should be one thing rather than another, one would not have been angry either. One would have accepted the fact, as one accepts the fact that a pea is green or a canary yellow. So be it, I should have said. But I had been angry because he was angry. Yet it seemed absurd, I thought, turning over the evening paper, that a man with all this power should be angry. Or is anger, I wondered, somehow, the familiar, the attendant sprite on power? Rich people, for example, are often angry because they suspect that the poor want to seize their wealth. The professors, or patriarchs, as it might be more accurate to call them, might be angry for that reason partly, but partly for one that lies a little less obviously on the surface. Possibly they were not "angry" at all; often, indeed, they were admiring, devoted, exemplary in the relations of private life. Possibly when the professor insisted a little too emphatically upon the inferiority of women, he was concerned not with their inferiority, but with his own superiority. That was what he was protecting rather hot-headedly and with too much emphasis, because it was a jewel to him of the rarest price. Life for both sexes—and I looked at them, shouldering their way along the pavement —is arduous,° difficult, a perpetual struggle. It calls for gigantic courage and strength. More than anything, perhaps, creatures of illusion as we are, it calls

---

*patriarchy:* Social organization in which the father is the leader of the family and men are the leaders of society.    *arduous:* Difficult to accomplish or achieve.

for confidence in oneself. Without self-confidence we are as babes in the cradle. And how can we generate this imponderable° quality, which is yet so invaluable, most quickly? By thinking that other people are inferior to oneself. By feeling that one has some innate° superiority—it may be wealth, or rank, a straight nose, or the portrait of a grandfather by Romney—for there is no end to the pathetic devices of the human imagination—over other people. Hence the enormous importance to a patriarch who has to conquer, who has to rule, of feeling that great numbers of people, half the human race indeed, are by nature inferior to himself. It must indeed be one of the chief sources of his power. But let me turn the light of this observation on to real life, I thought. Does it help to explain some of those psychological puzzles that one notes in the margin of daily life? Does it explain my astonishment the other day when Z, most humane, most modest of men, taking up some book by Rebecca West and reading a passage in it, exclaimed, "The arrant° feminist! She says that men are snobs!" The exclamation, to me so surprising—for why was Miss West an arrant feminist for making a possibly true if uncomplimentary statement about the other sex?—was not merely the cry of wounded vanity; it was a protest against some infringement of his power to believe in himself. Women have served all these centuries as looking-glasses° possessing the magic and delicious power of reflecting the figure of man at twice its natural size. Without that power probably the earth would still be swamp and jungle. The glories of all our wars would be unknown. We should still be scratching the outlines of deer on the remains of mutton bones and bartering flints for sheepskins or whatever simple ornament took our unsophisticated taste. Supermen and Fingers of Destiny would never have existed. The Czar and the Kaiser would never have worn their crowns or lost them. Whatever may be their use in civilised societies, mirrors are essential to all violent and heroic action. That is why Napoleon and Mussolini both insist so emphatically upon the inferiority of women, for if they were not inferior, they would cease to enlarge. That serves to explain in part the necessity that women so often are to men. And it serves to explain how restless they are under her criticism; how impossible it is for her to say to them this book is bad, this picture is feeble, or whatever it may be, without giving far more pain and rousing far more anger than a man would do who gave the same criticism. For if she begins to tell the truth, the figure in the looking-glass shrinks; his fitness for life is diminished. How is he to go on giving judgement, civilising natives, making laws, writing books, dressing up and speechifying at banquets, unless he can see himself at breakfast and at dinner at least twice the size he really is? So I reflected, crumbling my bread and stirring my coffee and now and again looking at the peo-

---

*imponderable:* Incapable of being understood or evaluated.   *innate:* Inherent, inborn.   *arrant:* Extreme, lacking moderation.   *looking glass:* An old fashioned term for a mirror.

ple in the street. The looking-glass vision is of supreme importance because it charges the vitality; it stimulates the nervous system. Take it away and man may die, like the drug fiend deprived of his cocaine. Under the spell of that illusion, I thought, looking out of the window, half the people on the pavement are striding to work. They put on their hats and coats in the morning under its agreeable rays. They start the day confident, braced, believing themselves desired at Miss Smith's tea party; they say to themselves as they go into the room, I am the superior of half the people here, and it is thus that they speak with that self-confidence, that self-assurance, which have had such profound consequences in public life and lead to such curious notes in the margin of the private mind.

But these contributions to the dangerous and fascinating subject of the psychology of the other sex—it is one, I hope, that you will investigate when you have five hundred a year of your own—were interrupted by the necessity of paying the bill. It came to five shillings and ninepence. I gave the waiter a ten-shilling note and he went to bring me change. There was another ten-schilling note in my purse; I noticed it, because it is a fact that still takes my breath away—the power of my purse to breed ten-shilling notes automatically. I open it and there they are. Society gives me chicken and coffee, bed and lodging, in return for a certain number of pieces of paper which were left me by an aunt, for no other reason than that I share her name.

My aunt, Mary Beton, I must tell you, died by a fall from her horse when she was riding out to take the air in Bombay. The news of my legacy reached me one night about the same time that the act was passed that gave votes to women. A solicitor's letter fell into the post-box and when I opened it I found that she had left me five hundred pounds a year for ever. Of the two—the vote and the money—the money, I own, seemed infinitely the more important. Before that I had made my living by cadging° odd jobs from newspapers, by reporting a donkey show here or a wedding there; I had earned a few pounds by addressing envelopes, reading to old ladies, making artificial flowers, teaching the alphabet to small children in a kindergarten. Such were the chief occupations that were open to women before 1918. I need not, I am afraid, describe in any detail the hardness of the work, for you know perhaps women who have done it; nor the difficulty of living on the money when it was earned, for you may have tried. But what still remains with me as a worse infliction than either was the poison of fear and bitterness which those days bred in me. To begin with, always to be doing work that one did not wish to do, and to do it like a slave, flattering and fawning, not always necessarily perhaps, but it seemed necessary and the stakes were too great to run risks; and then the thought of that one gift which it was death to hide—a small one but

_cadging:_ Begging.

dear to the possessor—perishing and with it myself, my soul—all this became like a rust eating away the bloom of the spring, destroying the tree at its heart. However, as I say, my aunt died; and whenever I change a ten-shilling note a little of that rust and corrosion is rubbed off; fear and bitterness go. Indeed, I thought, slipping the silver into my purse, it is remarkable, remembering the bitterness of those days, what a change of temper a fixed income will bring about. No force in the world can take from me my five hundred pounds. Food, house and clothing are mine for ever. Therefore not merely do effort and labour cease, but also hatred and bitterness. I need not hate any man; he cannot hurt me. I need not flatter any man; he has nothing to give me. So imperceptibly I found myself adopting a new attitude towards the other half of the human race. It was absurd to blame any class or any sex, as a whole. Great bodies of people are never responsible for what they do. They are driven by instincts which are not within their control. They too, the patriarchs, the professors, had endless difficulties, terrible drawbacks to contend with. Their education had been in some ways as faulty as my own. It had bred in them defects as great. True, they had money and power, but only at the cost of harbouring in their breasts an eagle, a vulture, for ever tearing the liver out and plucking at the lungs—the instinct for possession, the rage for acquisition which drives them to desire other people's fields and goods perpetually; to make frontiers and flags; battleships and poison gas; to offer up their own lives and their children's lives. Walk through the Admiralty Arch (I had reached that monument), or any other avenue given up to trophies and cannon, and reflect upon the kind of glory celebrated there. Or watch in the spring sunshine the stockbroker and the great barrister° going indoors to make money and more money and more money when it is a fact that five hundred pounds a year will keep one alive in the sunshine. These are unpleasant instincts to harbour, I reflected. They are bred of the conditions of life; of the lack of civilisation, I thought, looking at the statue of the Duke of Cambridge, and in particular at the feathers in his cocked hat, with a fixity that they have scarcely ever received before. And, as I realised these drawbacks, by degrees fear and bitterness modified themselves into pity and toleration; and then in a year or two, pity and toleration went, and the greatest release of all came, which is freedom to think of things in themselves. That building, for example, do I like it or not? Is that picture beautiful or not? Is that in my opinion a good book or a bad? Indeed my aunt's legacy unveiled the sky to me, and substituted for the large and imposing figure of a gentleman, which Milton recommended for my perpetual adoration, a view of the open sky.

So thinking, so speculating, I found my way back to my house by the river. Lamps were being lit and an indescribable change had come over London since the morning hour. It was as if the great machine after labouring all day

---

*barrister:* Lawyer.

had made with our help a few yards of something very exciting and beautiful —a fiery fabric flashing with red eyes, a tawny monster roaring with hot breath. Even the wind seemed flung like a flag as it lashed the houses and rattled the hoardings.

In my little street, however, domesticity prevailed. The house painter was descending his ladder; the nursemaid was wheeling the perambulator° carefully in and out back to nursery tea; the coal-heaver was folding his empty sacks on top of each other; the woman who keeps the green-grocer's shop was adding up the day's takings with her hands in red mittens. But so engrossed was I with the problem you have laid upon my shoulders that I could not see even these usual sights without referring them to one centre. I thought how much harder it is now than it must have been even a century ago to say which of these employments is the higher, the more necessary. Is it better to be a coal-heaver or a nursemaid; is the charwoman who has brought up eight children of less value to the world than the barrister who has made a hundred thousand pounds? It is useless to ask such questions; for nobody can answer them. Not only do the comparative values of charwomen and lawyers rise and fall from decade to decade, but we have no rods with which to measure them even as they are at the moment. I had been foolish to ask my professor to furnish me with "indisputable proofs" of this or that in his argument about women. Even if one could state the value of any one gift at the moment, those values will change; in a century's time very possibly they will have changed completely. Moreover, in a hundred years, I thought, reaching my own doorstep, women will have ceased to be the protected sex. Logically they will take part in all the activities and exertions that were once denied them. The nursemaid will heave coal. The shop-woman will drive an engine. All assumptions founded on the facts observed when women were the protected sex will have disappeared—as, for example (here a squad of soldiers marched down the street), that women and clergymen and gardeners live longer than other people. Remove that protection, expose them to the same exertions and activities, make them soldiers and sailors and engine-drivers and dock labourers, and will not women die off so much younger, so much quicker, than men that one will say, "I saw a woman today," as one used to say, "I saw an aeroplane." Anything may happen when womanhood has ceased to be a protected occupation, I thought, opening the door. But what bearing has all this upon the subject of my paper, Women and Fiction? I asked, going indoors.

**NOTES**

1."'Men know that women are an overmatch for them, and therefore they choose the weakest or the most ignorant. If they did not think

*perambulator:* Baby carriage.

so, they never could be afraid of women knowing as much as themselves.' . . . In justice to the sex, I think it but candid to acknowledge
that, in a subsequent conversation, he told me that he was serious in
what he said."—BOSWELL, *The Journal of a Tour to the Hebrides.*
2. "The ancient Germans believed that there was something holy in
women, and accordingly consulted them as oracles."—FRAZER,
*Golden Bough.*

## QUESTIONS

1. What was Woolf searching for in the British Museum? Be specific.
2. Explain some of the problems that Woolf encounters as she is
   researching her subject. How does she solve them?
3. Why was Woolf angry at the professor she sketched? Who is Professor
   von X.? Do you think he is a real, historical figure?
4. What emotion does Woolf find in Professor von X.'s writing about
   women? How does she explain this?
5. What does Woolf mean when she says, "Women have served all these
   centuries as looking-glasses possessing the magic and delicious power
   of reflecting the figure of man at twice its natural size"?
6. Does Woolf blame individual men for the way they think about
   women? If not, who does she blame?
7. How did the money that Woolf inherited from her aunt change her
   perception of men? Why?
8. Find some places in the essay where the author uses vivid details. Why
   do you think she does so? How would the essay have been different if
   she'd left them out?
9. Summarize Woolf's advice about writing an argument; then explain
   whether you agree with it.

## CONNECTIONS

1. How might Woolf respond to the argument in the *New York Herald*
   editorial that it is "the law of her nature" that has made woman "subject to man"?
2. Do Woolf and Julius Lester agree in their views about the roles that
   men and women are expected to play? Refer to specific lines from
   each author's essay to support your response.

# ∾ Barbie Doll

*Marge Piercy*

Marge Piercy was born in Detroit in 1936 into a working-class family. She earned a bachelor's degree from the University of Michigan and a master's from Northwestern University. Piercy has written more than a dozen novels and volumes of verse. Her novels include *Braided Lives* (1981), *Fly Away Home* (1984), *He, She, and It* (1991), and *The Longings of Females* (1994). Her collections of poems include *Breaking Camp* (1968), *Woman on the Edge of Time* (1976), *The Moon Is Always Female* (1980), and *My Mother's Body* (1985). Two selections of her work are included in this book: the following poem, "Barbie Doll," and the poem "To Be of Use" (included in Section 4); both come from the collection *To Be of Use* (1973).

**WARM-UP:** What toys did you play with as a child? Did they affect the way you saw the world? If so, in what way?

This girlchild was born as usual                                    1
and presented dolls that did pee-pee
and miniature GE stoves and irons
and wee° lipsticks the color of cherry candy.
Then in the magic of puberty, a classmate said:                    5
You have a great big nose and fat legs.

She was healthy, tested intelligent,
possessed strong arms and back,
abundant sexual drive and manual dexterity.
She went to and fro apologizing.                                   10
Everyone saw a fat nose on thick legs.

She was advised to play coy,
exhorted° to come on hearty,
exercise, diet, smile and wheedle.°
Her good nature wore out                                           15
like a fan belt.
So she cut off her nose and her legs
and offered them up.
In the casket displayed on satin she lay

---

4 *wee:* Tiny    13 *exhorted:* Strongly advised, admonished    14 *wheedle:* Entice by soft words or flattery

20       with the undertaker's cosmetics painted on,
       a turned-up putty nose,
       dressed in a pink and white nightie.
       Doesn't she look pretty? everyone said.

         Consummation at last.
25         To every woman a happy ending.

## QUESTIONS

1. What is the relationship between the toys that the girl received and the comment that her classmate made?
2. What contradictory advice did the girl receive about how to become desirable?
3. Consider the description of the girl (lines 7–9). What is the common thread between the characteristics listed?
4. Considering the context of this poem, explain the effect of the lines "Her good nature wore out / like a fan belt."
5. Look up "consummation" in a dictionary. What does it mean in the poem?
6. What is the tone of this poem?
7. How might the poem be different if the title was "G. I. Joe"?

## CONNECTIONS

1. Compare and contrast the girl described in "Barbie Doll" to any of the female characters presented in "The Quiet Girl" (Section 1).
2. Compare and contrast this poem to "Those Winter Sundays," included in Section 1.

# ❧ Men as Success Objects

*Warren Farrell*

Psychologist Warren Farrell is the only man elected three times to the board of the National Organization for Women (NOW) of New York City. Farrell has written several books and articles, including *The Liberated Man: Beyond Masculinity* (1974), the best-seller *Why Men Are the Way They Are: the Male–Female Dynamic* (1986), and *The Myth of Male Power: Why Men are the Disposable Sex* (1993), which defends the rights of men and retracts his earlier support of women's rights. Farrell's latest book is entitled *The Seven Greatest Myths About Men* (1997). The following article first appeared in 1988 in the November/December issue of *The Family Therapy Networker*.

**WARM-UP:** What criteria does society in general use to measure a man's level of success?

For thousands of years, marriages were about economic security and survival. Let's call this Stage I in our culture's conception of marriage. Beginning in the 1950s, marriages became focused on personal fulfillment and we entered into the era of the Stage II relationship. In Stage II, love was redefined to include listening to each other, joint parenting, sexual fulfillment, and shared decision making. As a result, many traditional marriages consummated in Stage I failed under the new Stage II expectations. Thus we had the great surge of divorces beginning in the '60s.

The increasing incidence of divorce altered the fundamental relationship between women, men, and the workplace. Before divorce became common, most women's income came from men, so discrimination in favor of a woman's husband benefited her. But, as the divorce rate mushroomed, the same discrimination often hurt her. Before divorce became a common expectation, we had two types of inequality—women's experience of unequal rights in the workplace and men's experience of unequal responsibility for succeeding in the workplace. To find a woman to love him, a man had to "make his mark" in the world. As women increasingly had to provide for themselves economically, we confined our examination of inequality between the sexes to inequality in the workplace. What was ignored was the effect of inequality in the homeplace. Also ignored was a man's feeling that no woman would love him if he volunteered to be a full-time house-husband instead of a full-time provider. As a result, we falsely assumed that the experience of inequality was confined to women.

Because divorces led to a change in the pressures on women (should she *become* a doctor, marry a doctor, or have a career and marry a doctor?), that change became "news" and her new juggling act got attention in the media. Because the underlying pressures on men did not change (women still married men who earned more than they did), the pressure on men to succeed did not change, and, therefore, received no attention. With all the focus on discrimination against women, few understood the sexism directed against men.

The feminist perspective on relationships has become like fluoride in water—we drink it without being aware of its presence. The complaints about men, the idea that "men are jerks," have become so integrated into our unconscious that even advertisers have caught on. After analyzing 1,000 commercials in 1987, researcher Fred Hayward found that when an ad called for a negative portrayal in a male-female interaction, an astonishing 100 percent of the time the "bad guy" was the man.

5      This anti-male bias isn't confined to TV commercials. A sampling of the cards in the "Love and Friendship" section of a greeting card store revealed these gems:
"If they can send one man to the moon, why can't they send them all?"
"When you unzip a man's pants . . . his brains fall out."
"If we can make penicillin out of moldy cheese . . . maybe we can make men out of the low-lifes in this town."
A visit to the bookstore turns up titles like *No Good Men.* Imagine *No Good Women* or *No Good Jews.* And what do the following titles have in common? *Men Who Can't Love; Men Who Hate Women and the Women Who Love Them; Smart Women/Foolish Choices; Successful Women, Angry Men: Peter Pan Syndrome.*

10     Feminism-as-fluoride has left us acknowledging the working mother ("Superwoman") without even being aware of the working father. It is by now well recognized that, even among men who do more housework or more childcare than their wives, almost never does the man truly share the 24-hour-a-day psychological responsibility of ministering to everyone's needs, egos, and schedules.

But it is not so widely recognized that, despite the impact feminism has had on the contemporary family, almost every father still retains 24-hour-a-day psychological responsibility for the family's financial well-being. Even women who earn more than their husbands tell me that they know their husbands would support their decision to earn as much or as little as they wish. If a woman marries a successful man, then she knows she will have an option to work or not, but not an obligation. Almost all men see bringing home a healthy salary as an obligation, not an option.

A woman today has three options:

*Option 1:* Full-time career.
*Option 2:* Full-time family.
*Option 3:* Some combination of career and family.

A man sees himself as having three "slightly different" options:

*Option 1:* Work full time.
*Option 2:* Work full time.
*Option 3:* Work full time.

The U.S. Bureau of the Census explains that full-time working males work an average of eight hours more per week on their jobs than full-time working females.

Since many women now earn substantial incomes, doesn't this relieve the pressure on men to be a wallet? No. Why? Because successful women do exactly what less-successful women do—"marry up," that is, marry a man whose income is greater than her own. According to statistics, if a women cannot marry up or marry someone with a high wage-earning potential, she does not marry at all. Therefore, a man often reflexively backs away from a woman he's attracted to when he discovers she's more successful than he is because he senses he's only setting himself up for rejection. Ultimately, she'll dump him for a more successful man. She may sleep with him, or live with him, but not marry him unless she spots "potential." Thus, of top female executives, 85 percent don't get married; the remaining 15 percent almost all marry up. Even successful women have not relaxed the pressure on men to succeed.

Ask a girl in junior high school about the boy whom she would "absolutely love" to ask her out to the prom and chances are almost 100 percent that she would tell you her fantasy boy is *both* good-looking *and* successful (a jock or student leader, or someone who "has potential"). Ask a boy whom he would absolutely love to ask out to the prom and chances are almost 100 percent his fantasy girl is good-looking. Only about 25 percent will also be interested in a girl's "strong career potential" (or her being a top female jock). His invisible curriculum, then, taught him that being good-looking is not enough to attract a good-looking girl—he must be successful *in addition* to being good-looking. This was his experience of inequality: "Good-looking boy does not equal good-looking girl." Why are boys willing to consider themselves unequal to girls' attention until they hit their heads against 21 other boys on a football field?

In part, the answer is because boys are addicted. In all cultures, boys are addicted to the images of beautiful women. And in American culture this is enormously magnified. Boys are exposed to the images of beautiful women about 10 million times per year via television, billboards, magazines, etc. In the process, the naturally beautiful girl becomes a *genetic celebrity.* Boys become addicted to the image of the quasi-anorexic female. To be the equal of this genetic celebrity, the adolescent boy must become an *earned celebrity* (by performing, paying on dates, etc.). Until he is an earned celebrity, he feels like a groupie trying to get a celebrity's attention.

Is there an invisible curriculum for girls and boys growing up? Yes. For girls, "If you want to have your choice among boys, you had better be beautiful." For boys, it's "You had better be handsome *and* successful." If a boy wants a romantic relationship with a girl he must not only be successful and perform, he must pay and pursue—risk sexual rejection. Girls think of the three Ps—performing, paying, and pursuing—as male power. Boys see the three Ps as what they must do to earn their way to female love and sexuality. They see these not as power, but as compensations for powerlessness. This is the adolescent male's experience of inequality.

### QUESTIONS

1. Farrell speaks of "two types of inequality—woman's experience of unequal rights in the workplace and men's experience of unequal responsibility for succeeding in the workplace." Are those two similar or "equal," in your opinion?
2. According to Farrell, why did the pressures upon women receive much attention while those upon men did not? Do you agree with his analysis of this point?
3. Offer examples of TV commercials, greeting cards, and book and magazine titles that demean women, rather than men. Would Farrell's essay have been more convincing or less convincing if he had mentioned such examples? Are these examples beside the point, given his argument?
4. Do you agree with Farrell's claim that "almost every father still retains 24-hour-a-day psychological responsibility for the family's financial well being"? If you disagree, do you feel that this claim *was* correct in 1988, when this essay was first published?
5. One of the statistics that Farrell offers is that 85% of top female executives do not marry, and almost all of the others marry men who make more money than they do. What does Farrell see as the cause of this? Could this statistic be interpreted differently?
6. In paragraph 14, Farrell writes, "The U.S. Bureau of the Census explains that full-time working males work an average of eight hours

more per week on their jobs than full-time working females." What is his point? Does this statistic demonstrate that point?

7. Do you agree with the author's claim about what young men want from their dream mates? Do you agree with his claim about what young women want?

8. Explain why, according to Farrell, young men see "performing, paying, and pursuing" as "compensations for powerlessness."

9. Do you find Farrell's essay convincing as a whole? Why or why not?

## CONNECTIONS

1. Both Warren Farrell and Julius Lester write about the difficulties of being male in U.S. culture. How are their conclusions similar? How are they different?

2. Explore both similarities and differences between Farrell's essay and the *New York Herald* editorial rejecting women's rights.

# ∽ Dancing in the Cracks between Worlds

*Tom Daly*

> Tom Daly is the founder and director of The Living Arts Foundation and the
> Men's Council Project, both headquartered in Boulder, Colorado. He holds a
> bachelor's degree in zoology and botany from the University of Colorado,
> Boulder; a master's degree in counseling and psychology from the University
> of Colorado, Denver; and a Ph.D. in fine arts and men's studies from The
> Union Institute in Cincinnati, Ohio. He has led men's groups since 1971, has
> taught classes from the junior high to postgraduate levels, and has published
> articles in such publications as *Harper's, Edges,* and *Man!* Daly travels
> around North America helping men to form men's councils, create male ini-
> tiations, and transmit rituals such as drum-dancing and the sweat lodge. The
> following essay was originally published in an anthology of writing by men
> about men, entitled *Wingspan: Inside the Men's Movement* (1992).

> **WARM-UP:** What have you heard, read, or experienced about the
> Men's Movement? What are your impressions of it?

1    Like most of the boys in the neighborhood I loved to hang out in the vacant
lots nearby. The lots represented a natural wilderness, a place where the
kids could get together to practice a kind of instinctive alchemy.° We could
transform thrown-away lumber into airplanes and swords, turn dogs and cats
into jungle beasts and dragons, and make cardboard boxes and dirt mounds
into forts and battleships. Behind the wall of lush weeds and grasses, we created a mythic realm where the forces of good and evil could play themselves
out with wild abandon. For me, it was a place of fundamental sacredness.
Rooted in rich Nebraska earth and my fertile imagination, I made up chants
and spells, swore oaths, created and inscribed runes,° and evoked the gods.
This was the happiest and healthiest period of my life.

About the time I left the primary grades, things began to change. I learned
that the sacred belonged in church, that stories of mythic heroes and fabulous
quests weren't for real, and that magic and witchcraft were bad. I learned that
being dirty and sweaty and loud and passionate weren't okay. And all this at a
time when my hormones were really beginning to kick in. I began a period of
profound confusion and self-consciousness that lasted well into manhood.

---

*alchemy:* Ability to transform one chemical element into another.    *runes:* Ancient written characters
or charms.

Somehow I made it through the usual rites of passage into manhood. I came to live in a man's body and have a man's name. I got good at sports and drank beer with the guys. I did the mandatory flirting with death by climbing mountains in Colorado and driving like a madman. I learned to hide my feelings and act as though I knew what I was doing at all times, especially around women. I fathered two children, paid taxes, voted, and had a decent job. I was miserable.

Something was missing, and I had no idea what it was. I felt a deep longing, but I was so busy making a living and being a nice guy that I couldn't really touch some essential part of myself. In fact, I had been trained not to. The world was pulling too hard on the outside for me to notice the inside. I had to find out from others what I really wanted. My family and friends, the advertisers and authorities were more than happy to tell me. I needed "stuff," endless stuff, that I had to work my ass off to get, to keep, and to maintain. I needed to follow a lot of written and often unwritten rules if I wanted to be really successful. And it was totally my fault if I didn't make it.

I was convinced that there weren't any other guys like me out there. I    5 never heard other guys expressing personal doubts about themselves, only complaining about their wives or girlfriends, talking sports, or expressing frustration about their jobs. I couldn't trust men; they were the competition. I found, however, that I could confide in certain women; they could understand my feelings. They could cry or express uncertainties. A deep part of me wanted that. I had been bonded to my mom; she had been my source of nourishment both physically and emotionally. I couldn't go to Dad for that stuff. If he and I talked at all, it was about how I was doing in school or at work and arguing about politics. So I found myself dependent on women for emotional needs, not really as adults, more as substitute mothers. I came to judge my manhood by comparison. All the cues about manhood were outside me, separate from my deeper self. With both men and women there was a constant need to keep checking. I felt manly if I could compete successfully with men and if I was very different from women.

I knew things weren't working, yet I kept trying to do more, and bigger, and better. Nothing seemed to be enough. After a divorce and a series of dead-end relationships with women, in desperation I reached out to a couple of men I knew at work. Slowly, but surely, I started to get the feeling that maybe there were other men like me and that I could talk to them about how I really felt. I began to trust those men more deeply and in the process started to trust myself more. I dropped some of my walls and the struggle to measure myself against others.

I read the works of Carlos Castaneda and Joseph Campbell and an interview with Robert Bly titled "What Do Men Really Want?" Something began to come alive in me: A more primitive, younger, and wilder side that had been suppressed for so long was awakening. I started to feel better about sweat and emotions and the passions of my youth. Suddenly, storytelling was okay again, warriorship was redefined and applauded, quests were real, and mystery and magic were natural. I found myself alone in the mountains on solo backpacking trips; I was rediscovering my roots in the earth and my roots in the mythic dimension. I began to see this as a quest for my true self.

Reading and being alone weren't enough; in fact, they just added to my frustration, my incompleteness. Here were mentors who spoke to a fundamental part of me, and yet I had no place to explore that, no place to live it. I began to see more gaps within myself and what those spaces might mean. I could feel the wounds of repression and disconnection from the child, the wild one, and the magician in me. I studied about rites of passage and initiations of men from all over the world. I read about Kalahari bushmen, Australian aborigines,° Plains Indians, and Siberian shamans. In the process I was reclaiming and honoring a lost part of my childhood and recovering my soul.

Inevitably, I was drawn to workshops and retreats that felt as though they might be enactments of the practices that I was reading about. At one such event I met some men of like spirit. We began to meet regularly and to explore these notions in a very concrete and experiential way. We met every two weeks and took weekend retreats together. We drummed, we danced, we did ceremony. We talked about our worst fears, deepest wounds, our greatest joys and our abiding passions. I came to know myself in ways I hadn't dreamed of. The six brothers that I met then were the first brothers of the Boulder Men's Council. Since that time, five years ago, the Men's Council has grown to include many like-spirited brothers.

10      The Men's Council is to me a place like the vacant lots of my childhood. And, like them, it is not vacant, but simply wild and uncivilized. It holds something that grows naturally out of the earth. The great mysteries are still alive there. This natural wilderness is the very soul of my being, my source. And as wonderful as that is, I'm not contemplating living there all the time, any more than I would try to live aboriginal dreamtime, Plains Indian spirituality, or Siberian shamanism. Yet, all these traditions have value for me and have something in common: a connection to the sacred that is earth-centered, that is lived out in real community, and that honors the mythic realms of reality.

The Men's Council encourages this dialogue between the wilderness and civilization, a dialogue that is certainly heating up. Wilderness was the first parent, and all cultures are its children. The children have now grown, but many of us lack respect for the elder and this threatens us all. I feel this struggle within myself. I am not a primitive man and yet I am also not a civilized

---

*aborigines:* Native, indigenous people.

man. And I find that I am not alone. Most of my Council brothers are also questers and wild men and warriors and pilgrims, spiraling in and out of a great labyrinth.° We are meeting and exploring ways to connect with our deepest selves and the earth, to bring that into our communities and to create a sustainable culture.

As we men gather to live out the truths of ourselves, we discover the value of our secular rites of passage and we cocreate new sacred ones that honor our manhood. Only when we have accepted ourselves and our brothers as men can we become fully humanized adults. This is not a one-time process. Nor can it be in this age. We are not conforming to a set of traditional beliefs or established doctrines. We are living in the mystery of what we will become. To do this, we need all our brothers. We must use the grief, the anger, the fear, and the wildness to take us down into our souls.

One of the beauties for me in this self-reclamation project is that I am now defining myself more from an internal place and can meet both men and women out of shared interest and not so much out of competition and dependency. Everything I do, be it writing for this book, changing my godson's diapers, or putting a supportive arm around a brother, is manly and comes more from myself. I can see the world with more clarity now, and paradoxically that makes the world far more mysterious. This awareness has a price. I feel the pain in others and in the earth. My choices seem infinitely more complex and difficult. Being adult and male is a huge responsibility. Fortunately, I now understand that this is not to be done alone. I have Council brothers and many sisters who enjoy this serious and blissful business of dancing in the cracks between worlds.

**QUESTIONS**

1. Consider the title of this essay: "Dancing in the Cracks between Worlds." What are those cracks? Which worlds are they between? Does the title carry positive or negative connotations?
2. Make a list of the elements Daly was taught to reject; make another list of the rituals he was expected to embrace as he became "a man."
3. Why did Daly feel, for a long time, that he couldn't trust other men? Why did he feel he could trust women?
4. What does the author need to connect to?
5. What do you think Daly means when he describes the vacant lot of his childhood as "wild and uncivilized"? Does he intend that description as a rejection or as a compliment?

*labyrinth:* Maze.

6. According to Daly, what is the price that accompanies awareness of the mystery of the world?
7. Identify places where Daly uses details effectively.

## CONNECTIONS

1. Compare and contrast Daly's essay with the one written by Warren Farrell.
2. Identify some similarities between Daly's essay and Willa Cather's story "The Enchanted Bluff" (included in Section 1).

# ◇ Cinderella's Stepsisters

## Toni Morrison

The first African American author to win the Nobel Prize for literature, Toni Morrison was born in Lorain, Ohio. She has taught English at various universities and has been an editor for a publishing company. Her novels include *Song of Solomon* (which won the National Book Critics Circle Award for fiction in 1978), *Tar Baby* (1981), *Beloved* (which won the Pulitzer Prize for fiction in 1987), and *Jazz* (1992). In 1992 she also published a nonfiction book entitled *Playing in the Dark: Whiteness and the Literary Imagination.* Her essays have appeared in several magazines. The following piece was first delivered as a commencement address at Barnard College and first published in *Ms.* magazine in 1979.

**WARM-UP:** Describe a situation in which you were "in charge" of others. How did you feel? How did you treat subordinates? If you've never had the experience of being in charge, describe a situation in which someone else had authority over you.

Let me begin by taking you back a little. Back before the days at college. To nursery school, probably, to a once-upon-a-time time when you first heard, or read, or, I suspect, even saw "Cinderella." Because it is Cinderella that I want to talk about; because it is Cinderella who causes me a feeling of urgency. What is unsettling about that fairy tale is that it is essentially the story of household—a world, if you please—of women gathered together and held together in order to abuse another woman. There is, of course, a rather vague absent father and a nick-of-time prince with a foot fetish. But neither has much personality. And there are the surrogate "mothers," of course (god- and step-), who contribute both to Cinderella's grief and to her release and happiness. But it is her stepsisters who interest me. How crippling it must have been for those young girls to grow up with a mother, to watch and imitate that mother, enslaving another girl.

I am curious about their fortunes after the story ends. For contrary to recent adaptations, the stepsisters were not ugly, clumsy, stupid girls with outsize feet. The Grimm collection describes them as "beautiful and fair in appearance." When we are introduced to them they are beautiful, elegant, women of status, and clearly women of power. Having watched and participated in the violent dominion° of another woman, will they be any less cruel

1

*dominion:* Control, subjugation.

when it comes their turn to enslave other children, or even when they are required to take care of their own mother?

It is not a wholly medieval problem. It is quite a contemporary one: feminine power when directed at other women has historically been wielded in what has been described as a "masculine" manner. Soon you will be in a position to do the very same thing. Whatever your background—rich or poor—whatever the history of education in your family—five generations or one—you have taken advantage of what has been available to you . . . and you will therefore have both the economic and social status of the stepsisters *and* you will have their power.

I want not to *ask* you but to *tell* you not to participate in the oppression of your sisters. Mothers who abuse their children are women, and another woman, not an agency, has to be willing to stay their hands. Mothers who set fire to school buses are women, and another woman, not an agency, has to tell them to stay their hands. Women who stop the promotion of other women in careers are women, and another woman must come to the victim's aid. Social and welfare workers who humiliate their clients may be women, and other women colleagues have to deflect their anger.

5      I am alarmed by the violence that women do to each other: professional violence, competitive violence, emotional violence. I am alarmed by the willingness of women to enslave other women. I am alarmed by a growing absence of decency on the killing floor of professional women's worlds. You are the women who will take your place in the world where *you* can decide who shall flourish and who shall wither; you will make distinctions between the deserving poor and the undeserving poor; where you can yourself determine which life is expendable and which is indispensable. Since you will have the power to do it, you may also be persuaded that you have the right to do it. As educated women the distinction between the two is first-order business.

I am suggesting that we pay as much attention to our nurturing sensibilities as to our ambition. You are moving in the direction of freedom and the function of freedom is to free somebody else. You are moving toward self-fulfillment, and the consequences of that fulfillment should be to discover that there is something just as important as you are and that just-as-important thing may be Cinderella—or your stepsister.

In your rainbow journey toward the realization of personal goals, don't make choices based only on your security and your safety. Nothing is safe. That is not to say that anything ever was, or that anything worth achieving ever should be. Things of value seldom are. It is not safe to have a child. It is not safe to challenge the status quo. It is not safe to choose work that has not been done before. Or to do old work in a new way. There will always be someone there to stop you. But in pursuing your highest ambitions, don't let your personal safety diminish the safety of your stepsister. In wielding the power that is deservedly yours, don't permit it to enslave your stepsisters. Let your might and your power emanate from that place in you that is nurturing and caring.

Women's rights is not only an abstraction, a cause; it is also a personal affair. It is not only about "us"; it is also about me and you. Just the two of us.

## QUESTIONS

1. What does Morrison's essay suggest about where we learn our values? Are all the values we learn good ones?
2. Explain what Morrison means when she claims that "feminine power when directed at other women has historically been wielded in what has been described as a 'masculine' manner." What is a "masculine" manner? What might a "feminine" manner be?
3. Relying on your own experiences, describe what relationships between women are often like.
4. Do you agree with Morrison that "the function of freedom is to free someone else"? Explain your position.
5. In the fifth paragraph, what does Morrison mean by "violence"?
6. Who is the audience for Morrison's essay?
7. What is Morrison's tone in this essay?
8. Identify sentence fragments in the opening paragraph; explain whether they are effective.
9. Explain your understanding of the last paragraph of the essay.

## CONNECTIONS

1. In light of the insights provided by Morrison in this essay, discuss the relationship between the narrator and the quiet girl from the selection by Maxine Hong Kingston (Section 1).
2. Does Virginia Woolf's view of the connection between anger and potential loss of power shed any light on the relationships described in "Cinderella's Stepsisters"?
3. Reread paragraph 45 of Paolo Freire's essay "The 'Banking' Concept of Education." Is its point similar to or different from Morrison's views of "the function of freedom"?

## ∼ Sizing Up the Sexes

### Christine Gorman

> Christine Gorman has published numerous science-based articles in both popular magazines and scientific journals—including an article she co-authored in 1996, entitled "Equilibrium and Kinetic Measurements Reveal Rapidly Reversible Binding of Ras to Ref," which appeared in *The Journal of Biological Chemistry*. The following essay appeared initially in *Time* magazine in 1992.

> **WARM-UP:** Do you think that the roles that men and women assume as adults are primarily molded by genetic differences, socio-environmental influences, or a combination of the two?

What are little boys made of?
What are little boys made of?
Frogs and snails
And puppy dogs' tails,
That's what little boys are made of.

What are little girls made of?
What are little girls made of?
Sugar and spice
And all that's nice,
That's what little girls are made of.
*Anonymous*

1    Many scientists rely on elaborately complex and costly equipment to probe the mysteries confronting humankind. Not Melissa Hines. The UCLA behavioral scientist is hoping to solve one of life's oldest riddles with a toybox full of police cars, Lincoln Logs and Barbie dolls. For the past two years, Hines and her colleagues have tried to determine the origins of gender differences by capturing on videotape the squeals of delight, furrows of concentration and myriad° decisions that children from 2½ to 8 make while playing. Although both sexes play with all the toys available in Hines' laboratory, her work confirms what most parents (and more than a few aunts, uncles and nursery-school teachers) already know. As a group, the boys favor sports cars, fire trucks and Lincoln Logs, while the girls are drawn more often to dolls and kitchen toys.

---

*myriad:* Innumerable.

But one batch of girls defies expectations and consistently prefers the boy toys. These youngsters have a rare genetic abnormality that caused them to produce elevated levels of testosterone, among other hormones, during their embryonic development. On average, they play with the same toys as the boys in the same ways and just as often. Could it be that the high levels of testosterone present in their bodies before birth have left a permanent imprint on their brains, affecting their later behavior? Or did their parents, knowing of their disorder, somehow subtly influence their choices? If the first explanation is true and biology determines the choice, Hines wonders, "Why would you evolve to want to play with a truck?"

Not so long ago, any career-minded researcher would have hesitated to ask such questions. During the feminist revolution of the 1970s, talk of inborn differences in the behavior of men and women was distinctly unfashionable, even taboo. Men dominated fields like architecture and engineering, it was argued, because of social, not hormonal, pressures. Women did the vast majority of society's childrearing because few other options were available to them. Once sexism was abolished, so the argument ran, the world would become a perfectly equitable,° androgynous place, aside from a few anatomical details.

But biology has a funny way of confounding° expectations. Rather than disappear, the evidence for innate° sexual differences only began to mount. In medicine, researchers documented that heart disease strikes men at a younger age than it does women and that women have a more moderate physiological response to stress. Researchers found subtle neurological differences between the sexes both in the brain's structure and in its functioning. In addition, another generation of parents discovered that, despite their best efforts to give baseballs to their daughters and sewing kits to their sons, girls still flocked to dollhouses while boys clambered into tree forts. Perhaps nature is more important than nurture after all.

Even professional skeptics have been converted. "When I was younger, I believed that 100% of sex differences were due to the environment," says Jerre Levy, professor of psychology at the University of Chicago. Her own toddler toppled that utopian° notion. "My daughter was 15 months old, and I had just dressed her in her teeny little nightie. Some guests arrived, and she came into the room, knowing full well that she looked adorable. She came in with this saucy little walk, cocking her head, blinking her eyes, especially at the men. You never saw such flirtation in your life." After 20 years spent studying the brain, Levy is convinced: "I'm sure there are biologically based differences in our behavior."

5

---

*equitable:* Fair, evenhanded.    *confounding:* Destroying, refuting.    *innate:* Inborn, inherent.    *utopian:* Ideal.

Now that it is O.K. to admit the possibility, the search for sexual differences has expanded into nearly every branch of the life sciences. Anthropologists have debunked° Margaret Mead's work on the extreme variability of gender roles in New Guinea. Psychologists are untangling the complex interplay between hormones and aggression. But the most provocative, if as yet inconclusive, discoveries of all stem from the pioneering exploration of a tiny 3-lb. universe: the human brain. In fact, some researchers predict that the confirmation of innate differences in behavior could lead to an unprecedented understanding of the mind.

Some of the findings seem merely curious. For example, more men than women are lefthanded, reflecting the dominance of the brain's right hemisphere. By contrast, more women listen equally with both ears, while men favor the right one.

Other revelations are bound to provoke more controversy. Psychology tests, for instance, consistently support the notion that men and women perceive the world in subtly different ways. Males excel at rotating three-dimensional objects in their head. Females prove better at reading emotions of people in photographs. A growing number of scientists believe the discrepancies° reflect functional differences in the brains of men and women. If true, then some misunderstandings between the sexes may have more to do with crossed wiring than cross-purposes.

Most of the gender differences that have been uncovered so far are, statistically speaking, quite small. "Even the largest differences in cognitive function are not as large as the difference in male and female height," Hines notes. "You still see a lot of overlap." Otherwise, women could never read maps and men would always be lefthanded. That kind of flexibility within the sexes reveals just how complex a puzzle gender actually is, requiring pieces from biology, sociology and culture.

10    Ironically, researchers are not entirely sure how or even why humans produce two sexes in the first place. (Why not just one—or even three—as in some species?) What is clear is that the two sexes originate with two distinct chromosomes. Women bear a double dose of the large X chromosome, while men usually possess a single X and a short, stumpy Y chromosome. In 1990 British scientists reported they had identified a single gene on the Y chromosome that determines maleness. Like some kind of biomolecular Paul Revere, this master gene rouses a host of its compatriots to the complex task of turning a fetus into a boy. Without such a signal, all human embryos would develop into girls. "I have all the genes for being male except this one, and my husband has all the genes for being female," marvels evolutionary psychologist Leda Cosmides, of the University of California at Santa Barbara. "The only difference is which genes got turned on."

*debunked:* Denounced, exposed as false.    *discrepancies:* Differences.

Yet even this snippet of DNA is not enough to ensure a masculine result. An elevated level of the hormone testosterone is also required during the pregnancy. Where does it come from? The fetus' own undescended testes. In those rare cases in which the tiny body does not respond to the hormone, a genetically male fetus develops sex organs that look like a clitoris and vagina rather than a penis. Such people look and act female. The majority marry and adopt children.

The influence of the sex hormones extends into the nervous system. Both males and females produce androgens, such as testosterone, and estrogens— although in different amounts. (Men and women who make no testosterone generally lack a libido.) Researchers suspect that an excess of testosterone before birth enables the right hemisphere to dominate the brain, resulting in lefthandedness. Since testosterone levels are higher in boys than in girls, that would explain why more boys are southpaws.

Subtle sex-linked preferences have been detected as early as 52 hours after birth. In studies of 72 newborns, University of Chicago psychologist Martha McClintock and her students found that a toe-fanning reflex was stronger in the left foot of 60% of the males, while all the females favored their right. However, apart from such reflexes in the hands, legs and feet, the team could find no other differences in the babies' responses.

One obvious place to look for gender differences is in the hypothalamus, a lusty little organ perched over the brain stem that, when sufficiently provoked, consumes a person with rage, thirst, hunger or desire. In animals, a region at the front of the organ controls sexual function and is somewhat larger in males than in females. But its size need not remain constant. Studies of tropical fish by Stanford University neurobiologist Russell Fernald reveal that certain cells in this tiny region of the brain swell markedly in an individual male whenever he comes to dominate a school. Unfortunately for the piscine pasha, the cells will also shrink if he loses control of his harem to another male.

Many researchers suspect that, in humans too, sexual preferences are controlled by the hypothalamus. Based on a study of 41 autopsied brains, Simon LeVay of the Salk Institute for Biological Studies announced last summer that he had found a region in the hypothalamus that was on average twice as large in the heterosexual men as in either women or homosexual men. LeVay's findings support the idea that varying hormone levels before birth may immutably stamp the developing brain in one erotic direction or another. 15

These prenatal fluctuations may also steer boys toward more rambunctious° behavior than girls. June Reinisch, director of the Kinsey Institute for Research in Sex, Gender and Reproduction at Indiana University, in a pioneering study of eight pairs of brothers and 17 pairs of sisters ages 6 to 18

*rambunctious:* Unruly, uncontrollable.

uncovered a complex interplay between hormones and aggression. As a group, the young males gave more belligerent answers than did the females on a multiple-choice test in which they had to imagine their response to stressful situations. But siblings who had been exposed in utero° to synthetic antimiscarriage hormones that mimic testosterone were the most combative of all. The affected boys proved significantly more aggressive than their unaffected brothers, and the drug-exposed girls were much more contentious° than their unexposed sisters. Reinisch could not determine, however, whether this childhood aggression would translate into greater ambition or competitiveness in the adult world.

While most of the gender differences uncovered so far seem to fall under the purview° of the hypothalamus, researchers have begun noting discrepancies in other parts of the brain as well. For the past nine years, neuroscientists have debated whether the corpus callosum, a thick bundle of nerves that allows the right half of the brain to communicate with the left, is larger in women than in men. If it is, and if size corresponds to function, then the greater crosstalk between the hemispheres might explain enigmatic phenomena like female intuition, which is supposed to accord women greater ability to read emotional clues.

These conjectures about the corpus callosum have been hard to prove because the structure's girth varies dramatically with both age and health. Studies of autopsied material are of little use because brain tissue undergoes such dramatic changes in the hours after death. Neuroanatomist Laura Allen and neuroendocrinologist Roger Gorski of UCLA decided to try to circumvent some of these problems by obtaining brain scans from live, apparently healthy people. In their investigation of 146 subjects, published in April, they confirmed that parts of the corpus callosum were up to 23% wider in women than in men. They also measured thicker connections between the two hemispheres in other parts of women's brains.

Encouraged by the discovery of such structural differences, many researchers have begun looking for dichotomies° of function as well. At the Bowman Gray Medical School in Winston-Salem, N.C., Cecile Naylor has determined that men and women enlist widely varying parts of their brain when asked to spell words. By monitoring increases in blood flow, the neuropsychologist found that women use both sides of their head when spelling, while men use primarily their left side. Because the area activated on the right side is used in understanding emotions, the women apparently tap a wider range of experience for their task. Intriguingly, the effect occurred only with spelling and not during a memory test.

---

*in utero:* "In the uterus".    *contentious:* Displaying a tendency to quarrel.    *purview:* Range, limits.
*dichotomies:* Divisions into two distinct groups.

Researchers speculate that the greater communication between the two sides of the brain could impair a woman's performance on certain highly specialized visual-spatial tasks. For example, the ability to tell directions on a map without physically having to rotate it appears stronger in those individuals whose brains restrict the process to the right hemisphere. Any crosstalk between the two sides apparently distracts the brain from its job. Sure enough, several studies have shown that this mental-rotation skill is indeed more tightly focused in men's brains than in women's.

But how did it get to be that way? So far, none of the gender scientists have figured out whether nature or nurture is more important. "Nothing is ever equal, even in the beginning," observes Janice Juraska, a biopsychologist at the University of Illinois at Urbana-Champaign. She points out, for instance, that mother rats lick their male offspring more frequently than they do their daughters. However, Juraska has demonstrated that it is possible to reverse some inequities by manipulating environmental factors. Female rats have fewer nerve connections than males into the hippocampus, a brain region associated with spatial relations and memory. But when Juraska "enriched" the cages of the females with stimulating toys, the females developed more of these neuronal connections. "Hormones do affect things—it's crazy to deny that," says the researcher. "But there's no telling which way sex differences might go if we completely changed the environment." For humans, educational enrichment could perhaps enhance a woman's ability to work in three dimensions and a man's ability to interpret emotions. Says Juraska: "There's nothing about human brains that is so stuck that a different way of doing things couldn't change it enormously."

Nowhere is this complex interaction between nature and nurture more apparent than in the unique human abilities of speaking, reading and writing. No one is born knowing French, for example; it must be learned, changing the brain forever. Even so, language skills are linked to specific cerebral centers. In a remarkable series of experiments, neurosurgeon George Ojemann of the University of Washington has produced scores of detailed maps of people's individual language centers.

First, Ojemann tested his patients' verbal intelligence using a written exam. Then, during neurosurgery—which was performed under a local anesthetic—he asked them to name aloud a series of objects found in a steady stream of black-and-white photos. Periodically, he touched different parts of the brain with an electrode that temporarily blocked the activity of that region. (This does not hurt because the brain has no sense of pain.) By noting when his patients made mistakes, the surgeon was able to determine which sites were essential to naming.

Several complex sexual differences emerged. Men with lower verbal IQs were more likely to have their language skills located toward the back of the brain. In a number of women, regardless of IQ, the naming ability was restricted to the frontal lobe. This disparity could help explain why strokes that affect the rear of the brain seem to be more devastating to men than to women.

25     Intriguingly, the sexual differences are far less significant in people with higher verbal IQs. Their language skills developed in a more intermediate part of the brain. And yet, no two patterns were ever identical. "That to me is the most important finding," Ojemann says. "Instead of these sites being laid down more or less the same in everyone, they're laid down in subtly different places." Language is scattered randomly across these cerebral centers, he hypothesizes, because the skills evolved so recently.

What no one knows for sure is just how hardwired the brain is. How far and at what stage can the brain's extraordinary flexibility be pushed? Several studies suggest that the junior high years are key. Girls show the same aptitudes for math as boys until about the seventh grade, when more and more girls develop math phobia. Coincidentally, that is the age at which boys start to shine and catch up to girls in reading.

By one account, the gap between men and women for at least some mental skills has actually started to shrink. By looking at 25 years' worth of data from academic tests, Janet Hyde, professor of psychology and women's studies at the University of Wisconsin at Madison, discovered that overall gender differences for verbal and mathematical skills dramatically decreased after 1974. One possible explanation, Hyde notes, is that "Americans have changed their socialization and educational patterns over the past few decades. They are treating males and females with greater similarity."

Even so, women still have not caught up with men on the mental-rotation test. Fascinated by the persistence of that gap, psychologists Irwin Silverman and Marion Eals of York University in Ontario wondered if there were any spatial tasks at which women outperformed men. Looking at it from the point of view of human evolution, Silverman and Eals reasoned that while men may have developed strong spatial skills in response to evolutionary pressures to be successful hunters, women would have needed other types of visual skills to excel as gatherers and foragers of food.

The psychologists therefore designed a test focused on the ability to discern and later recall the location of objects in a complex, random pattern. In series of tests, student volunteers were given a minute to study a drawing that contained such unrelated objects as an elephant, a guitar and a cat. Then Silverman and Eals presented their subjects with a second drawing containing additional objects and told them to cross out those items that had been added and circle any that had moved. Sure enough, the women consistently surpassed the men in giving correct answers.

30     What made the psychologists really sit up and take notice, however, was the fact that the women scored much better on the mental-rotation test while

they were menstruating. Specifically, they improved their scores by 50% to 100% whenever their estrogen levels were at their lowest. It is not clear why this should be. However, Silverman and Eals are trying to find out if women exhibit a similar hormonal effect for any other visual tasks.

Oddly enough, men may possess a similar hormonal response, according to new research reported in November by Doreen Kimura, a psychologist at the University of Western Ontario. In her study of 138 adults, Kimura found that males perform better on mental-rotation tests in the spring, when their testosterone levels are low, rather than in the fall, when they are higher. Men are also subject to a daily cycle, with testosterone levels lowest around 8 P.M. and peaking around 4 A.M. Thus, says June Reinisch of the Kinsey Institute: "When people say women can't be trusted because they cycle every month, my response is that men cycle every day, so they should only be allowed to negotiate peace treaties in the evening."

Far from strengthening stereotypes about who women and men truly are or how they should behave, research into innate sexual differences only underscores humanity's awesome adaptability. "Gender is really a complex business," says Reinisch. "There's no question that hormones have an effect. But what does that have to do with the fact that I like to wear pink ribbons and you like to wear baseball gloves? Probably something, but we don't know what."

Even the concept of what an innate difference represents is changing. The physical and chemical differences between the brains of the two sexes may be malleable° and subject to change by experience: certainly an event or act of learning can directly affect the brain's biochemistry and physiology. And so, in the final analysis, it may be impossible to say where nature ends and nurture begins because the two are so intimately linked.

## QUESTIONS

1. Where does Gorman provide an overview of the debate about gender differences? Is this placement effective?
2. Why were some researchers reluctant for a time to consider possible biological gender differences in human behavior?
3. Is U.S. society more equitable in terms of gender than it was 30 years ago? If so, what has accounted for that change?
4. Explain why Jerre Levy believes that the example of her daughter's "flirtation" supports the theory that "there are biologically based differences in our behavior." Do you feel that her example proves that point?

---

*malleable:* Changeable; soft.

5. What examples does Gorman provide to support the idea that there are significant differences between men's and women's brains? Are these major differences?
6. What point does Gorman support by quoting Janice Juraska and discussing Juraska's research?
7. Why does the author refer to the concept of gender as "a puzzle"?
8. Reread Gorman's conclusion. Does she lean toward nature, nurture, or a combination of both as the major influence on a person's gender role?

## CONNECTIONS

1. In Marge Piercy's "Barbie Doll," is it nature or nurture that shapes the main character's sense of femininity?
2. How does the transitional piece that introduces this section, Julius Lester's essay "Being a Boy," relate to Gorman's essay?
3. Explain the similarities between Gorman's essay's conclusion and the conclusion of Tom Daly's essay (earlier in this section).

# ～ From My Parents

*Noel Linayao*

> Noel Linayao was born in the Philippines in 1972. In 1978, his family moved
> to Japan; there, with other so-called military brats, he attended a Depart-
> ment of Defense school until his family relocated to the United States in
> 1986. A graduate of Silver Creek High School in East San Jose, California,
> Linayao first attended San Diego State University and later transferred to San
> Jose State University. When he wrote this essay, he was a junior majoring in
> computer graphics and enrolled in ROTC. After earning his bachelor's
> degree, Linayao hopes to get a military commission, serve four years of
> active duty (preferably in aviation), and then pursue a career in computer
> animation.

> **WARM-UP:** How do most of the members of your generation view
> gender roles? What do they see as a man's primary responsibilities? What
> about a woman's primary responsibilities? Do you agree with what the
> majority of your generation thinks about this issue?

"Get Ready!" the jumpmaster yells over the noise of the aircraft. We      1
respond with a loud and thunderous "Get Ready!" "Stand Up!" is the
next command. We echo back "Stand Up!" carrying about a hundred pounds
of ammunition, weapons, food, and other necessary equipment. "Hook
Up!" . . . "Check Static Line!" . . . "Check Equipment!" . . . "Sound off for
Equipment Check!" . . . "Stand in the Door!" . . . the light turns green . . . "Go!"
And one by one, soldiers exit the aircraft into a black void. This is the U.S.
Army's Airborne Jump School, and neither size nor gender prevents anyone
from attending and earning the coveted Airborne Jump Wings. Like Northern
Warfare Training or Air Assault School, I have seen many women complete
this school, some even surpassing their male counterparts, and this has reaffirmed my belief that women can accomplish anything that they set their
minds to.

Any notion or belief that I had concerning the roles of men and women
has come from my parents and the environment in which I was raised. I am a
product of a traditional Filipino Roman Catholic family who was raised in
Japan on a military base. I had arrived in Japan in the fall of 1978. My father
was in the U.S. Navy and my mother was a homemaker. Japan was where I was

exposed to the roles that gender places upon an individual. During Japanese Culture class, I was taught that Japan was notoriously known for its strong traditional views regarding women. People call each other by their family name there, so many women feel that they have lost a part of their being. In addition, women in Japan must play the role of being a homemaker. Japanese men believe that the homemaker should care for the children, watch over her husband's health, and pay attention to keeping the home in order. At six years of age, I accepted my mother for who she was, a mother and a homemaker.

As I grew older, the perception that I first had concerning my mother began to change. I had never noticed it before, but in small increments, my mother's role in the household was not what I first perceived it to be. My father was in the U.S. Navy; consequently, he was away six months out of the year. During those long trips, my mother had to assume both roles as the father and mother. It was on these long trips that I began seeing my mother not as the weaker sex, totally dependent on her spouse, but as a strong, independent woman who essentially raised four sons on her own.

My mother was never a quiet person; she was outgoing and extremely outspoken; she was never afraid to let others know what she truly felt. The longer I watched my mother, the traditional belief that I had about women began to fade. When my father returned, my mother reverted back and assumed her role as being the mother, but never as a subservient homemaker. My father also played a role in helping to shape my views on women. For example, he never treated my mother as a lesser individual, but instead he treated her as his equal. My parents helped one another out. My father helped cook, clean, essentially helped my mother with the domestic chores. They were a team: When one was at work, the other took over. They both had total respect for one another and that is what I was shown and taught to believe in.

5    Through my parents, I was brought up to believe that there is little or no difference in what a man or a woman can or cannot accomplish. I do not believe that a woman should sit at home and take on a conservative sex role. Instead, she should go out and find a career that she truly loves and excel in it. I was taught that a woman can do anything that a man can do, and at times, even better. Consequently, the women that I have dated and known have always been highly ambitious and independent individuals. People say that one dates someone like their mother. In the case of my girlfriend Sarah, this seems to be true. Sarah is strong-willed, ambitious, independent, and more importantly, the backbone of the relationship. She is amazed at how I actually turned out. I am the exact opposite of the stereotypical Filipino male that her friends had first thought me to be.

Looking back at my childhood, the biggest impact that I had concerning men and women came directly from my parents. Parents do have a profound effect on how our minds are shaped concerning roles between genders. For example, Sarah's brother-in-law is the exact opposite of me; he believes that the woman should take care of the children and do the chores around the house. His parents' roles had been defined in this way; therefore, I believe that this is what he perceives to be right. What parents display to their children concerning their roles in the relationship will help shape how the children will decipher those roles in the future.

## QUESTIONS

1. Is this essay's introduction effective? Why or why not? What should a good introduction do for an essay?
2. What is Linayao's thesis? Where does he state it? Does the thesis appear only once in the essay? Why?
3. Do you agree with this essay's thesis? Explain your answer.
4. Does this essay flow well? If you feel that it does, explain how the author succeeded in creating that flow. If you think that it doesn't, point to places where you feel that the flow of ideas was broken, and suggest ways to improve that aspect of the essay.
5. Does Linayao make effective use of details in this essay? Point to places in the essay where details make the writing vivid or places where you think more detail would have made the essay stronger.
6. Is this essay's conclusion effective? Why or why not?
7. Early in the essay, Linayao describes himself as "a product of a traditional Filipino Roman Catholic family." Does the rest of the essay challenge your belief about what such a family is like? Explain your answer.

## CONNECTIONS

1. Does this essay support Christine Gorman's views about the factors that affect the development of gender roles, or does it challenge those views?
2. Consider the experiences described in this student essay, as well as those described in Marge Piercy's poem "Barbie Doll" and in Warren Farrell's selection "Men as Success Objects." Which one is closest to your own experiences? Do you think that some of the attitudes described in those selections have become obsolete, or do they all still exist in our society today?

# 〜 Men Are from Earth—and So Are Women

## *Ellen Goodman*

Ellen Goodman, long-time syndicated columnist and associate editor of the *Boston Globe,* was born in Boston. After graduating from Radcliffe College, she worked for various newspapers and magazines. In 1980 she won the Pulitzer Prize for distinguished commentary; she has also been awarded the Hubert H. Humphrey Civil Rights Award. Her books include *Turning Points* (1979), *Keeping in Touch* (1985), and *Value Judgments* (1993). In the introduction to the latter, she states, "If I absolutely had to choose one word to describe my subject, the word would be: values." The following column was syndicated in more than four hundred newspapers across the country in 1995.

**WARM-UP:** Do you ever listen to talk radio or watch TV talk shows? What do you get out of such shows?

1   When I was a kid we didn't need books to tell us that men were from Mars and women were from Venus. We could see that they inhabited different worlds.

Women were at home; men in the office. Women wore the skirts; men wore the pants in the family. She raised the kids; he ran the world.

Now, after 30 years of emphasizing what we have in common, we're back to focusing on the differences between the sexes. The more similar our real lives, the more we seem to focus on the separateness of our emotional workings and biological wirings.

The pop talk now is all about the different languages we speak, the different ways our brains work, the difference in our feelings. We scan the latest research looking for evidence of gender gaps rather than common ground.

5   Deborah Tannen's book "You Just Don't Understand" has become proof that men and women can't communicate, even though her point was that we *can.* The complex new brain research has been reduced to a similar shorthand pronouncement that men and women "think differently."

We've become hooked again on notions of natural differences. But we should be more concerned with ways we are again nurturing differences.

A Yale researcher, Dr. Sally Shaywitz, who watched men and women sounding out words under a Magnetic Resonance Imaging machine, was struck by the alternate paths the male and female brain took to get to the same place. But today we're directing men and women to separate places.

Talk radio has become largely a guy thing. It's not only moved to the right, but also to the testosterone. The powerful hosts are mostly male, so are the callers and so are the listeners. It's become the turf of the angry white man.

Talk television, on the other hand, is largely a gal thing. The hosts may be more equally divided by gender—Ricki Lake and Montel Williams, Rolando and Geraldo, Sally Jesse Raphael and Maury Povich—but the viewers are mostly female.

The sexes are split and so are the subjects. Male talk radio is about political life. Female talk television is about personal life. The hot topics of the radio week are the balanced budget, food stamps, Congress. The hot topics of the television week are "man-stealers," "meddling mothers-in-law," "obese women."     10

I don't think that men naturally "evolved" from hunting mammoths to attacking Congress. Nor did the fittest of the female species survive gathering berries to be obsessed with man-stealing.

But the right-wing talk radio folks deliberately point their followers to the world, the arena of public policy, while the no-wing talk television hosts direct their audience to the home, the drama of private life. One sex gets marching orders, the other gets hankies.

In the end, keeping either men or women in single-sex slots may be equally destructive. But in the current rush of policy-making and unmaking, it's most troubling that the public voice is overwhelmingly male.

These men are arguing, faxing and forming what we call "public" opinion while the women are talking personally in the traditional living room of relationships. Men are told to worry about laws and women about their in-laws.

In the cacophony° of loud broadcast voices, women are uncomfortable in a shouting match. They're drowned out when speaking in their own voice. Indeed the year of the angry white man, typified by the sound of talk radio, may not signify a male backlash as much as it does a female retreat.     15

But public policy is not a boy-thing. Whether you believe in nature or nurture, governing is not done in one part of the brain or for one-half of the population.

Don't tell me that men are from Mars and women are from Venus. The last time I looked we were living here, together.

## QUESTIONS

1. Goodman writes that "the more similar our real lives, the more we seem to focus on the separateness of our emotional workings and

---

*cacophony:* Harsh or discordant sound.

biological wirings." In what ways are the "real lives" of men and women more similar today than they used to be? In what ways are they still different?

2. Goodman says that "we're back to focusing on the differences between the sexes." Do you believe we should emphasize similarities? differences? both? neither? Explain your response.

3. Based on this essay, do you believe that Goodman would prefer men and women to reverse roles in politics, business, and the home? Why or why not?

4. What concern does Goodman express in paragraphs 6 and 7?

5. Do you agree with Goodman's observations about talk radio and TV talk shows?

6. Do you agree that "in the current rush of policy-making and unmaking . . . the public voice is overwhelmingly male"?

7. Identify places where Goodman refers to other writers to support her argument, and explain whether or not these references are effective.

8. What is the tone of Goodman's essay?

9. Is this essay organized effectively? Justify your answer.

## CONNECTIONS

1. Is Goodman critical of essays like the one written by Christine Gorman? Explain your response.

2. Do you think Goodman would agree with Warren Farrell about society's pressures upon men? Support your answer with evidence from Goodman's text.

# Drafting, Organization, and the In-Class Essay

Advice about writing must always be linked to the specific writing situation. What may have been a good suggestion yesterday may not apply today, and what may have been good writing advice today may fail you tomorrow. For example, many students were taught in high school a basic formula for writing essays: the five-paragraph model (an introduction, followed by three "body" paragraphs, and a conclusion that typically just repeats the introduction). But this approach is too limiting; using the five-paragraph model for all writing situations is like trying to solve all math problems with one algebraic formula. The five-paragraph model assumes that *form* should determine *content*: All writing situations are thus reduced to something you can write three things about. But what if you have *four* points to make in support of your thesis? Or what if you're asked to write a ten-page paper? (By the old model, that would require paragraphs that are each two pages long!) Although the five-paragraph model works fine for some writing situations, most essays you will be assigned to write in college require a more complex approach, one that is developed as you write. This approach assumes that there is no one right way to organize an essay: *Content* should determine *form*. This is not to say that you should forget everything you've learned about organizing your points; rather, you should keep an open mind. Watch for an organization suggested by your prewriting—one that develops an idea rather than merely listing points.

Although you need to approach each writing situation with a fresh perspective, you will probably take some common general steps to create an essay. You will probably begin with some form of prewriting to generate ideas about the topic. Once you have some ideas, you may want to develop a thesis—a sentence or two that summarizes the main idea of the essay. It's a good idea to write the thesis at the top of the page you are working on or on an index card, so you can look at it as often as you need. Developing a thesis early in the writing process will help you focus your essay: Having it gives you direction. At this stage, though, you have yet to write the essay, so the thesis you develop will be tentative. You may need to revise it later, so that it will reflect all of the ideas present in your final draft.

Whether or not you develop a tentative thesis at this stage is your choice; do what feels most useful to you. In any case, your next step after prewriting is to write a rough draft.

## Drafting

A rough draft is your first attempt to create a developed and focused response to a writing situation. Think of it as a grain of sand, small and rough:

Once it enters and irritates an oyster, the grain of sand will become over time a highly polished pearl. Similarly, the first draft of your essay will probably be rough; however, once you have added layers of attention and work, the final version can become as polished as you want to make it.

The way to approach the first draft depends on the writing situation. In the case of a short essay, you may just begin writing—quickly, without pausing to edit and evaluate. The point is just to get your pen or pencil moving or your fingers typing, to produce something, a few pages that you can later revise and polish. However, if you are writing a long essay, perhaps one that includes researched material, you may want to create an outline.

*Outlining*    There are several benefits to developing a tentative outline before drafting. Produced quickly, an outline can help you see areas that need to be developed further through more thought and prewriting. It can also help you organize your thoughts and ideas before you begin writing a rough draft. Sometimes you will want to create a formal, detailed outline, like the following one, which could have helped the student to write the essay "Do I?!" included on page 204 of this text:

**Introduction:** details (white, church, music, rice, etc.)

**Body:**

I. Wedding day in the U.S.

    a. More important than the relationship

    b. Has to be big

      —dress

      —limos

      —reception

II. The cost

    a. Money

    b. Anxiety

Ill. Why get married that way?

    a. Why follow tradition?

IV. Why be with only one person?

    a. Freud (monogamy is unnatural)

    b. Humans were not designed for it

V. Answer: Dream of finding "the right one"

**Conclusion:** personal experience (more details to contrast introduction: jeans, Jamaican music, backyard, etc.)

At other times you will want to create an informal outline—little more than a list of sentences or ideas. If you take a prewriting list, for example, and reorder the points so that they flow from one to the next, building a direction for the essay overall, the result will be a simple outline.

Whether you decide to outline, however, depends on your needs as a writer. If you find that you need to know where you're heading with an essay before you begin writing or if you feel that writing without an outline is like driving on unfamiliar streets without a road map, then create an outline. If you feel that outlining restricts your creativity, then don't bother with it—just write a draft instead, letting it be as rough and uneven as it comes. You can always revise later.

*The First Sentence*    Can you "just write a draft," though? Many writers—whatever their skills—find the first sentence the most difficult to write. There are several ways to handle this problem. Some people spend a lot of time developing a good first sentence before they begin to write the rest of the essay. The danger in this approach, though, is obvious: If you cannot create a first sentence that you're pleased with, you may experience the dreaded writer's block. A more optimistic and practical approach is to think of the first sentence as your first step. You want to walk, but you don't know how. So you try, and you fall. But falling is not *failing*. So keep trying, keep writing until you've written your way across and down the page. Once you learn how to walk, you won't even remember your first fall! Similarly, once you've written one or two drafts of an essay, that first sentence will probably be long gone, either revised or thrown out.

Another method is to leave the introduction for last. Start writing any part of the essay that you feel comfortable with: Pick one idea from your prewriting or outline and get going. Afterward, think of a catchy way to lead your readers toward the points you've made. (For more advice on how to handle introductions and conclusions, two very important elements of any essay, see the discussion in Section 3.)

## Organization

A well-organized essay moves logically and smoothly from one idea to the next, without any tangents or gaps to distract from the flow. An essay, after all, is not just a cluster of isolated paragraphs floating in a sea of white space; it is more like a chain, with each paragraph acting as a link. The paragraphs can be connected in many ways, but there should be a reason for the order you choose, and that order should be made clear to the reader. Try to establish a logical progression—for example, from least important to most important idea; from past to present and into the future (chronological order, as exemplified by Julius Lester's essay "Being a Boy" and by Maxine Hong Kingston's short story "The Quiet Girl"); or from identifying a problem to proposing a solution (as in Michael Buenaflor's essay "It's Good to Know the Opposition").

In contrast, consider two other essays from the previous section: Patricia Hampl's "Memory and Imagination" and Paolo Freire's "The 'Banking' Concept of Education." Hampl's essay begins well enough with a description about a significant experience in her childhood, but toward the end of the essay she moves back and forth between advice about writing and views on the relationship between memoir, politics, and history. Some readers see in this a powerful "spiral" effect that reinforces ideas; others feel that the essay is just disorganized. Similarly, Freire's essay begins well but becomes repetitive: In paragraph 4, for example, the author makes a point about students being treated like empty vessels, but then he repeats the idea in paragraphs 16 and 23, among other places. Perhaps he does this purposely (we discuss the effective use of recurrence in Section 5 of this text), but this repetition, which is not subtle, might distract and annoy some readers.

Since there are many ways of organizing an essay, you may decide to focus more on organization during the revision stage, after you have already written a rough draft. (For more advice, see the section on editing and revision in Section 4.)

### In-Class Essays

Let's briefly discuss the in-class essay, because it is a special writing situation—one that is affected by a time limit. In other words, much of what we have already stated does not apply when you are writing an essay in class, when you do not have time to mull over an idea and revise your points for best effect. Think of the in-class essay, then, as a writing case composed of three parts: prewriting, drafting, and editing. The amount of time you dedicate to each part will be determined by the amount of time you are given to write the essay as a whole. We generally recommend the 10/70/20% approach: You should use about 10% of the time to prewrite, 70% to write the essay, and 20% to reread and edit it. This is only a suggestion, however, so feel free to adjust these percentages to fit your individual needs.

When you receive an assignment for an in-class essay, you should first read it carefully, underlining key words and making notes in the margins. Then read it over again, perhaps several times. As soon as you feel that you understand the assignment, prewrite, using whichever method works best for you—clustering, freewriting, listing. This is a very important step: Because your time is limited, you must generate ideas quickly.

As soon as you have generated ideas, take a moment to think about how they might be organized. Even if you usually don't outline, for in-class essays you should do so (although, because of the time limitations, the outline shouldn't be very detailed). You will need that quick way to determine the best order for the ideas you gathered during prewriting. Though you are given a limited time, remember that you are nonetheless expected to write a complete essay—with an introduction, paragraphs that explain and pursue ideas supporting a thesis, and a conclusion.

Finally, a very important step in writing the in-class essay is the editing. Since you've drafted the essay quickly, you are more likely to have misspelled words and committed grammatical errors. You should definitely spare time to reread the essay for correctness and clarity. We recommend that you just cross out the errors or confusing sentences and correct them directly above the line. Don't worry too much about messiness; most teachers will prefer a cross-out and a correction to no editing whatsoever. (Of course, remember that you cannot earn credit for anything that is illegible.)

### *Final Words*

Writing is always a combination of old habits and new tricks, familiar words and innovative ways of putting them together, old beliefs and new insights. Treating writing as a process will help you to understand that there's no single structure or formula to guide your hand. Once you become comfortable with this way of approaching composition, you will find that it offers true freedom of expression.

## Topics for Writing about Gender

1. Write an essay in which you first present Julius Lester's and Warren Farrell's views about manhood, and then follow them with your own views on the subject.
2. Write an essay describing your childhood and exploring the way in which the notions you learned about men and women affect your life today.
3. Write an essay describing a childhood experience in which you felt you were not being as "manly" or "womanly" as you were expected to be.
4. Informally interview older members of your family about how they were expected to be while growing up; ask, for example, about household chores, careers, expectations, and goals. Then, write an

essay that describes the differences between their experiences and your own; explain these differences in terms of generation, gender, culture, class, or other criteria that may apply.

5. Write an essay discussing a position in the workforce that you believe should be reserved only for males or only for females.

6. Write an essay exploring the roles of men and women in a culture other than that of the United States.

7. In an extended definition essay, explore various perceptions of the term "feminist."

8. Rewrite the poem "Barbie Doll," using the title "G. I. Joe" and "boy" as the main character.

9. Write an essay either supporting or opposing schools reserved for only one gender.

10. Write an essay modeled after Julius Lester's but presenting the flip side: Entitle it "Being a Girl."

11. Write an essay modeled after Warren Farrell's, entitling it "Women as ____ Objects" (fill in the blank).

12. Some people argue that platonic friendship between a man and a woman is impossible; in an essay, support or oppose this viewpoint.

## ∾ Taking the Manly Way Out

*Dave Barry*

> Dave Barry, a syndicated columnist at the *Miami Herald,* has won a Pulitzer
> Prize for his humorous writing. Recently, he has played in a band that
> includes writers Amy Tan (whose essay "Mother Tongue" appears in Section
> 6) and Stephen King. He is the author of several best-selling collections of
> essays, including *Dave Barry Turns 40* (1990), *Babies and Other Hazards of
> Sex* (1993), and more recently, *Dave Barry's Complete Guide to Guys* (1995).
> The following column appeared first in the *Miami Herald* and was reprinted
> in *Dave Barry Talks Back* (1991).

> **WARM-UP:** Describe a situation in which you experienced difficulty
> asking somebody out or being asked out on a date.

Today we're going to explore the mysterious topic of How Guys Think,     1
which has baffled women in general, and the editors of *Cosmopolitan*
magazine in particular, for thousands of years.

The big question, of course, is: How come guys never call? After successful
dates, I mean. You single women out there know what I'm talking about. You
go out with a guy, and you have a great time, and *he* seems to have a great
time, and at the end of the evening he says, quote, "Can I call you?" And you,
interpreting this to mean "Can I call you?", answer: "Sure!"

The instant you say this, the guy's body starts to dematerialize. Within a
few seconds you can stick a tire iron right through him and wave it around; in
a few more seconds he has vanished entirely, gone into the mysterious Guy
Bermuda Triangle, where whole squadrons of your dates have disappeared
over the years, never to be heard from again.

Eventually you start to wonder if there's something wrong with you, some
kind of emotional hang-up or personality defect that your dates are detecting.
Or possibly foot odor. You start having long, searching discussions with your
women friends in which you say things like: "He really seemed to like me" and
"I didn't feel as though I was putting pressure on him" and "Would you mind,
strictly as a friend, smelling my feet?"

This is silly. There's nothing wrong with you. In fact, you should interpret     5
the behavior of your dates as a kind of guy *compliment* to you. Because when
the guy asks you if he can call you, what he's really asking you, in Guy Code, is

will you marry him. Yes. See, your basic guy is into a straight-ahead, bottom-line kind of thought process that does not work nearly as well with the infinitely subtle complexities of human relationships as it does with calculating how much gravel is needed to cover a given driveway. So here's what the guy is thinking: If he calls you, you'll go out again, and you'll probably have another great time, so you'll probably go out again and have *another* great time, and so on until the only possible *option* will be to get married. This is classic Guy Logic.

So when you say "Sure!" in a bright cheery voice, you may think you're simply indicating a willingness to go out again, but as far as he's concerned you're endorsing a lifetime commitment that he is quite frankly not ready to make after only one date, so he naturally decided he can never see you again. From that day forward, if he spots you on the street, he'll spring in the opposite direction to avoid the grave risk that the two of you might meet, which would mean he'd have to ask you if you wanted to get a cup of coffee, and you might say yes, and pretty soon you'd be enjoying each other's company again, and suddenly a clergyman would appear at your table and YOU'D HAVE TO GET MARRIED AIEEEEEEE.

(You women think this is crazy, right? Whereas you guys out there are nodding your heads.)

So my advice for single women is that if you're on a date with a guy you like, and he asks whether he can call you, you should give him a nonthreatening answer, such as:

"No."

Or: "I guess so, but bear in mind that I'm a nun."

This will make him comfortable about seeing you again, each time gaining the courage to approach you more closely, in the manner of a timid, easily startled woodland creature such as a chipmunk. In a few years, if the two of you really do have common interests and compatible personalities, you may reach the point where he'll be willing to take the Big Step, namely, eating granola directly from your hand.

No matter how close you become, however, remember this rule: Do not pressure the guy to share his most sensitive innermost thoughts and feelings with you. Guys hate this, and I'll tell you why: If you were to probe inside the guy psyche, beneath that macho exterior and the endless droning about things like the 1978 World Series, you would find, deep down inside, a passionate, heartfelt interest in: the 1978 World Series. Yes. The truth is, guys don't *have* any sensitive innermost thoughts and feelings. It's time you women knew! All these years you've been agonizing about how to make the relationship work, wondering how come he never talks to you, worrying about all the anguished emotion he must have bottled up inside, and meanwhile he's fretting about how maybe he needs longer golf spikes. I'm sorry to have to tell you this. Maybe you *should* become a nun.

Anyway, I hope I've cleared up any lingering questions anybody might have regarding guys, as a gender. For some reason I feel compelled to end this with a personal note: Heather Campbell, if you're out there, I just want to say that I had a really nice time taking you to the Junior Prom in 1964, and I was a total jerk for never, not once, mentioning this fact to you personally.

### QUESTIONS

1. Barry suggests that men are afraid of commitments such as marriage. Do you agree?
2. Are women afraid of commitment?
3. According to Barry, how are women affected by rejection? Do you agree with his view? Does rejection affect men in the same way?
4. Considering Barry's discussion of "Guy Code," identify other code languages used by different groups.
5. Explain what Barry means by "Guy Logic." Do you agree that there is such a thing? What would "Girl Logic" be?
6. What does Barry mean—in the title and elsewhere—by "manly"?
7. What do you think was Barry's purpose in writing this essay? Did he succeed?
8. Do you find this essay insulting? funny? accurate? all three? Explain your answer.

### CONNECTIONS

1. List some similarities between the girl described in "Barbie Doll" and the rejected date in Barry's essay.
2. Compare and contrast Barry's views of dating with those of Julius Lester.

# Love and
# Other Metaphors

# Metaphors and Other Language Play

· · · · · · · · · · · · · · · · · · · · · · · ·

You've heard the term *metaphor* before—and, even if you're not sure yet what the term means, you've been using and creating metaphors and other figures of speech ever since you were a child. Figures of speech are the "special effects" of language, achieved by using words in unexpected ways. Most of us use figures of speech every day, unconsciously or consciously, when speaking and writing because they create images that illustrate the ideas we want to get across.

As Patricia Hampl points out in her essay "Memory and Imagination," a figure of speech is also "revealing of the self." The comparisons we draw reveal something about us: A woman would not be likely to derisively call a man a "dog" if she thought dogs were kinder and nobler than most humans; a small child, like the narrator of Sandra Cisneros's story "Eleven," will draw her analogies from a child's experiences and vocabulary ("it's just my body shaking like when you have the hiccups, and my whole head hurts like when you drink milk too fast," she says; "I want today to be far away already, far away like a runaway balloon"). A black man like Julius Lester might choose to reflect something about his life by comparing himself to "Bill McCord, who had girls after him like a cop-killer has policemen" and by comparing his ego to "a toilet-paper raincoat in the African rainy season."

Let's look at some of the most common figures of speech and (some that are the most fun to play with in one's own writing).

## Simile

A simile is a comparison that ties together two different things by saying one is *like* or similar to another (see the examples from Lester's essay). Making such comparisons can clarify an idea: To say that something is very big, for example, is not as specific as to say that it's as big as a house or as big as the sky. At the same time, like all figures of speech, similes spice up a description; in a poem included in this section, for example, Yehuda Amichai writes, "Love is finished again, like a profitable citrus season / or like an archaeological dig that turned up / from deep inside the earth / turbulent things that wanted to be forgotten." In a selection included in the previous section, Virginia Woolf writes "London was like a workshop. London was like a machine." Do these comparisons create positive associations? Do they add negative associations? In either case, they add complexity to the ideas being expressed.

If you don't think that you can come up with interesting similes of your own, try this game: First, think of an object. Use that object as the nucleus of a cluster, and cluster around it various qualities that the object possesses—for example, a tomato is red, juicy, full of seeds, round, shiny, soft, etc. Then, choose one of those qualities. On a separate piece of paper, write that quality as the nucleus of a new cluster, clustering around it as many objects as you can think of that possess that quality. If we choose "red" from the preceding list, let's say, the objects around it could be a bullfighter's cape, a cardinal, a cherry, a stop sign, a brick, etc. Now we can play with the association between the original object, the tomato, and one of the new objects we've come up with— for example, on the white plate, the tomato was as red as a cardinal in a snowy field.

## Metaphor

Metaphor compares two things by saying not that one is *like* the other but that one *is* the other. Describing a nun, for example, Patricia Hampl writes, "her face was a sallow green olive placed upon the jumbo ripe olive of her black habit." Another good example of metaphor comes from the Virginia Woolf piece mentioned previously: "The student by my side, for instance, who was copying assiduously from a scientific manual was," she writes, "extracting pure nuggets of the essential ore every ten minutes or so." The author presents knowledge as valuable by saying that it *is* gold—the "essential ore" worth mining for. In contrast, a person who calls a man a "dog" doesn't intend to say that the guy is a furry, four-legged animal; the metaphor is used in this case as an insult, to say that the man is somehow less than human.

## Analogy

By simply saying that one thing *is* another, a metaphor forces us to figure out for ourselves the many similarities between the two things; an analogy explains the various similarities. For example, in an essay included in this section, Francine du Plessix Gray analyzes the imagery we often associate with love—showing that the common analogy in our culture compares love to war.

Often, an analogy clarifies the relationship between two things by comparing it to the relationship between two other things with which we are more familiar. In "Earth's Body" (included in Section 5), Scott Russell Sanders draws an analogy when he writes, "A dog will bite a rag and shake it, first playfully, then earnestly, and at last furiously, with snarls and bristling hair, as though outraged by the limp cloth. Just so, in the dark hours, certainty of death seizes me by the throat."

We'll discuss analogies further when we present the special case of argumentative essays in Section 6, because people often use analogies in their arguments.

### Personification

A subset of metaphor, personification gives human characteristics to an inanimate object (in a sense asserting that the object is somehow human-like). Consider how many things are commonly personified as female: ships, cats, countries, the moon. Both intangibles and objects can be personified: time will tell, death knocks at the door, the rain is singing. The radio keeps silent. The stoplight winks its green eye. In an example from an essay included in Section 5, Annie Dillard writes, "What does a weasel think about? He won't say. His journal is tracks in clay, a spray of feathers, mouse blood and bone . . ." Calling those elements a "journal" is using a metaphor; suggesting that a weasel keeps a journal is an example of personification.

### Symbol

The green eye of a stoplight means something to most modern humans: It stands for our turn to cross the street, and therefore it's a symbol. A symbol is not so much a comparison but another way of denoting something. It stands for something other than itself. Some blue, red, and white strips of cloth, with a few white stars, signify the United States. The red piano book in Patricia Hampl's "Memory and Imagination" stands (as she tells us) for everything she wanted but didn't get as a child, which she can now "give" herself by fantasizing that she'd actually had it. In Willa Cather's "The Enchanted Bluff," the rock in the middle of the desert stands for all the childhood dreams of the boys who hope to explore it someday.

Symbols abound in the transitional piece between this section and the next, John Steinbeck's "The Chrysanthemums." The chrysanthemums mentioned in the title appear in the story, but the story is not about the flowers. As the story unfolds, it becomes clear that Steinbeck intends the flower to be a symbol. In other words, the chrysanthemum represents or is associated with something or someone else. But we don't want to spoil the story for you: You'll develop your own explanation of what the chrysanthemums stand for.

The use of figures of speech in writing ties in, then, with the use of examples and descriptive details: All of these engage the reader in a different way than the rational power of ideas does. Some writers use these techniques to try to disguise a lack of solid content; however, the best writers combine both content and imagery to convey their points as effectively as possible.

### Final Words

Using figures of speech presents challenges as well as benefits. There is always the possibility of falling into clichés ("she had roses in her cheeks"; "he was like a fish out of water")—we'll discuss clichés further in the next section. To avoid overused expressions, which add neither clarity nor spice to your writing, draw comparisons from your own experiences (who else will know them as well as you do?). Write that the tree was as tall as a child feels when riding on his father's shoulders. Write that her hair smelled the way sweaters do after a long night spent in a smoky bar. Make your own connections. Don't be like the conventional kids described by Gabriele Rico in "The Childhood Origins of Natural Writing," who want to sound just like everybody else.

Another challenge related to the use of figures of speech is their inherent ambiguity. This is both a drawback and an advantage. When someone says life is a game, for example, does that person mean that life has rules? that there is a start and a finish? that there are winners and losers in life? Or does the person mean that life should be fun and not be taken too seriously?

Perhaps the moral is this, then: A figure of speech that serves its intended purpose is usually quite clear, but it also opens up an area of creative tension, a place where writer and reader (or speaker and audience) meet. Those who think that reading is not an interactive process just don't understand that language is like a kaleidoscope: Its patterns are made of many colorful bits, and as you turn them around in your head, you change them.

# ∽ From the Song of Songs

The following selection comes from Chapter 8 verses 5–7 of a collection of poems (or "songs") from the Old Testament. These songs deal with various aspects of the love between a man and a woman. People have traditionally believed that the collection was written by King Solomon, but the editors of the Oxford Study Edition of the *New English Bible* (from which this translation is taken) state that scholarly estimates of the time of its writing vary from as early as the tenth century B.C. to as late as the fourth century B.C. Theologians have argued for many centuries about the metaphorical meanings of the Song of Songs.

**WARM-UP:** What do you think love is, according to the Bible? If you're not sure, what would you guess?

*Bridegroom*
. . . Under the apricot-trees I roused you,
there where your mother was in labour with you,
there where she who bore you was in labour.
Wear me as a seal upon your heart,
as a seal upon your arm;                                                  5
for love is strong as death,
passion cruel as the grave;
it blazes up like blazing fire,
fiercer than any flame.
Many waters cannot quench love,                                          10
no flood can sweep it away;
if a man were to offer for love
the whole wealth of his house,
it would be utterly scorned.

## QUESTIONS

1. What is the effect of lines 2 and 3 in this selection? What do they add to the selection overall?
2. Explain your understanding of line 4.
3. What is the image of love presented in this selection?
4. Note the repetition, the "doubling" effect in lines 1–7. How do you think this affects the points expressed in those lines? What's the effect, then, of lines 8–10?

5. Which words and images in this selection do not seem to be related to love? What is their effect?
6. Point out examples of metaphor and simile in this selection.

## CONNECTIONS

Compare the view of love expressed in this selection with the one presented in Kate Chopin's "The Story of an Hour."

# From The First Letter of Paul to the Corinthians (1 Corinthians 13)

Several letters included in the New Testament communicated the thoughts of the apostle Paul to various early Christian communities. The letters seem to have been written sometime between 48 and 58 A.D. "The First Letter of Paul to the Corinthians" was directed to the congregation Paul had founded in the Greek city of Corinth. The following selection, which actually begins with the last verse of chapter 12, focuses on Christian love.

**WARM-UP:** Complete the following, in a line or a paragraph: "Love is ..."

And now I will show you the best way of all.

I may speak in tongues of men or of angels, but if I am without love, I am a sounding gong or a clanging cymbal. I may have the gift of prophecy, and know every hidden truth; I may have faith strong enough to move moun tains; but if I have no love, I am no- thing. I may dole out all I possess, or even give my body to be burnt, but if I have no love, I am none the better.

Love is patient; love is kind and envies no one. Love is never boastful, nor conceited, nor rude; never selfish, not quick to take offence. Love keeps no score of wrongs; does not gloat over other men's sins, but delights in the truth. There is nothing love cannot face; there is no limit to its faith, its hope, and its endurance.

Love will never come to an end. Are there prophets? their work will be over. Are there tongues of ecstasy? they will cease. Is there knowledge? it will van- ish away; for our knowledge and our prophecy alike are partial, and the par-

1

2

3

4

5

6

7

8

9

10

tial vanishes when wholeness comes.
11    When I was a child, my speech, my
outlook, and my thoughts were all
childish. When I grew up, I had finished
12    with childish things. Now we see only
puzzling reflections in a mirror,° but
then we shall see face to face. My knowledge now is partial; then it will be
13    whole, like God's knowledge of me. In
a word, there are three things that last
for ever: faith, hope, and love; but the
greatest of them all is love.


## QUESTIONS

1. Point out examples of metaphor and personification in this selection.
2. Explain your understanding of the difference between love and faith.
3. Explain the meaning of the statement, "I may dole out all I possess, or even give my body to be burnt, but if I have no love, I am none the better"?
4. What characteristics does this selection ascribe to love?
5. When the verse says "Love will never come to an end," does it mean that love between individuals will last forever? that love itself is everlasting? or something else? Explain your position.
6. In line 10, what is the meaning of "wholeness"?


## CONNECTIONS

Compare and contrast the view of love presented in this selection with the view presented in the selection from the Song of Songs.

---

12 *"Now we see only puzzling reflections in a mirror"*: In ancient times, mirrors were made of polished metal and thus offered only imprecise, vague reflections.

# ∼ Sonnet #130

*William Shakespeare*

William Shakespeare, perhaps the most famous writer in the English language, was born in April 1564 into a middle-class family in Stratford-upon-Avon, England. As a youth, he attended the Stratford Grammar School, where the curriculum consisted of grammar, reading, writing, and recitation done almost entirely in Latin. In 1582, the eighteen-year-old Shakespeare married Anne Hathaway, who was eight years his senior. Shakespeare was thought to have been employed as a schoolmaster in his youth; he later joined an acting company, became a leading member of Lord Chamberlain's Men, and, by 1592, was established as a playwright in the theaters in London. When a plague forced the theaters to shut their doors from the summer of 1592 until June 1594, Shakespeare turned to writing poetry. He wrote most of his 154 sonnets from then until about 1599; they were published in 1606. Shakespeare died in 1616 and was buried in Holy Trinity Church in Stratford-upon-Avon.

**WARM-UP:** Make a list of clichéd similes that frequently appear in love songs and poems.

My mistress'° eyes are nothing like the sun;
Coral is far more red than her lips' red;
If snow be white, why then her breasts are dun;°
If hairs be wires,° black wires grow on her head.
I have seen roses damasked,° red and white,                    5
But no such roses see I in her cheeks;
And in some perfumes is there more delight
Than in the breath that from my mistress reeks.°
I love to hear her speak, yet well I know
That music hath a far more pleasing sound;                    10
I grant I never saw a goddess go;
My mistress, when she walks, treads on the ground.
And yet, by heaven, I think my love as rare
As any she belied° with false compare.

---

1 *mistress:* In Shakespeare's time, the term meant "beloved."   3 *dun:* A slightly brownish, dark gray color.   4 *wires:* In poetry written around Shakespeare's time, it was common to refer to the beloved's hair as "golden wires."   5 *damasked:* Variegated, patterned with one color over another   8 *reeks:* Here meaning "emanates, comes forth."   14 *belied:* Contradicted, unmasked as lies.

## QUESTIONS

1. Going through the sonnet line by line, make a list of the similes that would have been used if Shakespeare had been saying that his mistress *is* like all those things.
2. What is the tone of the poem? Does it change? If so, where does the shift occur?
3. Is the language of this poem detailed? If not, point out where you would add more details and explain why.
4. Note the rhyme pattern in the poem (which lines rhyme with which). Does this add something to the ideas expressed? Explain your response.
5. Explain your understanding of the last two lines of the poem.
6. What is the poem's message about romantic love?

## CONNECTIONS

Compare and contrast the style of this poem to that of the selection from the Song of Songs.

# ∼ Sonnet #43

## *Elizabeth Barrett Browning*

Elizabeth Barrett was born in 1806 and spent her childhood at Hope End, Great Britain. Largely self-educated at home, she translated ancient and Byzantine Greek poetry and published many works—including *The Battle of Marathon* (1820), *An Essay on Mind* (1826), and *The Seraphim and Other Poems* (1836)—before beginning, in 1844, a correspondence with another poet, Robert Browning, who she later married. She published several more volumes of verse, including *Sonnets from the Portuguese* (1850), in which the following sonnet appears. Elizabeth Barrett Browning died in 1861 in her husband's arms.

**WARM-UP:** Do you think that true love lasts forever? Explain your answer.

How do I love thee? Let me count the ways.
I love thee to the depth and breadth and height
My soul can reach, when feeling out of sight
For the ends of Being and ideal Grace.
I love thee to the level of everyday's                            5
Most quiet need, by sun and candle-light.
I love thee freely, as men strive for Right;
I love thee purely, as they turn from Praise.
I love thee with the passion put to use
In my old griefs, and with my childhood's faith.        10
I love thee with a love I seemed to lose
With my lost saints—I love thee with the breath,
Smiles, tears, of all my life!—and, if God choose,
I shall but° love thee better after death.

**QUESTIONS**

1. Are any words or combination of words repeated in the poem? If so, identify them; then explain what is emphasized by the repetition.
2. What is the tone of the poem? Does the tone change at any point? If so, where does the shift occur?

---

14 *but:* Here meaning "only."

3. Explain the difference between the two kinds of love described in the first two "ways" that the poem lists (one described in lines 2–4, the other in lines 5 and 6).
4. The speaker states that she (or he) loves "with childhood's faith." What *are* the characteristics of childhood faith, which are here ascribed to love?
5. Would you say that the speaker in this poem is a religious person? Find evidence in the text for your answer.
6. Explain your understanding of the last two lines of the poem (following the final dash).

## CONNECTIONS

1. Of the selections you have read in this chapter, which one does Barrett Browning's poem most resemble? in what way(s)?
2. Compare and contrast the attitude toward love expressed by the speaker in Barrett Browning's poem to that expressed in Shakespeare's poem. Explain and support your response by pointing to specific elements of the two poems.

# ∿ The Elusive Emotion

*Robert C. Solomon*

> Robert Solomon is Professor of Philosophy at the University of Texas at Austin. He is the author of numerous books, including *Continental Philosophy since the 1750s: The Rise and Fall of the Self* (1988) and *Ethics and Excellence: Cooperation and Integrity in Business* (1992); he recently coauthored *A Short History of Philosophy* (1996). Solomon has lectured around the country on the subject of love. The following is a selection from his book *About Love: Reinventing Romance for Our Times* (1988).

> **WARM-UP:** Do you see romantic love as a positive emotion? Why or why not?

## "I Love You"

What we call "love" is a social invention, a construction of concepts that   1
serve a very special function in our society. What we call "love" is not a universal phenomenon but a culture-specific interpretation of the universal phenomena of sexual attraction and its complications. Love may begin in biology, but it is essentially a set of ideas, ideas that may even turn against the biological impulses that are their source. The history of romantic love is the history of a special set of attitudes toward sex, even where sex is never mentioned, and if love seems so elusive° that is in part because sex is so obviously tangible. Love is, as Willard Gaylin keeps telling us, "so much more" than sex, but it is that "so much more" that is so elusive, and the reason is that it is our own doing and it changes even as we are looking at it.

"Love" is first of all a word, a word we are taught to honor, a word that we are urged to use. It is not long after "dating" that one feels compelled, as one has been taught, to describe what one feels as love. The timing is essential: unless you are exceedingly confident and/or resistant to humiliation, one does not proclaim love at a first meeting. One should be cautious about first saying it during sex; it may not be taken seriously. Waiting too long does not increase the impact but reduces it, like the climax of a movie gone on too long. But it is our saying "love"—not feeling it—that is responsible for the existence and importance of love in our society. How many people would be in love, wrote the writer and aphorist° La Rochefoucauld two centuries ago, if they had

---

*elusive:* Intangible, hard to comprehend or define.    *aphorist:* One who creates (or is fond of using) proverbs or sayings.

never heard the word? The answer is "none of us," for to love is not to experience a natural sensation but rather to participate in one of the great ongoing innovations of modern Western culture.

It should not surprise us then that the definitive moment in love is not the moment of meeting, the first longing look or the initial touch or caress. It is not making love or the feeling of love but the word "love"—or rather "three little words," one referring to self, the third to the other and the verb tying the two together in a novel and perhaps terrifying complex of intentions, obligations and social expectations. To be sure, love involves desire and feeling, but if love were just a desire or a feeling, there would be no need to announce it or even put a name on it, much less identify it as the most important event of our lives. We would not worry about the possibility of getting it wrong or wonder about whether or not it was "true." We would not feel so compelled to write poetry about it. There would be little cause for anxiety or embarrassment, much less sleepless nights and endless confusion. If love were, as the cynics say, nothing but "ignorance and deprivation" (Kingsley Amis in *Lucky Jim*) or "lust plus the ordeal of civility" (Freud), it would be hard to imagine why it should be so important, why it should matter so much *whom* one loved, much less whether one is loved in return, why it would be anything more than an itch in need of a scratch easily satisfied or forgotten. It would not be clear why the desire for love to last—not for a while but "forever"—should be so essential to the emotion, nor would it be at all evident why the emotion should be so desirable in the first place.

To say "I love you" is not to report a feeling and it is not just the expression of a feeling. It is an aggressive, creative, socially definitive act, which among other things places the other person in an unexpected and very vulnerable position. The question may involve a long period of deliberation and shy hesitation. We might just blurt it out without any preparation at all, surprising even ourselves. It may follow months of passion and companionship or it might come immediately upon meeting, following a strangely long, hypnotic "hello." It is not so terrible, of course, if he or she is willing and ready with the one acceptable response, namely, "I love you too." But nothing else will do. No excuses are appropriate. One cannot say "How interesting" or "How curious, I'm in love with someone too." "You'll get over it" is outright cruelty, and silence isn't much better. But from that moment on, nothing will ever be the same. From that moment on, there is no going back. (Imagine saying "I love you" to someone by mistake, and then trying to explain how it was that you "didn't mean it.") From that moment on, there will be the need to keep saying it, day after day, year after year.

5      Why is the phrase so significant? Because it signifies a decision and presents an invitation, perhaps a dilemma, which may well change the whole of

one's life. The phrase, like the emotion, is at its very heart *reciprocal*,° not that it cannot be rebuffed (it often is) but in that it is essentially a plea, even a demand, for a response in kind. It is the signal that changes a delightful friendship or a casual relationship into something much more—or, if it misfires, something much less. "I love you" is not just a phrase or an expression. It is not a description of how one feels. It is the opening to an unknown future, an invitation to a new way of life.

"I love you" does not always have the same meaning, and this, too, should tell us something about the elusive nature of love. The first time it is always a surprise, an invasion, an aggressive act, but once said, "I love you" can only be repeated. It is unthinkable that it should not be said again, and again, and again. When one has not said it for a while, this may itself precipitate a crisis. ("Now why haven't you said that in all of these months!") On the other hand, "I love you" can also serve as a threat ("Don't push me on this; you might lose me"), emotional blackmail ("I've said it, now you have to respond in kind"), a warning ("It's only because I love you that I'm willing to put up with this"), an apology ("I could not possibly have meant what I just said to you, to *you* of all people"). It can be an instrument—more effective than the loudest noise—to interrupt a dull or painful conversation. It can be a cry, a plea, a verbal flag ("Pay attention to me!") or it can be an excuse ("It's only because I love you . . ."). It can be a disguise ("I love you," he whispered, looking awkwardly askance° at the open door). It can be an attack ("How can you do this to me?") or even an end ("So that's that. With regrets, good-bye"). If this single phrase has so many meanings, how varied and variable must be the emotion.

But "I love you" is not a universal language. There is nothing like it in most societies, and so no emotion quite to compare with it. Some sort of sexual desire might be universal, but the set of ideas, demands, rituals and expectations that are synthesized in the words "I love you" are very special and, anthropologically speaking, quite rare. Love is elusive because we are trying to define a creative act in the making, trying to catch fully formed that which can be ours only in time, insisting on proof and assurances when it is in fact up to us whether "I love you" has any meaning at all.

## Other Cultures

In premarital relationships, a convention of love-making is strictly adhered to. True, this is a convention of speech rather than action. A boy declares that he will die if a girl refuses him her favours, but the Samoans laugh at stories of romantic love, scoff at fidelity to a long absent wife or

---

*reciprocal:* Shared, felt, or shown by both.     *askance:* With doubt or mistrust.

mistress, believe explicitly that one love will quickly cure another. . . . The composition of ardent love songs, the fashioning of long and flowery love letters, the invocation of the moon, the stars and the sea in verbal courtship, all serve to give Samoan love-making a close superficial resemblance to our own, yet . . . romantic love as it occurs in our civilization, inextricably° bound up with ideas of monogamy, exclusiveness, jealousy and undeviating fidelity does not occur in Samoa. . . . Even a passionate attachment to one person which lasts for a long period and persists in the face of discouragement but does not bar out other relationships, is rare among the Samoans. Marriage, on the other hand, is regarded as a social and economic arrangement in which the relative wealth, rank, skill of husband and wife must all be taken into consideration. . . . As Samoans lack the inhibitions and intricate specialization of sex feeling which make marriages of convenience unsatisfactory, it is possible to bulwark° marital happiness with other props.

—MARGARET MEAD, *The Coming of Age in Samoa*

So long as we think of love as something "natural," as a phenomenon as universal as hunger or mutual dependency or sexual impulses and appetites, we cannot possibly appreciate the extent to which romantic love is culturally defined and, consequently, the extent to which we are responsible for determining the rules and the context in which we love. Now, on the one hand, it would be ridiculous to overdo the claim and insist that we alone (perhaps with the French and a few other decadent European societies) believe in romantic love or even understand what it is. Quite obviously there have been stories that strike us as clearly romantic even in ancient times—in Sophocles and The Tale of Genji, in the Song of Solomon and the legend of the Taj Mahal. But to so expand the notion of romance that it includes every form of sexual obsession in every society and every desire to marry the girl or boy in the next house or hut obliterates all the distinctions worth making and ignores the very special conditions and demands of love that we take for granted in our society but are rare exceptions in most others. Our examples of famous lovers in the past and other cultures almost all find themselves in extremely fortunate circumstances. It is not just our luxurious notion of "romance" that leads us to look for love only among royalty and the aristocracy, for only such rare individuals had the leisure or the freedom to indulge in the luxury that we call "love." We, on the other hand, take the freedom, comfort and comparative leisure of our individualism for granted, not realizing that our common ability to see ourselves as individuals capable of love is

---

*inextricably:* So that it is impossible to separate or untangle.    *bulwark:* To fortify, protect.

the product of 5,000 years of history and an exceptionally benign° set of social circumstances—however much we may find to bitch and complain about.

It is this same lack of individuality, freedom of choice and leisure that explains the preponderance° of cultures without love as we might define it. It is not that these people lack an essential emotion, and it is certainly not the case that they are any less caring, less compassionate or less sensitive or tender in their relationships. It is not the case that they are any less sexually excited or satisfied; indeed, one of the most self-consciously romantic periods in modern Western life—nineteenth-century Victorian culture—used love as something of a substitute for sex. While it celebrated and encouraged marriage based on romance, it notoriously condemned the idea that married couples should enjoy sex together. The proper loving wife was advised to "close her eyes and think of England." It is perfectly desirable and clearly possible that two people living their lives together in an arranged marriage should come to love as well as honor one another, but such love does not strike us as "romantic." Two teenagers on some exotic South Seas island might dream of running away together, but such childish fantasies are not deemed worthy of more than amusement in such societies. Such love is not an end in itself, much less an emotion to be coveted. Sexual experimentation and enthusiasm may be fine, but marriage, especially, is considered far too important to depend on such whimsical factors.

All societies have sex, and given the consequences of sex, all societies have rules and practices that delineate the circumstances in which sex is permissible and in which it is not. And despite the perennial° warnings against our "permissive society," ours is far from the most or the least tolerant where sexual promiscuity and fidelity are concerned. Margaret Mead's classic description of sex in Samoa makes it clear (as did the voyeuristic descriptions and fantasies of earlier male explorers) that sex as such is plentiful and "no big deal." What we call "love" was considered by the Samoans as a relatively rare and amusing neurosis. Marriage had nothing to do with love not because it ignored love but because love as we think of it simply was not part of the equation. So, too, the great anthropologist Bronislaw Malinowski writes in his *Sexual Life of Savages* that many societies lack what we call romantic love because such idealization of a single person occurs only where there are substantial obstacles to erotic satisfaction, a theory more recently advanced by Philip Slater in his polemical° diagnosis of love as the result of making sex an artificially scarce commodity (*The Pursuit of Loneliness*). Where several possible sex partners are always available, so the argument goes, the intensity of

10

---

*benign:* Not damaging or dangerous; beneficial.     *preponderance:* Prevalence; dominance.     *perennial:* Immortal, everlasting.     *polemical:* Argumentative, quarrelsome.

romantic love seems quite beside the point. Of course teaching that sex is a sin is an effective way of restricting the acceptability if not the availability of many sex partners, and we should not be surprised to find that romantic love tends to flourish in societies that have been Christianized (as observations of recently converted societies in Africa and the South Pacific make quite clear). But it is not just sexual restriction that makes Christian societies particularly receptive to romantic love; the Christian emphasis on individuality and equality are at least as important, and we should not be surprised that the development of romantic love in Europe closely parallels some of the more dramatic changes in the conception of Christianity, for example the rising attention to the Virgin Mary in the twelfth century, at just the time when the status of women began to improve enormously, making courtly love—a precursor of romantic love—possible.

One of the factors making romantic love possible or impossible is the presence and importance of privacy. Now, on the one hand, virtually every society has some sense of the importance of privacy (Barrington Moore, *Privacy*, 1986), and most societies—from ancient Greece to the Fulani tribe in Africa and the Hopi in the American Southwest—insist that the sexual act be private, even if they exhibit enormous tolerance concerning sexual activities as such. But more important than such physical privacy is the conception of personal privacy in such matters as individual rights and personal choice. . . . In most societies this conception of the private and the personal does not exist; one's identity is solely defined by one's place in the society. In such societies it is to be expected that marriage too will be a matter of social determination. Romantic love has nothing to do with it and, consequently, has nothing to do with the life of such a society.

Another essential factor in romantic love, we noted, is equality. This alone explains why so few societies recognize romantic love, and why the few examples from ancient times typically involve women of the very highest social standing, queens like Guinevere and Sheba, for example. In most societies the unequal status of the sexes makes romantic love unthinkable, and marriage is mainly a matter of domination and submission. In our own past the ancient Hebrews had no concept of romantic love. The roles of men and women were thoroughly defined and unequal. Marriages were arranged rather than by choice, and arranged marriages strike us as the very antithesis° of romance, even leaving aside the awkward question about whether such marriages are in general as successful as romantically based marriages (the evidence suggests a clear yes). In Japan, too, marriage has never been romantic, not just because marriages were arranged but also because the role of the woman is so submis-

---

*antithesis:* Direct opposite, reverse.

sive, because she is discouraged from all of those talents that would make her an equal and interesting partner instead of a devoted and, in many cases, abused servant. As if to prove the point, the one place in Japanese history that romantic love did seem to flourish was in the "floating world" of the Tokagawa Shogunate. Those luscious depictions of mutually enjoyed intercourse in the classic art of the Shunga do not depict married couples but, for the most part, merchants and courtesans. The "floating world," built by a clever shogun to distract the rich but status-less merchant class from politics, was the one place in class-defined Japan where well-educated women could meet men on a more or less equal basis, and many love stories emerged as the result. Sexual freedom was a presupposition, but a more important foundation was equality, an equality not to be found in loveless marriage. We might note that such inequality in sexual matters is not necessarily a distinction between the sexes. In ancient Greece, where men and women were also distinctively unequal, homosexual relations too were asymmetrical and therefore not romantic. The standard relationship was between a man and a "youth." Their roles were different and so were their feelings: the man was the mentor and admired the beauty of his beloved; the youth was expected to be grateful, but not enamored. (There is an ironic twist in Plato's *Symposium,* where the youth Alcibiades turns this tradition upside down in his love for Socrates, his teacher and "beloved.") Romantic love demands, if not supposes, equality.

The perennial debate in anthropology and in discussions of "human nature" generally has to do with the relative importance of human differences versus cross-cultural similarities. What, in other words, is a matter of culture and what is a result of biology or "the human condition." With respect to romantic love, there are features of love that can be found in all societies—the importance of sex and the culture-bound preference of some partners as more desirable than others. But those features that constitute romantic love are quite specialized and can be found only in a small number of societies (though the number is rapidly growing). Yet lest we draw the moralistic conclusion that our romantic society is somehow "better" than those cultures without romance, let us remind ourselves that we have a long way to go before we can praise our invention for its contribution to social harmony or stability, much less happiness. Most of the world looks upon our romantic fantasies as a source of social chaos and irresponsibility, as the cause of much unhappiness and, to say the obvious, the reason behind our appalling divorce rate and the enormous numbers of older women, especially, who find themselves abandoned in a culture not particularly sensitive or responsible. Our emphasis on romance encourages vanity instead of camaraderie, seclusion instead of community, whimsicality instead of responsibility, emotional excitement instead of social stability. The result seems to be a culture that is fragmented, frustrated and lonely just as much as (and because) it is romantic. Until we reinvent a form of romantic love that answers such charges, we should be humble about our enthusiasm indeed.

## The History of Love

> The Western concept of love (in its heterosexual and humanistic aspects) was—if not "invented" or "discovered"—at least developed in the twelfth century as never before. Only at that late date was man able to begin thinking consecutively about ways of harmonizing sexual impulses with idealistic motives, of justifying amorous intimacy not as a means of preserving the race, or glorifying God, or attaining some ulterior metaphysical object but rather as an end in itself that made life worth living.
>
> —IRVING SINGER, *The Nature of Love, Vol. II*

We have said that love is historical, and what this means is that we can understand it only by understanding its history. Many of love's virtues represent the proudest achievements of our civilization—the respect for the individual and our protection of individual choices, the equalization of the sexes and the destruction of class distinctions in society, the delicate balance between sexual desire and expression and the need for privacy, subtlety and limitation, the pursuit of happiness. At the same time the long evolution of love means that we still carry with us much of the baggage of the past, including residual sex roles, inhibitions, and an overidealization that tends to confuse love with religion.

15      Love has developed through five thousand years of history, reaching fruition as "romantic" love only in the past century or so. Sexual desire may seem like something of a constant through history, but the objects of desire and the source, nature and vicissitudes° of that desire vary as much as societies and their philosophies. Romantic love is built out of those very modern ideas about the status of the sexes, the importance of sexual relations, the significance of marriage, the nature of personal identity and the meaning of life as well as the perennial promptings of biology. Strictly speaking, there is nothing in Plato's *Symposium* about *romantic* love. It takes modern thinking to feel modern love, and however rich the insights of the ancients or dazzling their poetry, the understanding of love is now up to us.

Romantic love is an amalgam of primitive, ancient, medieval and modern ideas about sex and its significance. Sexuality "fits" into different societies in different ways, and conceptions of love and marriage vary accordingly. However necessary heterosexual intercourse may be to the preservation of every society, sexual desire is virtually never limited to this reproductive end. It is

---

*vicissitudes:* Troubles, changes in fortune.

almost always tied to a network of philosophical ideas, whether the Platonic conception that all desire is ultimately a desire for Goodness and Beauty, the medieval doctrine that intimacy represents the union with God or the late Romantic philosophy that sex is the life force of the universe flowing through us all. What distinguishes romantic love is, more than anything else, its importance for its own sake—not as a means to have children, not as a celebration of God. It is the emotion itself (not the sex which prompts it) that is important, quite apart from its role or consequences in society. To celebrate love for its own sake meant giving primary attention and trump status to personal preferences and feelings, even when they were irrational and self-destructive and contrary to the good of everyone. How many societies have had the luxury of letting sex and marriage be determined on the basis of individual desire, satisfaction, emotion and enjoyment alone?

The history of romantic love begins to take form with the Greeks, with Plato in particular. Never mind that the relationships celebrated by the Greeks were strictly between men and excluded women or that erotic relations were typically unequal. What Plato added to the more primitive conceptions of the importance of sex was the concept of *idealization,* not only the idealization of one's lover but of love itself. Plato is often criticized for overidealizing love but, in retrospect, we can see that without that sense of idealization, we would not have a concept of love that was so much more than sexual desire; we might still be enamored of just a beautiful body rather than a beautiful person, and we would not care that the feeling last, as Plato says, "forever."

Christianity is not always considered a romantic religion, mainly because of the several centuries during which the church attacked sexual desire as such in all of its forms and expressions, even within marriage. But the history of erotic love has been determined not only by the fact that Christian thought demeaned sexual love but also by the Christian emphasis on the "inner" individual soul and the importance of such emotions as faith and devotion. The genius of Christianity was that it virtually invented the "inner" self and raised certain emotions to divine significance—think of Saint Augustine's *Confessions,*° for example. But following Plato, Christianity also co-opted° erotic love and turned it into something else, still the love of one's fellow man and perhaps the love of one's wife or husband, but no longer sexual, no longer personal, no longer merely human. In its positive presentation, love became a form of idealization, even worship, an attempt to transcend not only oneself and one's own self-interests but also the limited world of mere human relationships. The Christian conception of love aimed always "higher," toward not just virtue or happiness but perfection itself. It is with Christianity that love

---

*Confessions:* Autobiography discussing the religious conversion of Saint Augustine, written in the second century A.D.     *co-opted:* Absorbed, assimilated, appropriated.

becomes literally "divine"—not just exhilarating but an absolute in itself. But on the negative side, it must be said (and often has been) that the Christian conception of love could be brutal and inhuman, denying not only our "natural" impulses but even the conception of a loving marriage as such. Saint Paul's advice, "Better to marry than to burn," was one of the more generous sentiments governing this revised concept of love. Tertullian was not alone in insisting that even to look on one's wife with lust was a sin. Indeed all such desires become antithetical to love, not an expression of it. To Nietzsche's observation that Christianity is Platonism for the masses, we might add that because of Christianity, we now have psychoanalysis.

Christian theology may have encouraged and revered love above all else, but it was not erotic love that flourished. Alternative names for love—"caritas,"° "philia"° and "agape"°—may have clarified the scholarship but not the phenomenology of the emotion. When one looked lovingly at another, who could say whether the feeling was divine caritas or nasty eros, except that one knew that one *should* feel the former. An entire literature grew up, from which some of our favorite first-date dialogues are derived, distinguishing loving from sexual desire as if these were not only always distinguishable but even opposed. By the fourteenth century this confusion had become canonized as Platonic love, for which Plato (or at least Socrates) is indeed to blame. Platonic love substituted Christian faith for pagan wisdom. Love had become even more idealized than Socrates had urged, but what had been gained in spirituality was lost in the denial of the erotic passions and the importance of happy human relationships for their own sake.

20 It was in reaction to this insensitivity to human desires and affections that courtly love was directed in the twelfth century. Romantic love is often identified historically with courtly love—which is rightly recognized as its significant late medieval predecessor. But the two are quite distinct, as Irving Singer has argued in his *Nature of Love*. The two are often conflated,° and courtly love in particular is often reduced to the ridiculous image of the amorous but frustrated troubadour° singing pathetically before the (very tall) tower of some inevitably fair but also unavailable lady. But the point of courtly love was not frustration. It was a renewed appreciation of the beauty and importance of sex, but although the sexual consummation of love was the explicit goal of courtship, this was not, in an important sense, its purpose. Courtly love was an aspiration for perfection, using sex as its prod, encouraging good

---

*caritas:* Latin, meaning "charity" in the sense of kindness, love for one's fellow human beings. *philia:* Greek, meaning love for one's friends (platonic).   *agape:* Greek, meaning love of God.   *conflated:* Combined, blended.   *troubadour:* One of the poet-musicians who entertained audiences from the eleventh to the thirteenth centuries in parts of Europe, singing mostly about courtly love.

manners ("chivalry") and courage, articulateness and poetic creativity. The troubadours and other courtly types followed Plato but integrated much of Christianity as well (though the church took a dim view of the practice, considering it nothing more than a heretical rationalization for sex). Indeed, the paradigm° of courtly love began not as chaste and frustrated (if poetic) desire but as secret, adulterous and all-embracing illicit love (Lancelot and Guinevere, for example). Socially, courtly love was a plaything of the upper class. It was as much talk (and crooning) as action, and, perhaps most important, it was wholly distinct from, even opposed to, marriage. It is not at all surprising that the texts and theories of the male troubadours—Andreas Capellanus, especially—were typically drawn from the adulterous advice of Ovid. But their female counterparts—Eleanor of Aquitaine, for example—didn't take love and marriage any more seriously (in part because they were almost always already married).

Much of the history of our changing conceptions of love has to do with the effort to bring together and synthesize the idealization suggested by Plato and Christian love with the very real demands and desires of a couple in love. The virtue of courtly love was its effort to carry out this synthesis and at the same time introduce some sexual and aesthetic satisfaction into a world of arranged marriages based wholly on social, political and economic considerations. It is courtly love that also introduces the essential romantic conception of erotic love as good in itself, a conception that one does not find in the theology of *Symposium* and certainly does not find in Christian concepts of love. In his study, Singer formulates five general features of love that characterize the courtly: (1) that sexual love between men and women is *itself* an ideal worth striving for; (2) that love ennobles both lover and beloved; (3) that sexual love is an ethical and aesthetic achievement and not merely sexual in the narrow sense; (4) that love has to do with courtesy and courtship but not (necessarily) with marriage; and (5) that love involves a "holy oneness" between man and woman. The first feature signals a radical challenge to the traditional Christian view of love, while the third is a rebuke of the vulgar view that love is nothing but sexual desire. But it is the last feature listed that is perhaps most important for our contemporary conception of love. With its roots in Christian mysticism but ancient mythology too, this idea of a "union" between a man and a woman would become the central but most difficult (and therefore often "magical" or "mystical") theme of the romantic period.

Romantic love as such is part and parcel of Romanticism, a distinctively modern philosophy. It presupposes an unusually strong conception of self and individual autonomy and passion combined with a dramatic metaphysics

---

*paradigm:* Standard or ideal.

of unity—of which sexual unity in love is a particularly exciting and tangible example. The great German philosopher Hegel advocated a vision of the universe as a single unity, which he called "love." The romantic poet Shelley described two selves in love as "one soul of interwoven flame." Romantic love takes as its premise the idea of the expansion of individual self to include another—hardly necessary in those societies in which citizenship and other memberships provided all of the shared identity one could possibly imagine. It is the culmination of the notion of the "inner self," again not a virtue that would have been understood in less psychological or individualistic societies. In essence, romantic love came of age only when newly industrialized and increasingly anonymous societies fostered the economically independent and socially shrunken ("nuclear") family, when women as well as men were permitted considerable personal *choice* in their marriage partners, when romantic love novels spread the gospel to the multitude of women of the middle class (whereas courtly love had been the privilege of a few aristocratic heroines) and, philosophically most important, when the centuries-old contrast between sacred and profane love had broken down and been synthesized in a secular mode (like so many ideas in the Enlightenment). Romantic love depended on what the historian Robert Stone has called "affective individualism," an attitude to the individual and the importance of his or her emotions that did not and could not have arisen until modern times.

What is also particularly modern is the linkage between love and marriage. The two have not always been linked so essentially as "horse and carriage," as one popular song would have it. In Plato, for obvious reasons, the question of marriage did not even arise in considerations of eros. Ovid considered love and marriage as opposites, although the marriage of one's intended did provide a challenging obstacle and thereby an additional source of excitement. The long history of marriage as a sacrament has little to say about sexual love and sometimes has much to say against it, and by the time of courtly love, courtship typically provided an *alternative* to loveless marriage rather than a prelude to marriage or—almost unheard of—the content of marriage itself.

In fact, the history of romantic love would seem to indicate that love has its origins not only independent of marriage but as a rebellion *against* marriage. The classic chivalric romance of Camelot was not the story of Arthur and Guinevere but of Guinevere and Lancelot—illicit, illegal, clandestine and doomed. Tristan and Isolde were each married to someone else, and most of the romance in European literature has consisted of stories of mistresses and adultery, not successful marriages. The twelfth-century troubadours encouraged love outside of marriage as an escape valve for women trapped in loveless political marriages. Indeed, one French historian, Denis de Rougement, has insisted that the whole history of romantic love is one of pathological rebellion and self-destruction, quite opposed to that quiet, faithful form of marital love that he calls "conjugal." It is not until the seventeenth century, in Shakespeare's comedies, for example, that we start to see some synthesis of the ideals of love and marriage, the latter typically supplying the culmination of the former (as well as conclusion of the play). But Montaigne, Shakespeare's near contemporary, and Stendhal, the great nineteenth-century romantic, both thought that love and marriage did not mix, and given our current emphasis on the thrills of early love and the hassles of marriage, one might well conclude that the modern reconciliation has not yet taken effect either.

What we know as romantic love is the historical result of a long and painful synthesis between pagan eros, idealistic Christian love and modern philosophy. It is not just sexual, or even primarily sexual, but an idealistic updating of the pagan virtues of cultivation and sensuousness, Christian devotion and fidelity in the modern context of individual privacy, autonomy and affectivity. To think that romantic love is just a "natural" reaction of one person to another is to ignore the whole historical development that lies behind even the most ordinary love affair.

25

## QUESTIONS

1. What is the concept of "idealization" that Solomon cites?
2. What is Solomon's definition of love?
3. What was the early Christian attitude toward the body and "natural" impulses? Has this attitude changed?
4. According to Solomon, which aspects of Christianity make Christian societies "particularly receptive to romantic love"?
5. What was the point of "courtly love"? How did it differ from romantic love?
6. According to Solomon, are arranged marriages as successful as those based on romantic love?
7. What factors make romantic love possible?
8. According to Solomon, what does our "emphasis on romance" encourage? Do you agree with this view?
9. According to Solomon, what does the phrase "I love you" signify? Explain whether you agree or disagree.
10. According to Solomon, why is love elusive?

## CONNECTIONS

1. Find the points where Solomon discusses nineteenth-century Victorian views of love. Determine whether the poem by Elizabeth Barrett

Browning, which was written at that time, supports Solomon's assertions.

2. Reread the selection from Paul's letter to the Corinthians. Do Solomon's views about Christianity and love change your understanding of that passage?

# ~⁓ On Friendship

*Francine du Plessix Gray*

Born in 1930 in Poland, Francine du Plessix Gray emigrated to the United States in 1941. After studying at Bryn Mawr, Black Mountain College, and Barnard College, she worked as a journalist and an editor; she has also taught writing at Yale and Columbia University. She is the author of several books of both fiction and nonfiction, including *Divine Disobedience: Profiles in Catholic Radicalism* (1970) and *Soviet Women: Walking the Tightrope* (1990); she has also published articles in *Vogue, The New Yorker,* and other magazines. The following selection comes from her book *Adam and Eve and the City* (1987).

**WARM-UP:** What is the difference between love and friendship? Provide an example of each.

I saw Madame Bovary at Bloomingdale's the other morning, or rather, I saw          1
many incarnations of her. She was hovering over the cosmetic counters, clutching the current issue of *Cosmopolitan,* whose cover line read "New Styles of Coupling, Including Marriage." Her face already ablaze with numerous products advertised to make her irresistible to the opposite sex, she looked anguished, grasping, overwrought,° and terribly lonely. And I thought to myself: Poor girl! With all the reams of literature that have analyzed her plight (victimized by double standards, by a materialistic middle-class glutting on the excesses of romantic fiction), notwithstanding all these diagnoses, one fact central to her tragic fate has never been stressed enough: Emma Bovary had a faithful and boring husband and couple of boring lovers—not so intolerable a condition—but she did not have a friend in the world. And when I think of the great solitude which the original Emma and her contemporaries exude,° one phrase jumps to my mind. It comes from an essay by Francis Bacon, and it is one of the finest statements ever penned about the human need for friendship: "Those who have no friends to open themselves unto are cannibals of their own hearts."

In the past years the theme of friendship has been increasingly prominent in our conversations, in our books and films, even in our college courses. It is evident that many of us are yearning with new fervor for this form of bonding. And our yearning may well be triggered by the same disillusionment with the reign of Eros that destroyed Emma Bovary. Emma was eating her heart

*overwrought:* Extremely agitated.    *exude:* To emanate, spread around.

out over a fantasy totally singular to the Western world, and only a century old at that: the notion that sexual union between men and women who believe that they are passionately in love, a union achieved by free choice and legalized by marriage, tends to offer a life of perpetual bliss and is the most desirable human bond available on earth. It is a notion bred in the same frenzied climate of the romantic epoch that caused countless young Europeans to act like the characters of their contemporary literature. Goethe's *Werther* is said to have triggered hundreds of suicides. Numerous wives glutted on the fantasies of George Sand's heroines demanded separations because their husbands were unpoetic. And Emma Bovary, palpitating from that romantic fiction which precurses° our current sex manuals in its outlandish hopes for the satiation of desire, muses in the third week of her marriage: Where is "the felicity, the passion, the intoxication" that had so enchanted her in the novels of Sir Walter Scott?

This frenzied myth of love which has also led to the downfall of Cleopatra, Juliet, Romeo, and King Kong continues to breed, in our time, more garbled thinking, wretched verse, and nonsensical jingles than any emotion under the sun: "All You Need Is Love," or as we heard it in our high-school days, "Tell me you'll love me forever, if only tonight." As Flaubert put it, we are all victims of romanticism. And if we still take for granted its cult of heterosexual passion, it is in part because we have been victimized, as Emma was, by the propaganda machine of the Western novel. It was the power and the genius of the novel form to fuse medieval notions of courtly love with the idealization of marriage that marked the rise of the eighteenth-century middle class. (By "romantic love," I mean an infatuation that involves two major ingredients: a sense of being "enchanted" by another person through a complex process of illusion, and a willingness to totally surrender to that person.)

One hardly needs a course in anthropology to realize that this alliance of marriage and romantic love is restricted to a small segment of the Western world, and would seem sheer folly in most areas of this planet. The great majority of humans—be it in China, Japan, Africa, India, the Moslem nations —still engage in marriages prearranged by their elders or dictated by pragmatic reasons of money, land, tribal politics, or (as in the Socialist countries) housing shortages. Romantically motivated marriage as the central ingredient of the good life is almost as novel in our own West. In popular practice, it remained restricted to a narrow segment of the middle class until the twentieth century. And on the level of philosophical reflection, it was always friendship between members of the same sex, never any bonding of sexual affection, which from Greek times to the Enlightenment was held to be the cornerstone of human happiness. Yet this central role allotted to friendship for two thou-

---

*precurses:* Precedes.

sand years has been progressively eroded by such factors as the nineteenth-century exaltation° of instinct; science's monopoly on our theories of human sentiment; the massive eroticizing of society; and that twentieth-century celebration of the body that reaches its peak in the hedonistic° solitude of the multiple orgasm.

To Aristotle, friendship can be formed only by persons of virtue: A man's      5 capacity for friendship is the most accurate measure of his virtue; it is the foundation of the state, for great legislators care even more for friendship than they care for justice. To Plato, as we know, passionate affection untainted by physical relations is the highest form of human bonding. To Cicero, *Amicitia*° is more important than either money, power, honors, or health because each of these gifts can bring us only one form of pleasure, whereas the pleasures of friendship are marvelously manifold; and friendship being based on equity, the tyrant is the man least capable of forming that bond because of his need to wield power over others. Montaigne's essay, along with Bacon's, is the most famous of many that glorify our theme in the Renaissance. And like the ancients, he stresses the advantages of friendship over any kind of romantic and physical attachment. Love for members of the opposite sex, in Montaigne's words, is "an impetuous° and fickle flame, undulating and variable, a fever flame subject to fits and lulls." Whereas the fire of friendship produces "a general and universal warmth, moderate and even," and will always forge bonds superior to those of marriage because marriage's continuance is "constrained and forced, depending on factors other than our free will."

A century later, even La Rochefoucauld, that great cynic who described the imperialism of the ego better than any other precursor of Freud, finds that friendship is the only human bond in which the tyrannical cycle of our self-love seems broken, in which "we can love each other even more than love ourselves." One of the last classic essays on friendship I can think of before it loses major importance as a philosophical theme is by Ralph Waldo Emerson. And it's interesting to note that by mid-nineteenth century, the euphoric absolutes which had previously described this form of bonding are sobered by many cautious qualifications. A tinge of modern pragmatism sets in. Emerson tends to distrust any personal friendship unless it functions for the purpose of some greater universal fraternity.

Yet however differently these thinkers focused on our theme, they all seemed to reach a consensus on the qualities of free will, equity, trust, and selflessness unique to the affection of friendship. They cannot resist comparing it to physical passion, which yearns for power over the other, seeks possession

---

*exaltation:* Aggrandizement, abundant praise.    *hedonistic:* Focused solely on pleasure and happiness. *Amicitia:* Latin, meaning friendship.    *impetuous:* Impulsive, rash.

and the state of being possessed, seeks to devour, breeds on excess, can easily become demonic, is closely allied to the death wish, and is often a form of agi-tated narcissism° quite unknown to the tranquil, balanced rule of friendship. And rereading the sagas of Tristan and Iseult, Madame Bovary, and many other romantic lovers, it is evident that their passions tend to breed as much on a masturbatory excitement as on a longing for the beloved. They are in love with love, their delirium is involved with a desire for self-magnification through suffering, as evidenced in Tristan's words, "Eyes with joy are blinded. I myself am the world." There is confrontation, turmoil, aggression, in the often militaristic language of romantic love: Archers shoot fatal arrows or unerring shafts; the male enemy presses, pursues, and conquers; women sur-render after being besieged by amorous assaults. Friendship on the other hand is the most pacifist species in the fauna° of human emotions, the most stead-fast and sharing. No wonder then that the finest pacifist ideology in the West was devised by a religious group—the Quakers—which takes as its official name the Religious Society of Friends; the same temperate principle of frater-nal bonding informs that vow demanded by the Benedictine Order—the Oath of Stability—which remains central to the monastic tradition to this day. No wonder, also, that the kind of passionate friendship shared by David and Jonathan has inspired very few masterpieces of literature, which seem to thrive on tension and illicitness.° For until they were relegated to the dissect-ing rooms of the social sciences, our literary views of friendship tended to be expressed in the essay form, a cool, reflective mode that never provided friendship with the motive,° democratic, propagandistic force found by Eros in novel, verse, and stage. To this day, friendship totally resists commercial exploitation, unlike the vast businesses fueled by romantic love that support the couture,° perfume, cosmetic, lingerie, and pulp-fiction trades.

One should note, however, that most views of friendship expressed in the past twenty centuries of Western thought have dealt primarily with the male's capacity for affection. And they tend to be extremely dubious about the possi-bility of women ever being able to enjoy genuine friendships with members of their own sex, not to speak of making friends with male peers. Montaigne expressed a prejudice that lasts well into our day when he wrote, "The ordi-nary capacity of women is inadequate for that communion and fellowship which is the nurse of that sacred bond, nor does their soul feel firm enough to endure the strain of so tight and durable a knot." It is shocking, though not surprising, to hear prominent social scientists paraphrase that opinion in our own decades. Konrad Lorenz and Lionel Tiger, for instance, seem to agree that

narcissism: Egotism; excessive love of oneself.    fauna: Animal life (here used ironically).    illicitness: The quality of being forbidden, taboo.    motive . . . force: The force that propelled or generated some-thing.    couture: The business of creating custom-made women's clothing.

women are made eminently unsociable by their genetic programming; their bondings, in Lorenz's words, "must be considered weak imitations of the exclusively male associations." Given the current vogue for sociobiology, such assertions are often supported by carefully researched papers on the courtship patterns of Siberian wolves, the prevalence of eye contact among male baboons, and the vogue for gangbanging among chimpanzees.

Our everyday language reflects the same bias: "Fraternity" is a word that goes far beyond its collegiate context and embraces notions of honor, dignity, loyalty. "Sorority" is something we might have belonged to as members of the University of Oklahoma's bowling team in the early 1950s. So I think it is high time that the same feminist perspective that has begun to correct the biases of art history and psychoanalysis should be brought to bear on this area of anthropology. We have indeed been deprived of those official, dramatically visible rites offered to men in pub, poolroom, Elks, hunting ground, or football league. And having been brought up in a very male world, I'm ashamed to say it took me a decade of feminist consciousness to realize that the few bonding associations left to twentieth-century women—garden clubs, church suppers, sewing circles (often derided by men because they do not deal with power)—have been activities considerably more creative and life-enhancing than the competition of the poolroom, the machismo° of beer drinking, or the bloodshed of hunting.

Among both sexes, the rites and gestures of friendship seemed to have    10
been decimated° in the Victorian era, which brought a fear of homosexuality unprecedented in the West. (They also tended to decrease as rites of heterosexual coupling became increasingly permissive.) Were Dr. Johnson and James Boswell gay, those two men who constantly exhibited their affection for each other with kisses, tears, and passionate embraces? I suspect they were as rabidly straight as those tough old soldiers described by Tacitus begging for last kisses when their legion broke up. Since Freud, science has tended to dichotomize° human affection along lines of deviance and normalcy, genitality and platonic love, instead of leaving it as a graduated spectrum of emotion in which love, friendship, sensuality, sexuality, can freely flow into each other as they did in the past. This may be another facet of modern culture that has cast coolness and self-consciousness on our gestures of friendship. The 1960s brought us some hope for change, both in its general emotional climate and in our scientists' tendency to relax their definitions of normalcy and deviance. For one of the most beautiful signs of that decade's renewed yearning for friendship and community, particularly evident among the groups who marched in civil-rights or antiwar demonstrations, was the sight of men

---

*machismo:* Assertive, aggressive, or domineering expression of "maleness."    *decimated:* Devastated, wiped out;    *dichotomize:* Divide into two parts or groups.

clutching, kissing, embracing each other unabashedly as Dr. Johnson and James Boswell.

Which leads me to reflect on the reasons why I increasingly turn to friendship in my own life: In a world more and more polluted by the lying of politicians and the illusions of the media, I occasionally crave to hear and to tell the truth. To borrow a beautiful phrase from Friedrich Nietzsche, I look upon my friend as "the beautiful enemy" who alone is able to offer me total candor. I look for the kind of honest friend Emma Bovary needed: one who could have told her that her lover was a jerk.

Friendship is by its very nature freer of deceit than any other relationship we can know because it is the bond least affected by striving for power, physical pleasure, or material profit, most liberated from any oath of duty or of constancy. With Eros the *body* stands naked, in friendship our *spirit* is denuded. Friendship, in this sense, is a human condition resembling what may be humanity's most beautiful and necessary lie—the promise of an afterlife. It is an almost celestial sphere in which we most resemble that society of angels offered us by Christian theology, in which we can sing the truth of our inner thoughts in relative freedom and abundance. No wonder then that the last contemporary writers whose essays on friendship may remain classics are those religiously inclined, scholars relatively unaffected by positivism° or behaviorism,° or by the general scientificization of human sentiment. That marvelous Christian maverick, C. S. Lewis, tells us: "Friendship is unnecessary, like philosophy, like art, like the universe itself (since God did not *need* to create). It has no survival value; rather it is one of those things that give value to survival." And the Jewish thinker Simone Weil focuses on the classic theme of free consent when she writes: "Friendship is a miracle by which a person consents to view from a certain distance, and without coming any nearer, the very being who is necessary to him as food."

The quality of free consent and self-determination inherent in friendship may be crucial to the lives of twentieth-century women beginning their vocations. But in order to return friendship to an absolutely central place in our lives, we might have to wean ourselves in part from the often submissive premises of romantic passion. I suspect that we shall always need some measure of swooning and palpitating, of ecstasy and trembling, of possessing and being possessed. But, I also suspect that we've been bullied and propagandized into many of these manifestations by the powerful modern organism that I

---

*positivism:* A school of thought that holds that true knowledge is based on natural phenomena and their properties, as verified by scientific observation rather than faith.    *behaviorism:* A school of thought that holds that psychology should deal only with human behavior, because the human mind and consciousness cannot really be defined and examined.

call the sexual-industrial complex and that had an antecedent° in the novels that fueled Emma Bovary's deceitful fantasies. For one of the most treacherous aspects of the cult of romantic love has been its complex idealization and exploitation of female sexuality. There is now a new school of social scientists who are militantly questioning the notion that Western romantic love is the best foundation for human bonding, and their criticism seems much inspired by feminist perspectives. The Australian anthropologist Robert Brain, for instance, calls romantic love "a lunatic relic of medieval passions . . . the hand-maiden° of a moribund capitalistic culture and of an equally dead Puritan ethic."

What exactly would happen if we women remodeled our concepts of ideal human bonding on the ties of friendship and abandoned the premises of enchantment and possession? Such a restructuring of our ideals of happiness could be extremely subversive. It might imply a considerable de-eroticizing of society. It could bring about a minor revolution against the sexual-industrial complex that brings billions of dollars to thousands of men by brainwashing us into the roles of temptress and seductress, and estranges us from the plain and beautiful Quaker ideal of being a sister to the world. How topsy-turvy the world would be! Dalliance,° promiscuity, all those more sensationalized aspects of the Women's Movement that were once seen as revolutionary might suddenly seem most bourgeois and old-fashioned activities. If chosen in conditions of rigorous self-determination, the following values, considered up to now as reactionary, could suddenly become the most radical ones at hand: Virginity. Celibacy. Monastic communities. And that most endangered species of all, fidelity in marriage, which has lately become so exotically rare that it might soon become very fashionable, and provide the cover story for yet another publication designed to alleviate the seldom-admitted solitude of swinging singles: "Mick Jagger Is into Fidelity."

### QUESTIONS

1. Explain your understanding of the Francis Bacon statement quoted by du Plessix Gray.
2. Find and explain du Plessix Gray's definition of "romantic love." Do you agree with it? Why or why not?
3. What medium does the author blame for the perpetuation of romantic fantasies? Is this still accurate in our society today?

---

*antecedent:* Precedent, preliminary.    *handmaiden:* Something or someone whose function is to serve or assist.    *dalliance:* Frivolous action.

4. What is the effect of combining the names "Cleopatra, Juliet, Romeo, and King Kong" in a list of victims of love?

5. According to du Plessix Gray, what factors eroded the role of friendship in society?

6. Explain what du Plessix Gray means when she says that romantic lovers "are in love with love."

7. Traditionally, what group activities have cemented friendships between men? What activities have cemented friendships between women? Are those activities still relevant to our lives today, or have they been replaced by other bonding activities?

8. What does du Plessix Gray mean by "the sexual-industrial complex"?

9. Why is this author "increasingly turn[ing] to friendship in [her] life"? When and why do *you* turn to friendship, instead of romantic love?

10. Are the introduction and conclusion of this essay effective? Where does the author's thesis appear?

## CONNECTIONS

1. Compare and contrast du Plessix Gray's ideas about romantic love with those expressed in Robert Solomon's essay.

2. Discuss the common thread between this essay and Marge Piercy's poem "Barbie Doll."

3. Compare and contrast du Plessix Gray's views of romantic love and physical passion with those reflected in Julius Lester's "Being a Boy" (the transitional selection between Sections 1 and 2).

# ∼ In the Life

*Becky Birtha*

Becky Birtha has published two collections of short stories—*For Nights Like This One: Stories of Loving Women* (1983) and *Lovers' Choice* (1987)—as well as a poetry collection entitled *The Forbidden Poems* (1991). Stories from *Lover's Choice* have appeared in more than twenty college textbooks and other anthologies, including *We Are the Stories We Tell* (1989), *Woman on Woman* (1990), and *Daughters of Africa* (1991). Birtha received an Individual Fellowship in Literature from the Pennsylvania Council on the Arts in 1985 and a Creative Writing Fellowship Grant from the National Endowment for the Arts in 1988. The following selection comes from *Lovers' Choice*.

**WARM-UP:** Have you ever known an elderly couple who had been together for most of their lives? How did they behave toward each other?

Grace come to me in my sleep last night. I feel somebody presence, in the room with me, then I catch the scent of Posner's Bergamot Pressing Oil, and that cocoa butter grease she use on her skin. I know she standing at the bedside, right over me, and then she call my name.

"Pearl."

My Christian name Pearl Irene Jenkins, but don't nobody ever call me that no more. I been Jinx to the world for longer than I care to specify. Since my mother passed away, Grace the only one ever use my given name.

"Pearl," she say again. "I'm just gone down to the garden awhile. I be back."

I'm so deep asleep I have to fight my way awake, and when I do be fully woke, Grace is gone. I ease my tired bones up and drag em down the stairs, cross the kitchen in the dark, and out the back screen door onto the porch. I guess I'm half expecting Gracie to be there waiting for me, but there ain't another soul stirring tonight. Not a sound but singing crickets, and nothing staring back at me but that old weather-beaten fence I ought to painted this summer, and still ain't made time for. I lower myself down into the porch swing, where Gracie and I have sat so many still summer nights and watched the moon rising up over Old Mister Thompson's field.

I never had time to paint that fence back then, neither. But it didn't matter none, cause Gracie had it all covered up with her flowers. She used to sit right here on this swing at night, when a little breeze be blowing, and say she could tell all the different flowers apart, just by they smell. The wind pick up a scent, and Gracie say, "Smell that jasmine, Pearl?" Then a breeze come up from

1

5

another direction, and she turn her head like somebody calling her and say, "Now that's my honeysuckle, now."

It used to tickle me, cause she knowed I couldn't tell all them flowers of hers apart when I was looking square at em in broad daylight. So how I'm gonna do it by smell in the middle of the night? I just laugh and rock the swing a little, and watch her enjoying herself in the soft moonlight.

I could never get enough of watching her. I always did think that Grace Simmons was the prettiest woman north of the Mason-Dixon line. Now I've lived enough years to know it's true. There's been other women in my life besides Grace, and I guess I loved them all, one way or another, but she was something special—Gracie was something else again.

She was a dark brownskin woman—the color of fresh gingerbread hot out the oven. In fact, I used to call her that—my gingerbread girl. She had plenty enough of that pretty brownskin flesh to fill your arms up with something substantial when you hugging her, and to make a nice background for them dimples in her checks and other places I won't go into detail about.

Gracie could be one elegant good looker when she set her mind to it. I'll never forget the picture she made, that time the New Year's Eve party was down at the Star Harbor Ballroom. That was the first year we was in the Club, and we was going to every event they had. Dressed to kill. Gracie had on that white silk dress that set off her complexion so perfect, with her hair done up in all them little curls. A single strand of pearls that could have fooled anybody. Long gloves. And a little fur stole. We was serious about our partying back then! I didn't look too bad myself, with that black velvet jacket I used to have, and the pleats in my slacks pressed so sharp you could cut yourself on em. I weighed quite a bit less than I do now, too. Right when you come in the door of the ballroom, they have a great big floor to ceiling gold frame mirror, and if I remember rightly, we didn't get past that for quite some time.

Everybody want to dance with Gracie that night. And that's fine with me. Along about the middle of the evening, the band is playing a real hot number, and here come Louie and Max over to me, all long-face serious, wanting to know how I can let my woman be out there shaking her behind with any stranger that wander in the door. Now they know good and well ain't no strangers here. The Cinnamon & Spice Club is a private club, and all events is by invitation only.

Of course, there's some thinks friends is more dangerous than strangers. But I never could be the jealous, overprotective type. And the fact is, I just love to watch the woman. I don't care if she out there shaking it with the Virgin Mary, long as she having a good time. And that's just what I told Max and Lou. I could lean up against that bar and watch her for hours.

You wouldn't know, to look at her, she done it all herself. Made all her own dresses and hats, and even took apart a old ratty fur coat that used to belong to my great aunt Malinda to make that cute little stole. She always did her own hair—every week or two. She used to do mine, too. Always be teasing me about let her make me some curls this time. I'd get right aggravated. Cause you can't have a proper argument with somebody when they standing over your head with a hot comb in they hand. You kinda at they mercy. I'm sitting fuming and cursing under them towels and stuff, with the sweat dripping all in my eyes in the steamy kitchen—and she just laughing. "Girl," I'm telling her, "you know won't no curls fit under my uniform cap. Less you want me to stay home this week and you gonna go work my job and your job too."

Both of us had to work, always, and we still ain't had much. Everybody always think Jinx and Grace doing all right, but we was scrimping and saving all along. Making stuff over and making do. Half of what we had to eat grew right here in this garden. Still and all, I guess we *was* doing all right. We had each other.

Now I finally got the damn house paid off, and she ain't even here to appreciate it with me. And Gracie's poor bedraggled garden is just struggling along on its last legs—kinda like me. I ain't the kind to complain about my lot, but truth to tell, I can't be down crawling around on my hands and knees no more—this body I got put up such a fuss and holler. Can't enjoy the garden at night proper nowadays, nohow. Since Mister Thompson's land was took over by the city and they built them housing projects where the field used to be, you can't even see the moon from here, till it get up past the fourteenth floor. Don't no moonlight come in my yard no more. And I guess I might as well pick my old self up and go on back to bed.

Sometimes I still ain't used to the fact that Grace is passed on. Not even after these thirteen years without her. She the only woman I ever lived with— and I lived with her more than half my life. This house her house, too, and she oughta be here in it with me.

I rise up by six o'clock most every day, same as I done all them years I worked driving for the C.T.C. If the weather ain't too bad, I take me a walk— and if I ain't careful, I'm liable to end up down at the Twelfth Street Depot, waiting to see what trolley they gonna give me this morning. There ain't a soul working in that office still remember me. And they don't even run a trolley on the Broadway line no more. They been running a bus for the past five years.

I forgets a lot of things these days. Last week, I had just took in the clean laundry off the line, and I'm up in the spare room fixing to iron my shirts, when I hear somebody pass through that squeaky side gate and go on around to the back yard. I ain't paid it no mind at all, cause that's the way Gracie most often do when she come home. Go see about her garden fore she even come in the house. I always be teasing her she care more about them collards and string beans than she do about me. I hear her moving around out there while

15

I'm sprinkling the last shirt and plugging in the iron—hear leaves rustling, and a crate scraping along the walk.

While I'm waiting for the iron to heat up, I take a look out the window, and come to see it ain't Gracie at all, but two a them sassy little scoundrels from over the projects—one of em standing on a apple crate and holding up the other one, who is picking my ripe peaches off my tree, just as brazen as you please. Don't even blink a eyelash when I holler out the window. I have to go running down all them stairs and out on the back porch, waving the cord I done jerked out the iron—when Doctor Matthews has told me a hundred times I ain't supposed to be running or getting excited about nothing, with my pressure like it is. And I ain't even supposed to be *walking* up and down no stairs.

20    When they seen the ironing cord in my hand, them two little sneaks had a reaction all right. The one on the bottom drop the other one right on his padded quarters and lit out for the gate, hollering, "Look out, Timmy! Here come Old Lady Jenkins!"

When I think about it now, it was right funny, but at the time I was so mad it musta took me a whole half hour to cool off. I sat there on that apple crate just boiling.

Eventually, I begun to see how it wasn't even them two kids I was so mad at. I was mad at time. For playing tricks on me the way it done. So I don't even remember that Grace Simmons has been dead now for the past thirteen years. And mad at time just for passing—so fast. If I had my life to live over, I wouldn't trade in none of them years for nothing. I'd just slow em down.

The church sisters around here is always trying to get me to be thinking about dying, myself. They must figure, when you my age, that's the only excitement you got left to look forward to. Gladys Hawkins stopped out front this morning, while I was mending a patch in the top screen of the front door. She was grinning from ear to ear like she just spent the night with Jesus himself.

"Morning, Sister Jenkins. Right pretty day the good Lord seen fit to send us, ain't it?"

25    I ain't never known how to answer nobody who manages to bring the good Lord into every conversation. If I nod and say yes, she'll think I finally got religion. But if I disagree, she'll think I'm crazy, cause it truly is one pretty August morning. Fortunately, it don't matter to her whether I agree or not, cause she gone right on talking according to her own agenda anyway.

"You know, this Sunday is Women's Day over at Blessed Endurance. Reverend Solomon Moody is gonna be visiting, speaking on 'A Woman's Place in the Church.' Why don't you come and join us for worship? You'd be most welcome."

I'm tempted to tell her exactly what come to my mind—that I ain't never heard of no woman name Solomon. However, I'm polite enough to hold my tongue, which is more than I can say for Gladys.

She ain't waiting for no answer from me, just going right on. "I don't spose you need me to point it out to you, Sister Jenkins, but you know you ain't as young as you used to be." As if both of our ages wasn't common knowledge to each other, seeing as we been knowing one another since we was girls. "You reaching that time of life when you might wanna be giving a little more attention to the spiritual side of things than you been doing. . . ."

She referring, politely as she capable of, to the fact that I ain't been seen inside a church for thirty-five years.

". . . And you know what the good Lord say. 'Watch therefore, for ye know          30
neither the day nor the hour . . .' But, 'He that believeth on the Son hath everlasting life . . .'"

It ain't no use to argue with her kind. The Lord is on they side in every lit-
tle disagreement, and he don't never give up. So when she finally wind down and ask me again will she see me in church this Sunday, I just say I'll think about it.

Funny thing, I been thinking about it all day. But not the kinda thoughts she want me to think, I'm sure. Last time I went to church was on a Easter Sunday. We decided to go on accounta Gracie's old meddling cousin, who was always nagging us about how we unnatural and sinful and a disgrace to her family. Seem like she seen it as her one mission in life to get us two sinners inside a church. I guess she figure, once she get us in there, God gonna take over the job. So Grace and me finally conspires that the way to get her off our backs is to give her what she think she want.

Course, I ain't had on a skirt since before the war, and I ain't aiming to change my lifelong habits just to please Cousin Hattie. But I did take a lotta pains over my appearance that day. I'd had my best tailor-made suit pressed fresh, and slept in my stocking cap the night before so I'd have every hair in place. Even had one a Gracie's flowers stuck in my buttonhole. And a brand new narrow-brim dove gray Stetson hat. Gracie take one look at me when I'm ready and shake her head. "The good sisters is gonna have a hard time concen-
trating on the preacher today!"

We arrive at her cousin's church nice and early, but of course it's a big crowd inside already on accounta it being Easter Sunday. The organ music is wailing away, and the congregation is dazzling—decked out in nothing but the finest and doused with enough perfume to outsmell even the flowers up on the altar.

But as soon as we get in the door, this kinda sedate commotion break out          35
—all them good Christian folks whispering and nudging each other and try-
ing to turn around and get a good look. Well, Grace and me, we used to that. We just find us a nice seat in one of the empty pews near the back. But this busy buzzing keep up, even after we seated and more blended in with the crowd. And finally it come out that the point of contention ain't even the bottom half of my suit, but my new dove gray Stetson.

This old gentleman with a grizzled head, wearing glasses about a inch thick is turning around and leaning way over the back of the seat, whispering to Grace in a voice plenty loud enough for me to hear, "You better tell your beau to remove that hat, entering in Jesus' Holy Chapel."

Soon as I get my hat off, some old lady behind me is grumbling. "I declare, some of these children haven't got no respect at all. Oughta know you sposed to keep your head covered, setting in the house of the Lord."

Seem like the congregation just can't make up its mind whether I'm supposed to wear my hat or I ain't.

I couldn't hardly keep a straight face all through the service. Every time I catch Gracie eye, or one or the other of us catch a sight of my hat, we off again. I couldn't wait to get outa that place. But it was worth it. Gracie and me was entertaining the gang with that story for weeks to come. And we ain't had no more problems with Cousin Hattie.

40    Far as life everlasting is concerned, I imagine I'll cross that bridge when I reach it. I don't see no reason to rush into things. Sure, I know Old Man Death is gonna be coming after me one of these days, same as he come for my mother and dad, and Gracie and, just last year, my old buddy Louie. But I ain't about to start nothing that might make him feel welcome. It might be different for Gladys Hawkins and the rest of them church sisters, but I got a whole lot left to live for. Including a mind fulla good time memories. When you in the life,° one thing your days don't never be, and that's dull. Your nights neither. All these years I been in the life, I loved it. And you know Jinx ain't about to go off with no Old *Man* without no struggle, nohow.

To tell the truth, though, sometime I do get a funny feeling bout Old Death. Sometime I feel like he here already—been here. Waiting on me and watching me and biding his time. Paying attention when I have to stop on the landing of the stairs to catch my breath. Paying attention if I don't wake up till half past seven some morning, and my back is hurting me so bad it take me another half hour to pull myself together and get out the bed.

The same night after I been talking to Gladys in the morning, it take me a long time to fall asleep. I'm lying up in bed waiting for the aching in my back and my joints to ease off some, and I can swear I hear somebody else in the house. Seem like I hear em downstairs, maybe opening and shutting the icebox door, or switching off a light. Just when I finally manage to doze off, I hear somebody footsteps right here in the bedroom with me. Somebody tippy-toeing real quiet, creaking the floor boards between the bed and the dresser . . . over to the closet . . . back to the dresser again.

I'm almost scared to open my eyes. But it's only Gracie—in her old raggedy bathrobe and a silk handkerchief wrapped up around all them little

---

*"in the life"*: Expression referring to people who are living openly as gays or lesbians.

braids in her head—putting her finger up to her lips to try and shush me so I won't wake up.

I can't help chuckling. "Hey Gingerbread Girl. Where you think you going in your house coat and bandana and it ain't even light out yet. Come on get back in this bed."

"You go on to sleep," she say. "I'm just going out back a spell."                    45

It ain't no use me trying to make my voice sound angry, cause she so contrary when it come to that little piece of ground down there I can't help laughing. "What you think you gonna complish down there in the middle of the night? It ain't even no moon to watch tonight. The sky been filling up with clouds all evening, and the weather forecast say rain tomorrow."

"Just don't pay me no mind and go on back to sleep. It ain't the middle of the night. It's almost daybreak." She grinning like she up to something, and sure enough, she say, "This the best time to pick off them black and yellow beetles been making mildew outa my cucumber vines. So I'm just fixing to turn the tables around a little bit. You gonna read in the papers tomorrow morning bout how the entire black and yellow beetle population of number Twenty-seven Bank Street been wiped off the face of the earth—while you was up here sleeping."

Both of us is laughing like we partners in a crime, and then she off down the hall, calling out, "I be back before you even know I'm gone."

But the full light of day is coming in the window, and she ain't back yet.

I'm over to the window with a mind to holler down to Grace to get her            50
behind back in this house, when the sight of them housing projects hits me right in the face: stacks of dirt-colored bricks and little caged-in porches, heaped up into the sky blocking out what poor skimpy light this cloudy morning brung.

It's a awful funny feeling start to come over me. I mean to get my housecoat, and go down there anyway, just see what's what. But in the closet I can see it ain't but my own clothes hanging on the pole. All the shoes on the floor is mine. And I know I better go ahead and get washed, cause it's a whole lot I want to get done fore it rain, and that storm is coming in for sure. Better pick the rest of them ripe peaches and tomatoes. Maybe put in some peas for fall picking, if my knees'll allow me to get that close to the ground.


The rain finally catch up around noon time and slow me down a bit. I never could stand to be cooped up in no house in the rain. Always make me itchy. That's one reason I used to like driving a trolley for the C.T.C. Cause you get to be out every day, no matter what kinda weather coming down—get to see people and watch the world go by. And it ain't as if you exactly out in the weather, neither. You get to watch it all from behind that big picture window.

Not that I woulda minded being out in it. I used to want to get me a job with the post office, delivering mail. Black folks could make good money with the post office, even way back then. But they wouldn't out you on no mail route. Always stick em off in a back room someplace, where nobody can't see em and get upset cause some little colored girl making as much money as the white boy working next to her. So I stuck with the C.T.C. all them years, and got my pension to prove it.

The rain still coming down steady along about three o'clock, when Max call me up say do I want to come over to her and Yvonne's for dinner. Say they fried more chicken than they can eat, and anyway Yvonne all involved in some new project she want to talk to me about. And I'm glad for the chance to get out the house. Max and Yvonne got the place all picked up for company. I can smell that fried chicken soon as I get in the door.

55      Yvonne don't never miss a opportunity to dress up a bit. She got the front of her hair braided up, with beads hanging all in her eyes, and a kinda loose robe-like thing, in colors look like the fruit salad at a Independence Day picnic. Max her same old self in her slacks and loafers. She ain't changed in all the years I known her—cept we both got more wrinkles and gray hairs. Yvonne a whole lot younger than us two, but she hanging in there. Her and Max been together going on three years now.

Right away, Yvonne start to explain about this project she doing with her women's club. When I first heard about this club she in, I was kinda interested. But I come to find out it ain't no social club, like the Cinnamon & Spice Club used to be. It's more like a organization. Yvonne call it a collective. They never has no outings or parties or picnics or nothing—just meetings. And projects.

The project they working on right now, they all got tape recorders. And they going around tape-recording people story. Talking to people who been in the life for years and years, and asking em what it was like, back in the old days. I been in the life since before Yvonne born. But the second she stick that microphone in my face, I can't think of a blessed thing to say.

"Come on, Jinx, you always telling us all them funny old time stories."

Them little wheels is rolling round and round, and all that smooth, shiny brown tape is slipping off one reel and sliding onto the other, and I can't think of not one thing I remember.

60      "Tell how the Cinnamon & Spice Club got started," she say.

"I already told you about that before."

"Well tell how it ended, then. You never told me that."

"Ain't nothing to tell. Skip and Peaches broke up." Yvonne waiting, and the reels is rolling, but for the life of me I can't think of another word to say about it. And Max is sitting there grinning, like I'm the only one over thirty in the room and she don't remember a thing.

Yvonne finally give up and turn the thing off, and we go on and stuff ourselves on the chicken they fried and the greens I brung over from the garden.

By the time we start in on the sweet potato pie, I have finally got to remembering. Telling Yvonne about when Skip and Peaches had they last big falling out, and they was both determine they was gonna stay in the Club—and couldn't be in the same room with one another for fifteen minutes. Both of em keep waiting on the other one to drop out, and both of em keep showing up, every time the gang get together. And none of the rest of us couldn't be in the same room with the two a them for even as long as they could stand each other. We'd be sneaking around, trying to hold a meeting without them finding out. But Peaches was the president and Skip was the treasurer, you might say our hands was tied. Wouldn't neither one of em resign. They was both convince the Club couldn't go on without em, and by the time they was finished carrying on, they had done made sure it wouldn't.

Max is chiming in correcting all the details, every other breath come outa    65
my mouth. And then when we all get up to go sit in the parlor again, it come out that Yvonne has sneaked that tape recording machine in here under that African poncho she got on, and has got down every word I said.

When time come to say good night, I'm thankful, for once, that Yvonne insist on driving me home—though it ain't even a whole mile. The rain ain't let up all evening, and is coming down in bucketfuls while we in the car. I'm half soaked just running from the car to the front door.

Yvonne is drove off down the street, and I'm halfway through the front door, when it hit me all of a sudden that the door ain't been locked. Now my mind may be getting a little threadbare in spots, but it ain't wore out yet. I know it's easy for me to slip back into doing things the way I done em twenty or thirty years ago, but I could swear I distinctly remember locking this door and hooking the key ring back on my belt loop, just fore Yvonne drove up in front. And now here's the door been open all this time.

Not a sign a nobody been here. Everything in its place, just like I left it. The slipcovers on the couch is smooth and neat. The candy dishes and ash trays and photographs is sitting just where they belong, on the end tables. Not even so much as a throw rug been moved an inch. I can feel my heart start to thumping like a blowout tire.

Must be, whoever come in here ain't left yet.

The idea of somebody got a nerve like that make me more mad than    70
scared, and I know I'm gonna find out who it is broke in my house, even if it don't turn out to be nobody but them little peach-thieving rascals from round the block. Which I wouldn't be surprised if it ain't. I'm scooting from room to room, snatching open closet doors and whipping back curtains—tiptoeing down the hall and then flicking on the lights real sudden.

When I been in every room, I go back through everywhere I been, real slow, looking in all the drawers, and under the old glass doorstop in the hall, and in the back of the recipe box in the kitchen—and other places where I keep things. But it ain't nothing missing. No money—nothing.

In the end, ain't nothing left for me to do but go to bed. But I'm still feeling real uneasy. I know somebody or something done got in here while I was gone. And ain't left yet. I lay wake in the bed a long time, cause I ain't too particular about falling asleep tonight. Anyway, all this rain just make my joints swell up worse, and the pains in my knees just don't let up.

The next thing I know Gracie waking me up. She lying next to me and kissing me all over my face. I wake up laughing, and she say, "I never could see no use in shaking somebody I rather be kissing." I can feel the laughing running all through her body and mine, holding her up against my chest in the dark—knowing there must be a reason why she woke me up in the middle of the night, and pretty sure I can guess what it is. She kissing under my chin now, and starting to undo my buttons.

It seem like so long since we done this. My whole body is all a shimmer with this sweet, sweet craving. My blood is racing, singing, and her fingers is sliding inside my nightshirt. "Take it easy," I say in her ear. Cause I want this to take us a long, long time.

75    Outside, the sky is still wide open—the storm is throbbing and beating down on the roof over our heads, and pressing its wet self up against the window. I catch ahold of her fingers and bring em to my lips. Then I roll us both over so I can see her face. She smiling up at me through the dark, and her eyes is wide and shiny. And I run my fingers down along her breast, underneath her own nightgown. . . .

I wake up in the bed alone. It's still night. Like a flash I'm across the room, knowing I'm going after her, this time. The carpet treads is nubby and rough, flying past underneath my bare feet, and the kitchen linoleum cold and smooth. The back door standing wide open, and I push through the screen.

The storm is moved on. That fresh air feel good on my skin through the cotton nightshirt. Smell good, too, rising up outa the wet earth, and I can see the water sparkling on the leaves of the collards and kale, twinkling in the vines on the bean poles. The moon is rising high up over Thompson's field, spilling moonlight all over the yard, and setting all them blossoms on the fence to shining pure white.

There ain't a leaf twitching and there ain't a sound. I ain't moving either. I'm just gonna stay right here on this back porch. And hold still. And listen close. Cause I know Gracie somewhere in this garden. And she waiting for me.

## QUESTIONS

1. What do the names of the main characters suggest about them?
2. Describe the narrator. Based on this story, what can you tell about her personality? Support your answer with quotations from the text.

3. What is Pearl/Jinx's relationship to society as a whole like? Are her comments about society what you would have expected her to say?
4. What is Jinx angry at? Why?
5. List five words that describe Grace and Pearl's relationship.
6. Reread paragraphs 26 and 27. What point is Pearl making about the church?
7. Explain whether you think the introduction to the story is effective, pointing to specific words and phrases to support your opinion.
8. Is the conclusion of this story effective? Why or why not?
9. How do you feel about Birtha's writing style? Point to specific language in the story to support your response.

**CONNECTIONS**

1. Does this story support or undermine du Plessix Gray's thesis about romantic love and friendship?
2. Compare and contrast the voice of the narrator of this story with the voice of the narrator of Sandra Cisneros's story "Eleven," included in Section 1.

# ~ Do I?!

*Kristina Milam*

> Kristina Milam was born in Idaho Falls, Idaho, but moved often as a child, following her father's military career to places such as Italy and Newport, Rhode Island. After she graduated from high school in 1984, Milam went to work full-time as a bank teller. Later, she found work as an inventory control manager in a jewelry company, where she worked for five years before returning to school in 1994. Milam is now a student at Chabot College in Hayward, California; she intends to earn an associate's degree and then transfer to a four-year university to pursue a bachelor's degree and a teaching credential in history. In the meantime, Milam teaches Sunday school, works as a teaching assistant for a history instructor at Chabot College, and is contemplating marriage.

> **WARM-UP:** Do you tend to see the institution of marriage as one that adds to the happiness and well-being of those who enter into it? Why or why not?

Here comes the bride,
All dressed in white!

1      Every American girl is trained almost from birth to dream of the day when she will be the bride all dressed in white. She is taught to believe she wants a big church wedding. She dreams of choirs and rice. She believes that, if she can create the perfect wedding day, then she will have the perfect everlasting marriage. Regardless of the fact that her family has to take out a second mortgage on their home to afford all the trimmings. Some women even marry men they do not love simply to have the fancy wedding. They believe that if they get married all their problems will simply drift away. That leaves only one question: Why?

Couples starting out concentrate more on the single day of their wedding than on the content of their marriage. People are more concerned with the color of the bridesmaids' dresses than with the complexities of their relationship. We, as Americans, are led to believe that a wedding is supposed to be a grand gala. We tend to look down on people who have simple weddings or get married in Reno or Las Vegas. They did not have a "real" wedding. But a wedding should be a personal celebration, not a royal fashion show. The happiness of the couple should be more important than the approval of society.

It is human nature to want to celebrate and share good times with family and friends. We want to share our excitement and good fortune. What that entails is as different as every bride and groom. However, tradition has dictated to us and fashion has taught us what we should have at the "perfect wedding." The bride must be in a long flowing gown of white. The groom must wear a tuxedo. There must be sparkling bridesmaids, handsome groomsmen, and adorable children as the flower girl and ring bearer. They all must come in long limos or horse-drawn carriages. The reception afterwards must be a splendid event with champagne, cake, and dancing till dawn.

What we do not see in magazines is the bride having a nervous breakdown because the napkins are not perfect or the flowers are the wrong shade of pink. We do not see the parents going into debt to make the fairy tale come true. The couple is usually too distraught and too busy to truly enjoy the occasion. The illusion of perfection is so delicate that one precocious flower girl will bring the whole thing crashing down in their mind's eye. It is our insane need for this ritual that is our downfall.

In *Civilization and Its Discontents,* Sigmund Freud, who, ironically, was    5
married to the same woman all his life, takes a similar view of marriage. He writes that the joining of one man and one woman for life is against human nature: "Only the weaklings have submitted to such an extensive encroachment upon their sexual freedom, and stronger natures have only done so subject to compensatory conditions" (61). He believes present-day civilized people leave no room for the simple natural love of two human beings. This natural love needs no ceremony, no blessing from the civilized world. There is no need for a decadent wedding. Americans, especially women, have been taught to believe that their happiness is dependent upon finding that "special someone" and marrying with resplendent fanfare. Freud would take exception to that assumption. Freud professes that "Taboos, laws, and customs impose further restrictions, which affect both men and women" (59). He believes that marriage is an undue barrier to a person's happiness.

According to Freud, any monogamist° relationship also goes against human nature and instinct.

> It cuts off a fair number of people from sexual enjoyment, and so becomes the source of serious injustice. Present day civilization makes it plain that it will only permit sexual relationships on the basis of a solitary, indissoluble° bond between one man and one woman. (60)

---

*monogamist:* Here meaning "focused on one person at a time."    *indissoluble:* Incapable of being undone or broken.

The dilemma comes from the fact that humans are not monogamist creatures, but society expects them to be. Human nature is to procreate. The instinct is to insure survival of the species. And nowhere in that instinct is there a lace, taffeta, rhinestone-studded gown. So why do people do it?

Everyone likes to believe there is that one special person out there just for him or her. A wedding is a celebration of that hope. People want to believe in the best. They want to believe they will be one of the lucky ones. Even Freud believes happiness is subjective (41): "We . . . place ourselves, with our wants and sensibilities, in their conditions, and then examine what occasions we should find in them for experiencing happiness or unhappiness" (41). Humans need to be left to their own happiness. Traditions and society may dictate the wedding, but the heart dictates the outcome of the marriage.

Even though I believe that marriage-for-life was invented by cave men who were lucky to make it to twenty, I, too, will someday throw myself at the feet of tradition. Of course, I am going to be married wearing my jeans in my parents' backyard. We are going to have a barbecue and a Jamaican steel drum band. Wanna come?

## QUESTIONS

1. What is the thesis of Milam's essay?
2. Do you agree with her critique of the marriage rituals that are common in the United States?
3. Do you agree with her critique of the whole concept of monogamous relationships? On what are you basing your views?
4. Does Milam use details effectively in her essay? Explain your answer.
5. Is the essay well organized? Could its organization have been improved? If so, how?
6. Is the essay convincing as a whole? What could Milam have done to add to its persuasiveness?
7. Is the essay strengthened by the inclusion of Freud's views on marriage and monogamous relationships? Why or why not?

## CONNECTIONS

1. Compare and contrast the points raised in this essay with those made in Kate Chopin's "The Story of an Hour" or Marge Piercy's poem "Barbie Doll" (both included in Section 2).
2. Is Kristina Milam's critique directed at the same target as Francine du Plessix Gray's "On Friendship"?

## Say Yes

*Tobias Wolff*

Tobias Wolff was born in Birmingham, Alabama in 1945 and served in the
U.S. army in Vietnam between 1964 and 1968 (after being expelled from
prep school). His memoir about his childhood, *This Boy's Life* (1989), was
later made into a movie. He studied at Oxford and at Stanford and has
received numerous fellowships and prizes for his writing. His collections of
short stories include *In the Garden of the North American Martyrs* (1981) and
*Back in the World* (1985), in which the following selection appears.

**WARM-UP:** How would you characterize our culture's attitude toward
interracial relationships and marriages?

They were doing the dishes, his wife washing while he dried. He'd washed    1
the night before. Unlike most men he knew, he really pitched in on the
housework. A few months earlier he'd overheard a friend of his wife's congrat-
ulate her on having such a considerate husband, and he thought, *I try.* Helping
out with the dishes was a way he had of showing how considerate he was.

They talked about different things and somehow got on the subject of
whether white people should marry black people. He said that all things considered, he thought it was a bad idea.

"Why?" she asked.

Sometimes his wife got this look where she pinched her brows together
and bit her lower lip and stared down at something. When he saw her like this
he knew he should keep his mouth shut, but he never did. Actually it made
him talk more. She had that look now.

"Why?" she asked again, and stood there with her hand inside a bowl, not    5
washing it but just holding it above the water.

"Listen," he said, "I went to school with blacks, and I've worked with
blacks and lived on the same street with blacks, and we've always gotten along
just fine. I don't need you coming along now and implying that I'm a racist."

"I didn't imply anything," she said, and began washing the bowl again,
turning it around in her hand as though she were shaping it. "I just don't see
what's wrong with a white person marrying a black person, that's all."

"They don't come from the same culture as we do. Listen to them sometime—they even have their own language. That's okay with me, I *like* hearing
them talk"—he did; for some reason it always made him feel happy—"but it's
different. A person from their culture and a person from our culture could
never really *know* each other."

"Like you know me?" his wife asked.

10    "Yes. Like I know you."

"But if they love each other," she said. She was washing faster now, not looking at him.

Oh boy, he thought. He said, "Don't take my word for it. Look at the statistics. Most of those marriages break up."

"Statistics." She was piling dishes on the drainboard at a terrific rate, just swiping at them with the cloth. Many of them were greasy, and there were flecks of food between the tines of the forks. "All right," she said, "what about foreigners? I suppose you think the same thing about two foreigners getting married."

"Yes," he said, "as a matter of fact I do. How can you understand someone who comes from a completely different background?"

15    "Different," said his wife. "Not the same, like us."

"Yes, different," he snapped, angry with her for resorting to this trick of repeating his words so that they sounded crass, or hypocritical. "These are dirty," he said, and dumped all the silverware back into the sink.

The water had gone flat and gray. She stared down at it, her lips pressed tight together, then plunged her hands under the surface. "Oh!" she cried, and jumped back. She took her right hand by the wrist and held it up. Her thumb was bleeding.

"Ann, don't move," he said. "Stay right there." He ran upstairs to the bathroom and rummaged in the medicine chest for alcohol, cotton, and a Band-Aid. When he came back down she was leaning against the refrigerator with her eyes closed, still holding her hand. He took the hand and dabbed at her thumb with the cotton. The bleeding had stopped. He squeezed it to see how deep the wound was and a single drop of blood welled up, trembling and bright, and fell to the floor. Over the thumb she stared at him accusingly. "It's shallow," he said. "Tomorrow you won't even know it's there." He hoped that she appreciated how quickly he had come to her aid. He'd acted out of concern for her, with no thought of getting anything in return, but now the thought occurred to him that it would be a nice gesture on her part not to start up that conversation again, as he was tired of it. "I'll finish up here," he said. "You go and relax."

"That's okay," she said. "I'll dry."

20    He began to wash the silverware again, giving a lot of attention to the forks.

"So," she said, "you wouldn't have married me if I'd been black."

"For Christ's sake, Ann!"

"Well, that's what you said, didn't you?"

"No, I did not. The whole question is ridiculous. If you had been black we probably wouldn't even have met. You would have had your friends and I would have had mine. The only black girl I ever really knew was my partner in the debating club, and I was already going out with you by then."

"But if we had met, and I'd been black?"

"Then you probably would have been going out with a black guy." He picked up the rinsing nozzle and sprayed the silverware. The water was so hot that the metal darkened to pale blue, then turned silver again.

"Let's say I wasn't," she said. "Let's say I am black and unattached and we meet and fall in love."

He glanced over at her. She was watching him and her eyes were bright. "Look," he said, taking a reasonable tone, "this is stupid. If you were black you wouldn't be you." As he said this he realized it was absolutely true. There was no possible way of arguing with the fact that she would not be herself if she were black. So he said it again: "If you were black you wouldn't be you."

"I know," she said, "but let's just say."

He took a deep breath. He had won the argument but he still felt cornered. "Say what?" he asked.

"That I'm black, but still me, and we fall in love. Will you marry me?"

He thought about it.

"Well?" she said, and stepped close to him. Her eyes were even brighter. "Will you marry me?"

"I'm thinking," he said.

"You won't, I can tell. You're going to say no."

"Let's not move too fast on this," he said. "There are lots of things to consider. We don't want to do something we would regret for the rest of our lives."

"No more considering. Yes or no."

"Since you put it that way—"

"Yes or no."

"Jesus, Ann. All right. No."

She said. "Thank you," and walked from the kitchen into the living room. A moment later he heard her turning the pages of a magazine. He knew that she was too angry to be actually reading it, but she didn't snap through the pages the way he would have done. She turned them slowly, as if she were studying every word. She was demonstrating her indifference to him, and it had the effect he knew she wanted it to have. It hurt him.

He had no choice but to demonstrate his indifference to her. Quietly, thoroughly, he washed the rest of the dishes. Then he dried them and put them away. He wiped the counters and the stove and scoured the linoleum where the drop of blood had fallen. While he was at it, he decided, he might as well mop the whole floor. When he was done the kitchen looked new, the way it looked when they were first shown the house, before they had ever lived here.

He picked up the garbage pail and went outside. The night was clear and he could see a few stars to the west, where the lights of the town didn't blur them out. On El Camino the traffic was steady and light, peaceful as a river. He felt ashamed that he had let his wife get him into a fight. In another thirty years of so they would both be dead. What would all that stuff matter then? He thought of the years they had spent together, and how close they were, and how well they knew each other, and his throat tightened so that he could hardly breathe. His face and neck began to tingle. Warmth flooded his chest. He stood there for a while, enjoying these sensations, then picked up the pail and went out the back gate.

The two mutts from down the street had pulled over the garbage can again. One of them was rolling around on his back and the other had something in her mouth. Growling, she tossed it into the air, leaped up and caught it, growled again and whipped her head from side to side. When they saw him coming they trotted away with short, mincing steps. Normally he would heave rocks at them, but this time be let them go.

45   The house was dark when he came back inside. She was in the bathroom. He stood outside the door and called her name. He heard bottles clinking, but she didn't answer him. "Ann, I'm really sorry," he said. "I'll make it up to you, I promise."

"How?" she asked.

He wasn't expecting this. But from a sound in her voice, a level and definite note that was strange to him, he knew that he had to come up with the right answer. He leaned against the door. "I'll marry you," he whispered.

"We'll see," she said. "Go on to bed. I'll be out in a minute."

He undressed and got under the covers. Finally he heard the bathroom door open and close.

50   "Turn off the light," she said from the hallway.

"What?"

"Turn off the light."

He reached over and pulled the chain on the bedside lamp. The room went dark. "All right," he said. He lay there, but nothing happened. "All right," he said again. Then he heard a movement across the room: He sat up, but he couldn't see a thing. The room was silent. His heart pounded the way it had on their first night together, the way it still did when he woke at a noise in the darkness and waited to hear it again—the sound of someone moving through the house, a stranger.

## QUESTIONS

1. How would you characterize the male character in this story? As part of that description, would you call him a racist?
2. In your experience, are people of different races or cultures as separated into different groups as the husband in this story describes them?

3. The husband believes he "won the argument." Why do you think he believes this? Do you agree with him?
4. Does the husband in the story love his wife? Quote specific points in the story to support your answer.
5. What is the effect of the description of the two "mutts" included in the story?
6. Explain your understanding of the last paragraph of the story. What point(s) is the author making by using this ending?
7. Identify effective similes and metaphors in the story.

## CONNECTIONS

1. Compare and contrast the relationship between the husband and wife presented in this story with the relationship between the two lovers from Becky Birtha's "In the Life."
2. How would you relate this story to Christine Gorman's essay "Sizing up the Sexes"?

## 〜 The Unromantic Generation

*Bruce Weber*

> Bruce Weber, an editor of *The New York Times Magazine,* has written many
> articles about various aspects of popular culture—such as the theater, Holly-
> wood, fashion, and art—and has published in magazines such as *Vogue, The
> New Yorker,* and *American Artist.* In 1986, Weber edited *Look Who's Talking:
> An Anthology of American Short Stories.* The following essay appeared ini-
> tially in 1987 in *The New York Times Magazine.*

> **WARM-UP:** Prioritize the following in order of importance to you,
> and then explain your order: (a) being very well off financially, (b) ob-
> taining recognition from colleagues for contributions to your special
> field, (c) being successful in business, (d) raising a family, (e) falling in
> love, (f) developing a meaningful philosophy of life.

1    Here is a contemporary love story.
    Twenty-four-year-old Clark Wolfsberger, a native of St. Louis, and
Kim Wright, twenty-five, who is from Chicago, live in Dallas. They've been
going together since they met as students at Southern Methodist University
three years ago. They are an attractive pair, trim and athletic, she dark and lissome,° he broad-shouldered and square-jawed. They have jobs they took
immediately after graduating—Clark works at Talent Sports International, a
sports marketing and management company; Kim is an assistant account
executive at Tracy-Locke, a large advertising agency—and they are in love.
    "We're very compatible," she says.
    "We don't need much time together to confirm our relationship," he says.
5    When they speak about the future, they hit the two-career family notes
that are conventional now in the generations ahead of them. "At thirty, I'll
probably be married and planning a family," says Kim. "I'll stay in advertising.
I'll be a late parent."
    "By thirty, I'll definitely be married; either that or water-skiing naked in
Monaco," Clark says, and laughs. "No. I'll be married. Well-established in my
line of work. Have the home, have the dog. Maybe not a kid yet, but eventually. I'm definitely in favor of kids."
    In the month I spent last winter visiting several cities around the country,
interviewing recent college graduates about marriage, relationships, modern
romance, I heard a lot of this, life equations already written, doubt banished. I

---

*lissome:* Nimble, supple.

undertook the trip because of the impression so many of us have: that in one wavelike rush to business school and Wall Street, young Americans have succumbed to a culture of immediate gratification and gone deep-down elitist on us. I set out to test the image with an informal survey meant to take the emotional temperature of a generation, not far behind my own, that *seems* so cynical, so full of such "material" girls and boys.

The sixty or so people I interviewed, between the ages of twenty-two and twenty-six, were a diverse group. They spoke in distinct voices, testifying to a range of political and social views. Graduate students, lawyers, teachers, entertainers, business people, they are pursuing a variety of interests. What they have in common is that they graduated from college, are living in or around an urban center, and are heterosexual, mirrors of myself when I graduated from college in 1975. And yet as I moved from place to place, beginning with acquaintances of my friends and then randomly pursuing an expanding network of names and phone numbers, another quality emerged to the degree that I'd call it characteristic: they are planners. It was the one thing that surprised me, this looking ahead with certainty. They have priorities. I'd ask about love; they'd give me a graph.

This isn't how I remember it. Twelve years ago, who knew? I was three years away from my first full-time paycheck, six from anything resembling the job I have now. It was all sort of desultory° and hopeful, a time of dabbling and waiting around for some event that would sprout a future. Frankly, I had it in mind that meeting a woman would do it.

My cultural prototype was Benjamin Braddock, the character played by     10
Dustin Hoffman in Mike Nichols's 1967 film *The Graduate,* who, returning home after his college triumphs, finds the prospect of life after campus daunting in the extreme, and so plunges into inertia. His refrain "I'm just a little worried about my future," served me nicely as a sort of wryly understated mantra.°

What hauls Benjamin from his torpor° is love. Wisely or not, he responds to a force beyond logic and turns the world upside down for Elaine Robinson. And though in the end their future together is undetermined, the message of the movie is that love is meant to triumph, that its passion and promise, however naïve, are its strength, and that if we are lucky it will seize us and transform our lives.

Today I'm still single and, chastened by that, I suppose, a little more rational about what to expect from love. Setting out on my trip, I felt as if I'd be plumbing a little of my past. But the people I spoke with reminded me more of the way I am now than the way I was then. I returned thinking that young

---

*desultory:* Aimless, lacking a clear plan or purpose.     *mantra:* An invocation or incantation (here used ironically to mean something often repeated).     *torpor:* Extreme sluggishness, apathy.

people are older than they used to be, *The Graduate* is out of date, and for young people just out of college today, the belief that love is all you need no longer obtains.°

"Kim's a great girl; I love her," Clark Wolfsberger says. "But she's very career-oriented. I am, too, and with our schedules the way they are, we haven't put any restrictions on each other. I think that's healthy."

"He might want to go back to St. Louis," Kim Wright says. "I want to go back to Chicago. If it works out, great. If not, that's fine, too. I can handle it either way."

15    They are not heartless, soulless, cold, or unimaginative. They *are* self-preoccupied, but that's a quality, it seems to me, for which youthful generations have always been known. What distinguishes this generation from mine, I think, is that they're aware of it. News-conscious, media-smart, they are sophisticated in a way I was not.

They have come of age, of course, at a time when American social traditions barely survive. Since 1975, there have been more than a million divorces annually, and it is well publicized that nearly half of all marriages now end in divorce. Yet the era of condoned casual promiscuity and sexual experimentation—itself once an undermining of the nation's social fabric—now seems to be drawing to a close with the ever-spreading plague of sexually transmitted disease.

The achievements of feminist activism—particularly the infusion of women into the work force—have altered the expectations that the sexes have for each other and themselves.

And finally, the new college graduates have been weaned on scarifying forecasts of economic gloom. They feel housing problems already; according to *American Demographics* magazine, the proportion of young people living at home with their parents was higher in 1985 than in the last three censuses. They're aware, too, of predictions that however affluent they are themselves, they're probably better off than their children will be.

With all this in mind, today's graduates seem keenly aware that the future is bereft of conventional expectations, that what's ahead is more chaotic than mysterious. I've come to think it ironic that in a youth-minded culture such as ours, one that ostensibly° grants greater freedom of choice to young people than it ever has before, those I spoke with seem largely restrained. Concerned with, if not consumed by, narrowing the options down, getting on track, they are aiming already at a distant comfort and security. I spoke, on my travels, with several college counselors and administrators, and they concur that the immediate concerns of today's graduates are more practical than those of

---

*obtains:* Here meaning "applies."    *ostensibly:* Seemingly.

their predecessors. "I talk to them about sex," says Gail Short Hanson, dean of students at George Washington University, in Washington. "I talk about careers. And marriage, with women, because of the balancing act they have to perform these days. But love? I can't remember the last conversation I had about love."

Career-minded, fiercely self-reliant, they responded to me, a single man    20 with a good job, with an odd combination of comradeliness and respect. When the interviews were over, I fielded a lot of questions about what it's like to work at *The New York Times*. How did I get my job? Occasionally, someone would ask about my love life. Considering the subject of our discussions, I was surprised it happened so rarely. When it did, I told them I'd come reasonably close to marriage once, but it didn't work out. Nobody asked me why. Nobody asked if I was lonely.

Micah Materre, twenty-five, recently completed an internship at CBS News in Chicago and is looking for a job in broadcast journalism. Like many of the young people I talked to, she is farsighted in her romantic outlook: "I went out with a guy last fall. He had a good job as a stockbroker. He was nice to me. But then he started telling me about his family. And there were problems. And I thought, 'What happens if I fall in love and we get married? What then?'"

It may be a memory lapse, but I don't recall thinking about marriage much at all until I fell in love. I was twenty-nine; late, that's agreed. But the point is that for me (and for my generation as a whole, I believe, though you hate to make a statement like that), marriage loomed only as an outgrowth of happenstance; you met a person. Today's graduates, however, seem uneasy with that kind of serendipity.° All of the married couples I spoke with are delighted to be married, but they do say their friends questioned their judgment. "I heard a lot of reasons why I shouldn't do it," one recent bride told me. "Finally, I just said to myself, 'I feel happier than I've ever felt. Why should I give this up just because I'm young?'"

Most of them too young to remember the assassination of *either* Kennedy, they are old enough to have romantic pasts, to have experienced the trauma of failure in love. What surprised me was how easily so many of them accepted it; it seems a little early to be resigned to the idea that things fall apart. In each interview, I asked about past involvements. Were you ever serious about anyone? Any marital close calls? And virtually everyone had a story. But I heard very little about heartbreak or lingering grief. Instead, with an almost uniform equanimity,° they spoke of maturity gained, lessons learned. It isn't disillusionment exactly, and they *are* too young to be weary; rather, it sounds like determination.

---

*serendipity:* Lucky accident.    *equinimity:* Evenness, calm.

Twenty-five-year-old Peter Mundy of San Francisco, for example, says that until six months ago he'd had a series of steady girlfriends. "I'm down on romance," he says. "There's too much pain, too much pressure. There are so many variables, and you can't tell until you're in the middle of it whether it'll be positive. It's only in retrospect that you can see how things went wrong. In the meantime, you end up neglecting other things."

25    The prevalent notion is that chemistry is untrustworthy; partners need to be up to snuff° according to pretty rigorous standards. Ellen Lubin, twenty-six, of Los Angeles, for example, has just gotten engaged to the man she has been living with for two years. When she met him, she says: "I wasn't that attracted to him right away. But there were things about him that made me say, 'This is what I want in a man.' He's bright. He's a go-getter. He was making tons of money at the age of twenty-five. He's well-connected. He was like my mentor in coming to deal with life in the city."

At the end of *The Graduate*, Benjamin Braddock kidnaps his lady love at the altar, an instant after she has sealed her vows to someone else, and they manage to make their escape because Benjamin bolts the church door from the outside with a cross. That was the 1960s, vehement times. When I graduated, we were less obstreperous.° Sacraments we could take or leave. And marriage wasn't much of an issue. If we put it off, it wasn't for the sake of symbolism so much as that it didn't seem necessary. In the last few years, I've been to a number of weddings among my contemporaries, people in their thirties, and that impression of us is still with me. What we did was drift toward marriage, arriving at it eventually, and with some surprise. Some of us are still drifting.

Today's graduates have forged a new attitude entirely. In spite of the high divorce rate, many of those I spoke with have marriage in mind. Overwhelmingly, they see it as not only desirable, but inevitable. Because of the odds, they approach it with wariness and pragmatism. More cautious than their parents (for American men in 1985, the median age at the time of their first marriage was 25.5, the highest since the turn of the century; it was 23.3 for women, a record), they are methodical in comparison with me.

Perhaps that explains why I find the way they speak about marriage so unromantic. Men and women tend to couch their views in different terms, but they seem to share the perception that marriage is necessarily restricting. Nonetheless they trust in its rewards, whatever they are. Overall, it doesn't represent the kind of commitment that seems viable° without adequate preparation.

"I've been dating someone for a year and a half," says Tom Grossman, a twenty-four-year-old graduate of the University of Texas. "We don't talk about

---

*up to snuff:* Slang meaning "good enough." *obstreperous:* Defiant, unruly.   *viable:* Possible, conceivable.

marriage, and frankly I don't think it'll occur." Currently area sales manager in San Antonio for the John H. Harland Company, a check-printing concern, Grossman says he has professional success in mind first. "I want to be really well-off financially, and I don't want that struggle to interfere with the marriage. There are too many other stress factors involved. I want to be able to enjoy myself right away. And I never want to look back and think that if I hadn't gotten married, I could have accomplished more."

Many young women say they responded with some alarm to last year's *Newsweek* report on the controversial demographic study conducted at Harvard, which concluded that once past thirty, a woman faces rapidly dwindling chances of marrying. At a time when women graduates often feel it incumbent on them to pursue careers, they worry that the possibility of "having it all" is, in fact, remote. 30

Janie Russell, twenty-five, graduated from the University of North Carolina in 1983, left a serious boyfriend behind, and moved to Los Angeles to pursue a career in the film industry. Working now as a director of production services at New Visions Inc., like many other young women she believes the independence fostered by a career is necessary, not only for her own self-esteem but as a foundation for a future partnership. "I look forward to marriage," she says. "But this is a very selfish time for me. I have to have my career. I have to say to myself, 'I did this on my own.' It makes me feel more interesting than I would otherwise. Of course, what may happen is that I'll look up one day and say, 'O.K., husband, where are you?' And he won't be there."

About halfway through my trip I stopped interviewing married couples because they tended to say similar things. They consider themselves the lucky ones. As twenty-four-year-old Adam Cooper put it, at dinner with his wife, Melanee, also twenty-four, in their Chicago apartment: "The grass is not greener on the other side."

I came away thinking it is as true as ever: all happy families are the same. But the couples I spoke with seemed to me part of a generation other than their own, older even than mine. Calling the Coopers to arrange an interview, I was invited for "a good, home-cooked meal."

The next day, I met Micah Materre, who expressed the prevailing contemporary stance as well as anyone. Outgoing and self-possessed, she gave me a long list of qualities she's looking for in a man: good looks, sense of humor, old-fashioned values, but also professional success, financial promise, and a solid family background. "Why not?" she said. "I deserve the best." But as I was folding up my notebook, she added a plaintive note: "I'll get married, won't I? It's the American way, right?"

Very early on in my sexual experience I was flattered by a woman who told me she ordinarily wouldn't go to bed with men who were under twenty-six. 35

"Until then," she said, "all they're doing when they're with you is congratulating themselves." For whatever reason, she never returned my calls after that night. Not an untypical encounter, all in all. Congratulations to both of us.

We were a lusty, if callow,° bunch, not least because we thought we could afford to be. Encouraged by the expansive social mores spawned by the sexual revolution, fortified by the advent° of a widespread availability of birth control, and fundamentally unaware of germs, we interpreted sex, for our convenience, as pure pleasure shared by "consenting parties." If it feels good, do it. Remember that?

It is an attitude that the current generation inherited and put into practice at an early age. Asked about her circle of friends in Los Angeles, Lesley Bracker, twenty-three, puts it nonchalantly: "Oh, yeah, we were all sexually active as teen-agers. When we were younger, it was considered O.K. to sleep around."

Now, however, they are reconsidering. In general, on this topic, I found them shy. They hesitate to speak openly about their sex lives, are prone to euphemism ("I'm not exactly out there, you know, mingling"), and say they worry about promiscuity only because they have friends who still practice it. According to Laura Kavesh and Cheryl Lavin, who write a column about single life, "Tales from the Front," for the *Chicago Tribune* that is syndicated in some sixty other papers around the country, a letter from a reader about the virtues of virginity generated more supportive mail than anything that has appeared in the column in its two years of existence. I'm not about to say there's a new celibacy among the young, but my impression is that even if they're having twice as much sex as they say they're having, it's not as much as you would think.

The AIDS scare, of course, is of primary relevance. "I talk about AIDS on first dates, " says Jill Rotenberg, twenty-five, publishing manager of a rare-book company in San Francisco. "I talk about it all the time. I've spoken with the guy I'm dating about taking an AIDS test. Neither one of us is thrilled about condoms. But we use them. The first time we had sex, I was the one who had one in my wallet."

40    Not everyone is so vehement. But seriously or jokingly, in earnest tête-à-tête° or idly at dinner parties, they all talk about it. To some, the new concern is merely a source of disappointment. Several of the young people I spoke with express the sense of having been robbed. It's tough to find sex when you want it, tougher than it used to be, is the lament of many, mostly men. As it was put to me at one point, "I wish I'd been born ten years earlier."

---

*callow:* Immature.    *advent:* Coming about.    *tête-à-tête:* From the French, meaning "face-to-face," a private conversation between two people.

Jill Rotenberg says she feels betrayed: "I've had one long relationship in my life. He was my first lover, and for a long time my only one. So I feel I've had an untainted past. Now I feel I'm being punished anyway, even though I've been a good girl."

"I feel like I'm over the hurdle," says Douglas Ertman, twenty-two, of San Francisco, who got engaged last summer. "I'm really lucky to know that I'll have one sexual partner forever."

Most agree that the solution is monogamy, at least on a temporary basis. "Its a coupled-up society," says Alan Forman, twenty-six, a law student of George Washington University who, for the last several months, has been in a monogamous relationship. "Now more than ever. A lot of people I know are feeling the pressure to get hooked up with somebody."

I ask Forman and his girlfriend, twenty-four-year-old Debra Golden, about their future together. They say they don't know ("I'm too insecure to make a decision like that," she says), and I get the sense they never talk about it. Then she turns to him, genuinely curious. "Say you break up with me and go to New York next year," she says.

"I don't know," he says. "If I meet someone and I like her, what do I have     45
to do, ask her to take a blood test?"

A decade ago, one of the privileges that my contemporaries and I inferred° from our sexual freedom was more or less to deny that there might be, in the sexual act, an innately implied emotional exchange. It's no longer feasible, however, to explain away sex as frivolity, inconsequential gratification. And that has complicated things for all of as, of course, whatever age, single or not.

But for young people, it's an issue, like marriage, that has been raised early: what does sex mean, if it doesn't mean nothing?

It's clearly a struggle for them. In one of my first interviews, twenty-five-year-old Karl Wright of Chicago told me: "Maybe there's a silver lining in all this. Maybe AIDS will bring back romance." The more I think about that, the more chilling it gets.

Beverly Caro, a twenty-five-year-old associate in the Dallas law firm of Gardere & Wynne, graduated from Drake University, in Des Moines, in 1983, and attended law school there as well. Her office high above the street looks out on the city's jungle of futuristic skyscrapers. She had offers from firms in Denver and her hometown of Kansas City, Mo., she says, but chose to come to Dallas because "I see upward mobility here; that's what I was looking for."

Ms. Caro has an attractive, thoughtful manner and a soft voice, but like     50
many of her contemporaries, given the chance to discuss her personal goals,

---

*inferred:* Derived.

she speaks with a certitude that borders on defiance. Currently, she sees two men "somewhat regularly," she says. "I'd like to have a companion. A friend, I guess. But finding a man is not a top priority. I want to travel. I want to establish myself in the community. I don't see any drastic changes in my life by the time I turn thirty. Except that I'll be a property owner."

During my interviews, the theme of getting on track and staying there surfaced again and again. I came to think of it as the currency of self-definition. As a generation, they are not a particularly well-polled group, but certain figures bear out my impression.

According to annual surveys of 300,000 college freshmen conducted by the Higher Education Research Institute at the Graduate School of Education of the University of California at Los Angeles, young people today, by the time they *enter* college, are more inclined to express concrete life objectives than they've been for many years. Of those surveyed last fall, 73.2 percent cited being "very well off financially" as an essential or very important objective. That's up from 63.3 percent in 1980, 49.5 percent in 1975. Other objectives that the survey shows have risen in importance include "obtain recognition from colleagues for contributions to my special field"; "have administrative responsibility for the work of others"; "be successful in my own business"; and "raise a family." At the same time, the percentage of freshmen who consider it important to "develop a meaningful philosophy of life" has declined from 64.2 percent in 1975 to 40.6 percent last year.

Many of the people I spoke to feel the pressure of peer scrutiny. A status thing has evolved, to which many seem to have regretfully succumbed. Several expressed a weariness with meeting someone new and having to present themselves by their credentials. Yet, overwhelmingly, asked what they're looking for in a romantic partner, they responded first with phrases such as "an educated professional" and "someone with direction." They've conceded, more or less consciously, that unenlightened and exclusionary as it is, it's very uncool not to know what you want and not to be already chasing it.

"Seems like everyone in our generation has to be out there achieving," says Scott Birnbaum, twenty-five, who is the chief accountant for TIC United Corp., a holding company in Dallas.

55      Birnbaum graduated from the University of Texas in 1984, where, he says, "For me, the whole career-oriented thing kicked in." A native Texan with a broad drawl, he lives in the Greenville section of the city, an area populated largely by young singles. His apartment is comfortably roomy, not terribly well appointed. He shakes his head amiably as he points to the television set propped on a beer cooler. "What do I need furniture for?" he says. "Most of my time is taken up going to work."

Confident in himself professionally, Birnbaum was one of very few interviewees who spoke frankly about the personal cost of career success. Many speculated that they'll be worried if, in their thirties, they haven't begun to settle their love lives; this was more true of women than men. But Birnbaum confesses a desire to marry now. "It's kind of lonely being single," he says. "I'd hate to find myself successful at thirty without a family. Maybe once I'm married and have children, that might make being successful careerwise less important."

The problem, he goes on, is the collective outlook he's part and parcel of. "Here's how we think," he says. "Get to this point, move on. Get to that point, move on. Acquire, acquire. Career, career. We're all afraid to slow down for fear of missing out on something. That extends to your social life as well. You go out on a date and you're thinking, 'Hell, is there someone better for me?' I know how terrible that sounds but it seems to be my problem. Most of my peers are in the same position. Men and women. I tell you, it's tough out there right now."

When I returned to New York, I called Alex de Gramont, whom I'd been saving to interview last. I've known Alex for a long time, since he was a gawky and curious high school student and I was his teacher. Handsome now, gentle-looking, he's a literary sort, prone to attractive gloom and a certain lack of perspective. He once told me that his paradigm of a romantic, his role model, was Heathcliff, the mad, doomed passion-monger from Emily Brontë's *Wuthering Heights.*

A year out of Wesleyan University in Middletown, Conn., Alex has reasons to be hopeful. His book-length senior thesis about Albert Camus has been accepted for publication, and on the strength of it, he has applied to four graduate programs in comparative literature. But he's unenthusiastic, and he has applied to law schools, too. In the meantime, he is living with his parents in New Jersey.

He tells me that last summer he went to West Germany in pursuit of a woman he'd met when he was in college. He expected to live there with her, but he was back in this country in a couple of weeks. "Camus has a line," Alex says, "'Love can burn or love can last. It can't do both.'" Like Benjamin Braddock, Alex is a little worried about his future.

Dustin Hoffman is forty-nine. I'm thirty-three. Both of us are doing pretty well. Alex, at twenty-three, confesses to considerable unease. "Every minute I'm not accomplishing something, I feel is wasted," he says, sort of miserably. "I feel a lot of pressure to decide what to do with my life. I'm a romantic, but these are very unromantic times."

60

## QUESTIONS

1. What is the effect of referring to the younger generation as "unromantic"? What other word(s) could the author have used to describe the young people's attitude toward love?

2. Explain what Weber means when he writes "young Americans have succumbed to a culture of immediate gratification and gone deep-down elitist on us."

3. According to Weber, what factors "distinguish this generation" of young people from his own?

4. Do you agree with Weber that to "today's graduates . . . the future is bereft of conventional expectations, that what's ahead is more chaotic than mysterious"? If so, explain how this awareness affects your decisions, particularly those concerning love.

5. Explain whether you agree with Weber that young people today "are aiming already at a distant comfort and security"; support your response with an example.

6. Weber quotes several people he has interviewed. Do you believe that he interviewed a broad enough sample on which to base his conclusions?

7. What is Weber's attitude toward love? What is his attitude toward marriage?

8. Are the introduction and conclusion of this essay effective? Support your response by pointing to specific words, phrases, or ideas.

9. This essay was first published by the *New York Times* in 1987. Do you think that young people's attitudes toward love and sex have changed since then? If so, in what ways?

10. Weber mentions the film *The Graduate* as representative of his generation's attitude toward love. What film would you cite to represent *your* generation's attitudes toward love? Summarize the film and explain its relevance.

## CONNECTIONS

1. Compare and contrast the type(s) of evidence Weber uses to support his thesis with the types used by Francine du Plessix Gray and Robert Solomon.

2. Compare and contrast Weber's writing style to Benjamin Barber's in "Why America Skips School" (Section 1).

# ∼ Love Is Finished Again

*Yehuda Amichai*

One of the leading figures in modern Israeli literature, Yehuda Amichai was born in 1924 in Germany. Together with his Orthodox Jewish parents, in 1936 he moved to what was then Palestine, escaping the Holocaust. He has worked as a teacher and has fought in the numerous wars that have convulsed Israel. Although he has published novels, short stories, and plays as well, he is primarily recognized as a poet. The following selection comes from *The Selected Poetry of Yehuda Amichai* (1986), translated and edited by Chana Bloch and Stephen Mitchell.

**WARM-UP:** In one paragraph, complete the following: "A finished love is like . . ."

Love is finished again, like a profitable citrus season
or like an archaeological dig that turned up
from deep inside the earth
turbulent things that wanted to be forgotten.

Love is finished again. When a tall building                           5
is torn down and the debris° cleared away, you stand there
on the square empty lot, saying: What a small
space that building stood on
with all its many floors and people.

From the distant valleys you can hear                                  10
the sound of a solitary tractor at work
and from the distant past, the sound of a fork
clattering against a porcelain plate,
beating an egg yolk with sugar for a child,
clattering and clattering.                                             15

## QUESTIONS

1. Explain whether the simile used in the first line of this poem presents love in a positive light.

6 *debris:* Remains of something broken or destroyed.

2. What is the effect of comparing love to an archaeological dig? Explain your response.
3. What does Amichai's point about a building torn down imply about love?
4. How do lines 10 and 11 relate to the subject of love being finished?
5. How does the ending of the poem tie in with the subject of finished love?
6. What does the poem as a whole suggest that a person does when "love is finished"?

## CONNECTIONS

1. Is this poem's message about a "finished love" similar to the attitudes toward breakups expressed by the young people quoted in Bruce Weber's "The Unromantic Generation"?
2. In terms of both content and style, compare and contrast this poem to any of the other poems included in this book.

# Introductions and Conclusions: Hello, Good-bye

## Introductions

You're in front of the mirror. You look at yourself: no smudges, nothing out of place. Dark blue blazer. Hair slicked back. Eyes sparkling with . . . is that fear? You tone it down. You wipe your palms on a paper towel. There are five minutes left until the job interview; this is *the* job, and first impressions, you know well, are very important.

An essay's introduction is the first impression that the readers get. It has to be effective, if you want readers to give you their time or (when readers are forced to keep reading) if you want them to think of your writing as good. There is no one formula for a good introduction, just as there isn't one for a first impression: To make a good first impression in a bar you would wear different clothing than you would to look good for a job interview with a bank manager. The point is to consider what the members of your audience want and to write something that will attract them, intrigue them, make them read on.

Some possibilities:

- *Start with a brief story or description using vivid language:* We all like to be entertained. In an example of this type of introduction, Tom Daly opens his essay "Dancing in the Cracks between Worlds" (Section 2) with a description of the vacant lot where he used to play as a child. In this section, Bruce Weber begins his discussion of the "unromantic generation" by telling what he calls "a contemporary love story." Just remember that an introductory anecdote must have a point and that the connection between the anecdote and your essay's thesis should be readily apparent.
- *Start with a powerful quotation to introduce your topic:* Let someone else take over the difficult task of coming up with a first sentence! In "Sizing Up the Sexes," for example (Section 2), Christine Gorman starts her discussion of gender differences by quoting a whole nursery rhyme about what boys and girls are made of. Introductory quotations are often effective; however, avoid introducing an essay by quoting from a dictionary; it's been done so many times that the effect is trite.
- *Start with a question or a startling fact or statistic:* Most of us like to learn something new. For an example of this kind of introduction, reread the beginning of Benjamin Barber's "America Skips School" (Section 1), where Barber presents a report issued by the Department of Education Statistics. Barber uses the report to shock readers into

recognizing a problem, so he can then discuss the problem in detail and offer solutions.

- *In some situations, start with your thesis statement:* Many readers value clarity most and like to get to the point. Consider the first line of the selection from "The Elusive Emotion," included in this section: "What we call 'love' is a social invention, a construction of concepts that serve a very special function in our society." Because many people like to read about this topic and because this thesis challenges common claims about love, the introduction works. So don't force yourself to be "glitzy" if you're more of a "to-the-point" writer: Try to find something that will interest your audience and still fit your style.

If you're not going to start with the thesis, however, don't start with a cliché or some overly general remarks about the topic (something like "Love is difficult to define. It means many different things to many different people. Love has always been a difficult concept. As the song says . . .") Generalizations may help you to begin an essay, but they don't help a reader struggling to find interest in one. Instead, let your imagination play with the topic. If in your prewriting you come up with a good story that backs your thesis or some details that appeal to the reader's senses, save those for the introduction. Or find an analogy or a metaphor that clarifies the topic while making it more lively—that's what the first paragraph of this section attempts to do.

Consider the following introduction from a student essay, "When I Was a Boy," by LaSandra DeLeon:

> I used to be a boy. It wasn't until the third grade that I discovered I was a girl. Actually, I think I was a boy stuck inside a girl's body. You see, I always played games with the boys; we would play chase and baseball and my favorite was to catch as many bugs as I could during recess. Just like the boys, I used to tease the girls for playing stupid things like play-house, or dress-up. I *know* I wasn't a girl then.

Does it grab your attention? Why or why not? Does the author use any of the techniques we have mentioned? Check the introductions of essays that you like to see how those writers drew you in. Also, check introductions that left you cold or turned you off, and learn what to avoid. Make checking your introduction a conscious part of the revision of every essay.

## Conclusions

Talking about an applicant for a sales representative position, a manager once mentioned that the man hadn't "closed" the interview. "He didn't reiterate his strengths, or his enthusiasm for the job, or his conviction that he'd be good at it. He petered out." "Petering out" is an ineffective but much too common way for an essay to end. The conclusion, however, is what you leave your readers with—the last note that echoes after they look away from the page. In many ways, introductions and conclusions are similar: They both need to be striking and to underline your main point. However, while the introduction takes the world and focuses it toward the thesis (the point you want your readers to get from the essay), the conclusion is often an upside-down funnel—reiterating the thesis in some way but then discussing its significance, its implications for the bigger picture.

A technique writers often use is the one that Gabriele Rico and other teachers of writing call "coming full circle." In essays that come full circle, the conclusion echoes some theme or image from the introduction. (For examples illustrating this technique, see the essays by Pei Kuan, Ellen Goodman, and Kristina Milam in Sections 1, 2, 3, respectively.) This writing trick is used often because it works: It gives the essay a sense of completion; it reminds the readers where they started on this idea-trip, while pointing out that they are now actually in a different place because they've moved through the various points made within the essay. In truth, then, a more accurate metaphor to describe this progress would be a spiral rather than a circle: You end up in a similar place but not on the same plane where you started.

In both introductions and conclusions, try not to state the obvious: Phrases like "This essay will be about . . ." or "In conclusion . . ." appear like a writer's training wheels; they signal that you can't yet create an effective introduction or that you don't know how to make a smooth transition from the last point in the body of your essay to the conclusion. If you're used to writing such sentences, go ahead and do so as you draft, but then edit them out as you revise the essay.

A writing instructor once told her students that one easy way to strengthen an introduction is to cut out the first sentence or two from it. You'd be surprised how often that works—both for introductions and, in reverse, for conclusions: Cutting out the last sentence or two in a draft often means that the essay will end with something more concrete, rather than with one of the platitudes that often tempt us with their sound of superficial wisdom.

---

### What You Might Include in an Introduction or Conclusion:

- A brief story that relates to your thesis

- A vivid description that relates to your thesis

- A powerful quotation about your topic

- A startling fact or statistic

- The essay's thesis statement

## Topics for Writing about Love

• • • • • • • • • • • • • • • • • • • • • • • • • • •

1. Write an essay that presents the most common metaphors and symbols associated with love in this country, analyzing their messages about love.

2. Write an essay that defines "love" depending on the context in which it is used—for example, between family members, friends, or lovers.

3. Responding to Francine du Plessix Gray's and Robert Solomon's essays, write an essay that presents romantic love as a positive force.

4. Write an essay that explores the question of whether males and females view love differently.

5. Write an essay that explains why people should or should not get married.

6. Write an essay that discusses the benefits and disadvantages of arranged marriages.

7. Write an essay that evaluates the reasons why people get divorced.

8. Write an essay about the loss of a love you've experienced (whether the love of a family member, a friend, a lover, or someone else). Describe the process you went through, and compare your feelings with those expressed in Yehuda Amichai's poem "Love Is Finished Again."

9. If you, members of your family, or people you know come from a different country, write an essay exploring the differences between views of love in the United States and the views that exist in that other country.

10. In a letter to an imaginary pen pal from another country, describe Valentine's Day in the United States. Use your own experience with Valentine's Day to illustrate the points you are making about the general character of this holiday.

11. Interview people much older and much younger than you to find out how they define love. If the definitions are different, write an essay that presents these different views and explores some factors that might account for those differences.

# ∼ The Chrysanthemums

*John Steinbeck*

John Steinbeck (1902–1968) grew up in the Salinas Valley of California, where he worked for a while as a fruit picker. He studied biology and English at Stanford University but then dropped out to pursue writing as a career. His novels include *Of Mice and Men* (1937), *The Grapes of Wrath* (1939), which won a Pulitzer Prize, *Cannery Row* (1945), and *East of Eden* (1952). Steinbeck also wrote short stories; the following story is from a collection entitled *The Long Valley* (1938). In 1962, he received the Nobel Prize for Literature.

**WARM-UP:** Draw three clusters: one around the word "love," one around the word "respect," and one around the word "work." Do the clusters share any elements? If so, which ones?

The high grey-flannel fog of winter closed off the Salinas Valley from the sky and from all the rest of the world. On every side it sat like a lid on the mountains and made of the great valley a closed pot. On the broad, level land floor the gang plows bit deep and left the black earth shining like metal where the shares° had cut. On the foothill ranches across the Salinas River, the yellow stubble fields seemed to be bathed in pale cold sunshine, but there was no sunshine in the valley now in December. The thick willow scrub along the river flamed with sharp and positive yellow leaves.

It was a time of quiet and of waiting. The air was cold and tender. A light wind blew up from the southwest so that the farmers were mildly hopeful of a good rain before long; but fog and rain do not go together.

Across the river, on Henry Allen's foothill ranch there was little work to be done, for the hay was cut and stored and the orchards were plowed up to receive the rain deeply when it should come. The cattle on the higher slopes were becoming shaggy and rough-coated.

Elisa Allen, working in her flower garden, looked down across the yard and saw Henry, her husband, talking to two men in business suits. The three of them stood by the tractor shed, each man with one foot on the side of the little Fordson. They smoked cigarettes and studied the machine as they talked.

Elisa watched them for a moment and then went back to her work. She was thirty-five. Her face was lean and strong and her eyes were as clear as

*shares:* Plowshares, the parts of a plow that cut through the earth.

water. Her figure looked blocked and heavy in her gardening costume, a man's black hat pulled low down over her eyes, clod-hopper° shoes, a figured print dress almost completely covered by a big corduroy apron with four big pockets to hold the snips, the trowel and scratcher,° the seeds, and the knife she worked with. She wore heavy leather gloves to protect her hands while she worked.

She was cutting down the old year's chrysanthemum stalks with a pair of short and powerful scissors. She looked down toward the men by the tractor shed now and then. Her face was eager and mature and handsome; even her work with the scissors was overeager, overpowerful. The chrysanthemum stems seemed too small and easy for her energy.

She brushed a cloud of hair out of her eyes with the back of her glove, and left a smudge of earth on her cheek in doing it. Behind her stood the neat white farm house with red geraniums close-banked around it as high as the windows. It was a hard-swept looking little house with hard-polished windows, and a clean mud-mat on the front steps.

Elisa cast another glance toward the tractor shed. The strangers were getting into their Ford coupe. She took off a glove and put her strong fingers down into the forest of new green chrysanthemum sprouts that were growing around the old roots. She spread the leaves and looked down among the close-growing stems. No aphids° were there, no sowbugs or snails or cutworms. Her terrier fingers destroyed such pests before they could get started.

Elisa started at the sound of her husband's voice. He had come near quietly, and he leaned over the wire fence that protected her flower garden from cattle and dogs and chickens.

10    "At it again," he said. "You've got a strong new crop coming."

Elisa straightened her back and pulled on the gardening glove again. "Yes. They'll be strong this coming year." In her tone and on her face there was a little smugness.

"You've got a gift with things," Henry observed. "Some of those yellow chrysanthemums you had this year were ten inches across. I wish you'd work out in the orchard and raise some apples that big."

Her eyes sharpened. "Maybe I could do it, too. I've a gift with things, all right. My mother had it. She could stick anything in the ground and make it grow. She said it was having planters' hands that knew how to do it."

"Well, it sure works with flowers," he said.

15    "Henry, who were those men you were talking to?"

---

*clod-hopper shoes:* Large, heavy shoes.    *snips, the trowel and scratcher:* Gardening tools.    *aphids:* Small insects that suck the juices from plants.

· · · · · · · · · · · · · · · · · · · · · · · · · · · · · · · · · · · · ·

"Why, sure, that's what I came to tell you. They were from the Western Meat Company. I sold thirty head of three-year-old steers. Got nearly my own price, too."

"Good," she said. "Good for you."

"And I thought," he continued, "I thought how it's Saturday afternoon, and we might go into Salinas for dinner at a restaurant, and then to a picture show—to celebrate, you see."

"Good," she repeated. "Oh, yes. That will be good."

Henry put on his joking tone. "There's fights tonight. How'd you like to go to the fights?" 20

"Oh, no," she said breathlessly, "No, I wouldn't like fights."

"Just fooling, Elisa. We'll go to a movie. Let's see. It's two now. I'm going to take Scotty and bring down those steers from the hill. It'll take us maybe two hours. We'll go in town about five and have dinner at the Cominos Hotel. Like that?"

"Of course I'll like it. It's good to eat away from home."

"All right, then. I'll go get up a couple of horses."

She said, "I'll have plenty of time to transplant some of these sets, I guess." 25

She heard her husband calling Scotty down by the barn. And a little later she saw the two men ride up the pale yellow hillside in search of the steers.

There was a little square sandy bed kept for rooting the chrysanthemums. With her trowel she turned the soil over and over, and smoothed it and patted it firm. Then she dug ten parallel trenches to receive the sets. Back at the chrysanthemum bed she pulled out the little crisp shoots, trimmed off the leaves at each one with her scissors, and laid it on a small orderly pile.

A squeak of wheels and plod of hoofs came from the road. Elisa looked up. The country road ran along the dense bank of willows and cottonwoods that bordered the river, and up this road came a curious vehicle, curiously drawn. It was an old spring-wagon, with a round canvas top on it like the corner of a prairie schooner.° It was drawn by an old bay horse and a little grey-and-white burro.° A big stubble-bearded man sat between the cover flaps and drove the crawling team. Underneath the wagon, between the hind wheels, a lean and rangy mongrel dog walked sedately. Words were painted on the canvas, in clumsy, crooked letters. "Pots, pans, knives, sisors, lawn mores, Fixed." Two rows of articles, and the triumphantly definitive "Fixed" below. The black paint had run down in little sharp points beneath each letter.

Elisa, squatting on the ground, watched to see the crazy, loose-jointed wagon pass by. But it didn't pass. It turned into the farm road in front of her

*prairie schooner:* Covered wagon used by the pioneers who traveled cross-country. *burro:* Spanish, meaning donkey.

house, crooked old wheels skirling° and squeaking. The rangy dog darted from between the wheels and ran ahead. Instantly the two ranch shepherds flew out at him. Then all three stopped, and with stiff and quivering tails, with taut straight legs, with ambassadorial dignity, they slowly circled, sniffing daintily. The caravan pulled up to Elisa's wire fence and stopped. Now the newcomer dog, feeling outnumbered, lowered his tail and retired under the wagon with raised hackles° and bared teeth.

30    The man on the seat called out, "That's a bad dog in a fight when he gets started."

Elisa laughed. "I see he is. How soon does he generally get started?"

The man caught up her laughter and echoed it heartily. "Sometimes not for weeks and weeks," he said. He climbed stiffly down, over the wheel. The horse and the donkey dropped like unwatered flowers.

Elisa saw that he was a very big man. Although his hair and beard were greying, he did not look old. His worn black suit was wrinkled and spotted with grease. The laughter had disappeared from his face and eyes the moment his laughing voice ceased. His eyes were dark, and they were full of the brooding that gets in the eyes of teamsters and of sailors. The calloused hands he rested on the wire fence were cracked, and every crack was a black line. He took off his battered hat.

"I'm off my general road, ma'am," he said. "Does this dirt road cut over across the river to the Los Angeles highway?"

35    Elisa stood up and shoved the thick scissors in her apron pocket. "Well, yes, it does, but it winds around and then fords the river. I don't think your team could pull through the sand."

He replied with some asperity,° "It might surprise you what them beasts can pull through."

"When they get started?" she asked.

He smiled for a second. "Yes. When they get started."

"Well," said Elisa, "I think you'll save time if you go back to the Salinas road and pick up the highway there."

40    He drew a big finger down the chicken wire and made it sing. "I ain't in any hurry, ma'am. I go from Seattle to San Diego and back every year. Takes all my time. About six months each way. I aim to follow nice weather."

Elisa took off her gloves and stuffed them in the apron pocket with the scissors. She touched the under edge of her man's hat, searching for fugitive hairs. "That sounds like a nice kind of a way to live," she said.

---

*skirling:* Emitting a high, shrill tone.    *hackles:* Here, meaning the hair along the neck and back.
*asperity:* Roughness.

He leaned confidentially over the fence. "Maybe you noticed the writing on my wagon. I mend pots and sharpen knives and scissors. You got any of them things to do?"

"Oh, no," she said, quickly. "Nothing like that." Her eyes hardened with resistance.

"Scissors is the worst thing," he explained. "Most people just ruin scissors trying to sharpen 'em, but I know how. I got a special tool. It's a little bobbit° kind of thing, and patented. But it sure does the trick."

"No. My scissors are all sharp."                                                                             45

"All right, then. Take a pot," he continued earnestly, "a bent pot, or a pot with a hole. I can make it like new so you don't have to buy no new ones. That's a savings for you."

"No," she said shortly. "I tell you I have nothing like that for you to do."

His face fell to an exaggerated sadness. His voice took on a whining undertone. "I ain't had a thing to do today. Maybe I won't have no supper tonight. You see I'm off my regular road. I know folks on the highway clear from Seattle to San Diego. They save their things for me to sharpen up because they know I do it so good and save them money."

"I'm sorry," Elisa said irritably. "I haven't anything for you to do."

His eyes left her face and fell to searching the ground. They roamed about        50
until they came to the chrysanthemum bed where she had been working. "What's them plants, ma'am?"

The irritation and resistance melted from Elisa's face. "Oh, those are chrysanthemums, giant whites and yellows. I raise them every year, bigger than anybody around here."

"Kind of a long-stemmed flower? Looks like a quick puff of colored smoke?" he asked.

"That's it. What a nice way to describe them."

"They smell kind of nasty till you get used to them," he said.

"It's a good bitter smell," she retorted, "not nasty at all."                                                55

He changed his tone quickly, "I like the smell myself."

"I had ten-inch-blooms this year," she said.

The man leaned farther over the fence. "Look, I know a lady down the road a piece, has got the nicest garden you ever seen. Got nearly every kind of flower but no chrysanthemums. Last time I was mending a copper-bottom washtub for her (that's a hard job but I do it good), she said to me, 'If you ever run acrost some nice chrysanthemums I wish you'd try to get me a few seeds.' That's what she told me."

_bobbit:_ A small polishing wheel of felt or leather.

Elisa's eyes grew alert and eager. "She couldn't have known much about chrysanthemums. You *can* raise them from seed, but it's much easier to root the little sprouts you see there."

60    "Oh," he said. "I s'pose I can't take none to her, then."

"Why yes you can," Elisa cried. "I can put some in damp sand, and you can carry them right along with you. They'll take root in the pot if you keep them damp. And then she can transplant them."

"She'd sure like to have some, ma'am. You say they're nice ones?"

"Beautiful," she said. "Oh, beautiful." Her eyes shone. She tore off the battered hat and shook out her dark pretty hair. "I'll put them in a flower pot, and you can take them right with you. Come into the yard."

While the man came through the picket gate Elisa ran excitedly along the geranium-bordered path to the back of the house. And she returned carrying a big red flower pot. The gloves were forgotten now. She kneeled on the ground by the starting bed and dug up the sandy soil with her fingers and scooped it into the bright new flower pot. Then she picked up the little pile of shoots she had prepared. With her strong fingers she pressed them into the sand and tamped° around them with her knuckles. The man stood over her. "I'll tell you what to do," she said. "You remember so you can tell the lady."

65    "Yes, I'll try to remember."

"Well, look. These will take root in about a month. Then she must set them out, about a foot apart in good rich earth like this, see?" She lifted a handful of dark soil for him to look at. "They'll grow fast and tall. Now remember this: In July tell her to cut them down, about eight inches from the ground."

"Before they bloom?" he asked.

"Yes, before they bloom." Her face was tight with eagerness. "They'll grow right up again. About the last of September the buds will start."

She stopped and seemed perplexed.° "It's the budding that takes the most care," she said hesitantly. "I don't know how to tell you." She looked deep into his eyes, searchingly. Her mouth opened a little, and she seemed to be listening. "I'll try to tell you," she said. "Did you ever hear of planting hands?"

70    "Can't say I have, ma'am."

"Well, I can only tell you what it feels like. It's when you're picking off the buds you don't want. Everything goes right down into your fingertips. You watch your fingers work. They do it themselves. You can feel how it is. They pick and pick the buds. They never make a mistake. They're with the plant. Do

---

*tamped:* Drove down; pushed in.    *perplexed:* Puzzled, uncertain.

you see? Your fingers and the plant. You can feel that, right up your arm. They know. They never make a mistake. You can feel it. When you're like that you can't do anything wrong. Do you see that? Can you understand that?"

She was kneeling on the ground looking up at him. Her breast swelled passionately.

The man's eyes narrowed. He looked away self-consciously. "Maybe I know," he said. "Sometimes in the night in the wagon there—"

Elisa's voice grew husky. She broke in on him, "I've never lived as you do, but I know what you mean. When the night is dark—why, the stars are sharp-pointed, and there's quiet. Why, you rise up and up! Every pointed star gets driven into your body. It's like that. Hot and sharp and—lovely."

Kneeling there, her hand went out toward his legs in the greasy black trousers. Her hesitant fingers almost touched the cloth. Then her hand dropped to the ground. She crouched low like a fawning dog.

He said, "It's nice, just like you say. Only when you don't have no dinner, it ain't."

She stood up then, very straight, and her face was ashamed. She held the flower pot out to him and placed it gently in his arms. "Here. Put it in your wagon, on the seat, where you can watch it. Maybe I can find something for you to do."

At the back of the house she dug in the can pile and found two old and battered aluminum saucepans. She carried them back and gave them to him. "Here, maybe you can fix these."

His manner changed. He became professional. "Good as new I can fix them." At the back of his wagon he set a little anvil, and out of an oily tool box dug a small machine hammer. Elisa came through the gate to watch him while he pounded out the dents in the kettles. His mouth grew sure and knowing. At a difficult part of the work he sucked his underlip.

"You sleep right in the wagon?" Elisa asked.

"Right in the wagon, ma'am. Rain or shine I'm dry as a cow in there."

"It must be nice," she said. "It must be very nice. I wish women could do such things."

"It ain't the right kind of a life for a woman."

Her upper lip raised a little, showing her teeth, "How do you know? How can you tell?" she said.

"I don't know, ma'am," he protested. "Of course I don't know. Now here's your kettles, done. You don't have to buy no new ones."

"How much?"

"Oh, fifty cents'll do. I keep my prices down and my work good. That's why I have all them satisfied customers up and down the highway."

75

80

85

Elisa brought him a fifty-cent piece from the house and dropped it in his hand. "You might be surprised to have a rival some time. I can sharpen scissors, too. And I can beat the dents out of little pots. I could show you what a woman might do."

He put his hammer back in the oily box and shoved the little anvil out of sight. "It would be a lonely life for a woman, ma'am, and a scarey life, too, with animals creeping under the wagon all night." He climbed over the singletree, steadying himself with a hand on the burro's white rump. He settled himself in the seat, picked up the lines. "Thank you kindly, ma'am," he said. "I'll do like you told me; I'll go back and catch the Salinas road."

90    "Mind," she called, "if you're long in getting there, keep the sand damp."

"Sand, ma'am? . . . Sand? Oh, sure. You mean around the chrysanthemums. Sure I will." He clucked his tongue. The beasts leaned luxuriously into their collars. The mongrel dog took his place between the back wheels. The wagon turned and crawled out the entrance road and back the way it had come, along the river.

Elisa stood in front of her wire fence watching the slow progress of the caravan. Her shoulders were straight, her head thrown back, her eyes half-closed, so that the scene came vaguely into them. Her lips moved silently, forming the words "Good-bye—good-bye." Then she whispered, "That's a bright direction. There's a glowing there." The sound of her whisper startled her. She shook herself free and looked about to see whether anyone had been listening. Only the dogs had heard. They lifted their heads toward her from their sleeping in the dust, and then stretched out their chins and settled asleep again. Elisa turned and ran hurriedly into the house.

In the kitchen she reached behind the stove and felt the water tank. It was full of hot water from the noonday cooking. In the bathroom she tore off her soiled clothes and flung them into the corner. And then she scrubbed herself with a little block of pumice,° legs and thighs, loins and chest and arms, until her skin was scratched and red. When she had dried herself she stood in front of a mirror in her bedroom and looked at her body. She tightened her stomach and threw out her chest. She turned and looked over her shoulder at her back.

After a while she began to dress, slowly. She put on her newest underclothing and her nicest stockings and the dress which was the symbol of her prettiness. She worked carefully on her hair, penciled her eyebrows and rouged her lips.

---

*pumice:* A light, rough, porous stone used to scrub the skin clean.

Before she was finished she heard the little thunder of hoofs and the    95
shouts of Henry and his helper as they drove the red steers into the corral. She
heard the gate bang shut and set herself for Henry's arrival.

His step sounded on the porch. He entered the house calling, "Elisa,
where are you?"

"In my room, dressing. I'm not ready. There's hot water for your bath.
Hurry up. It's getting late."

When she heard him splashing in the tub, Elisa laid his dark suit on the
bed, and shirt and socks and tie beside it. She stood his polished shoes on the
floor beside the bed. Then she went to the porch and sat primly and stiffly
down. She looked toward the river road where the willow-line was still yellow
with frosted leaves so that under the high grey fog they seemed a thin band of
sunshine. This was the only color in the grey afternoon. She sat unmoving for
a long time. Her eyes blinked rarely.

Henry came banging out of the door, shoving his tie inside his vest as he
came. Elisa stiffened and her face grew tight. Henry stopped short and looked
at her. "Why—why, Elisa. You look so nice!"

"Nice? You think I look nice? What do you mean by 'nice'?"    100

Henry blundered on. "I don't know. I mean you look different, strong and
happy."

"I am strong? Yes, strong. What do you mean 'strong'?"

He looked bewildered. "You're playing some kind of a game," he said help-
lessly. "It's a kind of a play. You look strong enough to break a calf over your
knee, happy enough to eat it like a watermelon."

For a second she lost her rigidity. "Henry! Don't talk like that. You didn't
know what you said." She grew complete again. "I'm strong," she boasted, "I
never knew before how strong."

Henry looked down toward the tractor shed, and when he brought his    105
eyes back to her, they were his own again. "I'll get out the car. You can put on
your coat while I'm starting."

Elisa went into the house. She heard him drive to the gate and idle down
his motor, and then she took a long time to put on her hat. She pulled it here
and pressed it there. When Henry turned the motor off she slipped into her
coat and went out.

The little roadster° bounced along on the dirt road by the river, raising the
birds and driving the rabbits into the brush. Two cranes flapped heavily over
the willow-line and dropped into the river-bed.

---

*roadster:* Two-seat, convertible automobile.

Far ahead on the road Elisa saw a dark speck. She knew.

She tried not to look as they passed it, but her eyes would not obey. She whispered to herself sadly, "He might have thrown them off the road. That wouldn't have been much trouble, not very much. But he kept the pot," she explained. "He had to keep the pot. That's why he couldn't get them off the road."

110    The roadster turned a bend and she saw the caravan ahead. She swung full around toward her husband so she could not see the little covered wagon and the mismatched team as the car passed them.

In a moment it was over. The thing was done. She did not look back.

She said loudly, to be heard above the motor. "It will be good, tonight, a good dinner."

"Now you're changed again," Henry complained. He took one hand from the wheel and patted her knee. "I ought to take you in to dinner oftener. It would be good for both of us. We get so heavy out on the ranch."

"Henry," she asked, "could we have wine at dinner?"

115    "Sure we could. Say! That will be fine."

She was silent for a while; then she said, "Henry, at those prize fights, do the men hurt each other very much?"

"Sometimes a little, not often. Why?"

"Well, I've read how they break noses, and blood runs down their chests. I've read how the fighting gloves get heavy and soggy with blood."

He looked around at her. "What's the matter, Elisa? I didn't know you read things like that." He brought the car to a stop, then turned to the right over the Salinas River bridge.

120    "Do any women ever go to the fights?" she asked.

"Oh, sure, some. What's the matter Elisa? Do you want to go? I don't think you'd like it, but I'll take you if you really want to go."

She relaxed limply in the seat. "Oh, no. No. I don't want to go. I'm sure I don't." Her face was turned away from him. "It will be enough if we can have wine. It will be plenty." She turned up her coat collar so he could not see that she was crying weakly—like an old woman.

### QUESTIONS

1. What impression of the setting does this introduction create? Do any images in the first paragraph relate to other images in the story?
2. List various words used to describe Elisa. Are some of them repeated? What do these reveal about her character?

. . . . . . . . . . . . . . . . . . . . . . . . . . . . . . . . . . . . . . . .

3. Describe Henry and Elisa's relationship; focus on the interaction that takes place between them in the beginning and at the conclusion of the story.
4. Identify any symbols used in the story, and explain what they might represent.
5. Describe the character of the traveling man. How does he break through Elisa's defenses? What might his success reveal about Elisa?
6. What does the traveling repairman mean when he says that his life "ain't the right kind of life for a woman"? What reasons does he provide to support this claim?
7. What does Elisa mean when she says, "That's a bright direction there. There's a glowing there"?
8. In the conclusion of the story, why is Elisa "crying weakly—like an old woman"?

## CONNECTIONS

1. Compare and contrast Elisa Allen to Louise Mallard, the main character of Kate Chopin's "The Story of an Hour" (included in Section 2).
2. Compare and contrast the relationship between Henry and Elisa Allen to that of the husband and wife described in Tobias Wolff's "Say Yes."

# Work Is a Four-Letter Word

# Avoiding Clichés, Jargon, and Euphemisms

Imagine that you've just finished listening to an elaborate lecture when two students behind you start commenting on what you've just heard:

"Cool as a cucumber," says one of them. "I bet I'll get a cephalalgia out of it."

"Ha!" the second replies. "It was totally cognitively rewarding."

"More like cerebrally challenging," adds the other.

Fortunately, that's an unlikely scenario. Unfortunately, in an attempt to sound more impressive (especially in writing), people do sometimes use language that doesn't fit its context or is worn out, ambiguous, at times intentionally evasive. Three examples of such misused language are clichés, jargon, and euphemisms. A *cliché* is a word or phrase that has lost its freshness through overuse. Once referring to meaningless talk, *jargon* is associated today with the specialized language of a profession, trade, or discipline, such as law, medicine, and the sciences: We speak of or write using *technical jargon* or *scientific jargon*. Whereas clichés and jargon are generally used unintentionally or without intending ambiguity, *euphemisms* are intentionally evasive, often used to cover up unpleasant facts.

## Clichés

Dead as a doornail, pale as a ghost—a cliché is an expression that was once descriptive but has since lost its freshness and originality. Some clichés are proverbs or part of a proverb: *there's no smoke without fire; what goes around, comes around; stay on track; don't cry over spilt milk; the grass is always greener on the other side of the fence; don't count your chickens before they hatch.* While clichés are familiar to most of us, these clichés convey little meaning. People often use such clichés because they are ready-made and convenient, requiring no thought or originality. The danger of using a cliché, then, is that it can signal the reader that you are lazy or lack creativity.

Another common type of cliché appears in the form of a metaphor or simile—like *quick as a flash, fast as lightning, busy as a bee, blind as a bat.* Once original and witty, these expressions have been overused and have lost their freshness and ability to affect readers. Rather than using them, you should try to create your own similes (see "Metaphor and Other Language Play," in Section 3). A fresh simile may not be "as good as gold," but it's representative of you—of your creativity and ability to write well.

## *Jargon*

Members of a specialized group may use jargon with ease and familiarity; however, people outside of that group may then feel as though they are listening to (or reading) a foreign language. For example, if a lawyer discussed *involuntary conversion* with you, would you know that he or she meant "loss or destruction of property through theft, accident, or condemnation"? Or, if a doctor told you that you have a *bilateral perorbital hematoma* and a *cephalalgia,* would you understand that he or she was referring to a black eye and a headache?

Jargon, then, may be the specialized vocabulary used by experts who want to discuss a topic in detail, communicating nuances that outsiders to the field may not be aware of. As a student, for example, you will be introduced to the specialized language of various academic disciplines; should you become a graduate student, you will be expected to use the terminology of your discipline fluently—whether that discipline is anthropology, English, marketing, music, or physics. In this text, one example of specialized vocabulary used effectively occurs in Maxine Kumin's essay "Enough Jam for a Lifetime" (included in this section): The author uses cooking terminology such as "sheeting" and "dip and drip"; however, since she is not writing for cooking experts, she clearly defines those terms.

You should only use jargon, then, if you must—if the writing situation calls for specific terms or if you are a member of a specialized group writing to other members who expect you to use a certain vocabulary. Otherwise, in an attempt to use jargon to impress general, nonspecialized readers and to appear sophisticated and intelligent, you risk confusing your readers and sounding pretentious. This is what author Russell Baker points out through his parody "Little Red Riding Hood Revisited," which begins

> Once upon a time a small person named Little Red Riding Hood initiated plans for the preparation, delivery, and transportation of foodstuffs to her grandmother, a senior citizen residing at a place of residence in a forest of indeterminate dimension.
>
> In the process of implementing this program, her incursion into the forest was in mid-transportation process when it attained interface with an alleged perpetrator. This individual, a wolf, made inquiry as to the whereabouts of Little Red Riding Hood's goal as well as inferring that he was desirous of ascertaining the contents of Little Red Riding Hood's foodstuffs basket. . . .

Using more words than the original, this version of the story actually says less; big words don't always translate into better writing.

## Euphemisms

In contrast to clichés and jargon, euphemisms are used intentionally to disguise meaning. A euphemism is often a word or phrase used to replace another that is considered taboo, negative, offensive, or too direct. For example, people don't really rest much in a *rest room*, nor do they often powder their faces in a *powder room* or take a bath every time they enter a *bathroom*. Most of us use these terms because they provide an inoffensive way to discuss what one does with a toilet.

However, sometimes people use euphemisms not to avoid offending others but to affect the way others relate to a thing; for example, calling pornography *adult entertainment* or referring to prisons as *correctional facilities* makes them both seem positive and innocent; *termination* is a lot easier to approve of than *killing;* and *to put down* sounds less harsh than *to insult* or *to degrade*. In these examples, a mild, comfortable term is used to redefine something that many people might find uncomfortable. Unfortunately, the disturbing act or thing that the euphemism denotes has not changed—only the language used to discuss it has. While a euphemism may be used with good intentions (as, for example, when we talk about someone *passing away*), it evades the truth nonetheless.

Some groups go to great lengths to create euphemisms that present them in the best way possible. Businesspeople, for example, prefer the euphemism *downsizing* to *layoff*—and *layoff* to *firing*. Politicians and members of the military are also fond of euphemisms. In the recent Gulf War, which was euphemistically titled *Desert Storm*, U.S. missiles were called *smart bombs,* and the destruction of a target by a missile was called a *surgical strike*. When both American and Iraqi soldiers were killed in the *theater of operation,* it was called *collateral damage*. The intent of such language use is to cover up the truth about what occurs during a war, to make combat seem clinical, sanitary, neat, and safe.

# Final Words

· · · · · · · · · · · · · · · · · · · · · · · · · ·

If you have heard a fancy phrase before or are not sure precisely what the word or expression means, try to avoid using it (or at least consult a dictionary and consider carefully the context in which you want to use it). Prefer, instead, straightforward language and comparisons that you have created yourself, that will help readers see things the way you do.

# ∿ The Ant and the Grasshopper

*Aesop*

According to legend, Aesop was a Phrygian slave who lived in Greece at the time of King Croesus, sometime between the years 620 and 560 B.C. He is said to have been crippled or deformed in some way. He earned his freedom through his wit and cunning, later becoming a favorite advisor to the king. His popularity and outspokenness, however, earned him enemies as well as friends: He was killed by being hurled over a cliff in Delphi. According to *The Oxford Companion to English Literature,* however, Aesop, "to whom tradition attributes the authorship of the whole stock of Greek fables, is probably a legendary figure." Either way, the numerous tales known as Aesop's fables, personifying animals as characters, have survived through the centuries and are as relevant today as they were in ancient Greece.

**WARM-UP:** Do you believe that work is an important part of who we are? Should all people work? Why or why not?

1    One frosty autumn day an ant was busily storing away some of the kernels of wheat which he had gathered during the summer to tide him over the coming winter.

A grasshopper, half perishing from hunger, came limping by. Perceiving what the industrious ant was doing, he asked for a morsel from the ant's store to save his life.

"What were you doing all during the summer while I was busy harvesting?" inquired the ant.

"Oh," replied the grasshopper, "I was not idle. I was singing and chirping all day long."

5    "Well," said the ant, smiling grimly as he locked his granary door, "since you sang all summer, it looks as though you would have to dance all winter."

**QUESTIONS**

1. Are any descriptions in this fable particularly effective? If so, which ones?
2. In one sentence, summarize the main idea (or thesis) of the fable.
3. Would you count the grasshopper's "singing and chirping" as work? Why or why not? Would it have been considered work if he had gotten paid for it?
4. Should the ant have helped the grasshopper? Why or why not?

5. We often hear that most people in this country save much less of their money than people in other countries do. Are these people like the grasshopper? Explain your response.
6. Define "welfare"; in your opinion, is that what the grasshopper is asking for? Explain your response.

## CONNECTIONS

Would Michael Buenaflor (author of "It's Good to Know the Opposition," included in Section 1) agree with the ant's response to the grasshopper's request? Is there a stage in life when human beings *should* be "grasshoppers"? Is there a stage when they should be "ants"?

# ∽ The Gospel of Wealth

## Andrew Carnegie

> Born in 1835, Andrew Carnegie emigrated from Scotland to the United
> States at the age of thirteen and, at the age of sixteen, became one of the first
> American telegraph operators. He worked for the Pennsylvania Railroad for
> twelve years. Foreseeing the demand for iron and steel, he left the railroad to
> start the Keystone Bridge Works in 1873. When he sold his Carnegie Steel
> Company in 1901, it was producing twenty-five percent of the steel sold in
> the United States. Carnegie wrote several books, including *The Empire of
> Business* (1902) and *Problems of To-day: Wealth—Labor—Socialism* (1908).
> The following essay first appeared in the *North American Review* in 1889.
> Carnegie died in 1919, but his name lives on. He believed in sharing the
> immense wealth he accumulated; many institutions still reflect his influence
> today, including Carnegie Hall in New York and Carnegie-Mellon University
> in Pittsburgh.

**WARM-UP:** Freewrite for five minutes on the images you associate
with extremely wealthy people. What are the sources of those images?

1   The problem of our age is the proper administration of wealth, that the ties
of brotherhood may still bind together the rich and poor in harmonious
relationship. The conditions of human life have not only been changed, but
revolutionized, within the past few hundred years. In former days there was
little difference between the dwelling, dress, food, and environment of the
chief and those of his retainers. The Indians are today where civilized man
then was. When visiting the Sioux, I was led to the wigwam of the chief. It was
like the others in external appearance, and even within the difference was trifling between it and those of the poorest of his braves. The contrast between
the palace of the millionaire and the cottage of the laborer with us today measures the change which has come with civilization. This change, however, is
not to be deplored, but welcomed as highly beneficial. It is well, nay, essential,
for the progress of the race that the houses of some should be homes for all
that is highest and best in literature and the arts, and for all the refinements of
civilization, rather than that none should be so. Much better this great irregu-
larity than universal squalor. Without wealth there can be no Mæcenas.° The
"good old times" were not good old times. Neither master nor servant was as
well situated then as today. A relapse to old conditions would be disastrous to

---

*Mæcenas:* Ancient Roman politician and literary patron famous for his wealth.

both—not the least so to him who serves—and would sweep away civilization with it. But whether the change be for good or ill, it is upon us, beyond our power to alter, and, therefore, to be accepted and made the best of it. It is a waste of time to criticize the inevitable.

It is easy to see how the change has come. One illustration will serve for almost every phase of the cause. In the manufacture of products we have the whole story. It applies to all combinations of human industry, as stimulated and enlarged by the inventions of this scientific age. Formerly, articles were manufactured at the domestic hearth, or in small shops which formed part of the household. The master and his apprentices worked side by side, the latter living with the master, and therefore subject to the same conditions. When these apprentices rose to be masters, there was little or no change in their mode of life, and they, in turn, educated succeeding apprentices in the same routine. There was, substantially, social equality, and even political equality, for those engaged in industrial pursuits had then little or no voice in the State.

The inevitable result of such a mode of manufacture was crude articles at high prices. Today the world obtains commodities of excellent quality at prices which even the preceding generation would have deemed incredible. In the commercial world similar causes have produced similar results, and the race is benefited thereby. The poor enjoy what the rich could not before afford. What were the luxuries have become the necessaries of life. The laborer has now more comforts than the farmer had a few generations ago. The farmer has more luxuries than the landlord had, and is more richly clad and better housed. The landlord has books and pictures rarer and appointments more artistic than the king could then obtain.

The price we pay for this salutary° change is, no doubt, great. We assemble thousands of operatives in the factory, and in the mine, of whom the employer can know little or nothing, and to whom he is little better than a myth. All intercourse between them is at an end. Rigid castes are formed, and, as usual, mutual ignorance breeds mutual distrust. Each caste is without sympathy with the other, and ready to credit anything disparaging in regard to it. Under the law of competition, the employer of thousands is forced into the strictest economies, among which the rates paid to labor figure prominently, and often there is friction between the employer and the employed, between capital and labor, between rich and poor. Human society loses homogeneity.°

The price which society pays for the law of competition, like the price it pays for cheap comforts and luxuries, is also great; but the advantages of this law are also greater still than its cost—for it is to this law that we owe our wonderful material development, which brings improved conditions in its

5

---

*salutary:* Healthy, restorative.    *homogeneity:* Conformity, similarity.

train. But, whether the law be benign° or not, we must say of it, as we say of the change in the conditions of men to which we have referred: it is here; we cannot evade it; no substitutes for it have been found; and while the law may be sometimes hard for the individual, it is best for the race, because it insures the survival of the fittest in every department. We accept and welcome, therefore, as conditions to which we must accommodate ourselves, great inequality of environment; the concentration of business, industrial and commercial, in the hands of a few; and the law of competition between these, as being not only beneficial, but essential to the future progress of the race. Having accepted these, it follows that there must be great scope for the exercise of special ability in the merchant and in the manufacturer who has to conduct affairs upon a great scale. That this talent for organization and management is rare among men is proved by the fact that it invariably secures enormous rewards for its possessor, no matter where or under what laws or conditions. The experienced in affairs always rate the MAN whose services can be obtained as a partner as not only the first consideration, but such as render the question of his capital scarcely worth considering: for able men soon create capital; in the hands of those without the special talent required, capital soon takes wings. Such men become interested in firms or corporations using millions; and, estimating only simple interest to be made upon the capital invested, it is inevitable that their income must exceed their expenditure and that they must, therefore, accumulate wealth. Nor is there any middle ground which such men can occupy, because the great manufacturing or commercial concern which does not earn at least interest upon its capital soon becomes bankrupt. It must either go forward or fall behind; to stand still is impossible. It is a condition essential to its successful operation that it should be thus far profitable, and even that, in addition to interest on capital, it should make profit. It is a law, as certain as any of the others named, that men possessed of this peculiar talent for affairs, under the free play of economic forces must, of necessity, soon be in receipt of more revenue than can be judiciously expended upon themselves; and this law is as beneficial for the race as the others.

Objections to the foundations upon which society is based are not in order, because the condition of the race is better with these than it has been with any other which has been tried. Of the effect of any new substitutes proposed we cannot be sure. The Socialist or Anarchist who seeks to overturn present conditions is to be regarded as attacking the foundation upon which civilization itself rests, for civilization took its start from the day when the capable, industrious workman said to his incompetent and lazy fellow, "If

---

*benign:* Harmless, favorable.

thou dost not sow, thou shalt not reap," and thus ended primitive Communism by separating the drones from the bees. One who studies this subject will soon be brought face to face with the conclusion that upon the sacredness of property civilization itself depends—the right of the laborer to his hundred dollars in the savings-bank, and equally the legal right of the millionaire to his millions. Every man must be allowed "to sit under his own vine and figtree, with none to make afraid," if human society is to advance, or even to remain so far advanced as it is. To those who propose to substitute Communism for this intense Individualism, the answer therefore is: The race has tried that. All progress from that barbarous day to the present time has resulted from its displacement. Not evil, but good, has come to the race from the accumulation of wealth by those who have had the ability and energy to produce it. But even if we admit for a moment that it might be better for the race to discard its present foundation, Individualism—that it is a nobler ideal that man should labor, not for himself alone, but in and for a brotherhood of his fellows, and share with them all in common . . . even admit all this, and a sufficient answer is, This is not evolution, but revolution. It necessitates the changing of human nature itself—a work of eons, even if it were good to change it, which we cannot know.

It is not practicable in our day or in our age. Even if desirable theoretically, it belongs to another and long-succeeding sociological stratum.° Our duty is with what is practicable now—with the next step possible in our day and generation. It is criminal to waste our energies in endeavoring to uproot, when all we can profitably accomplish is to bend the universal tree of humanity a little in the direction most favorable to the production of good fruit under existing circumstances. We might as well urge the destruction of the highest existing type of man because he failed to reach our ideal as to favor the destruction of Individualism, Private Property, the Law of Accumulation of Wealth, and the Law of Competition; for these are the highest result of human experience, the soil in which society, so far, has produced the best fruit. Unequally or unjustly, perhaps, as these laws sometimes operate, and imperfect as they appear to the Idealist, they are, nevertheless, like the highest type of man, the best and most valuable of all that humanity has yet accomplished.

We start, then, with a condition of affairs under which the best interests of the race are promoted, but which inevitably gives wealth to the few. Thus far, accepting conditions as they exist, the situation can be surveyed and pronounced good. The question then arises—and if the foregoing be correct, it is the only question with which we have to deal—What is the proper mode of administering wealth after the laws upon which civilization is founded have

---

*stratum:* A layer, level, or gradation in an ordered system, representing a period or stage of development.

thrown it into the hands of the few? And it is of this great question that I believe I offer the true solution. It will be understood that fortunes are here spoken of, not moderate sums saved by many years of effort, the returns from which are required for the comfortable maintenance and education of families. This is not wealth, but only competence, which it should be the aim of all to acquire, and which it is for the best interests of society should be acquired.

This, then, is held to be the duty of the man of wealth: to set an example of modest, unostentatious living, shunning display or extravagance; to provide moderately for the legitimate wants of those dependent upon him; and, after doing so, to consider all surplus revenues which come to him simply as trust funds, which he is called upon to administer, and strictly bound as a matter of duty to administer in the manner which, in his judgment, is best calculated to produce the most beneficial results for the community—the man of wealth thus becoming the mere trustee and agent for his poorer brethren, bringing to their service his superior wisdom, experience, and ability to administer, doing for them better than they would or could do for themselves.

10    ... Those who would administer wisely must, indeed, be wise; for one of the serious obstacles to the improvement of our race is indiscriminate charity. It were better for mankind that the millions of the rich were thrown into the sea than so spent as to encourage the slothful, the drunken, the unworthy. Of every thousand dollars spent in so-called charity today, it is probable that nine hundred and fifty dollars is unwisely spent—so spent, indeed, as to produce the very evils which it hopes to mitigate° or cure. A well-known writer of philosophic books admitted the other day that he had given a quarter of a dollar to a man who approached him as he was coming to visit the house of his friend. He knew nothing of the habits of this beggar, knew not the use that would be made of this money, although he had every reason to suspect that it would be spent improperly. This man professed to be a disciple of Herbert Spencer; yet the quarter-dollar given that night will probably work more injury than all the money will do good which its thoughtless donor will ever be able to give in true charity. He only gratified his own feelings, saved himself from annoyance—and this was probably one of the most selfish and very worst actions of his life, for in all respects he is most worthy.

In bestowing charity, the main consideration should be to help those who will help themselves; to provide part of the means by which those who desire to improve may do so; to give those who desire to rise the aids by which they may rise; to assist, but rarely or never to do all. Neither the individual nor the race is improved by almsgiving.° Those worthy of assistance, except in rare cases, seldom require assistance....

---

*mitigate:* Alleviate, lessen.    *almsgiving:* Charity.

The best means of benefiting the community is to place within its reach the ladders upon which the aspiring can rise—free libraries, parks, and means of recreation, by which men are helped in body and mind; works of art, certain to give pleasure and improve the public taste; and public institutions of various kinds, which will improve the general condition of the people; in this manner returning their surplus wealth to the mass of their fellows in the forms best calculated to do them lasting good.

Thus is the problem of rich and poor to be solved. The laws of accumulation will be left free, the laws of distribution free. Individualism will continue, but the millionaire will be but a trustee for the poor, intrusted for a season with a great part of the increased wealth of the community, but administering it for the community far better than it could or would have done for itself. The best minds will thus have reached a stage in the development of the race in which it is clearly seen that there is no mode of disposing of surplus wealth creditable to thoughtful and earnest men into whose hands it flows, save by using it year by year for the general good. This day already dawns. Men may die without incurring the pity of their fellows, still sharers in great business enterprises from which their capital cannot be or has not been withdrawn, and which is left chiefly at death for public uses; yet the day is not far distant when the man who dies leaving behind him millions of available wealth, which was free to him to administer during life, will pass away "unwept, unhonored, and unsung," no matter to what uses he leaves the dross° which he cannot take with him. Of such as these the public verdict will then be: "The man who dies thus rich dies disgraced."

Such, in my opinion is the true gospel concerning wealth, obedience to which is destined some day to solve the problem of the rich and the poor, and to bring "Peace on earth, among men good will."

## QUESTIONS

1. Carnegie concludes his first paragraph by asserting that the change in economy is "beyond our power to alter." Challenge this assumption by preparing a list of occasions when people have been able to alter the "conditions of human life."
2. Discussing the "price which society pays for the law of competition," Carnegie argues that we must "accept" and "accommodate ourselves" to a "great inequality of environment." Does Carnegie have a bias or interest in people accepting this idea?
3. Are there other factors, besides a "peculiar talent for affairs," that might affect an individual's success at making money?

*dross:* Here meaning trivial or inferior matter, impurity.

4. What do you think about Carnegie's statement, "Those worthy of assistance, except in rare cases, seldom require assistance"?

5. In paragraph nine, Carnegie explains what he believes is the purpose of the "man of wealth." Create a list of wealthy characters from books, TV programs, movies, etc., and explain whether these examples support or contradict his belief.

6. In paragraph 12, Carnegie provides a list of benefits that the wealthy should provide for the poor. Explain how these benefits might help the poor.

7. Based on your own knowledge, what are some of the objections raised by those who feel that private individual charity is not the best way to help the poor?

8. What is the effect of the use of biblical references in this essay?

9. Identify some examples of euphemism in this selection.

## CONNECTIONS

1. How do you imagine that Henry and Elisa Allen, from John Steinbeck's "The Chrysanthemums," would respond to Carnegie's ideas about the nature of work? Would Harry and Elisa agree with each other?

2. Explain the relationship between Carnegie's views and those reflected in Aesop's fable.

# The Rite of Work: The Economic Man

*Sam Keen*

A regular contributor to *Psychology Today,* Sam Keen has earned degrees from Princeton University and Harvard Divinity School. He was nominated for an Emmy Award for his PBS series "The Enemy Within" and is the author of numerous books, including *To a Dancing God* (1970), *Telling Your Story: A Guide to Who You Are and Who You Can Be* (with Anne Valley Fox— 1973), *The Passionate Life* (1983), *Faces of the Enemy: Reflections of the Hostile Imagination* (1988), and *Fire in the Belly: On Being a Man* (1991). The following selection is taken from *Fire in the Belly,* which made Keen a prominent figure in the growing men's movement.

**WARM-UP:** What are some things that people do in order to fit it in at work?

*One does not work to live; one lives to work.*
——MAX WEBER,
*Capitalism and the Protestant Ethic*

*Have leisure and know that I am God.*
——PSALM 65

## The Bottom Line—Work and Worth

Preparations for the male ritual of work begin even before the age of     1
schooling. Long before a boy child has a concept of the day after tomorrow, he will be asked by well-meaning but unconscious adults, "What do you want to be when you grow up?" It will not take him long to discover that "I want to be a horse" is not an answer that satisfies adults. They want to know what men plan to do, what job, profession, occupation we have decided to follow at five years of age! Boys are taught early that they are what they do. Later, as men, when we meet as strangers on the plane or at a cocktail party we break the ice by asking, "What do you do?"

Formal preparation for the rites of manhood in a secular° society takes place first through the institution of schooling. Our indoctrination into the dominant myths, value system, and repertoire of heroic stories is homogenized° into the educational process. My fifteen-year-old nephew put the matter more accurately than any social scientist. "Schools," he said, "are designed

---

*secular:* Indifferent to or exclusive of religious rule.     *homogenized:* Made uniform, blended.

to teach you to take life sitting down. They prepare you to work in office buildings, to sit in rows or cubicles, to be on time, not to talk back, and to let somebody else grade you." From the first grade onward, schools teach us to define and measure ourselves against others. We learn that the world is composed of winners and losers, pass or fail.

The games that make up what we call physical education—football, basketball, and baseball—are minibattles that teach boys to compete in the game of life. Pregame pep talks, like salesmen's meetings, begin with the Vince Lombardi prayer: "Winning isn't the most important thing. It's the only thing." For many boys making the team, from Little League to college, provides the ritual form of combat that is central to male identity.

The first full-time job, like the first fight or first sex, is a rite of passage for men in our time. Boys have paper routes, but men have regular paychecks. Like primitive rites, work requires certain sacrifices and offers certain insignia° of manhood. In return for agreeing to put aside childish dalliance° and assume the responsibility for showing up from nine to five at some place of work, the initiate receives the power object—money—that allows him to participate in the adult life of the community.

5    Getting a credit card is a more advanced rite of passage. The credit card is for the modern male what killing prey was to a hunter. To earn a credit rating a man must certify that he has voluntarily cut himself off from childhood, that he has foregone the pleasure of languid° mornings at the swimming hole, and has assumed the discipline of a regular job, a fixed address, and a predictable character. The Visa card (passport to the good life) is an insignia of membership, a sign that the system trusts you to spend what you have not yet earned because you have shown good faith by being regularly employed. In modern America going into debt is an important part of assuming the responsibilities of manhood. Debt, the willingness to live beyond our means, binds us to the economic system that requires both surplus work and surplus consumption. The popular bumper sticker, "I owe, I owe, so off to work I go" might well be the litany° to express the commitment of the working man.

After accepting the disciplines of work and credit, a whole hierarchy of graduated symbolic initiations follows, from first to thirty-second degree. Mere employment entitles one to display the insignia of the Chevette. Acquiring the executive washroom key qualifies one for a Buick or Cadillac. Only those initiated into the inner sanctum of the boardroom may be borne in the regal Rolls-Royce. To the victors belong the marks of status and the repair bills. The right to wear eagle feathers or to sing certain sacred songs was recognized in American Indian tribes to signify the possession of a high degree of power and status, just as in contemporary society certain brand names and

*insignia:* Badges, citations.    *dalliance:* Play.    *languid:* Sluggish, lazy.    *litany:* Repetitive chant, list.

logos are tokens of class and rank. A man wears a Rolex not because it tells time more accurately than a $14.95 Timex but because, like a penis shield, it signifies an advanced degree of manhood. In a society where the marks of virtue are created by advertising, possession of stylish objects signifies power. For economic man a Ralph Lauren polo shirt says something very different than its Fruit of the Loom equivalent. The implicit message is that manhood can be purchased. And the expense of the luxury items we own marks our progress along the path of the good life as it is defined by a consumer society.

Within the last decade someone upped the ante on the tokens required for manhood. A generation ago providing for one's family was the only economic requirement. Nowadays, supplying the necessities entitles a man only to marginal respect. If your work allows you only to survive you are judged to be not much of a man. To be poor in a consumer society is to have failed the manhood test, or at least to have gotten a D–. The advertising industry reminds us at every turn that real men, successful men, powerful men, are big spenders. They have enough cash or credit to consume the best. Buying is status. "It's the cost of the toys that separates the men from the boys." The sort of man who reads *Playboy* or *The New Yorker* is dedicated to a life of voluntary complexity, conspicuous° consumption, and adherence to the demanding discipline of style.

The rites of manhood in any society are those that are appropriate and congruent° with the dominant myth. The horizon within which we live, the source of our value system, and the way we define "reality" are economic. The bottom line is the almighty dollar. Time is money, money is power, and power makes the world go round. In the same sense that the cathedral was the sacred center of the medieval city, the bank and other commercial buildings are the centers of the modern city.

Once upon a time work was considered a curse. As the result of Adam and Eve's sin we were driven from the Garden of Eden and forced to earn our bread by the sweat of our brows. Men labored because of necessity, but found the meaning and sweetness of life in free time. According to the Greeks, only slaves and women were bound to the life of work. Free men discovered the joys and dignity of manhood in contemplation and in the cultivation of leisure. Until the time of the Protestant Reformation° the world was divided between the realm of the secular, to which work and the common life belonged, and the realm of the sacred, which was the monopoly of the Church. Martin Luther changed all of this by declaring that every man and woman had a sacred vocation. The plowman and the housewife no less than the priest were called by God to express their piety° in the common life of the

---

*conspicuous:* Very obvious, striking.    *congruent:* Similar, compatible.    *Protestant Reformation:* Protest led by Martin Luther, a religious leader in sixteenth century Germany, against the established Roman Catholic church.    *piety:* Devotion.

community. Gradually the notion of the priesthood of all believers came to mean that every man and woman had a calling to meaningful secular work.

10      In the feudal era manhood involved being the lord of a manor, the head of a household, or at least a husbandman of the land. As the industrial revolution progressed men were increasingly pulled out of the context of nature, family, church, and community to find the meaning of their lives in trading, industry, the arts, and the professions, while women practiced their vocations by ministering to the needs of the home and practicing charity within the community. Gradually, getting and spending assumed the place of greatest importance, virtually replacing all of the old activities that previously defined manhood— hunting, growing, tending, celebrating, protesting, investigating. As "the bottom line" became our ultimate concern, and the Dow Jones the index of reality, man's world shrank. Men no longer found their place beneath the dome of stars, within the brotherhood of animals, by the fire of the hearth, or in the company of citizens. Economic man spends his days with colleagues, fellow workers, bosses, employees, suppliers, lawyers, customers, and other strangers. At night he returns to an apartment or house that has been empty throughout the day. More likely than not, if he is married with children, his wife has also been away at work throughout the day and his children have been tended and educated by another cadre° of professionals. If he is successful his security (*securus*—"free from care") rests in his investments (from "vestment"—a religious garment) in stocks, bonds, and other commodities whose future value depends upon the whims of the market.

Nowadays only a fortunate minority are able to find harmony between vocation and occupation. Some artists, professionals, businessmen, and tradesmen find in their work a calling, a lifework, an arena within which they may express their creativity and care. But most men are shackled to the mercantile society in much the same way medieval serfs were imprisoned in the feudal system. All too often we work because we must, and we make the best of a bad job.

In the secular theology of economic man Work has replaced God as the source from whom all blessings flow. The escalating gross national product, or at least the rising Dow Jones index, is the outward and visible sign that we are progressing toward the kingdom of God; full employment is grace; unemployment is sin. The industrious, especially entrepreneurs with capital, are God's chosen people, but even laborers are sanctified because they participate in the productive economy.

As a form of secular piety Work now satisfies many of the functions once served by religion. In the words of Ayn Rand, whose popular philosophy

---

*cadre:* Staff, personnel.

romanticized capitalism and sanctified selfishness, "Your work is the process of achieving your values. Your body is a machine but your mind is its driver. Your work is the purpose of your life, and you must speed past any killer who assumes the right to stop you. . . . Any value you might find outside your work, any other loyalty or love, can only be travelers going on their own power in the same direction."

We don't work just to make a living. Increasingly, the world of work provides the meaning of our lives. It becomes an end in itself rather than a means. A decade ago, only twenty-eight percent of us enjoyed the work we did. And yet, according to a Yankelovich survey, eighty percent of us reported that we would go right on working even if we didn't need the money. By the 1980s this profile changed. We are just as attached to our work, but now we are demanding that the workplace provide an outlet for our creativity. Yankelovich reports in 1988 that fifty-two percent of Americans respond "I have an inner need to do the very best job I can, regardless of the pay" and sixty-one percent when asked what makes for the good life say "a job that is interesting."

Something very strange has happened to work and leisure in the last generation. The great promise of emerging technology was that it would finally set men free from slavery and we could flower. As late as the 1960s philosophers, such as Herbert Marcuse, sociologists, and futurists were predicting a coming leisure revolution. We were just around the corner from a twenty-hour work week. Soon we would be preoccupied by arts, games, and erotic dalliance on leisurely afternoons. At worst we would have to learn to cope with "pleasure anxiety" and the threat of leisure.

Exactly the opposite happened. Work is swallowing leisure. The fast lane has become a way of life for young professionals who are giving their all to career. In the 1990s Americans may come more and more to resemble the Japanese—workaholics all, living to work rather than working to live, finding their identity as members of corporate tribes. . . .

Part of the problem is that work, community, and family are getting mixed up and lumped together. Increasingly, Americans live in places where they are anonymous, and seek to find their community at work. Companies, with the help of organizational development consultants, are trying to make the workplace the new home, the new family. The new motto is: humanize the workplace, make it a community; let communication flourish on all levels. The best (or is it the worst?) of companies have become paternalistic° or maternalistic,° providing their employees with all the comforts and securities of home. . . .

In short, the workplace is rapidly becoming its own culture that defines who we are. Like minisocieties, professions and corporations create their own

15

---

*paternalistic:* Relating to a father, fatherly.    *maternalistic:* Relating to a mother, motherly.

ritual and mythology. Doctors share a common story, a history of disease and cure, a consensus about the means of healing with other doctors. Businessmen share the language of profit and loss with other businessmen and acknowledge the same tokens of success. As economic organizations have grown larger than governments, employees render them a type of loyalty previously reserved for God, country, or family.

To determine what happens to men within the economic world we need to look critically at its climate, its ruling mood, its ethos, its aims, and its method. We should no more accept a profession's or a corporation's self-evaluation, its idealistic view of itself (we are a family, a "service" organization, dedicated to the highest ideals of quality, etc.) than we would accept the propaganda of any tribe or nation.

20       A recent critical study of the climate of corporate culture suggests it may be more like a tyrannical° government than a kindly family. Earl Shorris, in a neglected and very important book, suggests that the modern corporation represents a historically new form of tyranny in which we are controlled by accepting the definitions of happiness that keep us in harness for a lifetime. Herewith, in short, his argument:

> The most insidious° of the many kinds of power is the power to define happiness. . . .
>
> The manager, like the nobleman of earlier times, serves as the exemplary merchant: since happiness cannot be defined, he approximates his definition through the display of symbols, such as expense account meals, an expensive house, stylish clothing, travel to desirable places, job security, interesting friends, membership in circles of powerful people, advantages for his children, and social position for his entire family. . . .
>
> In the modern world, a delusion° about work and happiness enables people not only to endure oppression but to seek it and to believe that they are happier because of the very work that oppresses them. At the heart of the delusion lies the manager's definition of happiness: sweat and dirty hands signify oppression and a coat and tie signify happiness, freedom, and a good life.
>
> Blue-collar workers . . . resist symbolic oppression. One need only visit an assembly line and observe the styles of dress, speech, and action of the workers to realize the symbolic freedom they enjoy. . . . They live where they please, socialize with whomever they please, and generally enjoy complete freedom outside the relatively few hours they spend at

---

*tyrannical:* Despotic, unjust, abusive of power.   *insidious:* Corrupting, deceiving.   *delusion:* False assumption, deception.

their jobs. . . . No matter how much money a blue-collar worker earns, he is considered poor; no matter how much he enjoys his work, he is thought to be suffering. In that way, blue-collar wages are kept low and blue-collar workers suffer the indignity° of low status.

The corporation or the bureaucracy . . . becomes a place, the cultural authority, the moral home of a man. The rules of the corporation become the rules of society, the future replaces history, and the organization becomes the family of the floating man. . . . By detaching him from the real world of place, the corporation becomes the world for him.

Men abandoned the power to define happiness for themselves, and having once abandoned that power, do not attempt to regain it. . . .

The new rhetoric about the workplace as home and family needs to be balanced by an honest evaluation of the more destructive implications of the iron law of profit. Home and family are ends in themselves. They are, or should be, about sharing of love to no purpose. They file no quarterly reports. Business is an activity organized to make a profit. And any activity is shaped by the end it seeks. Certainly business these days wears a velvet glove, comporting itself with a new facade of politeness and enlightened personnel policies, but beneath the glove is the iron fist of competition and warfare.

The recent spate of best-selling books about business that make use of military metaphors tell an important story about economic life and therefore about the climate within which most men spend their days. Listen to the metaphors, the poetry of business as set forth in David Rogers's *Waging Business Warfare* from the jacket copy:

Become a master of strategy on today's corporate killing fields—and win the war for success. . . . How to succeed in battle: believe it: if you're in business, you're at war. Your enemies—your competitors—intend to annihilate° you. Just keeping your company alive on the battlefield is going to be a struggle. Winning may be impossible—unless you're a master of military strategy. . . . You can be—if you'll follow the examples of the great tacticians of history. Because the same techniques that made Genghis Khan, Hannibal, and Napoleon the incomparable conquerors they were are still working for Chrysler's Lee Iacocca, Procter & Gamble's John Smale, Remington's Victor Kiam, and other super-strategists on today's corporate killing fields. . . . Join them at the command post! Mastermind the battle! Clobber the enemy! Win the war!

Or, maybe to succeed you need to know *The Leadership Secrets of Attila the Hun?* Or listen to the language of Wall Street: corporate raiders, hostile

---

*indignity:* Insult, humiliation.     *annihilate:* Destroy.

takeovers, white knights, wolf packs, industrial spies, the underground economy, head-hunting, shark-repellent, golden parachutes, poison pills, making a killing, etc.

When we organize our economic life around military metaphors and words such as *war, battle, strategy, tactics, struggle, contest, competition, winning, enemies, opponents, defenses, security, maneuver, objective, power, command, control, willpower, assault* we have gone a long way toward falling into a paranoid worldview. And when men live within a context where their major function is to do battle—economic or literal—they will be shaped by the logic of the warrior psyche.

## The High Price of Success

25      At the moment the world seems to be divided between those countries that are suffering from failed economies and those that are suffering from successful economies. After a half century of communism the USSR, Eastern Europe, and China are all looking to be saved from the results of stagnation by a change to market economies. Meanwhile, in the U.S., Germany, and Japan we are beginning to realize that our success has created an underclass of homeless and unemployed, and massive pollution of the environment. As the Dow rises to new heights everyone seems to have forgotten the one prophetic insight of Karl Marx: where the economy creates a class of winners it will also create a class of losers, where wealth gravitates easily into the hands of the haves, the fortunes of the have-nots become more desperate.

On the psychological level, the shadow of our success, the flip side of our affluence, is the increasing problem of stress and burnout. Lately, dealing with stress and burnout has become a growth industry. Corporations are losing many of their best men to the "disease" of stress. Every profession seems to have its crisis: physician burnout, teacher burnout, lawyer burnout. Experts in relaxation, nutrition, exercise, and mediation are doing a brisk business.

But finally, stress cannot be dealt with by psychological tricks, because for the most part it is a philosophical rather than a physiological problem, a matter of the wrong worldview. Perhaps the most common variety of stress can best be described as "rustout" rather than burnout. It is a product, not of an excess of fire but of a deficiency of passion. We, human beings, can survive so long as we "make a living," but we do not thrive without a sense of significance that we gain only by creating something we feel is of lasting value—a child, a better mousetrap, a computer, a space shuttle, a book, a farm. When we spend the majority of our time doing work that gives us a paycheck but no sense of meaning we inevitably get bored and depressed. When the requirements of our work do not match our creative potential we rust out. The second kind of burnout is really a type of combat fatigue that is the inevitable result of living for an extended period within an environment that is experienced as a battle zone. If the competition is always pressing you to produce more and faster, if life is a battle, if winning is the only thing, sooner or later you are going to come down with battle fatigue. Like combat veterans returning from Vietnam, businessmen who live for years within an atmosphere of low-intensity warfare begin to exhibit the personality traits of the warrior. They become disillusioned and numb to ethical issues, they think only of survival and grow insensitive to pain. You may relax, breathe deeply, take time for R and R, and remain a warrior. But ultimately the only cure for stress is to leave the battlefield.

The feminist revolution made us aware of how the economic order has discriminated against women, but not of how it cripples the male psyche. In ancient China the feet of upperclass women were broken, bent backwards, and bound to make them more "beautiful." Have the best and brightest men of our time had their souls broken and bent to make them "successful"?

Let's think about the relation between the wounds men suffer, our over-identification with work, and our captivity within the horizons of the economic myth.

Recently, a lament° has gone out through the land that men are becoming too tame, if not limp. The poet Robert Bly, who is as near as we have these days to a traveling bard and shaman for men, says we have raised a whole generation of soft men—oh-so-sensitive, but lacking in thunder and lightning. He tells men they must sever the ties with mother, stop looking at themselves through the eyes of women, and recover the "wild man" within themselves.

I suspect that if men lack the lusty pride of self-affirmation, if we say "yes" too often but without passion, if we are burned out without ever having been on fire, it is mostly because we have allowed ourselves to be engulfed by a metabody, a masculine womb—The Corporation. . . .

At what cost to the life of our body and spirit do we purchase corporate and professional success? What sacrifices are we required to make to these upstart economic gods?

Here are some of the secrets they didn't tell you at the Harvard Business School, some of the hidden, largely unconscious, tyrannical, unwritten rules that govern success in professional and corporate life:

*Cleanliness is next to prosperity.* Sweat is lower class, lower status. Those who shower before work and use deodorant make more than those who shower after work and smell human throughout the day. As a nation we are proud that only three percent of the population has to work on the land—get soiled, be earthy—to feed the other ninety-seven percent.

30

---

*lament:* Mourn, complaint.

*Look but don't touch.* The less contact you have with real stuff—raw material, fertilizer, wood, steel, chemicals, making things that have moving parts—the more money you will make. Lately, as we have lost our edge in manufacturing and production, we have comforted ourselves with the promise that we can prosper by specializing in service and information industries. Oh, so clean.

*Prefer abstractions.* The further you move up toward the catbird seat, the penthouse, the office with the view of all Manhattan, the more you live among abstractions. In the brave new world of the market you may speculate in hog futures without ever having seen a pig, buy out an airline without knowing how to fly a plane, grow wealthy without having produced anything.

*Specialize.* The modern economy rewards experts, men and women who are willing to become focused, concentrated, tightly bound, efficient. Or to put the matter more poignantly,° we succeed in our professions to the degree that we sacrifice wide-ranging curiosity and fascination with the world at large, and become departmental in our thinking. The professions, like medieval castles, are small kingdoms sealed off from the outer world by walls of jargon. Once initiated by the ritual of graduate school, MBAs, economists, lawyers, and physicians speak only to themselves and theologians speak only to God.

*Sit still and stay indoors.* The world is run largely by urban, sedentary° males. The symbol of power is the chair. The chairman of the board sits and manages. As a general rule those who stay indoors and move the least make the most money. Muscle doesn't pay. Worse yet, anybody who has to work in the sun and rain is likely to make the minimum wage. With the exception of quarterbacks, boxers, and race car drivers, whose bodies are broken for our entertainment, men don't get ahead by moving their bodies.

*Live by the clock.* Ignore your intimate body time, body rhythms, and conform to the demands of corporate time, work time, professional time. When "time is money," we bend our bodies and minds to the demands of EST (economic standard time). We interrupt our dreams when the alarm rings, report to work at nine, eat when the clock strikes twelve, return to our private lives at five, and retire at sixty-five—ready or not. As a reward we are allowed weekends and holidays for recreation. Conformity to the sacred routine, showing up on time, is more important than creativity.

---

*poignantly:* Piercingly, to the point.    *sedentary:* Inactive, stagnant.

Instead of "taking our time" we respond to deadlines. Most successful men, and lately women, become Type A personalities, speed freaks, addicted to the rush of adrenaline, filled with a sense of urgency, hard driven, goal oriented, and stressed out. The most brutal example of this rule is the hundred-hour week required of physicians in their year of residency. This hazing ritual, like circumcision, drives home the deep mythic message that your body is no longer your own.

*Wear the uniform.* It wouldn't be so bad if those who earned success and power were proud enough in their manhood to peacock their colors. But no. Success makes drab. The higher you rise in the establishment the more colorless you become, the more you dress like an undertaker or a priest. Bankers, politicians, CEOs wear black, gray, or dark blue, with maybe a bold pinstripe or a daring "power tie." And the necktie? That ultimate symbol of the respectable man has obviously been demonically designed to exile the head from the body and restrain all deep and passionate breath. The more a corporation, institution, or profession requires the sacrifice of the individuality of its members, the more it requires uniform wear. The corp isn't really looking for a few good men. It's looking for a few dedicated Marines, and it knows exactly how to transform boys into uniform men. As monks and military men have known for centuries, once you get into the habit you follow the orders of the superior.

*Keep your distance, stay in your place.* The hierarchy of power and prestige that governs every profession and corporation establishes the proper distance between people. There are people above you, people below you, and people on your level, and you don't get too close to any of them. Nobody hugs the boss. What is lacking is friendship. I know of no more radical critique of economic life than the observation by Earl Shorris that nowhere in the vast literature of management is there a single chapter on friendship.

*Desensitize yourself.* Touch, taste, smell—the realm of the senses—receive little homage.° What pays off is reason, will-power, planning, discipline, control. There has, of course, recently been a move afoot to bring in potted plants and tasteful art to make corporate environments more humane. But the point of these exercises in aesthetics, like the development of communication skills by practitioners of organizational development, is to increase production. The bottom line is still profit, not pleasure or persons.

---

*homage:* Respect.

*Don't trouble yourself with large moral issues.* The more the world is governed by experts, specialists, and professionals, the less anybody takes responsibility for the most troubling consequences of our success-failure. Television producers crank out endless cop and killing tales, but refuse to consider their contribution to the climate of violence. Lawyers concern themselves with what is legal, not what is just. Physicians devote themselves to kidneys or hearts of individual patients while the health delivery system leaves masses without medicine. Physicists invent new generations of genocidal weapons which they place in the eager arms of the military. The military hands the responsibility for their use over to politicians. Politicians plead that they have no choice—the enemy makes them do it. Professors publish esoterica° while students perish from poor teaching. Foresters, in cahoots with timber companies, clear-cut or manage the forest for sustained yield, but nobody is in charge of oxygen regeneration. Psychologists heal psyches while communities fall apart. Codes of professional ethics are for the most part, like corporate advertisements, high sounding but self-serving.

When we live within the horizons of the economic myth, we begin to consider it honorable for a man to do whatever he must to make a living. Gradually we adopt what Erich Fromm called "a marketing orientation" toward our selves. We put aside our dreams, forget the green promise of our young selves, and begin to tailor our personalities to what the market requires. When we mold ourselves into commodities, practice smiling and charm so we will have "winning personalities," learn to sell ourselves, and practice the silly art of power dressing, we are certain to be haunted by a sense of emptiness.

35    Men, in our culture, have carried a special burden of unconsciousness, of ignorance of the self. The unexamined life has been worth quite a lot in economic terms. It has enabled us to increase the gross national product yearly. It may not be necessary to be a compulsive extrovert to be financially successful, but it helps. Especially for men, ours is an outer-directed culture that rewards us for remaining strangers to ourselves, unacquainted with feeling, intuition, or the subtleties of sensation and dreams.

Many of the personality characteristics that have traditionally been considered "masculine"—aggression, rationality—are not innate or biological components of maleness but are products of a historical era in which men have been socially assigned the chief roles in warfare and the economic order. As women increasingly enter the quasimilitary° world of the economic system they are likely to find themselves governed by the logic of the system. Some

---

*esoterica:* Knowledge limited to a small circle or group.    *quasimilitary:* Militaristic in some sense or to some degree.

feminists, who harbor a secret belief in the innate moral superiority of women, believe that women will change the rules of business and bring the balm° of communication and human kindness into the boardroom. To date this has been a vain hope. Women executives have proven themselves the equal of men in every way—including callousness. The difference between the sexes is being eroded as both sexes become defined by work. It is often said that the public world of work is a man's place and that as women enter it they will become increasingly "masculine" and lose their "femininity." To think this way is to miss the most important factor of the economic world. Economic man, the creature who defines itself within the horizons of work and consumption, is not man in any full sense of the word, but a being who has been neutralized, degendered, rendered subservient to the laws of the market. The danger of economics is not that it turns women into men but that it destroys the fullness of both manhood and womanhood.

## QUESTIONS

1. What is the female counterpart to the male experience Keen describes in the first paragraph of this selection?
2. Keen asserts that young boys are taught to compete in sports to learn the "ritual form of combat that is central to the male identity" and that is the dominant attitude in the workplace. What other things besides sports teach young boys competition? Do young girls receive similar conditioning? What do the activities that they are expected to participate in teach them?
3. Keen believes that the bank has replaced the church as the central focus of modern society; explain whether you agree or disagree. If Keen is correct, what does this shift in focus reveal about the interests of our society?
4. Keen explains that corporations are now given a "type of loyalty previously reserved for God, country, or family." What do the four institutions—corporations, religious organizations, country, and family—have in common?
5. In paragraph 21, Keen uses "velvet" and "iron" metaphorically. Explain how he creates balance using these contrasting metaphors and discuss whether or not the metaphors are clichés.
6. Keen paraphrases what he calls the "prophetic insight" of Karl Marx, the founder of Communism: "where the economy creates a class of winners it will also create a class of losers, where wealth gravitates

---

*balm:* Ointment—anything soothing or healing.

easily into the hands of the haves, the fortunes of the have-nots become more desperate." Do you agree with this view?

7. In paragraph 28, Keen asks, "Have the best and brightest men of our time had their souls broken and bent to make them 'successful'?" What are Keen's assumptions about these "successful" men?

8. Keen provides a list of ten "unwritten rules" that govern success in professional and corporate life. Offer some examples that illustrate or contradict Keen's rules.

### CONNECTIONS

1. Trace the similarities and differences between Keen's essay and the selection by Warren Farrell (included in Section 2).

2. Discuss the relationship between Robert Hayden's poem "Those Winter Sundays" (Section 1) and Keen's ideas about work.

3. Do any of the people interviewed in Bruce Weber's essay "The Unromantic Generation" (Section 3) appear to share Keen's views about work? Do the lifestyles of any of these people provide examples to support Keen's ideas?

# ∽ One Tree by the River

*Jeff Sawicki*

Jeff Sawicki was born in Naugatuck, Connecticut, and attended a Catholic school until the sixth grade, when he transferred to the public school system. After moving to California, he attended Foothill Junior College for two years and then enrolled in San Jose State University. He has coached football at the high school, junior college, and college level (including one year as an assistant coach at San Jose State). Along the way, he has also worked in a golf course pro shop and as an assistant superintendent at a country club, a truck driver, a health club instructor, a bartender, and a restaurant manager. He hopes to major in history and to earn a master's degree in physical education while continuing to coach football.

**WARM-UP:** Many people complain about today's white-collar jobs, which often require people to sit behind a desk, typing on a keyboard, for most of the day. Do you feel that workers were better off in earlier times, when labor was a more physical activity? Explain your answer.

I grew up in southern Connecticut in a small town of about 25,000 people.    1
The town sits nestled in the Naugatuck Valley, and, not surprisingly, it is called Naugatuck; I was once told in grammar school that the name means "One Tree by the River" in Algonquin, the language of the original Indian inhabitants. The nearest city was called Mattatuck, or "Two Trees by the River," but for the last two hundred years it's been named Waterbury, and somewhere through the intervening couple of centuries a few million trees managed to sprout along the river which runs beside, through, and (at least it did until the dam was built forty years ago) occasionally over both Waterbury and Naugatuck.

The Naugatuck of my youth was a typical blue-collar immigrant shop town of a kind which can be found all over New England. We had the Uniroyal Rubber Factory (where both the dreaded Chuck Taylor canvass-style basketball shoe and Naugahyde were developed), the chemical plant, where my grandfather worked away his life, finally contracting and dying of lung cancer (he is now buried across the river in sight of the plant, and in easy reach of the rotten-egg stench it emits on a seemingly regularly scheduled basis), and the Eastern Company Foundry, where my mother held her first job as a secretary, and by which I would walk every morning on my way to St. Hedwigs Catholic Grammar School.

Before I left, the older parts of town still had a faint feel of what it must have been like at the turn of the century, when a great flood of immigrants entered the Naugatuck Valley to find work in the factories, which, until recently, still lined the river's bank. My great grandparents came then, and lived in Union City's Polish neighborhood until the flood of '55 forced them to move further up Spring Street, into Naugatuck proper.

Each school day my sister Kari and I would be dropped off at my grandmother's house while my mother went to work at Waterbury Hospital. Kari and I would leave the house at 7:00 a.m. every morning, walk past the foundry, across the footbridge which spans the river just below the big bridge, then up the hill through Union City to school. And every morning without fail I would linger near that massive, drab, brown brick foundry, peeking inside through the same cracked window pane; I had to look through the cracks because the glass was no longer remotely transparent, but rather a solid piece of grime molded into the surrounding brick-work. When I looked inside I would see fifteen or twenty half-naked men, drenched with sweat and covered with dust, constantly shifting huge piles of sand by hand. They always looked hollow-eyed and weary, reminiscent of the pictures of Welsh coal miners I have seen in my youth. I remember always being afraid they would see me spying on them through the cracked glass, although I didn't really know why. Maybe it was because I was looking at something no child should ever see, the potentiality of a life spent working in a dark, dingy, hell-hot furnace without any hope of a break. The lives of these men I saw would surely be a forlorn° hope in the eyes of most people I know, but I see something noble in men who suffer through agonizing labor to feed their families and educate their children, so those children in turn will not have to shift sand piles in Hell to survive.

5      When I was thirteen, my mother sold the house I grew up in, and we moved across town to an apartment by the Hop Brook Golf Course. This was no country club, but a true blue-collar links with rocks in the fairway, brown grass on the "greens," and green grass in the sand traps. Like any such course, it had its share of characters, all of whom knew each other from the day they were born to the day they died.

Every day after school I would go to work in the tiny white-washed cinder block pro shop, and every day one or another of these men would come in and the same conversation would occur: "What's your name?" one of them would ask. "Jeff Sawicki," I would reply. "Pollock, huh?" "Yep!" Then I would ask his name. "Stanley Jacobowski." "Pollock, huh?" "Yep," would be his reply. "Saw-

---

*forlorn:* Abandoned, forsaken.

icki, you Bob's son and Ann Marie Witkoski's kid?" "Yep." "I knew your family way back."

Most of the new men back then worked in the foundries or at the chemical plant, regardless of where they came from; their sons followed them in when they were old enough, all working side by side, whether Pole, German, Italian, or, after the war, Black, together developing one identity. These sons are the men I knew growing up, they are the survivors, now in their seventies or eighties, who would tell me stories of how their fingers, hands, and backs had been ruined by their labor. Always they spoke to me, with pride, of their children, or grandchildren, who had gone on to college and "real" lives.

On the town green, next to the statue of the Civil War Federal, stands a somber gray granite block, much like a tombstone, on which are inscribed the names of some one hundred fifty or so Naugatuck men: names like Jacobowski, Wojack, Wozniak, Pascale, and Rodriguez, men who left the factories where they were killing themselves slowly, in hope of better lives for their children, only to be killed in a far quicker and less painless manner in some far-off place. This they did not only for their children, but for all of us.

My hometown is full of the children of those men, and it's nice to see those children, the people I call my friends, in their success; but in that success, and in the process of moving and becoming educated which led to it, many of them seem to have lost much of the moral ethic and élan° of their fathers and grandfathers. I do not pretend to understand why, but it seems for them the only thing worth working for is the latest BMW model. I much prefer the old folks back home; they still take a man at his word and his family's name means more than the type of car he drives.

My divorced mother working twelve hours a day to support two children, my grandfather working and dying in the chemical plant, those men I watched every day on my way to school, and those same men, ten years later and a hundred years older, that I talked to daily at Hop Brook taught me the value of hard work and sacrifice for the family and friends which I hold dear. They also taught me to judge a man by who he is and how he acts, not by where he's from, or what color he is.

It's interesting for me to note again the Indian name of the town, "One Tree by the River," and wonder if I am the only one to realize its symbolic significance: *We the People* of the town have truly become one, growing and spreading from the river's bank, each carrying the values instilled in us by our parents and those surrounding us.

I often wonder how much the men listed on the war memorial would have liked to see the river one last time.

---

*élan:* Spirit, vigor.

**QUESTIONS**

1. Explain Sawicki's attitude toward blue-collar work, as expressed in this essay. Point to specific lines in the essay that support your answer.
2. What is this essay's thesis? Is it clearly stated?
3. Does Sawicki use any clichés, euphemisms, or jargon in this essay? If you feel that he does, support your answer with specific examples.
4. Does this essay contain effective use of details? Point to specific parts of the essay to support your answer.
5. How would you characterize the author's voice in this essay?
6. Are the introduction and the conclusion of this essay effective? Would you have changed them in any way to improve them? Does Sawicki use the "full circle" effect?
7. Have you ever held a job that required physical labor? How did you feel about it? Did you learn to value such work? to resent it? both?
8. Do you agree with Sawicki that most people used to have a better work ethic and more spirit of self-sacrifice than they do today? On what do you base your beliefs about this subject?

**CONNECTIONS**

1. According to Sam Keen in the selection that precedes this essay, what grade would the workers described in this essay earn on the "manhood test"? Why?
2. Compare and contrast this essay with any of the other student essays included in this text, focusing on the stylistic concerns discussed so far: appropriate choice of words, use of details, use of figures of speech, avoidance of clichés and jargon.

# The Victimization of Women: Economic Realities

*Michael Parenti*

Michael Parenti was born in 1933 and earned a Ph.D. from Yale University in 1962. He has taught social science and political science at several colleges and universities, including Howard University, the University of Canterbury in New Zealand, and California State University—Northridge. A regular lecturer on radio and television programs, Parenti has written many books, including *Democracy for the Few* (1977), *Inventing Reality: The Politics of News Media* (1986), *The Sword and the Dollar: Imperialism, Revolution, and the Arms Race* (1989), and *Land of Idols: Political Mythology in America* (1994), from which the following selection is taken. Another selection from *Land of Idols* appears in the last section of this text.

**WARM-UP:** Create a list of jobs, duties, and tasks that people perform but for which they are not compensated monetarily. Mark which items on the list are usually designated for males and which for females. Also, mark which tasks are generally performed by people of the lower class, middle class, and upper class.

It is not men in toto° who are the oppressors of women, but "men in partic-  1
ular roles."[1] The mode of gender oppression often varies according to class and race, resulting in dramatic differences in the destinies of women. Bourgeois° feminist consciousness is both class bound and indifferent—or overtly° hostile—to the recognition of class differences and class conflict. The same Abigail Adams, who forthrightly argued woman's cause, expressed undiluted hostility toward the farmers of western Massachusetts who, facing ruinous taxes, foreclosures, and the prospect of debtors prison, took up arms in 1787. In a letter to Thomas Jefferson, she denounced Shay's Rebellion:° "Ignorant, restless desperados, without conscience or principles, have led a deluded° multitude to follow their standard, under pretense of grievances which have no existence but in their imaginations. Some of them were crying out for a paper currency, some for an equal distribution of property." Abigail Adams

---

*in toto:* Latin, meaning "on the whole"; totally, entirely.   *Bourgeois:* Here meaning "middle-class."
*overtly:* Openly, frankly.   *Shay's Rebellion:* (1786–87) Daniel Shay, a destitute farmer, led 1,200 debt-ridden farmers in western Massachusetts in protest marches against the government after it adjourned before taking action to halt farm foreclosures; troops were brought in to suppress the protests.
*deluded:* Misled, deceived.

called for the "most vigorous measures to quell° and suppress" economically oppressed women and men, these "mobbish insurgents" who dared to rebel against her class.[2]

Similarly, the French novelist George Sand, who defied nineteenth-century conventions by wearing men's clothes and demanding equality for women, denounced the revolutionary women and men of the Paris Commune who fought against the class privileges she herself enjoyed: "The mob . . . is composed in part of dupes and fools, in part of the most degraded and criminal elements of the population. . . . nothing but a lot of coarse clowns."[3] When push came to shove, the otherwise iconoclastic° Sand showed her bourgeois colors and class bigotry, demonstrating once again that wearing pants is no guarantee of wisdom or fairness.

In 1908, the labor militant Clara Zetkin sharply criticized "a great and very influential portion of the English Women's Righters" who opposed the "legal protection of female labor."[4] Anne Sullivan, teacher of Helen Keller, repeatedly tangled with Boston Brahmin° women, who advocated female suffrage° and abolitionism, yet treated their Irish servant girls like dirt.[5]

Through the nineteenth century in most states of the Union, women could not hold office or vote. They could not sit on juries. They were barred from medical schools, law schools, and postgraduate training either by law or custom. They did not have legal custody of their own children, or legal ownership of their own earnings, or of any property or inheritance acquired before or during marriage; these became the husband's property.[6]

5    Whatever else may be said of their lives, today affluent and professionally employed females are saved from many of the worst abuses inflicted upon working-class women (and men). Low-income females are far more heavily burdened by toil, drudgery, want, and illness. They enjoy far fewer opportunities for advanced education, leisure, travel, creative work, career advancement, and financial independence, and have less access to good maternal and medical services and child-care. As one class-conscious feminist puts it, "Working-class life is demeaning, not because its culture or values are inferior, but because of the lack of money, lack of opportunity, lack of job responsibility, lack of respect, lack of power—i.e., because of oppressive treatment of the working class by the higher classes."[7]

For many low-income Caucasian, African-American, and Latino women, work does not offer the self-development of a professional career.[8] One in four women workers of color are employed as domestics. Among their stingiest employers are the professional women who hire them in order to free themselves for career pursuits. One study showed that professional women

---

*quell:* To overpower, suppress.   *iconoclastic:* Challenging established beliefs or institutions.   *Brahmin:* Here meaning "upper-class."   *suffrage:* The right to vote.

regularly denied their domestic help the benefits they took for granted for themselves, such as paid holidays, paid sick leave, and regular raises. Only about half of them contributed to Social Security for their employees.[9] The study said nothing about affluent *male* professionals, who doubtless are no better employers than their female counterparts.

Mostly because of hard times, from 1970 to 1990 the number of women who have more than one job has increased almost 500 percent, from 636,000 to 3.1 million.[10] The mistreatment of women knows no class boundaries but is more pernicious° among economically deprived groups, as oppressive class conditions and gender mistreatment reinforce each other—even within the labor movement itself.[11] The double oppression of class and gender becomes a triple oppression when we include the racism that low-income women of color encounter. One statistic might suffice: premature death among Black females is nearly five times higher than for White females.[12]

The superexploitation faced by working women is a long-standing one, highlighted in a government report released in 1911:

> The low wages at which women will work form the chief reason for employing them at all. . . . A woman's cheapness is, so to speak, her greatest economic asset. She can be used to keep down the cost of production where she is regularly employed. . . . [S]he can be introduced as a strike breaker to take the place of men seeking higher wages, or the threat of introducing her may be used to avert such a strike. But the moment she organizes a union and seeks by organization to secure better wages she diminishes or destroys what is to the employer her chief value.[13]

Nowadays, women are less likely to be used as strikebreakers but their job marketability still rests on their relatively low wage demands. In 1992, women earned seventy-five cents for every dollar earned by men, up from sixty cents in previous years. This jump did not reflect any gain in women's wages, but losses in men's earnings because of the 1990–92 recession and the downgrading of higher paid male occupations.

The conditions of women varies greatly from country to country. In North America and Europe, almost all females attend secondary school. In Pakistan, only 17 percent are enrolled in school.[14] In Iran, women are denied an advanced education. Important government posts are closed to them. An Iranian male can divorce his wife at any time without informing her but she has no such option. "If women were given the right to divorce their husbands," according to the head of the Islamic Republic's Supreme Court, "being emotional by nature, they could make irrational decisions. This does not apply to

10

*pernicious:* Highly injurious.

men."[15] Iranian president Hashemi Rafsanjani concurred: "Men are stronger and more capable in all fields. Men's brains are larger."[16] Here is yet another head of state who cannot tell the difference between his brain and his ego.

Though woman's lot may differ from country to country, common patterns persist. In all countries, females are disproportionately concentrated in the lowest paying employments and greatly underrepresented in the more desirable positions. Across the globe, women grow approximately half the world's food, but own almost none of the land. In every country, be it Bangladesh or the United States, women take primary responsibility for child-rearing and other life-maintenance chores, unpaid labor that is essential for social production and biological reproduction. In every country, women with dependent children who lack spousal support are among the very poorest.[17]

To conclude, however, that men as a "class" exploit women as a "class" is to ignore class reality. Throughout the world, most men also suffer from the economic oppressions of capitalism and imperialism. Since they compose two-thirds of the work force, they make up most of the impoverished workers. And relatively few of the men who grow the other half of the world's food own any land. To some degree, men's desperate economic situation increases their abuse of women. True, abuse knows no class boundaries, but it occurs with greater frequency among unemployed or poor males taking out their frustrations by getting drunk and neglecting or abusing their female partners and children.[18] Class oppression fosters sexual oppression. Here again, low-income women have it the worst.

It should be evident by now that economic factors underlie much (but not all) of women's oppression. Yet some writers claim that poverty is essentially gender-based, noting that White women in the United States earn less than Black men.[19] Are we to conclude from this that White women are more economically oppressed than Black men? The data on income takes into account only persons with jobs and does not factor in unemployment, which is far worse for African-American males than for White or even Black females —being as high as 60 and 70 percent in inner-city neighborhoods. By every other indicator, be it high-school dropout rates, college attendance, homelessness, suicide, drug addiction, incarceration° rates, and death rates, African-American males do not fare as well as White females.[20]

Poverty is a class condition not fundamentally determined by gender or race—although both gender and race are major contributing factors. The economic vulnerability of women is brought home, literally, by the no-fault divorce laws. Intended to treat the sexes as equal before the law, no-fault divorce has had a disastrous effect on women and children. The new laws

---

*incarceration:* Imprisonment, confinement.

assume that women, including ones who have spent most of their lives as housewives and mothers, are independent and employable rather than dependent. The result is that only one in six divorced women are awarded any alimony, and only 13 percent of women with preschool children are granted child support. A year after divorce, men experience a 43 percent increase in their standard of living, while women suffer a 73 percent decline in theirs. Estimates of noncompliance° on child support range from 60 to 80 percent.[21] As a result, more than half the families headed by single mothers are low-income and most of the poor are children. With one of every five children in this country living in severely deprived conditions, there is an "infantilization" of poverty.[22] Much of this stems from a policy that pursues an abstract "gender equality," without making adequate allowance for economic realities, specifically the limited job marketability of females who have been long-term "homemakers." To highlight the economic factors that are interlaced with women's oppression is not to dismiss such oppression but to explain something about its virulence.°

1. Juliet Mitchell, *Women's Estate* (New York: Vintage, 1973), p. 163.
2. Abigail Adams to Thomas Jefferson, January 29, 1787: J. P. Boyd (ed.), *The Papers of Thomas Jefferson* (Princeton: Princeton University Press, 1955), pp. 86–87.
3. André Maurois, *Lelia, The Life of George Sand* (New York: Penguin, 1977, originally published 1953), p. 549. Referring passingly to the mass executions of the revolutionaries, Sand was concerned that the *wrong* people might be shot: "There have been a number of summary shootings. A great many innocent, or only half-guilty, persons are going to pay with their lives for the genuinely guilty, who will get off scot-free." Referring to Victor Hugo, who supported the communards, she writes, "Hugo seems really to have a screw loose. He has published a deal of wild nonsense": ibid., p. 550.
4. Meredith Tax, *The Rising of the Women* (New York: Monthly Review Press, 1980), p. 189.
5. Joseph Lash, *Helen and Teacher* (New York: Delacorte Press, Seymour Lawrence, 1980).
6. Kraditor, *The Ideas of the Woman Suffrage Movement*, p. 4; Barbara Ehrenreich and Deirdre English, *Witches, Midwives, and Nurses* (Old Westbury, NY: The Feminist Press, 1973).
7. Mary McKenney, "Class Attitudes and Professionalism," *Quest*, 3, Spring 1977, p. 54.
8. As one working-class female puts it: "I don't want to do the dirty, shitty job that [my husband) does. I'd rather stay here at home and have to struggle to make ends meet [and] take care of the kids": quoted in Bev Fisher, "Race and Class: Beyond Personal Politics," *Quest*, 3, Spring 1977, p. 10. On the class and racial limitations of the women's movement, see Angela Davis, *Women, Race & Class* (New York, Random House, 1981); bell hooks, *Feminist Theory, From Margin to Center* (Boston: South End Press, 1984).
9. The study by Doris McLaughlin, reported in *Time*, May 6, 1974, p. 81. On statistics regarding minority employment as domestics, see *1975 Handbook of Women Workers,*

*noncompliance:* Unwillingness to accept or conform.     *virulence:* Bitterness, malignancy.

U.S. Department of Labor, Employment Standards Administration, Women's Bureau, Bulletin 297 (Washington, DC: Government Printing Office), p. 106. In 1993, President Clinton's first nominee for U.S. Attorney General, Zoe Baird, was revealed to have hired illegal aliens as domestics and paid them below minimum wages and no benefits. She withdrew her name from nomination: *New York Times,* January 19, 1993.

10. *New York Times,* February 15, 1990.

11. On the struggles of working women, see Domitila Barrios de Chungara (with Moema Viezzer), *Let Me Speak! Testimony of Domitila, a Woman of the Bolivian Mines* (New York: Monthly Review Press, 1978); Heleieth Saffioti, *Women in Class Society* (New York: Monthly Review Press, 1978); Rosalyn Boxandall, Linda Gordon, Susan Reveryby (eds.), *America's Working Women* (New York: Random House, 1976); Nancy Seifer, *Nobody Speaks for Me!* (New York: Simon and Schuster, 1976); Haleh Afshar (ed.) *Women, Work, and Ideology in the Third World* (London: Tavistock Publications, 1985). On the struggles of women against sexism in the labor movement, see Tax, *The Rising of the Women.*

12. Davis, *Women, Race & Class;* Gloria Hull (ed.), *And Some of Us Are Brave* (New York: Feminist Press, 1982); Cherrie Moraga (ed.), *This Bridge Called Our Backs, Writings by Radical Women of Color* (Watertown, MA: Persephone Press, 1981). On premature deaths, see *Seattle Post-Intelligencer,* November 28, 1992.

13. John Andrews and W. D. P. Bliss, *History of Women in Trade Unions,* vol. 10, Bureau of Labor (Washington, DC: Government Printing Office, 1911), cited in Tax, *The Rising of the Women,* p. 92.

14. *Washington Post,* June 27, 1988. Education is no guarantee of equality. Japanese women are among the most educated females in the world, yet their primary role remains that of housewife and mother. Their husbands often address them as *gusai* ("dumb wife"), and the term "woman's wisdom" means shallow thinking. Making up 40 percent of Japan's work force, women are mostly in the lower-paid, dead-end jobs. Generally they earn half of what men make. Margaret Shapiro, "In Japan, the Son Still Rises," *Washington Post,* February 10, 1988.

15. Bahman Azad, "Iranian Women's Continuing Struggle," *People's Weekly World,* April 4, 1992.

16. *Washington Post,* December 15, 1991. More extreme examples of the mistreatment of women around the world are in the last section of this chapter.

17. *Washington Post,* June 27, 1988.

18. Mary Merva and Richard Fowles, *Effect of Diminished Economic Opportunity on Social Stress* (Washington, DC: Economic Policy Institute, 1992).

19. For instance, Catharine MacKinnon, "From Practice to Theory, or What is a White Woman Anyway," *Yale Journal of Law and Feminism,* 4, Fall 1991, p. 19.

20. *Washington Post,* January 18, 1990 and April 17, 1991; *Seattle Post-Intelligencer,* November 28, 1992; also the study of the American Council on Education, April 1989 on African-American college attendance.

21. Lenore Weitzman, *The Divorce Revolution* (New York: The Free Press, 1985).

22. Report by the Children's Defense Fund, summarized in *Oakland Tribune,* December 18, 1992.

## QUESTIONS

1. According to Parenti, how does "the mode of gender oppression" vary according to class and race?

2. What evidence does Parenti provide to show that upper-class women often oppress (or are indifferent to the struggles of) middle- or lower-class women? Is that evidence compelling?

3. What examples does Parenti provide to demonstrate his claim that "today affluent and professionally employed women are saved from many of the worst abuses inflicted upon working-class women (and men)"?

4. According to Parenti, what is the social reality of a woman's "job marketability"?

5. According to Parenti, does abuse exist in middle- and upper-class families? How does it differ from that found in lower-class families? Are the main causes of abuse economic?

6. Parenti dismisses the statistic that shows white women in the United States earning less than Black men; he adds the factor of unemployment and other indicators that compare the situation of *all* white women to that of *all* Black men. Does this render the first statistic irrelevant?

7. Who tends to benefit and who tends to suffer, economically, from divorce? Why?

8. Were you surprised by the figures Parenti presents on alimony and child support rates? Why or why not?

9. Talk to some women who are in the workforce. Do most of them feel that economically they are worse off than men?

## CONNECTIONS

1. How would Parenti respond to the points raised in the final paragraph of Sam Keen's essay?

2. Discuss the female character in Kate Chopin's "The Story of an Hour" (Section 2) in relation to Parenti's claims about gender, class, and work.

3. How does Toni Morrison's essay "Cinderella's Stepsisters" (Section 2) relate to the issues discussed in this selection from Parenti's book?

4. Reread the introduction to Warren Farrell's "Men as Success Objects" (Section 2). Does Parenti's examination of divorce support or contradict Farrell's views on this topic? Explain your response.

# ～ Larry Ross

## *Studs Terkel*

Studs Terkel was born in Chicago in 1912; he graduated from the University of Chicago in 1932 and from the University of Chicago Law School in 1934. Terkel has worked as a disk jockey, a radio commentator, and a TV emcee, among other occupations, but he is best known for his writing and for his collections of interviews, or oral histories, including *Hard Times: An Oral History of the Great Depression* (1970), *Talking to Self* (1977), *American Dreams: Lost and Found* (1980), *The Good War* (1984), *Race* (1992), and *Coming of Age* (1995). The following selection, "Larry Ross," first appeared in a collection of interviews entitled *Working* (1985).

**WARM-UP:** Write a paragraph that compares a particular workplace to something else.

1      The corporation is a jungle. It's exciting. You're thrown in on your own and you're constantly battling to survive. When you learn to survive, the game is to become the conqueror, the leader.

*"I've been called a business consultant. Some say I'm a business psychiatrist. You can describe me as an advisor to top management in a corporation." He's been at it since 1968.*

I started in the corporate world, oh gosh—'42. After kicking around in the Depression, having all kinds of jobs and no formal education, I wasn't equipped to become an engineer, a lawyer, or a doctor. I gravitated to selling. Now they call it marketing. I grew up in various corporations. I became the executive vice president of a large corporation and then of an even larger one. Before I quit I became president and chief executive officer of another. All nationally known companies.

Sixty-eight, we sold out our corporation. There was enough money in the transaction where I didn't have to go back in business. I decided that I wasn't going to get involved in the corporate battle any more. It lost its excitement, its appeal. People often ask me, "Why weren't you in your own business? You'd probably have made a lot of money." I often ask it myself, I can't explain it, except ...

Most corporations I've been in, they were on the New York Stock Exchange with thousands and thousands of stockholders. The last one—whereas, I was the president and chief executive, I was always subject to the board of directors, who had pressure from the stockholders. I owned a portion of the business, but I wasn't in control. I don't know of any situation in the corporate world where an executive is completely free and sure of his job from moment to moment.

Corporations always have to be right. That's their face to the public. When things go bad, they have to protect themselves and fire somebody. "We had nothing to do with it. We had an executive that just screwed everything up." He's never really ever been his own boss.

The danger starts as soon as you become a district manager. You have men working for you and you have a boss above. You're caught in a squeeze. The squeeze progresses from station to station. I'll tell you what a squeeze is. You have the guys working for you that are shooting for your job. The guy you're working for is scared stiff you're gonna shove him out of his job. Everybody goes around and says, "The test of the true executive is that you have men working for you that can replace you, so you can move up." That's a lot of boloney. The manager is afraid of the bright young guy coming up.

Fear is always prevalent in the corporate structure. Even if you're a top man, even if you're hard, even if you do your job—by the slight flick of a finger, your boss can fire you. There's always the insecurity. You bungle a job. You're fearful of losing a big customer. You're fearful so many things will appear on your record, stand against you. You're always fearful of the big mistake. You've got to be careful when you go to corporation parties. Your wife, your children have to behave properly. You've got to fit in the mold. You've got to be on guard.

When I was president of this big corporation, we lived in a small Ohio town, where the main plant was located. The corporation specified who you could socialize with, and on what level. (His wife interjects: "Who were the wives you could play bridge with.") The president's wife could do what she wants, as long as it's with dignity and grace. In a small town they didn't have to keep check on you. Everybody knew. There are certain sets of rules.

Not every corporation has that. The older the corporation, the longer it's been in a powerful position, the more rigid, the more conservative they are in their approach. Your swinging corporations are generally the new ones, the upstarts, the nouveau riche.° But as they get older, like duPont, General Motors, General Electric, they became more rigid. I'd compare them to the old, old rich—the Rockefellers and the Mellons—that train their children how to handle money, how to conserve their money, and how to grow with their money. That's what happened to the older corporations. It's only when they get in trouble that they'll have a young upstart of a president come in and try to shake things up.

nouveau riche: French, meaning a person newly rich and eager to show off their new wealth.

The executive is a lonely animal in the jungle who doesn't have a friend. Business is related to life. I think in our everyday living we're lonely. I have only a wife to talk to, but beyond that . . . When I talked business to her, I don't know whether she understood me. But that was unimportant. What's important is that I was able to talk out loud and hear myself—which is the function I serve as a consultant.

10     The executive who calls me usually knows the answer to his problem. He just has to have somebody to talk to and hear his decision out loud. If it sounds good when he speaks it out loud, then it's pretty good. As he's talking, he may suddenly realize his errors and he corrects them out loud. That's a great benefit wives provide for executives. She's listening and you know she's on your side. She's not gonna hurt you.

Gossip and rumor are always prevalent in a corporation. There's absolutely no secrets. I have always felt every office was wired. You come out of the board meeting and people in the office already know what's happened. I've tried many times to track down a rumor, but never could. I think people have been there so many years and have developed an ability to read reactions. From these reactions they make a good, educated guess. Gossip actually develops into fact.

It used to be a ploy for many minor executives to gain some information. "I heard that the district manager of California is being transferred to Seattle." He know there's been talk going on about changing district managers. By using this ploy—"I know something"—he's making it clear to the person he's talking to that he's been in on it all along. So it's all right to tell him. Gossip is another way of building up importance within a person who starts the rumor. He's in, he's part of the inner circle. Again, we're back in the jungle. Every ploy, every trick is used to survive.

When you're gonna merge with a company or acquire another company, it's supposed to be top secret. You have to do something to stem the rumors because it might screw up the deal. Talk of the merger, the whole place is in a turmoil.° It's like somebody saying there's a bomb in the building and we don't know where it is and when it's going to go off. There've been so many mergers where top executives are laid off, the accounting department is cut by sixty percent, the manufacturing is cut by twenty percent. I have yet to find anybody in a corporation who was so secure to honestly believe it couldn't happen to him.

They put on a front: "Oh, it can't happen to me. I'm too important." But deep down, they're scared stiff. The fear is there. You can smell it. You can see it on their faces. I'm not so sure you couldn't see it on my face many, many times during my climb up.

_turmoil:_ Chaos, disorder.

I always used to say—rough, tough Larry—I always said, "If you do a    15
good job, I'll give you a great reward. You'll keep your job." I'll have a sales
contest and the men who make their quota will win a prize—they'll keep their
jobs. I'm not saying there aren't executives who instill fear in their people. He's
no different than anybody walking down the street. We're all subject to the
same damn insecurities and neuroses°—at every level. Competitiveness, that's
the basis of it.

Why didn't I stay in the corporate structure? As a kid, through the Depression, you always heard about the tycoons,° the men of power, the men of industry. And you kind of dream that. Gee, these are supermen. These are the guys
that have no feeling, aren't subject to human emotions, the insecurities that
everybody else has. You get in the corporate structure, you find they all button
their pants the same way everybody else does. They all got the same fears.

The corporation is made up of many, many people. I call 'em the gray
people and the black—or white—people. Blacks and whites are definite colors, solid. Gray isn't. The gray people come there from nine to five, do their
job, aren't particularly ambitious. There's no fear there, sure. But they're not
subject to great demands. They're only subject to dismissal when business
goes bad and they cut off people. They go from corporation to corporation
and get jobs. Then you have the black—or white—people. The ambitious
people, the leaders, the ones who want to get ahead.

When the individual reaches the vice presidency or he's general manager,
you know he's an ambitious, dedicated guy who wants to get to the top. He
isn't one of the gray people. He's one of the black-and-white vicious people—
the leaders, the ones who stick out in the crowd.

As he struggles in this jungle, every position he's in, he's terribly lonely. He
can't confide and talk with the guy working under him. He can't confide and
talk to the man he's working for. To give vent to his feelings, his fears, and his
insecurities, he'd expose himself. This goes all the way up the line until he gets
to be president. The president *really* doesn't have anybody to talk to, because
the vice presidents are waiting for him to die or make a mistake and get
knocked off so they can get his job.

He can't talk to the board of directors, because to them he has to appear    20
as a tower of strength, knowledge, and wisdom, and have the ability to walk on
water. The board of directors, they're cold, they're hard. They don't have any
direct-line responsibilities. They sit in a staff capacity and they really play
God. They're interested in profits. They're interested in progress. They're
interested in keeping a good face in the community—if it's profitable. You
have the tremendous infighting of man against man for survival and clawing
to the top. Progress.

*neuroses:* Mental and emotional disorders.   *tycoons:* Businesspeople of exceptional wealth and power.

We always saw signs of physical afflictions because of the stress and strain. Ulcers, violent headaches. I remember one of the giant corporations I was in, the chief executive officer ate Gelusil by the minute. That's for ulcers. Had a private dining room with his private chef. All he ever ate was well-done steak and well-done hamburgers.

There's one corporation chief I had who worked, conservatively, nineteen, twenty hours a day. His whole life was his business. And he demanded the same of his executives. There was nothing sacred in life except the business. Meetings might be called on Christmas Eve or New Year's Eve, Saturdays, Sundays. He was lonesome when he wasn't involved with his business. He was always creating situations where he could be surrounded by his flunkies, regardless of what level they were, presidential, vice presidential . . . It was his life.

In the corporate structure, the buck keeps passing up until it comes to the chief executive. Then there ain't nobody to pass the buck to. You sit there in your lonely office and finally you have to make a decision. It could involve a million dollars or hundreds of jobs or moving people from Los Angeles, which they love, to Detroit or Winnipeg. So you're sitting at the desk, playing God.

You say, "Money isn't important. You can make some bad decisions about money, that's not important. What is important is the decisions you make about people working for you, their livelihood, their lives." It isn't true.

25      To the board of directors, the dollars are as important as human lives. There's only yourself sitting there making the decision, and you hope it's right. You're always on guard. Did you ever see a jungle animal that wasn't on guard? You're always looking over your shoulder. You don't know who's following you.

The most stupid phrase anybody can use in business is loyalty. If a person is working for a corporation, he's supposed to be loyal. This corporation is paying him less than he could get somewhere else at a comparable job. It's stupid of him to hang around and say he's loyal. The only loyal people are the people who can't get a job anyplace else. Working in a corporation, in a business, isn't a game. It isn't a collegiate event. It's a question of living or dying. It's a question of eating or not eating. Who is he loyal to? It isn't his country. It isn't his religion. It isn't his political party. He's working for some company that's paying him a salary for what he's doing. The corporation is out to make money. The ambitious guy will say, "I'm doing my job. I'm not embarrassed taking my money. I've got to progress and when I won't progress, I won't be here." The schnook° is the loyal guy, because he can't get a job anyplace else.

Many corporations will hang on to a guy or promote him to a place where he doesn't belong. Suddenly, after the man's been there twenty-five years, he's

---

*schnook:* Yiddish, meaning a stupid or unimportant person.

outlived his usefulness. And he's too old to start all over again. That's part of the cruelty. You can't only condemn the corporation for that. The man himself should be smart enough and intuitive enough to know he isn't getting any-place, to get the hell out and start all over. It was much more difficult at first to lay off a guy. But if you live in a jungle, you become hard, unfortunately.

When a top executive is let go, the king is dead, long live the king. Sud-denly he's a persona non grata.° When it happens, the shock is tremendous. Overnight. He doesn't know what hit him. Suddenly everybody in the organi-zation walks away and shuns him because they don't want to be associated with him. In corporations, if you back the wrong guy, you're in his corner, and he's fired, you're guilty by association. So what a lot of corporations have done is when they call a guy in—sometimes they'll call him in on a Friday night and say, "Go home now and come in tomorrow morning and clean out your desk and leave. We don't want any farewells or anything. Just get up and get the hell out." It's done in nice language. We say, "Look, why cause any trouble? Why cause any unrest in the organization? It's best that you just fade away." Imme-diately his Cadillac is taken away from him. His phone extension on the WATS line is taken away from him.* All these things are done quietly and—bingo! he's dead. His phone at home stops ringing because the fear of association continues after the severance. The smell of death is there.

We hired a vice president. He came highly recommended. He was with us about six months and he was completely inadequate. A complete misfit. Called him in the office, told him he was gonna go, gave him a nice severance pay. He broke down and cried. "What did I do wrong? I've done a marvelous job. Please don't do this to me. My daughter's getting married next month. How am I going to face the people?" He cried and cried and cried. But we couldn't keep him around. We just had to let him go.

I was just involved with a gigantic corporation. They had a shake-up two       30
Thursdays ago. It's now known as Black Thursday. Fifteen of twenty guys were let go overnight. The intelligent corporations say, "Clear, leave tonight, even if it's midweek. Come in Saturday morning and clean your desk. That's all. No good-bys or anything." They could be guys that have been there anywhere from a year to thirty years. If it's a successful operation, they're very generous. But then again, the human element creeps in. The boss might be vindictive° and cut him off without anything. It may depend what the corporation wants to maintain as its image.

And what it does to the ego! A guy in a key position, everybody wants to talk to him. All his subordinates are trying to get an audience with him to

---

*persona non grata:* Latin, meaning a person who is unacceptable or unwelcome.   *vindictive:* Hungry for revenge.

build up their own positions. Customers are calling him, everybody is calling him. Now his phone's dead. He's sitting at home and nobody calls him. He goes out and starts visiting his friends, who are busy with their own business, who haven't got time for him. Suddenly he's a failure. Regardless what the reason was—regardless of the press release that said he resigned—he was fired.

The only time the guy isn't considered a failure is when he resigns and announces his new job. That's the tipoff. "John Smith resigned, future plans unknown" means he was fired. "John Smith resigned to accept the position of president of X Company"—then you know he resigned. This little nuance you recognize immediately when you're in corporate life.

Changes since '42? Today the computer is taking over the world. The computer exposes all. There's no more chance for shenanigans and phoniness. Generally the computer prints out the truth. Not a hundred percent, but enough. It's eliminated a great deal of the jungle infighting. There's more facts for the businessman to work from, if the computer gives him the right information. Sometimes it doesn't. They have a saying at IBM: "If you put garbage in the computer, you'll take garbage out." Business is becoming more scientific with regard to marketing, finance, investments. And much more impersonal.

But the warm personal touch *never* existed in corporations. That was just a sham. In the last analysis, you've got to make a profit. There's a lot of family-held corporations that truly felt they were part of a legend. They had responsibilities to their people. They carried on as best they could. And then they went broke. The loyalty to their people, their patriarchy,° dragged 'em all down. Whatever few of 'em are left are being forced to sell, and are being taken over by the cold hand of the corporation.

35     My guess is that twenty corporations will control about forty percent of the consumer goods market. How much room is there left for the small guy? There's the supermarket in the grocery business. In our time, there were little mama-and-papa stores, thousands and thousands throughout the country. How many are there today? Unless you're National Tea or A & P, there's just no room. The small chains will be taken over by the bigger chains and they themselves will be taken over . . . The fish swallows the smaller fish and he's swallowed by a bigger one, until the biggest swallows 'em all. I have a feeling there'll always be room for the small entrepreneur, but he'll be rare. It'll be very difficult for him.

The top man is more of a general manager than he is an entrepreneur. There's less gambling than there was. He won't make as many mistakes as he did before in finance and marketing. It's a cold science. But when it comes to dealing with people, he still has to have that feel and he still has to do his own thinking. The computer can't do that for him.

---

*patriarchy:* Here meaning "fatherliness," paternalism.

When I broke in, no man could become an executive until he was thirty-five, thirty-six years old. During the past ten years there've been real top executives of twenty-six, twenty-seven. Lately there's been a reversal. These young ones climbed to the top when things were good, but during the last couple of years we've had some rough times. Companies have been clobbered and some have gone back to older men. But that's not gonna last.

Business is looking for the highly trained, highly skilled *young* executive, who has the knowledge and the education in a highly specialized field. It's happened in all professions and it's happening in business. You have your comptroller° who's highly specialized. You have your treasurer who has to know finance, a heavily involved thing because of the taxation and the SEC.° You have the manufacturing area. He has to be highly specialized in warehouse and in shipping—the ability to move merchandise cheaply and quickly. Shipping has become a horrendous problem because costs have become tremendous. You have to know marketing, the studies, the effect of advertising. A world of specialists. The man at the top has to have a general knowledge. And he has to have the knack of finding the right man to head these divisions. That's the difficulty.

You have a nice, plush lovely office to go to. You have a private secretary. You walk down the corridor and everybody bows and says, "Good morning, Mr. Ross. How are you today?" As you go up the line, the executives will say, "How is Mrs. Ross?" Until you get to the higher executives. They'll say, "How is Nancy?" Here you socialize, you know each other. Everybody plays the game.

A man wants to get to the top of the corporation, not for the money involved. After a certain point, how much more money can you make? In my climb, I'll be honest, money was secondary. Unless you have tremendous demands, yachts, private airplanes—you get to a certain point, money isn't that important. It's the power, the status, the prestige. Frankly, it's delightful to be on top and have everybody calling you Mr. Ross and have a plane at your disposal and a car and a driver at your disposal. When you come to town, there's people to take care of you. When you walk into a board meeting, everybody gets up and says hello. I don't think there's any human being that doesn't love that. It's a nice feeling. But the ultimate power is in the board of directors. I don't know anybody who's free. You read in the paper about stockholders' meetings, the annual report. It all sounds so glowing. But behind the scenes, a jungle.

I work on a yearly retainer with a corporation. I spend, oh, two, three days a month in various corporate structures. The key executives can talk to me and bounce things off me. The president may have a specific problem that I

*comptroller:* Controller or accountant.    *SEC:* The Securities and Exchange Commission.

will investigate and come back to him with my ideas. The reason I came into this work is that all my corporate life I was looking for somebody like me, somebody who's been there. Because there's no new problems in business today. There's just a different name for different problems that have been going on for years and years and years. Nobody's come up yet with a problem that isn't familiar. I've been there.

Example. The chief executive isn't happy with the marketing structure. He raises many questions which I may not know specifically. I'll find out, and come back with a proposal. He might be thinking of promoting one of his executives. It's narrowed down to two or three. Let's say two young guys who've been moved to a new city. It's a tossup. I notice one has bought a new house, invested heavily in it. The other rented. I'd recommend the second. He's more realistic.

If he comes before his board of directors, there's always the vise. The poor sonofabitch is caught in the squeeze from the people below and the people above. When he comes to the board, he's got to come with a firm hand. I can help him because I'm completely objective. I'm out of the jungle. I don't have the trauma that I used to have when I had to fire somebody. What is it gonna do to this guy? I can give it to him cold and hard and logical. I'm not involved.

I left that world because suddenly the power and the status were empty. I'd been there, and when I got there it was nothing. Suddenly you have a feeling of little boys playing at business. Suddenly you have a feeling—so what? It started to happen to me, this feeling, oh, in '67, '68. So when the corporation was sold, my share of the sale was such . . . I didn't have to go back into the jungle. I don't have to fight to the top. I've been to the mountain top. (Laughs.) It isn't worth it.

45      It was very difficult, the transition of retiring from the status position, where there's people on the phone all day trying to talk to you. Suddenly nobody calls you. This is psychological . . . (Halts, a long pause.) I don't want to get into that. Why didn't I retire completely? I really don't know. In the last four, five years, people have come to me with tempting offers. Suddenly I realized what I'm doing is much more fun than going into that jungle again. So I turned them down.

I've always wanted to be a teacher. I wanted to give back the knowledge I gained in corporate life. People have always told me I'd always been a great sales manager. In every sales group you always have two or three young men with stars in their eyes. They always sat at the edge of the chair. I knew they were comers.° I always felt I could take 'em, develop 'em, and build 'em. A lot of old fogies like me—I can point out this guy, that guy who worked for me, and now he's the head of this, the head of that.

Yeah, I always wanted to teach. But I had no formal education and no university would touch me. I was willing to teach for nothing. But there also, they

---

*comers:* Slang, referring to people showing promise or making rapid progress.

have their jungle. They don't want a businessman. They only want people in the academic world, who have a formalized and, I think, empty training. This is what I'd really like to do. I'd like to get involved with the young people and give my knowledge to them before it's buried with me. Not that what I have is so great, but there's a certain understanding, a certain feeling . . .

---

* Wide area telecommunications service. A prerogative granted important executives by some corporations: unlimited use of the telephone to make a call anywhere in the world.

## QUESTIONS

1. What analogy does Ross use throughout the interview to explain how he views the corporate world? What does this analogy reveal about his view of human nature?
2. Why had the corporate world "lost its excitement, its appeal," for Larry Ross?
3. According to Ross, what must a corporation do, "in the last analysis"? What gets in the way—and has to be eliminated—as a result?
4. Explain whether or not you agree with Ross's statement that "We're all subject to the same damn insecurities and neuroses—at every level." Provide examples to support your opinion.
5. According to Ross, what is one function of a corporate wife? Why do you think Ross views wives as he does?
6. Considering what Ross reiterates throughout the interview about emotions in the corporate world, why is the last line of the interview ironic?
7. Does Ross use any clichés, jargon, or euphemisms? If so, make a list of some of these.

## CONNECTIONS

1. Ross writes that, in working for a large corporation, "there are certain sets of rules" that must be followed. What are these rules? Are they similar to the "unwritten rules" of success described by Sam Keen?
2. What do you think Andrew Carnegie might have said about Ross's career?

# ∿ Enough Jam for a Lifetime

## *Maxine Kumin*

Maxine Kumin was born in 1925. She received both a bachelor's and a master's degree from Radcliffe College. As a visiting professor she has taught at numerous universities—including the University of Massachusetts at Amherst, Princeton, Brandeis, and Columbia. She has also worked both as a farmer in New Hampshire and as a poetry consultant for the Library of Congress. She has published numerous novels, children's books, short stories, poems, and essays. Her books include the short story collection *Why Can't We Live Like Civilized Human Beings?* (1982), the collection of essays entitled *In Deep: Country Essays* (1987), and the poetry collections *Nurture* (1989) and *Looking for Luck* (1992). She received the Pulitzer Prize for poetry in 1973 and the Poets Prize in 1993. Her articles have appeared in magazines such as *Country Journal, The Hudson Review,* and *Mademoiselle.* The following comes from her 1994 collection of essays entitled *Women, Animals, and Vegetables.*

**WARM-UP:** In a few paragraphs, explain why you either love or hate a particular type of housework. (Include a description of that activity.)

1    January 25. Three days of this hard freeze; 10 below at dawn and a sullen 2 above by midday. After the morning barn chores, I start hauling quart containers of wild blackberries up from the basement freezer. I am a little reluctant to begin.

Last August, when the berries were at their most succulent, I did manage to cook up a sizable batch into jam. But everything peaks at once in a New England garden, and I turned to the importunate° broccolis and cauliflowers and the second crop of bush beans, all of which wanted blanching and freezing straightaway. Also, late summer rains had roused the cucumber vines to new efforts. There was a sudden spurt of yellow squash as well.

Victor went on picking blackberries. Most mornings he scouted the slash pile° along upturned boulders, residue from when we cleared the last four acres of forage pasture. We've never had to fence this final field, for the brush forms an impenetrable° thicket on two sides and deep woods encircle the rest.

---

*importunate:* Tenacious, overly persistent in request or demand.    *slash pile:* Pile of debris or plant trimmings.    *impenetrable:* Here meaning incapable of being penetrated or pierced.

We've always had blackberries growing wild here and there on the property, good-sized ones, too. But never such largess, such abundance. I wondered what this bumper crop signified, after a drought-filled summer. Were the Tribulation and the Rapture at hand?

Long ago I wrote in a poem, "God does not want / His Perfect fruit to rot," 5
but that was before I had an addicted picker on my hands—whose enthusiasm became my labor. It is the habit of the deeply married to exchange vantage points.°

Even the horses took up blackberries as a snack. Like toddlers loose in a popcorn shop, they sidled down the brambly° row, cautiously curling their lips back so as to pluck a drooping cluster free without being stabbed in the muzzle by truly savage thorns. It was a wonderful sight.

Making jam—even though I complain how long it takes, how messy it is with its inevitable spatters and spills, how the lids and the jars somehow never match up at the end of the procedure—is rich with gratifications. I get a lot of thinking done. I puff up with feelings of providence.° Pretty soon I am flooded with memories.

My mother used to visit every summer during our pickling, canning, freezing, and jamming frenzy. She had a deep reservoir of patience, developed in another era, for repetitive tasks; she would mash the blender-buzzed, cooked berries through a strainer until her arms were as weary as a weightlifter's at the end of a grueling workout. She prided herself on extracting every bit of pulp from the purple mass.

I find myself talking to her as I work. I am not nearly as diligent,° I tell her, thumping the upended strainer into the kitchen scraps pile, destined for compost. I miss her serious attention to detail.

Scullery° work used to make my mother loquacious.° I liked hearing 10
about her childhood in the southwestern hilly corner of Virginia at the turn of the century, how the cooking from May to October was done in the summer kitchen, a structure loosely attached to the back of the house, much as many New England sheds and barns connect to the farmhouses they supplement. I liked hearing about my grandfather's matched pair of driving horses—Saddlebreds, I gather, from the one surviving snapshot that shows my mother's three youngest brothers lined up on one compliant° horse's back. My mother talked about the family pony that had a white harness for Sundays. I wonder aloud what a white harness was made of in the 1890s. Perhaps she had imagined this item, but fabricated it lovingly so long ago that it had become real.

---

*vantage points:* Positions or standpoints from which to view something.   *brambly:* Prickly.   *providence:* Divine guidance or care.   *diligent:* Steady, earnest, and energetic in one's efforts.   *Scullery:* Pantry, storeroom.   *loquacious:* Talkative.   *compliant:* Ready or disposed to accept or to conform.

One spectacular late summer day we took my mother down North Road along Stevens Brook in search of elderberries. We hiked up and down the sandy edge of the water in several locations before coming upon an enormous stand of the berries, ripe to bursting, branches bent double with the weight of them. After filling the five-gallon pail we had brought with us, greedily we started stuffing whole racemes° of berries into a spare grain bag.

I had not thought much about dealing with the booty until we had lugged it triumphantly home. Mother sat at the kitchen table well past midnight, stripping the berries from their slender finger filaments into my biggest cooking pot. Even so, the great elderberry caper took two more days to complete. We prevailed, eventually boiling the berries with some green apples from our own trees so that the released pectin would permit the mass to jell. I don't believe in additives and scorn commercial pectin, but I will lean on home-grown apples or rhubarb in order to thicken the berry soup.

It was amazing what those elderberries had reawakened in my mother; she was transported. There was the cold cellar, there stood the jars of pickled beets, the Damson plum conserve larded with hazelnuts; there, too, the waist-high barrel of dill pickles weighted down with three flatirons atop a washtub lid. Potatoes and sweet potatoes, carrots, onions, and apples were stored in areas appropriate to their needs—apples in the dark far corner which was the driest (and spookiest), and so on. There was the springhouse, where milk from the family cow cooled unpasteurized in a metal can set down in a cavity of rocks, and a butter churn which took hours of push-pulling the paddle to turn the cream into a finished product.

It was never an idyll° Mother described. She remembered sharply and wryly° the labor, the peonage° of childhood, when the most menial and least absorbing tasks were invariably° assigned to the smallest children, especially the girls. She could not escape the chores of housekeeping for the imagined dramas of field and barn. But interestingly, chickens seemed always to have been relegated° to the care of females.

15      Mother loathed the chickens that pecked her feet when she went into the coop to scatter their scratch. She detested egg gathering, having to shoo brood hens off their nests and then be quick about plucking the eggs into the basket; eggs from which fluff, feathers, and bits of crusty manure had to be removed. I never saw my mother eat an egg, boiled soft or hard, poached, or sunny-side up. They were a bit too close to nature for her taste.

---

*racemes:* Types of stem.    *idyll:* A descriptive work in poetry or prose that suggests a mood of peace and contentment.    *wryly:* Ironically, humorously.    *peonage:* The use of laborers who become servants by going into debt to their employers.    *invariably:* Without fail, always.    *relegated:* Banished, assigned.

Another kitchen thing I hear my mother say as I work, this cold January noon: "Warm the plates!" she croons to me from the Great Beyond. She abhorred° the common practice of serving hot food on cold china. *Common* is the epithet° she would have applied to it, a word that carried powerful connotations of contempt.

This wintry day, then, I reduce five gallons of blackberries to serviceable pulp, measure out three cups of sugar to every four of berry mash, and set it boiling. We will have successive batches on the stove the rest of this day. I have already rummaged for suitable jars from the cellar shelves and these I will boil for fifteen minutes on a back burner. Toward the end I will grow more inventive about jars, for there are never enough of the good, straight-sided variety.

But for now, the jam puts up lacy bubbles, rolling around the top third of my giant cooking pot at a full boil. Despite candy thermometers, the only way I trust to gauge when the jam is ready is dip and drip. From a decent height, off a slotted spoon, I perform this test until the royal stuff begins to form a tiny waterfall. This is known as sheeting; all the cookbooks describe it, but it's a delicate decision to arrive at. Stop too soon and you have a lovely blackberry sauce to serve over ice cream, sponge cake, or applesauce. Continue too long and you have a fatally overcooked mess of berry leather.

There is no quality control in my method. Every batch is a kind of revisionism.° It makes its own laws. But the result is pure, deeply colored, uncomplicated, and unadulterated blackberry jam, veritably° seedless, suitable for every occasion. After it has cooled, I pour melted paraffin° on top of it, tilting the glass to get an airproof seal. Modern science frowns on so casual an approach to shutting out microbes, but I don't apologize. If the wax shows a spot of mold growing on top after a few months on the shelf, I can always remove it, wipe the sides clean, and pour a new layer of wax over all.

My mother would go home from her summer visits with a package of pickles and jams for her later delectation.° When she died, there were several unopened jars in her cupboard. I took them back with me after the funeral. We ate them in her stead, as she would have wanted us to. Enough jam for a lifetime, she would say with evident satisfaction after a day of scullery duty. It was; it is.

20

## QUESTIONS

1. Does Kumin make jam only because she likes the taste? What other reasons might she have?

---

*abhorred:* Loathed, hated.    *epithet:* Abusive word, insult.    *revisionism:* Change in version.    *veritably:* Truly, genuinely.    *paraffin:* Wax.    *delectation:* Delight, enjoyment.

2. What is Kumin's attitude toward jam-making? Does her attitude change as she describes the labor of the process? If so, identify a line or two that shows a shift in her attitude.
3. What does Kumin appear to admire about her mother's attitude toward work?
4. For Kumin and for her mother, jam-making acts as a conduit to memory. Are there any particular activities that bring up memories for *you*?
5. Kumin writes with a lot of attention to detail. Are there passages where you feel her description is either too sparse or overdone? If so, which are those?
6. Does jam-making qualify as work? Explain your response.
7. In real life, Maxine Kumin makes jam and writes essays, poems, and stories. Do you consider her occupations useful? Does our society value such work?

**CONNECTIONS**

1. If you were to describe Kumin as one of the characters from the fable of the grasshopper and the ant, which one would you say she is? Why?
2. Compare Kumin's attitude toward jam-making to the attitude that Pearl/Jinx expresses toward her work in the story "In the Life" (included in Section 3).

# ∼ To Be of Use

*Marge Piercy*

For a biographical note about Marge Piercy, turn to page 117. The following comes from her 1973 poetry collection *To Be of Use.*

**WARM-UP:** Prepare a list of professions in which people create things necessary to survival and a list of professions in which people create things that are *not* necessities. Of the latter group, whom do you respect? Why?


The people I love the best                                            1
jump into work head first
without dallying° in the shallows
and swim off with sure strokes almost out of sight.
They seem to become natives of that element,                         5
the black sleek heads of seals
bouncing like half-submerged balls.

I love people who harness themselves, an ox to a heavy cart,
who pull like water buffalo, with massive patience,
who strain in the mud and the muck to move things forward,           10
who do what has to be done, again and again.

I want to be with people who submerge
in the task, who go into the fields to harvest
and work in a row and pass the bags along,
who are not parlor generals and field deserters                      15
but move in a common rhythm
when the food must come in or the fire be put out.

The work of the world is common as mud.
Botched, it smears the hands, crumbles to dust.
But the thing worth doing well done                                  20
has a shape that satisfies, clean and evident.
Greek amphoras° for wine or oil,
Hopi vases that held corn, are put in museums
but you know they were made to be used.
The pitcher cries for water to carry                                 25
and a person for work that is real.

---

3 *dallying:* Playing lightly, wasting time.   22 *amphoras:* Ancient jars or vases.

QUESTIONS

1. Explain the meaning of the line "The work of the world is common as mud."
2. Identify recurring words and images from this poem. How do they reinforce the point of the poem?
3. Are there any images that don't seem to fit in with others? If so, do they add or detract from the poem as a whole? In what way(s)?
4. Look up "field deserters" and "parlor generals" in a dictionary of expressions. What does Piercy mean in the sentence where she uses those terms?
5. What is Piercy's point in the lines about Greek amphoras and Hopi vases? Why are those objects placed in museums? What does the speaker see as their real value?
6. What do you consider "work that is real"?

CONNECTIONS

1. Does Piercy's poem support Andrew Carnegie's views about work?
2. Compare the writing style in Piercy's "To Be of Use" with the style of her poem "Barbie Doll" (included in Section 2).

# ∾ Federico's Ghost

## Martin Espada

Born in Brooklyn, New York, in 1957, Martin Espada is of Puerto Rican descent. He is the author of three books—*The Immigrant Iceboy's Bolero* (1982), *Rebellion Is the Circle of a Lover's Hands* (1990), and *Trumpets from the Islands of Their Eviction* (1994)—and has been the recipient of numerous writing fellowships. Now a tenant lawyer and supervisor of "Su Clinica," a legal services program administered by the Suffolk University Law School in Boston, Espada has worked as a radio journalist in Nicaragua, a welfare rights paralegal, an advocate for mentally ill patients, a night desk clerk in a transient hotel, an attendant in a primate nursery, a groundskeeper in a minor league ballpark, and a bouncer in a bar. The following poem first appeared in issue #30 of the magazine *River Styx* and was later reprinted in *Rebellion Is the Circle of a Lover's Hands.*

**WARM-UP:** In a descriptive paragraph, show what you have experienced, witnessed, heard, read, or imagined about the working conditions of farmworkers.

The story is     1
that whole families of fruitpickers
still crept between the furrows
of the field at dusk,
when for reasons of whiskey or whatever     5
the cropduster plane sprayed anyway,
floating a pesticide drizzle
over the pickers
who thrashed like dark birds
in a glistening white net,     10
except for Federico,
a skinny boy who stood apart
in his own green row,
and, knowing the pilot
would not understand in Spanish     15
that he was the son of a whore,
instead jerked his arm
and thrust an obscene finger.

The pilot understood.
He circled the plane and sprayed again,     20

watching a fine gauze of poison
drift over the brown bodies
that cowered and scurried on the ground,
and aiming for Federico,
25    leaving the skin beneath his shirt
wet and blistered,
but still pumping his finger at the sky.

After Federico died,
rumors at the labor camp
30    told of tomatoes picked and smashed at night,
growers muttering of vandal children
or communists in camp,
first threatening to call Immigration,
then promising every Sunday off
35    if only the smashing of tomatoes would stop.

Still tomatoes were picked and squashed
in the dark,
and the old women in camp
said it was Federico,
40    laboring after sundown
to cool the burns on his arms,
flinging tomatoes
at the cropduster
that hummed like a mosquito
45    lost in his ear,
and kept his soul awake.

## QUESTIONS

1. Why do you think Espada wrote this poem? What do you think he
   wanted to achieve? In your opinion, did he succeed?
2. The theme of revenge recurs throughout this poem. Identify some of
   its recurrences and explain who is seeking revenge upon whom and
   why.
3. In the first stanza, "dark birds" is contrasted with "white net." What
   might this indicate about the poem as a whole?
4. Note the verbs Espada used to describe the actions of the fruitpickers.
   What effect do those particular verbs create?
5. Describe Federico's personality; offer evidence from the poem to support your description.

**CONNECTIONS**

1. Compare and contrast the views of agricultural work presented in Espada's poem and John Steinbeck's "The Chrysanthemums," the transition piece between this section and the previous one.
2. How is Piercy's view of farm labor, presented in "To Be of Use," different from the one expressed in this poem?

# ~ Less Is More: A Call for Shorter Work Hours

*Barbara Brandt*

While working with Gordon Fellman on the book *The Deceived Majority: Politics and Protest in Middle America* (1973), Barbara Brandt left Brandeis University, where she was a graduate student in sociology, to become a commune organizer in Sommerville, Massachusetts. A longtime organizer and social activist, Brandt founded the Boston-area Urban Solar Energy Association and helped organize international conferences for The Other Economic Summit (TOES) in Toronto (1988) and Houston (1990). She is the author of several books, including *Whole Life Economics: Revaluing Daily Life* (1993). The following selection comes from a paper she prepared for the Boston-based Shorter Work-Time Group.

**WARM-UP:** When you were a child, what were your parents' occupations? How often were your parents working? What were they like when they came home from work? How did you feel toward your parents' work?

1    America is suffering from overwork. Too many of us are too busy, trying to squeeze more into each day while having less to show for it. Although our growing time crunch is often portrayed as a personal dilemma, it is in fact a major social problem that has reached crises proportions over the past 20 years.

The simple fact is that Americans today—both women and men—are spending too much time at work, to the detriment° of their homes, their families, their personal lives, and their communities. The American Dream promised that our individual hard work paired with the advance of modern technology would bring about the good life for all. Glorious visions of the leisure society were touted° throughout the '50s and '60s. But now most people are working more than ever before, while still struggling to meet their economic commitments. Ironically, the many advances in technology, such as computers and fax machines, rather than reducing our workload, seem to have speeded up our lives at work. At the same time, technology has equipped us with "conveniences" like microwave ovens and frozen dinners that merely enable us to adopt a similar frantic pace in our home lives so we can cope with more hours at paid work.

---

*detriment:* Loss, damage.    *touted:* Praised or publicized loudly.

A recent spate° of articles in the mainstream media has focused on the new problems of overwork and lack of time. Unfortunately, overwork is often portrayed as a special problem of yuppies and professionals on the fast track. In reality, the unequal distribution of work and time in America today reflects the decline in both standard of living and quality of life for most Americans. Families whose members never see each other, women who work a double shift (first on the job, then at home), workers who need more flexible work schedules, and unemployed and underemployed people who need more work are all casualties of the crisis of overwork.

Americans often assume that overwork is an inevitable fact of life—like death and taxes. Yet a closer look at other times and other nations offers some startling surprises.

Anthropologists have observed that in pre-industrial (particularly hunting and gathering) societies, people generally spend 3 to 4 hours a day, 15 to 20 hours a week, doing the work necessary to maintain life. The rest of the time is spent in socializing, partying, playing, storytelling, and artistic or religious activities. The ancient Romans celebrated 175 public festivals a year in which everyone participated, and people in the Middle Ages had at least 115.

In our era, almost every other industrialized nation (except Japan) has fewer annual working hours and longer vacations than the United States. This includes all of Western Europe, where many nations enjoy thriving economies and standards of living equal to or higher than ours. Jeremy Brecher and Tim Costello, writing in *Z Magazine* (Oct. 1990), note that "European unions during the 1980s made a powerful and largely successful push to cut working hours. In 1987 German metalworkers struck and won a 37.5-hour week; many are now winning a 35-hour week. In 1990, hundreds of thousands of British workers have won a 37-hour week."

In an article about work-time in the *Boston Globe,* Suzanne Gordon notes that workers in other industrialized countries "enjoy—as a statutory° right—longer vacations [than in the U.S.] from the moment they enter the work force. In Canada, workers are legally entitled to two weeks off their first year on the job. After two or three years of employment, most get three weeks of vacation. After 10 years, it's up to four, and by 20 years, Canadian workers are off for five weeks. In Germany, statutes guarantee 18 days minimum for everyone, but most workers get five or six weeks. The same is true in Scandinavian countries, and in France."

In contrast to the extreme American emphasis on productivity and commitment, which results in many workers, especially in professional-level jobs, not taking the vacations coming to them, Gordon notes that "in countries that

5

---

*spate:* Outburst.    *statutory:* Enacted, created, or regulated by law.

are America's most successful competitors in the global marketplace, all working people, whether lawyers or teachers, CEOs or janitors, take the vacations to which they are entitled by law. 'No one in West Germany,' a West German embassy's officer explains, 'no matter how high up they are, would ever say they couldn't afford to take a vacation. Everyone takes their vacation.'"

And in Japan, where dedication to the job is legendary, Gordon notes that the Japanese themselves are beginning to consider their national workaholism a serious social problem leading to stress-related illnesses and even death. As a result, the Japanese government recently established a commission whose goal is to promote shorter working hours and more leisure time.

10      Most other industrialized nations also have better family-leave policies than the United States, and in a number of other countries workers benefit from innovative time-scheduling opportunities such as sabbaticals.°

While the idea of a shorter workweek and longer vacations sounds appealing to most people, any movement to enact shorter work-time as a public policy will encounter surprising pockets of resistance, not just from business leaders but even from some workers. Perhaps the most formidable barrier to more free time for Americans is the widespread mind-set that the 40-hour workweek, 8 hour a day, 5 days a week, 50 weeks a year, is a natural rhythm of the universe. This view is reinforced by the media's complete silence regarding the shorter work-time and more favorable vacation and family-leave policies of other countries. This lack of information, and our leaders' reluctance to suggest that the United States can learn from any other nation (except workaholic Japan) is one reason why more Americans don't identify overwork as a major problem or clamor° for fewer hours and more vacation. Monika Bauerlein, a journalist originally from Germany now living in Minneapolis, exclaims, "I can't believe that people here aren't rioting in the streets over having only two weeks of vacation a year."

A second obstacle to launching a powerful shorter work-time movement is America's deeply ingrained work ethic, or its modern incarnation, the workaholic syndrome. The work ethic fosters the widely held belief that people's work is their most important activity and that people who do not work long and hard are lazy, unproductive, and worthless.

For many Americans today, paid work is not just a way to make money but is a crucial source of their self-worth. Many of us identify ourselves almost entirely by the kind of work we do. Work still has a powerful psychological and spiritual hold over our lives—and talk of shorter work-time may seem somehow morally suspicious.

---

*sabbaticals:* Breaks or changes from a work routine.    *clamor:* Shout, make noise.

Because we are so deeply a work-oriented society, leisure-time activities —such as play, relaxation, engaging in cultural and artistic pursuits, or just quiet contemplation and "doing nothing"—are not looked on as essential and worthwhile components of life. Of course, for the majority of working women who must work a second shift at home, much of the time spent outside of paid work is not leisure anyway. Also much of our non-work time is spent not just in personal renewal, but in building and maintaining essential social ties —with family, friends, and the larger community.

Today, as mothers and fathers spend more and more time on the job, we are beginning to recognize the deleterious° effects—especially on our young people—of the breakdown of social ties and community in American life. But unfortunately, our nation reacts to these problems by calling for more paid professionals—more police, more psychiatrists, more experts—without recognizing the possibility that shorter work hours and more free time could enable us to do much of the necessary rebuilding and healing, with much more gratifying and longer-lasting results.

15

Of course, the stiffest opposition to cutting work hours comes not from citizens but from business. Employers are reluctant to alter the 8-hour day, 40-hour workweek, 50 weeks a year because it seems easier and more profitable for employers to hire fewer employees for longer hours rather than more employees—each of whom would also require health insurance and other benefits—with flexible schedules and work arrangements.

Harvard University economist Juliet B. Schor, who has been studying issues of work and leisure in America, reminds us that we cannot ignore the larger relationship between unemployment and overwork: While many of us work too much, others are unable to find paid work at all. Schor points out that "workers who work longer hours lose more income when they lose their jobs. The threat of job loss is an important determinant of management's power on the shop floor." A system that offers only two options—long work hours or unemployment—serves as both a carrot and a stick. Those lucky enough to get full-time jobs are bribed into docile° compliance with the boss, while the spectre of unemployment always looms as the ultimate punishment for the unruly.

Some observers suggest that keeping people divided into "the employed" and "the unemployed" creates feelings of resentment and inferiority/superiority between the two groups, thus focusing their discontent and blame on each other rather than on the corporations and political figures who actually dictate our nation's economic policies.

Our role as consumers contributes to keeping the average work week from falling. In an economic system in which addictive buying is the basis of

---

*deleterious:* Harmful.    *docile:* Meek.

corporate profits, working a full 40 hours or more each week for 50 weeks a year gives us just enough time to stumble home and dazedly—almost automatically—shop; but not enough time to think about deeper issues or to work effectively for social change. From the point of view of corporations and policymakers, shorter work-time may be bad for the economy, because people with enhanced free time may begin to find other things to do with it besides mindlessly buying products. It takes more free time to grow vegetables, cook meals from scratch, sew clothes, or repair broken items than it does to just buy these things at the mall.

20    Any serious proposal to give employed Americans a break by cutting into the eight-hour work day is certain to be met with anguished cries about international competitiveness. The United States seems gripped by the fear that our nation has lost its economic dominance, and pundits,° policymakers, and business leaders tell us that no sacrifice is too great if it puts America on top again.

As arguments like this are put forward (and we can expect them to increase in the years to come), we need to remember two things. First, even if America maintained its dominance (whatever that means) and the economy were booming again, this would be no guarantee that the gains—be they in wages, in employment opportunities, or in leisure—would be distributed equitably between upper management and everyone else. Second, the entire issue of competitiveness is suspect when it pits poorly treated workers in one country against poorly treated workers in another; and when the vast majority of economic power, anyway, is in the control of enormous multinational corporations that have no loyalty to the people of any land.

Many people are experimenting with all sorts of ways to cope with grueling work schedules. Those with enough money use it to "buy time." They find child care, order take-out meals, and hire people to pick their children up from school and do the family shopping. Other options being pursued by both men and women include actively looking for good part-time jobs; sharing jobs; arranging more flexible work schedules; going into business for themselves; working at home; and scaling back on consumption in order to work fewer hours for lower pay. While these ideas work in some cases, they are often stymied° by a lack of support from employers, and they aren't available to many people, especially those with lower incomes.

But perhaps the major shortcoming of all these individual responses is precisely that: They are individual. The problem of overwork is a broad problem of our economic system. It cannot be solved by just one individual, family, or business. Individual approaches ignore the many larger causes of the problem.

---

*pundits:* People who give opinions in an authoritative manner.    *stymied:* Thwarted, blocked.

A number of solutions now discussed for the overwork crisis are actually steps in the wrong direction.

The conservative climate of the '80s and '90s has spawned a neotraditional   25
cultural movement that holds up the 1950s as a golden age from which we have unwisely strayed. Their simplistic solution to the complex set of social issues involved with overwork is to force women back into the home. While we all should support the right of any woman to freely choose home and family as her primary responsibility and source of fulfillment, we need to oppose social and economic policies that either seek to keep women at home or offer them only limited opportunity—low-paying, low-status, part-time jobs—outside the home. Such policies are not only unfair to women themselves, they are economically harmful to the many families supported by working women.

The idea of a four-day, 10-hour-a-day workweek has frequently been suggested as a superior alternative to the current five-day workweek. But this is no shortening of work hours, and it ignores the fact that many people who do paid work also need to care for home and family when they get home. Lengthening the workday would add considerably to the burden these people already carry.

Finally, we should be wary of programs supposedly aimed at helping working parents and their families when the ultimate outcome is to keep parents at work longer—day care for sick children and corporate day care centers open on weekends to accommodate parents who want to work extended hours, for example.

Now that public attention is beginning to take note of the mounting personal, economic, and social toll of overwork, it is time to treat overwork as a major political and social issue. To accomplish this, the Shorter Work-Time Group of Boston—a multicultural group of women's and labor activists—proposes a national campaign for shorter work hours that could foster a formidable alliance of unions, community groups, women's groups, and workers in all fields. To begin this campaign, we propose a 10-point plan that could help heal the problems of overwork in its many forms and enhance the quality of all our lives—at home, on the job, and in the community.

### 1. Establish a 6-hour day/30-hour week

We propose that a 6-hour day/30-hour week be made the new standard for "full-time work." This new policy would not only give America's workers more time to devote to our families, friends, and personal and community lives, but would also provide benefits to employers in increased efficiency and productivity, reduced accidents and absenteeism, improved morale, lower turnover, and retention of valuable employees.

So that workers do not suffer financially from reduction of their   30
work-time, we also propose that any reduction in hours be accompanied

by a corresponding increase in hourly income—that the six-hour day be compensated by what was formerly eight-hour pay. Since numerous studies have shown shortened workdays improve productivity, this would not be economically unrealistic.

**2. Extend paid vacations for all American workers**

American workers should enjoy what their counterparts around the world take for granted—four to six weeks of paid vacation each year. Vacation should be based on overall years in the work force rather than tied to the number of years a person has been employed in a particular firm.

**3. Improve family-leave policies**

The Family and Medical Leave Act . . . needs broad national support so that politicians would fear reprisals from an angry public if they did not support it. This bill would provide job security for people who have to leave work for extended periods in order to care for newborn children or seriously ill family members. Although it does not provide for pay during such leaves, paid leave should be an eventual goal.

**4. Establish benefits for all workers**

At present, employers of part-time and temporary workers are not legally required to provide health insurance, vacations, pensions, or any other benefits. This is especially insidious° because women and many low-income workers are most likely to hold part-time and temporary jobs. Congresswoman Pat Schroeder has introduced HR 2575, the Part-Time and Temporary Workers Protection Act, to rectify this situation at the national level.

**5. Discourage overtime work**

Since overtime is detrimental to workers, their families, and the other workers it replaces, we would like to see it eliminated as much as possible. This can be done by mandating the elimination of compulsory overtime and raising the pay rate to double time for voluntary overtime.

35    **6. Support alternative working arrangements**

We encourage business to increase flex-time and other innovative work-time arrangements that enable employees to better meet their personal and family needs.

**7. Acknowledge workaholism as a social disorder**

In Japan, they even coined a word—*karoshi* (death from overwork)—to show this is a serious disease.

**8. Promote awareness that our citizens and our nation as a whole will benefit from shorter work-time**

We need a public education campaign to raise public consciousness about the devastating effects that overwork is having on our health, our families,

---

*insidious:* Corrupting, deceiving.

our communities, and especially on our young people. American workers must have more time to care for their families and restore their communities. This does not mean sending women back home. It means giving all people the time and resources to create their own solutions. If we had more time for ourselves, for example, we would probably see a wide variety of child-care options. In some families, women would do this exclusively; in others, women and men would share child-care responsibilities; some people would hire paid help; and others would develop cooperative or community-based programs for their children; many people would take advantage of a mix of options. The same would probably occur with regard to a wide range of family and community issues.

**9. Look at how the issue of overwork influences the problems of underemployment and unemployment**

Because of increasing economic pressures, many corporations are developing a two-tier work force: a core of workers who enjoy good salaries, job security, and full benefits, and another group of lower paid part-time and temporary workers who have no benefits or job security.

**10. Challenge the assertion that we have to enslave ourselves to our jobs in order to keep America competitive**

Germany, for example, has mandated shortened work hours, and clearly has not lost its competitive edge in the world economy.

## ANNUAL VACATION TIME (in weeks)

|  | By law | By bargaining agreement |
|---|---|---|
| Austria | 4 | 4–5 |
| Denmark | — | 5 |
| Finland | 5 | 5–6 |
| France | 5 | 5–6 |
| Germany | 3 | 4–6 |
| Greece | 4 | — |
| Ireland | 3 | 4 |
| Italy | — | 4–6 |
| Netherlands | 3 | 4–5 |
| Portugal | 4 | — |
| Spain | 5 | 5 |
| Sweden | 5 | 5–8 |
| Switzerland | 4 | 4–5 |
| United States | — | 2–4 |
| United Kingdom | — | 4–6 |

*Source: "Reduction of Working Time in Europe,"* European Industrial Relations Review, *No 127,* August 1984:9–13.

## QUESTIONS

1. Why does Brandt characterize "overwork" as a crisis? Explain whether or not you agree with her.
2. Is the information Brandt presents about working conditions in other countries—shorter work weeks, longer vacations, better family-leave policies, etc.—"news" to you? If so, why, according to Brandt, is this so? Do you agree with her?
3. Identify the obstacles that, according to Brandt, are blocking the "shorter work-time movement."
4. Why does Brandt believe that "individual approaches ignore the many larger causes of the problem"?
5. Identify the solutions that Brandt offers for what she calls the "overwork crisis"; explain which ones you believe to be feasible.
6. Are women more likely than men to be overworked in the United States today? Offer specific evidence to support your answer.
7. Is the introduction of this selection effective? Explain your response.
8. Identify the sources of information that Brandt refers to in this essay; explain whether or not they support Brandt's argument.

## CONNECTIONS

1. Does Robert Hayden's poem "Those Winter Sundays" (Section 1) support Brandt's views? Explain your response.
2. In which ways do Brandt's views intersect points made by Larry Ross in his interview with Studs Terkel?

# ∽ The Future of Work

*James Robertson*

James Robertson is the author of several books, including *The Future of Work: Jobs, Self-Employment, and Leisure after the Industrial Age* (1985). He has taken part in numerous conferences on the subject of work in North America, Australia, and various European countries. He is also a trustee of the New Economics Foundation, headquartered in London. The following essay is based on a lecture delivered by Robertson in 1991 in Oxfordshire, Great Britain; it was first published in the anthology *Mindfulness and Meaningful Work* (1994), edited by Claude Whitmyer.

**WARM-UP:** List some activities that you perform—hobbies, chores, etc.—that seem like "work" but for which you are not monetarily compensated. Describe one of them and explain in which ways it is and is not "work."

As we reach the final years of the present millennium,° we are entering a 1 new phase of human history. The new postmodern patterns of life and thought will reflect the emergence of a one-world human community, in which people will relate in a new way to themselves, to one another, to nature, and to what is larger than all of those and provides the framework and context for them.

Many people today, conditioned as they are by the scientific worldview of the modern age, think of the future as something which already exists. For them the future is there, down the track, waiting to be reached. Their concern about it, if they have one, is to forecast it and prepare for it. But that is not good enough. We humans help to create the future, each one of us, whether we like it or not. We are responsible for choosing between different possible futures, and for helping to realize the future we prefer.

## A Brief History of Work

When thinking about the future of work and the transformation of work that is now in prospect, it is instructive to look back on how work has been organized in past ages. In ancient societies, such as classical Greece and Rome, most people worked as slaves. In medieval Europe, most people worked as serfs. In modern industrial societies, most people work as employees. At least

---

*millennium:* A period of 1,000 years.

in a formal legal sense this development reflects some progress towards greater freedom and equality. Nevertheless, in modern, as in ancient and medieval society, the organization of work still reflects and reinforces the domination of subordinates by superiors: then, of slaves by masters and serfs by lords; now, of employees by employers. The assumption still is that most people should work for people and organizations other than themselves and for purposes other than their own.

In the 1980s we heard a lot about the need to shake off a dependency culture. But the way people work, and what they regard as work, is at the heart of a culture. In the 1990s we must confront the need to change the way we organize and understand work, so that most people will no longer be compelled to depend either on an employer to give them work or on the state to give them the dole.°

5      In other words, the postmodern era must be one in which employment is no longer the dominant form of work. The transition to the new era must include a liberation of work. Employment must give way to "ownwork" as the norm to which most people aspire.

Ownwork, as I have said in my book *Future Work,* is "activity which is purposeful and important, and which people organize and control for themselves. It may be either paid or unpaid. It is done by people as individuals and household members; it is done by groups of people working together; and it is done by people, who live in a particular locality, working locally to meet local needs. For the individual and the household, ownwork may mean self-employment, essential household and family activities, productive leisure activities such as do-it-yourself or growing some of one's own food, and participation in voluntary work. For groups of people, ownwork may mean working together as partners, perhaps in a community enterprise or a cooperative, or in a multitude of other activities—with social, economic, environmental, scientific, or other purpose—in which they have a personal interest and to which they attach personal importance. For localities, the significance of ownwork is that it contributes to local self-reliance, an increased local capacity to meet local needs by local work, and a reduction of dependence on outside employers and suppliers."

I am suggesting that the new consciousness and new social order will involve, among other things, a transformation of the dominant form of work from employment to ownwork.

## The Context for the Transformation

The medieval-to-modern transition was from a morally and religiously based worldview and world order to a worldview and world order claiming to

---

*dole:* Handout, welfare.

be objectively scientific. So modern economic life including people's work choices and also their consumer choices and investment decisions is supposedly governed by value-free economic laws, not subject to ethical decision. (Don't mix ethics with economics, the economics professors tell their students.)

Now, nature abhors° a vacuum, and the resulting ethical vacuum in economic life has been filled with the values of greed and power and competition. Global ecological and social catastrophe now threatens. A fundamental change of direction is necessary to a new path of development. As more and more people have become aware of this, a world-wide "new economics" movement has come into existence in the 1980s, including The Other Economic Summits (TOES) held annually since 1984.

In the next ten or twenty or thirty years, the new economics movement    10
envisages° a transformation of economic life and thought. Today's conventional economic approach is amoral, dependency-creating for people, and destructive for the Earth. These characteristics can be traced back to the thinking of the founders of modern thought: Bacon, Galileo, Descartes, Hobbes, Newton, and Adam Smith, though, in my view, it is silly to blame them for it. The new ways of economic life and thought must be enabling for people, conserving if not positively enriching for the Earth, and ethically based. Those are the underlying principles of the new economics. I believe they will form part of a wider new consciousness and social order—ethical, developmental, and (to borrow Albert Schweitzer's phrase) with reverence for Life.

And that, I believe, is the wider context in which we should be aiming to create a new future for work.

## Redefining Work and the Workplace

There are two important alternative views of the future of work which must be discussed. First is the approach of those who focus on people working in companies, such as the work of economist Fred Blum with Hormel, a meat packing and canning firm in the United States, and the Scott Bader Commonwealth, the common ownership pioneer in Great Britain. Blum's approach reflects the modern view of work as something done in employing organizations. One of the strengths of this approach is that that is how most people still understand work in countries like ours today, as employment, having a job. So, in that sense, it reflects where we actually have to start from.

The other view of the future of work, as typified by the approach I take, emphasizes the need to redefine work to include many kinds of purposeful and useful and rewarding activity, unpaid as well as paid, in addition to work

*abhors:* Detests.    *envisages:* Envisions, imagines.

in employing organizations. I think we need to create new opportunities for increasing numbers of people to take up many kinds of ownwork. We need also to ask how it was that the firm or enterprise ever came to be regarded as the basic unit of economic activity and wealth creation. Why, when modern economic ideas took shape, was the household or the local community not regarded as the basic building block in the economy? Why did the term "workplace" come to be attached to factories and offices, and not to households or communities? And how should we now set about turning those industrial-age definitions and assumptions on their heads?

There are, of course, serious difficulties here. Most of the people who concern themselves today with "the world of work" don't understand this approach or see it as practical or relevant. They don't see how it addresses the problems of the many millions of people who are now in unsatisfactory jobs, or who, being unemployed, want jobs. Business, government, and the established foundations are unwilling to support action research into the potential for reconceptualizing and restructuring work in this way.

15    And yet, surely, only by exploring the possibility of replacing employment with ownwork as the norm shall we be able to understand what a new consciousness and a new social order, that puts people first and focuses on the development of human potential, will actually mean. Because work is such a central feature of social organization and culture, an ownwork society will differ fundamentally from an employment society.

Take the question of men's work and women's work. In preindustrial societies, most men and women worked around their homes and neighborhoods, as part of the local village community. Then, in industrial society the split between men's work and women's work widened. Men became "economically active" members of the "work force," going out to "workplaces" in "the world of work" to do paid, high-status, impersonal kinds of work, more or less unrelated to their own personal and family interests and concerns. Meanwhile, women stayed at home, "dependents" of their menfolk, looking after the home and family—doing unpaid, low-status work, but with much more direct personal involvement and concern. Many of the problems and injustices resulting from this split are still with us today. By contrast, the ownwork society will offer men and women alike a more equal and balanced share in both the formal and informal sectors of this dual economy.

Or, again, take technology. An ownwork society will involve the development of enabling technologies which people—either as individuals, or as cooperatives, or as local communities—can control and use to serve their own purposes. These will also be ecologically conserving technologies. Examples include soft energy and organic farming technologies. By contrast, the employment society develops technologies that dominate people and nature, and are designed to be used by employees in the interest of employers.

The ownwork approach also opens up important questions about money. Because, at least to some extent, ownwork delinks people's work from their incomes, it points towards what is known as the Basic Income Scheme—under which all citizens will receive an unconditional basic income from the community. It points also to the need for wider distribution of capital, so that people will become less dependent on employers to provide them with the means of production—material (including land, premises, and equipment) as well as financial. And it points to the need for some fundamental changes in taxation that will encourage people to take on useful work, unpaid as well as paid.

Then there is the question of people's attitudes to work. In an employment society most people work for purposes other than their own. They work because they have to, to get a living. In such condition, other things being equal, work is something to be minimized. Remember the Caribbean proverb, "If work were a good thing, the rich would have found a way to keep it to themselves." In an ownwork society, on the other hand, in which most people are able to work on their own chosen purposes, work will be what gives meaning to most people's lives—as it is today for the fortunate few. It isn't just because I was brought up in Scotland and Yorkshire with more than my fair share of the puritan work ethic, that I think good work should be a centrally valuable part of human life.

What I am saying, then, is that there are two valid, though in a significant    20
respect different, approaches to creating a people-centered future for work, the one starting from today's work situation, the other from the possibility of a different situation in the future. There is no need to argue that one is right and the other wrong. They complement one another. Together they point the way to a future for work in which increasing numbers of corporate organizations will make human and ecological values central, and also in which increasing numbers of people will be liberated from the need to work in the typical corporate structure of today.

## A Challenge to the World's Faiths

The teachings of all the world's religious faiths are opposed to the amoral economic orthodoxy° of modern times. Why is it that they have failed to challenge it more successfully? Why have they shown so much respect for supposedly value-free expert knowledge about economic matters? Why have they failed to halt the onward march of economic imperialism into almost every corner of our lives?

---

*orthodoxy:* Convention, established doctrine or belief.

Is it perhaps because the faiths—I'm thinking of Buddhism, Hinduism, Islam, and Judaism, as well as Christianity—have tended to see things in terms of two separate worlds: an ideal spiritual world; and a sinful, delusory° "real-life" world which is not important enough to be worth the trouble of transforming?

Of course many Christians have been deeply concerned about work and other economic questions. An example is Pope John Paul's encyclical° "Centesimus Annus." Like its predecessors back to "Rerum Novarum" a hundred years ago, this contains many pointers to the kind of future we now need to create for work and economic life. But the fact remains that religious teachings have not yet made significant impact on the way of economic life and thought, and on the path of economic development, which humankind has actually taken in the last few hundred years.

Two factors may now help to change this. The first is the increasingly evident bankruptcy of the modern worldview in the face of the global crisis of environment and development. The second is the collapse of communism and the destruction of its credibility as a transformative ideology. The collapse of communism does not mean the triumph of capitalism or, as one American pundit° would have us believe, the end of history. On the contrary, I believe it opens the way for the faiths to participate more actively in a new approach to this worldly transformation.

25        Some of us in the New Economics Foundation, with the backing of the WorldWide Fund for Nature (WWF) and Christian Aid, are now working to establish a new network of faiths and economic alternatives. This is bringing new understanding to those of us who are not active members of a faith.

I hope it will also be useful to people from the various faiths who want to grapple with the contradictions between their faith's teachings and the secular institutional values that shape most people's work and economic life today.

I hope it will help us all to participate more effectively in the transformation of today's dominant values and institutions for the new era in human history which now beckons.

#### QUESTIONS

1. Define "ownwork." Does housework qualify as work, by this definition? Does volunteer work qualify?
2. Look up "postmodern" in a dictionary; then explain what Robertson means by this term.

---

*delusory:* Deceptive.  *encyclical:* Here meaning a papal letter addressed to the bishops of a church. *pundit:* A person who gives opinions in an authoritative manner.

3. Robertson claims, "We humans help to create the future, each one of us, whether we like it or not." List events of the recent past that have changed the future (your present), and then describe how today might be different if some of these events had not happened.

4. List similarities and differences between slaves, serfs, and employees. Do you agree with Robertson that "At least in a formal legal sense this development (from slaves to employees) reflects some progress towards greater freedom and equality"? Do you believe that the only progress toward freedom and equality has been in the legal arena?

5. What does Robertson mean by an "ethical vacuum in economic life"? What does he claim are the results of this? Does he give evidence in support of this claim?

6. How does Robertson treat views opposing his?

7. Explain why you agree or disagree with the author's claim that "Today's conventional economic approach is amoral, dependency-creating for people, and destructive for the Earth."

8. Is Robertson suggesting, in his conclusion, that religion and business should be linked? Explain your response.

## CONNECTIONS

1. Compare and contrast Robertson's history of work to the histories presented by Andrew Carnegie and by Sam Keen. Whose is Robertson's version of history more similar to?

2. Would Robertson's concept of "ownwork" solve the crisis of overwork that Barbara Brandt identifies? Explain your response.

# The Real Work of Writing: Revision

Experienced writers—whether professional or not—tend to think of writing as a process rather than as a product. Good writing is rarely something that can be produced in one sitting: It requires several attempts to develop ideas and discover the best way to express them. Looking at writing as a process assumes that you will approach each situation with patience and thought, creating several drafts and mulling over paragraphs, sentences, and words before you can begin to consider your essay complete.

People who approach writing as a process tend to rewrite a lot. To understand *revision,* you should look carefully at the word itself. Following the prefix *re* is the word "vision"; re-vision means "re-seeing" a piece of writing, seeing it in another way, perhaps with a different focus or goal in mind.

Even if you are an adept writer—that is, you have, in the past, written essays with some success—you can do better still. Suppose that you've been assigned to write another essay. You sit down that night and, in a matter of hours (after some prewriting, thinking, and nail biting), you write a first draft. You know it isn't as good as it could be, but you are not sure what step to take next—only that you should not give up yet. Since you know from past experience that you are able to read your work more carefully and critically when you approach it with a fresh eye, you decide to leave the essay alone for now and to return to it the next day to work on it some more.

You return to the essay to reread it. In the process, you might notice a few misspellings or grammatical errors—but it's too soon to begin correcting those. Instead, it is at this point that you have to begin to re-see the essay as a whole.

Revision can often be difficult, as it may require you to delete, rewrite, or add entire paragraphs; nonetheless, it is often the most important phase of the writing process.

Try not to think of revision as a one-step operation. In its early stage of development, an essay usually needs improvement in more than one place and in more than one way. Sometimes the ideas need to be better developed. Sometimes tangential information needs to be deleted. Sometimes the essay needs to be organized more effectively. Sometimes the tone needs refining. Because so many different aspects of an essay may need revision, it is best to approach the draft in a different way each time you reread it.

## *The Mind, Spirit, and Body Method of Revision*

One way to reexamine an essay effectively is to use the "Mind, Spirit, and Body" method of revision, which incorporates editing as well. Just as a human being exists in several realms—in mind, spirit, and body—so, too, does an essay as a whole. The "mind" of an essay is its content, its ideas. The "spirit" of an essay is the way in which it affects its readers. Finally, the "body" of an essay is made up of its physical features, its grammar and mechanics.

When you revise using the mind, spirit, and body method, you need to reread your essay several times, focusing on each of the three elements individually, highlighting different aspects of the essay that can be improved. But don't assume that you can reread the essay only three times—once for each part of the process. Sometimes you may have to read a draft several times while focusing only on its mind, whereas other times you may find the spirit of your essay most lacking. Or maybe you will read a draft several times to focus on its body—especially when you feel that the essay is near completion.

*Mind*    An essay's mind, on the one hand, consists of ideas. It is the content and logic of an essay. On the other hand, the mind of an essay is also reflected in its clarity and organization. Rereading an essay for its mind is not always as simple as reading an essay from beginning to end, adding or deleting a point here and there. Rather, you will probably want to focus separately on the development of individual ideas and on their organization and flow.

*Developing Ideas*    A paragraph is a coherent unit of thought. We organize an essay into paragraphs in order to help readers follow our thinking (and sometimes to help ourselves follow our own thinking). An effective paragraph states an idea or identifies a subject in a topic sentence and then discusses it— explains it fully and supports it with sufficient evidence (examples, analogies, expert opinions, facts, statistics, etc.). In the end, developed paragraphs should support a developed thesis—the main idea of the essay overall.

Poorly developed paragraphs, in contrast, usually possess one of two characteristics: They are either too long or too short. When a paragraph tries to cover too many ideas or too much information, it may leave a reader confused. If this is the case, divide the paragraph at the point where it shifts topics, then add a transitional word or phrase between the newly-created sections. Make sure that each paragraph is focused on *one* central idea. On the other hand, a paragraph that is too short may contain an undeveloped idea or one that is closely related to another paragraph. In the former case, develop the paragraph by explaining your ideas more fully or by adding an example or some other type of evidence (doing some prewriting on an undeveloped idea at this point might help); in the latter case, consider combining related paragraphs so that the idea developed in both will be clearer.

The key word in the preceding sentence is "consider." Treat your essay as a work in progress; look at it from various angles; put yourself in the chair of a reader who is following your ideas from paragraph to paragraph, not knowing what to expect.

*Organizing Ideas*    If you think that your essay sounds repetitive or disjointed, try the following techniques:

- *Add or improve topic sentences:* A topic sentence (which often begins a paragraph but can be any sentence in a paragraph) states the main idea of a paragraph. Topic sentences should support the thesis of the essay as a whole, while acting as street signs—letting a reader know where he or she is headed.
- *Outline the essay in its current rough shape to detect any gaps or inconsistencies in thought:* With a detailed post-drafting outline, you may be able to see more clearly where your essay needs further development. Perhaps you will find a paragraph where an added example would make a point stronger. Perhaps you will find paragraphs that can be rearranged for enhanced effect. Or perhaps you will realize that parts of your essay no longer make sense even to you!
- *Rearrange the paragraphs:* By looking either at the outline or at the draft itself, you may realize that a certain paragraph doesn't naturally follow another. Ask yourself what the direction of the essay is—or should be. For example, one of my students once wrote an essay arguing that stores selling pornographic material should not be allowed in cities because of their negative impact on the communities. His first paragraph dealt with the impact of such stores on the streets where they're located; the second paragraph dealt with their impact on the society as a whole; and the third discussed the stores' impact on the cities in which they operate. Once the student looked at a list of his main points, he realized that by switching the second and the third paragraph he could achieve a clearer flow of ideas and end on a stronger note.
- *Add transitions between paragraphs:* Sometimes, the paragraphs of your essay may appear in an order that makes sense to you but that isn't clear to your readers. To clarify the relationship between paragraphs, add transitions. A transition can consist of a word, a phrase, a sentence— sometimes even a whole transitional paragraph. The more complex the relationship between two points, the more it needs to be explained clearly. For example, in this book we purposely refer to the readings included between sections as "transitions," because they connect or show a relationship between two different themes; by including these selections, we hope to develop an anthology that not only flows well but also demonstrates an interconnectedness between a wide range of ideas.

Regardless of the length of a piece of writing—whether book, essay, or paragraph—if you use transitions to coordinate its ideas, it will flow better.

Some transitional words or phrases used between paragraphs or ideas show addition (like "also," "besides," "furthermore," "in addition," "moreover,"), some compare ("in comparison," "likewise," "similarly"), some contrast ("but," "however," "in contrast," "on the other hand"), and some show more complex relationships. For example, in Julius Lester's essay "Being a Boy," take a look at the transitions connecting paragraphs 10 through 16. The paragraphs are linked to each other by the words "though," "after," "finally," "but," "that," "fortunately," and "now." Using these simple words, Lester weaves the various points together; instead of feeling like you're reading a list, you feel like you're following a stream of thought. And that is what transitions can do for your paper: help it to flow well.

---

### Ways to Revise an Essay's Organization

- Add or improve topic sentences for each paragraph.
- Outline the essay in its current rough shape to detect any gaps or inconsistencies in thought.
- Rearrange the paragraphs as needed.
- Add or clarify transitions between paragraphs.

---

*Spirit*    The spirit of an essay determines how the writing is likely to affect readers. How much spirit you will impart to an essay depends on the writing situation and on the goal of the essay. The spirit of the essay includes its **voice** (or style); it also refers to the personal and emotional involvement of the writer, which is reflected not only in the flow of the language but also in the **tone** of the essay.

*Voice*    When you read, you become aware of the style, or voice, of a particular piece of writing. Voice is easily demonstrated: Read any pieces by different authors included in this text, and you are likely to "hear" a different voice in each. For an example, look again at Paolo Freire's "The 'Banking' Concept of Education" (Section 1), Warren Farrell's "Men as Success Objects" (Section 2), Becky Birtha's "In the Life" (Section 3), and Barbara Brandt's "Less Is More: A Call for Shorter Work Hours" (Section 4). Or pick up one of your textbooks and read a few pages: What is the voice of a science textbook, a math book, a history book? What is the voice of this book?

Ask yourself, then, who or what do you sound like when you write? Of course, different writing situations will require you to assume a particular version of your voice; you probably wouldn't write a letter to your best friend in the same way as you would articulate an argument about abortion or a proposal to a supervisor to purchase a new photocopy machine.

In revising for style, you might start by looking at your introduction: Will it engage readers, make them want to read on? Or check the conclusion: Does it add anything to the essay? Look specifically at your use of language: Are some sentences too wordy? Do clichés, jargon, or euphemisms dull your writing or hamper meaning? Are there places just begging for more descriptive verbs, for a metaphor or simile? Are there places that could benefit from more detail?

*Tone*   The combination of an author's voice and the content of a piece becomes the tone (or attitude) of a piece of writing. Readers are likely to be affected by the tone (remember Virginia Woolf's response to Professor Von X.'s angry writing, in the selection included in Section 2). While you may have written an early draft of an essay in a tone that corresponded to your mood at the time, you should later reread your essay for tone. You need to be aware of the way your writing will affect readers and of the way you want readers to perceive you. If you draft an essay in anger, frustration, or boredom, readers will notice this. And since one of the main goals of piece of writing, after all, is to find an audience—and writing that is unaware of readers and offends them is not likely to be read—you should adjust the tone of an essay to affect readers positively.

*Body*   When revising the body of an essay, you are reading for grammatical and mechanical correctness—another aspect of your writing that will affect your readers. This step requires you to read your essay sentence by sentence, searching for errors. If the draft has been written on a computer, you should first spell-check it, then print it out and read it on paper ("hard copy"); the change in mediums will help to clarify your view of the real (rather than the hoped-for) text. If you are aware of specific errors that you tend to commit, then you should be on the lookout for those. You may need to review past essays for any recurring errors; then reread the essay in progress several times, looking specifically for a different error each time. Grammatical correctness is an important part of a completed essay and one which most readers (especially teachers) expect. It is only one part of the process but it affects the way in which the content and style of the essay will be perceived as well.

### Final Words

Looking at writing as a process assumes that you will approach a writing situation in different ways, at different times, with different purposes. You will prewrite, you will draft, you will revise, and, just when you feel that your essay is complete and ready to be turned in for evaluation, you will edit carefully for correctness and clarity. In the end, from smudges of white-out, crumpled and discarded pages, or ghosts of paragraphs deleted from your computer screen, a new and better essay will emerge.

## Topics for Writing about Work

1. Assuming Andrew Carnegie's attitudes from "The Gospel of Wealth," write a letter in response to a charity group or nonprofit organization, rejecting its request for a donation or grant.
2. Write an essay in which you first explain and then agree or disagree with Sam Keen's ideas about the "unwritten rules" of success.
3. Interview people who perform white-collar work; then write an essay showing how their views about their jobs contrast or compare to Sam Keen's and Larry Ross's perspectives.
4. Summarizing Michael Parenti's views on wage inequities, write an essay that offers various explanations for the existence of differences in pay rates according to gender, race, or class.
5. Write an essay explaining why artists or homemakers *are* workers.
6. Write a personal essay that describes the profession you intend to pursue and discusses it in terms of monetary compensation, intellectual stimulation, emotional satisfaction, and societal good.
7. Write an essay that describes a job you have had; without saying whether you loved or hated this job, try to convey one of those feelings through your description.
8. If you believe that unemployed people should be given work, any type of job, rather than welfare, write an essay explaining your reasons for that belief.
9. Set up an interview with one of the administrators, janitors, or office workers from the school you attend; then write an essay describing that person's job and that person's feelings about his or her work. You may want to reread Studs Terkel's interview with Larry Ross, included in this section, as a possible model for your essay.
10. Find a person who has an unusual job—a coroner, a stuntman, a prostitute, a circus clown—and interview him or her; then write an essay describing the experiences and decisions that brought him or her to that career.
11. Choose an essay that you have already submitted for this course. Reread it repeatedly; then write a critique that points to specific parts of the essay, explaining how they could have been improved through the use of the "Mind, Spirit, and Body" method of revision. Submit the earlier version of your essay together with the critique.

## ∾ Kids in the Mall: Growing Up Controlled

*William Severini Kowinski*

A freelance writer who has also been an editor at the *Boston Phoenix*, W. S. Kowinski has written articles for many newspapers and magazines, including *Esquire*, *The New York Times Magazine*, *American Film*, and *West*. The following essay appeared in his first book, *The Malling of America: An Inside Look at the Great Consumer Paradise* (1985).

**WARM-UP:** Do you enjoy spending time in shopping malls? Why or why not? Why do you think so many people spend so much time there?

Butch heaved himself up and loomed over the group. "Like it was different for me," he piped. "My folks used to drop me off at the shopping mall every morning and leave me all day. It was like a big free baby-sitter, you know? One night they never came back for me. Maybe they moved away. Maybe there's some kind of a Bureau of Missing Parents I could check with."

—RICHARD PECK
*Secrets of the Shopping Mall,*
a novel for teenagers

1   From his sister at Swarthmore, I'd heard about a kid in Florida whose mother picked him up after school every day, drove him straight to the mall, and left him there until it closed—all at his insistence. I'd heard about a boy in Washington who, when his family moved from one suburb to another, pedaled his bicycle five miles every day to get back to his old mall, where he once belonged.

These stories aren't unusual. The mall is a common experience for the majority of American youth; they have probably been going there all their lives. Some ran within their first large open space, saw their first fountain, bought their first toy, and read their first book in a mall. They may have smoked their first cigarette or first joint or turned them down, had their first kiss or lost their virginity in the mall parking lot. Teenagers in America now spend more time in the mall than anywhere else but home and school. Mostly it is their choice, but some of that mall time is put in as the result of two-

. . . . . . . . . . . . . . . . . . . . . . . . . . . . . . . . . . . . . . .

paycheck and single-parent households, and the lack of other viable° alternatives. But are these kids being harmed by the mall?

I wondered first of all what difference it makes for adolescents to experience so many important moments in the mall. They are, after all, at play in the fields of its little world and they learn its ways; they adapt to it and make it adapt to them. It's here that these kids get their street sense, only it's mall sense. They are learning the ways of a large-scale artificial environment: its subtleties and flexibilities, its particular pleasures and resonances, and the attitudes it fosters.

The presence of so many teenagers for so much time was not something mall developers planned on. In fact, it came as a big surprise. But kids became a fact of mall life very early, and the International Council of Shopping Centers found it necessary to commission a study, which they published along with a guide to mall managers on how to handle the teenage incursion.°

The study found that "teenagers in suburban centers are bored and come     5
to the shopping centers mainly as a place to go. Teenagers in suburban centers spent more time fighting, drinking, littering and walking than did their urban counterparts, but presented fewer overall problems." The report observed that "adolescents congregated° in groups of two to four and predominantly at locations selected by them rather than management." This probably had something to do with the decision to install game arcades, which allow management to channel these restless adolescents into naturally contained areas away from major traffic points of adult shoppers.

The guide concluded that mall management should tolerate and even encourage the teenage presence because, in the words of the report, "The vast majority support the same set of values as does shopping center management." *The same set of values* means simply that mall kids are already preprogrammed to be consumers and that the mall can put the finishing touches to them as hard-core, lifelong shoppers just like everybody else. That, after all, is what the mall is about. So it shouldn't be surprising that in spending a lot of time there, adolescents find little that challenges the assumption that the goal of life is to make money and buy products, or that just about everything else in life is to be used to serve those ends.

Growing up in a high-consumption society already adds inestimable pressure to kids' lives. Clothes consciousness has invaded the grade schools, and popularity is linked with having the best, newest clothes in the currently

---

*viable:* Here meaning "workable."     *incursion:* Raid, hostile entrance.     *congregated:* Gathered.

acceptable styles. Even what they read has been affected. "Miss [Nancy] Drew wasn't obsessed with her wardrobe," noted *The Wall Street Journal.* "But today the mystery in teen fiction for girls is what outfit the heroine will wear next." Shopping has become a survival skill and there is certainly no better place to learn it than the mall, where its importance is powerfully reinforced and certainly never questioned.

The mall as a university of suburban materialism, where Valley Girls and Boys from coast to coast are educated in consumption, has its other lessons in this era of change in family life and sexual mores° and their economic and social ramifications. The plethora° of products in the mall, plus the pressure on teens to buy them, may contribute to the phenomenon that psychologist David Elkin calls "the hurried child": kids who are exposed to too much of the adult world too quickly, and must respond with a sophistication that belies° their still-tender emotional development. Certainly the adult products marketed for children—form-fitting designer jeans, sexy tops for preteen girls— add to the social pressure to look like an adult, along with the home-grown need to understand adult finances (why mothers must work) and adult emotions (when parents divorce).

Kids spend so much time at the mall partly because their parents allow it and even encourage it. The mall is safe, it doesn't seem to harbor any unsavory° activities, and there is adult supervision; it is, after all, a controlled environment. So the temptation, especially for working parents, is to let the mall be their babysitter. At least the kids aren't watching TV. But the mall's role as a surrogate mother may be more extensive and more profound.

10    Karen Lansky, a writer living in Los Angeles, has looked into the subject and she told me some of her conclusions about the effects on its teenaged denizens° of the mall's controlled and controlling environment. "Structure is the dominant idea, since true 'mall rats' lack just that in their home lives," she said, "and adolescents about to make the big leap into growing up crave more structure than our modern society cares to acknowledge." Karen pointed out some of the elements malls supply that kids used to get from their families, like warmth (Strawberry Shortcake dolls and similar cute and cuddly merchandise), old-fashioned mothering ("We do it all for you," the fast-food slogan), and even home cooking (the "homemade" treats at the food court).

The problem in all this, as Karen Lansky sees it, is that while families nurture children by encouraging growth through the assumption of responsibility and then by letting them rest in the bosom of the family from the rigors of

*mores:* Attitudes, habits, or manners.   *plethora:* Abundance.   *belies:* Hides, covers up.   *unsavory:* Disagreeable, distasteful.   *denizens:* Inhabitants or people who frequent a place.

growing up, the mall as a structural mother encourages passivity and consumption, as long as the kid doesn't make trouble. Therefore all they learn about becoming adults is how to act and how to consume.

Kids are in the mall not only in the passive role of shoppers—they also work there, especially as fast-food outlets infiltrate the mall's enclosure. There they learn how to hold a job and take responsibility, but still within the same value context. When *CBS Reports* went to Oak Park Mall in suburban Kansas City, Kansas, to tape part of their hour-long consideration of malls, "After the Dream Comes True," they interviewed a teenaged girl who worked in a fast-food outlet there. In a sequence that didn't make the final program, she described the major goal of her present life, which was to perfect the curl on top of the ice-cream cones that were her store's specialty. If she could do that, she would be moved from the lowly soft-drink dispenser to the more prestigious ice-cream division, the curl on top of the status ladder at her restaurant. These are the achievements that are important at the mall.

Other benefits of such jobs may also be overrated, according to Laurence D. Steinberg of the University of California at Irvine's social ecology department, who did a study on teenage employment. Their jobs, he found, are generally simple, mindlessly repetitive and boring. They don't really learn anything, and the jobs don't lead anywhere. Teenagers also work primarily with other teenagers; even their supervisors are often just a little older than they are. "Kids need to spend time with adults," Steinberg told me. "Although they get benefits from peer relationships, without parents and other adults it's one-sided socialization. They hang out with each other, have age-segregated jobs, and watch TV."

Perhaps much of this is not so terrible or even so terribly different. Now that they have so much more to contend with in their lives, adolescents probably need more time to spend with other adolescents without adult impositions, just to sort things out. Though it is more concentrated in the mall (and therefore perhaps a clearer target), the value system there is really the dominant one of the whole society. Attitudes about curiosity, initiative, self-expression, empathy,° and disinterested learning aren't necessarily made in the mall; they are mirrored there, perhaps a bit more intensely—as through a glass brightly.

Besides, the mall is not without its educational opportunities. There are     15
bookstores, where there is at least a short shelf of classics at great prices, and other books from which it is possible to learn more than how to do sit-ups. There are tools, from hammers to VCRs, and products, from clothes to records, that can help the young find and express themselves. There are older

*empathy:* Understanding, emotional identification with something or someone.

people with stories, and places to be alone or to talk one-on-one with a kindred° spirit. And there is always the passing show.

The mall itself may very well be an education about the future. I was struck with the realization, as early as my first forays° into Greengate, that the mall is only one of a number of enclosed and controlled environments that are part of the lives of today's young. The mall is just an extension, say, of those large suburban schools—only there's Karmelkorn instead of chem lab, the ice rink instead of the gym: It's high school without the impertinence° of classes.

Growing up, moving from home to school to the mall—from enclosure to enclosure, transported in cars—is a curiously continuous process, without much in the way of contrast or contact with unenclosed reality. Places must tend to blur into one another. But whatever differences and dangers there are in this, the skills these adolescents are learning may turn out to be useful in their later lives. For we seem to be moving inexorably° into an age of pre-planned and regulated environments, and this is the world they will inherit.

Still, it might be better if they had more of a choice. One teenaged girl confessed to *CBS Reports* that she sometimes felt she was missing something by hanging out at the mall so much. "But I'm here," she said, "and this is what I have."

### QUESTIONS

1. Kowinski uses an anecdotal introduction, one that provides a detailed, specific example to demonstrate an idea. Do you find this more effective than, for example, the informative introduction that begins Paolo Freire's "The 'Banking' Concept of Education"? Explain your reasons.

2. What is ironic about Kowinski's statement that "Some [American youth] ran within their first large open space, saw their first fountain, bought their first toy, and read their first book in a mall"?

3. Do you agree with Karen Lansky's conclusions, paraphrased by Kowinski, about what the mall provides for teenagers? Why or why not?

4. Do you agree with Kowinski's evaluation of mall jobs and the way they affect teenagers' goals and views of their future?

*kindred:* Allied, having a similar nature or character.    *forays:* Excursions.    *impertinence:* Irrelevance.
*inexorably:* Unavoidably.

5. Kowinski claims that "mall kids are already programmed to be consumers," to be "hard-core, lifelong shoppers" who will not challenge "the assumption that the goal of life is to make money and buy products." Is this a dominant assumption in your life? Do you have other "goals of life"?

6. Is Kowinski merely looking for a somewhat mythical reality often called "the good old days"? Or do you find his critique justified and accurate?

7. Do you think that, as he researched this topic, Kowinski talked to the teenagers about whom he is writing? Should your answer to this question affect your views about this essay? Why or why not?

8. Several words recur throughout the essay. Identify these recurrences and explain their effect: Do they detract from or emphasize the main idea?

## CONNECTIONS

1. How would Paolo Freire, the author of "The 'Banking' Concept of Education" (included in Section 1), respond to Kowinski's idea of the "mall as a university of suburban materialism" and "a structured environment [that] encourages passivity and consumption"?

2. The teenagers discussed in Kowinski's essay seem to be shaped by the same societal influences that affect the "girlchild" of Marge Piercy's poem "Barbie Doll" (included in Section 2). Have those influences affected you? If so, in what ways?

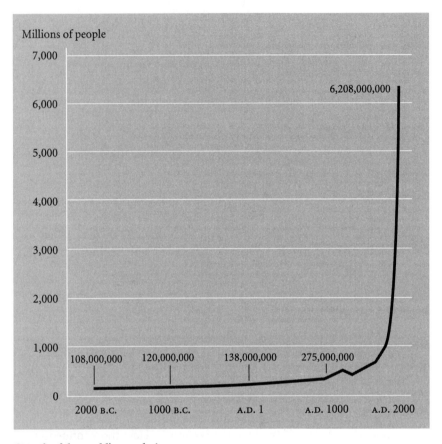

**Growth of the world's population**

The world's population grew slowly before A.D. 1. It then almost doubled by the year 1000. At its present rate of growth, the world's population will double in about 45 years. The world will have over 6 billion people by the year 2000. Source: WORLD BOOK estimates based on data from the United Nations. (Credit: From THE WORLD BOOK ENCYCLOPEDIA © 1997 World Book, Inc. By permission of the Publisher.)

# The Evolving Environment

# Meaningful Recurrence:
# Balanced Construction

• • • • • • • • • • • • • • • • • • • • • • • • • •

Often, when writers want to emphasize a point, they express it in such a way as to attract our attention not only through the strength of their ideas but also through the "sound" of the sentence (sentences can have a beat and a rhythm just as music does). All of us use this technique occasionally—especially when we are passionate about a subject (as Hamlet was when he intoned "To be or not to be" or Benjamin Barber is in his essay "America Skips School," when he counters the claim that all men are born free by saying, "In real life, as every parent knows, children are born fragile, born needy, born ignorant, born unformed, born weak, born foolish, born dependent—born in chains"). Many folk sayings also use a balanced construction: Consider "A penny saved is a penny earned," "Children should be seen, not heard," even Forrest Gump's "Stupid is as stupid does."

Parallel construction doesn't always draw attention to similarities between different elements; writers also use parallelism when they want to *contrast* two ideas. The similar grammatical form can accentuate the difference in content. This is called *juxtaposition.* One powerful example of juxtaposition is a sentence from Martin Luther King, Jr.'s "Letter from Birmingham Jail," written in 1963: Discussing the emerging Civil Rights movement in the United States, King wrote, "The nations of Asia and Africa are moving with jetlike speed toward gaining political independence, but we still creep at horse-and-buggy pace toward gaining a cup of coffee at a lunch counter." A selection from Ecclesiastes, the third reading in this section, also offers a string of juxtapositions: "a time to be born and a time to die; / a time to plant and a time to uproot; / a time to kill and a time to heal. . . ." The phrases in each of these examples are nearly parallel in structure, but the ideas they express are polar opposites—and that opposition is brought into focus by the sentence construction.

## *Recurrence within a Sentence*

When including in one sentence several ideas that you want to present as closely related, you should try to express them in similar grammatical form: Pair a verb with a verb, an adjective with an adjective, a noun with a noun, a clause with a clause (as the author of the book of Ecclesiastes did in the example just quoted). Annie Dillard uses this effect when she writes, in her essay "Living like Weasels" (included in this section), "I think it would be well, and proper, and obedient, and pure, to grasp your one necessity and not let it go, to dangle from it limp wherever it takes you." In this case, Dillard balances three adverbs—"well," "proper," and "obedient"—and two phrases—"to grasp your one necessity," "to dangle from it limp."

### Recurrence within a Paragraph

In the same way, when you present in one paragraph several sentences that are related, find ways to structure the whole sentences similarly. Note the following examples, taken from selections included in this section: In "Earth's Body," Scott Russell Sanders writes, "Heart pumps. Muscles twitch. Ears fill with indecipherable song." In "The Origins of Modern Vegetarianism," Paul Amato and Sonia Partridge quote an Australian saying: "If it moves, kill it; if it doesn't, cut it down." In a paragraph from "America Skips School" (included in Section 1), Benjamin Barber exclaims, "Because we believe in profits, we are consummate salespersons and efficacious entrepreneurs. Because we love sports, ours are the dream teams. Why can't a Chicago junior high school be as good as the Chicago Bulls? Because we cherish individuality and mobility," he continues, returning to the recurring construction, "we have created a magnificent (if costly!) car culture. . . ."

This kind of meaningful balance or pattern of recurrence should not be confused, however, with boring, unplanned repetition—as in "I ran home. Then I turned on the TV. Then I watched a show. Then I had dinner"—or "Because I was tired, I lay down. Because the bed was warm, I fell asleep. Because I was asleep, I started to dream." So, how can you tell the difference? Much of it depends on the amount of attention you invested in the sentence or paragraph. If the repetition happened accidentally, be wary. It may still be worth keeping, but you need to make that a conscious decision. Another factor is the level of significance of the point you are emphasizing through parallel construction. Save this "special effect" for ideas that you feel deserve and can withstand the spotlight that the parallelism puts on them. If you draw a reader's attention to something that's weak or unimportant, you will simply underscore those unwanted qualities.

### Recurrence within an Entire Selection

Recurrence, however, can refer to more than just a repetition within a sentence or paragraph. Ideas and symbols also recur, creating patterns or motifs that hold together an entire piece of writing, making it more cohesive. This occurs in essays and stories, in poems and plays—wherever the author wants to draw attention to a particular element of the whole in a more subtle, less explicit way (instead of telling the reader outright "this is important").

You've already encountered many such recurrences in various selections included in this book: for example, the recurrence of the word "strong" used to describe Elisa Allen in John Steinbeck's "The Chrysanthemums" (preceding Section 4); and of the words "structure" and "environment," used to emphasize the thesis in Kowinsky's essay "Kids in the Mall" (in Section 4); of the line "Love is finished again" in Yehuda Amichai's poem of the same name (in Section 3); or of the theme of similarities between the "quiet girl" and the narrator in Maxine Hong Kingston's "The Quiet Girl" (in Section 1).

Such meaningful repetitions, then, offer important clues about ideas that are significant in anything you read. Knowing this, you can begin to consider motifs and patterns that *you* can develop in your own writing.

# ∾ The Science of Place

*Winifred Gallagher*

> A graduate of the University of Pennsylvania, Winifred Gallagher is a science
> writer whose essays about human behavior have appeared in *The Atlantic
> Monthly, Rolling Stone, Discover,* and other magazines. Gallagher has also
> served as the psychology editor of *American Health.* The following selection
> is adapted from her 1993 book *The Power of Place: How Our Surroundings
> Shape Our Thoughts, Emotions, and Actions;* her most recently published
> book is *I.D.: How Heredity and Experience Make You Who You Are* (released
> in paperback under the title *Just the Way You Are*).

> **WARM-UP:** Think of various interiors in which you spend a lot of
> time. How does each one affect you?

1    Last spring, I spent several days sealed off from the sweet palmy swelter of
New Orleans in a series of frigid polyester conference rooms, listening to
men in white coats discuss the latest developments in brain science. Weary of
sci-fi scanning techniques and neurotransmitter balances, I treated myself to a
lecture by Mihaly Csikszentmihalyi, a professor of psychology at the University of Chicago best known for his improbable best-seller, *Flow;* despite its
easygoing title, this rather difficult, scholarly book methodically explores the
parameters of what the author terms "optimum experience" and the rest of us
call a good time. As I had hoped, Csikszentmihalyi was not concerned with
the workings of pills or the measurement of rats, and his introductory
remarks, which centered on his earliest forays° into his chosen area of inquiry,
went straight for the jugular of behavioral science. "As a small child, I wondered why most of the otherwise knowledgeable, accomplished adults who
surrounded me seemed to have almost no idea about how to live a satisfying
life," he said. "It was clear to me even then that the answer wasn't money or
power but, somehow, the ability to control and enjoy one's experience."

A bit of unaccustomed reflection on one dimension of our experience
suggests that the answer to that perennial child's question—If grown-ups
know so much, why aren't they happy?—is increasingly bound up with the
places in which we spend our lives. Many of the eclectic° researches that support this commonsensical idea are less discoveries than rediscoveries of principles that our forebears considered obvious. Throughout history, people of
all cultures have assumed that environment influences behavior. Now modern
science is confirming that our actions, thoughts, and feelings are indeed

---

*forays:* Raids, expeditions.    *eclectic:* Diverse, versatile.

shaped not just by our genes and neurochemistry, history and relationships, but also by our surroundings.

More than two thousand years ago, Hippocrates' observation that our well-being is affected by our settings was established as a cornerstone of Western medicine. The healers of antiquity had no idea that the malaria parasite is carried by mosquitoes, but they noted that the residents of hill towns were healthier than those from marshy regions, and concluded that the problem was the "bad air"—*mal aria*—of such places. Of all the environmental influences on a person's state, however, "it is chiefly the changes of seasons which produce diseases, and in the seasons the great changes from cold or heat," wrote the father of medicine, adding that "Such diseases as increase in the winter ought to cease in the summer, and such as increase in the summer ought to cease in the winter. . . ."

The centuries of literature on the relationship between mood and the seasons comprise a striking testimony to science's venerable association of behavior and environment. One of the most fundamental and enduring principles of classical medicine positively encouraged analogies between our internal and external climates. Physicians believed that the action of the four humors, or body fluids, determined everything from a person's constitution to his character. Because the balances of yellow bile, black bile, phlegm, and blood, which corresponded to the four elements of fire, earth, water, and air, were also related to summer, fall, winter, and spring, an individual's physiological and behavioral changes were inevitably viewed in the context of the sun's. In the second century A.D., Aretaeus prescribed that "Lethargics° are to be laid in the light and exposed to the rays of the sun, for the disease is gloom"; in the fourth century, Posidonius observed: "Melancholy occurs in autumn, whereas mania in summer."

Classical science's propensity° for viewing a person's state in its environmental context persisted down through the ages. In the seventeenth century, the English scholar Robert Burton, who suffered from bipolar disorder, in which profound depressions alternate with chaotic bursts of mania, compiled his exhaustive *Anatomy of Melancholy*. This text includes some stereotypical assumptions about climate and national as well as individual temperament that remain commonplace: "Hot countries are most troubled with . . . great numbers of madmen. . . . They are ordinarily so choleric° in their speeches, that scarce two words pass without railing or chiding in common talk, and often quarreling in their streets. . . . Cold air in the other extreme is almost as bad as hot. . . . In those northern countries, the people are therefore generally dull, heavy, and [include] many witches, which [some] ascribe to melancholy." Two hundred years later, this tendency to see connections between behavior and its setting still prevailed among the first practitioners of the infant science of psychiatry.

5

---

*lethargics:* People who exhibit exaggerated drowsiness, laziness, or indifference.    *propensity:* A natural inclination or preference.    *choleric:* Easily moved to anger.

Around the turn of the twentieth century, the wisdom of the ages concerning the relationship between place and state was eclipsed by technological and cultural changes so rapid and vast that social scientists still debate our ability to adjust to them. In one of the least remarked of these transformations, the Industrial Revolution drew the West indoors. Turning away from the natural world, huge populations gravitated toward a very different one made up of homes and workplaces that were warm and illuminated regardless of season or time of the day—although even on a rainy morning, it is brighter outside than inside with the lights on.

Society quickly adapted to its new indoor urban environment. Only a hundred years ago, the overwhelming majority of Americans lived in the country, while today, most cluster in metropolitan areas. Like other living things, however, our species has evolved over millions of years to respond to the cycles of the earth and sun with predictable biochemical and behavioral changes. Environmentally minded scientists have begun to question the trade-offs we unwittingly make in order to live sealed up inside an artificially heated, cooled, and lighted world that is structured around economic rather than biologic concerns. They point out, for example, that in the West, exposure to the sun's bright light has become erratic in duration and timing for the first time in history, and they suspect that the fact that most of us are no longer wakened by the dawn, drawn outdoors for much of the day by our way of life, and lulled to sleep by darkness helps explain why up to a third of us suffer from sleep or mood problems, or both. What is startling about that observation is not the idea that light has to do with mental and physical health, which was accepted a hundred years ago, but the fact that science forgot about it.

That the importance of light was obscured even from scientists has partly to do with a profound change in the modern Western attitude toward time itself. Over the millennia, our species developed a cyclical sense of time, still marked by recurring solstice° festivals, such as Christmas and Hanukkah, which bring light into the dark winter, and the spring celebrations, such as Easter and Passover, which celebrate the sun's return. The gradual replacement of this mode of time perception by the more recent historical, linear concept helped conceal seasonal mood shifts from modern medicine.

Just as society began to measure time by its own doings rather than nature's, individuals increasingly looked inward rather than outward for insights into their behavior. This propensity was encouraged by two milestones in twentieth-century science. First came Freudian theory, which emphasized the overwhelming importance of a person's internal psychological processes, heavily shaped by the past, in determining his ways. Metaphorically, the inward orientation of psychoanalysis, rooted in the thinking of its

_solstice:_ A point in time that marks the beginning of summer or winter.

early Eastern European forefathers, reflects something of the enclosed, restricted environment of the *shtetl*,° whose residents could not always move about freely. In such a culture, what psychoanalysts would later disparage° as a "flight into health" was not necessarily an option. Convinced of the therapeutic primacy of insight and inner change, Freudians were skeptical of the idea that altering one's milieu,° say, where one lived, might also have merit. That kind of thing was, they said, "running away from your problems," even though the people who ran away sometimes felt better.

As the psychoanalytic influence broadened, promoting soul searching as the royal road to wisdom and well-being, the rapid growth of psychopharmacology gave rise to another hypothesis, one in which all depended on inheriting the right neurochemistry. Both psychoanalysis and drugs, which are often seen as antithetical,° emphasize the individual's internal processes as the determinants of mental health, and pay little attention to the external environment, as earlier schools of thought had. . . .    10

Like those of other living things, our structure, development, and behavior rise from a genetic foundation sunk in an environmental context. Yet while we readily accept that a healthy seed can't grow into a plant without the right soil, light, and water, and that a feral° dog won't behave like a pet, we resist recognizing the importance of environment in our own lives. Nonetheless, says Hofer, "place, which is a good term in that there's not a lot of baggage to it, is important to human beings right from the beginning. Sperm and eggs are very clearly influenced by their immediate surroundings. When changes in the mucus of the uterine environment facilitate the process, sperm have a better chance of fertilizing the egg. In some way, the mother even decides which sperm gets to her ovum. During wartime, for example, X-bearing sperm are somehow favored.° And if an egg is not in the right spot, it can't form a placenta. The same principles apply when a zygote° is only a few cells as when a whole baby is interacting with its world. Nature and nurture cooperate in producing behavior, and the organism has a lot of say about what it's going to get out of its environment."

A good bit of that "say," however, depends on an organism's being in the right place at the right time. If it is not, despite normal genes, its physiological and behavioral development can be skewed. Siamese cats raised in a cold environment develop brown fur while those reared in a hot one are white, for example, and chicks incubated in an environment in which the eggs aren't rotated end up with malformed leg joints. Similarly, kittens raised in the dark stumble, fall, and collide when they are put in the light, and rats reared in dull

---

*shtetl:* Yiddish name for the small Jewish towns and villages that existed in Europe before World War II. *disparage:* Belittle, defame.    *milieu:* Setting, environment.    *antithetical:* Opposed, contrary.    *feral:* Wild, undomesticated.    *"X-bearing sperm . . . favored":* An X-bearing sperm will become a female. *zygote:* The cell created by the union of a sperm and an egg.

environments have smaller brains than those raised in complex ones. "When you're in that straitjacket of thinking in dichotomies° of nature or nurture, you're going to make mistakes," says Hofer. "We can talk about them as components of a system, but to see genes and environment in opposition—no. I wouldn't even say they interact, exactly. The proper analogy is closer to what happened when the Pilgrims arrived in America. They didn't simply duplicate England, although its culture exerted lots of influence. The United States is really a process that developed from what the settlers were predisposed to do and the new environment's enhancement of and constraints on that, from the climate to the presence of the Indians. It's impossible to say that one or the other determined the nation."

Hofer's enthusiasm for the subject of environment and behavior has developed over years of iconoclastic° research on our most important relationship; although the mother-infant bond has traditionally been considered a social one, his studies show that it is woven from the sensory strands of its physical, flesh-and-blood milieu. In laboratories and neonatal intensive care units, along power lines and in addiction treatment centers, in tropical forests and polar outposts, other researchers from disparate° disciplines are also uncovering hidden dimensions of the role our surroundings play in our well-being. An Olympian business, science requires gazing fearlessly into the dark, gaping, fire-breathing maw° of the nature of things and, in a facts-just-the-facts voice, reporting back only what can be measured, weighed, or counted. Although such objectivity and restraint are practical and elegant, scientists' formal discourse usually leaves out some of the juicy parts of their thinking. An untidy interdisciplinary subject such as the effects of places on behavior permits them to relax and indulge in some speculation, and to combine perspectives with those of peers from other fields.

These days, any big conference of scientists concerned with the future of our planet or species includes presentations and discussions of aspects of the relationship between people and places. At a recent annual meeting of the American Psychological Association, for example, two papers suggested something of the complexities to be revealed by increasingly sophisticated investigations of this feedback system. One study was an analysis of the ways in which lively and dull interiors affect mood and performance. When the subjects' responses to a stimulating, plant-filled, homey setting and a grim, institutional one were contrasted, the only reaction they all shared was a decline in vigorous activity and increased feelings of fatigue in the austere environment.

---

*dichotomies:* Here meaning two mutually exclusive groups.    *iconoclastic:* Here meaning going against established beliefs or institutions.    *disparate:* Different, diverse.    *maw:* Jaws, mouth.

This finding suggests that one reason staying in the hospital furthers recuperation is that it makes patients feel tired, which means it is easier for them to stay in bed and rest; they perk up when they get home because the environment there is so much more stimulating. More significant, however, the subjects' other responses to their surroundings varied according to certain of their personal traits, such as the tendency to "lose" oneself in a task or to be easily distracted. In other words, an everyday setting that inclines one individual to feel and function well can push another in the opposite direction. The next step in this research is the development of an "environmental sensitivity scale" or questionnaire that will systematically measure individual reactions to a range of ambient° conditions. Equipped with good data on which, or how many, people are sensitive to lighting, spatial arrangements, noise, and other ordinary features of our surroundings, architects, office managers, doctors, and the rest of us will be better able to create more supportive, personalized environments....

Like our choices about relationships or careers, our decisions about where    15
to live or work can have a significant if often unsuspected impact on our well-being, whether through subtle means, such as lighting and plants, or more directly, through agents such as allergens° or pollutants. Think for a moment about our chemical environment—the air we breathe, the water we drink. Over the past twenty years, it has been drastically altered by technology, but we don't understand the complex ways that the resulting changes could affect us. It is possible that chemical stressors are pushing certain people over the threshold for developing particular physical or psychological problems. In the future, a trip to the doctor may well involve an evaluation of such environmental components of our health.

Just as the world around us affects our behavior, our thoughts, emotions, and actions affect our surroundings. When asked to predict the most important environmental influence on behavior in the twenty-first century, researchers almost invariably give the same answer: urbanization, or making places citylike without necessarily making cities. Yet it would be equally accurate to say that urbanization is also the most important behavioral influence on the environment. The technological and social changes associated with this unprecedented worldwide development mean that before we superficially adjust to a new, lower status quo, our ever-adaptable species must understand what a good environment really is, in a community as well as a forest, in an office and school as well as a home. Burdened with increasingly complex social roles, we need places that support rather than fragment our lives, places

---

*ambient:* Surrounding.    *allergens:* Substances that cause allergies.

that balance the hard, standardized, and cost-efficient with the natural, personal, and healthful. To secure this kind of environmental quality in a rapidly changing world, we must put the principles emerging from the multidisciplinary science of places into practice on local and global levels.

In its hard-edged way, the research of environmentally minded scientists often confirms our own softer perceptions and intuitions, both individual and cultural, concerning the relationship between people and places. My own absorption in the subject began with the purchase of a small wooded property in upstate New York. From my first glimpse of the one-room schoolhouse commanding its sunlit site with all the authority of a small Greek temple, I knew I was home. Practitioners of the eponymous° Chinese form of geomancy° would attribute this feeling to the place's *feng shui,* or "wind and water." Not easy to nail down in Western terms, *feng shui* more or less corresponds to what we call ambience, or a place's distinctive atmosphere. Resting on a gentle shelf above a dirt road, the building is protected from bad weather by the low mountains behind it, while the rill° and brook that flow in front attract great blue herons, trout, deer, wildflowers, and other harbingers° of benign *chi,* a ubiquitous° energy that permeates places as well as people and other living things. According to Chinese tradition, the proper balance of *chi* ensures good *feng shui.* For whatever reason, this country place immediately struck me as just the thing to counter some of the environmental stress —bad *feng shui,* if you will—that life in a big city entails. My Manhattan street corner is a good example. Several times a day, the neighbors recoil from the shriek of tires, and even the crunch of metal, as two cars meet on a collision course at this intersection. The traffic isn't unusually heavy there, but two wide boulevards cross hard by an avenue coming in at a diagonal, resulting in three streaming rivers of undisciplined *chi* that converge just where the cars so often do.

Behavioral scientists don't employ *feng shui* terminology, but their method of analyzing environments in terms of the stimulation they afford boils down to much the same thing. Whether we think about *chi* or sensory input, we all seek a comfortable level of arousal from our settings, one that is neither so low as to court boredom nor so high as to invite anxiety. Over the course of a day, a week, and a year, most of us seek places that provide different degrees of stimulation. Arriving at the schoolhouse on Friday, I collapse and wait for the rhythms of nature to work their magic on my fried urban

---

*eponymous:* Relating to the person for whom something is named.    *geomancy:* The practice of finding hidden knowledge through the interpretation of geographical features.    *rill:* A very small brook. *harbingers:* Messengers, forerunners.    *ubiquitous:* Widespread, found everywhere.

nerves; after a few days of staring at the creek, I'm eager for the Broadway boogie-woogie again. Like weekenders from the time of ancient Rome, I have learned to regulate psychology with geography.

After discovering the benefits of running away from my problems, I began to exploit the therapeutic potential of my everyday surroundings at times when a flight into health wasn't feasible. Whether the strategy is to clean the house from one end to the other or walk a few miles of city streets, I've found that exposure to larger systems of physical organization, preferably while working the body, almost invariably brings glimmerings of hope and purpose. As William James observed while writing of another source for these two sustaining sensibilities, religion involves "the belief that there is an unseen order, and that our supreme good lies in harmoniously adjusting ourselves thereto." ...

If any one experience inclined me to spend several years exploring the    20 power of place, it was a trip through a part of America especially rich in geophysical peculiarities, where bumper stickers read: "Feel the Magic." The Four Corners area of the Southwest, of which Santa Fe is the unofficial capital, has a very old reputation among the Hopi, Navaho, Pueblo, and Spanish colonial cultures as a "sacred place" possessing special psychoactive properties. For hundreds of years, one of its top tourist attractions has remained the tiny village of Chimayo, the "Lourdes of America" that draws thousands of visitors each year during Holy Week. Long before Spanish missionaries dedicated a charming adobe chapel to the Madonna there, nearby Native Americans had believed that the springs and surrounding soil had special healing powers. This theory got some impressive support in the early nineteenth century, when a Christian visitor to the shrine saw a burst of light shoot from a spot on the ground. Since the auspicious° fireworks, piles of crutches, eyeglasses, and braces of those claiming to have been cured by the Virgin's "holy earth," exposed by a hole in the chapel's floor and free for the taking, have accumulated in the *santuario*.

At 3 A.M. on the morning after visiting Chimayo, I set off on a pilgrimage to a different kind of sacred place: the Jimez hot springs, carved into a mountain ridge in the high country above Los Alamos. My host on the freezing, moonless hike up to the site was an esteemed member of the Santa Clara Pueblo. Trusting entirely in what certainly seemed like his supernatural power to lead on through the pitch dark, up slippery slopes and across invisible logs spanning roaring streams, I finally glimpsed a tier of falls dropping into three natural basins in the obsidian cliffs. Plunging through steam clouds rising in the frigid air, we sank gratefully into the 100-degree water. At 4 A.M., our only

---

*auspicious:* Attended by favorable signs.

neighbors were some southern bikers and their girlfriends, who sported and mated, smoked pot and sipped Jack Daniel's in one of the pools below. Fearing that their raunchy behavior offended my companion, whose people consider this spot holy, I offered a prissy apology. Amused, he shook his head. "This place likes what they do," he said. "However, we usually come here to cleanse ourselves. Heal ourselves. As we tell our young people, sometimes you can't just watch the video. There are special things in the places all around us, but you may have to work hard to see them."

Bobbing gently above the vast valley as rose began to tint the sky behind the purply Sangre de Cristo range, I found that all the special things to see and otherwise sense fostered a special state of mind. Hardly for the first time, it struck me that we are only infinitesimal° flickers in the great scheme of things, but the emotion this inspired was altogether different from feeling like just another gnat during rush hour. This powerful perception of being a very small fish in a very big pond, called the "diminutive effect" by environmental psychologists, has been deliberately cultivated by the architects of Gothic cathedrals and Nazi stadiums alike. My sense of total immersion in the surroundings was further augmented by the wall of sound created by the thundering falls, and perhaps by certain unusual properties of a setting situated at a heady altitude in an area riddled with geophysical peculiarities. Certainly the sulfurous fumes exuded by the springs would have been familiar to the Delphic oracle,° said to have derived a good bit of her inspiration from whiffing volcanic gases. In short, some alchemy of natural grandeur framed in an unfamiliar Native American context, a few objective somethings-or-other, and a riot of neurochemicals set off by sleep deprivation, cold air, novelty, hot water, and some voyeurism produced an experience I'm happy enough to attribute to my presence in a magical place. Fortunately, speculating about some of its parts doesn't detract from the mystery of the whole.

The reluctance to dismiss heightened experiences in special places as entirely subjective is shared by James Lovelock, the British scientist who developed the "Gaia° hypothesis." This influential concept, which forms the core of my oldest daughter's high school biology course this year, approaches the earth and its processes as a unified living organism rather than as a grab bag of separate biological and geophysical systems. By profession, Lovelock is obliged to remain in the realm of the rational, but he doesn't discount the unusual experiences he has enjoyed in certain natural settings merely because science can't yet explain them. One such place is Brentor, an ancient volcanic site near his home.

---

*infinitesimal:* Extremely small.    *the Delphic oracle:* In ancient Greece, people consulted the priestess from the temple of Apollo in Delphi, to find out what the future would hold.    *Gaia:* Name given to the Earth by those who see it as one living organism.

Lovelock has written that when he climbs this strange hump command-ing a vista of the Atlantic, the Bodmin moor, and the Dartmoor cliffs, he sometimes experiences "a sense of presence. Not extrasensory, but something perceived by the senses that can neither be seen, heard, or felt in the usual way. It would be easy to attribute to this sensation the recognition of something sacred. A momentary contact with some entity larger and greater than the mind." Attempting to explain the derivation of this sensation, he cites a physi-cist colleague's special interpretation: the senses convey to the brain far more information than we can consciously be aware of; it is the totality of all that undifferentiated input that we perceive in a general way as ambience. At spe-cial places such as Brentor and the Jimez springs, this diffuse essence is some-how stronger and more poignant.

Soon after returning from New Mexico, I started to do the research for   25
this book. Every once in a while, someone who knew what I was up to would say something along these lines: All right then, where's the *best* place? There is no way to answer that question without asking "For whom?" The only univer-sal truth I've discovered during the past few years' work is that the recipe for the good life that Mihaly Csikszentmihalyi and all the rest of us imagined as children calls for being in the right place at the right time as often as we can manage.

## QUESTIONS

1. Gallagher weaves the ideas of Mihaly Csikszentmihalyi into her essay. What is Csikszentmihalyi's "answer" for living a satisfying life? Can you offer examples to illustrate his point?

2. What are some historical perceptions of the influence of environment on our lives, according to Gallagher?

3. Explain James Lovelock's "Gaia hypothesis," paraphrased by Gallagher in this essay.

4. What are some "sacred places" in the United States? Have you ever been in a place that felt to you somehow "magical," charged with a special energy? What factors do you think affected your mood there? Consider some of the factors that Gallagher mentions as she analyzes her own reaction to the Jimez hot springs.

5. What does Gallagher see as the difference between feeling like an "in-finitesimal flicker in the great scheme of things" and feeling like "just another gnat during rush hour"? Do you agree with her perception?

6. Gallagher quotes and paraphrases many scientists and scientific stud-ies. Are these sources convincing? Do you know of any other studies related to the influence of place in our lives?

7. Does this essay change the way you understand the definition of "environment"?

## CONNECTIONS

1. Explain the relationship between Gallagher's piece and William Kowinski's transitional piece "Kids in the Mall." Some issues to consider are urbanization, the move indoors, and the question of control.
2. Compare and contrast Gallagher's description of the environment around her cabin with Virginia Woolf's description of London (included in the selection from *The Magnifying Mirror*, in Section 2).

# ～ Dreaming Memories

## Guadalupe Medina

Guadalupe Medina was born in Mexico; she moved to the United States with her family when she was fourteen years old. In 1993, after graduating from Pioneer High School in San Jose, California, and receiving an "Abrazos & Books" scholarship (for academic performance and commitment to helping the Latino community), she enrolled at San Jose State University. As a leader in the group Universitarios del Corazón, dedicated to encouraging Latino youngsters to pursue a college education, she directed a summer program and interviewed prospective students. When she wrote the following selection, she was a nineteen-year-old second-semester freshman; she is now majoring in international business.

**WARM-UP:** Consider one particular environment in which you spent a long time as a child. Did that environment help shape the person you are today? If so, in what way?

I used to live in Mexico a long time ago. My memories go back in time, for   1
about fourteen years. I was five then. I lived in a small house made out of wood and clay. The old kitchen was made out of clay. The bedroom was made out of green painted wood: It was my mother's bedroom, my dad's, my sister's, my brother's, and mine, too. We had only one dark room to share; it had no big fancy windows to see the world through. And still every morning I was able to see the sun coming down through the holes in the roof of the house: warm sun in the spring and cold rain in the winter.

Our dark but cozy room had three beds and one dark brown chest of drawers. The chest of drawers separated our part of the room from that of my parents. In our part of the room we had two beds; one belonged to my brother and the other I shared with my little sister. For some reason, our bed was always on the door side; my sister used to call it "El rincón," the corner; it was and, since I remember, it has always been her favorite side of the bed. I slept on the other side, next to my brother's bed. His bed was always facing my parents', and the only object that separated us was the old brown chest of drawers. Back then, we did not own many things. The small kitchen had one table, with six chairs, a small stove, a refrigerator, and an old cabinet, which could hardly stand by itself.

My favorite place outside the house was the garden: the biggest part of home, and the place where I spent most of the day. The garden was full of plants: green palm-like plants, and red and yellow flowers, which looked like bells, and decorated the fence of the house. Mostly fruit trees and pink roses decorated our house. I used to call my garden the enchanted garden, because the lovely and sweet smell of the roses was always in every corner of the house. The fruit trees I loved the most. I spent most of the day climbing them to reach their fruit. But the reason I loved them the most was because fruit was the only thing I had to share with my little friends.

Sure I was poor, but I was so happy that I consider my childhood the most precious gift of my life. Back then I had nothing to worry about: Life seemed to be clear and beautiful, and everything was a new experience. Until one day my mom and dad decided they wanted to give their children a better life: a better house, a better place, a better future. Just as Tom Whitecloud said in his essay "Blue Winds Dancing," people are "always dissatisfied—getting a hill and wanting a mountain."

5     In a matter of three years my mom and dad were getting the hill. We were living in a bigger house made out of bricks and with shiny floors. The house had three bedrooms, a kitchen, a huge patio, and a garden twice as big as my enchanted one. In fact, our house was the biggest and most beautiful in around ten blocks. I was really happy that we had moved to a bigger house. But then things started to change. We did not spend as much time together as we did before. The closeness in which we had lived for many years was held captive in the walls that now separated our rooms. The shiny floors, which I had admired, because I thought they were for fancy houses and rich people, now made our house cold, unfamiliar and even unfriendly.

Soon, I realized that my dad was working twice as much as he did before. He was a trailer driver, and most of the time he was away from home. If we saw him more than three times a month, we were lucky. Sometimes he was away from home for months, and when he came back, he was so tired that the only thing he wanted to do was rest. My mom became both our mother and our father. She was the only one around all the time: She cooked, cleaned the house, bathed us, combed our hair; she did everything. We got so used to her that even when my dad was home, we only counted on my mother. When my dad realized that he was in some way losing us, he decided to work less, but things were getting so hard, that soon pesos just weren't enough. By that time, my brother and I were in junior high, and we needed books, uniforms, and money for school. But pesos on top of that hill were just not going to make it. Not when you know that on top of that mountain, heading North, there are green dollars that are probably easier to earn and are worth more than pesos.

The green mountain was thousands of miles away from home, and probably years away from being together. But that didn't matter; soon my dad immigrated to the United States. Claiming the mountain was the hardest thing we ever did—and still today, I feel that we haven't reached the top, yet. Two years later we reunited. We met each other for the second time in our lives. Once in the United States, we discovered things within ourselves and within each other that were not there before. We were together again, but between my father and us there were two years without communicating and two years of unshared feelings; no mountain of gold could ever replace those two years.

Climbing the mountain upwards meant leaving Mexico behind. It also meant separating myself from the memories of the little girl that now sleeps inside my body—a girl who dreams about a little warm and dark house, where feelings were shared, and where closeness occupied the sixth chair at the table on which I had my very first meal. Now as a grown woman, I understand that "Simplicity" is not seen through fancy windows, that "Closeness" does not sit at a big table, and that "Sharing" does not prefer to live in a big and beautiful house. But those feelings, reaching for dreams, will cross hills and mountains. Mountains that may be hard to climb up, and hard to reach to the top, the unknown and foggy top.

## QUESTIONS

1. Do you believe that the environment Medina describes as her first home was a good one for a child to grow up in? Why or why not?
2. Based on this essay, do you feel that Medina shares the appreciation that many Americans have for privacy? If not, what does she seem to value more?
3. Does Medina use details effectively? Does she offer too many? not enough? If you feel that the latter is true, where in the essay would you have liked to see more detail?
4. Does Medina use balanced grammatical construction and recurrence effectively? Look for examples of both in the text.
5. Medina quotes a line from an essay by Tom Whitecloud. Does she blend that quote well into the paragraph where she includes it? Does she refer to that quote again elsewhere in the essay? If so, what is the effect of those references?
6. Is the conclusion of this essay effective? Why or why not?
7. What figure(s) of speech does Medina use in her conclusion?

## CONNECTIONS

1. Does this essay support or challenge Winifred Gallagher's views— expressed in "The Science of Place"—about the impact of our surroundings on our feelings and thoughts?

2. Discuss similarities and differences between the first home environment that Medina describes and the home environment depicted in Robert Hayden's poem "Those Winter Sundays" (see Section 1).

# ∽ From Ecclesiastes

The following selection comes from the Old Testament book of Ecclesiastes (3:1–21), which has traditionally been attributed to King Solomon; however, the editors of the *Oxford Study Edition of the New English Bible* (1972), from which this selection was taken, write that the Hebrew used in the original is of the type used in the fourth and third centuries B.C., suggesting that the author of this portion of text lived later than Solomon.

**WARM-UP:** What would you assume is the Bible's view of the relationship between human beings and the environment? On what do you base your answer?

For everything its season, and for every activity under heaven its time:
a time to be born and a time to die;
a time to plant and a time to uproot;
a time to kill and a time to heal;
a time to pull down and a time to build up;
a time to weep and a time to laugh;
a time for mourning and a time for dancing;
a time to scatter stones and a time to gather them;
a time to embrace and a time to refrain from embracing;
a time to seek and a time to lose;
a time to keep and a time to throw away;
a time to tear and a time to mend;
a time for silence and a time for speech;
a time to love and a time to hate;
a time for war and a time for peace.

What profit does one who works get from all his labour? I have seen the business that God has given men to keep them busy. He has made everything to suit its time; moreover he has given men a sense of time past and future, but no comprehension of God's work from beginning to end. I know that there is nothing good for man except to be happy and live the best life he can while he is alive. Moreover, that a man should eat and drink and enjoy himself, in return for all his labours, is a gift of God. I know that whatever God does lasts for ever; to add to it or subtract from it is impossible. And he has done it all in such a way that men must feel awe in his presence. Whatever is has been already, and whatever is to come has been already, and God summons each event back in its turn. Moreover I saw here under the sun that, where justice ought to be, there was wickedness, and where righteousness ought to be, there was wickedness. I said to myself, 'God will judge the just man and the wicked equally; every activity and every purpose has its proper time.' I said to myself, 'In dealing with men it is God's purpose to test them and to see what they truly are. For man is a creature of chance and the beasts are creatures of chance, and one mischance awaits them all: death comes to both alike. They all draw the same breath. Men have no advantage over beasts; for everything is emptiness. All go to the same place: all came from the dust, and to the dust all return. Who knows whether the spirit of man goes upward or whether the spirit of the beast goes downward to the earth?' So I saw that there is nothing better than that a man should enjoy his work, since that is his lot. For who can bring him through to see what will happen next?

## QUESTIONS

1. Which elements of this selection could an environmental activist point to as support for a biblical environmentalism?
2. Which elements would seem to undermine an "environmentalist reading" of this selection?
3. Respond to the line "I know that whatever God does lasts for ever; to add to it or subtract from it is impossible." Do you believe this is true? If not, provide an example to support your response.
4. This text was probably written in the fourth or third century B.C. Since that time, humans have significantly altered their environment. Are the ideas from Ecclesiastes still relevant to our time and society? Explain your response.
5. In which way(s) do you profit from your labor? Are the words "profit" and "labour" used in this text in ways you usually hear them used? What else can "profit" and "labour" mean, aside from "paycheck" and "job"?

## CONNECTIONS

How does this selection relate to the ideas presented in Sam Keen's "The Rite of Work: The Economic Man," presented in Section 4?

# ∽ The Origins of Modern Vegetarianism

*Paul Amato and Sonia Partridge*

Paul Amato, Ph.D., teaches sociology at the University of Nebraska–Lincoln; he is currently finishing a book about the way young people's successes are affected by their families. Sonia Partridge is a psychologist practicing in Columbia, Missouri. The following selection comes from a book they co-authored in 1989: *The New Vegetarians: Promoting Health and Protecting Life.*

**WARM-UP:** Do you feel that more people should become vegetarians? Why or why not?

Vegetarians may be many things, but they are not lonely. A Gallup poll      1
conducted in 1985 for *American Health* magazine found that nearly nine million Americans call themselves vegetarians.[1] In addition, another 40 million adults are eating less meat and more plant foods than in the past. Similarly, a recent consumer study carried out by the National Restaurant Association found that customers are ordering fewer meat dishes and more salads, fresh fruits, and fruit juices than they used to.[2] The number of vegetarian restaurants is also increasing. The "Essential Guide" to vegetarian restaurants published by *Vegetarian Times* magazine in 1987 lists over 1000 entries; a 1978 edition listed only 350.[3] Clearly, the American diet is changing.

The growing mainstream status of vegetarianism is reflected in recent articles in popular magazines. For example, *Newsweek,* in 1986, referred to our healthier eating habits as "vegetarian chic,"[4] and *Time,* in 1988, praised the new vegetarian preferences of health-conscious young adults.[5] Indeed, many individuals have stopped eating meat for health reasons, although some have also been influenced by the animal liberation movement, religious beliefs, concerns about world hunger, or an awareness of the environmental damage caused by livestock production. But whatever their motives, one thing is clear: Vegetarianism can no longer be viewed as a fringe phenomenon.

The Gallup poll also revealed that nearly three fourths of Americans reject the notion that vegetarianism is merely a passing fad. A look at the historical record reveals that these people are correct. In fact, vegetarianism has a long, although not always illustrious, history in the West. A quick review of this history helps put present-day vegetarianism in perspective.

## A Quick History of Vegetarianism

It may surprise many people to hear that our early ancestors lived on a semivegetarian diet for several million years. Some anthropologists have fostered the stereotype of "man the hunter," but studies of contemporary "hunter–gatherers" suggest that early humans lived primarily on a diet of plant foods, with supplementation from animal flesh. Studies of tribal Australian aborigines° and the Kung-San of South Africa—groups that live under conditions similar to those of our ancestors—show that only about one fourth of their caloric intake derives from animal products. Nuts, seeds, fruits, and vegetables are the staple foods of these groups.[6] A view of early humans as *gatherers* rather than hunters is a more accurate portrayal.

5      Like most good ideas in the West, vegetarianism was developed by the ancient Greeks.[7] Pythagoras and Porphyry were the best-known practicing vegetarians, but the list of those who advocated° a vegetarian diet includes Diogenes, Plato, Epicurus, and Plutarch. The Greeks favored vegetarianism for a variety of reasons. Pythagoras and his followers believed that animals as well as humans have souls, and that after death, an animal may be reincarnated as a human and vice versa. According to this view, animals should not be killed and eaten because all souls have equal worth. Plato, in *The Republic,* described a vegetarian diet as being best suited for his ideal society. Plant foods were preferred, according to Plato, because they promote health and because they require less land to produce than do animal foods. Other Greek thinkers felt that eating animal flesh was naturally repugnant and should be rejected on aesthetic grounds.

The Romans borrowed many ideas from the Greeks, including vegetarianism, and in spite of their penchant° for feeding undesirables to the lions, vegetarian ideas survived throughout Roman times. The poet Ovid and the philosopher Seneca are examples of Romans who expounded° the cause of vegetarianism.

The fall of Rome and the spread of Christianity across Europe led to a "dark ages" in vegetarian thought. During this time, Christian thinkers such as Saint Augustine and Saint Thomas Aquinas provided intellectual rationalizations for the killing, eating, and general exploitation of animals by humans. They argued that only people have free will, rationality, and souls, and that animals were placed on earth for the convenience and use of humans—views that are still accepted by the majority of Christians today. However, the tradition of vegetarianism was kept alive in dark and dingy Christian abbeys° where monks abstained from meat to suppress their animal passions. (The belief that meat consumption is associated with base urges that hinder one's spiritual progress lingers on in the minds of some contemporary vegetari-

---

*aborigines:* Here, meaning native inhabitants.    *advocated:* Endorsed, recommended.    *penchant:* Strong inclination or liking.    *expounded:* Stated in detail or defended with arguments.    *abbeys:* Monasteries.

ans. . . .) The Benedictines, Trappists, and Cistercians are all examples of monastic° orders that practiced vegetarianism for a period of time.

During the 15th century, Europe discovered classical philosophy, art, and science. But it took the Europeans a little longer to rediscover vegetarianism. Leonardo da Vinci, visionary that he was, stood ahead of his time in being a confirmed vegetarian. As he wrote in his notebook:

> I have from an early age adjured° the use of meat, and the time will come when men such as I will look upon the murder of animals as they now look upon the murder of men.[8]

The vegetarian "Renaissance" can be said to have occurred during the late 18th and 19th centuries. During this period, Darwin's theory of evolution destroyed the notion that animals are fundamentally different from humans, and in so doing, challenged the religious and philosophical justification for eating them. The new view was that of a continuum of life, with humans and other animals separated in degree, but not in kind. The implications of the theory of evolution so upset Darwin that he stopped believing in God. He did not, however, give up eating meat.

The new view of animals as distantly related kin was incorporated into     10
the general humanitarian reform movements that occurred at this time. Indeed, many prominent vegetarians and animal welfare promoters were simultaneously involved in other struggles, such as the child welfare and anti-slavery movements. It was during this period that the first written works on vegetarianism by Europeans appeared. Leo Tolstoy and Percy Bysshe Shelley are examples of 19th-century writers who advocated a meatless lifestyle. For a while, people who abstained from eating flesh were said to be following the "Pythagorean diet." Later, the term "vegetarian" was coined from the Latin word "vegetus," meaning active or vigorous. (The term has misled many into thinking that vegetarians survive only on vegetables—an inaccurate view of vegetarian cuisine.)

Many Christian groups were at the forefront of the burgeoning° vege-tarian movement. The Bible Christian Church, founded by William Cowherd in 1809 in Manchester, England, played a major role in advocating and fur-thering the cause of vegetarianism. Members believed that Christ's teachings of mercy should be extended to animals as well as to people. They also believed that a vegetarian diet was healthier than one based on meat and that Christians have a duty to maintain good health in order to do God's work.

---

*monastic:* Relating to monasteries, monks, or nuns.     *adjured:* Here meaning "solemnly renounced."
*burgeoning:* Growing and expanding rapidly.

Members of this group later formed the Vegetarian Society in 1847—the first secular vegetarian organization in the West. They disseminated° information in the form of essays and lectures and taught that the adoption of vegetarianism would lead to universal brotherhood, an increase in happiness, and a more civilized society. This group still exists and is presently known as the Vegetarian Society of the United Kingdom.

The movement was carried on into the 20th century by vegetarian societies working at the grass-roots level, religious groups such as the Seventh-Day Adventists, and prominent figures such as George Bernard Shaw and Mohandas Gandhi. Vegetarian organizations formed in most Western countries, and newsletters, books, and other publications promoting the diet became common. In 1908 the International Vegetarian Union was formed, with its main function being to organize conferences at which vegetarians from around the world meet and share information. The union continues to be active today.

This orderly but gradual progression might have continued indefinitely had it not been for the social upheavals of the 1960s and 1970s. At this point in time, a variety of influences converged that had major implications for the course of vegetarianism: a new awareness of the importance of diet in maintaining health, an interest in Eastern philosophy and religion, a concern over the degradation of the environment through human "progress," a politically active stance in support of the rights of oppressed groups, the emergence of the peace movement, and a utopian belief in a perfectible society. All of these social trends provided pathways for new converts to the vegetarian cause. Out of this melange,° the modern era of vegetarianism emerged.

### The Environmental Movement

Most people are aware of the deleterious° effects of the automobile and heavy industry on the ecology of our planet. But few are aware that meat production has contributed greatly to environmental deterioration.

15    As Frances Moore Lappé pointed out in *Diet for a Small Planet,* there have been two population explosions in the 20th century: people in Third World countries and livestock in Western countries.[9] This increase in the number of livestock has been accompanied by a trend for livestock to spend all or part of their lives in feedlots° where they eat large quantities of grain and soybeans. (Cattle, for example, are fed about 22 pounds every day.) Feeding large numbers of animals in this fashion requires an enormous agricultural output. In fact, one half of the agriculture output in the United States every year goes to feed livestock.[10]

---

*disseminated:* Scattered, dispersed.    *melange:* Mixture (often of incongruous elements).    *deleterious:* Harmful, destructive.    *feedlots:* Plots of land on which livestock is raised and fattened.

Feedlot agriculture has placed a strain on our natural resources and the quality of our environment. For one thing, water resources are being squandered at an alarming rate. One half of the water consumed in the United States is used in livestock production.[11] (This includes water used directly by livestock and water used for the irrigation of crops to feed livestock.) Presently, about 2500 gallons of water are required to produce one pound of beef. This is an inefficient use of water to produce food, given that it takes about 15 times as much water to produce one pound of protein from beef as it does from soybeans. Not surprisingly, there is evidence that the heavy demand for water by the meat industry is leading to the depletion of unrenewable underground water reserves.

Approximately seven billion tons of topsoil are eroded every year in the United States. With the loss of topsoil, the fertility of the land and its yield are decreased. As it turns out, the majority of soil erosion is linked to overgrazing or the growing of food for livestock.[12] As they graze, cattle clear the land of vegetation and trample the ground, leaving the soil easily eroded by water and wind. Under natural conditions, the densities of ranging animals cause little harm, but the desire for profit has led owners to graze cattle in densities that frequently result in long-term soil damage. Consequently, overgrazing has been the major cause of desertification,° both in the United States and around the world. Large numbers of cattle are also grazed on public lands, including national parks, recreational areas, and military reservations—a practice that places our supposedly protected lands at risk.[13] In addition, corn, soybeans, and other crops grown in large quantities to feed livestock are among those that cause the most damage to the soil. Production of these crops could be lessened if they were not required for fattening up animals in feedlots. Furthermore, the clearing of land for livestock agriculture has resulted in massive deforestation. This loss of forest land has contributed further to soil erosion and the depletion of water reserves.

One might wonder what happens to the two billion tons of manure produced annually by farm animals. Much of the nitrogenous wastes turns into soluble ammonia and nitrates which leach° through the soil and contaminate the groundwater. This runoff encourages the growth of algae that deplete the water of oxygen and result in the death of aquatic life. Manure, however, is not the only problem. The dumping of unusable waste products such as viscera,° grease, and other by-products of the meat industry—much of which winds up in our water—is a cause for concern. The enormous quantity of waste generated gives the animal food industry the distinction of being one of the world's largest polluters of water.[14]

---

*desertification:* The process of turning arable land into desert.     *leach:* Dissolve out, drain.     *viscera:* Internal organs.

Our wildlife has also suffered as a direct consequence of livestock production, for the clearing of large tracts of land and forests for agriculture has
reduced the size and range of natural habitats. This problem is particularly
acute in the Amazon basin in Brazil where land is being cleared at a phenom-
enal rate for the grazing of cattle. (One might assume that the resulting beef
would help to feed the hungry people of Brazil, but most of the meat winds up
in hamburgers in American fast-food restaurants. Except for a few wealthy
landowners, the local people receive little benefit.)[15] Grazing animals alter the
ecological balance, placing wild plants and animals at risk. This behavior
underestimates our dependence on the ecosystem and reflects an attitude that
wildlife and forests stand in the way of progress. An Australian expression
aptly summarizes this view: if it moves, shoot it; if it doesn't, cut it down.

20      The damage inflicted on our environment by large-scale livestock production is, of course, unnecessary. Frances Moore Lappé described livestock as
"protein factories in reverse." As she pointed out, 16 pounds of grain and soy
fed to a cow yield only one pound of meat in return. And compared with the
one pound of meat it produces, the 16 pounds of grain have 21 times more
calories, 8 times more protein and a good deal more fiber.[16] In the United
States alone, 124 million tons of soybeans and grain are lost every year
through livestock production, averaging out to one cup of grain for every
human on earth every day.

Given the inequities° of food distribution in the world, it seems unlikely
that the United States could literally feed the world with its agricultural output. However, it is clear that the solution to the problem of hunger in the
Third World does not include an increase in livestock production. Meat consumption is a luxury available to people in affluent countries—and one that is
bought at the price of environmental damage and poor health. The world's
population cannot be supported on the high-meat diet common in Western
countries; instead, Third World countries will need to adopt the least wasteful
method of food production. The world will only be fed when a large proportion of its population lives as vegetarians.

Few people subscribe to the morality that an action is permissible simply
because one possesses the power to carry it out. As Mohandas Gandhi argued,
the fact that we are more intelligent than animals and have power over them
does not give us the right to exploit them. To the contrary, we are obligated to
protect them.[17] For individuals who agree with these ethical arguments, vegetarianism is mandatory.

---

*inequities:* Injustices.

1. Joel Gurin, "Are You a Semi-Vegetarian?" *American Health* (July/August 1985), pp. 37–43.

2. "Dining Out Becomes Healthier," *Vegetarian Times* (February 1986), p. 7.

3. "The Essential Guide to Dining, Leisure, Clubs, Products," *Vegetarian Times* (July 1987), pp. 27–75.

4. Ron Givens, "Going for the Greens," *Newsweek* (May 9, 1986), pp. 79–80.

5. Sheila Gribben and Andrea Sachs, "Vegetarians Hit the Fern Bars," *Time* (March 7, 1988), p. 84.

6. Gretel H. Pelto and Pertti, J. Pelto, *The Human Adventure* (New York: Macmillan, 1976), pp. 203–204.

7. Discussions of the history of vegetarianism can be found in: Keith Akers, *A Vegetarian Sourcebook* (Arlington, VA: Vegetarian Press, 1983), pp. 180–187; Daniel A. Dombrowski, *The Philosophy of Vegetarianism* (Amherst: The University of Massachusetts Press, 1984); Dudley Giehl, *Vegetarianism: A Way of Life* (New York: Harper and Row, 1979); James Turner, *Reckoning with the Beast: Animals, Pain, and Humanity in the Victorian Mind* (Baltimore: The Johns Hopkins University Press, 1980); "Vegetarianism," *Encyclopaedia Britannica* 22 (Chicago: William Bentor, 1969), pp. 935–945.

8. Leonardo da Vinci's notebook, quoted in Victoria Moran, "Leonardo da Vinci: A Portrait of a Renaissance Man" *Vegetarian Times* (October 1987) pp. 23–26.

9. Lappé, 1982, pp. 66–74.

10. *Ibid.*, p. 66.

11. Lappé, 1982, pp. 76–79; Akers, pp. 101–111.

12. Lappé, 1982, pp. 79–83; Akers, pp. 117–121.

13. Lynn Jacobs, "Amazing Grace: How the Livestock Industry Is Ruining the American West," *The Animals' Agenda* (January 1988), pp. 12–17.

14. Lappé, 1982, p. 84.

15. Frances Moore Lappé, *Food First: Beyond the Myth of Scarcity* (New York: Ballantine Books, 1978), pp. 84–53.

16. Lappé, 1982, p. 69.

17. Mohandas Gandhi, *The Story of My Experiments with Truth* (New York: Beacon Press, 1957).

## QUESTIONS

1. What are some common stereotypes of vegetarians? How does Amato and Partridge's historical account of vegetarianism challenge these stereotypes?

2. What is the relationship between vegetarianism and Darwin's theory of evolution?

3. How does human consumption of meat affect our environment?

4. The authors of this piece mention Frances Moore Lappé's contention that "there have been two population explosions in the 20th century: people in Third World countries and livestock in Western countries." This text focuses on the livestock population explosion. What do you

know about the human population explosion? Is it limited to Third World countries? Can it be sustained indefinitely? Are we seeing any effects of it today?

5. Many states, such as California, are continually faced with drought; people are required to conserve water and even threatened with fines for wasting water. Given Amato and Partridge's claim that "2,500 gallons of water are required to produce one pound of beef," do you think that people should be informed of this and encouraged to reduce their meat consumption to help reduce water use?

6. Are you a vegetarian? Why or why not? Are you aware of what you eat? Is it possible to be compassionate toward animals without being a vegetarian?

## CONNECTIONS

1. Does the biblical selection from Ecclesiastes support Amato and Partridge's views about Judeo-Christian ideas regarding the eating of meat?

2. Compare the writing style reflected in this selection with Winifred Gallagher's style in "The Science of Place," included in this section.

# The Obligation to Endure

*Rachel Carson*

Rachel Carson (1907–1964) was a biologist and an extremely influential author who helped to shape the American public's views regarding the need to protect our environment. She earned a bachelor's degree from the Pennsylvania College for Women in 1929 and a master's degree from Johns Hopkins University in 1932. Throughout her career, Carson received much recognition; she won a Westinghouse award for best science writing in a magazine in 1950 and the National Book Award for *The Sea Around Us* (1951), and she was elected to the American Academy of Arts and Letters in 1963. The following selection is taken from Carson's best-known work, *Silent Spring* (1962), which influenced president John F. Kennedy's decision to appoint a Science Advisory Committee to explore the writer's claims. The committee confirmed those claims and mandated that government agencies not only rethink their pesticide-related programs but also inform the public of decisions they make regarding pesticide use.

**WARM-UP:** Are you concerned about the use of pesticides in farms and gardens in the United States? Why or why not?

The history of life on earth has been a history of interaction between living   1
things and their surroundings. To a large extent, the physical form and the habits of the earth's vegetation and its animal life have been molded by the environment. Considering the whole span of earthly time, the opposite effect, in which life actually modifies its surroundings, has been relatively slight. Only within the moment of time represented by the present century has one species—man—acquired significant power to alter the nature of his world.

During the past quarter century this power has not only increased to one of disturbing magnitude but it has changed in character. The most alarming of all man's assaults upon the environment is the contamination of air, earth, rivers, and sea with dangerous and even lethal materials. This pollution is for the most part irrecoverable; the chain of evil it initiates not only in the world that must support life but in living tissues is for the most part irreversible. In this now universal contamination of the environment, chemicals are the sinister and little-recognized partners of radiation in changing the very nature of the world—the very nature of its life. Strontium 90, released through nuclear explosions into the air, comes to earth in rain or drifts down as fallout, lodges in soil, enters into the grass or corn or wheat grown there, and in time takes up its abode in the bones of a human being, there to remain until his death.

Similarly, chemicals sprayed on croplands or forests or gardens lie long in soil, entering into living organisms, passing from one to another in a chain of poisoning and death. Or they pass mysteriously by underground streams until they emerge and, through the alchemy° of air and sunlight, combine into new forms that kill vegetation, sicken cattle, and work unknown harm on those who drink from once pure wells. As Albert Schweitzer has said, "Man can hardly even recognize the devils of his own creation."

It took hundreds of millions of years to produce the life that now inhabits the earth—eons° of time in which that developing and evolving and diversifying life reached a state of adjustment and balance with its surroundings. The environment, rigorously shaping and directing the life it supported, contained elements that were hostile as well as supporting. Certain rocks gave out dangerous radiation; even within the light of the sun, from which all life draws its energy, there were short-wave radiations with power to injure. Given time— time not in years but in millennia—life adjusts, and a balance has been reached. For time is the essential ingredient; but in the modern world there is no time.

The rapidity of change and the speed with which new situations are created follow the impetuous and heedless° pace of man rather than the deliberate pace of nature. Radiation is no longer merely the background radiation of rocks, the bombardment of cosmic rays, the ultraviolet of the sun that have existed before there was any life on earth; radiation is now the unnatural creation of man's tampering with the atom. The chemicals to which life is asked to make its adjustment are no longer merely the calcium and silica and copper and all the rest of the minerals washed out of the rocks and carried in rivers to the sea; they are the synthetic creations of man's inventive mind, brewed in his laboratories, and having no counterparts in nature.

5    To adjust to these chemicals would require time on the scale that is nature's; it would require not merely the years of a man's life but the life of generations. And even this, were it by some miracle possible, would be futile, for the new chemicals come from our laboratories in an endless stream; almost five hundred annually find their way into actual use in the United States alone. The figure is staggering and its implications are not easily grasped—500 new chemicals to which the bodies of men and animals are required somehow to adapt each year, chemicals totally outside the limits of biologic experience.[1]

Among them are many that are used in man's war against nature. Since the mid-1940's over 200 basic chemicals have been created for use in killing

---

*alchemy:* Here meaning the ability to change one chemical element into another.    *eons:* Billions of years.    *heedless:* Careless, inconsiderate.

weeds, rodents, and other organisms described in the modern vernacular as "pests"; and they are sold under several thousand different brand names.

These sprays, dusts, and aerosols are now applied almost universally to farms, gardens, forests, and homes—nonselective chemicals that have the power to kill every insect, the "good" and the "bad," to still the song of birds and the leaping of fish in the streams, to coat the leaves with a deadly film, and to linger on in soil—all this though the intended target may be only a few weeds or insects. Can anyone believe it is possible to lay down such a barrage of poisons on the surface of the earth without making it unfit for all life? They should not be called "insecticides," but "biocides."

The whole process of spraying seems caught up in an endless spiral. Since DDT was released for civilian use, a process of escalation has been going on in which ever more toxic materials must be found. This has happened because insects, in a triumphant vindication of Darwin's principle of the survival of the fittest, have evolved super races immune to the particular insecticide used, hence a deadlier one has always to be developed—and then a deadlier one than that. It has happened also because, for reasons to be described later, destructive insects often undergo a "flareback," or resurgence, after spraying, in numbers greater than before. Thus the chemical war is never won, and all life is caught in its violent crossfire.

Along with the possibility of the extinction of mankind by nuclear war, the central problem of our age has therefore become the contamination of man's total environment with such substances of incredible potential for harm—substances that accumulate in the tissues of plants and animals and even penetrate the germ cells to shatter or alter the very material of heredity upon which the shape of the future depends.

Some would-be architects of our future look toward a time when it will 10 be possible to alter the human germ plasm° by design. But we may easily be doing so now by inadvertence,° for many chemicals, like radiation, bring about gene mutations. It is ironic to think that man might determine his own future by something so seemingly trivial as the choice of an insect spray.

All this has been risked—for what? Future historians may well be amazed by our distorted sense of proportion. How could intelligent beings seek to control a few unwanted species by a method that contaminated the entire environment and brought the threat of disease and death even to their own kind? Yet this is precisely what we have done. We have done it, moreover, for reasons that collapse the moment we examine them. We are told that the

---

*germ plasm:* The hereditary material of the germ cells (genes).   *inadvertence:* Lack of attention, oversight.

enormous and expanding use of pesticides is necessary to maintain farm production. Yet is our real problem not one of *overproduction?* Our farms, despite measures to remove acreages from production and to pay farmers *not* to produce, have yielded such a staggering excess of crops that the American taxpayer in 1962 is paying out more then one billion dollars a year as the total carrying cost of the surplus-food storage program. And is the situation helped when one branch of the Agriculture Department tries to reduce production while another states, as it did in 1958, "It is believed generally that reduction of crop acreages under provisions of the Soil Bank will stimulate interest in use of chemicals to obtain maximum production on the land retained in crops."[2]

All this is not to say there is no insect problem and no need of control. I am saying, rather, that control must be geared to realities, not to mythical situations, and that the methods employed must be such that they do not destroy us along with the insects.

The problem whose attempted solution has brought such a train of disaster in its wake is an accompaniment of our modern way of life. Long before the age of man, insects inhabited the earth—a group of extraordinarily varied and adaptable beings. Over the course of time since man's advent, a small percentage of the more than half a million species of insects have come into conflict with human welfare in two principal ways: as competitors for the food supply and as carriers of human disease.

Disease-carrying insects become important where human beings are crowded together, especially under conditions where sanitation is poor, as in time of natural disaster or war, in situations of extreme poverty and deprivation. Then control of some sort becomes necessary. It is a sobering fact, however, as we shall presently see, that the method of massive chemical control has had only limited success, and also threatens to worsen the very conditions it is intended to curb.

15    Under primitive agricultural conditions the farmer had few insect problems. These arose with the intensification of agriculture—the devotion of immense acreages to a single crop. Such a system set the stage for explosive increases in specific insect populations. Single-crop farming does not take advantage of the principles by which nature works; it is agriculture as an engineer might conceive it to be. Nature has introduced great variety into the landscape, but man has displayed a passion for simplifying it. Thus he undoes the built-in checks and balances by which nature holds the species within bounds. One important natural check is a limit on the amount of suitable habitat for each species. Obviously then, an insect that lives on wheat can build up its population to much higher levels on a farm devoted to wheat than

on one in which wheat is intermingled with other crops to which the insect is not adapted.

The same thing happens in other situations. A generation or more ago, the towns of large areas of the United States lined their streets with the noble elm tree. Now the beauty they hopefully created is threatened with complete destruction as disease sweeps through the elms, carried by a beetle that would have only limited chance to build up large populations and to spread from tree to tree if the elms were only occasional trees in a richly diversified planting.

Another factor in the modern insect problem is one that must be viewed against a background of geologic and human history: the spreading of thousands of different kinds of organisms from their native homes to invade new territories. This worldwide migration has been studied and graphically described by the British ecologist Charles Elton in his recent book *The Ecology of Invasions*. During the Cretaceous Period, some hundred million years ago, flooding seas cut many land bridges between continents and living things found themselves confined in what Elton calls "colossal separate nature reserves." There, isolated from others of their kind, they developed many new species. When some of the land masses were joined again, about 15 million years ago, these species began to move out into new territories—a movement that is not only still in progress but is now receiving considerable assistance from man.[3]

The importation of plants is the primary agent in the modern spread of species, for animals have almost invariably gone along with the plants, quarantine being a comparatively recent and not completely effective innovation. The United States Office of Plant Introduction alone has introduced almost 200,000 species and varieties of plants from all over the world. Nearly half of the 180 or so major insect enemies of plants in the United States are accidental imports from abroad, and most of them have come as hitchhikers on plants.

In new territory, out of reach of the restraining hand of the natural enemies that kept down its numbers in its native land, an invading plant or animal is able to become enormously abundant. Thus it is no accident that our most troublesome insects are introduced species.

These invasions, both the naturally occurring and those dependent on human assistance, are likely to continue indefinitely. Quarantine and massive chemical campaigns are only extremely expensive ways of buying time. We are faced, according to Dr. Elton, "with a life-and-death need not just to find new technological means of suppressing this plant or that animal"; instead we need the basic knowledge of animal populations and their relations to their surroundings that will "promote an even balance and damp down the explosive power of outbreaks and new invasions."

Much of the necessary knowledge is now available but we do not use it. We train ecologists in our universities and even employ them in our governmental agencies but we seldom take their advice. We allow the chemical death rain to fall as though there were no alternative, whereas in fact there are many, and our ingenuity could soon discover many more if given opportunity.

Have we fallen into a mesmerized° state that makes us accept as inevitable that which is inferior or detrimental, as though having lost the will or the vision to demand that which is good? Such thinking, in the words of the ecologist Paul Shepard, "idealizes life with only its head out of water, inches above the limits of toleration of the corruption of its own environment . . . Why should we tolerate a diet of weak poisons, a home in insipid° surroundings, a circle of acquaintances who are not quite our enemies, the noise of motors with just enough relief to prevent insanity? Who would want to live in a world which is just not quite fatal?"[4]

Yet such a world is pressed upon us. The crusade to create a chemically sterile, insect-free world seems to have engendered a fanatic zeal on the part of many specialists and most of the so-called control agencies. On every hand there is evidence that those engaged in spraying operations exercise a ruthless power. "The regulatory entomologists° . . . function as prosecutor, judge and jury, tax assessor and collector and sheriff to enforce their own orders," said Connecticut entomologist Neely Turner. The most flagrant abuses go unchecked in both state and federal agencies.

It is not my contention that chemical insecticides must never be used. I do contend that we have put poisonous and biologically potent chemicals indiscriminately into the hands of persons largely or wholly ignorant of their potentials for harm. We have subjected enormous numbers of people to contact with these poisons, without their consent and often without their knowledge. If the Bill of Rights contains no guarantee that a citizen shall be secure against lethal poisons distributed either by private individuals or by public officials, it is surely only because our forefathers, despite their considerable wisdom and foresight, could conceive of no such problem.

25    I contend, furthermore, that we have allowed these chemicals to be used with little or no advance investigation of their effect on soil, water, wildlife, and man himself. Future generations are unlikely to condone our lack of prudent concern for the integrity of the natural world that supports all life.

There is still very limited awareness of the nature of the threat. This is an era of specialists, each of whom sees his own problem and is unaware of or intolerant of the larger frame into which it fits. It is also an era dominated by industry, in which the right to make a dollar at whatever cost is seldom chal-

*mesmerized:* Hypnotized.    *insipid:* Dull, flat, tasteless.    *entomologists:* scientists who specialize in the study of insects.

lenged. When the public protests, confronted with some obvious evidence of damaging results of pesticide applications, it is fed little tranquilizing pills of half truth. We urgently need an end to these false assurances, to the sugar coating of unpalatable facts. It is the public that is being asked to assume the risks that the insect controllers calculate. The public must decide whether it wishes to continue on the present road, and it can do so only when in full possession of the facts. In the words of Jean Rostand, "The obligation to endure gives us the right to know."

1. "Report on Environmental Health Problems," *Hearings*, 86th Congress, Subcom. of Com. on Appropriations, March 1960, p. 170.
2. *The Pesticide Situation for 1957–58*, U.S. Dept of Agric., Commodity Stabilization Service, April 1958, p. 10.
3. Elton, Charles S., *The Ecology of Invasions by Animals and Plants*, New York: Wiley, 1958.
4. Shepard, Paul, "The Place of Nature in Man's World," *Atlantic Naturalist*, Vol. 13 (April–June 1958), pp. 85–89.

## QUESTIONS

1. Carson's title, taken from a quotation that appears at the end of the essay, seems to suggest that we are obligated to guarantee the survival of our species. Assuming that this should be our first goal as a species, what should be our second goal? our third?
2. Carson's first line is, "The history of life on earth has been a history of interaction between living things and their surroundings." Recall how you were taught history in school. Did those history courses correspond with Carson's contention?
3. Clarify what Carson sees as "man's war against nature."
4. Where does Carson concede (i.e, admit the truth of) a point raised by opponents to her argument? Why does she do it? What would the effect have been if she hadn't done so?
5. "This is an era of specialists," wrote Carson in 1962, "each of whom sees his own problem and is unaware of or intolerant of the larger frame into which it fits. It is also an era dominated by industry, in which the right to make a dollar at whatever cost is seldom challenged." Do her insights still apply today? What role do nonspecialists play in the arena of environmental concerns?
6. Carson complains that "life is asked to make its adjustment" to synthetic chemicals created by human beings. Although she generally means chemicals used for farming, all of us encounter every day other

"synthetic creations of man's inventive mind, brewed in his laboratories": We put them in our coffee, in our food, on our hair. Consider some such substances. How would their loss impact your life?

7. Identify effective uses of recurrence within Carson's selection.

8. How would you describe Carson's voice in this selection?

## CONNECTIONS

1. In the context of Carson's essay, consider the line from Ecclesiastes, "I know that whatever God does lasts for ever; to add to it or subtract from it is impossible." What have human beings added to their environment? What have they destroyed?

2. Analyze the connections between Carson's essay and "The Science of Place," by Winifred Gallagher. (Consider, in particular, the concept of "balance of nature.")

3. Explain the relationship between this essay and the poem "Federico's Ghost" (included in Section 4). What does the date of the poem's publication suggest about Carson's claims?

## ⁓ Brightest Heaven of Invention

*Charles T. Rubin*

> Charles T. Rubin was born in Cleveland, Ohio. He graduated from Western
> Reserve University in political science and philosophy, and he received his
> Ph.D. from Boston College. Rubin now teaches at Duquesne University in
> Pittsburgh, Pennsylvania, in the Department of Political Science, the Gradu-
> ate Center for Social and Public Policy, and the Environmental Science and
> Management Program; his research concentrates on the intersection be-
> tween political thought and public policy. The following selection comes
> from his book *The Green Crusade: Rethinking the Roots of Environmentalism,*
> published in 1994.

> **WARM-UP:** What are some of the criticisms that have been raised
> against the environmental movement during the last two decades?

*It is a mark of a mean capacity to spend much time on the things which concern the
body.*

—EPICTETUS, *Enchiridion* XLI[1]

*. . . it is possible to reach knowledge that will be of much utility in this life . . . and
so make ourselves the masters and possessors of nature. This would not only be
desirable to enable us to enjoy the fruits of agriculture and all the wealth of the
earth without labor, but even so in conserving health, the principal good and the
basis of all other goods in this life.*

—DESCARTES, *Discourse on Method* Part Six[2]

### Shadowy Beginnings

Poisoning, with its potential for subtle, drawn-out, or excruciating and con-      1
vulsive death, is, murder mysteries would have us believe, the method of
choice for intelligent killers bent on revenge. What is more calculatingly
deceptive than the gambit° that conceals poison in a favorite treat of the victim? To think that some slight but familiar enjoyment hides so great an evil
touches something deep. Fear of poisoning seems as universal as fear of death,
yet it is more likely to come out in some circumstances than in others. People
in battle or facing imminent threats like famine or disease do not generally
fear poison, fast or slow. One fears poison most when conditions are most
favorable to the poisoner (i.e., when there is a certain regularity, sufficiency,

*gambit:* Stratagem, calculated move.

and leisure in life). Speaking metaphorically, we can say that the evildoer has to be able to purchase the Turkish delight,° have time to spike it, and wait patiently, knowing that it will be consumed.

A comfortable middle class, therefore, is likely to be particularly susceptible to fear of poison, just as it will be the main consumer of the mystery stories that provide the vicarious° thrill of that fear. And that brings us to an unacknowledged master of the murder mystery, Rachel Carson.

Those who commend Rachel Carson and those who condemn her agree that it is impossible to conceive of today's environmental crusade without her best-selling *Silent Spring* (1962).[3] As her editor and biographer, Paul Brooks, wrote, it is "one of those rare books that change the course of history—not through incitement to war or violent revolution, but by altering the direction of man's thinking."[4] But the precise nature of her contribution is not easy to pin down. Was it her literary ability to evoke a sense of wonder at the beautiful complexities of nature? Yet such nature writing was a well-established and popular American genre since long before her best-selling *The Sea Around Us* (1951),[5] let alone *Silent Spring*. Was she the first to notice the problematic side of pesticide use? In fact, *Silent Spring* involved no original research but was a compendium° of over ten years of ongoing investigations by scientists and researchers. Was it her fanatical attacks on DDT and modern chemical technology that set the tone for the subsequent excesses of environmental fearmongering?° Yet she acknowledged the need for chemical insect control, making her position significantly more moderate than many who came after her. Was it by promoting regulation of pesticides that Carson left her mark? A 1962 government study was prompted by *Silent Spring;* it acknowledged that until the publication of that work, "people were generally unaware of the toxicity of pesticides."[6] But government regulation of pesticides was not, in fact, new. . . .

*Silent Spring* takes its name from the book's first chapter, in which Carson presents "A Fable for Tomorrow." An "evil spell" settles over a once beautiful and vibrant rural community; animals and human beings sicken and die, vegetation withers, livestock can no longer reproduce, there is no morning bird song. We have a mystery—"What has already silenced the voices of spring in countless towns in America? This book is an attempt to explain." But like any dramatic author, Carson has already foreshadowed the solution to the mystery in the fable. "No witchcraft, no enemy action had silenced the rebirth of new life in this stricken world. The people had done it themselves."[7]

5    The central theme of *Silent Spring* is that the thoughtless use of insecticides and herbicides (Carson called them "biocides," for she saw them as

---

*Turkish delight:* A kind of fruit candy.   *vicarious:* Substituted, imagined.   *compendium:* Summary.
*fearmongering:* Encouraging and generating fear.

indiscriminate destroyers of life) at least threatens the health of nature and humanity, and possibly puts life on earth itself in jeopardy. These miracles of modern science are systematically poisoning us, interfering with reproduction, and causing cancer. Even in the unlikely event that we do not come into much direct contact with these dangerous substances, Carson notes, they spread throughout the ecosystem, destroying life as they go and upsetting the balance of nature. While much of the power of the book, for all the facts and footnotes, depends on arousing fear at this threat of being poisoned, it is a two-pronged attack: direct threats to our health, and threats to the environment on which all life depends. Within this context, Carson conveys many of the teachings that have become staples of environmental arguments: about the balance of nature, the interconnections that make up ecosystems, the role of genetics in disease, and the subtle danger of small doses of toxins over a long period of time.

If arousing the fear of being directly poisoned could be called the "low road" taken by *Silent Spring,* then the vision of ecological fitness and a moral reevaluation of our relationship to nature is the "high road." But the ease with which Carson's brilliant writing allows the reader to travel down these paths also conceals pitfalls. Both cases depend on seriously flawed arguments. The result is that what Carson is against turns out to be much clearer than what she is for.

## Challenge and Response

Carson admits at the beginning of *Silent Spring* that there is an "insect problem" in need of "control." She makes quite clear that it was not her "contention that chemical pesticides must never be used."[8] Instead, she says, she seeks to provide more knowledge of the harm they can do and spur further research into their effects. She wants their use to be based on "realities" and not "mythical situations."[9]

Given the insidious effects Carson believes that even small doses of pesticides produce, and the way they spread, and the terrible toll they take on innocent animal life, it is understandable if by the end of the book, the reader has quite forgotten this opening admission. Perhaps she makes it only as the price of being heard, or because of the already "irrecoverable" and "irreversible" "contamination of air, earth, rivers, and sea with dangerous and even lethal materials."[10]

Yet Carson is quite enthusiastic about some methods for insect control; she sees great promise in "biological" techniques like the use of natural predators, lures, repellents, or the release of great numbers of sterilized males.[11] However problematic it might be to make any sharp distinction these days between "biological" and "chemical," it seems that Carson does not believe that nature is in all respects something we must let stand in whatever form it comes to us. She is, for example, against the wholesale application of herbicides to control plant growth at roadsides, but she is not against selective spraying to keep down large, woody plants and trees.[12] She is for the use of radiation to produce sterile male insects as a means of pest control, even though when she wants to foster our fear of poison, she likens the effects of pesticides to the effects of radiation.[13]

10    It seems Carson wants to strike *some* kind of balance on the question of pesticides, and the larger question of our relationship to nature, but the character of that balance, and the elements that enter into it, are not immediately clear. The scientists who developed the pesticides Carson excoriates° did not set out to create "biocides." Indeed, part of the impetus for their creation was a search for more specific poisons for use against pests. Whatever these scientists' extreme expectations about their ability to eliminate those pests,[14] their aim of providing a safe and secure food supply is not, it would seem, one that Carson objects to. Why did they go wrong—or more to the point, why have they failed to change direction? Carson summarizes the situation as she prepares to solve the mystery of who is poisoning us:

> Who has made the decision that sets in motion these chains of poisonings, this ever-widening wave of death that spreads out, like ripples when a pebble is dropped into a still pond? Who has placed in one pan of the scales the leaves that might have been eaten by the beetles and in the other the pitiful heaps of many-hued feathers, the lifeless remains of the birds that fell before the unselective bludgeon of insecticidal poisons? Who has decided—who has the *right* to decide—for the countless legions of people who were not consulted that the supreme value is a world without insects, even though it be also a sterile world ungraced by the curving wing of a bird in flight?[15]

The same thing keeps biocides on the market and produces scientists willing to develop and defend them: big business profits. Carson speaks of "an era dominated by industry, in which the right to make a dollar at whatever cost is seldom challenged."[16] Furthermore, "major chemical companies" are deeply involved in supplying funds to universities for pesticide research; "certain outstanding entomologists" support pesticides because they dare not "bite the hand that literally feeds them."[17] Having thus "poisoned the well" as regards her potential critics, Carson continued to put great weight on this ad hominem argument when they became her actual critics after the book was published.[18]

---

*excoriates:* Condemns or blames scathingly.

To deal with such problems, Carson speaks of increased government regulation of pesticide use, establishing zero-tolerances for pesticide residues in food, and substitution of relatively safer for more dangerous pesticides.[19] By implication, she also seems to believe that private funding of scientific research at universities should be limited. But such measures would clearly be only makeshift.° *Silent Spring* provides numerous examples of government regulatory agencies and researchers being part of the problem, not the solution.[20] No merely institutional or legal changes could be assured of providing the safer pest control Carson advocates, so long as the basic outlook of those who hold the offices and do the research does not change.

It is for this reason that Carson ultimately calls for a moral revaluation of our relationship with nature. It is widely and not unreasonably believed that Carson should be credited with bringing the public to understand nature in terms of ecology, food chains, the "web of life," and the "balance of nature," thus promoting greater respect for nature and more cautious interventions in it.[21] Indeed, this accomplishment reveals the moral vision that plays so prominent a role in her work, about which more shortly.

Whether they liked it or not, little of Carson's frightening message was lost on readers of the book. *Silent Spring,* wrote the noted anthropologist Loren Eisley in *Saturday Review,* is Rachel Carson's "account of those floods of insecticides and well-intentioned protective devices which have indiscriminantly slaughtered our wildlife of both forest and stream. Such ill-considered activities break the necessary food chains of nature and destroy the livelihoods of creatures not even directly affected by the pesticides."[22] Her book, added the *New York Times Book Review* in an essay aptly titled "There's Poison All Around," "is a cry to the reading public to help curb private and public programs which by use of poisons will end by destroying life on earth."[23] From the start, sympathetic reviews such as *Christian Century*'s "Elixers of Death" have pictured Carson as having made her case on the basis of "impeccable"° scientific credentials.[24] "[S]he is no hysterical Cassandra," noted *Commonweal* in "Varieties of Poison,"[25] but for all that *Christian Century* correctly noted that she had produced "a shocking and frightening book."[26]

Those who praised the book were often quite open about its essentially polemical° character: "No one is in a better position than Miss Carson to arouse the indignation of the public," noted *The Nation.*[27] While Lamont Cole, writing in *Scientific American,* was "glad this provocative book has been written," he admitted that it was not a "fair and impartial appraisal of all the evidence" but "a highly partisan selection of examples and interpretations that

15

---

*makeshift:* Rough-and-ready, shabby.  *impeccable:* Flawless, perfect.  *polemical:* Related to an argument or controversy.

support the author's thesis." This tactic is apparently justified, to his mind, by the fact that "the extreme opposite has been impressed on the public by skilled professional molders of public opinion."[28] Such hostility to the existing business, scientific, and governmental establishment, which is only now showing signs of abating among some environmentalists, created a sense that ecological PR needs to fight business PR. That, at least, is what *Commonweal* might have had in mind with this otherwise cryptic lead for its review: "*Silent Spring* represents a major breakthrough in the communications industry."[29]

Praise was not the only thing Carson met with. The book was widely and vociferously° criticized as well. Many such responses came more or less directly from the chemical industry she had attacked, and they often matched Carson in the intemperateness° of their tone, without her elegance of expression. Monsanto published a parody of the book, called "The Desolate Year," in its house organ, picturing the poverty and disease of a world without pesticides; 5,000 copies were sent to editors and book reviewers around the country.[30] The Nutrition Foundation, a trade group of food and chemical industries, developed a critical and widely distributed "Fact Kit."[31] The Velsicol Chemical Corporation is said to have made efforts to have Houghton Mifflin suppress the book, but that claim is debated.[32]

Carson's critics certainly used some unscientific arguments against her. *Chemical and Engineering News* claimed that she had ignored "the sound appraisals of such responsible, broadly knowledgeable scientists as the President of the National Academy of Sciences, the members of the President's Scientific Advisory Committee, the Presidents of the Rockefeller Foundation and Nutrition Foundation," as if mere arguments from authority would settle the issue.[33] But Carson herself may have invited them by suggesting that scientists who favor present pesticide practices "prostitute their professional work in order to win lucrative research fellowships," as a review in *The American City* put it. "This callous smear of the professional integrity of those who disagree with her is ugly. Miss Carson would be indignant if they countered that she based her writings on what would sell the most books rather than on what is fair and impartial analysis. But one suggestion follows another."[34]

Critics typically accused the book of being one-sided, presenting none of the benefits to health and food production that had been wrought by pesticide use. *Science* argued that the book was not "a judicial review or a balancing of the gains and losses; rather, it is the prosecuting attorney's impassioned plea for action against the use of these new materials which have received such widespread acceptance, acceptance accorded because of the obvious benefits their use has conferred."[35] Carson's attitude toward technology,

---

*vociferously:* Noisily, loudly.    *intemperateness:* The quality of being excessive or immoderate.

*Chemical and Engineering News* noted, would mean "disease, epidemics, starvation, misery and suffering incomparable and intolerable to modern man."[36]

Most seriously, Carson was accused of misrepresenting or misunderstanding the evidence she cited. A review in *Archives of Internal Medicine* asserted that *Silent Spring* "as science, is so much hogwash."[37] I have not been able to locate any review that attempted to take up her errors in the presentation of scientific material in any great detail. Still, the general points that are mentioned are far from trivial, such as Carson's assertion that birth-to-death exposure to "dangerous chemicals" is a new phenomenon,[38] or her failure to appreciate that the dose makes the poison.[39] Lamont Cole's generally favorable review treats this question in a very curious way: "Errors of fact are so infrequent, trivial and irrelevant to the main themes that it would be ungallant to dwell on them." He mentions one or two, but more to the point he finds two of Carson's main conceptual foundations highly suspect: her assumption that there is a "balance of nature," and that insects who exhibit resistance to pesticides will turn into super bugs.[40] Other Carson partisans and critics have pointed to different factual errors.[41]

As is so often the case, the controversy was not exactly bad for sales. Houghton Mifflin printed 100,000 copies, editorials and editorial cartoons on both sides appeared in newspapers across the country, the book was selected by Book of the Month Club, and Consumer's Union sponsored a special edition.[42] Within a short time, the book was published in at least 17 countries and 10 languages. Carson, having known since 1960 she was ill with the breast cancer that took her life in 1964, participated selectively but importantly in the intense controversy the book sparked, appearing on TV, testifying before congressional committees, and giving widely reported speeches on the occasion of receiving the awards that showered down on her.

What did this remarkable woman do to inspire such intense emotions and engage the imagination of not only the public at large but of politicians and policymakers? Carson's admirers have had two important insights into her accomplishments. On the one hand, they note that part of the effectiveness of her case was in overcoming scientific specialization so that she could give an overview of the problem posed by the increasing use of pesticides and herbicides.[43] It could be said that before Carson, scientists studied many problems: insecticide problems and herbicide problems, problems of human health effects and livestock health, impacts on this kind of plant or that kind of insect. It is only a slight exaggeration to say that after Carson, the public began to believe there was only one issue: the environmental problem.

In assessing Carson's contribution, her supporters are also on target when they admit that there was little new in *Silent Spring*. Instead, as her friend Shirley A. Biggs put it, "Her role was to put together a diffuse and variable body of data and to shape it into a clear account that would not only educate the public but also reach people in authority."[44] In other words, Carson was a wildly successful popularizer.[45]

## Selecting the Evidence

As capable as she was of making a clear and moving case, was she as capable of fulfilling the demand on a popularizer for accuracy and truthfulness? This question has been debated heatedly ever since the publication of the book. It is central to understanding how she so powerfully aroused our fear of being poisoned—the "low road" of *Silent Spring*.

Latter-day critics are able to point out that some of Carson's claims have not held up to subsequent research. For example, it is very unlikely that DDT is a carcinogen.[46] Changes of medical or scientific outlook subsequent to the book's publication mean that many parts must now be taken with a grain of salt. But it would hardly be Carson's fault if, having honestly presented the legitimate scientific opinions of her day, those opinions have since been abandoned. Yet *was* her presentation uniformly accurate? Her advocates have been able to take advantage of a characteristic critical blind spot. The main focus has always been on what Carson did *not* say, on her failure to admit the usefulness of pesticides in promoting human health and food production. Thus, despite much huffing and puffing about expert opinion disagreeing with Carson, critics rarely give specific or well-documented instances of where Carson was wrong *in terms of the evidence available to her at the time*. As Shirley Biggs notes, while there is often vague talk of exaggerations and errors, as of 1987 "[w]e at the Rachel Carson Council have yet to be shown a valid example, despite the sketchy state of much of the information available at the time. This accuracy shows the value of her very conservative approach."[47] It justifies calling her "'the greatest biologist since Darwin'" for the shift in our values and way of understanding the natural world that she helped bring about.[48]

25        It is beyond the scope of this work to examine all of Carson's sources and how she used them. But a closer look at her treatment of some of the human health effects of pesticides is in order, given the theme of poisoning. This theme was a "no lose" proposition for Carson, since no honest critic could deny that under some circumstances, the "biocides" she was discussing were indeed poisonous. In addition, we may focus on human health effects because, as Carson noted in a letter to Paul Brooks, "As I look over my reference material now, I am impressed by the fact that the evidence on this particular point outweighs by far, in sheer bulk and also significance, any other aspect of the problem."[49]

If the Rachel Carson Council had not yet seen a "valid" case of something not unreasonably called an "error," it is not for want of such examples. It is indeed possible to document material that is misrepresented or used out of context. The result is to make the harm of pesticides seem greater, more certain, or more unprecedented than the original source indicates.

A major theme of Carson's book is that one reason for the "silent spring" of the future is that pesticides obstruct reproduction. The culmination of a lengthy discussion of how DDT interferes with the ability of cells to produce energy is the remark, "Some indication of the possible effect on human beings is seen in medical reports of oligospermia, or reduced production of spermatozoa, among aviation crop dusters applying DDT."[50] Her citation (at the back of the book) is to a 1949 "letter to the Editor" of the *Journal of the American Medical Association* (JAMA).[51]

This short sentence reveals a great deal about Carson's rhetorical skill. While Carson says "reports," the citation is to a single report; because that report cites more than one case, the use of the plural is technically justified even if misleading to someone who does not check her references. Note also that "possible effect" is ambiguous; does it mean an effect that might be caused by DDT or a known effect of DDT (as in "it is possible to contract a cold from a handshake")? Finally, there is an ambiguity about how widespread the observation of oligospermia is. The sentence could imply the results of a large-scale study of crop dusters, but the source is nothing of the sort. It is a letter in the Queries and Minor Notes section of JAMA, where doctors sent in questions for referral to "competent authorities." In this case, a doctor from Phoenix writes to ask whether oligospermia he has noted in three crop dusters could be caused by DDT or its xylene solvent. The answer begins, "Neither xylene nor DDT is known specifically to impair spermatogenesis." It goes on to suggest that "real exposure to xylene" would produce symptoms sure to provoke "medical comment" and that the doctor investigate repeated low-dose exposure to carbon monoxide or pituitary gland malfunction. The answer notes in conclusion that an "adequate exploration" of this case might be "an outstanding contribution," since there is not much clinical data in the area.[52] In other words, the source cited denies the very connection Carson suggests, although with proper scientific caution it would not affirm that DDT could *not* be the cause. But that caution is quite different from Carson's attempt to represent this source as supporting her position that DDT is a "possible" cause of low sperm production.

Carson also discusses neurological effects of DDT exposure on human beings, citing reports by three British scientists who dosed themselves by exposure through the skin. The list of symptoms they experienced included aching limbs and joint pain that was "quite violent at times." Carson goes on

parenthetically,° "Despite this evidence, several American investigators conducting an experiment with DDT on volunteer subjects dismissed the complaint of headache and 'pain in every bone' as 'obviously of psychoneurotic
origin.'"[53] American investigators are thus presented as incompetent and
heartless. Note also that "the complaint" is grammatically ambiguous; it could
refer to a single complaint that many subjects reported or to a single complaint from one subject. The immediate reference to "volunteer subjects"
clearly suggests the former.

30     The source is a report whose publication in JAMA was authorized by the
Council on Pharmacy and Chemistry of the American Medical Association.[54]
It studied relatively low doses of DDT given to prisoners over an extended
period of time. One of its conclusions was that "During the entire study, no
volunteer complained of any symptom or showed, by the tests used, any sign
of illness that did not have an easily recognized cause clearly unrelated to
exposure to DDT." Further, "The results indicate that a large safety factor is
associated with DDT as it now occurs in the general diet."[55] These are two
propositions that Carson is entitled to dispute, but she does not so much as
mention them. What about the bone and joint pain? Do the researchers draw
their conclusions having ignored it? It is worth quoting the source of "the
complaint" at length, for it comes from a single individual:

> He had participated for 155 days and had received 138 doses of DDT. He
> had several complaints, including pain every day in every bone, occa-
> sional headache, and tearing of the right eye. He submitted to complete
> physical and laboratory examination, and all findings were normal. His
> complaints obviously were of psychoneurotic origin, and even the man
> himself did not seem to take them seriously.[56]

Thus does Carson manage to misrepresent, and by implication discredit, a
report whose conclusions decisively undercut her own.

    In other instances, Carson places her sources in a context that radically
changes their original meaning. One case can be found in connection with
another major example of how we are being poisoned, the carcinogenic properties of pesticides. She argues that pesticides act like radiation in impairing
cell division. Leukemia, she notes, is "one of the most common diseases to
result from exposure to radiation or to chemicals that imitate radiation." She
then discusses how benzene, a common insecticide solvent, "has been recognized in the medical literature for many years as a cause of leukemia."[57]
Immediately following, she points out how the "rapidly growing tissues of a

---

*parenthetically:* "In parentheses" or as an aside.

child would also afford conditions most suitable for the development of malignant cells." Indeed, Sir Macfarlane Burnet has shown an increasing incidence of early childhood leukemia. "According to this authority, 'The peak between three and four years of age can hardly have any other interpretation than exposure of the young organism to mutagenic stimulus° around the time of birth.'"[58] She then continues to discuss the carcinogenic effects of urethane, neither an insecticide nor a solvent but a chemical related to certain herbicides. One would be forgiven for believing, then, that Burnet and Carson have the same kinds of things in mind when they speak of "mutagenic stimulus."

The source here is an essay Burnet published in the *New England Journal of Medicine,* first delivered as a speech at the Harvard School of Public Health in 1958.[59] He documents a rising incidence of leukemia, particularly among children. While he does not doubt radiation can cause leukemia, he also suggests that in the United States, among urban whites, "Only an insignificant portion of the increase is due to ionizing radiation."[60] Hence, he believes, some other mutagenic stimulus must be found, just as Carson quotes him as saying.

Burnet admits he can only speculate about what that stimulus is. What is interesting is just how different his speculations are from Carson's. He argues that since the increase is not seen "in colored persons" in the United States, it seems unlikely that the stimulus is "some all pervading element associated with advancing civilization such as traces of carcinogens in the air from combustion processes of various types."[61]

It is the point of *Silent Spring* that "biocides" are precisely all-pervading elements of advancing civilization. Did this passage, then, give Carson any pause? What did she make of the fact that when Burnet discusses possible sources of "mutagenic chemicals," he talks about increased coffee and tea drinking, cigarette smoking, pharmaceuticals prescribed during pregnancy, and some hitherto unknown by-product from the production of artificial infant formula?[62] None of these sources is fully satisfactory for him; all of them are speculative. But he does not mention pesticides and herbicides at all.

We know what Carson made of this part of Burnet's argument. She suppressed it. She bracketed° his point with observations that made it appear that his thinking in the article cited moved in the same direction as her own. Furthermore, Carson claims to know what Burnet only speculates about and attributes that certainty to him as well. But Burnet's open-mindedness is precisely what characterizes the "meticulous" scientists among whose ranks Carson's defenders would like to place her.[63]

35

---

*mutagenic stimulus:* Factor that stimulates or increases the number of mutations in cells (often cancer-causing).    *bracketed:* Here meaning "surrounded."

Sometimes Carson neglects to tell the whole story in other ways. In making the case for the neurotoxic effects of organic phosphate insecticides, she notes that the "severe damage" they cause to the nervous system would make one expect them to be implicated in "mental disease."[64] A study from Australia supplies her that link, documenting mental illness in 16 individuals with "prolonged exposure" to such insecticides.[65] But Carson neglects to note some important qualifications on this study. The author admits he performed no statistical analysis showing that the apparent correlation between exposure and mental illness was not due to chance. When the author investigated two fruit-growing districts to see if an increase in "mental ill-health" could be found in the field, only 3 of 16 physicians surveyed reported any such increase. Of these, two could support their impression with case records.[66] In short, the study Carson uses to "nail down" her speculations is more speculative than she admits.

Carson does *not* misrepresent *all* her sources. Furthermore, there is no question that pesticides and herbicides can be extremely dangerous to human beings if misused or used carelessly. There would certainly be nothing wrong if Carson wished to disagree with or reinterpret her sources in light of her own understanding of the nature of the "biocide" problem. What is wrong is for her to have failed to do so openly. Of course, there would have been a cost to this kind of honesty. The book would be far less rhetorically powerful if Carson were frequently saying, "So-and-so reports his results that way, but I think they should be interpreted this way." As matters stand, her citations of authorities lead the reader to believe that scientific opinion is consistently on her side. As we have seen, that is not necessarily so. There are indeed "valid" examples of inaccuracies or mistakes to be found in *Silent Spring* and, further, these lapses do not occur at random but fit within a pattern that is necessary for Carson's case to be presented in the most effective and affecting way.

## Exit Humanity?

It is evident from Carson's obviously one-sided treatment of the topic—omitting any serious discussion of the benefits of pesticides—and by the less obvious pattern of distortion of her sources that she herself did not think that the facts of the matter spoke entirely for themselves. Since most people do not have to worry about acute pesticide poisoning, the "low road" fear had to be aroused by the presentation of threats whose subtlety makes them seem all the more insidious. That means her information had to be carefully selected and filtered. But there is another filter, the high road of her call for a moral revaluation of our relationship to nature, that Carson's supporters not only do not deny but celebrate. We turn now to that vision.

The idea of a "balance of nature," which Carson is often credited with popularizing, has had great persistence among the general public. Ironically, already in 1962 LaMonte Cole could assert that the balance of nature "is an obsolete concept among ecologists."[67] Nevertheless, one sees in Carson some of the reasoning that makes so many people think there is a delicate and static balance of nature, and that "upsetting" it is a particularly reckless thing to do. At the same time, a look at Carson's own metaphors and examples suggests some of the difficulties and ambiguities of this concept and that Carson herself may not have been clear on just how she wanted human beings to act in relationship to nature.[68]

Following the implications of the concern that we are both poisoners and poisoned, Carson suggests that the balance of nature can no more be ignored than a "man perched on the edge of a cliff" can defy the "law of gravity."[69] In other words, we face a dangerous situation in which the slightest misstep will bring final disaster. After all, it took "eons of time" for life to reach "a state of adjustment and balance with its surroundings" that we see around us.[70] In a moment, it would seem, humanity can disturb this delicate balance. And because "in nature nothing exists alone," such disturbance may be expected to have the most far-reaching consequences.[71]

If everything is connected to everything else in a finely tuned balance, then physically problematic and temporally remote consequences of pesticide use, on which Carson places a good deal of stress, become a plausible substitute for looking at positive immediate consequences such as prevention of epidemics or increased crop yields. The argument that small, repeated doses eventually can have widespread and dangerous consequences also becomes more plausible. Carson must develop this argument because however tragic the acute cases of pesticide poisoning she cites, they were relatively rare and often linked to flagrant misuse.

When nature comes to be seen as a seamless web and a delicate balance, human activity is more easily painted as the violation or destruction of that balance. Instead of a variety of potentially distinct human/nature relationships, each to be judged on its own merits, all interactions come to be viewed in light of the manifold impacts of the most intrusive and disruptive. Thus diverse situations come to be simplified into one "environmental crisis." Looking at the destruction we have shown ourselves capable of causing, we find it hard to see that there is any place for human beings within nature, leading some to wonder whether Carson has created an ideal of nature in which human beings have no place.[72]

Yet this notion of a natural balance of nature is precisely the one that has least ecological support. To her credit, it is not Carson's final word on the topic, however much the emotional force of some of her arguments depends on it. For she also likens the present interaction between humans and nature

40

to the "rumblings of an avalanche."[73] While this image retains the idea that small beginnings can have disastrous and unstoppable consequences, it makes human interventions seem less "unnatural." We are not the only cause of avalanches. Furthermore, nature recovers from avalanches; they are an ongoing aspect of ecosystem change.

Despite her sometime use of static imagery, at other times Carson recognizes that, if we are to speak of a "balance" at all, it is better understood in dynamic terms: "The balance of nature is not a *status quo;* it is fluid, ever shifting, in a constant state of adjustment. Man, too, is part of this balance."[74] Over time, changes, even vast changes, are normal. Species and habitats disappear. Life adjusts to hostile or dangerous situations and takes advantage of favorable conditions.[75]

45        Might it not be argued, then, that human beings, as participants in this ongoing, dynamic balance, are simply promoting the same kind of changes that are always going on in nature? Why any special concern about our modifications? Carson tries to explain the peculiar danger human actions pose even to the dynamic balance of nature. Human-induced changes, she argues, work much faster than nature normally works on its own.[76] Such speedy changes mean that ecosystems may not have time to adjust to them, and that in turn raises the specter of a dominolike collapse of the system as a whole.

This argument from collapse due to rapid change has proven increasingly popular. It is a staple, for example, with those concerned about the greenhouse effect. They admit that life on earth has flourished during periods even warmer than those they are projecting. But if we were to make a transition to such a warmer world in a mere hundred years, as opposed to hundreds of thousands, there would be no chance for various biota° to adjust to the change, with terrible consequences.

Still, we know that natural ecosystems can undergo vast and rapid changes due to things like volcanoes, earthquakes, fires, floods, and hurricanes, any of which can produce destruction on a scale that dwarfs just about anything humans can do at any speed. The question is, is the effect even of such great changes amplified over time and through space, as the avalanche metaphor suggests? Or does the balance of nature dampen the effects of such disturbances?

Carson is well aware that in fact the avalanche likeness is not entirely appropriate for what human beings are doing to nature. In yet another metaphor, she suggests how the consequences of our actions expand "like ripples when a pebble is dropped into a still pond."[77] But the ripples, even as they widen, have less and less of an impact on the still pond. What may be a tidal

---

*biota:* The plant and animal life of a region.

wave to the water strider next to the pebble's point of impact is hardly felt by the tadpole near shore. The sudden collapse of the ecosystem surrounding Mt. St. Helens did not cause a dominolike fall of surrounding and dependent systems, in turn spreading out an avalanche of destruction.

Is there any reason to believe that the way humans interact with nature is likely to weaken nature's ability to dampen the impact of our changes to it? Carson believes so, despite her use of the pebble metaphor: "Nature has introduced great variety into the landscape, but man has displayed a passion for simplifying it."[78] This argument is also now well established in environmental thinking. Carson associates what has come to be called "biodiversity" with ecosystem stability. The consequences of human-induced changes become more severe rather than less over time if the net result of those changes is to destabilize ecosystems by simplifying them.

Now, as we will see shortly, Carson is well aware that human activity can also create richer and more complex ecosystems. However, as plausible as the association of diversity and stability might seem, within the discipline of ecology it is not taken quite as a matter of course.[79] If diversity uniformly bred stability, it would be hard to understand how tropical rain forests, widely regarded as the greatest reservoirs of biological diversity, would be as fragile as they are said to be.

Thus, while the fear of poisoning that is the "low road" of *Silent Spring* is perfectly clear, the "high road," or Carson's attempt to popularize the significance of ecology and the "balance of nature," is less coherent. We began this examination by noting that Carson's advocates celebrate the existence of an informing moral vision in her work. It was not enough for her merely to catalog the various potential or actual dangers posed by the use of pesticides and heribicides. She also sought to provide an overarching lesson that could be learned from those particulars. But if that vision is clouded, how are we to know what to do or refrain from doing?

## Doing the Right Thing

Early in the book Carson notes that for the most part, the environment has shaped life on earth, and not vice versa. Over "the whole span of earthly time" the ability of life to modify its surroundings has been "relatively slight" —until humans came along.[80] And only in the last century have human beings gained "significant power" to "alter the nature of [their] world."[81] From this outlook, modern humans appear as a kind of rogue° species, an unnatural product of nature. We are back to the edge of the cliff. But later in

*rogue:* Mischievous, inclined to misbehave.

the book, when Carson discusses soils,° we get a different picture. Without soils, neither land plants nor land animals could survive. Yet soils are "in part a creation of life, born of a marvelous interaction of life and nonlife long eons ago."[82] This modification by life of its surroundings hardly seems "relatively slight," since it makes possible the natural world as we know it today. Compared with this accomplishment, it is human intervention that, so far, seems "relatively slight."

Still, Carson might say, it is human beings whose impact has been dangerous to life, rather than creative. For in "less than two decades," synthetic pesticides have become "so thoroughly distributed" that "for the first time in the history of the world, every human being is now subjected to contact with dangerous chemicals, from the moment of conception until death."[83] The implication is that there was a time when the "balance of nature" meant that human beings were not routinely exposed to potentially dangerous substances. Critics have pointed out what nonsense this statement is, since there have always been chemicals in the environment that, in some dose, are dangerous.[84] But more to the point, even Carson herself provides evidence that nature was not simply benign° prior to the last two decades, when she talks about pesticides "derived" from naturally occurring substances—some of which she knows to be extremely dangerous.[85] Nature was not a safe place that human actions made dangerous.

Perhaps human beings have used their ingenuity in such a way as to introduce entirely new kinds of dangers into nature. That seems to be the suggestion when Carson talks about "systemic insecticides," chemicals that kill insects by converting "plants or animals into a sort of Medea's robe° by making them actually poisonous."[86] Such insecticides produce "a weird world, surpassing the imaginings of the Brothers Grimm . . . where the enchanted forest of the fairy tales has become the poisonous forest where an insect that chews a leaf or sucks the sap of a plant is doomed."[87] Yet in the very next paragraph, Carson admits that the "hint" for such pesticides came from nature itself, where plants defend themselves by the synthesis of substances poisonous to their predators![88] The vision of nature as an "enchanted forest" where such things do not happen is, as Carson says, a "fairy tale"—but this fairy tale forms the basis for her excoriation of systemic insecticides.

55      Even if the human ability to modify nature is not as radically new as Carson sometimes makes out, even if nature is not "by nature" as safe as Carson sometimes suggests, it might still be true . . . that "nature knows best," and that human beings should therefore impose minimally on natural processes, lest

---

*soils:* The layer of earth in which plants can grow.    *benign:* Harmless.    *Medea's robe:* Reference to a Greek play in which a character kills another by giving her a beautiful poisoned robe; this expression, then, refers to something that looks good and promising but turns out to be deadly.

the balance of nature be disturbed. Clearly, this lesson is one Carson wants to get across, as the book's epigraph by E. B. White suggests. White laments that the human race "is too ingenious for its own good" in its efforts to "beat" nature "into submission." He hopes that we could accommodate ourselves "to this planet" and view it "appreciatively."[89] Yet we have seen how Carson admits that there is an "insect problem" in need of "control," and that there is a legitimate use of herbicides to control plant growth along highways. *Control* is very different from the *accommodation* White calls for.

The highway-spraying case is quite telling. Here, nature is being controlled not for some essential purpose like food but for creating marginal increases in safety and aesthetics by keeping large plants well back from the road. Such efforts may be important for many reasons, but they hardly represent an "accommodation" to planet earth.

Carson's stand on roadside spraying suggests in another way that nature does not always know best. Wholesale spraying is wrong in part because it destroys wildflowers that make the road beautiful.[90] But surely Carson knew two things about those roadside wildflowers: most of them are there *because* the road exists; many wildflowers do best on disturbed ground, which they take over and colonize. And that in turn is true because a great many North American wildflowers are aliens brought from Europe; they do well in disturbed ground because there they have less competition from native species. Finally, left to itself, the roadside would tend to exhibit ecological succession; the larger, woody plants that she is willing to see sprayed would force out many of the wildflowers that do well on open ground. In other words, in defending roadside wildflowers, Carson is defending a "natural" state that is in three ways a result of human intervention: the importation (accidental or otherwise) of the wildflowers, the building of the road, and the maintenance of conditions suitable for wildflower growth. It thus appears that human beings, while conquering nature, can at the same time *increase* biological diversity.

Carson's case shows how love of nature, which by all accounts she felt deeply, by no means guarantees that one has a clear view of the beloved. Careful writers about Carson have already recognized that her thinking about nature is more complex than at first meets the eye. Her failure to tease out the various strands of that complexity is probably a net rhetorical gain. It makes it possible for there to be "man" and "destruction" on one side of the ledger, and "nature" and "danger" on the other side. Because there is no clear picture of when humans intervene properly in nature, Carson can maintain both her pessimism about a future "where no birds sing" and her optimism that the right science and the right agricultural technology can provide many of the benefits of existing pesticides without their grave costs.

Carson's lack of clarity about humans' relationship to nature is summed up in her view of modern natural science. As much as she must rely on science for the better methods of pest control she wants to see put to work, she condemns its arrogance and seeks a new humility. She says that science must waken to the fact that in dealing with living beings, it is dealing with a world of "pressures and counterpressures . . . surges and recessions."[91] Only by taking this complexity into account will science be able "cautiously" to "guide" such "life forces" into "channels favorable to ourselves."[92]

> The "control of nature" is a phrase conceived in arrogance, born of the Neanderthal age of biology and philosophy, when it was supposed that nature exists for the convenience of man. The concepts and practices of applied entomology for the most part date from that Stone Age of science. It is our alarming misfortune that so primitive a science has armed itself with the most modern and terrible weapons, and that in turning them against the insects it has also turned them against the earth.[93]

Carson's last book is widely seen as an attempt to describe the kind of education children should have to produce the right relationship to nature. The title, *A Sense of Wonder,* already describes the essentials of that outlook.[94] Wonder, as she suggests, is indeed a good thing. But wonder and humility do not have to spring from the same sources as caution, nor would they necessarily have the same outcomes. Wonder is most consistent with a contemplative stance toward nature, a stance Carson clearly had an affinity for. Caution suggests an active stance. To channel nature cautiously is not to give up on control of nature; it is to control it better than we do now, as the slighting references to the stone age of philosophy and science suggest. Yet that age might have had a clearer picture than Carson of the difficulty of reconciling the activist and contemplative requirements she places on a more "modern" perspective.

60        By now, nothing can detract from *Silent Spring*'s immense contribution to the rise of the green crusade. But as our discussion suggests, it is not a fully coherent or completely worked out line of argument. While critical of the impact of the profit motive on government and science, it presents no complete critique of the American economic and political arrangements that produce such a result. While advocating humility toward nature, it maintains the necessity for human intervention, without fully articulating what constitutes legitimate and illegitimate intervention. While critical of one instantiation of modern science and technology, it relies on another.

1. Marcus Aurelius, *Meditations,* and Epictetus, *Enchiridion* (Chicago: Henry Regnery, 1956): 197.
2. René Descartes, *Discourse on Method,* trans. Laurence J. Lafleur (Indianapolis: Bobbs-Merrill, 1956): 40.
3. Rachel Carson, *Silent Spring,* 25th Anniversary Edition (Boston: Houghton Mifflin, 1962).

4. Paul Brooks, *The House of Life: Rachel Carson at Work* (Boston: Houghton Mifflin, 1972): 227.

5. Rachel Carson, *The Sea Around Us* (New York: Oxford University Press, 1951).

6. Frank Graham, Jr., *Since Silent Spring* (Boston: Houghton Mifflin, 1970): 78–79.

7. Carson, *Silent Spring*, 1–3. The book is said to have a "detective-story flavor" in Donald Fleming, "Roots of the New Conservation Movement," *Perspectives in American History*, vol. 6 (Cambridge: Cambridge University Press, 1972): 32.

8. Carson, *Silent Spring*, 12.

9. Ibid., 9.

10. Ibid., 6. Fleming suggests that since the book was written to "persuade and arouse," Carson had to "calculate her effects as never before, trim her sails to catch the prevailing winds" (Fleming, "New Conservation Movement," 29).

11. Carson, *Silent Spring*, 278–88.

12. Ibid., 75.

13. Ibid., 208–9.

14. Fleming, "New Conservation Movement," 29.

15. Carson, *Silent Spring*, 127.

16. Ibid., 13.

17. Ibid., 259.

18. Rachel Carson, "Rachel Carson Answers Her Critics," *Audubon Magazine* (September/October 1963): 313, 315.

19. Carson, *Silent Spring*, 183–84.

20. See her accounts of the Agriculture Department's gypsy moth and fire ant programs, *Silent Spring*, 157–68.

21. See, for example, Fleming, "New Conservation Movement," 30; Samuel P. Hays, *Beauty, Health and Permanence: Environmental Politics in the United States, 1955–1985* (Cambridge: Cambridge University Press, 1987): 6, 28; Robert C. Paehlke, *Environmentalism and the Future of Progressive Politics* (New Haven: Yale University Press, 1989): 29.

22. Loren Eiseley, "Using a Plague to Fight a Plague," *Saturday Review* 45 (September 29, 1962): 18–19.

23. Lorus Milne and Margery Milne, "There's Poison All Around," *New York Times Book Review* (September 23, 1962): 1.

24. "Elixers of Death," *Christian Century* 79 (December 19, 1962): 1564.

25. James Rorty, "Varieties of Poison," *Commonweal* 77 (December 14, 1962): 320.

26. "Elixers," *Christian Century*: 1564.

27. Marston Bates, "Man and Other Pests," *The Nation* 195 (October 6, 1962): 202.

28. LaMont C. Cole, "Rachel Carson's Indictment of the Wide Use of Pesticides," *Scientific American* (December 1962): 173. Contemporary writers, anxious to maintain Carson's reputation, have a hard time on this point. Her book is "calm and reasoned" but "Carson consciously wrote a polemic intended to stir people to political action." (Philip Shabecoff, *A Fierce Green Fire: The American Environmental Movement* [New York: Hill and Wang, 1993]: 109.) It is both an example of a " 'most profound sort of propaganda' " and "scientific evidence" that is "documented in impeccable detail" (Paehlke, *Progressive Politics*, 28).

29. Rorty, "Varieties of Poison," 320.

30. Graham, *Since Silent Spring*, 64–65.

31. Ibid., 58–59.

32. Compare Graham, *Since Silent Spring*, 49, with Elizabeth Whelan, *Toxic Terror: The Truth About the Cancer Scare* (Ottawa, Ill.: Jameson Books, 1985): 64.

33. William J. Darby, "Silence, Miss Carson," *Chemical and Engineering News* (October 1, 1962): 60.

34. "Rachel Carson vs. Pest Control," *The American City* (March 1963): 7.

35. I. L. Baldwin, "Chemicals and Pests," *Science* 137 (September 1962): 1042.

36. Darby, "Silence," 60.

37. Graham, *Since Silent Spring*, 56.

38. Ibid., 56–57.

39. Darby, "Silence," 62.

40. Cole, "Rachel Carson's Indictment," 173.

41. Frank Graham admits that Carson's claim that arsenic is the carcinogenic element in chimney soot is wrong, that she overstated the threat DDT posed to robins, and that she was wrong to think that insect pathogens do not cause disease in higher animals (Graham, *Since Silent Spring*, 67). Far more damagingly, Fleming points out that the whole idea that pesticides are concentrated as one moves up the food chain, which is crucial to Carson's arguments about distant and delayed effects, has "become increasingly dubious in the years that followed" (Fleming, *New Conservation Movement*, 31). There remains an unfortunate tendency to present vague criticisms of the book (e.g., the multi-point indictment in George Claus and Karen Bolander, *Ecological Sanity* [New York: David McKay, 1977]: 10). Unlike most of their impressively documented book, the charges in this instance are left completely unsubstantiated. On the other side, there is an equally unfortunate tendency simply to take her science for granted, as indicated in note 33, above.

42. Graham, *Since Silent Spring*, 69.

43. Gino J. Marco et al., *Silent Spring Revisited* (Washington, D.C.: American Chemical Society, 1987): 9.

44. Ibid., 5.

45. Paehlke's assessment seems just when he notes that one of her contributions "was her articulation of these vital sciences in language accessible to the educated public. Her style, a blend of scientific, political, and moral arguments . . . became the hallmark of popular environmentalism" (Paehlke, *Progressive Politics*, 28). The importance of popularization is also picked up by Claus and Bolander, *Sanity*, 9. Hays exhibits a stunning ability to miss the social forces he wants to describe when he claims that "even more influential" than Carson was a "widely reported administrative hearing about DDT in Wisconsin in 1968 and 1969" (Hays, *Beauty, Health*, 28).

46. Whelan, *Toxic Terror*, 78–85; Edith Efron, *The Apocalyptics* (New York: Simon and Schuster, 1984): 267–70.

47. Marco, *Silent Spring Revisited*, 8. The Rachel Carson Council is an organization that seeks to further Carson's work by the study of pesticides and chemical contaminants.

48. Ibid., 8.

49. Brooks, *House of Life*, 244.

50. Carson, *Silent Spring*, 207–8.

51. Ibid., 336.

52. "Occupational Oligospermia," *Journal of the American Medical Association* 140 (August 13, 1949): 1249.

53. Carson, *Silent Spring*, 193.

54. W. J. Hayes, Jr., W. F. Durham, and C. Cueto, Jr., "The Effect of Known Repeated Oral Doses of Chlorophenothane (DDT) in Man," *Journal of the American Medical Association* 162 (October 27, 1956): 890.

55. Ibid, 897.

56. Ibid., 893.

57. Carson, *Silent Spring*, 234.

58. Ibid., 234–35.

59. Sir Macfarlane Burnet, "Leukemia as a Problem of Preventive Medicine," *New England Journal of Medicine* 259 (August 28, 1958): 423–31.

60. Ibid., 427.

61. Ibid., 427.

62. Ibid., 429.

63. Marco, *Silent Spring Revisited*, 4.

64. Carson, *Silent Spring*, 197–98.

65. Ibid., 198.

66. S. Gershon and F. H. Shaw, "Psychiatric Sequelae of Chronic Exposure to Organophosphorus Insecticides," *Lancet* (June 24, 1961): 1372.

67. Cole, "Rachel Carson's Indictment," 176.

68. Vera L. Norwood, "The Nature of Knowing: Rachel Carson and the American Environment," *Signs: Journal of Women in Culture and Society* 12 (Summer 1987): 740–60.

69. Carson, *Silent Spring*, 5.

70. Ibid., 6.

71. Ibid., 51.

72. Norwood, "Nature of Knowing," 748.

73. Carson, *Silent Spring*, 262.

74. Ibid., 246.

75. Ibid., 6.

76. Ibid., 6–7.

77. Ibid., 127.

78. Ibid., 10.

79. Paul Colinvaux, *Why Big Fierce Animals are Rare: An Ecologist's Perspective* (Princeton: Princeton University Press, 1978): 123, 209. In general, Colinvaux's book is a highly readable presentation of how a professional ecologist looks at nature, and it is striking how different his view often is from the environmental popularizers who claim to be inspired by ecology. As Colinvaux himself puts it in his Preface, "Ecology is not the science of pollution, nor is it environmental science. Still less is it a science of doom. There is, however, an overwhelming mass of writings claiming that ecology is all of these things. I wrote this book in some anger to retort to this literature with an account of what one practicing ecologist thinks his subject is really about . . . I take the opportunity to brand as nonsense tales of destroying the atmosphere, killing lakes, and hazarding the world by making it simple" (vii). See also Mark Sagoff, "Fact and Value in Ecological Science," *Environmental Ethics* 7 (Summer 1985): 107–10.

80. Carson, *Silent Spring*, 5.
81. Ibid., 5.
82. Ibid., 53.
83. Ibid., 15.
84. Specifically on the issue of carcinogenicity, see Efron, *Apocalyptics*, 123–83.
85. Carson, *Silent Spring*, 17–18, 223.
86. Ibid., 32.
87. Ibid., 32–33.
88. Ibid., 33.
89. Ibid., vi.
90. Ibid., 69–70.
91. Ibid., 296.
92. Ibid., 296.
93. Ibid., 297.
94. Rachel Carson, *The Sense of Wonder* (Berkeley: Nature Company, [1956, 1984] 1990).

## QUESTIONS

1. What can you learn from this selection about the way in which you should present information from outside sources, as you include them in your essays? Consider Rubin's critique of Rachel Carson's techniques as well as his own methods of presenting such information in his writing.

2. Rubin accuses Rachel Carson of "poisoning the well" and "ad hominem argument" (meaning a personal attack on the opponent instead of a rebuttal of the opponent's claims) for claiming that some scientists support the use of pesticides because they receive funding from companies that sell pesticides. Do you agree with his characterization? Should Carson have left out that point?

3. Of what other unfair argumentation tactics does Rubin accuse Carson?

4. What does Rubin's use of language—phrases like "environmental crusade," "fanatical attack," "the subsequent excesses of environmental fearmongering"—reveal about his own agenda or perspective concerning environmentalism?

5. Do you agree with Rubin's analysis of the two metaphors he picks out of *Silent Spring*—the "man on the edge of a cliff" and the "rumblings of an avalanche"? Can you think of other possible interpretations for these metaphors?

6. Is it true, as Rubin claims, that natural disasters "can produce destruction on a scale that dwarfs just about anything humans can do at any speed"?

7. How would you describe Rubin's tone in this selection?

## CONNECTIONS

1. Based on the selections from Rachel Carson and Charles Rubin, do you agree with Rubin's conclusions about Carson's book? Why or why not?
2. Compare and contrast Rubin's introduction with the introduction of any other essay included in this text.

# ∾ The Greenhouse Affect°

*P. J. O'Rourke*

> P. J. O'Rourke was born in 1947; he earned his B.A. degree from the Miami
> University of Ohio and his M.A. from Johns Hopkins University. A reformed
> '60s liberal, he is currently a conservative humorist. After contributing for a
> number of years to *National Lampoon* magazine, he published several books,
> among them *Holidays in Hell* (1988), *Parliament of Whores* (1991), and *All
> the Trouble in the World: The Lighter Side of Overpopulation, Famine, Ecologi-
> cal Disaster, Ethnic Hatred, Plague, and Poverty* (1994). The following article
> appeared in 1990 in *Rolling Stone* magazine (for which O'Rourke is now the
> foreign affairs desk chief) and was included in *The* Rolling Stone *Environ-
> mental Reader*, published in 1992.

> **WARM-UP:** What is the stereotypical image of an environmentalist?
> Do you consider yourself an environmentalist? Explain your response.

1    If the great outdoors is so swell, how come the homeless aren't more fond
of it?

There. I wanted to be the one person to say a discouraging word about
Earth Day—a lone voice *not* crying in the wilderness, thank you, but hollering
in the rec room.

On April 22 [1990]—while everybody else was engaged in a great,
smarmy° fit of agreeing with himself about chlorofluorocarbons, while *tout le°*
rapidly-losing-plant-and-animal-species *monde°* traded hugs of unanimity°
over plastic-milk-bottle recycling, while all of you praised one another to the
ozone-depleted skies for your brave opposition to coastal flooding and every
man Jack and woman Jill told child Jason how bad it is to put crude oil on
baby seals—I was home in front of the VCR snacking high on the food chain.

But can any decent, caring resident of this planet possibly disagree with
the goals and aspirations embodied in the celebration of Earth Day? No.

5    That's what bothers me. Mass movements are always a worry. There's a
whiff of the lynch mob or the lemming° migration about any overlarge gathering of like-thinking individuals, no matter how virtuous their cause. Even a

---

*Affect:* The word is used here as a pun; in this context, O'Rourke should have written "effect"; however,
he is implying the word "affectation," which means an artificial attitude or behavior.    *smarmy:* Agreeable in a smug and false way.    *tout le . . . monde:* French, meaning "the whole world," everybody.
*unanimity:* Agreement, unison.    *lemming:* A rodent best known for mass migrations that sometimes
end in the sea, in mass drownings; to call someone a lemming is to accuse him or her of blindly following the herd.

band of angels can turn ugly and start looting if enough angels are hanging around unemployed and convinced that succubi° own all the liquor stores in heaven.

Whenever I'm in the middle of conformity, surrounded by oneness of mind, with people oozing concurrence on every side, I get scared. And when I find myself agreeing with everybody, I get really scared.

Sometimes it's worse when everybody's right than when everybody's wrong. Everybody in fifteenth-century Spain was wrong about where China is, and as a result, Columbus discovered Caribbean vacations. On the other hand, everybody in fifteenth-century Spain was right about heresies: They're heretical. But that didn't make the Spanish Inquisition more fun for the people who were burned at the stake.

A mass movement that's correct is especially dangerous when it's right about a problem that needs fixing. Then all those masses in the mass movement have to be called to action, and that call to action better be exciting, or the masses will lose interest and wander off to play arcade games. What's exciting? Monitoring the release into the atmosphere of glycol ethers used in the manufacture of brake-fluid anti-icing additives? No. But what about some violence, an enemy, someone to hate?

Mass movements need what Eric Hoffer—in *The True Believer,* his book about the kind of creepy misfits who join mass movements—calls a "unifying agent."

"Hatred is the most accessible and comprehensive of all unifying agents," writes Hoffer. "Mass movements can rise and spread without belief in a God, but never without belief in a devil." Hoffer goes on to cite historian F. A. Voigt's account of a Japanese mission sent to Berlin in 1932 to study the National Socialist movement. Voigt asked a member of the mission what he thought. He replied, "It is magnificent. I wish we could have something like it in Japan, only we can't, because we haven't got any Jews."

10

The environmental movement has, I'm afraid, discovered a unifying agent. I almost said "scapegoat," but scapegoats are probably an endangered species. Besides, all animals are innocent, noble, upright, honest and fair in their dealings and have a great sense of humor. Anyway, the environmental movement has found its necessary enemy in the form of that ubiquitous° evil —already so familiar to Hollywood scriptwriters, pulp-paperback authors, minority spokespersons, feminists, members of ACT UP, the Christic Institute and Democratic candidates for president: Big Business.

Now, you might think Big Business would be hard to define in this day of leveraged finances and interlocking technologies. Not so. Big Business is every

---

*succubi:* Demons.   *ubiquitous:* Widespread, found everywhere.

kind of business except the kind from which the person who's complaining draws his pay. Thus the rock-around-the-rain-forest crowd imagines record companies are a cottage industry. The Sheen family° considers movie conglomerates to be a part of the arts and crafts movement. And Ralph Nader thinks the wholesale lobbying of Congress by huge tax-exempt, public-interest advocacy groups is akin to working the family farm.

This is why it's rarely an identifiable person (and, of course, never you or me) who pollutes. It's a vague, sinister, faceless thing called industry. The National Wildlife Federation's booklet on toxic-chemical releases says, "Industry dumped more than 2.3 billion pounds of toxic chemicals into or onto the land." What will "industry" do next? Visit us with a plague of boils? Make off with our firstborn? Or maybe it will wreck the Barcalounger. "Once-durable products like furniture are made to fall apart quickly, requiring more frequent replacement," claims the press kit of Inform, a New York–based environmental group that seems to be missing a few sunflower seeds from its trail mix. But even a respectable old establishmentarian organization like the Sierra Club is not above giving a villainous and conspiratorial cast to those who disagree with its legislative agenda. "For the past eight years, this country's major polluters and their friends in the Reagan administration and Congress have impeded the progress of bills introduced by congressional Clean Air advocates," says the Sierra Club's 1989–90 conservation campaign press package. And here at *Rolling Stone*—where we are so opposed to the profit motive that we work for free, refuse to accept advertising and give the magazine away at newsstands—writer Trip Gabriel, in his *Rolling Stone* 571 article "Coming Back to Earth: A Look at Earth Day 1990," avers,° "The yuppie belief in the sanctity of material possessions, no matter what the cost in resource depletion, squared perfectly with the philosophy of the Reaganites—to exploit the nation's natural resources for the sake of business."

Sure, "business" and "industry" and "their friends in the Reagan administration and Congress" make swell targets. Nobody squirts sulfur dioxide into the air as a hobby or tosses PCBs [polychlorinated biphenyls] into rivers as an act of charity. Pollution occurs in the course of human enterprise. It is a by-product of people making things like a living, including yours. If we desire, for ourselves and our progeny, a world that's not too stinky and carcinogenic, we're going to need the technical expertise, entrepreneurial vigor and marketing genius of every business and industry. And if you think pollution is the fault only of Reaganite yuppies wallowing in capitalist greed, then go take a deep breath in Smolensk or a long drink from the river Volga.

15      Sorry, but business and industry—trade and manufacturing—are inherent to civilization. Every human society, no matter how wholesomely primi-

---

*Sheen family:* Reference to the family of Martin Sheen, an actor and political activist for liberal causes.
*avers:* Firmly asserts, declares.

tive, practices as much trade and manufacturing as it can figure out. It is the fruits of trade and manufacturing that raise us from the wearying muck° of subsistence and give us the health, wealth, education, leisure, and warm, dry rooms with Xerox machines—all of which allow us to be the ecology-conscious, selfless, splendid individuals we are.

Our ancestors were too busy wresting° a living from nature to go on any nature hikes. The first European ever known to have climbed a mountain for the view was the poet Petrarch. That wasn't until the fourteenth century. And when Petrarch got to the top of Mont Ventoux, he opened a copy of Saint Augustine's *Confessions* and was shamed by the passage about men "who go to admire the high mountains and the immensity of the oceans and the course of the heaven . . . and neglect themselves." Worship of nature may be ancient, but seeing nature as cuddlesome, hug-a-bear and too cute for words is strictly a modern fashion.

The Luddite° side of the environmental movement would have us destroy or eschew° technology—throw down the ladder by which we climbed. Well, nuts (and berries and fiber) to you, you shrub huggers. It's time we in the industrialized nations admitted what safe, comfortable and fun-filled lives we lead. If we don't, we will cause irreparable harm to the disadvantaged peoples of the world. They're going to laugh themselves to death listening to us whine.

Contempt for material progress is not only funny but unfair. The average Juan, Chang or Mobutu out there in the parts of the world where every day is Earth Day—or Dirt and Squalor Day anyhow—would like to have a color television too. He'd also like some comfy Reeboks, a Nintendo Power Glove and a Jeep Cherokee. And he means to get them. I wouldn't care to be the skinny health-food nut waving a copy of *50 Simple Things You Can Do to Save the Earth* who tries to stand in his way.

There was something else keeping me indoors on April 22 [1990]. Certain eco-doomsters are not only unreasonable in their attitude toward business, they're unreasonable in their attitude toward reason. I can understand harboring mistrust of technology. I myself wouldn't be inclined to wash my dog in toluene° or picnic in the nude at Bhopal. But to deny the validity of the scientific method is to resign your position as a sentient° being. You'd better go look for work as a lungwort° plant or an Eastern European Communist-party chairman.

---

*muck:* Slimy dirt, filth.    *wresting:* Achieving something with difficulty, by force or by great labor. *Luddite:* One who believes that technology is detrimental to society; reference to a group of nineteenth-century British workers who destroyed industrial machinery in protest against dislocation of the workers.    *eschew:* Avoid.    *toluene:* A chemical solvent.    *sentient:* Conscious and capable of feeling.    *lungwort:* A European herb once used to treat ailments of the lungs.

20          For example, here we have the environmental movement screeching like
New Kids on the Block fans because President Bush asked for a bit more scientific research on global warming before we cork everybody's Honda, ban
the use of underarm deodorants and replace all the coal fuel in our electrical-
generating plants with windmills. The greenhouse effect is a complex hypothesis. You can hate George Bush as much as you like and the thing won't get
simpler. "The most dire predictions about global warming are being toned
down by many experts," said a *Washington Post* story last January [1990]. And
that same month the *New York Times* told me a new ice age was only a couple
of thousand years away.

On the original Earth Day, in 1970—when the world was going to end
from overcrowding instead of overheating—the best-selling author of *The
Population Bomb,* Dr. Paul Ehrlich, was making dire predictions as fast as his
earnestly frowning mouth could move. Dr. Ehrlich predicted that America
would have water rationing by 1974 and food rationing by 1980; that hepatitis
and dysentery rates in the United States would increase by 500 percent due to
population density; and that the oceans could be as dead as Lake Erie by 1979.
Today Lake Erie is doing better than Perrier, and Dr. Ehrlich is still pounding
sand down a rat hole.

Now, don't get me wrong: Even registered Republicans believe ecological
problems are real. Real solutions, however, will not be found through pop hysteria or the merchandising of panic. Genuine hard-got knowledge is required.
The collegiate idealists who stuff the ranks of the environmental movement
seem willing to do absolutely anything to save the biosphere° except take science courses and learn something about it. In 1971, American universities
awarded 4,390 doctorates in the physical sciences. After fifteen years of youthful fretting over the planet's future, the number was 3,551.

It wouldn't even be all that expensive to make the world clean and prosperous. According to the September 1989 issue of *Scientific American,* which
was devoted to scholarly articles about ecological issues, the cost of achieving
sustainable and environmentally healthy worldwide economic development
by the year 2000 would be about $729 billion. That's roughly fourteen dollars
per person per year for ten years. To translate that into sandal-and-candle
terms, $729 billion is less than three-quarters of what the world spends annu-
ally on armaments.

The Earth can be saved, but not by legislative fiat.° Expecting President
Bush to cure global warming by sending a bill to Congress is to subscribe to
that eternal fantasy of totalitarians and Democrats from Massachusetts: a law
against bad weather.

---

*biosphere:* The environment in which life forms can flourish, including those life forms.    *fiat:* Authoritative or arbitrary decision, decree.

Sometimes I wonder if the fans of eco-Armageddon even want the          25
world's problems to get better. Improved methods of toxic-chemical incinera-
tion, stack scrubbers for fossil fuel power plants, and sensible solid-waste
management schemes lack melodramatic appeal. There's nothing apocalyptic
about gasohol.° And it's hard to picture a Byronic hero sorting his beer bottles
by color at the recycling center. The beliefs of some environmentalists seem to
have little to do with the welfare of the globe or of its inhabitants and a lot to
do with the parlor primitivism of the Romantic Movement.

There is this horrible idea, beginning with Jean Jacques Rousseau and still
going strong in college classrooms, that natural man is naturally good. All we
have to do is strip away the neuroses, repressions and Dial soap of modern
society, and mankind will return to an Edenic state.° Anybody who's ever met
a toddler knows this is soy-protein baloney. Neolithic man was not a guy who
always left his campsite cleaner than he found it. Ancient humans trashed half
the map with indiscriminate use of fire for slash-and-burn agriculture and
hunting drives. They caused desertification through overgrazing and firewood
cutting in North Africa, the Middle East and China. And they were responsible for the extinction of mammoths, mastodons, cave bears, giant sloths, New
World camels and horses and thousands of other species. Their record on
women's issues and minority rights wasn't so hot either. You can return to
nature, go back to leading the simple, fulfilling life of the hunter-gatherer if
you want, but don't let me catch you poking around in my garbage cans for
food.

Then there are the beasts-are-our-buddies types. I've got a brochure from
the International Fund for Animal Welfare containing a section called "High-
lights of IFAW's History," and I quote: "1978—Campaign to save iguanas
from cruelty in Nicaraguan marketplaces—people sew animals' mouths
shut."

1978 was the middle of the Nicaraguan civil war. This means that while
the evil dirt sack Somoza was shooting it out with the idiot Marxist Sandin-
istas, the International Fund for Animal Welfare was flying somebody to
besieged Managua to check on lizard lips.

The neo-hippie-dips, the sentimentality-crazed iguana anthropomorph-
izers,° the Chicken Littles, the three-bong-hit William Blakes—thank God
these people don't actually go outdoors much, or the environment would be
even worse than it is already.

But ecology's fools don't upset me. It's the wise guys I'm leery of. Tyranny          30
is implicit in the environmental movement. Although Earth Day participants

---

*gasohol:* Environmentally friendly gasoline (containing ethyl alcohol).  *Edenic state:* The unspoiled
state of existence that preceded the "fall" from the garden of Eden, described in the Bible.  *anthropo-
morphizers:* People who attribute human characteristics to nonhuman subjects.

are going to be surprised to hear themselves accused of fascist tendencies, dictatorship is the unspoken agenda of every morality-based political campaign. Check out Moslem fundamentalists or the right-to-lifers. Like abortion opponents and Iranian imams,° the environmentalists have the right to tell the rest of us what to do because they are morally correct and we are not. Plus the tree squeezers care more, which makes them an elite—an aristocracy of mushiness. They know what's good for us even when we're too lazy or shortsighted to snip plastic six-pack collars so sea turtles won't strangle.

## QUESTIONS

1. What does O'Rourke present as his motivation for writing this essay? Is that motivation reflected in the content and tone of the piece? Is this essay a useful addition to the debate about environmental concerns? Why or why not?

2. Do you agree with O'Rourke that "mass movements are always a worry . . . no matter how virtuous their cause"? Can you think of some mass movements that you would like to be associated with? Are there any that you feel threatened by?

3. Look up the words "fascist" and "dictatorship" in a dictionary. Do the denotative meanings of these terms fit mass movements such as those of Earth Day participants, as O'Rourke claims? Explain your answer.

4. O'Rourke speaks of the "faceless thing called industry." What other similar "faceless" things do people use as targets for their anger or frustration?

5. Is O'Rourke correct when he says that "it's rarely an identifiable person . . . who pollutes"? Can you think of specific industries, companies, even individuals who have been designated by the environmental movement as polluters?

6. Does O'Rourke, like Rachel Carson, concede some points to his opposition? If so, where, and what is the effect of those concessions?

7. What is your definition of "environmentalist"? Is it different from O'Rourke's?

8. Do we have to choose between environmentalism and technological progress? Can we have both? If so, how?

9. How would you characterize the author's voice in this selection?

---

*imams:* Muslim leaders or rulers.

**CONNECTIONS**

1. O'Rourke states that people concerned about the environment see nature as "cuddlesome, hug-a-bear and too cute for words." Consider some of the other writers included in this chapter. Do they bear out his statement? Is the statement borne out by your own experiences?
2. Like William Kowinski, in the essay serving as a transition into this section, O'Rourke discusses materialism. How are the two writers' perceptions of this subject different?
3. How might O'Rourke respond to Amato and Partridge's claim that "the desire for profit has led owners [of livestock] to graze cattle in densities that frequently result in long-term soil damage"?

## ～ A Modest Proposal: The Sequel

*Robert F. Jones*

Robert F. Jones was born in 1934. In 1956, he received his B.A. degree from
the University of Michigan; he then served in the Navy from 1956 to 1959.
He has been a senior writer for both *Time* and *Sports Illustrated* and has
published five novels (among them *Slade's Glacier* in 1981 and *Blood Tide* in
1990) and three nonfiction works. His stories and essays have appeared in
numerous anthologies. The following is reprinted from the collection *Sacred
Trusts: Essays on Stewardship and Responsibility* (1993), edited by Michael
Katakis.

**WARM-UP:** Some people are very concerned about the rapid growth
of the human population around the world. What ways of stemming this
growth do they advocate? Do you agree with the methods proposed?

*There was a time when meadow, grove and stream,*
*The earth, and every common sight,*
*To me did seem*
*Appareled in celestial light,*
*The glory and the freshness of a dream.*
*It is not now as it hath been of yore;—*
*Turn whereso'er I may,*
*By night or day,*
*The things which I have seen I now can see no more.*

—WILLIAM WORDSWORTH,
"Intimations of Immortality"

1    I travel a lot to the wilder corners of the world. Or perhaps I should say, to
what once were its wilder corners. They are wild no more. Turn whereso'er
I may—from East Africa to Central America, from my home in Vermont to
the Rocky Mountains or the once-verdant° islands of the North Pacific coast
—meadows are disappearing under asphalt or the plow, groves topple to the
unmuffled yowl of chain saws, and crystalline streams, where not too long ago
I fished alone (for silver trout and brighter dreams), now run dark with
eroded, clear-cut earth, glistening here or there with evanescent° tendrils of

---

*verdant:* Green with plants.    *evanescent:* Fragile, tending to vanish like vapor.

diesel oil. The most common sight on this fin de siècle° planet of ours, to me and many others who have loved it in all its wild, fresh, glorious diversity, seems to be ruin. You can bet on it: the things we have seen we now can see no more. As Joni Mitchell observed: "Don't it always seem to go that you don't know what you've got till it's gone? They paved paradise, put up a parking lot."

But it's too easy merely to lament these losses, even to write odes° or lyrics about them, and thus feel righteous for being on nature's side. The problem is graver than that. Scientists believe there have been five "major extinction spasms" on the planet over the course of the 3.5 billion years since life began. These great setbacks to evolution, one of which (at the end of the Paleozoic era some 245 million years ago) wiped out 96 percent of the earth's sea-dwelling species along with the dinosaurs that dominated the land, were caused by natural phenomena: meteor impacts and/or climate changes. Edward O. Wilson, the Pultzer-prize-winning Harvard scientist who is one of the world's leading authorities on everything from the lives of the ants to the death of nature, believes we are now in the midst of the sixth such spasm—this one attributable entirely to man. In *The Diversity of Life* (Cambridge, Mass.: Harvard University Press, 1992), Wilson describes how human population pressures, particularly in the developing nations of the so-called Third World, are destroying other species of life at a disastrous rate. Human beings are literally overwhelming nature. By the year 2020—less than a human generation from now—no fewer than 20 percent of the earth's existing species of plants and animals will be extinct, by Wilson's *conservative* estimate.

No one knows with anything like certainty just how many species—from microbes and molds through insects and flowers to eagles and elephants and whales—there are on our once-green and rich planet. Estimates range from ten to thirty million to as high as a hundred million. Tropical forests contain more than half of the species of life on earth, and already half of those fecund° woodlands have been cut down for human use. Exotic hardwoods have been harvested to panel posh homes and offices from Tokyo to Manhattan to Oslo. The grain fields and grazing lands that replace the forests will erode in a generation or two, leaving bare lifeless bedrock. By 2020, even the half of the woodlands that remains—some eight million square kilometers—will be cut in half again, or perhaps by as much as 90 percent. Wilson estimates conservatively that because of this runaway destruction of the earth's tropical forests, the planet is losing twenty-seven thousand species a year: seventy-four a day, or a little more than three species an hour (even while we sleep).

And extinction is forever.

---

*fin de siècle:* French, meaning "end of the century."    *odes:* Complex poems.    *fecund:* Fruitful, productive, fertile.

5      Humankind is clearly the cause of this disaster. As Wilson notes: "Human beings—mammals of the 50 kilogram weight class and members of a group, the primates, otherwise noted for scarcity—have become a hundred times more numerous than any other land animal of comparable size in the history of life. By ever conceivable measure, humanity is ecologically abnormal."

When I was born in 1934, the population of the United States was about 123 million; of the earth, just over 2 billion. In 1992, as I write this, those numbers have increased to 245 million and 5.4 billion, respectively. By the year 2000, demographers project figures of 268 million and more than 6 billion, and by 2025—when nearly all of the environmental damage will have been done (we should live so long!)—the United States will contain nearly 313 million human beings, while the planet sags under the weight of more than 8 billion. By 2050, only two generations down the road, the world total could reach 15 billion. . . .

If things are bad now—not just in terms of waning biodiversity but in the rapidly eroding quality of human existence itself—they will only get worse in the years ahead. The conditions of life we associate with the developing nations of Africa, Latin America, and south Asia—famine, overcrowding, lawlessness, pestilence, corruption, and brutality—will almost inevitably become part of our own lives. Visionary artists in various media have already given us glimpses, as through a glass darkly, of what the future might hold if we continue to proliferate° as wantonly as we are right now: in books like Aldous Huxley's *Brave New World*, George Orwell's *1984*, and Russell Hoban's *Riddley Walker* and, more viscerally, through the busy, nightmarish scenes of such films as *Blade Runner*, *Brazil*, and *The Terminator*.

Ironically, it is the well-meaning philosophy of humanism that has led us to this sorry pass. By placing man at the center of the universe and by bending every technological and scientific effort, especially in the realm of medicine, to the end of prolonging individual human lives, humanism and its works have ensured our domination of the planet and all the millions of other creatures on it. Yet even as we blithely,° mindlessly, inexorably° destroy the hard-won balance of nature, each of us smugly proclaiming him- or herself a "people person," we remain, as far as we know so far, the only animal capable of reflecting on nature or even of conceiving of such an entirety. At a time when humankind's numbers have never been higher, when we dominate the earth with our wasteful, wastrel° ways as no other animal has before, we continue to prate about "the sanctity of human life" as if it were something rare and therefore precious. It certainly is to the self-preoccupied individual who proclaims

---

*proliferate:* Multiply.   *blithely:* Casually, heedlessly.   *inexorably:* Inevitably, unavoidably.   *wastrel:* One who scatters his resources foolishly.

"Screw off, Jack, *I'm* all right!" But in terms of species survival, we've long since passed the point where individual lives are rare and precious. After all, as humanistic liberalism teaches us, no single individual regardless of gender, race, creed, sexual preference, or place of national origin is any better or worse than another. All people are created equal. Given a decent chance in the way of nutrition, education, and opportunity, each of us can be just as successful as the other.

Meanwhile, to provide this heaven on earth for each human being, we dim the skies with poisons, fell forests, and befoul rivers and even the oceans. Deserts spread like skin cancers across the face of the continents, and other species die, unnamed, unmourned, forever. What, if anything, can be done to correct this tragedy in progress?

The last time human beings were in ecological balance with the planet was        10
in the seventeenth century. At that time, 1650 to be precise, the human population was only five hundred million worldwide (less than that of sub-Saharan Africa today, and only half that of China). What a time that was! Shakespeare was not long dead, John Donne had caught the bard's falling star, Robert Herrick was out a-maying with the fair Corinna, while Andrew Marvell and his coy mistress tore their "pleasures with rough strife,/ Through the iron gates of life." The interior of Africa, with its teeming herds of Pleistocene° wildlife, remained a ghastly blank, punily nibbled at around the edges by Arab and European traders in ivory and slaves (many of whom paid for their temerity with death by fever or worse). The interior of North America too was still virtually pristine, the realm of Stone Age Indian tribes living in symbiosis° with some thirty million bison and plentiful antelope, deer, elk, wild sheep, and bears both black and grizzly; the skies darkened in spring and fall to the seemingly limitless flights of the passenger pigeon. Those few intrepid° (and often greedy) Europeans who tussled with the Indians usually ended up with a stone-headed arrow or spear through their vitals and their scalps drying on a lodgepole.

In Central and South America, Spain's so-called conquest had not made much of an impact except on the Aztec and Incan civilizations (which were looted and wiped out). Most of the tropical forest still stood intact as it had for eons, with its millions upon millions of life forms still breeding, changing, and speciating,° all the while fueling the great photosynthetic° engine of the planet by absorbing sunlight and giving back oxygen—the very fuel of life itself in all its variety.

The mid-Pacific cultures of Polynesia, Micronesia, and Melanesia were still intact as well, along with all the sea's riches of marine life. In south Asia,

*Pleistocene:* The Ice Age, which lasted until about 10,000 years ago.   *symbiosis:* Mutual dependence. *intrepid:* Resolute, fearless; enduring.   *speciating:* Forming new biological species.   *photosynthetic:* Capable of turning chemical compounds into carbohydrates, using the energy of light.

tigers, leopards, rhinoceroses, gaur,° nilghai, musk deer, gibbons, and orang-
utans, along with wild elephants and many smaller species, still lived in self-
sustaining numbers while humankind waged its greedy wars and led its silly,
messy, short, brutish, and nasty individual lives harmlessly in their midst. At
the poles, Antarctica lay "undiscovered" save by myriads of marine and avian
animals along with the rich stew of microscopic life that fed them, while in the
Arctic a few hardy Inuit thrived in harmony with nature's hot/cold heart,
blessedly ignorant of snowmobiles, satellite TV, liquor, and money—or of
measles, tuberculosis, and gonorrhea.

We will never return to a world like that, no matter how hard we try. Even
if by some miracle we could undo history, retool the human mindset that it's
produced, and somehow reduce human numbers to five hundred million
again without further damaging the nonhuman life that remains on the
planet, it would not be the same. We know too much now about our own
human propensity° for messing things up. Perhaps that was the inarticulate
subtext of Wordsworth's ode, "Intimations of Immortality." We are indeed the
spoilers.

Sometimes, in my more bitter moods, I wake at night with the three-
o'clock willies, remembering the things I've seen through more than half a
century wandering this earth: too many trout streams destroyed; too many
grouse covers° exchanged for cheap housing tracts; vast reaches of African or
Asian or American or Australian game lands laid waste to make room for the
crops and factories and tin-roofed hovels of the never-ending onslaught of
people; vistas of dying reefs and the dead white carapaces of sea urchins,
beneath the sea's surface in the Florida Keys, or off the so-called Coral Coast
of East Africa, or in the South Pacific, or the Caribbean; an empty cigarette
packet resting on a sludge of diesel waste blown by Russian trawlers on a reef
near Havana where thousands of fish—sergeant majors, wrasses, French
angels, parrotfish of rainbow colors—once teemed. At these times, I imagine a
few things that might at least keep our numbers in check, and might even
reduce them somewhat. I present them here as my modest proposal, or proposals, for I can imagine a number of alternatives.

15      None of these ideas is new, nor are any politically correct. Most of them
fly in the face of humanistic decency, and sometimes even I shudder on thinking them. But an old German folk song, learned at my mother's knee, gives me
courage: "Die Gedanken sind frei . . ." Thoughts are free, no one can forbid
them. At least not yet.

*Require licenses for having children.* After all, we require licenses for many
other things: driving a motor vehicle, flying an airplane, practicing medicine

---

*gaur:* East Indian wild oxes.   *propensity:* Inclination or decided preference.   *grouse covers:* Hideaways
from which hunters hunt game birds (grouses).

or law, selling alcoholic beverages, hunting, fishing, even marriage itself. We're used to the idea of licensing by now; it's an old friend, even (or perhaps especially) in places like Africa, South America, and Asia, where "baby licenses" are most needed. License requirements should be at least as strict as those applied by New York's Sullivan Law for getting a pistol permit: applicants must have a well-paying job, live in a decent neighborhood, never have been arrested for even a minor infraction, be of sound mind and body, and append three vouchers in writing from respectable fellow citizens (lawyers, police officers, or politicians). As in the hunter safety courses now mandatory in all of the United States, prospective moms and dads would be required to attend a series of parenting classes, culminating in a battery of stringent tests—oral, written (no multiple-choice or true/false questions), and "hands-on." For this last, they would be observed by hidden monitors over a long, rainy weekend in a crowded one-bedroom apartment as they care for a pair of carefully selected and coached teenage "problem children"—the sort who watch MTV with the volume at full blast, leave dirty clothes and dishes lying around everywhere, whine incessantly, pick sullenly at their food, and when asked if they'd like to do something—anything—reply, "Not really." Those wishing to have children could repeat this parent safety course up to three times if they failed the first time. But three strikes is out. A final failure would result in mandatory sterilization at government expense.

*Provide free birth control for all.* The U.S. Food and Drug Administration dragged its feet for thirty-five years before finally approving Depo-Provera, a synthetic version of progesterone,° that, if injected in 150-milligram doses once every three months, prevents conception in all but 0.3 percent of women using it.

Another alternative is the Norplant implant, small rods placed under the skin of the upper arm that prevent conception for up to five years and are effective in all but 0.05 percent of cases. The United Nations and various national governments in countries with runaway birth rates could inject or implant these devices at no cost to the women involved and perhaps even offer bonuses to women who elect this procedure. The same goes for vasectomies.

*Pay bonuses for abortions.* For that 0.05 to 0.3 percent of women who get pregnant anyway, the World Health Organization, with contributions of money and medical manpower, could provide free, safe abortions around the globe. With a little extra financial cost—much less than it would take to provide famine relief to millions of starving children—the WHO could pay hefty bonuses to these women, perhaps even implant them with sterility rods.

*Encourage alternative means of sexual-gratification.* The human sex drive     20
is powerful, often overriding reason or even the fear of death, as witness the

---

*progesterone:* One of the female hormones.

number of men shot out of the saddle each year by irate husbands or Frankie-and-Johnnie scenarios of women's revenge on men they feel have done them wrong. Fortunately, the sex drive is infinitely mutable°. . . . Since only hetero-sexual congress° produces offspring, perhaps the UN and Madison Avenue could join forces to produce tastefully persuasive advertising worldwide—in newspapers and magazines, on radio and TV—extolling° the joys of homo-sexuality (both male and female), onanism,° sadomasochism, and bestiality. Even fetishism could be encouraged. . . .

*Reverse societal attitudes concerning life and death.* Rather than discouraging dangerous activities and the consumption of substances deemed hazardous to health, governments, religious leaders, and trend setters around the globe might promote such things. The aim, after all, is a reduction of the human population and its deleterious° effect on the planet. The more bungee-jumping and hel-metless motorcycle riding, the better. With a little "hidden persuasion" in the right places, Russian roulette might supplant golf and tennis as a popular week-end diversion. Speed limits on the world's highways could be abolished, freeing traffic cops to shoot more innocent bystanders. The Food and Drug Adminis-tration and similar agencies in other countries could busy themselves establish-ing mandatory minimum levels for carcinogens° in all foods and drugs. Seatbelts and airbags could be banned in all vehicles; tax-free unfiltered ciga-rettes could be made available to everyone (especially schoolchildren). As more and more farms fail, plowshares might be hammered into weapons° and dis-tributed at cost to the young. Knife fighting and spearsmanship could replace rope climbing and volleyball in high school gym classes. By banning all health foods and recommending high-fat diets, along with excessive consumption of beer or wine with meals (including breakfast), a sizable slimming in human numbers might be accomplished. Free ice cream and nitrate-laden hot dogs at every ball game!

*Let AIDS and other epidemics save the planet.* It's a horrific idea—almost unthinkable—yet many people familiar with the peak-and-valley dynamics of animal populations have wondered if this latest visitation by the biblical horseman Pestilence° is not just a natural corrective to human overpopula-tion. When any species becomes too abundant for its habitat, some blight usu-ally comes along to pare the population back to its environment's carrying

---

*mutable:* Capable of change or of being changed.    *congress:* Here, meaning coming together. *extolling:* Celebrating, glorifying.    *onanism:* Masturbation or sex interrupted in order to prevent impregnation.    *deleterious:* Having a harmful effect.    *carcinogens:* Substances that can cause cancer. *"plowshares might be . . . weapons":* Reversed allusion to the biblical description of a peaceful time when swords would be melted and reshaped into plowshares.    *Pestilence:* The bubonic plague (or any virulent, devastating, contagious disease).

capacity. Tularemia° in rabbits, mange° in foxes, various epizootics° in water-fowl. Epidemics have ravaged human populations throughout history: the Black Death (bubonic plague) killed from a third to a half of Europe's population in the fourteenth century, and more recently the Spanish influenza pandemic of 1918 wiped out twenty million people worldwide. But none of them, so far, has caused more than a momentary check to human population growth. Tragic as it may be to millions of individuals, it seems highly unlikely (given a planetary human population of nearly six billion) that AIDS will reduce human numbers significantly.

"Many persons concerned about wildlife had high hopes for AIDS at first," a woman wildlife researcher told me in East Africa a couple of years ago, "as a kind of deus ex machina,° cruel as it is to say so, that would solve Africa's over-population problem. But I'm afraid that it's not to be. AIDS can't catch up with the birthrate." The World Health Organization recently estimated that HIV, the virus that causes AIDS, is spreading in Asia—at least in some nations—with the rapidity it showed in black Africa in the early 1980s. More than a million people in India are infected, the WHO says, and the Indian Health Organization projects 20 to 50 million infected by the year 2000, out of a total Indian population of 860 million. Already, more Indians test HIV positive than all the current cases in Europe and about as many as in the United States. But by the time the projected big numbers come into play, preventive measures and improved treatments, perhaps even a cure, will probably have reduced the AIDS impact on world population to a mere blip on the growth charts. No deus ex machina can save nature. Only humankind, its major threat, can do so.

*Alphaville,* Jean-Luc Godard's 1965 *nouvelle vague*° film, starring Eddie   25
Constantine and the luscious Anna Karina, posited a future in which people went around assassinating one another for no good reason. It made for exciting, surprise-a-minute cinema, but governments could achieve the same effect —paring of excessive human population—by subsidizing vendettas and blood feuds wherever they exist. Organizations idled by the end of the Cold War, such as the CIA, KGB, $RI_5$, Sureté, and Savak—accomplished provocateurs° all—might even trigger a few where none existed before. Idle hands are the devil's workshop. Such a program might even enhance family values. As Mark Twain so ably demonstrated in the feud chapters of *Huckleberry Finn,* nothing brings blood kin together more loyally than a little letting of it by the neighbors.

---

*Tularemia, mange, epizootics:* Types of diseases.   *deus ex machina:* In ancient Greek and Roman drama, a god, introduced into a play to resolve the entanglements of the plot.   *nouvelle vague:* French, meaning "new wave."   *provocateurs:* Agitators, people who cause trouble.

*Set up an opium den on every corner.* Nor does anything short of castration dull the sex drive like the fruit of the poppy.

*Give Dr. Kevorkian a Nobel prize.* As the old song says, suicide is painless. And think of the good you'll be doing for trees, weeds, birds, bugs, mosses, spores, and fungi, not to mention the porpoises, penguins, and possums now threatened by mankind's inexorable° destruction of the planet. The Michigan "suicide doctor" deserves to be as honored as Mother Teresa or Bishop Desmond Tutu.

Back in 1729, that great misanthrope° and essayist Jonathan Swift offered "A Modest Proposal" to solve Ireland's overpopulation problems. "It is a melancholy object to those who walk through this great town," he wrote from Dublin, "or travel in the country, when they see the streets, the roads, and cabin doors, crowded with beggars of the female sex, followed by three, four, or six children, all in rags and importuning° every passenger for an alms. These mothers, instead of being able to work for their honest livelihood, are forced to employ all their time in strolling to beg sustenance for their helpless infants; who, as they grow up, either turn thieves for want of work, or leave their dear native country to fight for the pretender in Spain, or sell themselves to the Barbadoes."

The good dean's solution was both practical and economical: "I have been assured by a very knowing American of my acquaintance in London, that a young healthy child, well nursed, is at a year old a most delicious, nourishing, and wholesome food, whether stewed, roasted, baked, or boiled; and I make no doubt that it will equally serve in a fricassee° or a ragout°."

30    This American proposes nothing so heartless as a boiled baby in every pot, but unless mankind learns to control its runaway population—learns responsible stewardship of what's left of the natural world, recognizes its kinship with all living things, the air, the waters, the very earth itself—the end result will be no less heartless than what Swift so cynically suggested. It is time for humankind the despoiler to become humankind the preserver. After all, extinction is forever.

Or as a great comedian of a bygone era, Mort Sahl, used to say in ending his act: "Is there anyone here I haven't offended?"

### QUESTIONS

1. Jones makes reference to outside sources: works by scientists, writers, filmmakers. Consider and discuss his motives for including such references in this essay.

---

*inexorable:* Relentless.   *misanthrope:* One who hates or mistrusts humankind.   *importuning:* Insisting upon a demand; troubling.   *fricassee and ragout:* Types of food (dishes).

2. Jones's explanation of "humanism" makes it sound egotistical and selfish. How do you understand the term?

3. According to Jones, how are human beings different from other animals?

4. If you could return to the way life was in the seventeenth century, when, Jones says, "human beings were in ecological balance with the planet," would you want to? Why or why not?

5. Do you think Jones is serious when he proposes each of his solutions to human overpopulation? Would you agree with any of Jones's proposals? If so, which? What are your objections to the ones you would reject?

6. What does the title of Jones's essay allude to?

7. Is Jones's "shock" technique successful? What do you feel after reading this essay? Whom do you think Jones has in mind as his intended audience?

## CONNECTIONS

1. The selection from Ecclesiastes included in this section states that everything has a "season." What "season" would Jones place the human species in?

2. Earlier in this section, Rachel Carson ends her essay with a quotation from Jean Rostand: "The obligation to endure gives us the right to know." How might Jones respond to that statement?

# ～ Living like Weasels

*Annie Dillard*

Annie Dillard was born in 1945; she earned both her B.A. and M.A. degrees from Hollins College in Virginia. At the age of 29, Dillard published her first book, *Pilgrim at Tinker Creek* (1974); in 1975, she was awarded the Pulitzer Prize for general nonfiction writing. From 1974 to 1981, she was also a contributing editor for *Harper's Magazine*. She has since published essays, poetry, short stories, literary criticism, prose narratives, and a memoir. Currently, Dillard is writer-in-residence at Wesleyan University. The following essay first appeared in her 1982 collection entitled *Teaching a Stone to Talk*.

**WARM-UP:** Are there any animals that you especially identify with? Explain why.

1    A weasel is wild. Who knows what he thinks? He sleeps in his underground den, his tail draped over his nose. Sometimes he lives in his den for two days without leaving. Outside, he stalks rabbits, mice, muskrats, and birds, killing more bodies than he can eat warm, and often dragging the carcasses home. Obedient to instinct, he bites his prey at the neck, either splitting the jugular vein at the throat or crunching the brain at the base of the skull, and he does not let go. One naturalist refused to kill a weasel who was socketed into his hand deeply as a rattlesnake. The man could in no way pry the tiny weasel off, and he had to walk half a mile to water, the weasel dangling from his palm, and soak him off like a stubborn label.

And once, says Ernest Thompson Seton—once, a man shot an eagle out of the sky. He examined the eagle and found the dry skull of a weasel fixed by the jaws to his throat. The supposition is that the eagle had pounced on the weasel and the weasel swiveled and bit as instinct taught him, tooth to neck, and nearly won. I would like to have seen that eagle from the air a few weeks or months before he was shot: was the whole weasel still attached to his feathered throat, a fur pendant? Or did the eagle eat what he could reach, gutting the living weasel with his talons before his breast, bending his beak, cleaning the beautiful airborne bones?

I have been reading about weasels because I saw one last week. I startled a weasel who startled me, and we exchanged a long glance.

Twenty minutes from my house, through the woods by the quarry and across the highway, is Hollins Pond, a remarkable piece of shallowness, where I like to go at sunset and sit on a tree trunk. Hollins Pond is also called Murray's Pond; it covers two acres of bottomland near Tinker Creek with six inches of water and six thousand lily pads. In winter, brown-and-white steers stand in the middle of it, merely dampening their hooves; from the distant shore they look like miracle itself, complete with miracle's nonchalance.° Now, in summer, the steers are gone. The water lilies have blossomed and spread to a green horizontal plane that is terra firma° to plodding blackbirds, and tremulous° ceiling to black leeches, crayfish, and carp.

This is, mind you, suburbia. It is a five-minute walk in three directions to rows of houses, though none is visible here. There's a 55 mph highway at one end of the pond, and a nesting pair of wood ducks at the other. Under every bush is a muskrat hole or a beer can. The far end is an alternating series of fields and woods, fields and woods, threaded everywhere with motorcycle tracks—in whose bare clay wild turtles lay eggs.

So. I had crossed the highway, stepped over two low barbed-wire fences, and traced the motorcycle path in all gratitude through the wild rose and poison ivy of the pond's shoreline up into high grassy fields. Then I cut down through the woods to the mossy fallen tree where I sit. This tree is excellent. It makes a dry, upholstered bench at the upper, marshy end of the pond, a plush jetty° raised from the thorny shore between a shallow blue body of water and a deep blue body of sky.

The sun had just set. I was relaxed on the tree trunk, ensconced° in the lap of lichen, watching the lily pads at my feet tremble and part dreamily over the thrusting path of a carp. A yellow bird appeared to my right and flew behind me. It caught my eye; I swiveled around—and the next instant, inexplicably, I was looking down at a weasel, who was looking up at me.

Weasel! I'd never seen one wild before. He was ten inches long, thin as a curve, a muscled ribbon, brown as fruitwood, soft-furred, alert. His face was fierce, small and pointed as a lizard's; he would have made a good arrowhead. There was just a dot of chin, maybe two brown hairs' worth, and then the pure white fur began that spread down his underside. He had two black eyes I didn't see, any more than you see a window.

The weasel was stunned into stillness as he was emerging from beneath an enormous shaggy wild rose bush four feet away. I was stunned into stillness twisted backward on the tree trunk. Our eyes locked, and someone threw away the key.

Our look was as if two lovers, or deadly enemies, met unexpectedly on an overgrown path when each had been thinking of something else: a clearing

5

10

---

*nonchalance:* The appearance of being unconcerned or indifferent;   *terra firma:* Latin, meaning "solid ground," dry land.   *tremulous:* Quivering, trembling.   *jetty:* A structure that extends into a body of water, usually so boats can land next to it.   *ensconced:* Installed, settled.

blow to the gut. It was also a bright blow to the brain, or a sudden beating of brains, with all the charge and intimate grate of rubbed balloons. It emptied our lungs. It felled the forest, moved the fields, and drained the pond; the world dismantled and tumbled into that black hole of eyes. If you and I looked at each other that way, our skulls would split and drop to our shoulders. But we don't. We keep our skulls. So.

He disappeared. That was only last week, and already I don't remember what shattered the enchantment. I think I blinked, I think I retrieved my brain from the weasel's brain, and tried to memorize what I was seeing, and the weasel felt the yank of separation, the careening splashdown into real life and the urgent current of instinct. He vanished under the wild rose. I waited motionless, my mind suddenly full of data and my spirit with pleadings, but he didn't return.

Please do not tell me about "approach-avoidance conflicts." I tell you I've been in that weasel's brain for sixty seconds, and he was in mine. Brains are private places, muttering through unique and secret tapes—but the weasel and I both plugged into another tape simultaneously, for a sweet and shocking time. Can I help it if it was a blank?

What goes on in his brain the rest of the time? What does a weasel think about? He won't say. His journal is tracks in clay, a spray of feathers, mouse blood and bone: uncollected, unconnected, loose-leaf, and blown.

I would like to learn, or remember, how to live. I come to Hollins Pond not so much to learn how to live as, frankly, to forget about it. That is, I don't think I can learn from a wild animal how to live in particular—shall I suck warm blood, hold my tail high, walk with my footprints precisely over the prints of my hands?—but I might learn something of mindlessness, something of the purity of living in the physical senses and the dignity of living without bias or motive. The weasel lives in necessity and we live in choice, hating necessity and dying at the last ignobly in its talons. I would like to live as I should, as the weasel lives as he should. And I suspect that for me the way is like the weasel's: open to time and death painlessly, noticing everything, remembering nothing, choosing the given with a fierce and pointed will.

15    I missed my chance. I should have gone for the throat. I should have lunged for that streak of white under the weasel's chin and held on, held on through mud and into the wild rose, held on for a dearer life. We could live under the wild rose wild as weasels, mute and uncomprehending. I could very calmly go wild. I could live two days in the den, curled, leaning on mouse fur, sniffing bird bones, blinking, licking, breathing musk, my hair tangled in the roots of grasses. Down is a good place to go, where the mind is single. Down is

out, out of your ever-loving mind and back to your careless senses. I remember muteness as a prolonged and giddy fast, where every moment is a feast of utterance received. Time and events are merely poured, unremarked, and ingested directly, like blood pulsed into my gut through a jugular vein. Could two live that way? Could two live under the wild rose, and explore by the pond, so that the smooth mind of each is as everywhere present to the other, and as received and as unchallenged, as falling snow?

We could, you know. We can live any way we want. People take vows of poverty, chastity, and obedience—even of silence—by choice. The thing is to stalk your calling in a certain skilled and supple way, to locate the most tender and live spot and plug into that pulse. This is yielding, not fighting. A weasel doesn't "attack" anything; a weasel lives as he's meant to, yielding at every moment to the perfect freedom of single necessity.

I think it would be well, and proper, and obedient, and pure, to grasp your one necessity and not let it go, to dangle from it limp wherever it takes you. Then even death, where you're going no matter how you live, cannot you part. Seize it and let it seize you up aloft even, till your eyes burn out and drop; let your musky flesh fall off in shreds, and let your very bones unhinge and scatter, loosened over fields, over fields and woods, lightly, thoughtless, from any height at all, from as high as eagles.

## QUESTIONS

1. What were your associations with the word "weasel" before you read Dillard's essay? What do you associate with the word now, after having read this essay?
2. What does Dillard think she can learn from weasels? Have you ever learned something from watching an animal? If so, what did you learn?
3. Explain what Dillard means when she says "the weasel lives in necessity and we live in choice, hating necessity and dying at the last ignobly in its talons." Do you agree with her?
4. Dillard writes that "mindlessness [is] the purity of living in the physical senses and the dignity of living without bias or motive." How does this contrast with *mindfulness?* In your opinion, which is a better way to live in our society? Why?
5. Point to some effective uses of detail in this essay.
6. Find some examples of effective juxtapositions in this essay and explain their effect.

**CONNECTIONS**

1. Explain how Dillard's claim, "the thing is to stalk your calling . . . to grasp your one necessity," echoes a statement from Ecclesiastes. Does it also relate to other essays you have read in earlier sections?

2. Rachel Carson argued that humans and the rest of nature must achieve a balance for both to survive in harmony. Does Dillard's description of Hollins Pond reveal a harmonious balance between humans and nature? Or does one side dominate the other?

# ～ Starfish

*Mary Oliver*

Mary Oliver was born in 1935. Though she attended both Ohio State University and Vassar College, she graduated from neither. She won the Pulitzer Prize for poetry for her 1984 book *American Primitive* and the National Book Award for her *New and Selected Poems* (1992). She has also published *A Poetry Handbook* (1994) and numerous other books of poems (most recently *Blue Pastures* in 1995). She is writer-in-residence at Sweet Briar College in Virginia. The following poem appeared in 1986 in her collection entitled *Dream Work*.

**WARM-UP:** Today in the United States, we tend to live fairly controlled and artificial lives. Our ancestors, who used to be less protected against nature, also used to fear it more. What elements of nature are *you* afraid of? Are there any animals or plants, for example, that you would like to see eliminated? Explain your answer.

In the sea rocks,                                                    1
   in the stone pockets
      under the tide's lip,
         in water dense as blindness

they slid                                                            5
   like sponges,
      like too many thumbs.
         I knew this, and what I wanted

was to draw my hands back
   from the water—what I wanted                                10
      was to be willing
         to be afraid.

But I stayed there,
   I crouched on the stone wall
      while the sea poured its harsh song            15
         through the sluices,°

while I waited for the gritty lightning
   of their touch, while I stared
      down through the tide's leaving
         where sometimes I could see them—            20

*sluices:* Here meaning channels.

their stubborn flesh
   lounging on my knuckles.
      What good does it do
         to lie all day in the sun

25     loving what is easy?
      It never grew easy,
         but at last I grew peaceful:
           all summer

my fear diminished
30     as they bloomed through the water
      like flowers, like flecks
         of an uncertain dream,

while I lay on the rocks, reaching
   into the darkness, learning
35       little by little to love
         our only world.

## QUESTIONS

1. Why does Oliver say she wanted "to be willing / to be afraid"?
2. A shift takes place in the way that the starfish are described in this poem: Note the earlier similes and metaphors as well as the later ones. What do you notice about them?
3. Explain what Oliver means when she asks, "What good does it do / to lie all day in the sun / loving what is easy?"
4. Point to some examples of parallel construction within a sentence in this poem, and explain their effect (given the overall context).
5. Do you see the actions of the poem's speaker as exaggerated? Do you agree that we should go out of our way to understand and accept aspects of the environment that we find threatening or unpleasant? Why or why not?

## CONNECTIONS

1. Compare and contrast Oliver's reaction to the starfish with Annie Dillard's reaction to the weasel she accidentally encounters.
2. Based on his essay "The Greenhouse Affect," how do you think P. J. O'Rourke might respond to this poem?

# 〜 Earth's Body

## Scott Russell Sanders

Scott Russell Sanders was born in 1945. He received a B.A. degree from
Brown University in 1967 and a Ph.D. from Cambridge University in 1971.
Since 1971, he has been teaching at Indiana University, Bloomington; his
writing has appeared in *Harper's*, the *New York Times*, and *Best American
Essays*. The following essay comes from *Staying Put: Making a Home in a
Restless World* (1993), one of several collections of personal essays that Scott
Russell Sanders has published.

**WARM-UP:** Do you believe that young people are more likely to be
concerned about the environment, to feel connected to nature, than
older adults are? Why or why not?

Seal tight your roof and walls and they will shelter you from weather, but     1
they will not shield you from fear. Fear comes on me now in this twitching
hour between midnight and dawn. I cannot say exactly which hour, because I
am afraid to look at a clock. My back aches and shoulders throb from splitting
a cord of oak, which was a foolish way for a man of forty-six to spend a day in
August. Here in southern Indiana, August is a slow oven. The bones bake, the
blood thins, the mind oozes into holes.

Even with windows gaping, the house catches no breeze. The only stir of
breath comes from my wife, my daughter, my son, and me. Kept awake by the
heat or my panicky heart, I tossed for a spell on damp sheets, cooking in my
own juice, until dread snatched me out of bed. I put on a loose pair of shorts,
all the clothing I could bear, and crept downstairs. Now I huddle in the
kitchen, the lights on, tea steeping. I trace the grain in the table—also oak, like
the wood I split all day—running my finger along the curved lines as though
one of them might lead me out of the pit.

Surely you know the place I am talking about. You have skidded down the
slope toward oblivion, for shorter or longer stays. And so you realize the pit is
not a gap in something solid, like a hole in rock, but the absence of all solidity,
the square root of nowhere and nothing. I go there too often, never willingly,
usually dragged from bed by the scruff of my neck.

A dog will bite a rag and shake it, first playfully, then earnestly, and at last
furiously, with snarls and bristling hair, as though outraged by the limp cloth.
Just so, in the dark hours, certainty of death seizes me by the throat. The grip is
hesitant to begin with, a teasing nibble, then the teeth clamp tight and I am

lifted and shaken like the flimsiest rag. It is a dance I have known since child-hood, this midnight shimmy with dread, and yet each time it sweeps me up my belly churns and muscles jerk as though for the first time. Nothing else in my life—not the tang of blackberries or the perfume of lilacs, not even the smack of love—is so utterly fresh, so utterly convincing, as this fear of annihilation.

5    Such alarm over the quenching of mind's wavery flame! Is this any way for a grown man to feel? Suitable or not, it is what I do feel. I rehearse this midnight panic because I cannot separate the bright thread of fear from the story I have to tell, which is about making oneself at home on the earth, know-ing the earth as one body knows another.

I sip the tea while staring at the kitchen window. The glass gives back the reflection of a balding man with taut lips, shadows in the hollows of checks and in gashes beside a crooked nose, black sockets where the eyes should be. No comfort there. The image is thinner and more fragile than the glass on which it hovers. I shift in my chair and the face disappears.

I raise a hand to my check, feel the stubble of whiskers, the slick of sweat, the nub of skull. Stubborn, those whiskers. Shaved morning after morning, they are not discouraged. They will persevere after my heart and lungs have quit. I take a dish towel from the drawer, sniff sunlight in the air-dried cloth, and wipe my face. Immediately the sweat begins to bead again, on skin that draws closer each year to the contours of the skull.

If you are older than thirty or so, you have shared this moment. You have studied the cracks in your face, the slump in your belly, the leaching of color from your hair. You have traced erosion under the tips of your fingers and in the icy pools of mirrors. No perception is more commonplace; and no emo-tion is more futile than fussing about it. Like any tree or hill, like any house heaved up into the weather, our bodies wear down. Inside the furrowing skin, slowly but implacably,° nerves unravel, cell walls buckle, messages go astray. Like gravity, like entropy, the rules of decay are printed in small type on our ticket of admission into the world.

The body is scarcely more durable than the reflection of a shadowy face in the night window. So where am I to turn during these unclocked hours before dawn? If there is no room for hope in the cramped house of the skin, and no security in the glimmerings of the mind, then what abides? Does anything persist, any knot more stubborn than bone, any force more steadfast than thought? The question drives me to set down my mug of tea, extinguish the kitchen light, and go outside into the dark.

10    I might have walked into a cave, the dark is so deep. No light shines from the neighboring houses, nor from the moon, long since gone down, nor from the

*implacably:* Relentlessly.

stars, blanked out by clouds. My eyes could be shut, for all the news they gather. Descending the steps into our back yard, I push against the darkness as against the weight of black water.

My eyes may be empty, but my ears quickly fill. The air sizzles with insect song. Crickets and grasshoppers warn and woo, rubbing their musical legs. They make the sound of beans rattling in a pan, tiny bells ringing on the ankles of dancers, fingers raked over the teeth of combs, waves rolling cobbles on the shore. Dozens of species combine to make this amorous hullabaloo. If I were to focus on the chirp of the snowy tree cricket, as one might pick out the oboe from an orchestra, and if I were to count the number of beats in fifteen seconds, then add that number to thirty-seven, the sum would roughly equal the temperature in Fahrenheit. I have tried this many times, and insect and thermometer usually agree within a few degrees. But on this muggy night I do not care to know the temperature, much as I admire the crickets for keeping track.

I hear no human sounds, amorous or otherwise, except the brief wail of a baby and the long wail of a siren. Cats bicker, without much enthusiasm. Now and again birds pipe up fretfully, as if reminding all within earshot that their trees are occupied. They will not be singing for some while yet. When baby, siren, cats, and birds fall silent, the insects own the air.

Listening, I cease to feel the weight of black water. I let myself walk out onto the lawn, trusting that the earth will uphold me, even though I cannot see the ground. The soil, baked hard by August, is lumpy under my bare feet. It smells of dust, dry and dull, as though it has never known the lushness of spring. The brittle grass licks my soles with a thousand feathery tongues. From the depths of my churchly childhood, the words of Isaiah (40: 6–8) rise up:

> *All flesh is grass,*
> *    and all its beauty is like the flower of the field.*
> *The grass withers, the flower fades,*
> *    when the breath of the Lord blows upon it;*
> *    surely the people is grass.*
> *The grass withers, the flower fades;*
> *    but the word of our God will stand for ever.*

Whoever composed that verse must have spent time down in the pit, wondering what does not fade, what will stand forever.

In lines that are familiar even to the unchurchly, Jesus converted Isaiah's warning into a promise: "Consider the lilies, how they grow; they neither toil nor spin; yet I tell you, even Solomon in all his glory was not arrayed° like one of these. But if God so clothes the grass which is alive in the field today and

---

*arrayed:* Decorated, embellished.

tomorrow is thrown into the oven, how much more will he clothe you, O men of little faith!" (Luke 12: 27–28). Indeed, grass has been well clothed for more than a hundred million years. Persistent, nourishing grass! Brother to corn, sister to rice, cousin to wheat! In the darkness, the voices of Isaiah and Jesus speak to me like rival angels, one saying *Look how grass withers under the breath of August,* the other saying *Yes, but look how it pushes up numberless fresh blades each May.*

15    My frisky mind keeps darting off, loping through a lifetime of books, raiding memory, jumping ahead into the future, visiting countries where I have never set foot, zigzagging through the cosmos. And why not? When the fiddling of a cricket is tuned to the temperature, which is driven by the weather, which is linked to the earth's tilting spin, which is governed by all the matter in the universe, why shouldn't one's mind gambol° about? Only risky, roving thought can be adequate to such a world.

While my mind rushes hither and yon, however, my body stays put. For the flesh there is no past or future, there is only this instant of contact, here, now. Heart pumps. Muscles twitch. Ears fill with indecipherable song. I lift my face and swallow some of the boggy° air. With it comes the fruity smell of oak, released like a long held secret from the pile of split logs. I smell the rank sweetness of the compost bin, where apple cores and watermelon rinds deliquesce° back toward dirt. I stroke the limestone blocks that hem in the wildflower bed. The flowers have faded but the stones endure, sandpapery to the touch. All the while, August heat clings to my limbs like damp wool.

As my eyes open their shutters to the dark, I dimly make out the twin trunks of our backyard maples. I shuffle to the nearer tree and read the braille of the bark with my fingers. Roots hump beneath my feet. Overhead, leaves form a canopy of black lace. I press my check and chest against the sharp ridges of the bark and wrap my arms around the trunk. My hands do not meet, the maple is so stout.

Once again, my mind sets off on its rambles. I remember hugging my Mississippi grandmother, her dresses made from flour sacking,° her waist larger than the circle of my child's arms. I think of the goitrous,° trembling, marvelous woman who taught me in high school biology class the parts of trees—heartwood and sapwood, phloem and cambium, stomata, rootlet, bud. I remember stroking the creamy flanks of sycamores on the banks of the Mahoning before that river was dammed. I think of the women in northern India who preserved their forest from loggers by hugging trees. Over our dead bodies, the women said, and meant it. Their struggle came to be known as *Chipko,* a Hindi expression meaning "embrace our trees."

---

*gambol:* Skip and leap playfully.    *boggy:* Wet and spongy, marshlike.    *deliquesce:* Melt away, become liquid.    *flour sacking:* The rough cloth from which bags are made to hold flour.    *goitrous:* Swollen.

If Ruth were to wake and come to the window and see me clasping a maple, would she be jealous? Would she fear losing me to the wood nymphs? Would she think I had become a druid?° Or would she merely laugh at her ridiculous, moody husband? I do the laughing for her. My guffaw° spreads ripples of silence through the crowd of insects. The spell broken, I unclasp the tree and stand back, hitching up my baggy shorts. I am comforted, although by whom or what I cannot say.

Comforted, I lie down on the lawn, and the blades prick the skin of my       20
back and legs. I loaf and invite my soul. It is too dark for observing a spear of summer grass, yet I cannot help but remember Whitman's *Song of Myself:*

> *A child said* What is the grass? *fetching it to me with full hands;*
> *How could I answer the child? I do not know what it is any more than he.*

Grass might be "the beautiful uncut hair of graves," Whitman speculates, yet he goes on to affirm that

> *The smallest sprout shows there is really no death,*
> *And if ever there was it led forward life, and does not wait at the end to*
>    *arrest it,*
> *And ceas'd the moment life appear'd.*
> *All goes onward and outward, nothing collapses,*
> *And to die is different from what any one supposed, and luckier.*

Instead of whistling in the dark, I sing. Lying there on my six feet of earth, I am reassured not so much by Whitman's words as by the shapely energy they appeal to—the chorusing crickets, the surging trees, the vigorous grass. My skin carries the bite marks of bark. My throat carries the aroma of cooking compost. My ears ring with the night gossip of birds. The darkness brims over with life. Thus I scratch my way up out of the pit into the arms of the world.

As I enter the kitchen, the clock—no longer terrifying—chimes four. I have been in the yard long enough for my tea to cool to the sultry temperature of the air. I carry the mug back outside and sit at the picnic table to wait for dawn to pump light into the world.

There is a species of poem called an *aubade*, which is a morning song, usually a lament of lovers forced to part at dawn, although it may be merely a celebration of sunrise, as in these lines from Robert Browning:

> *The year's at the spring,*
> *And day's at the morn;*

---

*druid:* Member of an ancient Celtic priesthood that was considered to have a strong connection with nature.   *guffaw:* Loud burst of laughter.

*Morning's at seven;*
*The hill-side's dew-pearled;*
*The lark's on the wing;*
*The snail's on the thorn;*
*God's in His heaven—*
*All's right with the world!*

I know that little lyric because it was stitched in red on a sampler that hung upon the wall of my childhood bedroom. I read those lines a thousand times as I lay in bed, terrified of sleep, wondering if I would ever wake, wondering if the world would still be there at dawn, trying to persuade myself that I would surface again from the black water and that morning would clean up whatever mess had been left by the previous day.

We didn't have larks where I grew up, but we did have roosters to announce the day, as well as dew to glisten and thorns to bristle and snails to leave opalescent° tracks in the first fight. So my midwestern mornings were charged with as much hope and grandeur as any English morning witnessed by Robert Browning. But my neighborhood had more troubling features as well—including bombs and bullies, suicides and drunks—that led me to doubt whether all really was right with the world. Amid the tumult of my teenage years, when I became certain that much in the world was miserably wrong, the lyric lost its charm, and God moved from heaven without leaving a forwarding address. Ever since, I have been trying to find where divinity resides.

Which brings me to the other sort of dawn song, the erotic verses that do not appear in red stitches on children's bedroom walls. *Aubade* is a French word pronounced roughly "oh-bod," and that is also roughly what it means. Oh bod! Glorious, desirable body! Not all examples are suitable for family entertainment, but there is a mild and famous one in *Romeo and Juliet.* The young lovers, secretly married, have spent their first night together—offstage —and as the scene opens Juliet is pleading:

*Wilt thou be gone? it is not yet near day:*
*It was the nightingale, and not the lark,*
*That pierced the fearful hollow of thine ear;*
*Nightly she sings on yond pomegranate-tree:*
*Believe me, love, it was the nightingale.*

Whether it is actually dawn or not is of some consequence to Romeo because he has been exiled for killing a man and must depart the realm before daylight on pain of death. Thus he replies:

---

*opalescent:* Iridescent, many-colored.

*It was the lark, the herald of the morn,*
*No nightingale: look, love, what envious streaks*
*Do lace the severing clouds in yonder east:*
*Night's candles are burnt out, and jocund° day*
*Stands tiptoe on the misty mountain tops.*
*I must be gone and live, or stay and die.*

Juliet insists that dawn is not breaking, and Romeo says, very well, I'll stay, death is a small price to pay for a few more minutes of bliss; whereupon she admits that it really is day and bids him go. He does go, after another exchange of metaphors, and the lovers are reunited only once again, and even more famously, in the tomb.

Dawn delivers me from the tomb. Nightly I am under sentence of death,   25 and daily the sentence is relaxed. Not revoked, mind you—merely stayed. In the darkness, I cling to trees, dig my fingers in the dirt, to keep from being dragged away. In the brightness I can ease my grip. Sun resurrects the weighty world. A king reveals his royalty, a saint her holiness, by restoring sight to the blind. Just so, the dawn for me is holy balm.

This dawn, the one I wait for at the picnic table, comes stealthily. Clouds diffuse the sunrise. No bucket of yellow spills over the eastern horizon, but instead light seeps evenly through the whole dome, as if the sky were on a rheostat.° Against the gathering brightness, the fretted edges of trees, the tangle of poles and wires, and the roof lines of my neighbors' houses begin to show. It is not so wild a landscape as the one I touched in the darkness, yet neither is it wholly tame. The crickets keep wooing. Crows and jays banter raucously° as they flounce from perch to perch. Bats, not yet ready to call it a night, flicker by on the trail of mosquitoes. Black-eyed Susans stare, tomatoes ripen, rhubarb wags its elephant ears. Beside the rhubarb patch a blue spruce, planted there after bearing our tinsel indoors one Christmas, extrudes° fresh needles from the tips of twigs. A squirrel slinks onto a limb over my head to fuss at me for invading the yard. All of this—not to mention the work of worms under my feet, the bacteria in my belly, the rising of the sun itself— goes on without anybody's say-so. Power lines and roof lines banish the eagles, alas, along with the fringed gentian,° the grizzly, and the faint tracery of comets, but they do not shut out, cannot shut out, the greater life by which we live. Dawn gives back to my eyes this delectable presence. If Ruth has reason to be jealous, it is not of another woman, nor of a dryad,° but of the seductive creation.

---

*jocund:* Cheerful, joyful.   *rheostat:* An instrument used to regulate electric currents.   *raucously:* Boisterously, stridently.   *extrudes:* Puts out, expels.   *gentian:* A type of colorful flower.   *dryad:* Imaginary creature (nymph) who lives in the woods.

Earth is sexy, just as sex is earthy. Each of us is a landscape of plains and peaks, valleys and thickets. I speak in metaphors, as through a garbled phone line, but what I mean is plain and simple: body and land are one flesh. They are made of the same stuff. Their beauty is one beauty, their wounds the same wounds. They call to us in the same perennial voice, crying, *Come see, come touch, come listen and smell, and O come taste.* We explore them alike, honor or abuse them alike. The health or sickness of one is inseparable from that of the other. There is no division between where we live and what we are.

The boys I knew while growing up in farm country spoke appreciatively about the lay of the land and spoke boastfully about this girl or that as a good lay, thereby confusing two passions. Such confusion—along with the whole sad history of men bullying women and animals and soil—has led some earnest people to conclude that the earth *is* female, innocent and fruitful, and not only in the imaginations of adolescent boys. To claim the earth as female might well make women feel powerful, a worthy consequence, but it also has the effect of making men seem like intruders on the planet. The claim is false, as well as dangerous. My body, no less than my wife's, is made of the earth. The radioactivity in my bones still ticks from the formation of the planet. Like Ruth, I carry within me the legacy of a thousand generations of genes. In my moody cycles, along with all other men, I might even be swayed by the moon —the scientists are still debating that point. I am certainly swayed by sunrise and starfire, by wind and rain, by my fellow creatures, by the whole procession of the year. I belong here, and so do we all, men and women.

Earth is our mother, as even bumper stickers remind us, but it is also our father; it is our brother and sister, husband and wife, male as well as female. In loving this gorgeous planet, we are freed from the half-life, the polarity of gender. I do not mean to belittle the marriage of man and woman, which is a joy to me, but to enlarge it. We think of sex too narrowly, as though it were a mere magnetism of groin to groin. The sensuous attraction that pulls us into bed is a special case of the greater attraction that binds us, nerves and belly and brain, to the flesh of the earth.

30     I realize it may seem odd to others that I find the earth voluptuous.° But there it is. What am I to make of it? I have never been tempted to go naked to a party or to bask in the buff° on a crowded beach. When a Supreme Court justice remarked not long ago that a society of nudists might wish to rent the Hoosierdome° in Indianapolis and convene there in the altogether—acres of skin in plastic seats—I did not find the prospect enticing. But I have often felt

---

*voluptuous:* Here, meaning full of pleasure for the senses.  *in the buff:* Naked.  *Hoosierdome:* An enclosed sports arena.

like shucking my clothes on the peaks of mountains, in the privacy of rivers, in the shadowy depths of woods. Not only felt like it, I am bound to confess, but have done so, when weather and solitude permitted. Psychiatrists may well have a label for this impulse, since they have a label for most of our desires, healthy or otherwise. Without benefit of a label, I acknowledge the impulse as part of who I am.

I first disrobed in the wild at the age of five, soon after my family had moved into the arsenal, that paradise of bombs, where deer were as common as rabbits. One afternoon I came upon a fawn bedded down in the woods behind our house. The deer, no bigger than I was, did not know enough to fear me, and so it lay there observing me calmly with slick brown eyes. It wore only a birthday suit of dappled fur, which invited my fingers, and I felt a powerful urge to cuddle against that tawny creature in my own birthday suit of simple skin. And so, there being at the age of five fewer barricades between wish and act, I wriggled out of my clothes and knelt down and lay my head on the velvety fur. The fawn shivered but did not bolt. I was launched on a lifetime of courtship.

I have not met another fawn on such intimate terms. Now and again, however, and well beyond the age of five—right up to my present age, in fact —I have been lured out of my clothes by waterfalls or wildflowers or stars. By giving in to this urge I have broken the laws of several states, ranging from Maine to Oregon. Before undressing, I always make sure there are no sheriffs in the vicinity—nor anybody else, for that matter, since I do not wish to impose my rapture° on strangers. It *is* rapture. When I first read King Lear° and I came to the storm scene on the heath° where the crazed old man, already stripped of the crown by his own hand, shouts "Off, off, you lendings!" and begins tearing at his clothes, I understood his frenzy. He has lost his kingdom, lost his daughters, all but lost his mind. What pleasures, what consolations remain for him except those that flow in through the channels of the senses? In grief or joy, a hard rain and a wild field call for peeling away the husks, stripping down to what Lear calls the "poor, bare, forked animal" of the body. My house is surrounded by scruffy lawns and buckled sidewalks, nothing so desolate as a heath. Near home I keep my clothes on, out of regard for my neighbors, and yet no thunderstorm passes without tempting me to dance naked in the street.

No promise of thunderstorms today, alas. Dry, dry, and hot. Between the withered blades of grass in my yard the dirt has cracked. Even in the heat, numberless lives still burn in the air and wood and soil, and I still feel a yen to

---

*rapture:* The sensation of being carried away by overwhelming emotion.   *King Lear:* A play by William Shakespeare in which a king is betrayed by two of his three daughters, who crave his crown. *heath:* Here, meaning a wide open area of uncultivated land.

get up and dance. So I do. My shorts are floppy as a clown's, my shuffle as clumsy. I am no Lear, no Romeo, neither hero nor king, merely a man who aches from a day of splitting wood and a night of fear and longing. The lover I dance with seems not to care.

In the memorable phrasing of The Letter to the Hebrews (11:1), "faith is the assurance of things hoped for, the conviction of things not seen." By that measure, and by most others, I am a man of little faith. In the dark night of the soul, I reach out to assure myself of things not seen. I must lay my hands on the side of the tree, must feel the prick of grass on my skin, must smell the dirt, must sing to myself a brave lullaby in order to sustain my hopes.

35    What do I hope for? Eternal life, I suppose. By that I mean something besides immortality—although, like all creatures not maddened by pain, I am hooked on the habit of living. The eternal life I seek is not some after time, some other place, but awareness of eternity in this moment and this place. What I crave is contact with the force that moves and shapes all there is or has been or will be.

The earth and our own bodies, by casting shadows, seem to be the opposite of light. But if you have gazed up through the leaves of a tree at the sky, if you have watched the jeweled crests of waves, or held a shimmering fish in your hand, or lifted your palm against the sun and seen ruby light blazing through the flesh of your squeezed fingers, you know that matter is filled with fire. Matter *is* fire, in slow motion. Einstein taught us as much, and bomb testers keep proving it with cataclysmic° explosions. The resistant stuff we touch and walk on and eat, the resistant stuff we are, blood and bone, is not the opposite of light but light's incarnation.

The Taoist° book of wisdom, *The Secret of the Golden Flower,* speaks about a condition of utter clarity and selflessness as "living midnight." I don't know a word of the original Chinese, and I might well misread the translation, but I am haunted by this phrase. Living midnight: to face oblivion, to drown in the annihilating water, to dwell without fear or fret at the still center. Hardest of all is to live *through* midnight, to accept the knowledge of one's own private extinction and still return to daylight charged with passion and purpose.

The man who dances in the backyard with an invisible lover, and then comes in the house humming to breakfast with his family, is the same one who was shaken like a rag by dread in the depths of the night.

"Hi, Pop," Eva says as I enter the kitchen.

40    "Morning, old guy," says Jesse.

---

*cataclysmic:* Disastrous, catastrophic.    *Taoist:* Related to Taoism, a Chinese mystical philosophy established in the sixth century B.C.

"Did you have a bad night?" asks Ruth, who notices whenever I leave bed early.

"Not so bad," I answer, and then, considering, I add, "a good night, really."

I kiss their shining heads, each in turn. Their faces, so dear and mysterious, tilt up to me. Their skin glows from sleep. No, not only from sleep. They glow steadily, my wife and daughter and son, this morning as always, with a radiance that my wakefulness helps me to see.

This is no happy ending, merely an interlude, a reprieve. My vision will dim once more, and I will have to clear my sight. Dread will seize me by the throat. When the need comes on me, I will go outside.

The sudden fierce grip of fear was once thought to be the mischievous   45
work of Pan, the god of wildness, and thus we still speak of feeling panic. I may be perverse, but I find myself soothed rather than frightened by wildness. I am reassured to feel one juice flowing through my fingers and the branches of the maple and the flickering grass. Pantheism° has taken a beating since the rise of the great monotheistic religions. I believe there is only one power, one shaping urge, but I also believe that it infuses everything—the glistening track of the snail along with the gleaming eye of the fawn, the grain in the oak, the froth on the creek, the coiled proteins in my blood and in yours, the mind that strings together these words and the mind that reads them.

The only sure antidote to oblivion is the creation. So I loop my sentences around the trunks of maples, hook them into the parched soil, anchor them to rock, to moon and stars, wrap them tenderly around the ankles of those I love. From down in the pit I give a tug, to make sure my rope of words is firmly hooked into the world, and then up I climb.

## QUESTIONS

1. What is the cause of the fear that Sanders describes at the beginning of this essay?
2. Sanders states that he has been "trying to find where divinity resides." In this essay, where does Sanders locate divinity?
3. After rereading Sanders' description of the women in northern India who "preserved their forests from loggers by hugging trees," consider popular characterizations of North American "tree-huggers." Do their actions enhance or detract from their message? In what other ways might people protest logging? Would those ways be as effective?
4. Describing his childhood in a rough neighborhood, Sanders explains that both his natural environment and his social environment

*pantheism:* The worship of different gods from various creeds or cultures, often nature gods.

affected his perception of the world. How did the environment affect him? How has your environment, both social and natural, affected you?

5. After you've read this essay once, read it again, marking as many similes and metaphors as you can find. Choose one that you particularly like; then discuss its connotations, its implications.

6. Find a few examples of parallel construction within sentences and paragraphs in this essay.

7. Consider the way Sanders introduces elements from other writers' texts. How does he keep the reader from getting confused by these inclusions? What kind of information does he provide for each quotation he includes?

### CONNECTIONS

1. Of the pieces you have already read in this section, which most resembles Sanders' in its tone? Explain your answer.

2. Explain how part of this essay relates to Tom Daly's essay "Dancing in the Cracks between Worlds," included in Section 2.

3. Both Mary Oliver (in her poem "Starfish") and Scott Russell Sanders discuss fears they have. What does each of them fear? What are the relationships between their fears and nature?

# ◇ I Hate Trees

*Rosa Ehrenreich*

Rosa Ehrenreich graduated from Harvard University in 1991 and continued her studies at Oxford University in England. She has written numerous articles, including "What Campus Radicals?" which appeared in *Harper's Magazine* in 1991 and has since been anthologized in various college composition textbooks. She is also the author of a book entitled *A Garden of Paper Flowers: An American in Oxford.* The following opinion piece appeared in the "You Said It" column of *Mademoiselle* magazine in February 1995.

**WARM-UP:** Do you participate in any concrete way(s) in the attempt to protect the environment? Do most people around you participate in similar ways?

Yes, it's true. I detest, loathe and despise trees. Here's why: Yesterday, I went out to buy stationery, and every kind I found was not only made of recycled paper but had something printed on it, like "earth friendly!" in childlike writing.

I went into a fit of rage so uncontrollable that I had to leave the store before I flipped out and flung my newspaper into the trash can instead of the recycling bin. After all, what have trees ever done for us? They don't work on assembly lines. They don't write poems. And when was the last time you saw a tree rush into a burning building to save a child or air-drop food into a famine-ridden country?

Trees have every right to hang out unmolested. But recall Dr. Seuss's Lorax, who spoke for the trees, "for the trees have no tongues." This isn't true today—every tree has a tongue. In fact, they have protectors running around in natural cotton T-shirts. A recent *Times Mirror* poll showed that 56 percent of Americans believe that improving the global environment should be a top priority for the nation. The U.S. has spent $2 trillion on environmental protection. Hell, trees have recycling laws; they even have Rainforest Crunch° ice cream.

But what about people? You know, all 5.3 billion of us. What about the 15.7 million American children who live below the poverty line? Or the 1.5 million Sudanese who were killed in the recent civil war? Or the 5 million

---

*Rainforest Crunch ice cream:* Reference to brands of ice cream that advertise their attempt to help preserve the rain forests by commercializing products that are gathered from it, without endangering its plants or animals.

African children who die each year from treatable or preventable illnesses? Who speaks for them? Who has even heard of them?

5        You don't see 56 percent of Americans campaigning for human rights. Nah, we're too busy sipping cappuccino from our refillable plastic mugs. That's the danger of environmentalism. For many of us, its an easy way to feel good: "Look at me, I'm recycling!"

There's nothing wrong with recycling. I recycle (so I lied about hating it; shoot me). And it's okay to buy Rainforest Crunch. Just don't let caring about trees become a substitute for what's harder—caring about people.

The next time you buy earth-friendly paper, use it to write to your senator, or write a letter for Amnesty International.° Use a recycled envelope to send a check to a cause you care about. Speak for the trees—but speak for people, too.

## QUESTIONS

1. Is Ehrenreich's introduction, claiming that she "detest[s], loathe[s] and despise[s] trees, effective? Would you guess that the title succeeded in getting people to read the essay?
2. What is Ehrenreich's critique of many people's concern for the environment? Do you agree with her?
3. What specific actions does Ehrenreich advocate?
4. Late in the essay, does the author's statement that "there's nothing wrong with recycling" strengthen or weaken her argument? Why?
5. Are there any particular details in the essay that leave a striking impression—details without which the essay would have been weaker? Why are they effective?
6. Do you feel that activists should focus their attention on one cause at a time? Can a person struggle successfully for several changes in society?

## CONNECTIONS

1. How are Ehrenreich's views of environmental activists similar to P. J. O'Rourke's? How are they different?
2. In "The Origins of Modern Vegetarianism," Amato and Partridge state that many of the people who supported vegetarianism and animal rights in the eighteenth and nineteen centuries also supported child welfare, the struggle for the abolition of slavery, and other "radical" causes. What does Ehrenreich's essay suggest about that trend?

---

*Amnesty International:* A watchdog organization that monitors and struggles to improve human rights around the world.

# Summary, Paraphrase, Quotation, and (for All) Attribution

. . . . . . . . . . . . . . . . . . . . . . . . . . . .

### Summary and Paraphrase

In a *summary* you are condensing information from a source into fewer words than the original had used (enough, however, to reflect the meaning of the source faithfully), and restating it in your own words. Two examples of summary are Charles Rubin's presentation of Rachel Carson's views, in his essay "Brightest Heaven of Invention," and Robert Jones' presentation of Edward O. Wilson's views (p. 399), in his essay "A Modest Proposal: The Sequel" (both included in this section). Jones, for example, writes,

> Edward O. Wilson, the Pulitzer-prize-winning Harvard scientist who is one of the world's leading authorities on everything from the lives of the ants to the death of nature, believes we are now in the midst of the sixth such spasm—this one attributable entirely to man. In *The Diversity of Life* . . . Wilson describes how human population pressures, particularly in the developing nations of the so-called Third World, are destroying other species of life at a disastrous rate. Human beings are literally overwhelming nature. By the year 2020—less than a human generation from now—no fewer than 20 percent of the earth's existing species of plants and animals will be extinct, by Wilson's *conservative* estimate.

You can *paraphrase* information by presenting it in your own words but in about as many words as the original. For example, if we were to paraphrase John F. Kennedy's line "Ask not what your country can do for you, ask what you can do for your country," we could say that President Kennedy told his fellow citizens to be more concerned with their ability to help their country than with the advantages they might gain from it.

### Quotation

Often, paraphrasing and summarizing will show your readers that you have understood the original source, and will prevent your paper from sounding like a collection of other people's sentences (that's the impression created by a paper that uses too many quotations). However, if you look at the preceding Kennedy quotation and its paraphrase, you'll certainly notice that the original version is much more powerful. That's a good reason to quote something directly. A *quotation,* a word-for-word copy of someone else's writing, should strengthen your essay by allowing your sources to speak in their own voices, especially when those voices are quite powerful or controversial. Be careful, however, to let your readers know that you are using a source's own words—either by placing those words between quotation marks (if the text you are quoting takes up four lines or less), or by setting them off in a separate paragraph, indented ten spaces from the left margin (if the quotation takes up more than four lines in your essay). If you are quoting a few lines from a poem, use slashes to show where one line ends and the next one begins (note the quotation from Ecclesiastes on page 331).

Also be careful to quote your sources so that you don't misrepresent the authors' views. Otherwise, if your readers should track down a source and discover that the quoted material presented an inaccurate picture of what the original author wrote (as Charles Rubin found when researching Rachel Carson's sources), your entire essay will lose credibility.

### Attribution

As you've noticed, writers often quote each other, inviting other people's voices into their text. However, imagine having a telephone conversation with someone you know, when suddenly you hear a different voice. Having no idea who this person is, would you keep talking? Probably not—or at least not for long, and not without the expectation that the person would soon be identified. Well, that's very similar to the effect that an unintroduced quotation has on your readers: They know they are reading someone else's words, but they have no idea *whose*, nor why they should care what this person claims.

What's worse is if you use someone else's words or ideas without giving that person credit; that's simply stealing. This kind of theft is called *plagiarism*. Plagiarism, whether done intentionally or accidentally, consists of allowing your reader to believe that certain words or ideas come from you when in fact those words or ideas come from material you encountered during your research. The penalties for plagiarism can be severe—including a grade of F on an assignment, a failing grade in the course, or even expulsion from the college or university.

Each time you incorporate someone else's words or ideas into your essays, you have to tell your reader whom they came from. That process of identifying your sources is called *attribution*. And you need to attribute effectively not only quotations but also paraphrases and summaries.

At the least, a proper attribution identifies the author; it may also contain other information.

- *The name of the author:* For example, note the last line of Rachel Carson's essay included in this section: Carson writes, *"In the words of Jean Rostand, 'The obligation to endure gives us the right to know.'"* Use an author's full name the first time you refer to him or her, and at least his or her *last* name from then on. Never refer by first name only to anyone you quote or paraphrase.

- *The author's credentials:* Let the readers know why they should give weight to what the author says. You probably wouldn't need to say "the famous playwright William Shakespeare," or "the inventor of the theory of relativity, Albert Einstein," since these people are so widely recognized, but most of your sources (unfamiliar to your readers) will benefit from some additional identification. In Winifred Gallagher's essay "The Science of Place," for example, the author is casual but thorough in the following attribution to her source; she provides information that lets us know why we should find the source credible: ". . . I treated myself to a lecture by Mihaly Csikszentmihalyi, *a professor of psychology at the University of Chicago best known for his improbable best-seller,* Flow . . ." she writes, proceeding to weave his ideas into her essay through both quotations and summary, along with quotations from "the father of medicine," Hippocrates, and "the English scholar" Robert Burton. Robert Jones also cites credentials in his introduction of Edward O. Wilson, quoted earlier in this discussion.

- *The title of the piece you are quoting or paraphrasing:* For example, let us "preview" for you the transitional piece connecting this section and the following one (which focuses on various issues in American culture): *In this selection, entitled "Discoveries," anthropologist Michael Dorris* discusses Native American environmental attitudes in the context of his broader analysis of the colonization of North America. (One note about formatting titles: Underline or italicize the titles of long works such as books, magazines and newspapers, and movies and plays; place within quotation marks the titles of shorter works such as most poems, short stories, essays, and songs.)

Awareness of two additional elements can help you create effective attributions. The first element is punctuation: An introduction that is *not* a complete sentence should be followed by a comma (as in "*According to Rubin,* 'We know what Carson made of this part . . .'"); an introduction that is a complete sentence should be followed by a colon (for example, "*Carson believes that we may one day regret our use of pesticides on the environment:* 'Future historians may well be amazed by our distorted sense of proportion'"). The second element is the verb that might appear in an introduction to a quotation or paraphrase. Although the generic verb "to say" is an easy way out, a more accurate descriptive verb will make it clear whether the person you are referring to is "admitting" or "arguing," "declaring" or "describing," "implying" or "insisting," "rejecting" or "reporting." As you read various selections in this text, note the various verbs that writers use to reveal a source's purpose.

### Final Words

In addition to the in-text attribution we have just discussed, in formal research papers you will also be expected to document any outside sources on a "Works Cited" or "Bibliography" page following the essay. This process is addressed in detail at the end of the next section, as part of our discussion of writing a research paper. Whether you provide such formal documentation or not, however, you always need to introduce your sources clearly within the text of the essay itself.

---

**What to Include in a Sentence or Phrase Introducing Material from an Outside Source**

- The full name of the person you are quoting or paraphrasing (or the last name only, if the reference is clear and you've already mentioned the full name in your paper).

- If needed, the credentials of the person being cited.

- Usually, the title of the work from which you are quoting or paraphrasing (unless, of course, you're referring to an interview you have conducted): Underline or italicize the titles of book-length works, magazines, or newspapers; place within quotation marks the titles of poems, short stories, essays, and songs.

---

## Topics for Writing about the Environment

1. William Kowinski writes that the "value system of the mall" is really the dominant one of the whole society." In an essay, explain whether or not you agree with this statement, supporting your perspective with examples from your observations, experiences, and reading.
2. Write an essay describing and analyzing one part of the environment of the school you attend, as well as the influence this environment seems to have on you. You could focus on a particular classroom, the library, or the campus as a whole.
3. After doing some reading on the subject, write an essay in which you present the arguments raised by those who feel that human over-population is the core threat to our environment. Explain why you agree or disagree with that view.

4. Write a letter to Robert Jones in which you respond to his proposals.

5. Robert Jones claims that we humans have a "propensity for messing things up." Write an essay that considers whether or not this is true; support your perspective with detailed examples.

6. According to Charles Rubin, Rachel Carson "speaks of increased government regulation of pesticide use, establishing zero-tolerances for pesticide residues in food, and substitution of relatively safer for more dangerous pesticides." Write an essay that addresses situations in which government regulation is a problem or cases in which it presents a solution.

7. Charles Rubin complains that Carson's attempt to explain what she means by the "balance of nature" is incoherent and murky. Where else, besides between humans and nature, is the concept of balance murky? Discuss this in one (or more) of the following pairs: work and play; male and female; right and wrong; private and public.

8. Write an essay modeled on Annie Dillard's "Living like Weasels," reflecting on an encounter (physical or mental) that you have had with a particular kind of animal or plant ("Living like___").

9. Write an essay explaining the current debate over animal rights and taking a side on this issue. (You may focus on the use of animals for food and clothing, their use in the area of medical research, their treatment when kept as pets and in zoos—or all of the above.)

10. Write an essay that takes issue with the views expressed in P. J. O'Rourke's "The Greenhouse Affect."

11. Compare and contrast the writing styles of two different authors included in this section, focusing on various elements of writing that have been discussed in your class so far during this term (word choice, use of figures of speech like metaphors and similes, use of balanced construction and recurrence in sentences, type of introduction or conclusion, and so forth). Support your claims with examples from the texts you choose to discuss.

## ∽ Discoveries

*Michael Dorris*

> A writer and anthropologist, Michael Dorris was the founder and chairman of the Department of Native American Studies at Dartmouth College and the author of the *New York Times* bestseller *The Broken Cord* (1989), which won the National Book Critics Circle Award for nonfiction as well as the Heartland Prize. Dorris was born in 1945 and died in 1997; he held a B.A. degree from Georgetown University and master's degree in philosophy from Yale University. He is best known for his novels, such as *A Yellow Raft in Blue Waters* and *The Crown of Columbus* (1991) (the latter coauthored with his wife, Louise Erdrich). He also wrote a children's book (*Morning Girl,* 1992), short stories (some of which are collected in *Working Men,* 1993), and numerous articles that have appeared in publications ranging from the *New York Times* to *Seventeen.* The following essay first appeared in the *Georgia Review* in 1992 and was included in the anthology *Paper Trail* (1994).

> **WARM-UP:** Human beings follow a variety of religions, speak a variety of languages, and follow a wide variety of customs. Overall, do you see this as a positive or a negative development? Why?

1   Multiculturalism as a topic has become almost cliché, a bow to each federally recognized ethnic population, a dutiful list of their respective accomplishments and contributions to the modern world. The word *mosaic* is often used, or, in Canada, the homier *patchwork quilt*. However, perspective, in discussing the various patches, is problematic, for it presumes a kind of omniscience° that only God or objective history can achieve. An individual, ultimately, speaks *from* a patch, *as* a patch. There is a way of viewing the mishmash of America from an African American point of view, or from a Chicano or Puerto Rican or Russian émigré. Each vantage has its own *ad*vantage, its own unique illumination.

    Half a millennium ago, my ancestors on my father's side, Modocs who lived in the lava flats of northern California, were going about their lives—hunting, fishing, falling in love, mourning their dead, completely unaware of

---

*omniscience:* The power of having complete knowledge and understanding of everything.

· · · · · · · · · · · · · · · · · · · · · · · · · · · · · · · · · · · · · ·

an Atlantic Ocean, much less any human beings on the other side of it. Irish peasants—my mother's people—toiling the rocky fields of the western county of Roscommon, speaking Gaelic and worrying when the next attack from the sea might come, had little notion of Spain, much less the possibility of America. Somewhere in the tree of my particular lineage there were French farmers, Swiss shepherds, German professors, Coeur d'Alene° salmon fisher-men, all innocent of the complications of contact, oblivious° of each others' priorities and concerns, insular, ethnocentric,° proud . . . and unfathomable° to a contemporary person.

These were men and women whose world was infinitely smaller, easier, but ultimately, I would argue, less interesting in its homogeneity° than our own. When their worlds inadvertently° collided, well into the eighteenth and nineteenth centuries, they were probably at least as confused as they were enlightened, as terrified by newness as they were fascinated by it. They no doubt mistrusted the strange, yearned for the security of the "old days," often wished each other gone. But somehow, fortuitously° (for me), there were among them people who dared to look beyond the boundaries of their own birthplaces, who not only accepted but embraced the possibilities of differ-ence, who joined together to forge something new.

In contemporary America we are assembled from many lands and diverse backgrounds, and seem alternately to periodically examine and celebrate, crit-icize and revise, maybe even learn from the process of our ongoing union. At our best, we seek the truth, and through that lens to avoid the mistakes and blindnesses of our respective forebears. We commemorate, we remember, we say Kaddish,° we hope. We are the unlikely survivors of an inexorable° process beyond any of our controls, and we feel an odd mixture of shame and pride, relief and regret. We are the chain of dancers on the beach at the end of Fed-erico Fellini's 8½, and we are, potentially, in our thoughtfulness, our willing-ness to listen to each other, our curiosity and our mutual compassion, the best chance for a better and more harmonious next five hundred years of world history.

There are, among Native American people I know and respect, many who    5
were angry at the attention lavished on the 1992 quincentennial.° These indi-viduals profess an aversion to Columbus and all that he stands for; they're

---

*Coeur d'Alene:* Native American tribe from Idaho.    *oblivious:* Unaware, inattentive.    *ethnocentric:* Believing that one's race or ethnic group is superior to others.    *unfathomable:* Impossible to compre-hend.    *homogeneity:* The quality of being of uniform composition throughout.    *inadvertently:* Unin-tentionally, accidentally.    *fortuitously:* Luckily.    *Kaddish:* Jewish prayer of mourning.    *inexorable:* Relentless.    *quincentennial:* The 500-year anniversary (in this case, the anniversary of the arrival of Columbus in America).

embittered descendants of tribes whose lands were stolen, whose populations were decimated, whose religions were outlawed and held in contempt, whose books were burned, whose skin color reviled. And they are right to be angry. Mythologizing and glorifying—or deprecating—a complicated past does no justice to anyone. It buries, in its fear of clarity, hard facts and sad realities. It absolves without any confession of guilt, and it does not heal.

There are, among my non-Indian friends, those who resent any cloud cast over the international orgy of self-congratulation, of blissful dismissal of every history save that of the conquerors. "To the victors belong the spoils," they crow. And they are wrong, wrong as the extollers of Manifest Destiny,° wrong as those who would remake the world in the image of a single culture or society or faith. Our diversity, as a species, has always been our salvation. Why do we struggle to deny and suppress it? And what do we forfeit in so doing?

Who were, after all, the societies that greeted Europeans five, four, three hundred years ago? What were their motives, their important elements, their contrasts with the norms of Old World nations that attempted to dominate and destroy them?

Imagine the scene: it is an autumn day in the late fifteenth century. On a beach with rose-colored sand, somewhere in the Caribbean, two groups of people, the hosts and their visitors, are about to meet for the first time. Emerging from a small landing boat is a group of men exhausted from a long and frightening ocean voyage. They didn't trust where they were going and now they don't know where they've arrived—but it doesn't look at all like the India described by Marco Polo. They come from Spain and Portugal and Genoa, are Christian and Jewish. The more superstitious and uneducated among them feared that, by sailing west across the Atlantic, they would fall off the edge of the planet.

The men seek treasure and adventure, fame and glory, but the people who greet them—if in fact they are "people" at all—seem, though handsome, quite poor. They are not dressed in fine brocade encrusted with precious jewels, as one would expect of subjects of the great Khan. They are, in fact, not dressed at all, except for a few woven skirts and dabs of ochre.° Are they demons? Are they dangerous? Do they know where the gold is hidden?

10     Watching the boat draw near is a cluster of men, women, and children. They speak a dialect of the Arawak language and are delighted to receive new

---

*extollers of Manifest Destiny:* Supporters of the U.S. policy that argued that it was the "destiny" of the United States to stretch from coast to coast, thus justifying the country's Western expansion.    *ochre:* A yellow earthy pigment.

guests, especially ones who aren't painted white—signifying death. Strangers arrive often, anxious to barter parrot feathers or new foods or useful objects made of stone or shell. These particular visitors look rather strange, it's true: their bodies are covered with odd materials, not at all suited for the warm climate, and they communicate with each other in a tongue as indecipherable° as Carib or Nahuatl.

Up close there are more surprises. The group includes no women and some among the hosts speculate why this may be the case. Have their clan mothers expelled these men, banned them to wander alone and orphaned? Has their tribe suffered some disaster? And another thing: they have the strong odor of people who have not had their daily bath. Are they from some simple and rude society that doesn't know how to comport itself?

But all this notwithstanding, guests are guests and should be treated with hospitality. They must be offered food and shelter, must be entertained with stories and music, before the serious business of trade begins.

The earth was much larger than Christopher Columbus imagined, its human population far more diverse. The land mass he encountered on his transatlantic voyages was thoroughly inhabited by more than one hundred million people, from the frigid steppes° of Patagonia at the farthest extremity of South America to the dark arboreal forests of Newfoundland. In the inhospitable Arctic, Inuits foraged for much of the year in small nuclear or extended family groups, assembling sporadically to carry on the necessary business of marriage, remembrance, or collective action, and only when the availability of food was at its peak. In the lush and verdant jungles of Yucatán and Guatemala, the Mayas had invented agriculture, writing, and an accurate calendar fifteen hundred years before the birth of Christ. Organized in complex, class-oriented societies, they subsisted on a nutritionally balanced diet based on maize, squashes, and beans. In the Andes of northwestern South America early Quechuas domesticated the potato, engineered an intricate system of roads and bridges, and formed a nation in which the state owned all property except houses and movable household goods, and taxes were collected in labor.

The Western Hemisphere was home to literally hundreds of cultures whose people spoke a multiplicity of dialects and languages derived from at least ten mutually exclusive linguistic families. Many societies had well-developed traditions of science and medicine—some 40 percent of the

---

*indecipherable:* Unreadable, mysterious.    *steppes:* Broad level stretches of land without trees.

modern world's pharmacopoeia° was utilized in America before 1492—and literature, visual art, and philosophy flourished in a variety of contexts. Yet beyond a shared geography, there were few common denominators; due to the haphazard nature and long process by which in-migrating peoples distributed themselves throughout the continents, the Western Hemisphere thrived as a living laboratory of disparate° lifestyles, linguistic variety, and cultural pluralism.

15          Obviously, no single group was directly aware of more than a fraction of the other extant° societies—and there was no conception of an overarching group identity. "We" was the family, the community, the tribe, and "they" were everyone else, known and unknown. The fact of cultural diversity, however, was manifest. Within a day's walk of virtually every indigenous° population could be found at least one and probably more than one unrelated community whose inhabitants, relative to the visitor, spoke a totally foreign and incomprehensible language, adhered to a unique cosmology,° dressed in unusual clothing, ate exotic foods, and had a dissimilar political organization with peculiar variations of age and gender roles.

A native person in most regions of precontact° America could and undoubtedly did believe that he or she belonged to the smartest, most tasteful, most accomplished, and most handsome human constellation in the universe, but clearly not the only one. Pluralism, in whichever way it was construed° and explained, was inescapably the norm.

It is little wonder, therefore, that for Europeans of the fifteenth and sixteenth centuries, America proved to be much more than a single new world: it was an unimagined universe. The sheer heterogeneity° of Western Hemisphere societies challenged every cherished medieval assumption about the orderly nature of human origin and destiny. It was as if a whole new set of potential operating rules were revealed—or, even more disconcerting, the cultural hodgepodge of America was an ego-threatening intimation that there were no dependable rules at all. Imagine the shock! To have believed for a thousand years that everything and everybody of consequence was known and neatly categorized and then suddenly to open a window and learn that all along one had been dwelling in a small house with no perspective on the teeming and chaotic city that surrounded one's accustomed neighborhood— no map or dictionary provided. How did Cain and Abel fit into this new, com-

---

*pharmacopoeia:* Collection of medicinal drugs.    *disparate:* Very distinct, different.    *extant:* Existent. *indigenous:* Native.    *cosmology:* Doctrine about the origin and structure of the universe.    *precontact:* Preceding the first contact between Europeans and Native Americans.    *construed:* Understood.    *heterogeneity:* The quality of being mixed or made up of dissimilar elements (the opposite of homogeneity).

plicated schema? Which Old Testament patriarch begat° the Lakota or the Chibcha? How did the Comanche get from the Tower of Babel to Oklahoma?

The contrasts between the Old World and the Americas were staggering. With only a few minor exceptions, virtually all Europeans spoke languages that sprang from a single linguistic family. Moreover, in the larger context, Europe's vaunted religious and philosophical divisions were basically variations on a concordant° theme. Everyone from the Baltic to the Balkans to the British Isles professed belief in the same divinity or, in the case of European Jewry, His father.

As side effects of this theological unity, Latin became a lingua franca° for intellectuals from all sectors, and the Mosaic° code formed the basis for practically every ethical or legal philosophy. The broad assumption of male dominance reigned uncontested, from individual marriage contracts to the leadership hierarchy of emergent nation-states. The Bible—in particular, the book of Genesis—was regarded as a literally true and factually accurate accounting of the origin of everything.

Significantly, in the Adam and Eve story, creation is intentional; a personalized, anthropomorphic° God formed a man in His image and then threw in a woman, made out of a nonessential rib, for His company and pleasure. His word was law and His only token competition came from a fallen angel, also of His manufacture. After devising, in six days, a universe whose primary purpose was to exist as a backdrop and amusement park for man, the Divinity set up a test for the objects of his invention—a test that the Divinity, being omniscient as well as omnipotent,° must have known all along man would fail.     20

Man did.

A nonbeliever attempting to analyze this saga might well find parts of it, while interesting, a bit bizarre. Why were men and women so disproportionately blessed? Why did God go to all the trouble? For all its paradox, however, the Genesis story did fulfill a function for the Hebraic culture to whom it was initially addressed. It authenticated divine sponsorship for the law of the land and proffered° the explanation, so necessary for a poor, threatened minority population, that life was supposed to be pain, that man deserved what he got, and that the only true happiness and peace would come to the just after death.

The disparate creation stories Native Americans believed about themselves—be they emergence myths or earth-diver tales, divine births or great floods—are every bit as pregnant with particular meaning for their specific

*begat:* Generated, sired.   *concordant:* Common.   *lingua franca:* A common language.   *Mosaic:* Jewish.   *anthropomorphic:* Human characteristics.   *omnipotent:* All-powerful.   *proffered:* Offered.

audiences as was Genesis for the Israelites. Take, for example, a tale found in several Northwest Coast repertoires: According to legend, one day Raven, the androgynous° culture hero/Trickster, spies a bush containing a new kind of berry. They are purple and luscious, bursting with sweet juice, and Trickster can't resist. He/she begins to gobble them up and doesn't stop until every one is consumed. His/her breast feathers are stained and his/her belly is bloated, but Raven staggers to the side of a cliff, spreads his/her wings, and careens off into the air.

Suddenly Raven is seized by terrible stomach cramps and immediately experiences the worst case of diarrhea in history. It's terrible: everywhere Raven flies, his/her droppings land, until finally the attack is over, the pain subsides, and with a sigh of relief Raven looks down at the earth to see the mess he/she has made. And there we are, come to life: human beings! Raven beholds these ridiculous creatures, made out of his/her excrement, and laughs. And the ridiculous creatures squint up at Raven—and laugh back!

25 A society with this irreverent code has a very different self-concept than one with solemn Genesis as its primary referent.° The Raven tale is supposed to be funny, is aimed to entertain and thus be memorable. Creation itself, the story implies, was a totally random act—a fluke. Additionally, the first encounter between creator and createe is maddening for both. Theirs is a relationship without mutual culpability,° without guilt, affection, or even clear purpose. As a matter of fact, subsequent chapters in the cycle demonstrate that the joking relationship between Raven and humanity persists and becomes even more perverse over time.

The universe based on such stories was conceived in large part as irrational, not a product of cause and effect, stimulus and response. Events occurred without great purpose and had to be dealt with on their own terms —pragmatically and intelligently. A plague of locusts, an earthquake, a misfortune did not take place because an individual or a people failed to satisfy a demanding and ambiguous Zeus or Jupiter or Jehovah, but rather were regarded as haphazard disruptions in the inevitable course of existence. Humor and fatalism,° as opposed to responsibility and recrimination,° were the appropriate attitudes toward misfortune. The gods, like everything else, were inscrutable.° Harmony, in human communities or in nature as a whole, was best preserved through balance and established customs, and both people

---

*androgynous:* Having both male and female characteristics.    *referent:* The thing that a symbol stands for.    *culpability:* The quality of deserving blame or guilt.    *fatalism:* The belief that events are preordained and human beings cannot change them.    *recrimination:* Bitter response, retaliation.    *inscrutable:* Hard to grasp or interpret.

and divinities were but elements in a grand, interrelated panorama that encompassed all things.

Practically speaking, prior to the so-called Age of Discovery, Europeans had little contact with populations substantively dissimilar to themselves—certainly not enough to shake their entrenched ethnocentrism. Relations with central or eastern Asia, or sub-Saharan Africa, were rare, and usually filtered through the Islamic societies occupying the southern and eastern perimeters of the Mediterranean. Although Arabs were regarded in certain respects as exotic and the polar opposite of Christians, they were, nevertheless, comprehensible; generally similar in terms of skin pigmentation, patriarchal orientation, and even religious derivation, their customs fell within the range of at least plausible behavior. They were ideal "heathens" because they tended to embrace skewed versions of the values revered by Europeans: messianic° and orthodox monotheism, territorial conquest, the accumulation of material wealth. In so doing, they provided a neat and precise contrast that, point by point, helped both groups define themselves (i.e., "this," not "that"). Throughout the Middle Ages, Europeans regarded rumored tales of a world beyond Granada or Cairo or Damascus, be they authored by Herodotus or Pliny, as odd to the point of science fiction and largely irrelevant to the daily lives of ordinary people.

This reassuring order suffered a severe blow when the first boatloads of Spanish and Portuguese sailors failed to topple off the edge of the world—pinpointed, predictably, just beyond the sight of Christendom's western shore —as they ventured far to the south and east. Verifying the immensity of Africa and the Orient, each continent bursting with undeniably non-European peoples and cultures, was traumatic enough news, yet not altogether a surprise. Alexander, after all, had been to India, and the spice route to Cathay° was well worn. But with the dramatic materialization of the Western Hemisphere, the dazzling implications of global heterogeneity could no longer be avoided.

The argument for the centrality of Europe was forced to alter its traditional rationalizations in order to account for all else that turned out to exist. An initial solution, analogous to that of the ostrich sticking its head into the sand at the first sign of trouble, was abject denial. If new data didn't fit into old orthodoxy, then it couldn't be accurate. Later as the diversity of humanity became increasingly manifest, the working definition of "true human being" became more rigid, more narrow, and long theological debates took place on

---

*messianic:* Idealistic, marked by a desire to convert, to remedy through action.    *Cathay:* Old name for China.

. . . . . . . . . . . . . . . . . . . . . . . . . . . . . . . . . . . . .

such esoterica° as whether or not natives of America and Australia even had souls.

30      This condescending approach was hard to maintain in the face of the intelligence and industry evident in New World cities, bountiful agriculture, science, art, and, especially, wealth reported by conquistadors° like Cortés and Pizarro. Indeed, the empire civilizations of Meso- and Latin America—those of the Aztec and Inca, especially—were probably easiest for Europeans to appreciate. Though the customs varied and the religions were unfamiliar to the early Spanish explorers, at least the motivating goals were recognizable: a thirst for conquest, the accumulation of wealth, a consolidation of political power in the hands of a single leader and his coterie.° The larger nation-states must have been reminiscent of Moorish analogs,° with their swarthy-looking populations, exploitable treasure, and grand capitals. Their wealth was obvious and marketable, their existing labor force was already organized and ready to be co-opted,° and their belief systems posed familiar challenges for Christian conversion.

Smaller, tribally based cultures of North America, on the other hand, must have struck Europeans as utterly bizarre upon first encounter. By and large these groups maintained no standing armies, practiced a mind-boggling variety of inordinately° flexible religions, were nonliterate, vague regarding the precise boundaries of their territory, and very often passed property and authority through a female line of descent. Few North American societies sought to impose ideology on neighboring cultures, insisting that the freedom of the individual predominated over the power of the state. Leadership tended to spring from expertise or proven ability rather than from dynastic heredity, and in any given tribe there might exist a multiplicity of "chiefs"— each a specialist in a limited arena of group life and none of them supreme over all others.

Furthermore, most native North American peoples considered land to be an abstract commodity similar in kind to air or water or fire—something necessary for human survival but above personal ownership. While the notion of a group or a person's rights to use a certain piece of property was widespread, there was almost no corresponding idea of "title," or land owned exclusively and permanently by those who didn't directly work it. Concepts of accumulation varied widely, from those who held all nonpersonal items in common, to

---

esoterica: Here meaning items not relevent to the general public.   conquistadors: Participants in the 16th century Spanish conquest of the Americas.   coterie: Intimate, exclusive group of people with a common interest.   analogs: Counterparts (things that are similar or analogous).   co-opted: Taken over, appropriated.   inordinately: Excessively.

• • • • • • • • • • • • • • • • • • • • • • • • • • • • • • • • • •

Northwest Coast "potlatch" societies like the Kwakiutl and Nootka where family status depended on formal giveaways of property—to the point of temporary impoverishment.

Armed conflict could occur between tribes, parts of tribes, or individuals for a variety of reasons, but usually the hostilities lasted no longer than a single season or encounter, and loss of life was minimal. As a rule, there was no insistence upon "total victory" or the complete annihilation of an enemy. Battles were fought for personal reasons—revenge, honor, or greed—and once these limited objectives had been achieved, the reason for a prolonged hostile action no longer existed. Last year's antagonists might be next year's hunting partners.

As competition with European invaders became increasingly intense, few indigenous societies mounted effective resistance, and those that did were soon vanquished°. Not only had most Native American cultures by and large failed to invent effective weaponry or support standing military forces, they were almost immediately devastated by an unseen foe that, according to some demographers, wiped out 95 percent of the precontact population. A pandemic° of diseases that had long existed in the Old World but never previously in the New—influenza, smallpox, measles, tuberculosis, and cholera prime among them—was inadvertently carried to the Western Hemisphere by the first European visitors, and in a matter of several generations virulent bacteria spread throughout the indigenous population. Often by the time the first Spanish or British arrived in the interior of the continents, most Indians were already dead, the straggling survivors traumatized and in despair. The lands that, in their naivete, some European chroniclers called "empty," were in fact only recently depleted of their previous inhabitants.

Early European explorers in America, continually confronted with the unexpected, soon began to seek the miraculous, as well as the familiar, in their journeys. They sent home reports of the Seven Golden Cities of Cibola, of fountains whose waters restored eternal youth, of warrior queens who rode upon giant armadillos. Feudal-type agricultural societies, like those of the Cherokee or Creek, were labeled "civilized," and those whose dress, customs, and lifestyles seemed most foreign were "savage."

Rather, they were simply "different," part of the mosaic of human possibility and potential, the laboratory of cultural experiment, that characterized the America of 1491. Collectively, its tribes offered legacies of tremendous

*vanquished:* Conquered, defeated.    *pandemic:* Here meaning "outbreak."

contribution to the contemporary world, from cultivated crops (corn, beans, squash, tomatoes, potatoes, manioc°) to political structures (models of representative government, gender equality) to philosophical approaches toward environmental conservation and peaceful coexistence. Many of the ideas and ideals first developed among its native peoples remain viable, sane options for a world that becomes, through technology, increasingly small, increasingly homogeneous. Diversity, that multifaceted reflection of human ingenuity, has become something of an endangered commodity—just when, perhaps, our stripped and exhausted planet needs it most.

Let us return, at last, to that hypothetical first meeting with which we began. In historical retrospect, is it unambiguously clear which group was "advanced," which was "primitive"? *Barbarous*—a term many Europeans and their Western Hemisphere descendants eventually used to describe Native American societies—is a relative, superficial designate, as it has been since the days when ancient Greeks judged the sophistication of foreigners on the basis of whether or not they grew beards. The Arawaks of the Caribbean never went to the moon or built a telephone, but they also never waged a war, never depleted the ozone layer with fluorocarbons. They were not saints, but neither were they devils. History remembers them most as beautiful, gentle, and impossible to enslave, not as conquerors or missionaries or industrialists.

Yes, the boys from the boat obviously fulfilled their ambitions: they "won." But in the long run, if we as a species delimit our imaginations, forget or lose touch with the thesaurus of our marvelously diversified past, did *we?*

In conclusion, the plaster stereotypes must be abandoned, not only because they are simplistic and ill informed, but more so because they are far less intellectually engaging, less interesting, less stimulating, and less challenging than the living, breathing, often exasperating, and always complicated reality.

### QUESTIONS

1. Do you agree with Dorris's assertion that "Our diversity, as a species, has always been our salvation"? Why or why not?
2. Explain why Dorris feels that the native inhabitants of the Western hemisphere were more aware of "the fact of cultural diversity" than their European counterparts.

*manioc:* Plant with a starchy edible root.

3. Why did the European "discoverers" consider most Native American tribes to be barbarous, according to Dorris?
4. What is your reaction to the creation myth that Dorris recounts in this essay?
5. Explain whether or not you agree with Dorris's analysis of the biblical story of creation (see paragraph 22).
6. Reread the last three paragraphs of this essay. Is the final paragraph necessary? What, if anything, does it add to the rest of the essay? Explain your response.

## CONNECTIONS

Reread the three paragraphs that follow the line "Our ancestors were too busy wresting a living from nature to go on any nature hikes," from P. J. O'Rourke's essay "The Greenhouse Affect" (included in Section 5). How would Michael Dorris respond to the points that O'Rourke makes in that passage?

# Issues in
# American Culture

# The Argumentative Essay:
# Convincing an Audience (The Clean Way . . .)

· · · · · · · · · · · · · · · · · · · · · · · · · · · ·

When you hear the word *argument,* you might think of a heated dispute between two people—about anything from balancing the federal budget to deciding which is the best college football team; the dispute seems unresolvable, and the participants seem piqued if not downright angry. Or you might recall Tobias Wolff's "Say Yes" (included in Section 3), which describes a quarrel that could result in a divorce. If you think of argumentation in this way, you are likely to want to avoid it.

But that isn't the only way to think of argumentation. In the context of effective argumentative writing, an argument is a balanced discussion of an issue. The goal is not to annihilate your opponents but to inform them about the varying perspectives on an issue and persuade them to agree with (or at least move closer to) your perspective. In writing an argumentative essay, you can control the terms, tone, and direction of the discussion, making it reasonable and fair rather than irrational and divisive.

Although the argumentative essay is usually treated as a special writing case, it really shouldn't be. Nearly all essays are by nature argumentative. Any time you state an opinion or write a thesis, you are creating an argumentative situation: Not all people will agree with your claim. An essay that pretends not to be argumentative is pretending that its thesis is absolute, that there is only one way to understand a situation; and so the reasons and evidence it offers in support of the thesis are likely to be biased, one-sided. In contrast, a good argumentative essay will make it clear that any thesis or claim is only one point of view among many. A good argumentative essay, then, will provide an overview of its subject; discuss at least two perspectives on that subject; support one of those views with sufficient reasons and evidence; and refute (answer or prove wrong) the other points of view, explaining why they are not as valid as the one that the essay is arguing for.

## *Finding Common Ground*
## *through the Introduction and Concessions*

Although your argumentative essay will refute most of the points raised by those who disagree with you, it should also reflect some common ground between the different positions. A "common ground" element is something on which you and your opponents can agree. Including such elements in your argument will make it easier for those who at first disagree with your claim to later move toward agreeing with you; it underscores the fact that there are bridges between two positions, that there are ways to find a compromise without "betraying your side." To establish common ground, try to find values that you and your audience share.

*Introductions*   If you write something offensive or biased in an introduction, people might just stop reading your essay, or at least might not consider its claim with an open mind. The introduction of an argumentative essay is a good place to establish some common ground with those who are about to disagree with you; think of an introduction as a handshake—not a stab.

If you were writing an essay in favor of the death penalty, for example, you wouldn't do well to begin by stating that all murderers should be fried in the electric chair. This would immediately lose the audience you most want to persuade—those who disagree with you. Instead, it would be more effective to stress the point that one human taking the life of another is wrong; people on both sides of the debate are likely to agree with you. Or, for another example, if you were to argue that Native Americans should have the right to consume peyote for religious purposes, you wouldn't want to begin by describing the hallucinogenic effects of the cacti. However, a description of a Catholic priest or a Jewish rabbi sipping wine during a religious ritual would give your audience a more familiar frame of reference into which to place the image of a Native American shaman ingesting peyote. Again, the point is to establish some common ground before you give your audience any reason to be skeptical about your argument.

*Concessions*   Once you have stated your claim, however, you can continue to establish common ground throughout the essay by making concessions. A concession is an acknowledgment of a good point in an argument made by those you otherwise disagree with. Consider the following examples of a concession. In her essay "The Obligation to Endure" (Section 5), Rachel Carson concedes that the earth has always contained elements hostile to life—that humans are not the only source of danger to themselves and to other animals and plants. Had she not stated this, her opponents would have done so, and this would have made her appear unwilling to accept limitations to her claim (that some substances created by humans pose great danger to all life on our planet). In turn, in his critique of Carson, Charles Rubin concedes that "there is no question that pesticides and herbicides can be extremely dangerous to human beings if misused or used carelessly."

Another example of a concession occurs in "The Conservative Case for Abortion" (included in this section), when Jerry Muller, who otherwise argues in support of legal abortion, states that "the right-to-life movement has done our society a service by insisting upon the humanity and moral worth of the unborn child." His next sentence begins with the word "but"—yet he has found some common ground with his opponents, without compromising his general claim.

## Supporting a Claim, Organizing an Argument

The claim of an argument is its thesis—the main idea or opinion that the essay is attempting to support. Like any other essay, an argumentative essay needs to flow well and to provide sufficient evidence to back up its claim.

*Support*   As you begin to plan your essay, make a list of the points you want to raise in support of your claim. Make a separate list of the reasons your opponents would offer for disagreeing with you. It's very important to be aware of the opposition's arguments; if you're not sure what they are, you should explore those positions either by talking to people or by doing some background reading. Once you have prepared the second list, you should try to answer (rebut) your opponents point by point, explaining why you disagree with them (yet keeping in mind that it's desirable to find some common ground).

The types of evidence used in an argumentative essay are no different from those used in any other essay; they include examples, anecdotes, quotations from experts, statistics, analogies, and so forth. For a discussion about using and documenting evidence, see "Research: Writing from Increased Knowledge," at the end of this section.

*Organization*   Once you have your prewriting lists, the issue of where to place the various points becomes an organizational question. Many writers choose to present their strongest ideas first and answer their opponents only at the end of their essays. Keep in mind, however, that unless you explain and either concede or refute early on the points raised by your opponents, you might create the impression that you are either biased or uninformed about other views; by the time you get around to dealing with the arguments of the opposition, you might find that impression hard to dispel. Better, then, to tackle your opponents' points from the beginning and to end with any additional points that go beyond the refutation.

If you do choose to refute your opponents first, should you list all their points and then all your answers, or should you follow each one of their points with your rebuttal? Our advice would be to do the latter, since presenting your opponents' entire position might give it some credibility that it wouldn't have if you pointed out the problems in each of its components, one by one.

## Language in Argument

In all essays, your choice of language impacts the clarity and the credibility of your views. In argumentative writing it's even more important to be precise and to avoid loaded words, particularly because some arguments depend on the meaning of a term.

*Defining Words*    At the beginning of this section, we explained what we mean by the term *argument:* not an emotional quarrel but a reasonable debate. Had we not defined our term, you might have thought that everything we have written so far about argumentation was very strange—after all, reasonable debate is *not* the technique that most people employ when they yell at each other about who got to a parking spot first! Defining your subject is therefore the key to having a reasonable argument. In the process, you will sometimes find that there *is* no disagreement; you and your "opponents" were simply talking about two different things.

For example, a student once asked an instructor whether she was a feminist. The instructor answered by asking the student to define the term. When he didn't, she explained, "If you mean am I a man-hater who thinks that women are the better gender, as some people define feminists, then—no. If you mean do I think that men and women should have the same opportunities to do anything they can do, should be paid equally when they perform the same job, and should share equally in family responsibilities, which is how I define the term, then—yes." The student seemed to be opposed to people who fit the first definition—but not those who fit the latter.

A similar situation might affect the controversy over affirmative action. Many of those who support affirmative action also firmly *oppose* quotas based on gender or race. Those who might have assumed these people to be "the enemy" in the fight against quotas may find that the argument dissolves—or takes a more interesting tack—once the two sides agree on a definition of "affirmative action."

Many of the writers included in this text take particular care to define concepts that are important to their thesis: Later in this section, for example, you will find essays that define terms like *fantasy, student athlete,* and *conservative.*

*Loaded Words*    At an art exhibit, once, a painter presented a white canvas with a single word printed on it in simple black letters. The word was *Jew.* What was the artist's message? That depends on how you read and understand the word. One thing the artist *was* therefore saying is that *Jew* is a loaded word.

A word's "load" consists not of its denotations—its explicit meanings—but of its connotations: all of the associations that it brings up in the mind of a user or a reader. For most people, words like *family, love,* and *freedom* carry positive loads; *fear, suicide,* and *war* bring up negative ones. What the word *religious* means to an atheist is different from what it means to a Christian, a Muslim, a Hindu, a Jew, or a believer of some other religion. Is *religious* synonymous with *moral* or *ethical?* Or does it mean "uneducated," "deceived," "exploited," describing a user of "the opiate of the masses," as Karl Marx defined religion? The load, the set of connotations carried by the word, derives from each person's background—from their life experiences and education.

Most words are loaded to some degree. Some have cultural loads; *capitalism,* for example, carries negative connotations in some countries and positive ones in others. Other words carry special personal connotations for members of smaller groups: *cat,* for example, may mean little more than a furry, four-legged animal to you, but to a cat lover it probably connotes much more. Finally, some words carry very personal loads in the vocabulary of particular individuals: For a teenager who nearly got trampled by a crowd at a rock concert, the word *crowd* or *concert* might bring up very different associations than it would for a person who'd had fun at such an event.

In the hands of speakers or writers who understand the power of language, loaded words can become dangerous ammunition. Words that suggest a particular load to people with a common cultural background can be used to manipulate those people. In the United States, a politician who calls an opponent a "communist," for example, is not just trying to tell the listeners that the opponent believes in communal ownership of property; the politician is trying to discredit the opponent by associating him or her with something that has negative connotations in the United States. In Eastern Europe, on the other hand, the term *landowner* makes some people uncomfortable even today, because the communist regimes had associated it for so long with greedy, overly rich exploiters of the poor. Or, to use an example from this section, Erling Jorstad's "Pluralism: Finding the Boundaries for Religious Freedom" attempts to define the term *cult;* as Jorstad explains, most of the definitions of the term carry negative connotations. Because of this, during the debates that followed the Waco incident, some people objected strongly to the Branch Davidians being referred to as a "cult."

Because connotations can strongly affect us, whether on a conscious or unconscious level, all users of language—in other words all human beings—need to be aware of the importance of careful word choice. Given that awareness, if people realize that someone is trying to manipulate them with loaded terms, they will probably become distrustful. If your goal is to persuade those who originally oppose your views but still keep the respect of those who are aware of the way language can be misused, you have to consider your words carefully.

## Avoiding Argumentative Deceit

In basketball a player can commit five personal fouls before being kicked out of the game—in essence for "unsportsmanlike conduct." In argumentation a single unethical argument made by a writer might cause a reader to dismiss an entire essay. The following are some common "fouls" in argumentation; you should avoid them in your own writing and point them out when you find them in other writers' presentations.

*Red Herring*   This foul is often committed by politicians: It is the strategy of ignoring a point that one cannot answer effectively and instead raising a different issue, simply to change the subject. Obviously, to a critical audience, a person using this "technique" will appear insincere and unprepared.

*Ad Hominem*   *Ad hominem,* Latin for "to the man or person," is an attack on the character of an opponent rather than an answer to the argument that the person is making. An ad hominem argument is often easy to identify; P. J. O'Rourke's essay "The Greenhouse Affect" (Section 5), for example, is sprinkled with ad hominem fallacies: People critical of the role that business plays in the environment are called "eco-doomsters"; people concerned about environmental degradation are called "fans of eco-Armageddon"; and, at one point, the author refers to a typical environmentalist as a "skinny health-food nut waving a copy of *50 Simple Things You Can Do to Save the Earth.*" Since O'Rourke's goal in this essay seems to be first to amuse and only secondly to persuade, he can allow himself to be offensive; obviously that would backfire in a serious attempt to persuade one's opponents.

However, an ad hominem argument isn't always so easy to spot. Charles Rubin (see Section 5) accuses Rachel Carson of using ad hominem arguments and "poisoning the well" (which essentially means the same thing: "smearing" the source of the argument instead of answering the argument itself) when she writes that the scientists who disagreed with her views were receiving money from big business. Clearly Carson's implication is that the scientists are not objective but are biased toward business interests. Rubin believes that Carson should have answered the objections raised by those scientists, rather than "smearing" the scientists' reputations. If these scientists were indeed sponsored by big business, however, is Carson wrong to mention it? The issue is not so clear-cut; however, an argument is always stronger if it focuses on an opponent's points rather than on his or her character.

*Strawperson*   Pretending to present an opponent's views, people sometimes paint an exaggerated, inaccurate picture in an attempt to refute the opposing position. This exaggerated depiction of an opponent is called a "strawperson." For example, as Ellen Goodman pointed out in one of her columns, to say that

Lorena Bobbitt (the woman who cut off her husband's penis and threw it away) represents the majority of U.S. feminists is to create a "straw opponent" instead of dealing with the average men and women who would describe themselves as feminists. Similarly, if you were to present Robert Jones's position from "A Modest Proposal: The Sequel" (included in Section 5) as a typical one for the average supporter of controlled human population growth, you would be attacking a strawperson—and those who advocate more moderate measures would note that you failed to refute their arguments.

## Avoiding Logical Fallacies

When people use loaded language or ad hominem arguments, they are usually well aware of what they are doing. In contrast, *logical fallacies*, or errors in reasoning, generally occur when people don't fully consider what they are saying (or writing). Following are explanations of the most common logical fallacies.

*Non Sequitur*   A *non sequitur* (Latin for "does not follow") is a conclusion that does not logically follow from a condition previously stated, or that is based on irrelevant evidence. In a sense, any fallacious reasoning is a non sequitur; however, the term is reserved for cases that include a completely illogical leap, a clear gap in reasoning. For example, if you were to say something like "Vegetables taste bad, so I am fat," you would be committing a non sequitur. Perhaps you meant that because you don't like vegetables you end up eating a lot of meat and bread and sweets, which make you fat; however, if you didn't spell that out, the gap in reasoning would confuse your audience. Or consider the non sequitur of a person who argues, "I do not deserve a ticket for speeding, officer; I've been a good driver all of my life and haven't had a speeding ticket in twenty-five years." The fact that a person has had a history of good driving does not mean that he or she should not be penalized for breaking a law.

*Faulty Analogy*   As Section 3 explained, an analogy points out a similarity between two distinct, complex relationships. Although an analogy is often an effective way to make a point, it does not *prove* anything. A faulty analogy occurs when someone assumes that two things that are alike in one way must necessarily be alike in another. Here's an example: During a heated discussion about the distribution of condoms on high school campuses, a student once asked, "How come a kid can't get an aspirin at school without a parent's permission but *can* get a condom without it?" To which another student answered, "If you don't take an aspirin once, you don't die. But if you don't use a condom once, you might." And there are many other ways in which aspirins and condoms are different . . . Using analogies in an argument can be persuasive—but it's usually easy to point out that their relevance is fairly limited.

*Post Hoc*    The name *post hoc* is abbreviated from the Latin *post hoc, ergo propter hoc,* which means "after the fact, therefore because of it." A post hoc argument is also known as faulty cause-and-effect reasoning. This occurs when someone mistakes a sequential relationship for a causal relationship. For example, some politicians are fond of pointing out that following the establishment of various welfare programs, the structure of the American family seems to be falling apart. They argue that welfare has caused that destruction; however, many other factors (or a combination of them) could have caused it, and simply saying that one followed the other is not the same as demonstrating that one *caused* the other.

A textual example of a post hoc argument occurs in Christine Gorman's essay "Sizing Up the Sexes" (included in Section 2). Gorman quotes Jerre Levy, who offers an anecdote about her fifteen-month-old daughter's flirtation as evidence that not all the differences between the sexes are caused by the environment. The sequential relationship between the aspects of the anecdote is clear and could be stated as "Levy's daughter was born female; Levy's daughter is very young; Levy's daughter flirts"; therefore, Levy suggests, females are inherently flirtatious. This reasoning, however, fails to consider a fact that Gorman discusses in her essay as well: that we have learned a lot from our environment by the time we are fifteen months old. Like a non sequitur, a post hoc argument leaves a gap in reasoning.

*Slippery Slope*    Like a post hoc fallacy, a slippery slope argument involves causal relationships. A slippery slope fallacy occurs when someone claims that if we take one action we will be forced to continue in that direction, as though we had stepped out onto a slippery incline and, unable to stop ourselves, would now slide down it uncontrollably. Slippery slope arguments, then, generally appeal to fear. Consider the following examples: "If the government takes away our right to own a gun, then it will soon take away all of our rights." "If we send troops to Bosnia, Somalia, Haiti, etc., then we will soon be in an all-out war." "If we ask welfare recipients to work, we'll end up creating poorhouses like those in nineteenth-century England." None of these statements is necessarily true; a writer would have to provide several cause-and-effect statements to explain how one step would lead to the other.

The argument becomes a slippery slope when we generalize, assuming that the possibility of slipping is true for everyone, and when we forget that steps taken in one direction can often be slowed down, stopped, or even reversed. ("Guy logic" hits a slippery slope, for example, in Dave Barry's essay

"Taking the Manly Way Out," when the author explains that a man who enjoys a date with a woman will end up thinking, "If she calls you, you'll go out again, and you'll probably have another great time, so you'll probably go out again and have *another* great time, and so on until the only possible *option* will be to get married.")

*Hasty Generalization*   A hasty generalization occurs when someone reaches a conclusion based on insufficient evidence. Maybe it rained the last time you washed your car, for example, but to conclude at that point that it will rain every time you wash your car would be to make a hasty generalization. One occurrence does not provide enough evidence for a reasonable conclusion.

In general, generalizations are problematic: If your claim is overly broad, as generalizations are, it can easily be proven wrong; one contradictory example will do it. Therefore, be careful to qualify, or limit, your claim; instead of claiming that all professional athletes are paid too much, say that *many* (maybe most) are overpaid; instead of claiming that the media present only negative images of African Americans, offer enough evidence to support the argument that the media *usually* do so.

If you use your personal experience in an argumentative essay, you need to back it up with further evidence, in order to avoid making a hasty generalization. Personal experience gives you additional authority in speaking about a subject, but it might represent an unusual situation. In "Being a Boy," for example, Julius Lester describes incidents from his childhood to demonstrate his claim that being a boy is difficult; however, if he had intended to write a formal argumentative essay, Lester would have had to back up his claim with other types of evidence as well.

*False Dilemma*   Posing a false dilemma is also known as the "either/or" fallacy. A false dilemma occurs when someone suggests that only two alternatives exist. For example, if in the previous paragraph we had stated that an author can either use *only* personal evidence in an essay or *no* personal experience at all, we would have been guilty of this fallacy—of not pointing out that other options are available. Similarly, if someone were to refer to the Aesop fable included in Section 4 of this text and argue that because the grasshopper starved we must all become ants, that person would be creating a false dilemma.

Another example of a false dilemma appears in the title of Martin Luther King, Jr.'s book *Chaos or Community: Where Do We Go from Here?* (which includes an essay that follows in this section). This title implies that we as a society have only two options: chaos or community; in reality, other possible alternatives exist. One could argue that the United States today appears to be somewhere in between chaos and community, in a sort of social limbo.

## Final Words

At the beginning of this section we stated that nearly all essays are by nature argumentative and, therefore, that you should consider the argumentative essay simply as a writing situation in which awareness of opposing views is heightened in order to explain better why *your* view is correct. A good argumentative essay will contain all the aspects of writing that we have discussed in this book—accurate and detailed language, effective organization, balanced and recurring ideas and images, strong introductions and conclusions, and so forth—but a good argumentative essay will also discuss various perspectives on an issue, provide evidence to support one of the perspectives, and refute the other ones.

The essays that follow in this section—some clearly argumentative, some not—should provide interesting starting points for argumentative essays of your own. There are many opinions on the subjects discussed under the title "Issues in American Culture"; we invite you to add your voice to the conversation. As Langston Hughes wrote in 1943, "America is a land in transition. And we know it is within our power to help in its further change toward a finer and better democracy than any citizen has known before."

# Letter to Peter Collinson, Member of Parliament for Weymouth

*Benjamin Franklin*

A diplomat, author, printer, scientist, and inventor, Benjamin Franklin (1706–1790) is one of those numbered among the Founding Fathers of the United States. As a politician, he signed the Declaration of Independence and negotiated with France and Great Britain on behalf of the newly formed government of the United States. Besides experimenting with electricity and lightning, Franklin invented bifocal eyeglasses, the efficient Franklin stove, and the lightning rod. Franklin also wrote prolifically; his works include numerous letters and pamphlets, scientific treatises, the long-lived *Poor Richard's Almanack,* and his own autobiography, *The Autobiography of Benjamin Franklin.* The following letter, written to his friend Peter Collinson on May 9, 1753, was first published by *Gentleman's Magazine* in January 1834, after Franklin's death.

**WARM-UP:** What is your position on the immigration issue? Are you concerned about the number of people now emigrating to the United States? Why or why not?

Philadelphia, May 9, 1753

Sir,

I thank you for the kind and judicious remarks you have made on my lit-   1
tle piece.° I have often observed with wonder that temper of the poorer English labourers which you mention, and acknowledge it to be pretty general. When any of them happen to come here, where labour is much better paid than in England, their industry seems to diminish in equal proportion. But it is not so with the German labourers: they retain the habitual industry and frugality° they bring with them, and receiving higher wages, an accumulation arises that makes them all rich. When I consider that the English are the offspring of Germans, that the climate they live in is much of the same temperature, when I see nothing in nature that should create this difference, I am tempted to suspect it must arise from constitution; and I have sometimes

---

*my little piece:* Apparently a reference to an earlier letter, now missing, from Franklin to Collinson.
*frugality:* Economy in the expenditure of resources.

doubted whether the laws peculiar to England, which *compel the rich to maintain the poor,* have not given the latter a dependence that very much lessens the care of providing against the wants of old age.

I have heard it remarked that the *poor* in *Protestant* countries, on the Continent of Europe, are generally more industrious than those of *Popish*° countries. May not the more numerous foundations in the latter for relief of the poor, have some effect towards rendering them less provident? To relieve the misfortunes of our fellow-creatures is concurring with the Deity,—it is god-like; but if we provide encouragement for laziness, and supports for folly, may it not be found fighting against the order of God and Nature, which perhaps has appointed want and misery as the proper punishments for, and cautions against, as well as necessary consequences of, idleness and extravagance? Whenever we attempt to amend the scheme of Providence, and to interfere with the government of the world, we had need be very circumspect, lest we do more harm than good. In New England they once thought *blackbirds* useless, and mischievous to the corn. They made efforts to destroy them. The consequence was, the blackbirds were diminished; but a kind of worm which devoured their grass, and which the blackbirds used to feed on, increased prodigiously;° then, finding their loss in grass much greater than their saving in corn, they wished again for their blackbirds.

We had here some years since a Transylvanian Tartar, who had travelled much in the East, and came hither merely to see the West, intending to go home through the Spanish West Indies, China, &c. He asked me one day, what I thought might be the reason that so many and such numerous nations, as the Tartars in Europe and Asia, the Indians in America, and the Negroes in Africa, continued a wandering, careless life, and refused to live in cities, and cultivate the arts they saw practised by the civilized parts of mankind? While I was considering what answer to make him, he said, in his broken English, "God make man for Paradise. He make him for live lazy. Man make God angry. God turn him out of Paradise, and bid workee. Man no love workee; he want to go to Paradise again; he want to live lazy. So all mankind love lazy." However this may be, it seems certain that the hope of becoming at some time of life free from the necessity of care and labour, together with fear of penury,° are the main springs of most people's industry.° To those, indeed, who have been educated in elegant plenty, even the provision made for the poor may appear misery; but to those who have scarce ever been better provided for, such provision may seem quite good and sufficient. These latter then have nothing to fear worse than their present condition, and scarce hope for any thing better than a parish maintenance. So that there is only the difficulty of

---

*Popish:* Roman Catholic.    *prodigiously:* Immensely, extraordinarily.    *penury:* Severe poverty.    *industry:* Diligent labor.

getting that maintenance allowed while they are able to work, or a little shame they suppose attending it, that can induce them to work at all; and what they do will only be from hand to mouth.

The proneness of human nature to a life of ease, of freedom from care and labour, appear strongly in the little success that has hitherto attended every attempt to civilize our American Indians. In their present way of living, almost all their wants are supplied by the spontaneous productions of nature, with the addition of very little labour, if hunting and fishing may indeed be called labour, where game is so plenty. They visit us frequently, and see the advantages that arts, sciences, and compact societies procure us. They are not deficient in natural understanding; and yet they have never shown any incli-nation to change their manner of life for ours, or to learn any of our arts. When an Indian child has been brought up among us, taught our language, and habituated to our customs, yet if he goes to see his relatives, and makes one Indian ramble with them, there is no persuading him ever to return. And that this is not natural to them merely as Indians, but as men, is plain from this, that when white persons, of either sex, have been taken prisoners by the Indians, and lived awhile with them, though ransomed by their friends, and treated with all imaginable tenderness to prevail with them to stay among the English, yet in a short time they become disgusted with our manner of life, and the care and pains that are necessary to support it, and take the first opportunity of escaping again into the woods, from whence there is no redeeming them. One instance I remember to have heard, where the person was brought home to possess a good estate; but finding some care necessary to keep it together, he relinquished it to a younger brother, reserving to himself nothing but a gun and a watch-coat, with which he took his way again into the wilderness.

*  *  *  *  *

So that I am apt to imagine that close Societies subsisting by labour and art, arose first not from choice but from necessity, when numbers being driven by war from their hunting-grounds, and prevented by seas, or by other nations, from obtaining other hunting-grounds, were crowded together into some narrow territories, which without labour could not afford them food. However, as matters now stand with us, care and industry seem absolutely necessary to our well-being. They should therefore have every encouragement we can invent, and not one motive to diligence be subtracted, and the support of the poor should not be by maintaining them in idleness, but by employing them in some kind of labour suited to their abilities of body, &c. as I am informed begins to be of late the practice in many parts of England, where workhouses are erected for that purpose. If these were general, I should think the poor would be more careful, and work voluntarily to lay up something for themselves against a rainy day, rather than run the risk of being obliged to work at the pleasure of others for a bare subsistence, and that too under confinement. The little value *Indians* set on what we prize so highly, under the name of learning, appears from a pleasant passage that happened some years since, at a treaty between some Colonies, and the Six Nations. When every thing had been settled to the satisfaction of both sides, and nothing remained but a mutual exchange of civilities, the English Commissioners told the Indians that they had in their country a college for the instruction of youth, who were there taught various languages, arts, and sciences; that there was a particular foundation in favour of the Indians to defray the expense of the education of any of their sons, who should desire to take the benefit of it: and said, if the Indians would accept the offer, the English would take half a dozen of their brightest lads, and bring them up in the best manner. The Indians, after consulting on the proposals, replied; that it was remembered that some of their youths had formerly been educated at that college, but that it had been observed that for a long time after they returned to their friends, *they were absolutely good for nothing;* being neither acquainted with the true methods of killing deer, catching beavers, or surprising an enemy. The proposition they looked on, however, as a mark of kindness, and good will of the English, to the Indian nations which merited a grateful return: and therefore, if the English gentlemen would send a dozen or two of their children to Opondago, the Great Council would take care of their education, bring them up in what was really the best manner, and make men of them.

I am perfectly of your mind that measures of great temper are necessary with the *Germans;* and am not without apprehensions that, through their indiscretion, or ours, or both, great disorders may one day arise among us. Those who come hither are generally the most stupid of their own nation, and as ignorance is often attended with credulity, when knavery° would mislead it; and with suspicion when honesty would set it right; and as few of the English understand the German language, and so cannot address them either from the press or the pulpit°, 'tis almost impossible to remove any prejudices they may entertain. Their clergy have very little influence on the people, who seem to take a pleasure in abusing and discharging the minister on every trivial occasion. Not being used to liberty, they know not how to make a modest use of it. And as Kolben says of the young Hottentots, that they are not esteemed men until they have shown their manhood by *beating their mothers,* so these seem not to think themselves free, till they can feel their liberty in abusing and insulting their teachers. Thus they are under no restraint from ecclesiastical° government; they behave, however, submissively enough at present to the *civil*

---

knavery: Dishonesty, trickery.    pulpit: Here referring to the church as an institution.    ecclesiastical: Church-related.

government, which I wish they may continue to do, for I remember when they modestly declined intermeddling in our *elections,* but now they come in droves and carry all before them,° except in one or two counties. Few of their children in the country know English. They import many books from Germany; and of the six printing-houses in the provinces, two are entirely German, two half German, half English, and but two entirely English. They have one German newspaper, and one half German. Advertisements intended to be general, are now printed in Dutch and English. The signs in our streets have inscriptions in both languages, and in some places only German. They begin of late to make all their bonds, and other legal instruments in their own language, which (though, I think, it ought not to be) are allowed good in our courts, where the German business so increases, that there is continued need of interpreters: and, I suppose, in a few years, they will also be necessary in the Assembly to tell one half of our legislators what the other half say. In short, unless the stream of their importation could be turned from this to other colonies, as you very judiciously propose, they will soon so outnumber us, that all the advantages we have, will, in my opinion, be not able to preserve our language, and even our government will become precarious. The French, who watch all advantages, are now themselves making a German settlement, back of us in the Illinois country, and by means of these Germans they may in time come to an understanding with ours; and, indeed, in the last war, our Germans showed a general disposition that seemed to bode us no good. For when the English, who were not Quakers, alarmed by the danger arising from the defenceless state of our country, entered unanimously into an association, and within this government and the low countries, raised, armed, and disciplined near ten thousand men, the Germans, except a very few in proportion to their number, refused to engage in it: giving out, one amongst another, and even in print, that if they were quiet, the French, should they take the country, would not molest them; at the same time abusing the Philadelphians for fitting out privateers° against the enemy: and representing the trouble, hazard, and expense of defending the province, as a greater inconvenience than any that might be expected from a change of government. Yet I am not for refusing to admit them entirely into our Colonies. All that seems to me necessary is, to distribute them more equally, mix them with the English, establish English schools, where they are now too thick settled: and take some care to prevent the practice lately fallen into by some of the ship-owners of sweeping the German gaols° to make up the number of their passengers. I say, I am not against the admission of Germans in general, for they have their virtues;—

---

*carry all before them:* Elect, as in "carry the election". *privateers:* Armed private ships hired to sail against an enemy. *gaols:* Jails.

their industry and frugality is exemplary. They are excellent husbandmen;° and contribute greatly to the improvement of a country.

I pray God to preserve long to Great Britain the English laws, manners, liberties, and religion. Notwithstanding the complaints so frequent in your public papers, of the prevailing corruption and degeneracy of the people, I know you have a great deal of virtue still subsisting among you; and I hope the Constitution is not so near a dissolution, as some seem to apprehend. . . .

### QUESTIONS

1. Who or what does Franklin blame for the lack of industriousness he perceives in English immigrants?
2. Explain in your own words what Franklin means by his statement, "God and Nature . . . perhaps has appointed want and misery as the proper punishments for, and cautions against, as well as necessary consequences of, idleness and extravagance." Do you agree with him? Explain your position.
3. Reread the analogy about the destruction of the blackbirds. Pay attention to its context in this letter. What is Franklin suggesting by that analogy?
4. According to Franklin, what are the "main springs of most people's industry"? Explain why you do or do not agree with him.
5. Franklin claims that most people's inclination is to secure "a life of ease." Do you agree? What are you doing to secure "a life of ease"?
6. What is Franklin's attitude toward Native Americans? Point to specific words in his letter to support your response.
7. Explain why Franklin is concerned about the pervasiveness of the German language in the colonies.
8. Of the various solutions proposed for dealing with the influx of German immigrants, which does Franklin support?
9. Does some of Franklin's reasoning about German immigrants seem similar to arguments you might hear today about legal and illegal immigration? If so, identify those arguments.
10. Do you believe that it's important for a country to have one common language in which the society functions? Why or why not?

### CONNECTIONS

1. Compare and contrast Franklin's views on welfare with those expressed by Andrew Carnegie (Section 4).

---

*husbandmen:* Farmers.

2. Does Franklin's letter support Michael Dorris's claims (from his essay "Discoveries") about how Native Americans were viewed by the Europeans who encountered them early in our history?

## "Graph: Number of Legal Immigrants Admitted to the United States Annually Since 1820"
from *World Book Encyclopedia,* 1997

**WARM-UP:** Do you feel that the United States should place stricter limits on the number of immigrants allowed into the country? Explain your answer.

**Number of legal immigrants admitted to the United States annually since 1820**

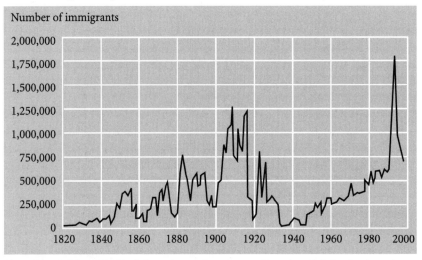

Figures from 1989 through 1992 include people granted permanent residence through the Immigration and Control Act of 1986. Source: U.S. Immigration and Naturalization Service. (Credit: From THE WORLD BOOK ENCYCLOPEDIA © 1997 World Book, Inc. By permission of the Publisher.)

| Year | Number of immigrants | Year | Number of immigrants |
|------|----------------------|------|----------------------|
| 1820 | 8,400 | 1920 | 430,000 |
| 1830 | 23,300 | 1930 | 241,700 |
| 1840 | 84,100 | 1940 | 70,800 |
| 1850 | 370,000 | 1950 | 249,200 |
| 1860 | 153,600 | 1960 | 265,400 |
| 1870 | 387,200 | 1970 | 373,300 |
| 1880 | 457,300 | 1980 | 530,600 |
| 1890 | 455,300 | 1990 | 1,536,500 |
| 1900 | 448,600 | 1995 | 720,500 |
| 1910 | 1,041,600 | | |

## QUESTIONS

1. What does the graph show about the number of immigrants who have entered the United States legally over time?

GRAPH    467

2. Are you familiar with the Immigration Reform and Control Act of 1986? If not, turn to a library for more information about it.
3. What are some of the arguments raised by people who feel that immigration into the United States should be severely restricted?
4. Are there specific conditions that people must meet today in order to be allowed to enter the United States as legal immigrants? Do some research to find out the most current information on this topic.

## CONNECTIONS

1. Based on Michael Dorris's essay (which introduces this section) and Benjamin Franklin's letter (which precedes this graph), how would you characterize the two authors' views on immigration?

# ～ The U.S. Declaration of Independence

*Thomas Jefferson*

The Continental Congress selected a committee of five people to write the document that would establish the United States as a nation. However, lawyer, architect, scientist, farmer, musician, educator, and philosopher Thomas Jefferson is credited with drafting the document, which required (revisions included) seventeen days to complete. Because some of his ideas (including a clause calling for the abolition of slavery) were not accepted by the committee, Jefferson had to revise the text several times to appease the committee and to persuade the Continental Congress to sign the document. That document, the Declaration of Independence, was adopted on July 4, 1776.

**WARM-UP:** The Declaration of Independence includes the famous phrase "all men are created equal." Explain what you believe the phrase means.

1   When in the Course of human events, it becomes necessary for one people to dissolve the political bands which have connected them with another, and to assume among the Powers of the earth, the separate and equal station to which the Laws of Nature and of Nature's God entitle them, a decent respect to the opinions of mankind requires that they should declare the causes which impel them to the separation.

We hold these truths to be self-evident, that all men are created equal, that they are endowed by their Creator with certain unalienable° Rights, that among these are Life, Liberty and the pursuit of Happiness. That to secure these rights, Governments are instituted among Men, deriving their just powers from the consent of the governed. That whenever any Form of Government becomes destructive of these ends, it is the Right of the People to alter or to abolish it, and to institute a new Government, laying its foundation on such principles and organizing its powers in such form, as to them shall seem most likely to effect their Safety and Happiness. Prudence, indeed, will dictate that Governments long established should not be changed for light and transient causes; and accordingly all experience hath shown, that mankind are more disposed to suffer, while evils are sufferable, than to right themselves by abolishing the forms to which they are accustomed. But when a long train of abuses and usurpations, pursuing invariably the same Object evinces° a design to reduce them under absolute Despotism,° it is their right, it is their

*unalienable:* Inalienable, incapable of being surrendered.   *evinces:* Displays clearly, reveals.   *Despotism:* Tyranny, unjust absolute power.

duty, to throw off such Government, and to provide new Guards for their future security.—Such has been the patient sufferance of these Colonies; and such is now the necessity which constrains them to alter their former Systems of Government. The history of the present King of Great Britain is a history of repeated injuries and usurpations,° all having in direct object the establishment of an absolute Tyranny over these States. To prove this, let Facts be submitted to a candid world.

He has refused his Assent to Laws, the most wholesome and necessary for the public good.

He has forbidden his Governors to pass Laws of immediate and pressing importance, unless suspended in their operation till his Assent should be obtained; and when so suspended, he has utterly neglected to attend to them.

He has refused to pass other laws for the accommodation of large districts of people, unless those people would relinquish the right of Representation in the Legislature, a right inestimable to them and formidable to tyrants only.

5

He has called together legislative bodies at places unusual, uncomfortable, and distant from the depository of their Public Records, for the sole purpose of fatiguing them into compliance with his measures.

He has dissolved Representative Houses repeatedly, for opposing with manly firmness his invasions on the rights of the people.

He has refused for a long time, after such dissolutions, to cause others to be elected; whereby the Legislative Powers, incapable of Annihilation°, have returned to the People at large for their exercise; the State remaining in the mean time exposed to all the dangers of invasion from without, and convulsions within.

He has endeavored to prevent the population of these States; for that purpose obstructing the Laws of Naturalization of Foreigners; refusing to pass others to encourage their migration hither, and raising the conditions of new Appropriations of Lands.

He has obstructed the Administration of Justice, by refusing his Assent to Laws for establishing Judiciary Powers.

10

He has made Judges dependent on his Will alone, for the tenure of their offices, and the amount and payment of their salaries.

He has erected a multitude of New Offices, and sent hither swarms of Officers to harass our People, and eat out their substance.

He has kept among us, in times of peace, Standing Armies without the Consent of our legislature.

He has affected to render the Military independent of and superior to the Civil Power.

---

*usurpations:* Wrongful seizures of property or authority.    *Annihilation:* Destruction, elimination.

15    He has combined with others to subject us to a jurisdiction foreign to our constitution, and unacknowledged by our laws; giving his Assent to their acts of pretended Legislation:

For quartering large bodies of armed troops among us:

For protecting them, by a mock Trial, from Punishment for any Murders which they should commit on the Inhabitants of these States:

For cutting off our Trade with all parts of the world:

For imposing taxes on us without our Consent:

20    For depriving us in many cases, of the benefits of Trial by Jury:

For transporting us beyond Seas to be tried for pretended offences:

For abolishing the free System of English Laws in a neighbouring Province, establishing therein an Arbitrary government, and enlarging its Boundaries so as to render it at once an example and fit instrument for introducing the same absolute rule into these Colonies:

For taking away our Charters, abolishing our most valuable Laws, and altering fundamentally the Forms of our Governments:

For suspending our own Legislatures, and declaring themselves invested with Power to legislate for us in all cases whatsoever.

25    He has abdicated Government here, by declaring us out of his Protection and waging War against us.

He has plundered our seas, ravaged our Coasts, burnt our towns, and destroyed the lives of our people.

He is at this time transporting large armies of foreign mercenaries to compleat the works of death, desolation and tyranny, already begun with circumstances of Cruelty & perfidy° scarcely paralleled in the most barbarous ages, and totally unworthy the Head of a civilized nation.

He has constrained our fellow Citizens taken Captive on the High Seas to bear Arms against their Country, to become the executioners of their friends and Brethren, or to fall themselves by their Hands.

He has excited domestic insurrections° amongst us, and has endeavored to bring on the inhabitants of our frontiers, the merciless Indian Savages, whose Known rule of warfare, is an undistinguished destruction of all ages, sexes and conditions.

30    In every stage of these Oppressions We have Petitioned for Redress° in the most humble terms: Our repeated Petitions have been answered only by repeated injury. A Prince, whose character is thus marked by every act which may define a Tyrant, is unfit to be the ruler of a free People.

Nor have We been wanting in attention to our British brethren. We have warned them from time to time of attempts by their legislature to extend an

---

*perfidy:* Treachery.    *insurrections:* Rebellions, revolts.    *Redress:* Compensation.

unwarrantable jurisdiction over us. We have reminded them of the circumstances of our emigration and settlement here. We have appealed to their native justice and magnanimity,° and we have conjured them by the ties of our common kindred to disavow these usurpations, which, would inevitably interrupt our connections and correspondence. They too have been deaf to the voice of justice and of consanguinity.° We must, therefore, acquiesce° in the necessity, which denounces our Separation, and hold them, as we hold the rest of mankind, Enemies in War, in Peace Friends.

We, therefore, the Representatives of the United States of America, in General Congress, Assembled, appealing to the Supreme Judge of the world for the rectitude° of our intentions, do, in the Name, and by Authority of the good People of these Colonies, solemnly publish and declare, That these United Colonies are, and of Right ought to be Free and Independent States, that they are Absolved from all Allegiance to the British Crown, and that all political connection between them and the State of Great Britain, is and ought to be totally dissolved; and that as Free and Independent States, they have full Power to levy War, conclude Peace, contract Alliances, establish Commerce, and to do all other Acts and Things which Independent States may of right do. And for the support of this Declaration, with a firm reliance on the Protection of Divine Providence, we mutually pledge to each other our Lives, our Fortunes and our sacred Honor.

### QUESTIONS

1. What is the effect of the first paragraph of this document? Is it an effective introduction? Why or why not?
2. What are the "Laws" referred to in "the Laws of Nature and of Nature's God"?
3. According to this declaration, what is the reason for the existence of governments? And from what do governments derive their "just powers"?
4. Explain the authors' comments regarding immigration to the colonies.
5. Of the "Facts" listed (in paragraphs 3 to 29) to support the colonies' decision to establish an independent government, do any resemble criticisms you have heard about the United States' present government?

---

*magnanimity:* Ability to reject cruelty and revenge, and to make sacrifices for worthy ends.  *consanguinity:* A close relation or connection.  *acquiesce:* Accept or comply passively.  *rectitude:* Moral integrity.

6. What is the overall tone of the piece? Are there any places where the tone changes? If so, where?

7. How aware of its audience is the Declaration? Whom does the Declaration address? Do you think that the Declaration affected all the members of its audience in the same way?

8. Are the arguments of the opposition (those who wanted the colonies to remain British) presented? Should they have been? Must an argument such as this one be inclusive? Why or why not?

9. Does the Declaration contain any concessions? If so, identify one.

10. Reread the last sentence of the Declaration. Does the pledge it refers to still apply today? Should it?

11. The United States Constitution, drafted in 1787 and put into effect in 1789, established the newly independent country's laws and government. Although amended after the Civil War, the original article 1, section 2, clause 3 of the Constitution read:

> Representatives and direct Taxes shall be apportioned among the several States which may be included within this Union, according to their respective Numbers, which shall be determined by adding to the whole Number of free Persons, including those bound to Service for a Term of Years, and excluding Indians not taxed, three fifths of all other Persons.

The 1840 publication of James Madison's notes on the debates from the Constitutional Convention of 1787 revealed that the euphemism "all other Persons" referred to slaves. Now reread the "Warm-up" you wrote for this reading. Does your knowledge about the "three fifths" clause support or contradict your interpretation of the famous phrase "all men are created equal"? Explain your answer.

## CONNECTIONS

1. Does the Declaration address any issues or concerns brought up by Benjamin Franklin in his letter to Peter Collinson written twenty-three years earlier? If so, which ones?

2. Compare the views about Native Americans reflected in the Declaration with those discussed in Michael Dorris's "Discoveries."

# Declaration of Sentiments and Resolutions

## Elizabeth Cady Stanton

One of the first activists for women's rights in the United States, Elizabeth Cady Stanton (1815–1902) was educated at New York's Johnstown Academy, an institution for males to which she was admitted under special arrangement. Stanton studied law but was later denied admission to the New York Bar because of her gender. In the face of such prejudice, Stanton dedicated her life to the abolition of laws that denied women equal rights. In 1848, Stanton and Lucretia Mott helped to organize the Seneca Falls Convention (where Stanton read the following declaration). Then Stanton formed a close partnership with Susan B. Anthony to work for women's suffrage. Stanton's other work includes *A Woman's Bible* (1895), the three-volume *History of Woman's Suffrage* (1896), and her autobiographical *Eighty Years and More* (1898).

**WARM-UP:** When you hear the term "women's movement," what do you think of? What do you believe it stands for? When do you believe the women's movement originated?

When, in the course of human events, it becomes necessary for one portion of the family of man to assume among the people of the earth a position different from that which they have hitherto occupied, but one to which the laws of nature and of nature's God entitle them, a decent respect to the opinions of mankind requires that they should declare the causes that impel them to such a course.

We hold these truths to be self-evident: that all men and women are created equal; that they are endowed by their Creator with certain inalienable° rights; that among these are life, liberty, and the pursuit of happiness; that to secure these rights governments are instituted, deriving their just powers from the consent of the governed. Whenever any form of government becomes destructive of these ends, it is the right of those who suffer from it to refuse allegiance to it, and to insist upon the institution of a new government, laying its foundation on such principles, and organizing its powers in such form, as to them shall seem most likely to effect their safety and happiness. Prudence, indeed, will dictate that governments long established should not be changed for light and transient causes; and accordingly all experience hath shown that mankind are more disposed to suffer, while evils are sufferable, then to right

1

---

*inalienable:* Incapable of being surrendered or transferred.

themselves by abolishing the forms to which they were accustomed. But when a long train of abuses and usurpations, pursuing invariably the same object evinces a design to reduce them under absolute despotism, it is their duty to throw off such government, and to provide new guards for their future security. Such has been the patient sufferance of the women under this government, and such is now the necessity which constrains them to demand the equal station to which they are entitled.

The history of mankind is a history of repeated injuries and usurpations on the part of man toward woman, having in direct object the establishment of an absolute tyranny over her. To prove this, let facts be submitted to a candid world.

He has never permitted her to exercise her inalienable right to the elective franchise.

5      He has compelled her to submit to laws, in the formation of which she had no voice.

He has withheld from her rights which are given to the most ignorant and degraded men—both natives and foreigners.

Having deprived her of this first right of a citizen, the elective franchise, thereby leaving her without representation in the halls of legislation, he has oppressed her on all sides.

He has made her, if married, in the eye of the law, civilly dead.

He has taken from her all right in property, even to the wages she earns.

10     He has made her, morally, an irresponsible being, as she can commit many crimes with impunity,° provided they be done in the presence of her husband. In the covenant of marriage, she is compelled to promise obedience to her husband, he becoming, to all intents and purposes, her master—the law giving him power to deprive her of her liberty, and to administer chastisement.

He has so framed the laws of divorce, as to what shall be the proper causes, and in case of separation, to whom the guardianship of the children shall be given, as to be wholly regardless of the happiness of women—the law, in all cases, going upon a false supposition of the supremacy of man, and giving all power into his hands.

After depriving her of all rights as a married woman, if single, and the owner of property, he has taxed her to support a government which recognizes her only when her property can be made profitable to it.

He has monopolized nearly all the profitable employments, and from those she is permitted to follow, she receives but a scanty remuneration.° He closes against her all the avenues to wealth and distinction which he considers

---

*impunity:* Exemption from punishment or harm.    *remuneration:* Payment.

most honorable to himself. As a teacher of theology, medicine, or law, she is not known.

He has denied her the facilities for obtaining a thorough education, all colleges being closed against her.

He allows her in Church, as well as State, but a subordinate position, claiming Apostolic authority° for her exclusion from the ministry, and, with some exceptions, from any public participation in the affairs of the Church.

He has created a false public sentiment by giving to the world a different code of morals for men and women, by which moral delinquencies which exclude women from society, are not only tolerated, but deemed of little account in man.

He has usurped° the prerogative of Jehovah himself, claiming it as his right to assign for her a sphere of action, when that belongs to her conscience and to her God.

He has endeavored, in every way that he could, to destroy her confidence in her own powers, to lessen her self-respect, and to make her willing to lead a dependent and abject° life.

Now, in view of this entire disfranchisement of one-half the people of this country, their social and religious degradation—in view of the unjust laws above mentioned, and because women do feel themselves aggrieved,° oppressed, and fraudulently deprived of their most sacred rights, we insist that they have immediate admission to all the rights and privileges which belong to them as citizens of the United States.

In entering upon the great work before us, we anticipate no small amount of misconception, misrepresentation, and ridicule; but we shall use every instrumentality within our power to effect our object. We shall employ agents, circulate tracts, petition the State and National legislatures, and endeavor to enlist the pulpit° and the press in our behalf. We hope this Convention will be followed by a series of Conventions embracing every part of the country.

## Resolutions

Whereas, The great precept of nature is conceded to be, that "man shall pursue his own true and substantial happiness." Blackstone in his Commentaries° remarks, that this law of Nature being coeval° with mankind, and dictated by God himself, is of course superior in obligation to any other. It is

---

*Apostolic authority:* Spiritual authority derived from the example of the apostles.    *usurped:* Unjustly taken over.    *abject:* Miserable, degrading.    *aggrieved:* Suffering from an infringement or denial of rights.    *pulpit:* Here referring to the clergy and the church as an institution.    *Blackstone in his Commentaries:* Sir William Blackstone (1723–1780) described the history of English law in his book *Commentaries on the Laws of England.*    *coeval:* Of the same or equal age or duration.

binding over all the globe, in all countries and at all times; no human laws are of any validity if contrary to this, and such of them as are valid, derive all their force, and all their validity, and all their authority, mediately and immediately, from this original; therefore,

*Resolved,* That such laws as conflict, in any way, with the true and substantial happiness of woman, are contrary to the great precept° of nature and of no validity, for this is "superior in obligation to any other."

*Resolved,* That all laws which prevent woman from occupying such a station in society as her conscience shall dictate, or which place her in a position inferior to that of man, are contrary to the great precept of nature, and therefore of no force or authority.

*Resolved,* That woman is man's equal—was intended to be so by the Creator, and the highest good of the race demands that she should be recognized as such.

25

Resolved, That the women of this country ought to be enlightened in regard to the laws under which they live, that they may no longer publish their degradation by declaring themselves satisfied with their present position, nor their ignorance, by asserting that they have all the rights they want.

*Resolved,* That inasmuch as man, while claiming for himself intellectual superiority, does accord to woman moral superiority, it is preeminently° his duty to encourage her to speak and teach, as she has an opportunity, in all religious assemblies.

*Resolved,* That the same amount of virtue, delicacy, and refinement of behavior that is required of woman in the social state, should also be required of man, and the same transgressions should be visited with equal severity on both man and woman.

*Resolved,* That the objection of indelicacy and impropriety,° which is so often brought against woman when she addresses a public audience, comes with a very ill-grace from those who encourage, by their attendance, her appearance on the stage, in the concert, or in feats of the circus.

*Resolved,* That woman has too long rested satisfied in the circumscribed limits which corrupt customs and a perverted application of the Scriptures have marked out for her, and that it is time she should move in the enlarged sphere which her great Creator has assigned her.

30

Resolved, That it is the duty of the women of this country to secure to themselves their sacred right to the elective franchise.

*Resolved,* That the equality of human rights results necessarily from the fact of the identity of the race in capabilities and responsibilities.

---

*precept:* Principle intended as a general rule.   *preeminently:* Predominantly, primarily.   *impropriety:* An improper or indecorous act or remark.

*Resolved therefore,* That, being invested by the Creator with the same capabilities, and the same consciousness of responsibility for their exercise, it is demonstrably the right and duty of woman, equally with man, to promote every righteous cause by every righteous means; and especially in regard to the great subjects of morals and religion, it is self-evidently her right to participate with her brother in teaching them, both in private and in public, by writing and by speaking, by any instrumentalities proper to be used, and in any assemblies proper to be held; and this being a self-evident truth growing out of the divinely implanted principles of human nature, any custom or authority adverse to it, whether modern or wearing the hoary° sanction of antiquity, is to be regarded as a self-evident falsehood, and at war with mankind.

[At the last session Lucretia Mott offered and spoke to the following resolution:]

*Resolved,* That the speedy success of our cause depends upon the zealous and untiring efforts of both men and women, for the overthrow of the monopoly of the pulpit, and for the securing to woman an equal participation with men in the various trades, professions, and commerce.

## QUESTIONS

1. What position does Stanton take in the introduction?
2. Identify the line where Stanton first mentions women. Explain whether the lines preceding it suggest that Stanton was referring to the condition of women.
3. What does Stanton claim in the third paragraph? Explain whether she provides supporting evidence for this claim in the declaration.
4. Which, if any, of the "facts" listed (in paragraphs 4 through 18) remain facts today?
5. Does Stanton provide evidence to support the claim that women are equal to men? Does she refute the claim that men are superior to women? Should she have done either?
6. What does the additional resolution in the final paragraph, contributed by Lucretia Mott, bring to this argument?
7. Many citizens of this country have never heard of Elizabeth Cady Stanton and the Seneca Falls Convention. Did you learn about them in any history courses you've taken? Do you think they should be discussed in such courses? Why or why not?

---

*hoary:* Gray or white with age.

**CONNECTIONS**

1. Reread the *New York Herald* editorial (from Section 2). Explain whether or not the editorial effectively refutes Stanton's "Declaration."
2. Why did Stanton model her "Declaration of Sentiments and Resolutions" after the United States' Declaration of Independence? How precisely does Stanton follow the Declaration of Independence?

# ∽ Genetic Labeling and the Old Eugenics

## *Ruth Hubbard and Elija Wald*

> Ruth Hubbard was born in 1924. She is Professor of Biology Emerita at
> Harvard University and serves on the boards of directors of the Council for
> Responsible Genetics and the Massachusetts chapter of the American Civil
> Liberties Union. She has published several books, including *The Politics of
> Women's Biology* (1990); the following selection comes from her book
> *Exploding the Gene Myth: How Genetic Information Is Produced and Manipu-
> lated by Scientists, Physicians, Employers, Insurance Companies, Educators,
> and Law Enforcers* (1993). The coauthor of the book, Elija Wald, is a free-
> lance writer and musician.

> **WARM-UP:** Some people see the new advance in genetics as an oppor-
> tunity to control and perhaps eliminate human illnesses and the associ-
> ated misery that they cause; other people fear that our knowledge of
> genetics will be used to discriminate against some of us. In which direc-
> tion do you tend to lean? Do you see improved understanding of genetic
> influences as a positive or a negative development?

## The Birth of Eugenics

A desire to understand the present and foresee the future has existed in vir-    1
tually all cultures. People have consulted shamans, oracles, priests,
witches, or astrologers, whose diagnostic tools range from direct heavenly
communications to the interpretation of dreams, tea leaves, or the movements
of the stars.

Most such soothsayers° spend their lives supporting the status quo. A
prophet who promises the wealthy that their future will be miserable is not
going to have a pleasant or lucrative career. One who harps on social injustices
or the virtues of the poor is considered a fool or a dangerous agitator. Every
royal court has had its magicians and prophets, and they have spent most of
their time telling the king that he is singularly well favored by the stars and
will go down in history as an exemplary° monarch.

With the rise of the merchant classes and the scientific renaissance, the
power of kings and magicians went into decline, and the industrial revolution
put them virtually out of business. The early industrial barons believed in reason and cold, hard facts. Yet, like the kings before them, they were not interested in hearing bad news. Now, science was used to explain that those on top

---

*soothsayer:* Prophets, fortune-tellers.    *exemplary:* Ideal, worthy of serving as an example.

of the heap were there because of their innate superiority to the masses, who were on the bottom because they were of inferior stock.

A fine example of using of science to explain social status can be seen in the following paragraph from *Heredity in Relation to Eugenics*, published in 1913 by Charles Benedict Davenport, a professor of biology at Harvard and later at the University of Chicago:

> Pauperism is a result of complex causes. On one side it is mainly environmental in origin as, for instance, in the case when a sudden accident, like death of the father, leaves a widow or family of children without means of livelihood, or a prolonged disease of the wage earner exhausts savings. But it is easy to see that in these cases heredity also plays a part; for the effective worker will be able to save enough money to care for his family in case of accident; and the man of strong stock will not suffer from prolonged disease. Barring a few highly exceptional conditions poverty means relative inefficiency and this in turn usually means mental inferiority.[1]

5    Hereditarianism produced beautifully self-fulfilling prophecies. Anyone who succeeded was, ipso facto,° a superior person. Since the children of the wealthy and educated usually turn out to be wealthy and educated, while the children of the poor tend to remain poor, it was quite clear to hereditarians that talent ran in the family. As for the social and natural scientists who produced the body of hereditarian theory, they were not only demonstrating the worthiness of their patrons but also proving their own superiority over the backward peoples who had failed to create the wonders of modern science.

The term *eugenics*, which means "wellborn," was coined in 1883 by Francis Galton, who came from a distinguished British upper-class family and was a cousin of Charles Darwin. Galton wrote that he invented it in order to have "a brief word to express the science of improving the stock, which is by no means confined to questions of judicious° mating, but which, especially in the case of man, takes cognizance° of all the influences that tend in however remote a degree to give the more suitable races or strains of blood a better chance of prevailing speedily over the less suitable than they otherwise would have had."[2] Given that Galton had little doubt about who represented "the more suitable races or strains of blood," class and race biases were there from the start of the eugenics movement. Galton later helped to found the English Eugenics Society and became its honorary president.

Many people have come to associate eugenic thinking with political conservatism because the early British and American eugenicists tended to be

*ipso facto:* Latin, meaning "by the very nature of the case."  *judicious:* Discreet, wise.  *cognizance:* Awareness.

conservative and incorporated their class, race, and imperialist° biases into the scientific and political programs of the eugenics movement. But, particularly when we come to look at contemporary hereditarian and eugenic thinking in the next chapter, it is important to remember that support for eugenics has come from across the political spectrum. In the nineteenth century, not only conservative followers of the Reverend Thomas Malthus but also progressives and liberal believers in meritocracy° believed that eugenics held promise for human betterment.

In 1912, near the start of a long career as a geneticist, Hermann J. Muller wrote: "The intrinsic° interest of these questions [about heredity] is matched by their extrinsic importance, for their solution would help us to predict the characteristics of offspring yet unborn and would ultimately enable us to modify the nature of future generations."[3] Muller was a politically progressive idealist, who tried to emigrate to the Soviet Union in the early 1930s because he wanted to help build a better world.

Until World War II, many distinguished biologists and social scientists in Great Britain and the United States supported eugenics, or at least did not express their opposition to it. As late as 1941, when eugenic extermination practices were in full force in Nazi Germany, the distinguished British biologist Julian Huxley—brother of Aldous Huxley, the author of *Brave New World* —wrote an article called "The Vital Importance of Eugenics," which begins: "Eugenics is running the usual course of many new ideas. It has ceased to be regarded as a fad, is now receiving serious study, and in the near future will be regarded as an urgent practical problem."[4] Later in the article, he argued that society must "ensure that mental defectives shall not have children." In a not unusual blurring of eugenic and economic considerations, he defined as mentally defective "someone with such a feeble mind that he cannot support himself or look after himself unaided."

Huxley hesitated to prescribe whether "racial degeneration" should be counteracted by "prohibition of marriage" or by "segregation in institutions" combined with "sterilization for those who are at large," but he stated as though it were an established fact that most "mental defects" are hereditary. Actually, though most instances of mental retardation among the middle and upper classes have a genetic component, this is not the case among poor people, where inadequate nutrition and prenatal care, lead poisoning, and substandard school systems play a considerable part.[5]

Like Muller, Huxley did not limit his concern to those persons who were demonstrably afflicted with "mental defects." He looked forward to a future

10

*imperialist:* One who advocates one nation extending or imposing political, economic, and social control over another nation.   *meritocracy:* A system that rewards those who are most talented or capable. *intrinsic:* Characteristic or belonging to the essential nature of something.

when it would become possible "to diagnose the carriers of the defect [who are] apparently normal," since "if these could but be detected, and then discouraged or prevented from reproducing, mental defects could very speedily be reduced to negligible proportions among our population."

It is shocking to realize that at the very moment when the Nazis were sterilizing and killing adults and children who had been diagnosed as disabled or mentally ill, Huxley could voice regret that it was "very difficult to envisage° methods for putting even a limited constructive program [of eugenics] into effect . . . due as much to difficulties in our present socioeconomic organization as to our ignorance of human heredity, and most of all to the absence of a eugenic sense in the public at large."

Huxley was by no means alone. Eugenics societies on both sides of the Atlantic were organizing "eugenic fairs" to educate the public about the menace of inherited defects, and warning the upper classes about the dangers of "class suicide" because they were having too few children while poor people were having too many.

European eugenicists tended to be preoccupied with class differences, but in the United States ethnic and racial concerns were at the top of the agenda. Lewis Terman, one of the principal engineers and advocates of IQ testing, expressed some of these in an article he published in 1924, in which he worried that

> the fecundity° of the family stocks from which our most gifted children come appears to be definitely on the wane. . . . It has been figured that if the present differential birth rate continues 1,000 Harvard graduates will, at the end of 200 years, have but 56 descendants, while in the same period, 1,000 South Italians will have multiplied to 100,000.[6]

## Genetic Labeling

15    To formulate eugenic policies, it is necessary first to label certain physical or mental traits and social behaviors as aberrant° and then to assume that they are transmitted biologically from parents to their children. Such labels can easily be exploited for ideological and political ends. An extreme example is the invention of *drapetomania,* a hereditary mental disease said to be prevalent among black slaves in the South, which manifested itself in an irresistible urge to run away from their masters.

There was no evidence whatsoever for the biological nature or genetic transmission of many of the traits that eugenicists said were inherited. Take the label "feebleminded." Class, race, ethnic, and linguistic differences have

---

*envisage:* Envision.    *fecundity:* Quality of being fruitful.    *aberrant:* Deviating from the norm.

often led to people's, and especially children's, mental capacities being judged lower than average. Many instances of slow or arrested mental development have their origins in infectious diseases or physical, psychological, or social traumas and hence are not inherited biologically, though members of the same family may share them because they share these experiences.

When we come to such labels as "alcoholism" or "pauperism°," difficulties of assigning causes are compounded by problems of description and definition. How much does one have to drink to be an alcoholic? How poor does one have to be, and for how long, before one is a pauper?

Even where diagnosis is relatively unambiguous, the eugenic approach only confuses and obscures the issues. In the early part of this century, *pellagra*, a chronic condition characterized by skin eruptions, digestive and nervous disturbances, and eventual mental deterioration, reached epidemic proportions in parts of the southern United States. Many people believed it to be infectious in origin, like syphilis. Charles Davenport and his colleagues agreed, but argued that by virtue of genetic predisposition pellagra is acquired preferentially by certain kinds of people. With uncanny precision, Davenport specified that "when both parents are susceptible to the disease, at least 40 percent, probably not far from 50 percent, of their children are susceptible."[7]

Around the same time Joseph Goldberger, an American epidemiologist,° showed that pellagra results front a lack of a vitamin found in grains and fresh vegetables, which he called the *pellegra preventive* (or *PP) factor*. His PP-factor was later renamed nicotinamide or niacin and identified as a member of the vitamin B complex. Though Goldberger published his findings in 1916, nutrition programs that could have prevented many cases of pellagra were not instituted until the beginning of the New Deal, in 1933. The conservative Republican administrations of the 1920s, averse to spending money on health and nutrition, were supported in their inertia° by the assertions of Davenport's adherents that pellagra was hereditary and could not be remedied by social programs.

The old eugenics reached its ultimate extreme in the Nazi extermination programs. Initially, these were directed against the same sorts of people eugenicists had targeted in Great Britain and the United States—people labeled as having physical or mental disabilities. Later, these programs were expanded to include Jews, homosexuals, Gypsies, Eastern European "Slavs," and other "inferior" types.

The Nazis referred to their procedures as "selection and eradication," to emphasize that they were doing nothing random or haphazard. They were proud of the fact that the exterminations were scientifically planned and carried out and that, even in the death camps, "eradication" was always preceded by "selection."

20

*pauperism:* Poverty.   *epidemiologist:* Scientist who studies diseases.   *inertia:* Reluctance to move or change.

The theoretical underpinnings of the Nazi extermination programs, and the enthusiastic sponsorship and support they received from German geneticists, anthropologists, psychiatrists, and other members of the so-called healing professions, have been described in grisly detail by Stephan Chorover,[8] Robert J. Lifton,[9] Benno Müller-Hill,[10] and Robert Proctor.[11] It is important to realize that the Nazis drew directly on eugenic arguments and programs developed by scientists and politicians in Great Britain and the United States. They just made these policies more inclusive and implemented them more decisively than British and American eugenicists may have intended.

In the United States, Charles Davenport was one of the most active supporters of eugenics. He persuaded the Carnegie Institution of Washington, D.C. to set up the Station for the Experimental Study of Evolution at Cold Spring Harbor on Long Island and became its first director in 1904. Part of the station's mission was to organize a central data bank in which to store genetic information on large numbers of individuals. In 1910, with funding from John D. Rockefeller, Jr. and from Mrs. E. H. Harriman, an heiress to the Harriman railroad fortune, Davenport opened the Eugenics Record Office at Cold Spring Harbor. He appointed Harry W. Laughlin, a Princeton Ph.D., as its superintendent, and recruited graduates of Radcliffe, Vassar, and the Ivy League schools to go and interview large numbers of so-called mental and social defectives.

Trained for a few weeks, in courses offered at Cold Spring Harbor and at a comparable institution administered by the psychologist Henry H. Goddard at Vineland, New Jersey, these upper-class field-workers descended on poor communities in New York and New Jersey. Despite their scant training, and the class and ethnic differences between themselves and their subjects, the field-workers were considered competent to diagnose, by sight alone, such varied "hereditary" conditions as "dementia°," "shiftlessness," "criminalism," and "feeblemindedness."[12] After identifying a range of "mental defects," they turned these "data" into pedigree charts and scientific reports.

25    Despite the apparent vagueness of the terminology, Davenport and his associates felt that they could categorize these conditions with mathematical precision. For instance, with reference to "shiftlessness," Davenport wrote:

> Let us take "shiftlessness" as an important element in poverty. Then classifying all persons in . . . two families as very shiftless, somewhat shiftless, and industrious the following conclusions are reached. When both parents are *very* shiftless practically all children are "very shiftless" or "somewhat shiftless." Out of 62 offspring, 3 are . . . "industrious" or about 5 per cent. When both parents are shiftless in some degree about 15 per cent of

---

*dementia:* Mental illness.

the known offspring are recorded as industrious. When one parent is more or less shiftless while the other is industrious only about 10 per cent of the children are "very shiftless." It is probable that . . . shiftlessness . . . [is] due to the absence of something which can be got back into the offspring only by mating with industry°.[13]

Despite the shoddiness of this science, Davenport's Eugenics Record Office and its staff were major resources for the two legislative programs that became cornerstones of U.S. eugenic policies: the involuntary sterilization laws and the Immigration Restriction Act of 1924.

## Involuntary Sterilization

Following Galton's original suggestions, eugenics programs were of two kinds, positive and negative. Positive eugenics was intended to encourage the "fit" (read: healthy, successful, well-to-do) to have many children. Negative eugenics was meant to prevent the "unfit" (an extremely elastic category) from having any.

Laughlin and Davenport favored the sterilization of people they referred to as "hereditary paupers, criminals, feebleminded, tuberculous, shiftless, ne'er-do-wells,"[14] but they did not originate the notion. As early as 1897, the Michigan legislature considered—and defeated—a bill to sterilize people of "bad heredity." A subsequent, compulsory sterilization bill, aimed at "idiots and imbecile children," was passed by the Pennsylvania legislature in 1905, but vetoed by Governor Samuel Pennypacker with the strong message that it was not only "illogical" but "violates the principles of ethics."[15] The first compulsory° sterilization law that was actually enacted passed the Indiana legislature in 1907. But even before that, in 1899, a Dr. Harry Sharp began to perform involuntary vasectomies at the Indiana State Reformatory at Jeffersonville on inmates whom he judged to be "hereditary criminals" or "otherwise genetically defective."[16]

The British geneticist J. B. S. Haldane, in his *Heredity and Politics,* gives an example of the standards used to make such judicial determinations. He quotes a Judge G. B. Holden of the superior Court in Yakima County, Washington, as follows:

On January 30, 1922, John Hill pleaded guilty to the crime of grand larceny. The theft was of a number of hams, which he took by stealth

---

*mating with industry:* Mating with a person who has a strong work ethic.   *compulsory:* Mandatory, forced.

because of his impoverished condition. . . . Hill is a Russian beet sugar laborer, with a wife, and five children all under age of eleven years. He is robust physically, about forty years of age, and his wife some years his junior. Hill, his wife and five children are all mentally subnormal, even for their situation in life. . . . It was apparent that he could not provide them with the common necessities of life. . . . He was forced to steal to prevent them from starvation, or to apply for public aid. The case was brought to the attention of the authorities through the discovery of the theft of the hams, since which time he and his family are partially dependent upon public charity . . . ; with more children the extent of demand for public charity will be increased.[17]

30      Judge Holden found Hill guilty of grand larceny and gave him an indeterminate sentence of "not less than six months, nor more than fifteen years, imprisonment in the state penitentiary," to be suspended if he agreed to be sterilized. "Under these conditions," continues Judge Holden, "the operation was suggested to him, and after explanation . . . he consented."[18]

Haldane remarks that Judge Holden did not say what tests he used to determine that Hill and his family were mentally defective, and goes to cite another of the judge's statements, this one about a burglar named Chris McCauley, whom he sentenced to compulsory sterilization: "This man, about thirty-five years of age, is subnormal mentally and has every appearance and indication of immorality. He has a strain of Negro blood in his veins, and has a disgusting and lustful appearance."[19]

Haldane summarizes the situation by suggesting that "Hill would not have been sterilized had he possessed an independent income," nor would McCauley have been, "had his complexion been lighter and his appearance more in conformity with Judge Holden's aesthetic standards."[20]

By 1931, some thirty states had compulsory sterilization laws on their books, aimed mostly at the "insane" and "feebleminded." These categories were loosely defined to include many recent immigrants and others who were functionally illiterate or knew little or no English and who therefore did poorly on IQ tests. The laws also were often extended to so-called sexual perverts, drug fiends, drunkards, epileptics, and others deemed ill or degenerate. Although most of these laws were not enforced, by January 1935 some twenty thousand people in the United States had been forcibly sterilized, most of them in California. The California law was not repealed until 1979 and, according to Phillip Reilly, a physician and attorney, in 1985 "at least nineteen states had laws that permitted the sterilization of mentally retarded persons (Arkansas, Colorado, Connecticut, Delaware, Georgia, Idaho, Kentucky, Maine, Minnesota, Mississippi, Montana, North Carolina, Oklahoma, Oregon, South Carolina, Utah, Vermont, Virginia, and West Virginia)."[21]

## Eugenic Immigration Policies

While the eugenicists diagnosed individuals with "hereditary defects" in virtually all ethnic groups, they found that certain groups had a much higher proportion of "defectives" than others. For this reason, eugenics was an explicit factor in the Immigration Restriction Act of 1924. This act was designed to decrease immigration to the United States from southern and eastern Europe, so as to tilt the population balance in favor of U.S. residents of British and northern European descent. The number of people allowed to immigrate into the United States from any country each year was restricted to 2 percent of the U.S. residents who had been born in that country, as listed in the census of 1890.

That thirty-four-year-old census date was chosen deliberately because it set as a baseline the composition of the U.S. population prior to the major immigrations from southern and eastern Europe at the end of the nineteenth century. In the 1930s and early 1940s, this legislation prevented the immigration of countless Jews who were attempting to flee the Nazis, because they had been born in eastern Europe.

Harry Laughlin of the Eugenics Record Office was one of the most important lobbyists and witnesses in favor of the Immigration Restriction Act at the congressional hearings that preceded its passage and was dignified with the title of "expert eugenical agent" by the House Committee on Immigration and Naturalization.

1. Charles Benedict Davenport. *Heredity in Relation to Eugenics.* New York: Henry Holt and Company, 1913, p. 80.
2. Francis Galton. *Inquiries into Human Faculty.* London: Macmillan, 1883, pp. 24–25.
3. H. J. Muller. "Principles of Heredity." [1912] In H. J. Muller, ed. *Studies in Genetics.* Bloomington: University of Indiana Press, 1962, pp. 6–17.
4. Julian Huxley. "The Vital Importance of Eugenics." *Harper's Monthly,* vol. 163, August 1941, pp. 324–331.
5. Rodger Hurley. *Poverty and Mental Retardation: A Causal Relationship.* New York: Random House, 1969.
6. Lewis M. Terman. "The Conservation of Talent." *School and Society,* vol. 19, 1924, pp. 359–364.
7. Allan Chase. *The Legacy of Malthus: The Social Costs of the New Scientific Racism.* New York: Knopf, 1977, p. 214.
8. Stephan L. Chorover. *From Genesis to Genocide.* Cambridge: MIT Press, 1979.
9. Robert J. Lifton. *The Nazi Doctors.* New York: Basic Books, 1986.
10. Benno Müller-Hill. *Murderous Science.* Oxford: Oxford University Press, 1988.
11. Robert N. Proctor. *Racial Hygiene: Medicine under the Nazis.* Cambridge: Harvard University Press, 1988.
12. Chase. *The Legacy of Malthus,* p. 121.
13. Davenport. *Heredity in Relation to Eugenics,* pp. 80, 82.
14. Chase. *The Legacy of Malthus,* p. 124.

15. Ibid., p. 124.
16. Ibid., p. 125.
17. J. B. S. Haldane. *Heredity and Politics.* New York: W. W. Norton and Co., 1938, pp. 103–104.
18. Ibid., p. 104.
19. Ibid., pp. 104–105.
20. Ibid., p. 105.
21. Phillip R. Reilly. *The Surgical Solution: A History of Involuntary Sterilization in the United States.* Baltimore: Johns Hopkins University Press, 1992, p. 148.

## QUESTIONS

1. Do the first few paragraphs of this selection create an effective introduction?
2. What is the thesis of this selection?
3. According to the authors, what was science supposed to "prove" and support during the industrial revolution?
4. What does "eugenics" mean?
5. According to the authors, which side of the political spectrum (liberal or conservative) was interested in eugenics?
6. Explain how the Station for the Experimental Study of Evolution at Cold Spring Harbor propagated a post hoc fallacy.
7. According to the authors, are the main causes of mental retardation among poor people primarily genetic? If not, what are they?
8. Are the authors making a faulty analogy when they compare British and U.S. interests in eugenics with Nazi eugenic practices?
9. What was the impact of genetic theories on immigration into the United States during the first half of the twentieth century?
10. Where do the authors respond to counterarguments raised by people who disagree with their thesis? Do they do this enough in the essay? Do you think that the authors are biased?

## CONNECTIONS

1. This essay includes various statements made by eugenicists about poor people. Would Andrew Carnegie have supported any of those statements? Find specific lines in Carnegie's essay (Section 4) to support your response.
2. Discuss the connection between this essay and the "three fifths" clause of the constitution (quoted in Question 11 on page 472).
3. Do the attitudes expressed by Benjamin Franklin (in the letter included in this section) seem to support the views of eugenicists?

## ∽ Racism and the White Backlash

*Martin Luther King, Jr.*

Martin Luther King, Jr., was ordained as a Baptist minister and earned a Ph.D. from Boston University in 1955. The leading figure of the Civil Rights movement of the 1950s and '60s, King was an impressive orator (most students in the United States today read or listen to his "I Have a Dream" speech). He also wrote several books, including *Stride toward Freedom: The Montgomery Story* (1958), *The Measure of a Man* (1959), *Why We Can't Wait* (1963), and the one from which the following selection was taken, *Where Do We Go from Here: Chaos or Community?* (1967). King received numerous awards for his work, including the Nobel Peace Prize in 1964. Still, despite his focus on nonviolence, he was imprisoned fourteen times. He was assassinated in Memphis, Tennessee, in 1968.

**WARM-UP:** What characteristics and attitudes do you associate with Martin Luther King, Jr.?

It is time for all of us to tell each other the truth about who and what have    1
brought the Negro to the condition of deprivation against which he struggles today. In human relations the truth is hard to come by, because most groups are deceived about themselves. Rationalization and the incessant° search for scapegoats are the psychological cataracts that blind us to our individual and collective sins. But the day has passed for bland euphemisms. He who lives with untruth lives in spiritual slavery. Freedom is still the bonus we receive for knowing the truth. "Ye shall know the truth, and the truth shall set you free."

It would be neither true nor honest to say that the Negro's status is what it is because he is innately° inferior or because he is basically lazy and listless or because he has not sought to lift himself by his own bootstraps. To find the origins of the Negro problem we must turn to the white man's problem. As Earl Conrad says in a recent book, *The Invention of the Negro*: "I have sought out these new routes in the unshakable conviction that the question involved there cannot be and never could be answered merely by examining the Negro himself, his ghettos, his history, his personality, his culture. For the answer to how the Negro's status came to be what it is does not lie essentially in the world of the Negro, but in the world of the white." In short, white America must assume the guilt for the black man's inferior status.

---

*incessant:* Unceasing, continual.    *innately:* Inherently, by nature.

Ever since the birth of our nation, white America has had a schizophrenic° personality on the question of race. She has been torn between selves—a self in which she proudly professed the great principles of democracy and a self in which she sadly practiced the antithesis° of democracy. This tragic duality has produced a strange indecisiveness and ambivalence° toward the Negro, causing America to take a step backward simultaneously with every step forward on the question of racial justice, to be at once attracted to the Negro and repelled by him, to love and to hate him. There has never been a solid, unified, and determined thrust to make justice a reality for Afro-Americans.

The step backward has a new name today. It is called the "white backlash." But the white backlash is nothing new. It is the surfacing of old prejudices, hostilities, and ambivalences that have always been there. It was caused neither by the cry of Black Power nor by the unfortunate recent wave of riots in our cities. The white backlash of today is rooted in the same problem that has characterized America ever since the black man landed in chains on the shores of this nation. The white backlash is an expression of the same vacillations,° the same search for rationalizations, the same lack of commitment that have always characterized white America on the question of race.

5      What is the source of this perennial° indecision and vacillation? It lies in the "congenital deformity" of racism that has crippled the nation from its inception. The roots of racism are very deep in America. Historically it was so acceptable in the national life that today it still only lightly burdens the conscience. No one surveying the moral landscape of our nation can overlook the hideous and pathetic wreckage of commitment twisted and turned to a thousand shapes under the stress of prejudice and irrationality.

This does not imply that all white Americans are racists—far from it. Many white people have, through a deep moral compulsion, fought long and hard for racial justice. Nor does it mean that America has made no progress in her attempt to cure the body politic of the disease of racism, or that the dogma° of racism has not been considerably modified in recent years. However, for the good of America, it is necessary to refute the idea that the dominant ideology in our country even today is freedom and equality while racism is just an occasional departure from the norm on the part of a few bigoted extremists.

What is racism? Dr. George Kelsey, in a profound book entitled *Racism and the Christian Understanding of Man*, states that:

> Racism is a faith. It is a form of idolatry. . . . In its early modern beginnings, racism was a justificatory device. It did not emerge as a faith. It

---

*schizophrenic:* Here referring to something that exhibits contradictory or antagonistic qualities. *antithesis:* Opposite. *ambivalence:* Uncertainty. *vacillations:* Indecisions. *perennial:* Enduring, constant. *dogma:* Point of view put forth as authoritative without adequate grounds.

arose as an ideological justification for the constellations of political and economic power which were expressed in colonialism and slavery. But gradually the idea of the superior race was heightened and deepened in meaning and value so that it pointed beyond the historical structure of relation, in which it emerged, to human existence itself.

In her *Race: Science and Politics,* Ruth Benedict expands on the theme by defining racism as "the dogma that one ethnic group is condemned by nature to hereditary inferiority and another group is destined to hereditary superiority. It is the dogma that the hope of civilization depends upon eliminating some races and keeping others pure. It is the dogma that one race has carried progress throughout human history and can alone ensure future progress."

Since racism is based on the dogma "that the hope of civilization depends upon eliminating some races and keeping others pure," its ultimate logic is genocide.° Hitler, in his mad and ruthless attempt to exterminate the Jews, carried the logic of racism to its ultimate tragic conclusions. While America has not literally sought to eliminate the Negro in this final sense, it has, through the system of segregation, substituted a subtle reduction of life by means of deprivation.

If a man asserts that another man, because if his race, is not good enough        10
to have a job equal to his, or to eat at a lunch counter next to him, or to have access to certain hotels, or to attend school with him, or to live next door to him, he is by implication affirming that that man does not deserve to exist. He does not deserve to exist because his existence is corrupt and defective.

Racism is a philosophy based on a contempt for life. It is the arrogant assertion that one race is the center of value and object of devotion, before which other races must kneel in submission. It is the absurd dogma that one race is responsible for all the progress of history and alone can assure the progress of the future. Racism is total estrangement. It separates not only bodies, but minds and spirits. Inevitably it descends to inflicting spiritual or physical homicide upon the out-group.

Of the two dominant and contradictory strains in the American psyche,° the positive one, our democratic heritage, was the later development on the American continent. Democracy, born in the eighteenth century, took from John Locke of England the theory of natural rights and the justification of revolution and imbued° it with the ideal of a society governed by the people. When Jefferson wrote the Declaration of Independence, the first government of the world to be based on these principles was established on American soil. A contemporary description of Benjamin Franklin might have described the

---

*genocide:* The deliberate and systematic destruction of a racial, political, or social group.   *psyche:* Soul, mind.   *imbued:* Permeated.

new nation: "He has torn lightning from the sky; soon he will tear their sceptres from the kings." And Thomas Paine in his enthusiasm declared, "We have the power to begin the world all over again."

Yet even amid these electrifying expressions of the rights of man, racism —the myth of inferior peoples—was flourishing here to contradict and qualify the democratic ideal. Slavery was not only ignored in defining democracy, but its enlargement was tolerated in the interests of strengthening the nation.

For more than two hundred years before the Declaration of Independence, Africa had been raped and plundered by Britain and Europe, her native kingdoms disorganized, and her people and rulers demoralized. For a hundred years afterward, the infamous trade continued in America virtually without abatement,° even after it had ceased to be legal on this continent.

15    In fact, this ghastly blood traffic was so immense and its profits were so stupendous that the economies of several European nations owe their growth and prosperity to it and New England rested heavily on it for its development. Beard declared it was fair to say of whole towns in New England and Great Britain: "The stones of your houses are cemented with the blood of African slaves." Conservatively estimated, several million Africans died in the calloused transfer of human merchandise to the New World alone.

It is important to understand that the basis for the birth, growth, and development of slavery in America was primarily economic. By the beginning of the seventeenth century, the British Empire had established colonies all along the Atlantic seaboard from Massachusetts to the West Indies to serve as producers of raw materials for British manufacturing, a market for goods manufactured in Britain, and a source of staple cargoes for British shipping engaged in world trade. So the colonies had to provide an abundance of rice, sugar, cotton, and tobacco. In the first few years of the various settlements along the East Coast, so-called indentured servants,° mostly white, were employed on plantations. But within a generation the plantation operators were demanding outright and lifetime slavery for the Africans they imported. As a function of this new economic policy, Africans were reduced to the status of property by law, and this status was enforced by the most rigid and brutal police power of the existing governments. By 1650 slavery had been legally established as a national institution.

Since the institution of slavery was so important to the economic development of America, it had a profound impact in shaping the social-political-legal structure of the nation. Land and slaves were the chief forms of private property, property was wealth and the voice of wealth made the law and determined politics. In the service of this system, human beings were reduced to

*abatement:* Decrease in degree or intensity.    *indentured servants:* People used as slaves for a limited amount of time.

propertyless property. Black men, the creators of the wealth of the New World, were stripped of all human and civil rights. And this degradation was sanctioned and protected by institutions of government, all for one purpose: to produce commodities for sale at a profit, which in turn would be privately appropriated.

It seems to be a fact of life that human beings cannot continue to do wrong without eventually reaching out for some rationalization to clothe their acts in the garments of righteousness. And so, with the growth of slavery, men had to convince themselves that a system which was so economically profitable was morally justifiable. The attempt to give moral sanction to a profitable system gave birth to the doctrine of white supremacy.

Religion and the Bible were cited and distorted to support the status quo. It was argued that the Negro was inferior by nature because of Noah's curse upon the children of Ham. The Apostle Paul's dictum became a watchword: "Servant, be obedient to your master." In this strange way theology became a ready ally of commerce. The great Puritan divine Cotton Mather culled the Bible for passages to give comfort to the plantation owners and merchants. He went so far as to set up some "Rules for the Society of Negroes," in which, among other things, Negroes disobedient to their masters were to be rebuked° and denied attendance at church meetings, and runaway slaves were to be brought back and severely punished. All of this, he reasoned, was in line with the Apostle Paul's injunction that servants should be obedient to their masters.

Logic was manipulated to give intellectual credence° to the system of slav-    20
ery. Someone formulated the argument for the inferiority of the Negro in the shape of a syllogism°:

> All men are made in the image of God;
> God, as everybody knows, is not a Negro;
> Therefore the Negro is not a man.

Academicians eventually climbed on the bandwagon and gave their prestige to the myth of the superior race. Their contribution came through the so-called Teutonic Origins theory, a doctrine of white supremacy surrounded by the halo of academic respectability. The theorists of this concept argued that all Anglo-Saxon institutions of any worth had their historical roots in the Teutonic tribe institutions of ancient Germany, and furthermore that "only the Teutonic race had been imbued with the ability to build stable governments." Historians from the lofty academic towers of Oxford, like Bishop William Stubbs and Edward A. Freeman, expounded the Teutonic Origins theory in British intellectual circles. It leaped the Atlantic and found lodging in the

---

*rebuked:* Reprimanded, turned back.    *credence:* Credibility.    *syllogism:* An argument in which a conclusion is drawn from given conditions.

mind of Herbert Baxter Adams, one of the organizers of the graduate school at Johns Hopkins University and founder of the American Historical Association. He expanded Freeman's views by asserting that the Teutonic Origins theory really had "three homes—England, Germany and the United States." Pretty soon this distorted theory dominated the thinking of American historians at leading universities like Harvard, Cornell, Wisconsin, and Columbia.

Even natural science, that discipline committed to the inductive method, creative appraisal, and detached objectivity, was invoked and distorted to give credence to a political position. A whole school of racial ethnologists° developed using such terms as "species," "genus," and "race." It became fashionable to think of the slave as a "species of property." It was during this period that the word "race" came into fashion.

Dr. Samuel G. Morton, a Philadelphia physician, emerged with the head-size theory which affirmed that the larger the skull, the superior the individual. This theory was used by other ethnologists to prove that the large head size of Caucasians signified more intellectual capacity and more native worth. A Dr. Josiah C. Nott, in his *Collections on the Natural History of the Caucasian and Negro Races,* used pseudoscientific evidence to prove that the black man was little above the level of an ape. A Frenchman, Count Arthur de Gobineau, in his book *The Inequality of the Human Races,* vigorously defended the theory of the inferiority of the black man and used the experience of the United States as his prime source of evidence. It was this kind of "science" that pervaded the atmosphere in the nineteenth century, and these pseudo scientists became the authoritative references for any and all seeking rationalization for the system of slavery.

Generally we think of white supremacist views as having their origins with the unlettered, underprivileged, poorer-class whites. But the social obstetricians who presided at the birth of racist views in our country were from the aristocracy: rich merchants, influential clergymen, men of medical sciences, historians, and political scientists from some of the leading universities of the nation. With such a distinguished company of the elite working so assiduously° to disseminate racist views, what was there to inspire poor, illiterate, unskilled white farmers to think otherwise?

25      Soon the doctrine of white supremacy was implied in every textbook and preached in practically every pulpit. It became a structural part of the culture. And men then embraced this philosophy, not as the rationalization of a lie, but as the expression of a final truth. In 1857 the system of slavery was given its ultimate legal support by the Supreme Court of the United States in the

---

*ethnologists:* Scientists who deal with comparative studies of cultures.   *assiduously:* Diligently, persistently.

Dred Scott decision, which affirmed that the Negro had no rights that the white man was bound to respect.

The greatest blasphemy° of the whole ugly process was that the white man ended up making God his partner in the exploitation of the Negro. What greater heresy° has religion known? Ethical Christianity vanished and the moral nerve of religion atrophied.° This terrible distortion sullied° the essential nature of Christianity.

Virtually all of the Founding Fathers of our nation, even those who rose to the heights of the Presidency, those whom we cherish as our authentic heroes, were so enmeshed° in the ethos of slavery and white supremacy that not one ever emerged with a clear, unambiguous stand on Negro rights. No human being is perfect. In our individual and collective lives every expression of greatness is followed, not by a period symbolizing completeness, but by a comma implying partialness. Following every affirmation of greatness is the conjunction "but." Naaman "was a great man," says the Old Testament, "but . . ."—that "but" reveals something tragic and disturbing—"but he was a leper." George Washington, Thomas Jefferson, Patrick Henry, John Quincy Adams, John Calhoun, and Abraham Lincoln were great men, but—that "but" underscores the fact that not one of these men had a strong, unequivocal belief in the equality of the black man.

No one doubts the valor and commitment that characterized George Washington's life. But to the end of his days he maintained a posture of exclusionism toward the slave. He was a fourth-generation slaveholder. He only allowed Negroes to enter the Continental Army because His Majesty's Crown was attempting to recruit Negroes to the British cause. Washington was not without his moments of torment, those moments of conscience when something within told him that slavery was wrong. As he searched the future of America one day, he wrote to his nephew: "I wish from my soul that the legislature of this State could see the policy of gradual abolition of slavery. It might prevent much future mischief." In spite of this, Washington never made a public statement condemning slavery. He could not pull away from the system. When he died he owned, or had on lease, more than 160 slaves.

Here, in the life of the father of our nation, we can see the developing dilemma of white America: the haunting ambivalence, the intellectual and moral recognition that slavery is wrong, but the emotional tie to the system so deep and pervasive that it imposes an inflexible unwillingness to root it out.

Thomas Jefferson reveals the same ambivalence. There is much in the life of Jefferson that can serve as a model for political leaders in every age; he came

30

---

*blasphemy:* Insult to something considered sacred.   *heresy:* Dissent from a dominant religious theory or practice.   *atrophied:* Wasted away, shriveled.   *sullied:* Tarnished.   *enmeshed:* Entangled.

close to the ideal "philosopher-king" that Plato dreamed of centuries ago. But in spite of this, Jefferson was a child of his culture who had been influenced by the pseudo-scientific and philosophical thought that rationalized slavery. In his *Notes on Virginia*, Jefferson portrayed the Negro as inferior to the white man in his endowments of body, mind, and imagination, although he observed that the Negro appeared to be superior at picking out tunes on the "banjar." Jefferson's majestic words, "all men are created equal," meant for him, as for many others, that all *white* men are created equal.

Yet in his heart Jefferson knew that slavery was wrong and that it degraded the white man's mind and soul. In the same *Notes on Virginia* he wrote: "For if a slave can have a country in this world, it must be any other in preference to that in which he is born to live and labor for another.... Indeed I tremble for my country when I reflect that God is just, that his justice cannot sleep forever ... the Almighty has no attribute which can take sides with us in such a contest." And in 1820, six years before his death, he wrote these melancholy words: "But the momentous question [slavery] like a fire-bell in the night, awakened and filled me with terror. I considered it at once as the knell of the Union.... I regret that I am now to die in the belief that the useless sacrifice of themselves by the generation of 1776, to acquire self-government and happiness to their country, is to be thrown away by the wise and unworthy passion of their sons, and that my only consolation is to be that I live not to weep over it."

This strange duality toward the Negro and slavery vexed° the mind of Abraham Lincoln for years. Few men in history have anchored their lives more deeply in moral convictions than Abraham Lincoln, but on the question of slavery Lincoln's torments and vacillation were tenacious.°

As early as 1837, as a State Legislator, Lincoln referred to the injustice and impracticality of slavery. Later he wrote of the physical differences between blacks and whites and made it clear that he felt whites were superior. At times he concluded that the white man could not live with the Negro. This accounted for his conviction that the only answer to the problem was to colonize the black man—send him back to Africa, or to the West Indies or some other isolated spot. This view was still in his mind toward the height of the Civil War. Delegation after delegation—the Quakers above all, great abolitionists like Charles Sumner, Horace Greeley, and William Lloyd Garrison— pleaded with Lincoln to free the slaves, but he was firm in his resistance. Frederick Douglass, a Negro of towering grandeur, sound judgment, and militant initiative, sought, without success, to persuade Lincoln that slavery, not merely the preservation of the union, was at the root of the war. At the time, Lincoln could not yet see it.

---

*vexed:* Annoyed, troubled.    *tenacious:* Persistent.

A civil war raged within Lincoln's own soul, a tension between the Dr. Jekyll of freedom and the Mr. Hyde of slavery, a struggle like that of Plato's charioteer with two headstrong horses each pulling in different directions. Morally Lincoln was for black emancipation, but emotionally, like most of his white contemporaries, he was for a long time unable to act in accordance with his conscience.

But Lincoln was basically honest and willing to admit his confusions. He 35 saw that the nation could not survive half slave and half free; and he said, "If we could first know where we are and whither we are tending, we could better judge what to do and how to do it." Fortunately for the nation, he finally came to see "whither we are tending." On January 1, 1863, he issued the Emancipation Proclamation, freeing the Negro from the bondage of chattel slavery. By this concrete act of courage his reservations of the past were overshadowed. The conclusion of his search is embodied in these words: "In giving freedom to the slave, we assure freedom to the free—honourable alike is what we give and what we preserve."

The significance of the Emancipation proclamation was described by Frederick Douglass in these words:

> Unquestionably, for weal or for woe, the First of January is to be the most memorable day in American Annals. The Fourth of July was great, but the First of January, when we consider it in all its relations and bearings, is incomparably greater. The one had respect to the mere political birth of a nation; the last concerns the national life and character, and is to determine whether that life and character shall be radiantly glorious with all high and noble virtues, or infamously blackened, forevermore....

But underneath, the ambivalence of white America toward the Negro still lurked with painful persistence. With all the beautiful promise that Douglass saw in the Emancipation Proclamation, he soon found that it left the Negro with only abstract freedom. Four million newly liberated slaves found themselves with no bread to eat, no land to cultivate, no shelter to cover their heads. It was like freeing a man who has been unjustly imprisoned for years, and on discovering his innocence sending him out with no bus fare to get home, no suit to cover his body, no financial compensation to atone for his long years of incarceration and to help him get a sound footing in society; sending him out with only the assertion: "Now you are free." What greater injustice could society perpetrate? All the moral voices of the universe, all the codes of sound jurisprudence,° would rise up with condemnation at such an act. Yet this is exactly what America did to the Negro. In 1863 the Negro was given abstract freedom expressed in luminous rhetoric.° But in an agrarian° economy he was

*jurisprudence:* A system or body of law.   *rhetoric:* Here meaning speech, discourse.   *agrarian:* Agricultural.

given no land to make liberation concrete. After the war the government granted white settlers, without cost, millions of acres of land in the West, thus providing America's new white peasants from Europe with an economic floor. But at the same time its oldest peasantry, the Negro, was denied everything but a legal status he could not use, could not consolidate, could not even defend. As Frederick Douglass came to say, "Emancipation granted the Negro freedom to hunger, freedom to winter amid the rains of heaven. Emancipation was freedom and famine at the same time."

The inscription on the Statue of Liberty refers to America as the "mother of exiles." The tragedy is that while America became the mother of her white exiles, she evinced° no motherly concern or love for her exiles from Africa. It is no wonder that out of despair and estrangement the Negro cries out in one of his sorrow songs: "Sometimes I feel like a motherless child." The marvel is, as Frederick Douglass once said, that Negroes are still alive.

In dealing with the ambivalence of white America, we must not overlook another form of racism that was relentlessly pursued on American shores: the physical extermination of the American Indian. The South American example of absorbing the indigenous Indian population was ignored in the United States, and systematic destruction of a whole people was undertaken. The common phrase, "The only good Indian is a dead Indian," was virtually elevated to national policy. Thus the poisoning of the American mind was accomplished not only by acts of discrimination and exploitation but by the exaltation° of murder as an expression of the courage and initiative of the pioneer. Just as Southern culture was made to appear noble by ignoring the cruelty of slavery, the conquest of the Indian was depicted as an example of bravery and progress.

40        Thus through two centuries a continuous indoctrination° of Americans has separated people according to mythically superior and inferior qualities while a democratic spirit of equality was evoked as the national ideal. These concepts of racism, and this schizophrenic duality of conduct, remain deeply rooted in American thought today. This tendency of the nation to take one step forward on the question of racial justice and then to take a step backward is still the pattern. Just as an ambivalent nation freed the slaves a century ago with no plan or program to make their freedom meaningful, the still ambivalent nation in 1954 declared school segregation unconstitutional with no plan or program to make integration real. Just as the Congress passed a civil rights bill in 1868 and refused to enforce it, the Congress passed a civil rights bill in 1964 and to this day has failed to enforce it in all its dimensions. Just as the

---

*evinced:* Displayed.   *exaltation:* Aggrandizement, glorification.   *indoctrination:* Brainwashing.

Fifteenth Amendment in 1870 proclaimed Negro suffrage, only to permit its *de facto*° withdrawal in half the nation, so in 1965 the Voting Rights Law was passed and then permitted to languish only with factional and halfhearted implementation.

The civil rights measures of the 1960s engraved solemn rights in the legal literature. But after writing piecemeal and incomplete legislation and proclaiming its historic importance in magnificent prose, the American Government left the Negro to make the unworkable work. Against entrenched segregationist state power, with almost total dependence economically on those they had to contend with, and without political experience, the impoverished Negro was expected to usher in an era of freedom and plenty.

When the war against poverty came into being in 1964, it seemed to herald a new day of compassion. It was the bold assertion that the nation would no longer stand complacently° by while millions of its citizens smothered in poverty in the midst of opulence.° But it did not take long to discover that the government was only willing to appropriate such a limited budget that it could not launch a good skirmish against poverty, much less a full-scale war.

Moreover, the poverty program, which in concept elated the Negro poor, became so embroiled in political turmoil that its insufficiencies were magnified and its operations paralyzed. Big-city machines felt threatened by it and small towns, especially in the South, directed it away from Negroes. Its good intentions and limited objectives were frustrated by the skillful maneuvers of experienced politicians. The worst effect of these manipulations was to cast doubt upon the program as a whole and discredit those Negroes involved directly in its administration.

In 1965 the President presented a new plan to Congress—which it finally passed in 1966—for rebuilding entire slum neighborhoods. With other elements of the program it would, in his words, make the decaying cities of the present into "the masterpieces of our civilization." This Demonstration Cities plan is imaginative; it embodies social vision and properly defines racial discrimination as a central evil. However, the ordinary Negro, though no social or political analyst, will be skeptical. He will be skeptical, first, because of the insufficient funds assigned to the program. He will be skeptical, second, because he knows how many laws exist in Northern states and cities prohibiting discrimination in housing, in education, and in employment; he knows how many overlapping commissions exist to enforce the terms of these laws—and he knows how he lives. The ubiquitous° discrimination in his daily life tells him that laws on paper, no matter how imposing their terms, will not guarantee that he will live in "the masterpiece of civilization."

---

*de facto:* Latin, meaning "in fact, in practice." *complacently:* Indifferently, smugly. *opulence:* Great wealth. *ubiquitous:* Present everywhere.

45        Throughout our history, laws affirming Negro rights have consistently been circumvented° by ingenious evasions which render them void in practice. Laws that affect the whole population—draft laws, income-tax laws, traffic laws—manage to work even though they may be unpopular; but laws passed for the Negro's benefit are so widely unenforced that it is a mockery to call them laws. There is a tragic gulf between civil rights laws passed and civil rights laws implemented. There is a double standard in the enforcement of law and a double standard in the respect for particular laws.

All of this tells us that the white backlash is nothing new. White America has been backlashing on the fundamental God-given and human rights of Negro Americans for more than three hundred years. With all of her dazzling achievements and stupendous material strides, America has maintained its strange ambivalence on the question of racial justice.

## QUESTIONS

1. What, according to King, are the two "selves" between which "white America" has been torn?
2. According to King, what is a "white backlash"? Is a "white backlash" taking place today?
3. What evidence does King provide to refute the claim that "the dominant ideology in our country . . . today is freedom and equality"?
4. What was the main reason for the growth of slavery in the United States? Why did racism develop initially?
5. According to King, who is responsible for the creation and spread of the doctrine of white supremacy? Why did so many people support those views?
6. According to Frederick Douglass, why was the Emancipation Proclamation a declaration of "freedom to hunger, freedom to winter amid the rains of heaven" for Black people?
7. In paragraph 37, King compares newly liberated slaves to "a man who had been unjustly imprisoned for years" and is suddenly set free. Is this analogy faulty?
8. Is King criticizing the teachings of the Bible in this essay? Explain your answer.
9. Point out some examples of the use of metaphor in this selection and discuss the connotations of one such metaphor.

---

*circumvented:* Avoided, bypassed.

**CONNECTIONS**

1. Compare and contrast the "scientific" analysis of the inferiority of certain races (discussed by King in this essay) to the early analyses of the status of Native Americans discussed by Michael Dorris in "Discoveries."

2. How might King have responded to Elizabeth Cady Stanton's claim, in paragraph 29 of her declaration about "a perverted application of the Scriptures"?

# Affirmative Action: The Price of Preference

*Shelby Steele*

Shelby Steele was born in Chicago in 1946. He earned a master's degree in sociology from Southern Illinois University in 1971 and a Ph.D. in English from the University of Utah in 1974. Currently on leave from his position as professor of English at San Jose State University, Steele is a Hoover Fellow at Stanford University. He has published articles in many newspapers and magazines, including *American Scholar,* the *Washington Post,* and *New Republic.* He is best known for his book *The Content of Our Character: A New Vision of Race in America* (1990), which includes the following essay (the selection originally appeared in the *New York Times Magazine* under the title "A Negative Vote on Affirmative Action").

**WARM-UP:** Do you believe affirmative action should be maintained, abolished, or reformed? If your answer is the last of these, what reforms would you suggest?

1    In a few short years, when my two children will be applying to college, the affirmative action policies by which most universities offer black students some form of preferential treatment will present me with a dilemma. I am a middle-class black, a college professor, far from wealthy, but also well-removed from the kind of deprivation that would qualify my children for the label "disadvantaged." Both of them have endured racial insensitivity from whites. They have been called names, have suffered slights, and have experienced firsthand the peculiar malevolence° that racism brings out in people. Yet, they have never experienced racial discrimination, have never been stopped by their race on any path they have chosen to follow. Still, their society now tells them that if they will only designate themselves as black on their college applications, they will likely do better in the college lottery than if they conceal this fact. I think there is something of a Faustian bargain° in this.

Of course, many blacks and a considerable number of whites would say that I was sanctimoniously° making affirmative action into a test of character. They would say that this small preference is the meagerest recompense for centuries of unrelieved oppression. And to these arguments other very obvious facts must be added. In America, many marginally competent or flatly incompetent whites are hired everyday—some because their white skin suits

---

*malevolence:* Intense ill will or hatred.    *Faustian bargain:* Exchanging one's soul for profit.    *sanctimoniously:* Insincerely, hypocritically.

the conscious or unconscious racial preference of their employer. The white children of alumni are often grandfathered° into elite universities in what can only be seen as a residual benefit of historic white privilege. Worse, white incompetence is always an individual matter, while for blacks it is often confirmation of ugly stereotypes. The Peter Principle° was not conceived with only blacks in mind. Given that unfairness cuts both ways, doesn't it only balance the scales of history that my children now receive a slight preference over whites? Doesn't this repay, in a small way, the systematic denial under which their grandfather lived out his days?

So, in theory, affirmative action certainly has all the moral symmetry that fairness requires—the injustice of historical and even contemporary white advantage is offset with black advantage; preference replaces prejudice, inclusion answers exclusion. It is reformist and corrective, even repentant and redemptive. And I would never sneer at these good intentions. Born in the late forties in Chicago, I started my education (a charitable term in this case) in a segregated school and suffered all the indignities that come to blacks in a segregated society. My father, born in the South, only made it to the third grade before the white man's fields took permanent priority over his formal education. And though he educated himself into an advanced reader with an almost professorial authority, he could only drive a truck for a living and never earned more than ninety dollars a week in his entire life. So yes, it is crucial to my sense of citizenship, to my ability to identify with the spirit and the interests of America, to know that this country, however imperfectly, recognizes its past sins and wishes to correct them.

Yet good intentions, because of the opportunity for innocence they offer us, are very seductive and can blind us to the effects they generate when implemented. In our society, affirmative action is, among other things, a testament to white goodwill and to black power, and in the midst of these heavy investments, its effects can be hard to see. But after twenty years of implementation, I think affirmative action has shown itself to be more bad than good and that blacks—whom I will focus on in this essay—now stand to lose more from it than they gain.

In talking with affirmative action administrators and with blacks and whites in general, it is clear that supporters of affirmative action focus on its good intentions while detractors emphasize its negative effects. Proponents talk about "diversity" and "pluralism"; opponents speak of "reverse discrimination," the unfairness of quotas and set-asides. It was virtually impossible to find people outside either camp. The closest I came was a white male manager

*grandfathered:* Here meaning "admitted on the basis of family connections". *Peter Principle:* A kind of "Murphy's Law" that states that people tend to be promoted until they reach a level at which they are incompetent.

at a large computer company who said, "I think it amounts to reverse discrimination, but I'll put up with a little of that for a little more diversity." I'll live with a little of the effect to gain a little of the intention, he seemed to be saying. But this only makes him a halfhearted supporter of affirmative action. I think many people who don't really like affirmative action support it to one degree or another anyway.

I believe they do this because of what happened to white and black Americans in the crucible° of the sixties when whites were confronted with their racial guilt and blacks tasted their first real power. In this stormy time white absolution and black power coalesced° into virtual mandates for society. Affirmative action became a meeting ground for these mandates in the law, and in the late sixties and early seventies it underwent a remarkable escalation of its mission from simple anti-discrimination enforcement to social engineering by means of quotas, goals, timetables, set-asides and other forms of preferential treatment.

Legally, this was achieved through a series of executive orders and EEOC° guidelines that allowed racial imbalances in the workplace to stand as proof of racial discrimination. Once it could be assumed that discrimination explained racial imbalances, it became easy to justify group remedies to presumed discrimination, rather than the normal case-by-case redress° for proven discrimination. Preferential treatment through quotas, goals, and so on is designed to correct imbalances based on the assumption that they always indicate discrimination. This expansion of what constitutes discrimination allowed affirmative action to escalate into the business of social engineering in the name of anti-discrimination, to push society toward statistically proportionate racial representation, without any obligation of proving actual discrimination.

What accounted for this shift, I believe, was the white mandate to achieve a new racial innocence and the black mandate to gain power. Even though blacks had made great advances during the sixties without quotas, these mandates, which came to a head in the very late sixties, could no longer be satisfied by anything less than racial preferences. I don't think these mandates in themselves were wrong, since whites clearly needed to do better by blacks and blacks needed more real power in society. But, as they came together in affirmative action, their effect was to distort our understanding of racial discrimination in a way that allowed us to offer the remediation of preference on the basis of mere color rather than actual injury. By making black the color of preference, these mandates have reburdened society with the very marriage of color and preference (in reverse) that we set out to eradicate. The old sin is reaffirmed in a new guise.

---

*crucible:* Vessel or container in which things are melted together.    *coalesced:* Blended together, united.
*EEOC:* Equal Employment Opportunity Commission.    *redress:* Compensation, correction.

But the essential problem with this form of affirmative action is the way it leaps over the hard business of developing a formerly oppressed people to the point where they can achieve proportionate representation on their own (given equal opportunity) and goes straight for the proportionate representation. This may satisfy some whites of their innocence and some blacks of their power, but it does very little to truly uplift blacks.

A white female affirmative action officer at an Ivy League university told me what many supporters of affirmative action now say: "We're after diversity. We ideally want a student body where racial and ethnic groups are represented according to their proportion in society." When affirmative action escalated into social engineering, diversity became a golden word. It grants whites an egalitarian fairness (innocence) and blacks an entitlement to proportionate representation (power). *Diversity* is a term that applies democratic principles to races and cultures rather than to citizens, despite the fact that there is nothing to indicate that real diversity is the same thing as proportionate representation. Too often the result of this on campuses (for example) has been a democracy of colors rather than of people, an artificial diversity that gives the appearance of an educational parity between black and white students that has not yet been achieved in reality. Here again, racial preferences allow society to leapfrog over the difficult problem of developing blacks to parity with whites and into a cosmetic diversity that covers the blemish of disparity—a full six years after admission, only about 26 percent of black students graduate from college.

Racial representation is not the same thing as racial development, yet affirmative action fosters a confusion of these very different needs. Representation can be manufactured; development is always hard-earned. However, it is the music of innocence and power that we hear in affirmative action that causes us to cling to it and to its distracting emphasis on representation. The fact is that after twenty years of racial preferences, the gap between white and black median income is greater than it was in the seventies. None of this is to say that blacks don't need policies that ensure our right to equal opportunity, but what we need more is the development that will let us take advantage of society's efforts to include us.

I think that one of the most troubling effects of racial preferences for blacks is a kind of demoralization, or put another way, an enlargement of self-doubt. Under affirmative action the quality that earns us preferential treatment is an implied inferiority. However this inferiority is explained—and it is easily enough explained by the myriad° deprivations that grew out of our oppression—it is still inferiority. There are explanations, and then there is the fact. And the fact must be borne by the individual as a condition apart from

*myriad:* Innumerable.

10

the explanation, apart even from the fact that others like himself also bear this condition. In integrated situations where blacks must compete with whites who may be better prepared, these explanations may quickly wear thin and expose the individual to racial as well as personal self-doubt.

All of this is compounded by the cultural myth of black inferiority that blacks have always lived with. What this means in practical terms is that when blacks deliver themselves into integrated situations, they encounter a nasty little reflex in whites, a mindless, atavistic° reflex that responds to the color black with alarm. Attributions may follow this alarm if the white cares to indulge them, and if they do, they will most likely be negative—one such attribution is intellectual ineptness. I think this reflex and the attributions that may follow it embarrass most whites today, therefore, it is usually quickly repressed. Nevertheless, on an equally atavistic level, the black will be aware of the reflex his color triggers and will feel a stab of horror at seeing himself reflected in this way. He, too, will do a quick repression, but a lifetime of such stabbings is what constitutes his inner realm of racial doubt.

The effects of this may be a subject for another essay. The point here is that the implication of inferiority that racial preferences engender in both the white and black mind expands rather than contracts this doubt. Even when the black sees no implication of inferiority in racial preferences, he knows that whites do, so that—consciously or unconsciously—the result is virtually the same. The effect of preferential treatment—the lowering of normal standards to increase black representation—puts blacks at war with an expanded realm of debilitating doubt, so that the doubt itself becomes an unrecognized preoccupation that undermines their ability to perform, especially in integrated situations. On largely white campuses, blacks are five times more likely to drop out than whites. Preferential treatment, no matter how it is justified in the light of day, subjects blacks to a midnight of self-doubt, and so often transforms their advantage into a revolving door.

15      Another liability of affirmative action comes from the fact that it indirectly encourages blacks to exploit their own past victimization as a source of power and privilege. Victimization, like implied inferiority, is what justifies preference, so that to receive the benefits of preferential treatment one must, to some extent, become invested in the view of one's self as a victim. In this way, affirmative action nurtures a victim-focused identity in blacks. The obvious irony here is that we become inadvertently invested in the very condition we are trying to overcome. Racial preferences send us the message that there is more power in our past suffering than our present achievements—none of which could bring us a *preference* over others.

---

*atavistic:* Related to an earlier age.

When power itself grows out of suffering, then blacks are encouraged to expand the boundaries of what qualifies as racial oppression, a situation that can lead us to paint our victimization in vivid colors, even as we receive the benefits of preference. The same corporations and institutions that give us preference are also seen as our oppressors. At Stanford University minority students—some of whom enjoy as much as $15,000 a year in financial aid—recently took over the president's office demanding, among other things, more financial aid. The power to be found in victimization, like any power, is intoxicating and can lend itself to the creation of a new class of super-victims who can feel the pea of victimization under twenty mattresses. Preferential treatment rewards us for being underdogs rather than for moving beyond that status—a misplacement of incentives that, along with its deepening of our doubt, is more a yoke than a spur.

But, I think, one of the worst prices that blacks pay for preference has to do with an illusion. I saw this illusion at work recently in the mother of a middle-class black student who was going off to his first semester of college. "They owe us this, so don't think for a minute that you don't belong there." This is the logic by which many blacks, and some whites, justify affirmative action—it is something "owed," a form of reparation. But this logic overlooks a much harder and less digestible reality, that it is impossible to repay blacks living today for the historic suffering of the race. If all blacks were given a million dollars tomorrow morning it would not amount to a dime on the dollar of three centuries of oppression, nor would it obviate° the residues of that oppression that we still carry today. The concept of historic reparation grows out of man's need to impose a degree of justice on the world that simply does not exist. Suffering can be endured and overcome, it cannot be repaid. Blacks cannot be repaid for the injustice done to the race, but we can be corrupted by society's guilty gestures of repayment.

Affirmative action is such a gesture. It tells us that racial preferences can do for us what we cannot do for ourselves. The corruption here is in the hidden incentive *not* to do what we believe preferences will do. This is an incentive to be reliant on others just as we are struggling for self-reliance. And it keeps alive the illusion that we can find some deliverance in repayment. The hardest thing for any sufferer to accept is that his suffering excuses him from very little and never has enough currency to restore him. To think otherwise is to prolong the suffering.

Several blacks I spoke with said they were still in favor of affirmative action because of the "subtle" discrimination blacks were subject to once on the job. One photojournalist said, "They have ways of ignoring you." A black

*obviate:* Cancel, prevent.

female television producer said, "You can't file a lawsuit when your boss doesn't invite you to the insider meetings without ruining your career. So we still need affirmative action." Others mentioned the infamous "glass ceiling" through which blacks can see the top positions of authority but never reach them. But I don't think racial preferences are a protection against this subtle discrimination; I think they contribute to it.

20    In any workplace, racial preferences will always create two-tiered populations composed of preferreds and unpreferreds. This division makes automatic a perception of enhanced competence for the unpreferreds and of questionable competence for the preferreds—the former earned his way, even though others were given preference, while the latter made it by color as much as by competence. Racial preferences implicitly mark whites with an exaggerated superiority just as they mark blacks with an exaggerated inferiority. They not only reinforce America's oldest racial myth but, for blacks, they have the effect of stigmatizing the already stigmatized.

I think that much of the "subtle" discrimination that blacks talk about is often (not always) discrimination against the stigma of questionable competence that affirmative action delivers to blacks. In this sense, preferences scapegoat the very people they seek to help. And it may be that at a certain level employers impose a glass ceiling, but this may not be against the race so much as against the race's reputation for having advanced by color as much as by competence. Affirmative action makes a glass ceiling virtually necessary as a protection against the corruptions of preferential treatment. This ceiling is the point at which corporations shift emphasis from color to competency and stop playing the affirmative action game. Here preference backfires for blacks and becomes a taint that holds them back. Of course, one could argue that this taint, which is, after all, in the minds of whites, becomes nothing more than an excuse to discriminate against blacks. And certainly the result is the same in either case—blacks don't get past the glass ceiling. But this argument does not get around the fact that racial preferences now taint this color with a new theme of suspicion that makes it even more vulnerable to the impulse in others to discriminate. In this crucial yet gray area of perceived competence, preferences make whites look better than they are and blacks worse, while doing nothing whatever to stop the very real discrimination that blacks may encounter. I don't wish to justify the glass ceiling here, but only to suggest the very subtle ways that affirmative action revives rather than extinguishes the old rationalizations for racial discrimination.

In education, a revolving door; in employment, a glass ceiling.

I believe affirmative action is problematic in our society because it tries to function like a social program. Rather than ask it to ensure equal opportunity we have demanded that it create parity between the races. But preferential treatment does not teach skills, or educate, or instill motivation. It only passes out entitlement by color, a situation that in my profession has created an unrealistically high demand for black professors. The social engineer's assumption is that this high demand will inspire more blacks to earn Ph.D.'s and join the profession. In fact, the number of blacks earning Ph.D.'s has declined in recent years. A Ph.D. must be developed from preschool on. He requires family and community support. He must acquire an entire system of values that enables him to work hard while delaying gratification. There are social programs, I believe, that can (and should) help blacks *develop* in all these areas, but entitlement by color is not a social program; it is a dubious reward for being black.

It now seems clear that the Supreme Court, in a series of recent decisions, is moving away from racial preferences. It has disallowed preferences except in instances of "identified discrimination," eroded the precedent that statistical racial imbalances are *prima facie*° evidence of discrimination, and in effect granted white males the right to challenge consent degrees that use preference to achieve racial balances in the workplace. One civil rights leader said, "Night has fallen on civil rights." But I am not so sure. The effect of these decisions is to protect the constitutional rights of everyone rather than take rights away from blacks. What they do take away from blacks is the special entitlement to more rights than others that preferences always grant. Night has fallen on racial preferences, not on the fundamental rights of black Americans. The reason for this shift, I believe, is that the white mandate for absolution from past racial sins has weakened considerably during the eighties. Whites are now less willing to endure unfairness to themselves in order to grant special entitlements to blacks, even when these entitlements are justified in the name of past suffering. Yet the black mandate for more power in society has remained unchanged. And I think part of the anxiety that many blacks feel over these decisions has to do with the loss of black power they may signal. We had won a certain specialness and now we are losing it.

But the power we've lost by these decisions is really only the power that grows out of our victimization—the power to claim special entitlements under the law because of past oppression. This is not a very substantial or reliable power, and it is important that we know this so we can focus more exclusively on the kind of development that will bring enduring power. There is talk now that Congress will pass new legislation to compensate for these new limits on affirmative action. If this happens, I hope that their focus will be on development and anti-discrimination rather than entitlement, on achieving racial parity rather than jerry-building° racial diversity.

I would also like to see affirmative action go back to its original purpose of enforcing equal opportunity—a purpose that in itself disallows racial preferences. We cannot be sure that the discriminatory impulse in America has yet

25

---

*prima facie:* Latin, meaning "apparent" or "self-evident."     *jerry-building:* Building cheaply and flimsily.

been shamed into extinction, and I believe affirmative action can make its greatest contribution by providing a rigorous vigilance in this area. It can guard constitutional rather than racial rights, and help institutions evolve standards of merit and selection that are appropriate to the institution's needs yet as free of racial bias as possible (again, with the understanding that racial imbalances are not always an indication of racial bias). One of the most important things affirmative action can do is to define exactly what racial discrimination is and how it might manifest itself within a specific institution. The impulse to discriminate *is* subtle and cannot be ferreted out unless its many guises are made clear to people. Along with this there should be monitoring of institutions and heavy sanctions brought to bear when actual discrimination is found. This is the sort of affirmative action that America owes to blacks and to itself. It goes after the evil of discrimination itself, while preferences only sidestep the evil and grant entitlement to its *presumed* victims.

But if not preferences, then what? I think we need social policies that are committed to two goals: the educational and economic development of disadvantaged people, regardless of race, and the eradication from our society— through close monitoring and severe sanctions—of racial, ethnic, or gender discrimination. Preferences will not deliver us to either of these goals, since they tend to benefit those who are not disadvantaged—middle-class white women and middle-class blacks—and attack one form of discrimination with another. Preferences are inexpensive and carry the glamour of good intentions —change the numbers and the good deed is done. To be against them is to be unkind. But I think the unkindest cut is to bestow on children like my own an undeserved advantage while neglecting the development of those disadvantaged children on the East Side of my city who will likely never be in a position to benefit from a preference. Give my children fairness; give disadvantaged children a better shot at development—better elementary and secondary schools, job training, safer neighborhoods, better financial assistance for college, and so on. Fewer blacks go to college today than ten years ago; more black males of college age are in prison or under the control of the criminal justice system than in college. This despite racial preferences.

The mandates of black power and white absolution° out of which preferences emerged were not wrong in themselves. What was wrong was that both races focused more on the goals of these mandates than on the means to the goals. Blacks can have no real power without taking responsibility for their own educational and economic development. Whites can have no racial innocence without earning it by eradicating discrimination and helping the disadvantaged to develop. Because we ignored the means, the goals have not been reached, and the real work remains to be done.

---

*absolution:* Acquittal, forgiveness.

## QUESTIONS

1. Is Steele's introduction effective? Explain your response.
2. Reread the first paragraph of the essay; based on that paragraph, explain how Steele might define "racial discrimination." Do you agree with that definition? If not, how would you define the term?
3. What is this essay's thesis?
4. Steele writes that "white incompetence is always an individual matter, while for blacks it is often confirmation of ugly stereotypes." Explain whether or not you agree with this assessment.
5. Where does Steele present arguments that his opponents might raise? Is his presentation effective? What are those arguments?
6. After discussing the opponents and proponents of affirmative action, the author quotes a manager who seems to fall somewhere in the middle. Reread the manager's words and Steele's explanation of them. Do you agree with Steele's reading? Why or why not?
7. What, according to Steele, is the main problem with affirmative action?
8. According to Steele, what are the effects of affirmative action on the status of African Americans today? Do you agree?
9. How does Steele account for the subtle discrimination that some black professionals still feel?
10. Do you agree with Steele that "racial preferences implicitly mark whites with an exaggerated superiority just as they mark blacks with an exaggerated inferiority"?
11. What does Steele call for in the final pages of this essay? Do you agree that these reforms would help women and ethnic minorities more than the current affirmative action policies do?
12. Is the essay as a whole an example of effective argumentation? Why or why not?

## CONNECTIONS

1. Compare and contrast Steele's views on race relations in the United States with the views expressed by Martin Luther King, Jr., in the essay "Racism and the White Backlash."
2. Compare and contrast Steele's writing style with that of any other author included in this anthology.

# ✎ Myths of Political Quietism

*Michael Parenti*

> For a biographical note on Parenti, turn to page 273. Like the selection
> included in Section 4, the following essay comes from his book *Land of Idols*
> (1994).

> **WARM-UP:** Do you think that it's possible for an individual to have a
> significant impact on U.S. society today? Can you think of individuals
> who have? Are we, as a country, better off today because of their efforts?

1    In our society, there exists a number of notions that foster political quietism°
and inaction. Since they seldom are developed into well-articulated ideolo-
gies, they fail to catch the attention of philosophers, social critics, and political
theorists.[1] These notions have been widely disseminated by political leaders
and news pundits° and are familiar refrains in the conversation of ordinary
citizens. Their effect, if not their intent, is to discourage popular struggle and
encourage an acceptance of existing politico-economic conditions. For that
reason, they need to be critically examined.

## "You Can't Fight City Hall"

Many people believe it is futile to try to effect meaningful political
change, a view summed up in the adage, "You can't fight city hall."[2] We are
advised not to expect government to respond to our demands. As conservatives and anarchists alike would say, government cannot solve problems; government *is* the problem. Certainly, in many areas of public life, government is
a negative force, an instrument of coercive power that helps to intensify rather
than mitigate° the inequities suffered by millions of people at home and
abroad. Government in the hands of the privileged and powerful will advance
the interests of the privileged and powerful—unless democratic forces can
mobilize a countervailing° power. And that is the question.

The privileged and powerful are those who own the banks, corporations,
factories, mines, news and entertainment industries, and agribusiness firms of
this country. They are what is meant by the "owning class" or the "rich." The
"ruling elites" or "ruling class" are the politically active portion of the owning
class. They and their faithful acolytes° and scribes compose the Business

---

*quietism:* Lack of uproar or outcry.    *pundits:* People who give opinions in an authoritative manner.
*mitigate:* Mollify, alleviate.    *countervailing:* Counteracting.    *acolytes:* People who assist or followers.

Roundtable, Business Council, Trilateral Commission, and the Council on Foreign Relations, organizations started by the Rockefellers, Mellons, Morgans and other economic royalists. They are the people who become the secretaries of state, defense, and treasury, the national security advisors and CIA directors. Indeed, they become presidents, vice presidents, and senators. For the very top positions of state, the ruling class is largely self-recruiting.[3]

Within a political system in which wealth and class play such a dominant role, there seems to be little opportunity for progressive betterment. Popular sentiment is often denied a hearing. People are repeatedly deceived or distracted with a never-ending panorama of pop culture and media puffery.° Dissidents are harassed, suppressed, and sometimes even assassinated. In time, people lapse into cynicism and sour resignation. "People are not likely to start a fight," notes Schattschneider, "if they are certain that they are going to be severely penalized for their efforts. In this situation repression may assume the guise of a false unanimity."[4] Indeed, some commentators treat political discouragement and quietude as symptomatic of contentment, arguing that we are too happy with our abundance and freedom to engage in political struggle.[5]

Yet, that is not the whole picture. Despite the powerful array of forces against them, many people still organize, agitate, protest, resist, and fight back —sometimes with an impressive measure of success. In recent decades we have witnessed a number of powerful democratic movements: the civil rights protests to enfranchise African Americans in the South and end lynch-mob rule and segregation, the civil liberties struggle against McCarthyism and government harassment of dissidents, the movement to end the Vietnam war, the anti-imperialist solidarity for El Salvador and Nicaragua, the attempts to build alternative educational and informational institutions, the movement for a nuclear freeze and an end to the arms race, and the struggles for women's rights, gay rights, ecology, and environmentalism. During those same years, we have seen long and bitter labor struggles valiantly fought by coal miners, steel workers, farm workers, airline employees, newspaper staffs, bus drivers, teachers, university staff, hospital workers, and others.

While probably none of these mass movements and labor struggles have met with unqualified success, all have made a difference. All have had an impact in limiting how far the rich and powerful can go in advancing their otherwise uncompromising pursuit of profit and privilege.

The conventional view is that power is antithetical° to freedom, a threat to it. This can be true of *state* power and other forms of institutionalized authority. However, *popular* power and freedom are not antithetical but complementary: If you do not have the power to limit the abuses of wealth and position,

*puffery:* Hype.   *antithetical:* Opposed, contradictory.

you do not have much freedom. In order to wrest democratic gains from entrenched interests, the people must mobilize a countervailing power. "The concessions of the privileged to the unprivileged," wrote John Stuart Mill in 1869, "are so seldom brought about by any better motive than the power of the unprivileged to extort them. . . ."[6] In 1857, Frederick Douglass wrote: "Power concedes nothing without a demand. It never has, and it never will."[7]

The goal of popular action is not only to limit or rebuff state power but to make it work for democratic ends as opposed to plutocratic° ones. Rather than saying "you cannot fight city hall," we might better say that we cannot afford not to. It is often frustrating and sometimes dangerous to challenge those who own and control the land, capital, and technology of society. But, in the long run, it is even more dangerous not to do so. As history shows, people frequently endeavor to resist the disadvantages imposed upon them by unjust socioeconomic conditions. They may be propelled by a vision of a better life for all or by the necessities of their own material conditions. Inequities and iniquities° can become so oppressive that submission no longer guarantees survival and the people have nothing to lose in resisting. This is not to say they will always rebel against oppression, but the right combination of anger, hope, and organization sometimes can galvanize° them to perform remarkable deeds.

Even in the most desperate circumstances, as exist under slavery, resistance can have an effect. Reflecting on his experience as a slave, Frederick Douglass observed that defiance of any sort was a "fearful hazard."

> Nevertheless, when a slave has nerve enough to exercise it, and boldly approaches his master, with a well-founded complaint against an overseer, though he may be repulsed, and may even have that of which he complains repeated at the time, and though he may be beaten by his master, as well as by his overseer, for his temerity,° in the end the policy of complaining is generally vindicated by the relaxed rigor of the overseer's treatment. The latter becomes more careful, and less disposed to use the lash upon such slaves thereafter. . . . The overseer very naturally dislikes to have the ear of the master disturbed by complaints; and either upon this consideration or upon advice and warning privately given him by his employers, he generally modifies the rigor of his rule. . . .[8]

10    Regarding their own interests, the worst thing people can do is to do nothing, to lapse into political quietism. In 1983, the Reagan administration's welfare chief, Linda McMahon, justified the savage cuts in human services imposed on the poorest and politically weakest element of the population, by

---

*plutocratic:* Related to aristocracy or the wealthy.    *iniquities:* Gross injustices.    *galvanize:* Stimulate or excite as if by an electric shock.    *temerity:* Daring, courage.

noting that their effects must have been tolerable because "We're not seeing riots. We're not seeing people rushing the doors of Congress and the White House."[9] The image of disabled and underemployed subsistence workers hopping jets to storm the capital is almost amusing. Not so the idea that the government can do what it likes to the most vulnerable among us as long as they don't take to the streets and inconvenience the rulers.

Compliant passivity is the goal of all rulers who seek to preserve their entrenched privileges against the claims of the disadvantaged. It is what they usually mean by "stability" and "order."

## "Plus ça change, plus c'est la même chose"

The old French saying, "The more it changes, the more it is the same thing," resembles the American one about not being able to fight city hall. But it goes a step further in its cynicism, arguing that it does not much matter what changes are effected because the same kinds of outrages will prevail— albeit with new players in new costumes. By this view, history becomes nothing more than a dreary repetition of human folly and injustice.

Much of history does seem to fit that description. Many times hopeful developments end in misery and mishap. New policies and leaders seem to bring the same old results. And like Victor Hugo, one is left to ask, "Will the future ever arrive?" Furthermore, when things do change in a significant way, it can be for the worse—as with global ecology, the scale and proficiency of military destructiveness, the neo-imperialist impoverishment of weaker nations, and the abuses of power imposed by technologies of surveillance and violence. So one is tempted to conclude, "*plus ça change, plus c'est misérable.*"

Yet, many things have improved through democratic struggle. The conditions of labor, never really secure in a capitalist society, have advanced dramatically in some western countries since the Industrial Revolution, when sickened and undernourished children toiled in factories from dawn to dusk. The transition from slavery to serfdom to "free labor" to organized labor represents a net gain in the human condition. Who among us, even a low-paid worker, would trade their lot for that of a slave in ancient Rome or the antebellum° South or even for an industrial worker of an earlier time—for whom such things as collective bargaining, arbitration, formal grievances, occupational safety, job benefits, unemployment insurance, seniority, and medical coverage were but a chimera.°

Likewise, the condition of women has improved—at least in some countries—through decades of struggle. In nineteenth-century America, women

15

---

*antebellum:* Pre–Civil War.    *chimera:* Illusion, fabrication of the mind.

in various states had no property rights in marriage. Most were granted no social identity other than that which they gained from their families or from marital association with a man. They could not vote or occupy public office. They had no entry into the job market except for a few low-paying occupations. They had no access to legal birth control and safe abortions. But whatever gains have been won, women who struggle against injustice are understandably loath to be told, "You've come a long way." What they hear in such reassurances is that they should be content with their present lot. Given their justifiable sense of outrage regarding the continuing injustices they face in present-day society, politically aware women are understandably inclined to do the opposite: emphasize the abuses they endure and ignore the accomplishments, claiming they are as oppressed as ever. But the truth is, as bad as women have it today in the United States, they had it worse in yesteryear—as we are well reminded whenever reactionism threatens to plunge us back to yesteryear, and whenever we observe the condition of women in a host of other countries.

Much the same can be said about racial oppression. Thus, note the victorious struggles against lynch-mob rule, segregation in public accommodations, electoral disfranchisement, and the like. But when a White supremacist senator like Strom Thurmond of South Carolina declares in a tone devoid of° admiration: "No one has made more progress than the nigra people" (as I once heard him say at a Senate committee hearing), African Americans are not inclined to sit back and be quietly grateful—which is what the senator wants them to be. Not surprisingly, some militants are inclined to do just the opposite, to deny that anything has really changed. "We are still on the plantation, living under the whip," is the way I heard one community leader put it. Such assertions manifest an imperfect appreciation of the unspeakable horrors of antebellum slavery and deny the courageous struggles won by generations of oppressed people against slavery and segregation.

Not only among those who fight for gender and racial equality but throughout the entire Left, it is too often taken as a badge of militancy to be as negative as possible, dismissing every gain as a crumb and a subterfuge°—and even a disguised oppression. While the powers that be try to transform every policy vice into a virtue, the understandable but inaccurate inclination of protestors is to change every virtue into a vice. It is one thing to be uncompromising in one's dedication to justice and democracy and something else to be unwilling to see that incremental gains are important steps to further struggles, that victories can be and have been won, and that these accomplishment—though incomplete and insufficient—sometimes bring a real better-

*devoid of:* empty of, lacking in.    *subterfuge:* Deception, deceitful scheme.

ment to the lives of millions of people. (This is not to deny that some gains are vastly inadequate in solving the horrendous problems faced by underprivileged peoples.)

The supermilitant who so thoroughly grasps the larger picture as to see nothing significantly good in any immediate struggle, ends up in a state of noisy inaction, eschewing° coalitions, or worse, becoming a divisive force, "outlefting" everyone else but accomplishing little.

Only by ignoring the differences in content among various oppressions can we assert that no "real" change has been achieved. To assert that a woman is "raped" every time a man casts a salacious glance her way may be an effective rhetorical device to highlight the subtler forms of male aggression, but it simultaneously diminishes the seriousness of rape by so expanding and diluting its meaning. It reduces content to form. While the basic *form* of man-victimizing-woman cannot be denied both in the act of visual harassment and the act of criminal sexual violence, the *content* is markedly different in the respective instances. To reduce content to form is to reduce reality to polemic.° It may make us more militant-sounding but not more effective and durable in fighting for social justice.

Let nothing said above detract from the understanding that it was *mili-* tancy in labor struggles, civil rights, and women's rights that generated the kind of agitation and popular force from which change did occur. Changes have been won through struggle against a money-dominated politico-economic system that seldom operates democratically on its own. But such past victories should not be read as a call for complacency. In this plutocracy, many democratic gains have yet to be won and past gains are ever in danger of being rolled back.     20

1. One exception might be philosopher Barrows Dunham's attempts to treat such views in his *Man Against Myth* (Boston: Little, Brown, 1947).
2. "You can't fight city hall," is an expression that was heard much more frequently in the 1940s and 1950s than today, perhaps because the municipalities of the nation have themselves so declined in political influence, media visibility, and budgetary solvency.
3. For a more detailed treatment of the ruling class, see Michael Parenti, *Democracy for the Few,* 5th ed. (New York: St. Martin's Press, 1988), pp. 196–200.
4. E. E. Schattschneider, *The Semi-Sovereign People* (New York: Holt, Rinehart & Winston, 1960), p. 8.
5. Among those who argue that public apathy is either symptomatic of contentment or desirable for stability are: Heinz Eulau, "The Politics of Happiness," *Antioch Review,* 16, 1956, pp. 259–264; Seymour Lipset, *Political Man* (Garden City, NY: Doubleday, 1960), pp. 179–219; and Samuel Huntington and Michael Crozier,

*eschewing:* Avoiding.     *polemic:* Discussion or quarrel, without substance.

*The Crisis of Democracy* (New York: New York University Press, 1975). This latter title is a report to the Trilateral Commission. The same opinion is propagated by conservative journalists. For example, George Will writes, "Low [voter] turnouts often are signs of social health. Low political energy can be a consequence of consensus about basics": *Washington Post,* September 5, 1991.

6. John Stuart Mill, *The Subjugation of Women* (Cambridge, MA: MIT Press, 1972), p. 72.
7. Philip Foner (ed.), *The Life and Writings of Frederick Douglass,* vol. 2, 1850–1860 (New York: International Publishers, 1950), p. 437.
8. Frederick Douglass, *My Bondage and My Freedom,* 1855 edition (New York: Dover Publications, 1969) p. 84.
9. *Washington Post,* editorial, February 17, 1983.

## QUESTIONS

1. Explain the meaning of the title "Myths of Political Quietism."
2. Explain what Parenti means by "owning class" and "ruling class." What is the difference between the two?
3. Do you agree with Parenti's claim that under our system "there seems to be little opportunity for progressive betterment"? What do you base your answer on?
4. What are some of the popular democratic movements that, according to Parenti, have been organized recently in our country?
5. According to Parenti, what is "the worst thing people can do" in regard to their government and their interests?
6. In what areas has our society changed for the better?
7. What does Parenti accuse many leftist/progressive activists of doing? Based on your experience, do you feel that his accusations are justified?
8. Does Parenti offer any concessions in the second part of the reading, "Plus ça change, plus c'est le même chose"?
9. Is this selection an example of effective argumentation? Why or why not? Would you change anything to make the essay more persuasive?

## CONNECTIONS

1. Compare and contrast Parenti's ideas and writing style with those of Paolo Freire (whose essay appears in Section 1).
2. Compare and contrast Parenti's discussion of progressive activists with P. J. O'Rourke's critique of the same (included in Section 5).

# ∽ American Classic

## *Louis Simpson*

Born in Jamaica in 1923, Louis Simpson became a U.S. citizen as a young man. He earned a Ph.D. from New York City's Columbia University in 1953 and worked in publishing and in the export trade before turning to writing and teaching. He has taught at Columbia, at the University of California–Berkeley, and at the State University of New York at Stony Brook. Best known as a poet, Simpson has published more than fifteen books of poems, including *At the End of the Open Road,* which won the Pulitzer Prize for poetry in 1964, *People Live Here: Selected Poems 1949–1983* (1983), and the recent *There You Are* (1995). He has also published an autobiography (*North of Jamaica,* 1972), as well as a memoir entitled *The King My Father's Wreck* (1995). The following poem first appeared in the collection *Caviare at the Funeral* (1980).


It's a classic American scene—                                    1
a car stopped off the road
and a man trying to repair it.

The woman who stays in the car
in the classic American scene                                     5
stares back at the freeway traffic.

They look surprised, and ashamed
to be so helpless . . .
let down in the middle of the road!

To think that their car would do this!                           10
They look like mountain people
whose son has gone against the law.

But every night they set out food
and the robber goes skulking back to the trees.
That's how it is with the car . . .                              15

it's theirs, they're stuck with it.
Now they know what it's like to sit
and see the world go whizzing by.

In the fume of carbon monoxide and dust
20    they are not such good Americans
as they thought they were.

The feeling of being left out
through no fault of your own, is common.
That's why I say, an American classic.

## QUESTIONS

1. What are the implications of comparing the people whose car has broken down with people "whose son has gone against the law"?
2. Why do you think the poet says that the two in the broken-down car "are not such good Americans / as they thought they were"?
3. Explain the last stanza of the poem. Why does the poet call the scene "an American classic"?
4. Do you agree that "the feeling of being left out / through no fault of your own, is common"? Have you ever felt that way? If so, in what context(s)?
5. Explain the paradox, the contradiction, in the last two sentences of the poem.

## CONNECTIONS

Which of the characters or authors you have read (or read about) so far in this text feel "left out" in some way?

# Get off My Jock:
## A Definition of What It Means to Be a Student Athlete

*Darron D. Reese*

Darron Reese was born in 1969 in Oakland, California. He attended nearby Mt. Diablo High School, where he participated in track, football, and wrestling and where he won the P. J. Kramer Award for outstanding athletic and academic achievement combined. After graduating from high school in 1988, Reese attended Diablo Valley College, participated in the state championships in track, and earned an associate's degree in two years. He is currently pursuing a bachelor's degree in recreation, with an option in youth science administration, at California State University–Hayward. As a member of the university's track team, Reese qualified for the national championships. He has been employed full-time as an emergency road-service dispatcher for the past several years and intends to earn a master's degree in public administration and then work as a teacher or a coach.

**WARM-UP:** What are some of the stereotypes associated with student-athletes? Do you know any student-athletes? What are they like?

There are many misunderstandings about what it means to be a student athlete. These misunderstandings make for some of the most interesting debates in high schools and colleges across America. As a student athlete myself, I have sat in many classes, heard many debates, and read many articles on the subject. Through this process, I've learned that those who say student athletes have it easy or "get breaks" don't fully understand how much time and energy goes into being one. While student athletes are often seen wearing their uniforms and competing in games, they are often overlooked when it comes to the preparation and dedication to their sports, along with the academic loads they too must carry, just as other students.

Some of the major misconceptions that I've run into are that student athletes party a lot, skip class, hang out in cliques, and are scholastically lazy. For example, I commonly hear people say that student athletes, or "Jocks," just like to party, fight, do drugs, and chase members of the opposite sex. It is also said that they hang out in their little cliques and don't associate with anyone else on campus, thinking that they're "God's gift to the earth." There is also the misconception that student athletes have no respect for professors, so they cut classes to go out and do Lord knows what, which leads to the notion that "Jocks are scholastically lazy."

The majority of these stereotypical notions transpire through the media's portrayal of the student athlete in movies such as "Animal House," "Revenge of the Nerds," "Back to School," and "Wildcats." Unfortunately, these movies may present various truths about the lifestyles of *some* student athletes.

*The Random House College Dictionary* defines "student" as "a person formally engaged in learning, especially one enrolled in an institution of secondary or higher education." It defines "athlete" as "a person trained to compete in contests involving physical agility, stamina, or strength; a trained competitor in a sport, exercise, or game requiring physical skills." Bringing the two definitions together to form student athlete, you have a person "formally engaged in learning" while blessed with the skills required in order "to compete in contests involving physical agility, stamina, or strength."

> Student-athletes operate on schedules with limited flexibility—typically attending classes in the morning and early afternoons, participating in sports-related activities during the afternoons and early evenings, and devoting evenings to study or other necessary daily activities. Generally, student-oriented services such as counseling, workshops, and other programs are conducted during times when student-athletes are involved in practice or conditioning and therefore have difficulty using these services (Jordan and Denson 95).

5    The day-to-day life of a student athlete has its ups and downs. One of the downs, for example, is if the athlete is living off-campus.

In my first quarter at California State University, Hayward, I commuted from West Pittsburg, CA (a one-and-a-half hour drive in traffic), not only for school: my job was also in Hayward, so it was a seven-day-a-week headache. I would wake up at 5:30 in the morning and leave at 6:15, when it would still be dark outside, in order to make it to my 8:00 class. I had three classes with one one-hour break in the whole day. I would finish classes at 1:10 pm. Track practice would begin at 2:00, and the fifty minutes in between were spent with the athletic trainer.

Practice ran overtime nearly every session (and, as glamorous as it may seem, there is a lot of hard work involved when striving to be the best at whatever you do). In four out of the five of these practices, I would train every last piece of energy out of my body. I would work until either my muscles would cramp up or I would vomit. There were even times when I would work out so hard, I just couldn't stand up anymore.

Having to be at work at five—in order to make money for tuition, books, and gas—I'd wrestle myself up from the cold hard ground and wobble to my truck. I would arrive at the job site at 5:01, tired, hungry, light-headed, grumpy, and, worst of all, musty.

Keeping my distance from co-workers, I would get off work at 11:00 even more stressed, trying not to think about my hour's drive home only to sit down in front of homework that I didn't understand because I was too tired in class to pay attention.

Within this lifestyle there was no time for girlfriends or talking on the phone. There was no time to stop and enjoy an ice cream cone, spend time with family or go for a walk in the park. I didn't even have time to go see professors during their office hours. And, because of this type of schedule, it was virtually impossible for me to make appointments with tutors, counselors, or academic advisors.

The above examples illustrate how the term student athlete can easily get misinterpreted. They also show how it can lead to the notion that student athletes are scholastically lazy. It is true that student athletes may miss a few classes, as all students do, but please don't contend that they are lazy when they could either be at work, tired, on a road trip, tending to family problems, or flat out sick.

An article that appeared in the January 8th, 1990 issue of *U.S. News and World Report* reported that a study conducted by the NCAA Presidents Commission found that athletes devote an average of thirty hours a week to their sport (Brownlee 50). This can cause serious problems mentally, physically, emotionally, and nutritionally.

> The Center for Counseling and Student Development, in conjunction with the Department of Intercollegiate Athletics, has developed a unique program in response to these concerns. Student Services for Athletes (SSA) is a program that recognizes the special challenges that student-athletes face and endeavors to provide existing student services to student-athletes at times and locations more convenient to them (Jordan and Denson 95).

The program will provide, in addition to regular tutoring services, "(1) academic monitoring, (2) consultation services with the university community, (3) outreach through workshops and special programs, and (4) personal counseling" (Jordan and Denson).

More programs such as SSA are needed, because student athletes all across America are dealing with the same types of problems (even ones with husbands or wives, kids, and full-time jobs).

Another thing that's overlooked is how much of an inconvenience it can be when student athletes go on the road. For example, they will take their textbooks with them to study for quizzes, midterms, and even finals during these long and very uncomfortable bus or van rides, not to mention sleeping in hotels and eating take-out food every weekend.

But despite the many obstacles involved, there are also lots of valuable things that one can learn from being a student athlete. No! not partying, fighting, or skipping class, but learning how to interact socially with peoples of all races. You learn that no matter how good you think you are, there's always someone out there better than you. You learn how to lose with pride and hold your chin up high. You learn about responsibility, relationships, and life, along with setting and achieving goals (athletically, scholastically, personally). You learn about rent. You learn how to deal with life's ups and downs (which were mentioned earlier). You learn about respect and self-respect, and that you must earn it. You learn not to underestimate others. All of these things are values, and being a student athlete helps to put you in touch with your own personal beliefs and value system.

In 1982 the U.S. Department of Education sponsored a study of the social-psychological behavior of high school students. The students were observed and then classified into four groups. The type 1 students had strong involvement in both academics and athletics. The type 2 students had high involvement in academics. The type 3 students had high involvement in athletics, while the type 4 students lacked involvement in both (Snyder and Spreitzer 520). The results of this two-year study revealed that type 1 students "had high scores in self-esteem, leadership, internal locus of control, and assimilation of the conventional values of the high school. In short, the findings indicated that students who can perform the joint roles of scholar and athlete are outstanding in terms of social psychological attributes" (Snyder and Spreitzer 520).

Before defining student athlete in my own words, the one thing I want to leave you with is that no matter how much publicity, recognition, or glory individual athletes receive, you should remember that Jocks too are still human and deal with the same day-to-day problems as everyone else. The way they handle these problems is entirely up to them. Therefore, it is important to try not to stereotype all athletes or a specific athletic program based on the judgments or actions of *one* individual (or from what is seen in the movies).

So what, then, is a student athlete? The answer is simple. A student athlete is one who, by being a student, is in constant search for knowledge and growth. A student athlete is one who, by being an athlete, uses his or her God-given ability to explore his or her physical limits, taking on all challenges. A successful student athlete knows how to deal with life's day-to-day obstacles in a mature and responsible manner. A successful athlete *knows* that he or she is a success in life. Without this inner sense of knowledge and self respect, he or she will never be able to gain the respect of others. And it is only with this self-respect and knowledge of self that a truly successful student athlete can deal with misplaced myths and stereotypes.

## Works Cited

Brownlee, Shannon. "The Myth of the Student-Athlete (College Sports Versus Education)." *U.S. News and World Report* 8 Jan. 1990: 50–53.

Jordon, Janice M., and Eric L. Denson. "Student Services for Athletes: A Model for Enhancing the Student-Athlete Experience." *Journal of Counseling and Development* 69 (1990): 94–97.

Knapp, Terry J., and J. F. Raney. "Student-Athletes and Academic Course Work: A Ten Year Summary." *Perceptual and Motor Skills* 71 (1990): 793–95.

*Random House College Dictionary.* 5th ed. 1975.

Snyder, Eldon E., and Elmer Spreitzer. "Social Psychology Concomitants of Adolescents' Role Identities as Scholars and Athletes: A Longitudinal Analysis." *Youth and Society* 23 1992: 507–24.

### QUESTIONS

1. Is the title of this essay effective? Why or why not?
2. In the context of an argumentative essay, is Reese's introduction effective? Why or why not?
3. Does Reese present claims that opponents of his viewpoint would make about this subject? If so, what are those claims?
4. Is Reese's use of personal experience to support his claim effective? Why or why not?
5. Find an example of the use of recurrence (effective repetition) in this essay.
6. As you read this essay, do you feel that you are hearing Reese's voice? Or has this student author taken on the voice of his sources?
7. What logical fallacy does Reese imply that his opponents are guilty of?
8. Do you find Reese's argument convincing? Why or why not?
9. What suggestions would you offer Reese for improving this essay?

### CONNECTIONS

1. Of the essays you have read so far during this term, which other ones seek to dispel a stereotype?
2. Compare and contrast Reese's writing style with that of Kristina Milam, the student who wrote the essay "Do I?!" (included in Section 3).

# Crimes against Humanity

## Ward Churchill

Born in 1947, Ward Churchill, a métis ("mixed-blood") descendant of Creek and Cherokee peoples, is the coordinator of the American Indian Movement (AIM) for the state of Colorado. Churchill graduated from Sangamon State University in Illinois with a degree in communications. He has written several books, most recently *Fantasies of the Master Race: Literature, Cinema, and the Colonization of American Indians* (1992), *Struggle for the Land: Indigenous Resistance to Genocide, Ecocide and Expropriation in Contemporary America* (1993), and *Indians Are Us: Culture and Genocide in Native North Americans* (1994). Churchill presently teaches at the Center for Studies of Ethnicity and Race in America, at the University of Colorado at Boulder. The following essay was first published in *Z Magazine* in March 1993.

**WARM-UP:** What do you know about the current status or conditions of indigenous peoples in the United States?

1    During the past couple of seasons, there has been an increasing wave of controversy regarding the names of professional sports teams like the Atlanta "Braves," Cleveland "Indians," Washington "Redskins," and Kansas City "Chiefs." The issue extends to the names of college teams like Florida State University "Seminoles," University of Illinois "Fighting Illini," and so on, right on down to high school outfits like the Lamar (Colorado) "Savages." Also involved have been team adoption of "mascots," replete with feathers, buckskins, beads, spears and "warpaint" (some fans have opted to adorn themselves in the same fashion), and nifty little "pep" gestures like the "Indian Chant" and "Tomahawk Chop."

A substantial number of American Indians have protested that use of native names, images and symbols as sports team mascots and the like is, by definition, a virulently° racist practice. Given the historical relationship between Indians and non-Indians during what has been called the "Conquest of America," American Indian Movement leader (and American Indian Anti-Defamation Council founder) Russell Means has compared the practice to contemporary Germans naming their soccer teams the "Jews," "Hebrews," and "Yids," while adorning their uniforms with grotesque caricatures of Jewish faces taken from the Nazis' anti-Semitic propaganda of the 1930s. Numerous

---

*virulently:* Viciously, maliciously.

demonstrations have occurred in conjunction with games—most notably during the November 15, 1992 match-up between the Chiefs and Redskins in Kansas City—by angry Indians and their supporters.

In response, a number of players—especially African Americans and other minority athletes—have been trotted out by professional team owners like Ted Turner, as well as university and public school officials, to announce that they mean not to insult but to honor native people. They have been joined by the television networks and most major newspapers, all of which have editorialized that Indian discomfort with the situation is "no big deal," insisting that the whole thing is just "good, clean fun." The country needs more such fun, they've argued, and "a few disgruntled Native Americans" have no right to undermine the nation's enjoyment of its leisure time by complaining. This is especially the case, some have argued, "in hard times like these." It has even been contended that Indian outrage at being systematically degraded —rather than the degradation itself—creates "a serious barrier to the sort of intergroup communication so necessary in a multicultural society such as ours."

Okay, let's communicate. We are frankly dubious° that those advancing such positions really believe their own rhetoric, but, just for the sake of argument, let's accept the premise that they are sincere. If what they say is true, then isn't it time we spread such "inoffensiveness" and "good cheer" around among *all* groups so that *everybody* can participate *equally* in fostering the round of national laughs they call for? Sure it is—the country can't have too much fun or "intergroup involvement"—so the more, the merrier. Simple consistency demands that anyone who thinks the Tomahawk Chop is a swell pastime must be just as hearty in their endorsement of the following ideas— by the logic used to defend the defamation of American Indians—[to] help us all really start yukking it up.

First, as a counterpart to the Redskins, we need an NFL team called "Niggers" to honor Afro-Americans. Half-time festivities for fans might include a simulated stewing of the opposing coach in a large pot while players and cheerleaders dance around it, garbed in leopard skins and wearing fake bones in their noses. This concept obviously goes along with the kind of gaiety attending the Chop, but also with the actions of the Kansas City Chiefs, whose team members—prominently including black team members—lately appeared on a poster looking "fierce" and "savage" by way of wearing Indian regalia. Just a bit of harmless "morale boosting," says the Chiefs' front office. You bet.

So that the newly-formed Niggers sports club won't end up too out of sync while expressing the "spirit" and "identity" of Afro-Americans in the

*dubious:* Doubtful.

above fashion, a baseball franchise—let's call this one the "Sambos"—should be formed. How about a basketball team called the "Spearchuckers"? A hockey team called the "Jungle Bunnies"? Maybe the "essence" of these teams could be depicted by images of tiny black faces adorned with huge pairs of lips. The players could appear on TV every week or so gnawing on chicken legs and spitting watermelon seeds at one another. Catchy, eh? Well, there's "nothing to be upset about," according to those who love wearing "war bonnets" to the Super Bowl or having "Chief Illiniwik" dance around the sports arenas of Urbana, Illinois.

And why stop there? There are plenty of other groups to include. "Hispanics"? They can be "represented" by the Galveston "Greasers" and San Diego "Spics," at least until the Wisconsin "Wetbacks" and Baltimore "Beaners" get off the ground. Asian Americans? How about the "Slopes," "Dinks," "Gooks," and "Zipperheads"? Owners of the latter teams might get their logo ideas from editorial page cartoons printed in the nation's newspapers during World War II: slant-eyes, buck teeth, big glasses, but nothing racially insulting or derogatory, according to the editors and artists involved at the time. Indeed, this Second World War-vintage stuff can be seen as just another barrel of laughs, at least by what current editors say are their "local standards" concerning American Indians.

Let's see. Who's been left out? Teams like the Kansas City "Kikes," Hanover "Honkies," San Leandro "Shylocks," Daytona "Dagos," and Pittsburgh "Polacks" will fill a certain social void among white folk. Have a religious belief? Let's all go for the gusto and gear up the Milwaukee "Mackerel Snappers" and Hollywood "Holy Rollers." The Fighting Irish of Notre Dame can be rechristened the "Drunken Irish" or "Papist Pigs." Issues of gender and sexual preference can be addressed through creation of teams like the St. Louis "Sluts," Boston "Bimbos," Detroit "Dykes," and the Fresno "Fags." How about the Gainesville "Gimps" and Richmond "Retards," so the physically and mentally impaired won't be excluded from our fun and games?

Now, don't go getting "overly sensitive" out there. None of this is demeaning or insulting, at least not when it's being done to Indians. Just ask the folks who are doing it, or their apologists like Andy Rooney in the national media. They'll tell you—as in fact they *have* been telling you—that there's been no harm done, regardless of what their victims think, feel, or say. The situation is exactly the same as when those with precisely the same mentality used to insist that Step 'n' Fetchit was okay, or Rochester on the Jack Benny Show, or Amos and Andy, Charlie Chan, the Frito Bandito, or any of the other cutesy symbols making up the lexicon° of American racism. Have we communicated yet?

lexicon: Vocabulary, terminology.

Let's get just get a little bit real here. The notion of "fun" embodied in rituals like the Tomahawk Chop must be understood for what it is. There's not a single non-Indian example used above which can be considered socially acceptable in even the most marginal sense. The reasons are obvious enough. So why is it different where American Indians are concerned? One can only conclude that, in contrast to the other groups at issue, Indians are (falsely) perceived as being too few, and therefore too weak, to defend themselves effectively against racist and otherwise offensive behavior.

Fortunately, there are some glimmers of hope. A few teams and their fans have gotten the message and have responded appropriately. Stanford University, which opted to drop the name "Indians" from Stanford, has experienced no resulting dropoff in attendance. Meanwhile, the local newspaper in Portland, Oregon, recently decided its long-standing editorial policy prohibiting use of racial epithets should include derogatory team names. The Redskins, for instance, are now referred to as "the Washington team," and will continue to be described in this way until the franchise adopts an inoffensive moniker° (newspaper sales in Portland have suffered no decline as a result).

Such examples are to be applauded and encouraged. They stand as figurative beacons in the night, proving beyond all doubt that it is quite possible to indulge in the pleasure of athletics without accepting blatant racism into the bargain.

On October 16, 1946, a man named Julius Streicher mounted the steps of a gallows. Moments later he was dead, the sentence of an international tribunal composed of representatives of the United States, France, Great Britain, and the Soviet Union having been imposed. Streicher's body was then cremated, and—so horrendous were his crimes thought to have been—his ashes dumped into an unspecified German river so that "no one should ever know a particular place to go for reasons of mourning his memory."

Julius Streicher had been convicted at Nuremberg, Germany, of what were termed "Crimes Against Humanity." The lead prosecutor in his case—Justice Robert Jackson of the United States Supreme Court—had not argued that the defendant had killed anyone, nor that he had personally committed any especially violent act. Nor was it contended that Streicher had held any particularly important position in the German government during the period in which the so-called Third Reich had exterminated some 6,000,000 Jews, as well as several million Gypsies, Poles, Slavs, homosexuals, and other untermenschen (subhumans).

---

*moniker:* Name or nickname.

15      The sole offense for which the accused was ordered put to death was in having served as publisher/editor of a Bavarian tabloid entitled *Der Stürmer* during the early-to-mid 1930s, years before the Nazi genocide° actually began. In this capacity, he had penned a long series of virulently anti-Semitic editorials and "news" stories, usually accompanied by cartoons and other images graphically depicting Jews in extraordinarily derogatory fashion. This, the prosecution asserted, had done much to "dehumanize" the targets of his distortion in the mind of the German public. In turn, such dehumanization had made it possible—or at least easier—for average Germans to later indulge in the outright liquidation of Jewish "vermin." The tribunal agreed, holding that Streicher was therefore complicit in genocide and deserving of death by hanging.

During his remarks to the Nuremberg tribunal, Justice Jackson observed that, in implementing its sentences, the participating powers were morally and legally binding themselves to adhere forever after to the same standards of conduct that were being applied to Streicher and the other Nazi leaders. In the alternative, he said, the victorious allies would have committed "pure murder" at Nuremburg—no different in substance from that carried out by those they presumed to judge—rather than establishing the "permanent benchmark for justice" which was intended.

Yet in the United States of Robert Jackson, the indigenous American Indian population had already been reduced, in a process which is ongoing to this day, from perhaps 12.5 million in the year 1500 to fewer than 250,000 by the beginning of the 20th century. This was accomplished, according to official sources, "largely through the cruelty of [Euro-American] settlers" and an informal but clear governmental policy which had made it an articulated goal to "exterminate these red vermin" or at least whole segments of them.

Bounties had been placed on the scalps of Indians—any Indians—in places as diverse as Georgia, Kentucky, Texas, the Dakotas, Oregon, and California, and had been maintained until resident Indian populations were decimated° or disappeared altogether. Entire peoples such as the Cherokee had been reduced to half their size through a policy of forced removal from their homelands east of the Mississippi River to what were then considered less preferable areas in the West.

Others, such as the Navajo, suffered the same fate while under military guard for years on end. The United States Army had also perpetrated a long series of wholesale massacres of Indians at places like Horseshoe Bend, Bear River, Sand Creek, the Washita River, the Marias River, Camp Robinson, and Wounded Knee.

---

*genocide:* Intentional and systematic destruction of a racial, political, or cultural group.    *decimated:* Destroyed.

Through it all, hundreds of popular novels—each competing with the    20
next to make Indians appear more grotesque, menacing, and inhuman—were
sold in the tens of millions of copies in the U.S. Plainly, the Euro-American
public was being conditioned to see Indians in such a way as to allow their
eradication to continue. And continue it did until the Manifest Destiny° of the
U.S.—a direct precursor° to what Hitler would subsequently call Lebens-
raumpolitik (the politics of living space)—was consummated.

By 1900, the national project of "clearing" Native Americans from their
land and replacing them with "superior" Anglo-American settlers was complete; the indigenous population had been reduced by as much as 98 percent
while approximately 97.5 percent of their original territory had "passed" to
the invaders. The survivors had been concentrated, out of sight and mind of
the public, on scattered "reservations," all of them under the self-assigned
"plenary" (full) power of the federal government. There was, of course, no
Nuremberg-style tribunal passing judgment on those who had fostered such
circumstances in North America. No U.S. official or private citizen was ever
imprisoned—never mind hanged—for implementing or propagandizing
what had been done. Nor had the process of genocide afflicting Indians been
completed. Instead, it merely changed form.

Between the 1880s and the 1980s, nearly half of all Native American children were coercively transferred from their own families, communities, and
cultures to those of the conquering society. This was done through compulsory attendance at remote boarding schools, often hundreds of miles from
their homes, where native children were kept for years on end while being systematically "deculturated" (indoctrinated to think and act in the manner of
Euro Americans rather than as Indians). It was also accomplished through a
pervasive foster home and adoption program—including "blind" adoptions,
where children would be permanently denied information as to who they
were/are and where they'd come from—placing native youths in non-Indian
homes.

The express purpose of all this was to facilitate a U.S. governmental policy
to bring about the "assimilation" (dissolution) of indigenous societies. In
other words, Indian cultures as such were to be caused to disappear. Such policy objectives are directly contrary to the United Nations 1948 Convention on
Punishment and Prevention of the Crime of Genocide, an element of international law arising from the Nuremberg proceedings. The forced "transfer of
the children" of a targeted "racial, ethnical, or religious group" is explicitly
prohibited as a genocidal activity under the Convention's second article.

---

*Manifest Destiny:* A nineteenth-century belief that the White people had the duty and right to control
and develop the entire North American continent.    *precursor:* Predecessor, forerunner.

Article II of the Genocide Convention also expressly prohibits involuntary sterilization as a means of "preventing births among" a targeted population. Yet, in 1975, it was conceded by the U.S. government that its Indian Health Service (IHS), then a subpart of the Bureau of Indian Affairs (BIA), was even then conducting a secret program of involuntary sterilization that had affected approximately 40 percent of all Indian women. The program was allegedly discontinued, and the IHS was transferred to the Public Health Service, but no one was punished. In 1990, it came out that the IHS was inoculating Inuit children in Alaska with Hepatitis-B vaccine. The vaccine had already been banned by the World Health Organization as having demonstrated correlation with the HIV-Syndrome which is itself correlated to AIDS. As this is written, a "field test" of Hepatitis-A vaccine, also HIV-correlated, is being conducted on Indian reservations in the northern plains region.

25    The Genocide Convention makes it a "crime against humanity" to create conditions leading to the destruction of an identifiable human group, as such. Yet the BIA has utilized the government's plenary° prerogatives to negotiate mineral leases "on behalf of" Indian peoples, paying a fraction of standard royalty rates. The result has been "super profits" for a number of preferred U.S. corporations. Meanwhile, Indians, whose reservations ironically turned out to be in some of the most mineral-rich areas of North America, which makes us the nominally° wealthiest segment of the continent's population, live in dire poverty.

By the government's own data in the mid-1980s, Indians received the lowest annual and lifetime per capita incomes of any aggregate° population group in the United States. Concomitantly, we suffer the highest rate of infant mortality, death by exposure and malnutrition, disease, and the like. Under such circumstances, alcoholism and other escapist forms of substance abuse are endemic° in the Indian community, a situation which leads both to a general physical debilitation of the population and a catastrophic accident rate. Teen suicide among Indians is several times the national average.

The average life expectancy of a reservation-based Native American man is barely 45 years; women can expect to live less than three years longer.

Such itemizations could be continued at great length, including matters like the radioactive contamination of large portions of contemporary Indian Country, the forced relocation of traditional Navajos, and so on. But the point should be made: Genocide, as defined in international law, is a continuing fact of day-to-day life (and death) for North America's native peoples. Yet there has been—and is—only the barest flicker of public concern about, or even

---

*plenary:* Complete, absolute. *nominally:* Theoretically; in name only. *aggregate:* Sum total. *endemic:* Epidemic, rampant.

consciousness of, this reality. Absent any serious expression of public outrage, no one is punished and the process continues.

A salient° reason for public acquiescence° before the ongoing holocaust in Native North America has been a continuation of the popular legacy, often through more effective media. Since 1925, Hollywood has released more than 2,000 films, many of them rerun frequently on television, portraying Indians as strange, perverted, ridiculous, and often dangerous things of the past. Moreover, we are habitually presented to mass audiences one-dimensionally, devoid of recognizable human motivations and emotions; Indians thus serve as props, little more. We have thus been thoroughly and systematically dehumanized.

Nor is this the extent of it. Everywhere, we are used as logos, as mascots, as    30
jokes: "Big Chief" writing tablets, "Red Man" chewing tobacco, "Winnebago" campers, "Navajo" and "Cherokee" and "Pontiac" and "Cadillac" pickups and automobiles. There are the Cleveland "Indians," the Kansas City "Chiefs," the Atlanta "Braves," and the Washington "Redskins" professional sports teams— not to mention those in thousands of colleges, high schools, and elementary schools across the country—each with their own degrading caricatures and parodies of Indians and/or things Indian. Pop fiction continues in the same vein, including an unending stream of New Age manuals purporting to expose the inner works of indigenous spirituality in everything from pseudo-philosophical to do-it-yourself styles. Blond yuppies from Beverly Hills amble about the country claiming to be reincarnated 17th-century Cheyenne Ushamans ready to perform previously secret ceremonies.

In effect, a concerted, sustained, and in some ways accelerating effort has gone into making Indians unreal. It is thus of obvious importance that the American public begin to think about the implications of such things the next time they witness a gaggle of face-painted and war-bonneted buffoons doing the "Tomahawk Chop" at a baseball or football game. It is necessary that they think about the implications of the grade-school teacher adorning their child in turkey feathers to commemorate Thanksgiving. Think about the significance of John Wayne or Charlton Heston killing a dozen "savages" with a single bullet the next time a western comes on TV. Think about why Land-o-Lakes finds it appropriate to market its butter with the stereotyped image of an "Indian princess" on the wrapper. Think about what it means when non-Indian academics profess—as they often do—to "know more about Indians than Indians do themselves." Think about the significance of charlatans like Carlos Castaneda and Jamake Highwater and Mary Summer Rain and Lynn Andrews churning out "Indian" best-sellers, one after the other, while Indians typically can't get into print.

---

*salient:* Notable, remarkable.    *acquiescence:* Agreement, consent.

Think about the real situation of American Indians. Think about Julius Streicher. Remember Justice Jackson's admonition.° Understand that the treatment of Indians in American popular culture is not "cute" or "amusing" or just "good, clean, fun."

Know that it causes real pain and real suffering to real people. Know that it threatens our very survival. And know that this is just as much a crime against humanity as anything the Nazis ever did. It is likely that the indigenous people of the United States will never demand that those guilty of such criminal activity be punished for their deeds. But the least we have the right to expect—indeed, to demand—is that such practices finally be brought to a halt.

### QUESTIONS

1. Is the introduction of this essay effective? What purpose do the first three paragraphs serve?
2. Explain whether you find Russell Means's analogy (cited in paragraph 2) to be true or false, and why.
3. In the third paragraph, what is Churchill implying about criticisms of Native American protests?
4. What effect does a sports team hope to create when it chooses a name and a mascot to represent itself? Cite examples to support your response.
5. What was your initial reaction to the team names Churchill suggests: "Sambos," "Greasers," "Kikes," "Honkies," "Papist Pigs," "Bimbos," "Retards"? What motivated you to react as you did?
6. Why does Churchill describe the example of Julius Streicher in such great detail? Is this amount of detail (four paragraphs) necessary? Is it effective? Explain your response.
7. Quote Churchill's definition of the word "deculturated." How is the practice of "deculturation" different from the "melting pot" ideal?
8. Summarize Churchill's description of the conditions of life on Native American reservations today. Were you aware of this situation before reading this essay? If so, where did you get your information? If not, why do you believe you were unaware?
9. Find places in the essay where Churchill offers quotations or statistics without attributing them to any specific sources. What effect does the absence of attributions have on the essay as a whole?
10. Why do you believe Churchill chose to write the essay in the first-person-plural point of view ("we")? Explain whether you find the

*admonition:* Warning.

technique effective in this essay; then discuss other writing situations in which you believe it would or would not be appropriate to use this point of view.

11. Find the paragraph in the essay where Churchill loops back to the introduction. Does the conclusion restate the introduction? summarize it? echo it? add anything new to the essay? In this essay, is the technique effective or not?

12. Find examples of recurrence in this essay. Do you feel that the author uses the technique effectively? Why or why not?

13. Explain whether you believe the essay justifies its last line.

## CONNECTIONS

How would you characterize Churchill's voice in this selection? Do you find it effective? Are there other voices in this book similar to Churchill's? If so, which ones?

# ～ The Meaning of a Word

*Gloria Naylor*

Gloria Naylor was born in 1950 in New York City. She served as a missionary for the Jehovah's Witnesses from 1967 to 1975 and then worked as a hotel telephone operator while earning a bachelor's degree from Brooklyn College of the City University of New York. Naylor then went on to pursue graduate work in African American studies at Yale University and to publish four novels: *The Women of Brewster Place* (1982), which won the American Book Award for fiction and was later made into a movie for television; *Linden Hills* (1985); *Mama Day* (1988); and *Bailey's Cafe* (1992). Naylor has also edited the 1995 anthology *Children of the Night: The Best Short Stories by Black Writers, '67 to the Present* and has published a number of essays, including the following selection, which first appeared in the *New York Times* in 1986.

**WARM-UP:** Think of a group to which you feel that you belong—cultural, professional, religious, social, etc. Are there any words that the group's members use differently than people outside of the group would do? If so, what are the words and, more important, why do you think this happens?

1    Language is the subject. It is the written form with which I've managed to keep the wolf away from the door and, in diaries, to keep my sanity. In spite of this, I consider the written word inferior to the spoken, and much of the frustration experienced by novelists is that awareness that whatever we manage to capture in even the most transcendent° passages falls far short of the richness of life. Dialogue achieves its power in the dynamics of a fleeting moment of sight, sound, smell, and touch.

I'm not going to enter the debate here about whether it is language that shapes reality or vice versa. That battle is doomed to be waged whenever we seek intermittent° reprieve° from the chicken and egg dispute. I will simply take the position that the spoken word, like the written word, amounts to a nonsensical arrangement of sounds or letters without a consensus that assigns "meaning." And building from the meanings of what we hear, we order reality. Words themselves are innocuous;° it is the consensus that gives them true power.

I remember the first time I heard the word *nigger.* In my third-grade class, our math tests were being passed down the rows, and as I handed the papers

---

*transcendent:* Surpassing the usual limits; spiritual.    *intermittent:* Not continuous.    *reprieve:* Temporary relief.    *innocuous:* Innocent, harmless.

to a little boy in back of me, I remarked that once again he had received a much lower mark than I did. He snatched his test from me and spit out that word. Had he called me a nymphomaniac° or a necrophiliac,° I couldn't have been more puzzled. I didn't know what a nigger was, but I knew that whatever it meant, it was something he shouldn't have called me. This was verified when I raised my hand, and in a loud voice repeated what he had said and watched the teacher scold him for using a "bad" word. I was later to go home and ask the inevitable question that every black parent must face—"Mommy, what does 'nigger' mean?"

And what exactly did it mean? Thinking back, I realize that this could not have been the first time the word was used in my presence. I was part of a large extended family that had migrated from the rural South after World War II and formed a close-knit network that gravitated around my maternal grandparents. Their ground-floor apartment in one of the buildings they owned in Harlem was a weekend mecca° for my immediate family, along with countless aunts, uncles, and cousins who brought along assorted friends. It was a bustling and open house with assorted neighbors and tenants popping in and out to exchange bits of gossip, pick up an old quarrel, or referee the ongoing checkers game in which my grandmother cheated shamelessly. They were all there to let down their hair and put up their feet after a week of labor in the factories, laundries, and shipyards of New York.

Amid the clamor, which could reach deafening proportions—two or three conversations going on simultaneously, punctuated by the sound of a baby's crying somewhere in the back rooms or out on the street—there was still a rigid set of rules about what was said and how. Older children were sent out of the living room when it was time to get into the juicy details about "you-know-who" up on the third floor who had gone and gotten herself "p-r-e-g-n-a-n-t!" But my parents, knowing that I could spell well beyond my years, always demanded that I follow the others out to play. Beyond sexual misconduct and death, everything else was considered harmless for our young ears. And so among the anecdotes of the triumphs and disappointments in the various workings of their lives, the word *nigger* was used in my presence, but it was set within contexts and inflections that caused it to register in my mind as something else.

In the singular, the word was always applied to a man who had distinguished himself in some situation that brought their approval for his strength, intelligence, or drive:

"Did Johnny really do that?"

"I'm telling you, that nigger pulled in $6,000 of overtime last year. Said he got enough for a down payment on a house."

5

---

*nymphomaniac:* Female with excessive sexual desires.    *necrophiliac:* One obsessed with or erotically stimulated by corpses.    *mecca:* Here meaning a gathering place.

When used with a possessive adjective by a woman—"my nigger"—it became a term of endearment for husband or boyfriend. But it could be more than just a term applied to a man. In their mouths it became the pure essence of manhood—a disembodied force that channeled their past history of struggle and present survival against the odds into a victorious statement of being: "Yeah, that old foreman found out quick enough—you don't mess with a nigger."

10        In the plural, it became a description of some group within the community that had overstepped the bounds of decency as my family defined it: Parents who neglected their children, a drunken couple who fought in public, people who simply refused to look for work, those with excessively dirty mouths or unkempt households were all "trifling niggers." This particular circle could forgive hard times, unemployment, the occasional bout of depression—they had gone through all of that themselves—but the unforgivable sin was lack of self-respect.

A woman could never be a *nigger* in the singular, with its connotation of confirming worth. The noun *girl* was its closest equivalent in that sense, but only when used in direct address and regardless of the gender doing the addressing. *Girl* was a token of respect for a woman. The one-syllable word was drawn out to sound like three in recognition of the extra ounce of wit, nerve, or daring that the woman had shown in the situation under discussion.

"G-i-r-l, stop. You mean you said that to his face?"

But if the word was used in a third-person reference or shortened so that it almost snapped out of the mouth, it always involved some element of communal disapproval. And age became an important factor in these exchanges. It was only between individuals of the same generation, or from an older person to a younger (but never the other way around), that "girl" would be considered a compliment.

I don't agree with the argument that use of the word *nigger* at this social stratum° of the black community was an internalization of racism. The dynamics were the exact opposite: the people in my grandmother's living room took a word that whites used to signify worthlessness or degradation and rendered it impotent. Gathering there together, they transformed *nigger* to signify the varied and complex human beings they knew themselves to be. If the word was to disappear totally from the mouths of even the most liberal of white society, no one in that room was naïve enough to believe it would disappear from white minds. Meeting the word head-on, they proved it had absolutely nothing to do with the way they were determined to live their lives.

15        So there must have been dozens of times that the word *nigger* was spoken in front of me before I reached the third grade. But I didn't "hear" it until it

*stratum:* Layer.

was said by a small pair of lips that had already learned it could be a way to humiliate me. That was the word I went home and asked my mother about. And since she knew that I had to grow up in America, she took me in her lap and explained.

## QUESTIONS

1. Do you find Naylor's introduction effective? What tone does she set in the first two paragraphs? Why might she have chosen that tone?
2. What is Naylor's thesis? Is its placement in the essay effective?
3. Enter the "debate" Naylor points out in paragraph 2: Explain whether you think "language . . . shapes reality" or reality shapes language, and provide an example from your experience to support your response.
4. Paragraphs 4 and 5 present a context in which the words "nigger" and "girl" had often been used around the author. Would the essay have been as effective if those paragraphs had been omitted? Why or why not?
5. What type of evidence does Naylor use to support her thesis? Is this evidence sufficient?
6. Where does Naylor mention views that oppose her own? Does she do justice to the opposition?
7. How does Naylor explain the fact that the word "nigger" could have a variety of meanings, depending on context?
8. What audience does Naylor seem to be writing for? On what do you base your answer?
9. Have you heard the word "nigger" used around you in real life (rather than in movies or on TV)? Having read Naylor's essay, do you perceive that word differently? If so, in what way(s)?

## CONNECTIONS

1. Compare the way Naylor defines words to the way Robert Solomon defines the word *love* in his essay "The Elusive Emotion," included in Section 3.
2. Does Gloria Naylor's thesis support or contradict the main point that Ward Churchill makes about language in his essay, which precedes this selection?

# ∼ Mother Tongue

*Amy Tan*

Amy Tan was born in Oakland, California, in 1952 and grew up in the San Francisco Bay Area. After attending high school in Switzerland, she returned to the United States to eventually earn a master's degree in linguistics from San Jose State University. Tan worked as a free-lance business writer before turning to fiction writing at the age of 35. Besides essays, Tan has published three novels—*The Joy Luck Club* (1989), *The Kitchen God's Wife* (1991), and *The Hundred Secret Senses* (1995)—and two books for children. Tan's work has been translated into twenty languages, and *The Joy Luck Club* was adapted into a Hollywood motion picture. The following essay first appeared in 1990 in the *Threepenny Review*.

**WARM-UP:** Do your parents use language differently than you do? If so, in what way(s)? Under what circumstances does one version or the other allow for more effective communication?

1   I am not a scholar of English or literature. I cannot give you much more than personal opinions on the English language and its variations in this country or others.

I am a writer. And by that definition, I am someone who has always loved language. I am fascinated by language in daily life. I spend a great deal of my time thinking about the power of language—the way it can evoke an emotion, a visual image, a complex idea, or a simple truth. Language is the tool of my trade. And I use them all—all the Englishes I grew up with.

Recently, I was made keenly aware of the different Englishes I do use. I was giving a talk to a large group of people, the same talk I had already given to half a dozen other groups. The nature of the talk was about my writing, my life, and my book, *The Joy Luck Club*. The talk was going along well enough, until I remembered one major difference that made the whole talk sound wrong. My mother was in the room. And it was perhaps the first time she had heard me give a lengthy speech, using the kind of English I have never used with her. I was saying things like, "The intersection of memory upon imagination" and "There is an aspect of my fiction that relates to thus-and-thus"—a speech filled with carefully wrought grammatical phrases, burdened, it suddenly seemed to me, with nominalized forms, past perfect tenses, conditional phrases, all the forms of standard English that I had learned in school and through books, the forms of English I did not use at home with my mother.

Just last week, I was walking down the street with my mother, and I again found myself conscious of the English I was using, the English I do use with her. We were talking about the price of new and used furniture and I heard myself saying this: "Not waste money that way." My husband was with us as well, and he didn't notice any switch in my English. And then I realized why. It's because over the twenty years we've been together I've often used that same kind of English with him, and sometimes he even uses it with me. It has become our language of intimacy, a different sort of English that relates to family talk, the language I grew up with.

So you'll have some idea of what this family talk I heard sounds like, I'll    5
quote what my mother said during a recent conversation which I videotaped and then transcribed. During this conversation, my mother was talking about a political gangster in Shanghai who had the same last name as her family's, Du, and how the gangster in his early years wanted to be adopted by her family, which was rich by comparison. Later, the gangster became more powerful, far richer than my mother's family, and one day showed up at my mother's wedding to pay his respects. Here's what she said in part:

> Du Yusong having business like fruit stand. Like off the street kind. He is Du like Du Zong—but not Tsung-ming Island people. The local people call putong, the river east side, he belong to that side local people. That man want to ask Du Zong father take him in like become own family. Du Zong father wasn't look down on him, but didn't take seriously, until that man big like become a mafia. Now important person, very hard to inviting him. Chinese way, came only to show respect, don't stay for dinner. Respect for making big celebration, he shows up. Mean gives lots of respect. Chinese custom. Chinese social life that way. If too important won't have to stay too long. He come to my wedding. I didn't see, I heard it. I gone to boy's side, they have YMCA dinner. Chinese age I was nineteen.

You should know that my mother's expressive command of English belies° how much she actually understands. She reads the *Forbes* report, listens to *Wall Street Week,* converses daily with her stockbroker, reads all of Shirley MacLaine's books with ease—all kinds of things I can't begin to understand. Yet some of my friends tell me they understand 50 percent of what my mother says. Some say they understand 80 to 90 percent. Some say they understand none of it, as if she were speaking pure Chinese. But to me, my mother's English is perfectly clear, perfectly natural. It's my mother tongue. Her language, as I hear it, is vivid, direct, full of observation and imagery. That was the language that helped shape the way I saw things, expressed things, made sense of the world.

Lately, I've been giving more thought to the kind of English my mother speaks. Like others, I have described it to people as "broken" or "fractured"

*belies:* Contradicts, does not accurately reflect.

English. But I wince when I say that. It has always bothered me that I can think of no way to describe it other than "broken," as if it were damaged and needed to be fixed, as if it lacked a certain wholeness and soundness. I've heard other terms used, "limited English," for example. But they seem just as bad, as if everything is limited, including people's perceptions of the limited English speaker.

I know this for a fact, because when I was growing up, my mother's "limited" English limited *my* perception of her. I was ashamed of her English. I believed that her English reflected the quality of what she had to say. That is, because she expressed them imperfectly her thoughts were imperfect. And I had plenty of empirical° evidence to support me: the fact that people in department stores, at banks, and at restaurants did not take her seriously, did not give her good service, pretended not to understand her, or even acted as if they did not hear her.

My mother had long realized the limitations of her English as well. When I was fifteen, she used to have me call people on the phone to pretend I was she. In this guise, I was forced to ask for information or even to complain and yell at people who had been rude to her. One time it was a call to her stockbroker in New York. She had cashed out her small portfolio and it just so happened we were going to go to New York the next week, our very first trip outside California. I had to get on the phone and say in an adolescent voice that was not very convincing, "This is Mrs. Tan."

10    And my mother was standing in the back whispering loudly, "Why he don't send me check, already two weeks late. So mad he lie to me, losing me money."

And then I said in perfect English, "Yes, I'm getting rather concerned. You had agreed to send the check two weeks ago, but it hasn't arrived."

Then she began to talk more loudly. "What he want, I come to New York tell him front of his boss, you cheating me?" And I was trying to calm her down, make her be quiet, while telling the stockbroker, "I can't tolerate any more excuses. If I don't receive the check immediately, I am going to have to speak to your manager when I'm in New York next week." And sure enough, the following week there we were in front of this astonished stockbroker, and I was sitting there red-faced and quiet, and my mother, the real Mrs. Tan, was shouting at his boss in her impeccable° broken English.

We used a similar routine just five days ago, for a situation that was far less humorous. My mother had gone to the hospital for an appointment, to find out about a benign brain tumor a CAT scan° had revealed a month ago. She said she had spoken very good English, her best English, no mistakes, Still, she said, the hospital did not apologize when they said they had lost the CAT scan

---

*empirical:* Derived from experience or observation.    *impeccable:* Flawless.    *CAT scan:* A computerized image made from an X-ray.

and she had come for nothing. She said they did not seem to have any sympathy when she told them she was anxious to know the exact diagnosis, since her husband and son had both died of brain tumors. She said they would not give her any more information until the next time and she would have to make another appointment for that. So she said she would not leave until the doctor called her daughter. She wouldn't budge. And when the doctor finally called her daughter, me, who spoke in perfect English—lo and behold—we had assurances the CAT scan would be found, promises that a conference call on Monday would be held, and apologies for any suffering my mother had gone through for a most regrettable mistake.

I think my mother's English almost had an effect on limiting my possibilities in life as well. Sociologists and linguists probably will tell you that a person developing language skills are more influenced by peers. But I do think that the language spoken in the family, especially in immigrant families which are more insular,° plays a large role in shaping the language of the child. And I believe that it affected my results on achievement tests, IQ tests, and the SAT. While my English skills were never judged as poor, compared to math, English could not be considered my strong suit. In grade school I did moderately well, getting perhaps B's, sometimes B-pluses, in English and scoring perhaps in the sixtieth or seventieth percentile on achievement tests. But those scores were not good enough to override the opinion that my true abilities lay in math and science, because in those areas I achieved A's and scored in the ninetieth percentile or higher.

This was understandable. Math is precise; there is only one correct answer. Whereas, for me at least, the answers on English tests were always a judgment call, a matter of opinion and personal experience. Those tests were constructed around items like fill-in-the-blank sentence completion, such as, "Even though Tom was ____, Mary thought he was ____." And the correct answer always seemed to be the most bland combinations of thoughts, for example, "Even though Tom was shy, Mary thought he was charming," with the grammatical structure "even though" limiting the correct answer to some sort of semantic° opposites, so you wouldn't get answers like, "Even though Tom was foolish, Mary thought he was ridiculous." Well, according to my mother, there were very few limitations as to what Tom could have been and what Mary might have thought of him. So I never did well on tests like that.

The same was true with word analogies, pairs of words in which you were supposed to find some sort of logical, semantic relationship—for example, "*Sunset* is to *nightfall* as ____ is to ____." And here you would be presented with a list of four possible pairs, one of which showed the same kind of relationship: *red* is to *stoplight, bus* is to *arrival, chills* is to *fever, yawn* is to *boring.* Well, I could never think that way. I knew what the tests were asking, but I

15

---

*insular:* Isolated.    *semantic:* Relating to meaning in language.

could not block out of my mind the images already created by the first pair, "*sunset* is to *nightfall*"—and I would see a burst of colors against a darkening sky, the moon rising, the lowering of a curtain of stars. And all the other pairs of words—red, bus, stoplight, boring—just threw up a mass of confusing images, making it impossible for me to sort out something as logical as saying: "A sunset precedes nightfall" is the same as "a chill precedes a fever." The only way I would have gotten that answer right would have been to imagine an associative situation, for example, my being disobedient and staying out past sunset, catching a chill at night, which turns into feverish pneumonia as punishment, which indeed did happen to me.

I have been thinking about all this lately, about my mother's English, about achievement tests. Because lately I've been asked, as a writer, why there are not more Asian Americans represented in American literature. Why are there few Asian Americans enrolled in creative writing programs? Why do so many Chinese students go into engineering? Well, these are broad sociological questions I can't begin to answer. But I have noticed in surveys—in fact, just last week—that Asian students, as a whole, always do significantly better on math achievement tests than in English. And this makes me think that there are other Asian-American students whose English spoken in the home might also be described as "broken" or "limited." And perhaps they also have teachers who are steering them away from writing and into math and science, which is what happened to me.

Fortunately, I happen to be rebellious in nature and enjoy the challenge of disproving assumptions made about me. I became an English major my first year in college, after being enrolled as pre-med. I started writing nonfiction as a freelancer the week after I was told by my former boss that writing was my worst skill and I should hone my talents toward account management.

But it wasn't until 1985 that I finally began to write fiction. And at first I wrote using what I thought to be wittily crafted sentences, sentences that would finally prove I had mastery over the English language. Here's an example from the first draft of a story that later made its way into *The Joy Luck Club,* but without this line: "That was my mental quandary° in its nascent° state." A terrible line, which I can barely pronounce.

20      Fortunately, for reasons I won't get into today, I later decided I should envision a reader for the stories I would write. And the reader I decided upon was my mother, because these were stories about mothers. So with this reader in mind—and in fact she did read my early drafts—I began to write stories using all the Englishes I grew up with: the English I spoke to my mother, which for lack of a better term might be described as "simple"; the English she used with me, which for lack of a better term might be described as "broken";

*quandary:* Dilemma or doubt.    *nascent:* Coming or having recently come into existence.

my translation of her Chinese, which could certainly be described as "watered down"; and what I imagined to be her translation of her Chinese if she could speak in perfect English, her internal language, and for that I sought to preserve the essence, but neither an English nor a Chinese structure. I wanted to capture what language ability tests can never reveal: her intent, her passion, her imagery, the rhythms of her speech and the nature of her thoughts.

Apart from what any critic had to say about my writing, I knew I had succeeded where it counted when my mother finished reading my book and gave me her verdict: "So easy to read."

## QUESTIONS

1. How does Tan define "a writer"? How do you define one?
2. How did Tan feel, when growing up, about her mother's way of speaking English? How does she feel about it as she writes this essay?
3. Why is Tan reluctant to refer to her mother's English as "broken" or "limited"?
4. What is Tan implying in her examples about the stock portfolio and the CAT scan?
5. Why does Tan claim that she experienced difficulty with tests designed to measure a student's command of standard English? What evidence does Tan provide to support her criticism(s) of the tests?
6. Why did Tan decide to become an English major?
7. Whom does Tan envision as the audience for her writing? How does assuming an audience help Tan to write? Do you imagine an audience when you write? Why or why not?
8. Do you feel that it's important for young people growing up in the United States to learn to use standard English correctly? Why or why not?
9. Aside from newly arrived immigrants, who else might be judged by his or her use (or misuse) of language? Support your response by providing examples of circumstances in which such a judgment might take place.

## CONNECTIONS

1. How does Tan's essay relate to the ideas about language presented in Gabriele Rico's "The Childhood Origins of Natural Writing" (included in Section 1)?
2. Compare and contrast Tan's experiences in school with those of the narrator of Maxine Hong Kingston's "The Quiet Girl" (included in Section 1).

## The Cure for Prejudice: Education

*Kevin O'Kelley*

> Kevin O'Kelley was born in Ford Hood, Texas, in 1957. In 1975, he dropped
> out of the University of Washington in Seattle and moved to Los Angeles.
> Now a student majoring in environmental science at San Jose State Univer-
> sity, O'Kelley is married with children and employed as a production
> supervisor at a large manufacturing facility. He was impelled to return to
> school, as he puts it, "initially by fear of the new trend in business manage-
> ment—corporate downsizing"; however, he now finds "education itself to
> be a goal, not merely the means to an end. My studies," he says, "are no
> longer fueled by beer but by a real desire to learn everything possible from
> every professor."

> **WARM-UP:** Do you believe that students should be required to fulfill
> a general education requirement en route to studying a major? Are there
> some general education subjects that you feel are unnecessary? Are there
> some that you believe students should study more often?

1    "To know me is to love me." Each of us believes this to be true of ourselves. We think, "If only somebody will take the trouble to *really* get to
know me, they will see how truly lovable I am." Very few of us, however, make
the leap to the corollary:° "To know another person is to love that person."
Certain rare individuals are able to achieve this understanding. Will Rogers
was one such person. He was famous for his statement, "I never met a man I
didn't like." The explanation for this, according to Richard Ketchum, a biographer of Rogers, is that Rogers had a sincere "old-fashioned belief in the virtues
of the common man, seasoned with a benevolent tolerance for the human
condition" (349). He respected others and listened to them with his whole
attention. Ketchum writes that Rogers' "inclination was to see the positive side
of human nature" (349). His liking for people was a direct result of his interest
in them. As we know, the feeling was reciprocated. Rogers was one of the most
beloved men in America. We have seen the same principle work as well with

---

*corollary:* Something that naturally follows, accompanies, or parallels.

nations as with individuals. Many, many times in history two nations, divided perhaps by language or social customs, and once hating and fearing each other, have learned to know each other and have ended up as firm allies, as a result of a new mutual understanding. In this century alone we see amazing developments in Europe. Nations which have warred against each other incessantly° for centuries are now united in the European Union, which is fostered by open borders and by unfettered° opportunities for travel and commerce.

We see the same principle at work when we study prejudice in our country. When we examine published accounts of prejudice, we see that those who prejudge an entire group of people—based solely on race, gender, or class distinctions—simply do not know or understand the groups against whom they are prejudiced. It is clear when reading the *New York Herald* editorial about the Women's Rights Convention of 1852 that the writer didn't know women at all! When he writes that "the majority of women are flimsy, flippant, and superficial," he shows us that he doesn't have the faintest clue what women are really like. Similarly, when we read of the nineteenth century scientists who "proved" the inferiority of the Black man, we see their absolute and total ignorance of the subject.

In her book *Exploding the Gene Myth* professor Ruth Hubbard chronicles a 1910 study performed by Charles Davenport of the Carnegie Institution, in which Davenport was investigating the lives of the poor, with the aim of proving the hereditary nature of such "mental defects" as "shiftlessness," "criminalism," and "feeblemindedness." To gather this data, Davenport sent whom to investigate? Rich white kids from Ivy League schools. If he had searched the world over, he could have found no one less qualified to do the research. The results of his study demonstrate that the scholars had absolutely no understanding of the people they were investigating, and their report is therefore (predictably) nothing but class prejudice, jazzed up with academic-sounding language (18). The correlation between unfamiliarity and prejudice is clear. I believe that class prejudice can exist only in the presence of ignorance and that understanding this provides us with a possible approach in our efforts to eliminate prejudice from our society.

Given the circularity of the equation ("I don't like your kind because I don't know any of you" and "I don't want to know you because I don't like your kind"), our options are limited. We cannot force a person to begin liking a member of a different group. We can, however, in some cases, educate an individual so that he or she learns to understand the other group a little better, hoping that this knowledge will begin the process of ending the preexisting

---

*incessantly:* Continually.     *unfettered:* Unrestricted.

prejudices. During the last twenty years or so, our nation's schools have made bold efforts in this area. Here at San Jose State University, the General Education requirements include three units of cultural diversity education, under the general heading of Cultural Pluralism.

5        The aim of the General Education portion of the curriculum of our university (and, indeed, of most institutions of higher learning) is twofold: to enable the student to better function in society; and to enrich society by producing a well-educated, clear-thinking citizen. The Mission Statement of San Jose State University includes a list of six goals, only one of which relates to teaching "an in-depth knowledge of a major field of study." The other goals are concerned with the student's future interaction with the community and include teaching "skills in communication and critical thinking," "responsible citizenship," and "multicultural and global perspective." We live in California, one of the most culturally diverse places on the planet Earth. A walk around campus is like taking a Cook's Tour of the World. By helping a student to overcome his or her prejudices, through the study of other cultures and the use of critical thinking skills, we both enable the student to better cope with life and we enrich society, thus serving both of the university's aims.

A proposal was recently made to increase the GE requirements at SJSU to six units of cultural diversity education. This led to howls from the student body. To many students, the GE requirements are distractions from the primary reason they are attending college: to attain certain marketable skills and knowledge. They believe that the subjects they take in the field of their major are subjects that they will actually use, while the others are not. Well, I have news for them. Cultural diversity is a subject they will deal with every day, and not merely at work. In terms of actual benefit in their lives, at work, in their children's schools, and even at the grocery store, an understanding of cultural diversity may be one of the most important elements of their college education.

The quantity of cultural diversity education desirable is subjective, but, given its importance in a student's future life, three units is a very meager amount. Requiring two classes of three units each, for a total of six units, would better serve to reinforce the lessons. Rather than being merely a subject that a student needs to get through, an item to be checked off on the GE checklist, cultural diversity would be a subject the student would really learn. If we require six units of study in American history, it makes sense to spend at least that much effort studying the American present.

Requiring any study of America's cultural diversity bothers many people. A popular sentiment is that such study is divisive and emphasizes our differences rather than our commonalities, thereby leading to strife. The theory here is that a harmonious society is one in which our differences are eliminated. This argument begs the question. Because the advocate wishes for a homogeneous society, he or she insists that we ignore the fact that we do, in fact, live in an extremely diverse society. By ignoring our differences, some hope that the differences will eventually just go away. But wishing will not make it so. Since the minority cultural elements of our society refuse to "just go away," this approach will not work. We can achieve true harmony, despite our differences, if we all learn to play the same tune and then practice together. I submit that the song we sing together will be considerably more sweet than the one-note dirge of a totally homogeneous society.

Trudy Rubin, a distinguished journalist and editorialist, published an essay in the *Philadelphia Inquirer* in 1991 titled "Multiculturalism is Misguided." In this essay she laments recent trends in multicultural education. She writes that "the hopes invested in 'multiculturalism' are woefully misguided, especially since they are so often driven by a hostility toward the study of Western civilization. Many of the academic backers of multiculturalism seem to believe that Western liberal thought has spawned only imperialism, racism and sexism" (582). She believes that the many solid and admirable traits of Western culture are overlooked or denigrated° in an orgy of political correctness designed to bolster minority cultures at the expense of that of the majority. This is a point well worth considering. If we take the easy road out— oversimplifying cultural interactions with facile° categorizations (white people are bad, black people are good; settlers were bad, Native Americans are good; men are bad, women are good; etc.)—we would be doing students a grave disservice; we would merely be substituting one set of prejudices for another. That multicultural education has potential pitfalls, however, is no reason to eschew° it. Universities have made extensive efforts to find materials which discuss the issues fairly, and modern university curricula invariably include studies in critical thinking. There is no doubt that students are enriched by study of the accomplishments of Western civilization. It is a logical extension to see that students will also be enriched by study of the accomplishments of other cultures.

Proponents of monoculturalism believe in the theory of "the melting    10
pot." If we blend all the cultures present in our country into one amalgam,° a new alloy will emerge, stronger than any single culture by itself. We know from experience, however, that cultures don't behave this way; cultures have a life of their own. Ignoring the evident fact that we live in a mixture of vibrant cultures is a form of blindness. Martin Luther King, Jr., wrote in his essay "Racism and the White Backlash" that "In human relations the truth is hard to come by, because most groups are deceived about themselves" (67). To achieve the truth that Dr. King seeks, we must un-deceive ourselves, and see America

---

*denigrated:* Belittled, defamed.   *facile:* Superficial.   *eschew:* Avoid.   *amalgam:* A mixture of different elements, a combination.

as it really is today. Our mixture of cultures, and our mutual lack of under-standing of each other's cultures, has led to rampant and widespread preju-dice. We know that the most effective tool at eradicating prejudice is education. Let us therefore commit ourselves to learning about each other, that we may end this blight on our country. Educators who propose that we study our various cultural components have opened their eyes and are making this effort. If we want to obey the dictum° of Socrates to "know thyself," this study is imperative.° A study of minority cultures is not a study of other peo-ple; it is a study of America.

A token three units of cultural diversity education in a four-year univer-sity education is merely a sop° to our collective guilt, a first step on a road that many of us are reluctant to travel. It is not a dedicated effort at reforming our society. Let us now take the second step. Let us determine the amount of cul-tural diversity education actually required of a student, by looking realistically at the needs of society and the needs of the future citizen. I am confident that an honest appraisal of these needs will result in a realization that we need to greatly expand this area of undergraduate education.

Very few of us are like Will Rogers. He was a natural, and we have to work at it. Well, just because something is hard work is no reason for Americans to avoid it. As a nation, we embrace new challenges and rise to whatever the occasion demands. Today, our nation needs the universities to lead us, through extensive education, out of the morass° of racial, gender, and class prejudice which bogs us down. As Dr. King wrote: "Freedom is still the bonus we receive for knowing the truth. 'Ye shall know the truth, and the truth shall set you free'" (67).

## Works Cited

Hubbard, Ruth, and Elija Wald. *Exploding the Gene Myth: How Genetic In-formation Is Produced and Manipulated by Scientists, Physicians, Employers, Insurance Companies, Educators, and Law Enforcers.* Boston: Beacon, 1993.

Ketchum, Richard M. *Will Rogers: His Life and Times.* New York: American Heritage, 1973.

King, Martin L., Jr. *Where Do We Go from Here: Chaos or Community?* New York: Harper & Row, 1967.

*New York Herald.* Editorial. 12 Sept. 1852.

Plato. "Charmides." *Great Treasury of Western Thought.* Ed. Mortimer J. Adler. New York: R. R. Bowker, 1977.

---

*dictum:* Pronouncement, statement.    *imperative:* Essential, crucial.    *sop:* A bribe or conciliatory gift.
*morass:* Marsh, swamp—here meaning something that confuses or impedes.

Rubin, Trudy. "Multiculturalism Is Misguided." *Patterns for College Writing: A Rhetorical Reader and Guide.* Ed. Laurie G. Kirszner and Stephen Mandell. 6th ed. New York: St. Martin's, 1995.
San Jose State University. "Mission Statement." San Jose, CA: San Jose State University, 1994.

## QUESTIONS

1. Is O'Kelley's introduction effective? Why or why not?
2. Is O'Kelley's analogy in the introduction—"We have seen the same principle work as well with nations as with individuals"—false? Explain your response.
3. Explain whether you agree with O'Kelley's discussion of "prejudice."
4. Does O'Kelley commit the fallacy of hasty generalization in his discussion of the *New York Herald* editorial? If so, when?
5. Is O'Kelley's use of the "Mission Statement" effective? Why?
6. Explain whether you accept O'Kelley's arguments concerning "cultural diversity education." If so, are these good reasons to increase the number of cultural diversity units required?
7. Where does O'Kelley bring in and discuss views opposing his argument? Is the placement (in terms of organization) effective? Are his refutations sound?
8. How well does O'Kelley handle quotations? Are the quotations always clearly attributed to a source? clearly documented?
9. Explain whether you agree with O'Kelley when he writes, "A study of many cultures is not a study of other people; it is a study of America."
10. Is O'Kelley's conclusion effective? Why or why not?

## CONNECTIONS

1. Explain whether or not O'Kelley's thesis supports Michael Parenti's argument from "Myths of Political Quietism."
2. Explain how this essay relates to the three that precede it in this section: "Crimes against Humanity," "The Meaning of a Word," and "Mother Tongue."

# ∿ Why Are Americans Afraid of Dragons?

*Ursula K. LeGuin*

Ursula Kroeber LeGuin was born in Berkeley, California, in 1929. She
attended Radcliffe College and Columbia University and then studied in
Paris on a Fulbright Fellowship. After marrying historian Charles A. LeGuin
in 1951, she taught at Mercer University in Georgia and at the University of
Idaho. She then moved to Portland, Oregon, and began to write fantasy and
science fiction. LeGuin is the author of more than a dozen novels for adults
and children, three volumes of short fiction, and numerous poems and
essays. She won the National Book Award for *The Farthest Shore* in 1972, and
the Hugo and the Nebula science fiction awards twice—for *The Dispossessed*
in 1975 and for *The Left Hand of Darkness* in 1976. She is a coeditor of the
*Norton Book of Science Fiction* (1993). The following essay first appeared in
1974 in the journal *PNLA Quarterly.*

**WARM-UP:** Do you ever read fiction (novels, short stories, poems)?
Why or why not? Why do some people believe that reading fiction is a
worthwhile activity?

1    This was to be a talk about fantasy. But I have not been feeling very fanciful
lately, and could not decide what to say; so I have been going about picking people's brains for ideas. "What about fantasy? Tell me something about
fantasy." And one friend of mine said, "All right, I'll tell you something fantastic. Ten years ago, I went to the children's room of the library of such-and-
such a city, and asked for *The Hobbit;* and the librarian told me, 'Oh, we keep
that only in the adult collection; we don't feel that escapism is good for
children.'"

My friend and I had a good laugh and shudder over that, and we agreed
that things have changed a great deal in these past ten years. That kind of
moralistic censorship of works of fantasy is very uncommon now, in the children's libraries. But the fact that the children's libraries have become oases in
the desert doesn't mean that there isn't still a desert. The point of view from
which that librarian spoke still exists. She was merely reflecting, in perfect
good faith, something that goes very deep in the American character: a moral
disapproval of fantasy, a disapproval so intense, and often so aggressive, that I
cannot help but see it as arising, fundamentally, from fear.

So: Why are Americans afraid of dragons?

Before I try to answer my question, let me say that it isn't only Americans
who are afraid of dragons. I suspect that almost all very highly technological

peoples are more or less antifantasy. There are several national literatures which, like ours, have had no tradition of adult fantasy for the past several hundred years: the French, for instance. But then you have the Germans, who have a good deal; and the English, who have it, and love it, and do it better than anyone else. So this fear of dragons is not merely a Western, or a technological, phenomenon. But I do not want to get into these vast historical questions; I will speak of modern Americans, the only people I know well enough to talk about.

In wondering why Americans are afraid of dragons, I began to realize that    5
a great many Americans are not only antifantasy, but altogether antifiction. We tend, as a people, to look upon all works of the imagination either as suspect, or as contemptible.

"My wife reads novels. I haven't got the time."

"I used to read that science fiction stuff when I was a teenager, but of course I don't now."

"Fairy stories are for kids. I live in the real world."

Who speaks so? Who is it that dismisses *War and Peace, The Time Machine,* and *A Midsummer Night's Dream* with this perfect self-assurance? It is, I fear, the man in the street—the hardworking, over-thirty American male —the men who run this country.

Such a rejection of the entire art of fiction is related to several American    10
characteristics: our Puritanism,° our work ethic, our profit-mindedness, and even our sexual mores.

To read *War and Peace* or *The Lord of the Rings* plainly is not "work"—you do it for pleasure. And if it cannot be justified as "educational" or as "self-improvement," then, in the Puritan value system, it can only be self-indulgence or escapism. For pleasure is not a value, to the Puritan; on the contrary, is a sin.

Equally, in the businessman's value system, if an act does not bring in an immediate, tangible profit, it has no justification at all. Thus the only person who has an excuse to read Tolstoy or Tolkien is the English teacher, because he gets paid for it. But our businessman might allow himself to read a best-seller now and then: not because it is a good book, but because it is a best-seller—it is a success, it has made money. To the strangely mystical mind of the money-changer, this justifies its existence; and by reading it he may participate, a little, in the power and mana° of its success. If this is not magic, by the way, I don't know what is.

The last element, the sexual one, is more complex. I hope I will not be understood as being sexist if I say that, within our culture, I believe that this

---

*Puritanism:* Strictness in matters of religion or conduct.    *mana:* Here meaning prestige.

antifiction attitude is basically a male one. The American boy and man is very commonly forced to define his maleness by rejecting certain traits, certain human gifts and potentialities, which our culture defines as "womanish" or "childish." And one of these traits or potentialities is, in cold sober fact, the absolutely essential human faculty of imagination.

Having got this far, I went quickly to the dictionary.

15    The *Shorter Oxford Dictionary* says: "Imagination. 1. The action of imagining, or forming a mental concept of what is not actually present to the senses; 2. The mental consideration of actions or events not yet in existence."

Very well; I certainly can let "absolutely essential human faculty" stand. But I must narrow the definition to fit our present subject. By "imagination," then, I personally mean the free play of the mind, both intellectual and sensory. By "play" I mean recreation, re-creation, the recombination of what is known into what is new. By "free" I mean that the action is done without an immediate object of profit—spontaneously. That does not mean, however, that there may not be a purpose behind the free play of the mind, a goal; and the goal may be a very serious object indeed. Children's imaginative play is clearly a practicing at the acts and emotions of adulthood; a child who did not play would not become mature. As for the free play of an adult mind, its result may be *War and Peace,* or the theory of relativity.

To be free, after all, is not to be undisciplined. I should say that the discipline of the imagination may in fact be the essential method or technique of both art and science. It is our Puritanism, insisting that discipline means repression° or punishment, which confuses the subject. To discipline something, in the proper sense of the word, does not mean to repress it, but to train it—to encourage it to grow, and act, and be fruitful, whether it is a peach tree or a human mind.

I think that a great many American men have been taught just the opposite. They have learned to repress their imagination, to reject it as something childish or effeminate,° unprofitable, and probably sinful.

They have learned to fear it. But they have never learned to discipline it at all.

20    Now, I doubt that the imagination can be suppressed. If you truly eradicated it in a child, he would grow up to be an eggplant. Like all our evil propensities, the imagination will out. But if it is rejected and despised, it will grow into wild and weedy shapes; it will be deformed. At its best, it will be mere ego-centered daydreaming; at its worst, it will be wishful thinking, which is a very dangerous occupation when it is taken seriously. Where literature is concerned, in the old, truly Puritan days, the only permitted reading

---

*repression:* Here meaning exclusion of some desires or impulses.    *effeminate:* Womanish.

was the Bible. Nowadays, with our secular° Puritanism, the man who refuses to read novels because it's unmanly to do so, or because they aren't true, will most likely end up watching bloody detective thrillers on the television, or reading hack Westerns or sports stories, or going in for pornography, from *Playboy,* on down. It is his starved imagination, craving nourishment, that forces him to do so. But he can rationalize such entertainment by saying that it is realistic—after all, sex exists, and there are criminals, and there are baseball players, and there used to be cowboys—and also by saying that it is virile,° by which he means that it doesn't interest most women.

That all these genres are sterile, hopelessly sterile, is a reassurance to him, rather than a defect. If they were genuinely realistic, which is to say genuinely imagined and imaginative, he would be afraid of them. Fake realism is the escapist literature of our time. And probably the ultimate escapist reading is that masterpiece of total unreality, the daily stock market report.

Now what about our man's wife? She probably wasn't required to squelch her private imagination in order to play her expected role in life, but she hasn't been trained to discipline it, either. She is allowed to read novels, and even fantasies. But, lacking training and encouragement, her fancy is likely to glom on to very sickly fodder,° such things as soap operas, and "true romances," and nursy novels, and historico-sentimental novels, and all the rest of the baloney ground out to replace genuine imaginative works by the artistic sweatshops of a society that is profoundly distrustful of the uses of the imagination.

What, then, are the uses of the imagination?

You see, I think we have a terrible thing here: a hardworking, upright, responsible citizen, a full-grown, educated person, who is afraid of dragons, and afraid of hobbits, and scared to death of fairies. It's funny, but it's also terrible. Something has gone very wrong. I don't know what to do about it but to try and give an honest answer to that person's question, even though he often asks it in an aggressive and contemptuous tone of voice. "What's the good of it all?" he says. "Dragons and hobbits and little green men—what's the *use* of it?"

The truest answer, unfortunately, he won't even listen to. He won't hear it. The truest answer is, "The use of it is to give you pleasure and delight."    25

"I haven't got the time," he snaps, swallowing a Maalox pill for his ulcer and rushing off to the golf course.

So we try the next-to-truest answer. It probably won't go down much better, but it must be said: "The use of imaginative fiction is to deepen your understanding of your world, and your fellow men, and your own feelings, and your destiny."

---

*secular:* Nonreligious.    *virile:* Vigorous, forceful.    *fodder:* Nourishment.

To which I fear he will retort, "Look, I got a raise last year, and I'm giving my family the best of everything, we've got two cars and a color TV. I understand enough of the world!"

And he is right, unanswerably right, if that is what he wants, and all he wants.

30      The kind of thing you learn from reading about the problems of a hobbit who is going to drop a magic ring into an imaginary volcano has very little to do with your social status, or material success, or income. Indeed, if there is any relationship, it is a negative one. There is an inverse correlation between fantasy and money. That is a law, known to economists as Le Guin's Law. If you want a striking example of Le Guin's Law, just give a lift to one of those people along the roads who own nothing but a backpack, a guitar, a fine head of hair, a smile, and a thumb. Time and again, you will find that these waifs have read *The Lord of the Rings*—some of them can practically recite it. But now take Aristotle Onassis, or J. Paul Getty: could you believe that those men ever had anything to do, at any age, under any circumstances, with a hobbit?

But, to carry my example a little further, and out of the realm of economics, did you ever notice how very gloomy Mr. Onassis and Mr. Getty and all those billionaires look in their photographs? They have this strange, pinched look, as if they were hungry. As if they were hungry for something, as if they had lost something and were trying to think where it could be, or perhaps what it could be, what it was they've lost.

Could it be their childhood?

So I arrive at my personal defense of the uses of the imagination, especially in fiction, and most especially in fairy tale, legend, fantasy, science fiction, and the rest of the lunatic fringe. I believe that maturity is not an outgrowing, but a growing up: that an adult is not a dead child, but a child who survived. I believe that all the best faculties of a mature human being exist in the child, and that if these faculties are encouraged in youth they will act well and wisely in the adult, but if they are repressed and denied in the child they will stunt and cripple the adult personality. And finally, I believe that one of the most deeply human, and humane, of these faculties is the power of imagination: so that it is our pleasant duty, as librarians, or teachers, or parents, or writers, or simply as grownups, to encourage that faculty of imagination in our children, to encourage it to grow freely, to flourish like the green bay tree, by giving it the best, absolutely the best and purest, nourishment that it can absorb. And never, under any circumstances, to squelch it, or sneer at it, or imply that it is childish, or unmanly, or untrue.

For fantasy is true, of course. It isn't factual, but it is true. Children know that. Adults know it too, and that is precisely why many of them are afraid of fantasy. They know that its truth challenges, even threatens, all that is false, all that is phony, unnecessary, and trivial in the life they have let themselves be forced into living. They are afraid of dragons, because they are afraid of freedom.

So I believe that we should trust our children. Normal children do not    35
confuse reality and fantasy—they confuse them much less often than we adults do (as a certain great fantasist pointed out in a story called "The Emperor's New Clothes"). Children know perfectly well that unicorns aren't real, but they also know that books about unicorns, if they are good books, are true books. All too often, that's more than Mummy and Daddy know; for, in denying their childhood, the adults have denied half their knowledge, and are left with the sad, sterile little fact: "Unicorns aren't real." And that fact is one that never got anybody anywhere (except in the story "The Unicorn in the Garden," by another great fantasist, in which it is shown that a devotion to the unreality of unicorns may get you straight into the loony bin). It is by such statements as, "Once upon a time there was a dragon," or "In a hole in the ground there lived a hobbit—it is by such beautiful non-facts that we fantastic human beings may arrive, in our peculiar fashion, at the truth.

## QUESTIONS

1. According to LeGuin, why do many people in the United States have "a moral disapproval of fantasy"?
2. Explain how the four characteristics LeGuin identifies in paragraph 10 contribute to some people's fear of dragons.
3. Why does LeGuin refer to a dictionary? Does it add to or detract from her argument?
4. How does LeGuin define the word *discipline* in paragraphs 17–19? What is your definition of the word?
5. Is LeGuin's description of a "typical" American man and woman exaggerated?
6. According to LeGuin, why is "imaginative fiction" good for us?
7. According to LeGuin, what is an "adult"? Explain whether or not you agree with her.
8. Explain what LeGuin means when she states that "fantasy is true." Do you agree with her?
9. Most of us in this country watch a lot of movies and TV shows, which also tell fictional stories. Do we get "enough" fantasy that way? Is there something to be gained from reading fiction that can't be gotten from *watching* fiction? Explain your answers.

**CONNECTIONS**

1. Having read LeGuin's discussion of Puritan attitudes toward work, would you say that Andrew Carnegie (see Section 4) subscribed to Puritan views? Explain your response.
2. How might Warren Farrell (see Section 2) respond to LeGuin's description of a typical U.S. male?

# ∾ It's Failure, Not Success

*Ellen Goodman*

> For a biographical note on Ellen Goodman, turn to page 144. The following
> selection first appeared in the *Boston Globe* in 1977 and is included in the
> essay collection *Close to Home* (1979).

**WARM-UP:**  What advice, both good and bad, have you received about
how to become successful?

I knew a man who went into therapy about three years ago because, as he put     1
it, he couldn't live with himself any longer. I didn't blame him. The guy was
a bigot, a tyrant and a creep.

In any case, I ran into him again after he'd finished therapy. He was still a
bigot, a tyrant and a creep, *but . . .* he had learned to live with himself.

Now, I suppose this was an accomplishment of sorts. I mean, nobody else
could live with him. But it seems to me that there are an awful lot of people
running around and writing around these days encouraging us to feel good
about what we should feel terrible about, and to accept in ourselves what we
should change.

The only thing they seem to disapprove of is disapproval. The only judgment they make is against being judgmental, and they assure us that we have
nothing to feel guilty about except guilt itself. It seems to me that they are all
intent on proving that I'm OK and You're OK, when in fact, I may be perfectly
dreadful, and you may be unforgivably dreary, and it may be—gasp!—*wrong*.

What brings on my sudden attack of judgmentitis is success, or rather,     5
*Success!*—the latest in a series of exclamation-point books all concerned with
How to Make it.

In this one, Michael Korda is writing a recipe book for success. Like the
other authors, he leapfrogs right over the "Shoulds" and into the "Hows." He
eliminates and edits out moral questions as if he were Fannie Farmer and the
subject was the making of a blueberry pie.

It's not that I have any reason to doubt Mr. Korda's advice on the way to
achieve success. It may very well be that successful men wear handkerchiefs
stuffed neatly in their breast pockets, and that successful single women should
carry suitcases to the office on Fridays whether or not they are going away for
the weekend.

He may be realistic when he says that "successful people generally have
very low expectations of others." And he may be only slightly cynical when he

writes: "One of the best ways to ensure success is to develop expensive tastes or marry someone who has them."

And he may be helpful with his handy hints on how to sit next to someone you are about to overpower.

10    But he simply finesses° the issues of right and wrong—silly words, embarrassing words that have been excised° like warts from the shiny surface of the new how-to books. To Korda, guilt is not a prod,° but an enemy that he slays on page four. Right off the bat, he tells the would-be successful reader that:

- It's OK to be greedy.
- It's OK to look out for Number One.
- It's OK to be Machiavellian° (if you can get away with it).
- It's OK to recognize that honesty is not always the best policy (provided you don't go around saying so).
- And it's always OK to be rich.

Well, in fact, it's not OK. It's not OK to be greedy, Machiavellian, dishonest. It's not always OK to be rich. There is a qualitative difference between succeeding by making napalm° or by making penicillin. There is a difference between climbing the ladder of success, and machete-ing a path to the top.

Only someone with the moral perspective of a mushroom could assure us that this was all OK. It seems to me that most Americans harbor ambivalence toward success, not for neurotic° reasons, but out of a realistic perception of what it demands.

Success is expensive in terms of time and energy and altered behavior— the sort of behavior he describes in the grossest of terms: "If you can undermine your boss and replace him, fine, do so, but never express anything but respect and loyalty for him while you're doing it."

This author—whose *Power!* topped the best-seller list last year—is intent on helping rid us of that ambivalence which is a signal from our conscience. He is like the other "Win!" "Me First!" writers, who try to make us comfortable when we should be uncomfortable.

15    They are all Doctor Feelgoods,° offering us placebo° prescriptions instead of strong medicine. They give us a way to live with ourselves, perhaps, but not a way to live with each other. They teach us a whole lot more about "Failure!" than about success.

---

*finesses:* Evades, trick.   *excised:* Removed.   *prod:* Incitement to act.   *Machiavellian:* Deceitful, manipulative.   *napalm:* Chemical used in incendiary bombs.   *neurotic:* Emotionally unstable. *Doctor Feelgoods:* People who offer encouraging but incomplete or inaccurate advice.   *placebo:* An inert or innocuous substance.

## QUESTIONS

1. Is Goodman's introduction effective? Why or why not?
2. Identify Goodman's thesis statement. Does it get reiterated in the essay? If so, where?
3. Why does Goodman take issue with Michael Korda's book?
4. Explain what Goodman means in the line, "They give us a way to live with ourselves, perhaps, but not a way to live with each other."
5. Explain the ironic effect of the sentence that concludes this essay.
6. What action do you imagine Goodman would like her audience to take?

## CONNECTIONS

1. Is Goodman's writing style in this piece similar to the style in the essay by her included in Section 2? If so, in what way(s)?
2. Compare Goodman's views of success with those discussed by Sam Keen in his essay, included in Section 4.
3. Would Ursula K. LeGuin agree or disagree with Goodman's assessment of "success"? Quote LeGuin to support your response.

# Dow Recycles Reality

*Mark Crispin Miller*

Mark Crispin Miller was born in 1949 in Chicago and earned degrees from Northwestern University and Johns Hopkins University. He has taught at the University of Pennsylvania and at Johns Hopkins and has published essays on film, television, advertising, and music in magazines such as *Mother Jones, The Nation, The New Republic,* and the *New York Review of Books,* as well as in the anthology *Boxed In: The Culture of TV* (1987). He has also written a book, *Spectacle* (1992), about the relationship between the media and the military during the Gulf War. The following essay was initially published in September 1990 in *Esquire* magazine.

**WARM-UP:** Find an advertisement in a newspaper or magazine and explain how its designers use words and images to promote the product advertised.

1    "That's my Dad." In the preteen voice-over there's just the trace of an apologetic chuckle. It's understandable. This "Dad" is an overt° dork. Pitching at a (Dow) company softball game, he gives up a base hit, then tries to block it with his foot. Note the look of nitwit concentration, recalling Dagwood Bumstead or Curly Howard hard at work. Dad, too, is a diverting stooge, with that potent Dow logo stamped across his cap, and his togs steeped in the brilliant white and orange of that logo. (In fact, the whole bright ball field is decked out in the same festive colors.)

"Good thing he's got a *real* job!" jokes Dad's young son, " . . . at Dow!" As the subject shifts from softball to the corporation, this cherub° drops the mild, ironic tone and starts promoting Dow's environmentalism in a kind of earnest kidspeak. Dad is (spoken haltingly) "a . . . plastics . . . recycling . . . engineer!" Dad "figures out ways" to turn plastic trash "into neat stuff like those picnic tables—and Brad's bat 'n' ball!"

With this last phrase, there appears tiny "Brad," apparently a baby brother, whacking a home run—and then there's Dad again, oafishly° striking out: "My Dad may be a lousy ballplayer," his son concludes, "but he's a *neat guy!*" The boy then grasps Dad's hand and gazes up, with filial° pathos,° into the engineer's weak, boyish face, sighing, "I'm *real proud* o' ya, Dad!" "*Proud* of

---

*overt:* Apparent; outright.    *cherub:* An innocent-looking, usually chubby and rosy angel.    *oafishly:* Foolishly.    *filial:* Related to being a son or a daughter.    *pathos:* Emotion, feeling.

me?" Dad gasps, and the camera cranes up and back to reveal the father-son communion amid the Dow-sponsored gaiety, as that hearty female voice, so reminiscent of "the Sixties" (the Seekers), breaks, as usual, into: "Dow . . . lets you do *great thiiiiiings!*"

Devised for Earth Day, this ad, like most "Green ads," tries to dim our awareness of foul air, mounting garbage, ozone depletion. Implicitly, Dow's sponsorship of this old-fashioned sunny fete° assures us that Dow, prolific° maker of (among other goodies) Styrofoam, pesticide, and chemical fertilizer, wants us all to live as we did before the rise of agribusiness, freeways, and fast food. The child, too, is reassuring. If this cool young Aryan is so moved by Dad's daily responsibilities, then Dad/Dow must be doing a heroic job indeed, with that "plastics recycling."

Not that plastic poses any danger! Certainly, each and every one of us          5
should go on using tons of it: Dad is there to help Dow make *more* plastics. And why not? Isn't plastic just as wholesome as whatever grows on trees? Among the items displayed on the child's left in one frame is a large green apple, placed there as if to blur the crucial difference between nature's bounty and the corporation's goods.

And Dow's TV spots work to sanitize not just its wares but its very image. In this ad Dow seems not huge and lethal, but goofily benign, like that awkward boy/dad in his special hat and corporate colors. By softening "Dad," our usual symbol of authority, Dow appears also to champion the weak and innocent: "Brad" belts a homer while Dad strikes out—just as, in other Dow ads, the effectual° one is not some steel-gray CEO, but a slightly rumpled backpacker; a lanky college student grinning on a humble bike; a slim and saintly Ph.D. gone home to save her Grandpa's farm. Dow projects itself as "caring"—yet its power seems all-pervasive.° In the final shot, that white-and-orange umbrella placed protectively above the faulty employee and his adoring son.

What Dow is selling here, then, is not just a profitable myth about plastics but the sense (which will become *our* sense, if we don't watch out) that certain dissident° impulses of the past have been absorbed—by Dow. In its ads, the young are on Dow's side—not like, say, twenty years ago. Back then, one of Dow's products—napalm—made the company notorious, through horrifying images of children burned and screaming. Those who saw, and haven't forgotten, may not feel comforted by Dow's knowing hikers, tykes, and Ph.D.s. Younger viewers, on the other hand, have no way of spotting the lie, since TV, thanks to Dow and others, has no memory.

---

*fete:* Celebration.   *prolific:* Productive, abundant.   *effectual:* Producing or able to produce a desired effect.   *all-pervasive:* Found everywhere.   *dissident:* Disagreeing with an established belief or group.

## QUESTIONS

1. Is Miller's introduction effective? What is his tone in the introduction?
2. What is Miller's thesis? Is its placement in the essay effective?
3. According to the author, how does the Dow advertisement attempt to create positive associations around plastics in general and around the Dow corporation in particular?
4. What are some of the key details that Miller zooms in on? Would you have noticed them in the advertisement otherwise? If you had seen the advertisement on TV, do you think that these details would have affected you in the way Miller suggests?
5. Why is the father in this ad presented as "goofily benign"?
6. What is Miller implying in the final line of paragraph 6, when he writes "In the final shot, white-and-orange umbrella is placed protectively above the faulty employee and adoring son"?
7. Does Miller use loaded language anywhere in the essay? If so, does it detract from the essay's effectiveness?
8. Explain the point that Miller makes in his conclusion.
9. Have you ever been annoyed or offended by a televised advertisement? If so, describe the advertisement and explain why it was annoying or offensive.

## CONNECTIONS

1. Does this essay support or contradict Ellen Goodman's statements about American views of success?
2. Note the placement of the thesis and of the evidence supporting the thesis in this essay. Then examine the placement of the thesis and evidence in Gloria Naylor's essay "The Meaning of a Word" and explain which organization you find more effective.
3. Name some selections you have read so far in this text whose overall style and tone resemble those of Miller's essay.

# Future Schlock

*Neil Postman*

Neil Postman was born in Brooklyn, New York, in 1931. After working as an elementary and secondary school teacher, Postman wrote *Teaching as a Subversive Activity* (1969) and *The Soft Revolution* (1971), which established him as a leading advocate of educational reform. A popular lecturer on the effects of mass media on U.S. culture and politics, Postman has published articles in *The Atlantic Monthly* and in *The Nation;* his recent books include *Technopoly: The Surrender of Culture to Technology* (1992), *How to Watch TV News* (1992), and *The End of Education: Redefining the Value of School* (1995). He is currently teaching at New York University, where he chairs the Department of Culture and Communication. The following essay comes from *Conscientious Objections: Stirring up Trouble about Language, Technology, and Education* (1988).

**WARM-UP:** What role has television played in your life? Did you watch TV a lot when you were a child? What have you learned by watching it?

Human intelligence is among the most fragile things in nature. It doesn't take much to distract it, suppress it, or even annihilate° it. In this century, we have had some lethal examples of how easily and quickly intelligence can be defeated by any one of its several nemeses:° ignorance, superstition, moral fervor, cruelty, cowardice, neglect. In the late 1920s, for example, Germany was, by any measure, the most literate, cultured nation in the world. Its legendary seats of learning attracted scholars from every corner. Its philosophers, social critics, and scientists were of the first rank; its humane traditions an inspiration to less favored nations. But by the mid-1930s—that is, in less than ten years—this cathedral of human reason had been transformed into a cesspool of barbaric irrationality. Many of the most intelligent products of German culture were forced to flee—for example, Einstein, Freud, Karl Jaspers, Thomas Mann, and Stefan Zweig. Even worse, those who remained were either forced to submit their minds to the sovereignty° of primitive superstition, or—worse still—willingly did so: Konrad Lorenz, Werner Heisenberg, Martin Heidegger, Gerhardt Hauptmann. On May 10, 1933, a huge bonfire was kindled in Berlin and the books of Marcel Proust, André Gide, Emile Zola, Jack London, Upton Sinclair, and a hundred others were

1

---

*annihilate:* Destroy.  *nemeses:* Formidable rivals or opponents.  *sovereignty:* Power, supremacy.

committed to the flames, amid shouts of idiot delight. By 1936, Joseph Paul Goebbels, Germany's Minister of Propaganda, was issuing a proclamation which began with the following words: "Because this year has not brought an improvement in art criticism, I forbid once and for all the continuance of art criticism in its past form, effective as of today." By 1936, there was no one left in Germany who had the brains or courage to object.

Exactly why the Germans banished intelligence is a vast and largely unanswered question. I have never been persuaded that the desperate economic depression that afflicted Germany in the 1920s adequately explains what happened. To quote Aristotle: Men do not become tyrants in order to keep warm. Neither do they become stupid—at least not *that* stupid. But the matter need not trouble us here. I offer the German case only as the most striking example of the fragility of human intelligence. My focus here is the United States in our own time, and I wish to worry you about the rapid erosion of our own intelligence. If you are confident that such a thing cannot happen, your confidence is misplaced, I believe, but it is understandable.

After all, the United States is one of the few countries in the world founded by intellectuals—men of wide learning, of extraordinary rhetorical° powers, of deep faith in reason. And although we have had our moods of anti-intellectualism, few people have been more generous in support of intelligence and learning than Americans. It was the United States that initiated the experiment in mass education that is, even today, the envy of the world. It was America's churches that laid the foundation of our admirable system of higher education; it was the Land-Grant Act of 1862 that made possible our great state universities; and it is to America that scholars and writers have fled when freedom of the intellect became impossible in their own nations. This is why the great historian of American civilization Henry Steele Commager called America "the Empire of Reason." But Commager was referring to the United States of the eighteenth and nineteenth centuries. What term he would use for America today, I cannot say. Yet he has observed, as others have, a change, a precipitous° decline in our valuation of intelligence, in our uses of language, in the disciplines of logic and reason, in our capacity to attend to complexity. Perhaps he would agree with me that the Empire of Reason is, in fact, gone, and that the most apt term for America today is the Empire of Shlock.

In any case, this is what I wish to call to your notice: the frightening displacement of serious, intelligent public discourse in American culture by the imagery and triviality of what may be called show business. I do not see the decline of intelligent discourse in America leading to the barbarisms that flourished in Germany, of course. No scholars, I believe, will ever need to flee America. There will be no bonfires to burn books. And I cannot imagine any proclamations forbidding once and for all art criticism, or any other kind of

*rhetorical:* Related to the art or skill of speaking and writing effectively.   *precipitous:* Steep, abrupt.

criticism. But this is not a cause for complacency, let alone celebration. A culture does not have to force scholars to flee to render them impotent. A culture does not have to burn books to assure that they will not be read. And a culture does not need a Minister of Propaganda issuing proclamations to silence criticism. There are other ways to achieve stupidity, and it appears that, as in so many other things, there is a distinctly American way.

To explain what I am getting at, I find it helpful to refer to two films,     5
which taken together embody the main lines of my argument. The first film is of recent vintage and is called *The Gods Must Be Crazy*. It is about a tribal people who live in the Kalahari Desert plains of southern Africa, and what happens to their culture when it is invaded by an empty Coca-Cola bottle tossed from the window of a small plane passing overhead. The bottle lands in the middle of the village and is construed° by these gentle people to be a gift from the gods, for they not only have never seen a bottle before but have never seen glass either. The people are almost immediately charmed by the gift, and not only because of its novelty. The bottle, it turns out, has multiple uses, chief among them the intriguing music it makes when one blows into it.

But gradually a change takes place in the tribe. The bottle becomes an irresistible preoccupation. Looking at it, holding it, thinking of things to do with it displace other activities once thought essential. But more than this, the Coke bottle is the only thing these people have ever seen of which there is only one of its kind. And so those who do not have it try to get it from the one who does. And the one who does refuses to give it up. Jealousy, greed, and even violence enter the scene, and come very close to destroying the harmony that has characterized their culture for a thousand years. The people begin to love their bottle more than they love themselves, and are saved only when the leader of the tribe, convinced that the gods must be crazy, returns the bottle to the gods by throwing it off the top of a mountain.

The film is great fun and it is also wise, mainly because it is about a subject as relevant to people in Chicago or Los Angeles or New York as it is to those of the Kalahari Desert. It raises two questions of extreme importance to our situation: How does a culture change when new technologies are introduced to it? And is it always desirable for a culture to accommodate itself to the demands of new technologies? The leader of the Kalahari tribe is forced to confront these questions in a way that Americans have refused to do. And because his vision is not obstructed by a belief in what Americans call "technological progress," he is able with minimal discomfort to decide that the songs of the Coke bottle are not so alluring that they are worth admitting envy, egotism, and greed to a serene culture.

The second film relevant to my argument was made in 1967. It is Mel Brooks's first film, *The Producers*. *The Producers* is a rather raucous° comedy

*construed:* Interpreted.     *raucous:* Boisterous, loud, unruly.

that has at its center a painful joke: An unscrupulous theatrical producer has figured out that it is relatively easy to turn a buck by producing a play that fails. All one has to do is induce dozens of backers to invest in the play by promising them exorbitant° percentages of its profits. When the play fails, there being no profits to disperse, the producer walks away with thousands of dollars that can never be claimed. Of course, the central problem he must solve is to make sure that his play is a disastrous failure. And so he hits upon an excellent idea: he will take the most tragic and grotesque story of the century—the rise of Adolf Hitler—and make it into a musical.

Because the producer is only a crook and not a fool, he assumes that the stupidity of making a musical on this theme will be immediately grasped by audiences and that they will leave the theater in dumbfounded rage. So he calls his play *Springtime for Hitler,* which is also the name of its most important song. The song begins with the words:

Springtime for Hitler and Germany;
Winter for Poland and France.

10     The melody is catchy, and when the song is sung it is accompanied by a happy chorus line. (One must understand, of course, that *Springtime for Hitler* is no spoof of Hitler, as was, for example, Charlie Chaplin's *The Great Dictator.* The play is instead a kind of denial of Hitler in song and dance; as if to say, it was all in fun.)

The ending of the movie is predictable. The audience loves the play and leaves the theater humming *Springtime for Hitler.* The musical becomes a great hit. The producer ends up in jail, his joke having turned back on him. But Brooks's point is that the joke is on us. Although the film was made years before a movie actor became President of the United States, Brooks was making a kind of prophecy about that—namely, that the producers of American culture will increasingly turn our history, politics, religion, commerce, and education into forms of entertainment, and that we will become as a result a trivial people, incapable of coping with complexity, ambiguity, uncertainty, perhaps even reality. We will become, in a phrase, a people amused into stupidity.

For those readers who are not inclined to take Mel Brooks as seriously as I do, let me remind you that the prophecy I attribute here to Brooks was, in fact, made many years before by a more formidable social critic than he. I refer to Aldous Huxley, who wrote *Brave New World* at the time that the modern monuments to intellectual stupidity were taking shape: Nazism in Germany, fascism in Italy, communism in Russia. But Huxley was not concerned in his book with such naked and crude forms of intellectual suicide. He saw beyond them, and mostly, I must add, he saw America. To be more specific, he foresaw that the greatest threat to the intelligence and humane creativity of our cul-

---

*exorbitant:* Excessive.

ture would not come from Big Brother and Ministries of Propaganda, or gulags° and concentration camps. He prophesied, if I may put it this way, that there is tyranny lurking in a Coca-Cola bottle; that we could be ruined not by what we fear and hate but by what we welcome and love, by what we construe to be a gift from the gods.

And in case anyone missed his point in 1932, Huxley wrote *Brave New World Revisited* twenty years later. By then, George Orwell's *1984* had been published, and it was inevitable that Huxley would compare Orwell's book with his own. The difference, he said, is that in Orwell's book people are controlled by inflicting pain. In *Brave New World,* they are controlled by inflicting pleasure.

The Coke bottle that has fallen in our midst is a corporation of dazzling technologies whose forms turn all serious public business into a kind of *Springtime for Hitler* musical. Television is the principal instrument of this disaster, in part because it is the medium Americans most dearly love, and in part because it has become the command center of our culture. Americans turn to television not only for their light entertainment but for their news, their weather, their politics, their religion, their history—all of which may be said to be their serious entertainment. The light entertainment is not the problem. The least dangerous things on television are its junk. What I am talking about is television's preemption of our culture's most serious business. It would be merely banal° to say that television presents us with entertaining subject matter. It is quite another thing to say that on television all subject matter is presented as entertaining. And that is how television brings ruin to any intelligent understanding of public affairs.

Political campaigns, for example, are now conducted largely in the form   15
of television commercials. Candidates forgo precision, complexity, substance —in some cases, language itself—for the arts of show business: music, imagery, celebrities, theatrics. Indeed, political figures have become so good at this, and so accustomed to it, that they do television commercials even when they are not campaigning, as, for example, Geraldine Ferraro for Diet Pepsi and former Vice-Presidential candidate William Miller and the late Senator Sam Ervin for American Express. Even worse, political figures appear on variety shows, soap operas, and sitcoms. George McGovern, Ralph Nader. Ed Koch, and Jesse Jackson have all hosted "Saturday Night Live." Henry Kissinger and former President Gerald Ford have done cameo roles on "Dynasty." Tip O'Neill and Governor Michael Dukakis have appeared on "Cheers." Richard Nixon did a short stint on "Laugh-In." The late Senator from Illinois, Everett Dirksen, was on "What's My Line?" a prophetic question if ever there was one. What *is* the line of these people? Or, more precisely, *where* is the line that one ought to be able to draw between politics and entertainment? I would suggest that television has annihilated it.

*gulags:* Prison labor camps.    *banal:* Dull, lacking originality or freshness.

It is significant, I think, that although our current President, a former Hollywood movie actor, rarely speaks accurately and never precisely, he is known as the Great Communicator; his telegenic° charm appears to be his major asset, and that seems to be quite good enough in an entertainment-oriented politics. But lest you think his election to two terms is a mere aberration,° I must remind you that, as I write [1988], Charlton Heston is being mentioned as a possible candidate for the Republican nomination in 1988. Should this happen, what alternative would the Democrats have but to nominate Gregory Peck? Two idols of the silver screen going one on one. Could even the fertile imagination of Mel Brooks have foreseen this? Heston giving us intimations° of Moses as he accepts the nomination; Peck re-creating the courage of his biblical David as he accepts the challenge of running against a modern Goliath. Heston going on the stump as Michelangelo; Peck countering with Douglas MacArthur. Heston accusing Peck of insanity because of *The Boys from Brazil.* Peck replying with the charge that Heston blew the world up in *Return to Planet of the Apes. Springtime for Hitler* could be closer than you think.

But politics is only one arena in which serious language has been displaced by the arts of show business. We have all seen how religion is packaged on television, as a kind of Las Vegas stage show, devoid of ritual, sacrality,° and tradition. Today's electronic preachers are in no way like America's evangelicals of the past. Men like Jonathan Edwards, Charles Finney, and George Whitefield were preachers of theological depth, authentic learning, and great expository° power. Electronic preachers such as Jimmy Swaggart, Jim Bakker, and Jerry Falwell are merely performers who exploit television's visual power and their own charisma for the greater glory of themselves.

We have also seen "Sesame Street" and other educational shows in which the demands of entertainment take precedence over the rigors of learning. And we well know how American businessmen, working under the assumption that potential customers require amusement rather than facts, use music, dance, comedy, cartoons, and celebrities to sell their products.

Even our daily news, which for most Americans means television news, is packaged as a kind of show, featuring handsome news readers, exciting music, and dynamic film footage. Most especially, film footage. When there is no film footage, there is no story. Stranger still, commercials may appear anywhere in a news story—before, after, or in the middle. This reduces all events to trivialities, sources of public entertainment and little more. After all, how serious can a bombing in Lebanon be if it is shown to us prefaced by a happy United

---

*telegenic:* Attractive to television viewers.    *aberration:* Deviation from the norm.    *intimations:* Suggestions.    *sacrality:* Sacredness.    *expository:* Conveying information or explaining what is difficult to understand.

Airlines commercial and summarized by a Calvin Klein jeans commercial? Indeed, television newscasters have added to our grammar a new part of speech—what may be called the "Now . . . this" conjunction, a conjunction that does not connect two things, but disconnects them. When newscasters say, "Now . . . this," they mean to indicate that what you have just heard or seen has no relevance to what you are about to hear or see. There is no murder so brutal, no political blunder so costly, no bombing so devastating that it cannot be erased from our minds by a newscaster saying, "Now . . . this." He means that you have thought long enough on the matter (let us say, for forty seconds) and you must now give your attention to a commercial. Such a situation is not "the news." It is merely a daily version of *Springtime for Hitler,* and in my opinion accounts for the fact that Americans are among the most ill-informed people in the world. To be sure, we know *of* many things; but we know *about* very little.

To provide some verification of this, I conducted a survey a few years back on the subject of the Iranian hostage crisis. I chose this subject because it was alluded to on television *every day for more than a year.* I did not ask my subjects for their opinions about the hostage situation. I am not interested in opinion polls; I am interested in knowledge polls. The questions I asked were simple and did not require deep knowledge. For example, Where is Iran? What language do the Iranians speak? Where did the Shah come from? What religion do the Iranians practice, and what are its basic tenets°? What does "Ayatollah" mean? I found that almost everybody knew nothing about Iran. And those who did know something said they had learned it from *Newsweek* or *Time* or the *New York Times.* Television, in other words, is not the great information machine. It is the great disinformation machine. A most nerve-wracking confirmation of this came some time ago during an interview with the producer and the writer of the TV mini-series *Peter the Great.* Defending the historical inaccuracies in the drama—which included a fabricated meeting between Peter and Sir Isaac Newton[5]—the producer said that no one would watch a dry, historically faithful biography. The writer added that it is better for audiences to learn something that is untrue, if it is entertaining, than not to learn anything at all. And just to put some icing on the cake, the actor who played Peter, Maximilian Schell, remarked that he does not believe in historical truth and therefore sees no reason to pursue it.

I do not mean to say that the trivialization of American public discourse is all accomplished on television. Rather, television is the paradigm° for all our attempts at public communication. It conditions our minds to apprehend the world through fragmented pictures and forces other media to orient

*tenets:* Principles or beliefs that members of a group hold to be true.     *paradigm:* Example, pattern.

themselves in that direction. You know the standard question we put to people who have difficulty understanding even simple language: we ask them impatiently, "Do I have to draw a picture for you?" Well, it appears that, like it or not, our culture will draw pictures for us, will explain the world to us in pictures. As a medium for conducting public business, language has receded in importance; it has been moved to the periphery° of culture and has been replaced at the center by the entertaining visual image.

Please understand that I am making no criticism of the visual arts in general. That criticism is made by God, not by me. You will remember that in His Second Commandment, God explicitly states that "Thou shalt not make unto thee any graven image, nor any likeness of anything that is in Heaven above, or that is in the earth beneath, or the waters beneath the earth." I have always felt that God was taking a rather extreme position on this, as is His way. As for myself, I am arguing from the standpoint of a symbolic relativist. Forms of communication are neither good nor bad in themselves. They become good or bad depending on their relationship to other symbols and on the functions they are made to serve within a social order. When a culture becomes overloaded with pictures; when logic and rhetoric lose their binding authority; when historical truth becomes irrelevant; when the spoken or written word is distrusted or makes demands on our attention that we are incapable of giving; when our politics, history, education, religion public information, and commerce are expressed largely in visual imagery rather than words, then a culture is in serious jeopardy.

Neither do I make a complaint against entertainment. As an old song has it, life is not a highway strewn with flowers. The sight of a few blossoms here and there may make our journey a trifle more endurable. But in America, the least amusing people are our professional entertainers. In our present situation, our preachers, entrepreneurs, politicians, teachers, and journalists are committed to entertaining us through media that do not lend themselves to serious, complex discourse. But these producers of our culture are not to be blamed. They, like the rest of us, believe in the supremacy of technological progress. It has never occurred to us that the gods might be crazy. And even if it did, there is no mountaintop from which we can return what is dangerous to us.

We would do well to keep in mind that there are two ways in which the spirit of a culture may be degraded. In the first—the Orwellian—culture becomes a prison. This was the way of the Nazis, and it appears to be the way of the Russians. In the second—the Huxleyan—culture becomes a burlesque.° This appears to be the way of the Americans. What Huxley teaches is

---

*periphery:* External boundary, outskirts.    *burlesque:* Mockery or caricature.

that in the Age of Advanced Technology, spiritual devastation is more likely to come from an enemy with a smiling countenance° than from one whose face exudes° suspicion and hate. In the Huxleyan prophecy, Big Brother does not watch us, by his choice; we watch him, by ours. When a culture becomes distracted by trivia; when political and social life are redefined as a perpetual round of entertainments; when public conversation becomes a form of baby talk; when a people become, in short, an audience and their public business a vaudeville act, then—Huxley argued—a nation finds itself at risk and culture-death is a clear possibility. I agree.

## QUESTIONS

1. What is the point of Postman's introductory example about Nazi Germany? Does Postman claim that the United States will become like Germany in the '30s?
2. Do you agree that show business has become more important than intellectual debate in the United States today? Support your answer with specific examples.
3. Why does Postman summarize the films *The Gods Must Be Crazy* and *The Producers*?
4. Do you agree that the television is, as Postman claims, "the command center of our culture"?
5. Who or what does the author blame for the "dumbing down" of America? Do you agree with his analysis?
6. What point is Postman making in paragraph 16, when he describes Charlton Heston and Gregory Peck running for President of the United States?
7. Expand on Postman's point that "we know *of* many things; but we know *about* very little."
8. Is Postman's use of the survey about the Iranian hostage crisis, discussed in paragraph 20, effective? Does it add to or detract from the argument?
9. Explain what Postman means by the term "symbolic relativist."
10. What is Postman's thesis?
11. What is Postman's tone? Is it consistent throughout the piece? Do you find it appropriate for the topic?
12. What action do you imagine Postman would like his audience to take after reading this essay?

---

*countenance:* Face or facial expression.    *exudes:* Oozes, emits.

**CONNECTIONS**

1. Compare and contrast Postman's views about television with those expressed in Benjamin Barber's essay "America Skips School" (included in Section 1).
2. Does Mark Crispin Miller's essay support Postman's argument? If so, explain how.

# ～ The Price of Privacy

*Anna Quindlen*

Anna Quindlen was born in Philadelphia in 1953. She earned a B.A. degree from Barnard College in 1974. Until 1995, she was a widely syndicated columnist with the *New York Times;* her column "Public & Private" won the Pulitzer Prize in 1992. Both her collections of columns and her two novels, *Object Lessons* (1991) and *One True Thing* (1994), have been best-sellers; she has also written a children's book, *The Tree That Came to Stay* (1992). In 1995 Quindlen gave up writing her column in order to concentrate on writing fiction. The following essay appeared in the *New York Times* in September 1994.

**WARM-UP:** Do you feel that the people of the area you live in are bound together as a community? Why? What creates a "sense of community"?

The city was haunted. Not by the little girl who is said to bounce a red ball     1
through the halls of the Dakota, many decades after death. Not by weeping Olive Thomas, the long-ago Ziegfeld Follies star who has been sighted, vaguely transparent, in the New Amsterdam Theater.

This newest ghost was a contemporary one, a young woman in a brightly colored running suit. Her face was not spectral°; it appeared on posters taped to the door of nearly every coffee shop and deli in lower Manhattan. On Sept. 20 she was discovered dead in a storage trailer on the outskirts of the Village. She had been strangled.

For a week after the discovery no one came forward to claim her, to say who she was, what she did, how she lived, who cared for her and who might have killed her. It was not only her death that was haunting, but a kind of rootlessness among us that that death suggests, the notion that the anonymity° of the city is only a shade removed from invisibility, and that the price of privacy may be to die alone.

Like so many things about the city, good and bad, this rootlessness has spread to the exurbs,° the suburbs, even the rural areas once known for a kind of suffocating neighborliness. In this world it was not only possible but unsurprising when, a year ago, two little girls were left alone to fend for themselves while their parents went to Mexico. No one in the quiet Chicago suburb knew

---

*spectral:* Ghostly.   *anonymity:* The quality or state of being anonymous or unknown.   *exurbs:* Districts located beyond a city's suburbs.

the family well. Minding our own business, it seems, has become a cardinal virtue.

5        The world is still a great repository of connection among unlikely cohorts, and none more so than in the city: doorman, deli man, co-workers, apartment house neighbors. And then there is the great covey° of familiar strangers, those seen day after day without introduction or information. Some called the police to say that the dead woman was one of those, that they knew the face but not the name.

Sometimes old people die in this fashion, no one left to claim them. Sometimes street people, too, who have left their identities with their sanity or sobriety in some long-abandoned home. But this woman was neither.

For many of us, who had once been new to the city, without much in the way of friends or connections, she suggested the ghost of years long past our younger selves. Haunted by the vacuum surrounding her death, strangers spun yarns to cover her. Perhaps a tourist not yet missed by her family far away. Or a student still unknown to classmates whose answering machine was filling up with messages from home.

Neither, it turned out, was correct. Tuesday the woman whose body was found in the trailer was identified as Carol Ann Artutis, 23, who lived just across the river in New Jersey. No family member or friend came forward to identify her; police found her by the fingerprints on an application she had filed to become a private investigator. On a question about next of kin, she had written "none."

As the facts of her life were filled in by police and the search for her murderer usurped° the search for her identity, she left an apparition behind. No spectral child, it was instead a glimpse into our own lives, in which a message on an answering machine passes as communication, in which eye contact is a gift given carefully and infrequently, in which human beings sometimes fade from view as surely as any phantasm.

### QUESTIONS

1. What writing strategy does Quindlen use in her introduction and conclusion?
2. Identify Quindlen's thesis.
3. Explain whether or not you agree with Quindlen regarding "the price of privacy."
4. Do you agree with the author's claim, "The world is still a great repository of connection among unlikely cohorts . . ."?

---

*covey:* Flock, bunch.    *usurped:* Seized, took over.

5. Of the stories and scenarios that Quindlen uses to illustrate her main point, which touches you the most? Which do you find the most persuasive? Why?
6. Do you agree with the author's view of anonymity in the United States?
7. Quindlen mentions that the woman she writes about was strangled; however, crime is not her main focus in this essay. Do you think that the kind of anonymity she describes affects the crime rate in our society? If so, how?

## CONNECTIONS

How does Quindlen's essay relate to Bruce Weber's "The Unromantic Generation" (Section 3) and Guadalupe Medina's "Dreaming Memories" (Section 5)?

# ∼ The Conservative Case for Abortion

## Jerry Z. Muller

Jerry Z. Muller was born in 1954; he is now an assistant professor of history at the Catholic University of America. Concerned with history, political science, and culture, Muller has authored several books—including *The Other God That Failed: Hans Freyer and the Deradicalization of German Conservatism* (1987) and *Adam Smith in His Time and Ours: Designing the Decent Society* (1993)—and has published several articles in newspapers, magazines, and journals—including "Four Cheers for Liberalism?" "The 'Homosexual Moment' on U.S. College Campuses," "A Conservative Defense of the Humanities Endowment," and the selection reprinted here, which is adapted from an essay originally published in *The New Republic.*

**WARM-UP:** What does the term *conservative* mean to you?

1    The current struggles over abortion are usually treated as conflicts between rival interpretations of individual rights: the "right to choose" of the woman who has conceived the fetus, or the "right to life" of the fetus. But there is a third position that is largely overlooked. Essentially conservative and "pro-family," it favors abortion as the right choice to promote healthy family life under certain circumstances.

This argument, which emphasizes the social function of the family over the rights of the individual, begins with the assumption that the possibility of choice matters less than the choice made. It argues that the choice to give birth to a child isn't always the right one. In fact, under some conditions, choosing to give birth may be socially dysfunctional, morally irresponsible or even cruel: inimical° to the forces of stability and bourgeois° responsibility conservatives cherish.

The prime obstacle to the right-to-life movement is not feminism; it is the millions of more or less conservative middle-class parents who know that, if their teen-age daughter were to become pregnant, they would advise her to get an abortion rather than marry out of necessity or go through the trauma of giving birth and then placing the child up for adoption. Many people— young, unmarried women loath° to bring a child into a family-less environment; parents of a fetus known to be afflicted by a disease that will make its life painful and short; parents who know that the birth of a fetus with severe

---

*inimical:* Unfriendly, hostile.    *bourgeois:* Middle-class.    *loath:* Unwilling, reluctant.

defects will mean pain for them and their other children—all choose abortion, not because they fetishize° choice but because they value the family.

The right-to-life movement has done our society a service by insisting upon the humanity and moral worth of the unborn child. But it has turned a legitimate moral concern into a moral absolute. It has made biological life not one good to be fought for, but the only good, to which all other considerations must be subordinated.

## Not a Fate but a Vocation

One of those considerations is the creation and preservation of families.    5
The pro-life movement is at odds with the assumptions of middle-class family formation. These families believe that the bearing and rearing of children is not an inexorable° fate but a voluntary vocation, and that, like any other vocation, it is to be pursued methodically using the most effective means available. Such a conception of the family includes planning when children are to be born and how many are to be born. It seeks to increase the chances of successfully socializing and educating children to help them find fulfilling work and spiritual lives. The technological repertoire° of today's family planning includes abortion to prevent out-of-wedlock childbirth, artificial contraception within marriage and voluntary sterilization when families have reached their desired size.

This vision of the family is a conception that those who seek to conserve modern society ought to fortify rather than undermine. It is under attack from many quarters, including the individualism and hedonism° of much of our popular and elite culture and the emphasis on career advancement among both men and women. But it is also threatened by the right-to-life movement.

The ideology of middle-class family formation maintains that families are not just another lifestyle option but an essential part of a modern society. Conservatives have long assumed that government should promote those social norms that encourage the creation of decent men and women and discourage those that experience has shown to be harmful. This logic lies at the heart of conservative debates on public policy, including recent proposals to reform welfare to discourage out-of-wedlock births.

The right-to-life movement stands as a barrier to such reform, contending that the removal of government subsidies for the bearing of out-of-wedlock children will cause women to resort more frequently to abortion. But

---

*fetishize:* Turn into a fixation or obsession.   *inexorable:* Unstoppable.   *repertoire:* List or supply of skills or devices.   *hedonism:* The doctrine that pleasure or happiness is the sole or chief good in life.

is it more important to minimize abortion or to minimize the birth of children to women who are unprepared to provide the familial structure needed for children to became responsible adults?

The pro-choice movement also condemns "welfare caps" because they reduce the choices facing women, and all choices are to be protected—including, in the words of liberal feminist Iris Young, "the freedom of all citizens to bear and rear children, whether they are married or not, whether they have high incomes or not."

10    For the right-to-life movement, of course, no fact about the potentially miserable outcome of the fetus's birth affects the imperative° that it be born. Beginning from different commitments, therefore, feminists and pro-lifers converge in rejecting the conservative assumption that the troubling social effects of out-of-wedlock births justify government attempts to limit them.

## Poor Children Out of Wedlock

The current right-to-life strategy calls for "chipping away" at the liberal abortion culture to "save" as many babies as possible. Because pro-lifers can have the greatest impact on legislation affecting the poor, the success of the movement is now measured in the lives of poor children born out of wedlock.

Indeed, the anti-abortion movement may already have helped increase the number of children born out of wedlock. The percentage of out-of-wedlock births in the United States rose from 18.4 percent in 1980 to 30.1 percent of all births in 1992, according to recent reports from the National Center for Health Statistics. During the same period, the proportion of nonmarital pregnancies ending in abortion declined, from 60 percent in 1980 to 46 percent in 1991. This trend may be due either to the increased difficulty of obtaining abortions or to increased preference for carrying babies to term. Either way, it marks a partial victory for the pro-life movement.

The second thrust of the current right-to-life strategy is the prohibition of abortion late in pregnancy, on the plausible assumption that even those with doubts about entirely prohibiting abortion regard the fetus as subject to ever greater respect as it develops. Here, too, the effect is tragic. Late-term abortions are rare and, when they do occur, it is frequently because the parents have discovered that their prospective child suffers from a serious birth defect or malformation. Yet it is these fetuses whom the pro-life movement now aims to "save." A bill now before Congress tries to force women to give birth to such babies.

The public is genuinely ambivalent on the question of abortion. It adheres to the tenets° of middle-class family life, yet without hearing those

---

*imperative:* Here meaning "necessity, obligation."    *tenets:* Beliefs, convictions.

tenets articulated. To focus on the conflict between the right-to-life move-ment and middle-class family values is to call into question the terms in which the abortion debate is usually cast. It should be understood as a three-way debate: among liberals, who believe that to let each of us do as we like will work out for the best; pro-lifers, who cling to one ultimate good at the expense of all others; and those committed to conserving middle-class fami-lies, sometimes at the expense of "choice," sometimes at the expense of "life." The third group lays best claim to the title "conservative."

## QUESTIONS

1. According to Muller, what is "[t]he prime obstacle to the right-to-life movement"?
2. What does Muller see as an important and justifiable reason for peo-ple to sometimes choose abortion?
3. According to Muller, which segment of the population has so far been affected the most by the right-to-life movement? Why?
4. Does Muller create a false dilemma in paragraph 8?
5. Muller twice places the word "save" (as used by the right-to-life movement in relation to babies) within quotation marks; find both instances, and explain why Muller doesn't think those babies are really saved.
6. Why does Muller describe his argument as "conservative"? What, according to him, are conservatives defending?
7. Muller writes that the public "adheres to the tenets of middle-class family life, yet without hearing those tenets articulated." What tenets is Muller referring to?
8. Is the introduction of this essay effective? Would you have introduced this topic differently? If so, how?
9. Does Muller do a good job of presenting and refuting his opponents' ideas and beliefs? Explain your position.

## CONNECTIONS

1. Name several characters from the selections you have read in this book so far who seem to fit Muller's definition of middle-class people. Which characters do not fit that description?
2. Both Ursula K. LeGuin's and Muller's arguments depend on the defi-nition of a word. Which words do they define? Of these two authors, which one uses the definition more effectively?

## ∼ Pluralism: Finding the Boundaries for Religious Freedom

*Erling Jorstad*

Erling Jorstad earned his bachelor's degree at Saint Olaf College in North-field, Minnesota, his master's degree at Harvard, and his Ph.D. at the University of Wisconsin–Madison. He is now retired after 38 years of teaching in the history and religious studies departments at Saint Olaf College. He has been a frequent speaker at church and clergy conferences. Through such books as *That New-Time Religion: The Jesus Revival in America* (1973), *Holding Fast/Pressing On: Religion in America in the 1980s* (1990), and *Popular Religion in America: The Evangelical Voice* (1995), Jorstad has documented and analyzed the impact of religion on U.S. society. The following selection comes from his 1986 book *Being Religious in America: The Deepening Crisis over Public Faith.*

**WARM-UP:** Do you think that religious groups are either too involved or not involved enough in politics in the United States?

1    In a nation that justly prides itself on protecting an immense variety of religious expressions, few events could match that of the trial of the Rev. Sun Myung Moon and his Unification Church in the early 1980s. Consider these facts:

1. Moon came from an uneducated peasant family in Korea.

2. The sacred book of the church he founded, titled *Divine Principle,* is, two experts say, "a bizarre mixture of pseudo-science, numerology, Korean shamanism, and evangelical Christianity."[1]

3. The book teaches that a second messiah, the Lord of the Second Advent, will come from Korea to complete the unfinished ministry of Jesus Christ. Moon's followers believe he is that figure.

4. His church, deeply entrenched in Korea and Japan, gives to its leaders between 70 and 100 million dollars a year for its ministry.[2]

5. The best estimate of the total number of full-time disciples of Rev. Moon in the United States is between 5000 and 7000.

6. He first attracted national publicity in the early 1970s for claiming Richard Nixon was God's gift to save the world from communism.[3]

7. He has been repeatedly charged and taken to court for allegedly turning earnest young adult converts into mindless, zealous zombies.

8. He has been charged by the federal government and convicted of income tax evasion.

9. As the implications of his trial became known nationally, he received support through several *amicus curiae* (friends of the court) briefs to help persuade the appeals courts to acquit Rev. Moon. These included Roman Catholic bishops, the National Council of Churches, Moral Majority, Christian Voice, the National Association of Evangelicals, the African Methodist Episcopal Church, the Southern Christian Leadership Conference, the American Civil Liberties Union, the National Bar Association, the Church of Jesus Christ of Latter-Day Saints, the American Association of Christian Schools, the National Conference of Black Mayors, The Presbyterian Church, U.S.A., The American Baptist Churches in the U.S., the Christian Legal Society, and other similar organizations.[4]

Putting these items together may well lead us to conclude it could happen "only in America." That familiar phrase may well help us understand how so controversial a group of religious seekers could win such heartfelt support from the leaders of organized religion in this country. And this trial, occurring "only in America," leads us to raise some questions over the deepening crisis that the new religions and extreme religious pluralism raise for us today.

## The Question We Consider

1. If it is true that a nation has no more religious freedom than the degree to which it allows its most deviant believers to flourish, then how far are we willing to go to protect that freedom? Do we want to redefine the boundaries?

2. How can the rewards of active participation in mainline religious life be made more compelling to the largest absentee group from those churches— the young adults?

3. What are, or should be, the limits on the extent to which seekers can claim freedom of expression of religion when their actions violate the law?

5

## Affirmations

Perhaps the most helpful way to go about exploring these questions would be for me to make some personal affirmations.

1. Religious freedom . . . flourishes because the United States is a secular state, not an established religious state. As founding father James Madison envisioned it, the state is independent of the church or ecclesiastical° control, and the churches are independent of state or political control.

*ecclesiastical:* Church-related.

2. The religious pluralism that such freedom creates is not the same thing as secularism. In a secular state we do not reject faith. Many people today cannot understand that. They would tolerate dissenter groups, but would also insist that ours is a nation based on specific religious absolutes—the ones from their own particular religious tradition.

3. Americans reject the new religions, such as the Unification Church, not so much for their theology, but because those bodies are so communal and collectivist. Most Americans prefer a more individualistic and privatized faith. For example, Unificationists met hostility because outsiders thought they were attempting to undermine both American youth and, eventually, American freedom. Unification doctrine° was not at stake.[5]

10    4. Mainline churches often fail to attract or hold adults because these churches do not teach that the joys and rewards of religious life require dedication and sacrifice—which many adults are willing to make.

## The Coming of the New Religions

What, then, is the deepening crisis in pluralism? How did we get into such a situation?

We start by defining some terms. The first is *cults*. Are cults groups such as Jim Jones and Peoples' Temple? Or are cults smooth-talking radio preachers foretelling the end of the world but in the meantime asking you to please send in your monthly pledge? Or are cults composed of worshipful converts devoted to a charismatic leader who claims new religious insights and powers and full control over their lives?

Specialists differ widely over precise definitions, because each of them sees a different part of the whole. Some use the term *cult* in a critical manner; any cult is *ipso facto°* dangerous, or at least wrong. Others see these bodies as the beginning of an entirely new direction in world religion. The participants are willing to make a radical break with existing religious communities in favor of something totally new. Other observers suggest that cults are simply new church bodies being formed, which is in harmony with the great tradition of American religious innovation.

What I say is this: For all their differences, the cults that appeared in the last two decades—the Unification Church, Scientology, the Children of God, The Way International, Hare Krishna, and Divine Light Mission—do have several features in common. Ronald Enroth summarizes:

> Most such groups respect their leaders highly. The Moonies border on deification. They depart from revealed truth, false teaching. As a sociolo-

---

*doctrine:* The body of principles that make up a belief system.    *ipso facto:* Latin, meaning "by its very nature."

gist, I see an adversarial stance *vis a vis* the social institutions of our society. There is also a degree of control at work, not only in the Eastern religions or more exotic cult groups, but also in some groups that claim to be evangelical. Most such groups believe, too, that they are in some way exclusively correct and superior to all other faiths.[6]

These groups offer their followers an all-encompassing way of living   15
which becomes strongly critical of mainline values. Made up largely of younger adults, the new religions create new family structures and loyalties within their own ranks, often at the expense of ties to their families of origin. The new religious seekers participate in extended communal relationships, including shared earnings and property. They devote intensive energies and much time recruiting new members and raising funds. They have created new symbol systems and liturgies° for their worship, emphasizing group and ecstatic° forms of expression.

All of these qualities elicit the hostility and criticisms of the larger society. One observer chastises "their frequent messianic intolerance and their lack of community and grass-roots support."[7] They have chosen to repudiate° those religious and social values most Americans cherish, such as the nuclear family, private property, and the traditional church. Thus they become religious in ways that are not traditionally middle-class American.

Their presence creates a problem, bordering on a crisis, because they are not simply some oddball, misfit unstable "weirdos" waiting for the next fad to join. Instead, the recruits are largely young, stable adults of the educated, professional, white middle class in all sections of the country.

Those who study the new religions disagree, however, over the extent to which the recruits understand the traditional religions they are rejecting. Enroth and Melton write that "some 80–85% of the people who join cults come from non-religious or nominally religious homes."[8] But another watcher, Walter Martin, states that "seventy-eight percent of people who are today in cults came out of professing Christian churches."[9]

Altogether, some 5000 new religions—ranging from a handful of seekers to groups with several thousand members—flourish in the United States. They have the funds, the energy, and the vision to continue their programs for the foreseeable future. As such, they stand in judgment of the major denominations, a judgment intensified not only by their considerable resources but by their apparently strange, often nonconformist expressions of faith. Such behavior provokes resistance.

Perhaps the greatest lure they possess is their ability to offer emotional   20
rewards and the fulfillment of personal needs, qualities which the mainline

---

*liturgies:* Rituals of worship.    *ecstatic:* Marked by a state of overwhelming emotion or trance.    *repudiate:* Renounce, reject.

denominations often fail to provide. Younger seekers criticize the existing churches for not really practicing what they preach. They also claim that the mainline churches are too shallow. Their indictment reads something like this: The mainliners lack an outreach to the oppressed and ignored; their spirituality seems superficial; they fail to create a sense of warmth and acceptance.[10]

The new religions offer programs that apparently meet the personal needs of these seekers. The leader serves as a father figure, the group becomes a surrogate family, and the daily routine becomes a welcome ordering of life. Enroth reports that new members state "they valued being a part of a group that was doing something important. Moonies have told me they couldn't care less about Rev. Moon's doctrines and that they would probably have left if they hadn't made such good friends."[11] Surely, then, the changing definition of religion and this form of expressive ethics have brought on the crisis we are exploring here.

## Unificationism

Some observers of the new religions disagree with my contention we have a crisis here. They point out that the number of participants is extremely small, that the Unification Church has no more than 7000 members, and similar groups acknowledge a high turnover rate.[12] Furthermore, these observers state, the "cult phenomenon" is really a media event created by television and exposé° journalists for its human interest and visual appeal.

Another argument is also raised. Don't such groups serve as a safety valve, attracting those people who wouldn't do well anyway in the competitive, young, upwardly mobile world of today's America? Where's the harm? If those 2000 folks in rural Oregon like to wear orange pajamas and worship a nonverbal guru who likes to ride around in a Rolls Royce, and they all stick to their own turf, why not? The statistics show that over 90% of those who join a new religion return home within two years.[13] So why all the fuss? Those who did remain found themselves the dupes of an imposter who was finally forced to leave Oregon and the United States by state and federal officials.

To answer these criticisms and to address the questions raised at the start of this chapter, we will look more closely at the Unification Church. In the last 15 years it has been the most controversial of all new bodies, and to this day its programs raise important questions for us. Furthermore, the Unificationists or "Moonies" stand out because they seek to influence national public policy and because they have substantial financial resources.[14]

25    Why all of this occurred is not easily summarized. In my estimation, Rev. Moon attracted very strong support at the beginning in the United States

---

*exposé:* The exposure or revelation of something negative.

because of his appealing vision of the one Unificationist world family. He took that vision directly into the American political world during the early 1970s, calling on America to be the unrelenting leader in a spiritual and militaristic sense to stop atheistic communism. The Unification Church openly (and legally) spent huge sums to persuade the public to support the anticommunist foreign policy of President Nixon. But to many Americans that seemed an unwarranted intrusion by a foreigner into domestic politics.

The Unificationists also received sharp criticism for their theology. After a careful study by a research team, the National Council of Churches of Christ concluded that such teachings were not Christian. Similar conclusions were reached by Japan's Catholic Bishops and the French Episcopal Conference.[15] Coupled with that were the stories from ex-Moonies, the dropouts from recruitment programs. They told the media of Unificationist demands for submission to the leaders, of coercive° spiritual and physical discipline and routine, of intense fasting and prayer, of being required to sell flowers in public centers for very long periods, of being forced to ignore their families and former friends. Most Americans looked critically at the mass marriages, prepared in the traditional Korean manner by the Rev. Moon himself.[16] All in all, this new religion seemed no way for Americans to express their faith.

By way of reply, the Unificationists started to spend very large amounts of money to build respectability among professional groups. They sponsored conferences among scientists, college teachers, and ministers to explain their cause and to win good will. These were held at posh hotels, with all the participants receiving full funding for transportation, room, and board. No other new religious body had such resources. Critics argued this was no way to win respectability. And the money, coming largely from the gifts of members of Asian churches, gave the Unification Church, some said, an unfair advantage over the voluntaristic activities of the North American churches.

Despite strong criticism, the Unificationists continue to pursue their stated objectives. They have moved directly into mainstream American political life with the purchase and management of the *Washington Times,* a daily newspaper. From the outset, the editors made it clear they sought to influence American policy making, especially to make it more actively resistant to any form of what they perceived as communist expansion overseas or at home. The *Times* also directed programs to raise funds for clothing, food, and medicine for the *contra* army in Nicaragua in the mid-1980s. Another Unificationist program in the political arena gave some $500,000 to fund a political-religious action program, the Coalition for Religious Freedom, which focused on supporting political office seekers who support Unificationist positions on church/state issues. Part of that fund was sent to another

*coercive:* Intended to force and dominate.

political lobby, created during the 1984 presidential campaign, the Americans Concerned for Traditional Values . . .[17] Other Unificationist money, some $3,500,000, was spent to send books, cassettes, tapes, and other printed information to a variety of organized religious bodies, especially to ministers.

All of this proves to be very controversial for many Americans. Yet, paradoxically, while this was occurring many religious leaders from every cluster of doctrinal, ethnic, and regional loyalties supported the right of Rev. Moon to pursue his programs. For all his upsetting qualities, Rev. Moon was seen by these leaders as less a threat to religious pluralism than was the ongoing harassment and intimidation they felt was being directed at him by the Internal Revenue Service (IRS). This harassment, however well-intentioned, could destroy religious freedom in this country, they believed.

30     The issue even today is extremely complicated and volatile. After several years of deliberations over the finances of the Unification Church, the IRS brought the church to trial, claiming Rev. Moon had failed to pay taxes on $162,000 in income from stocks and a bank account. Moon replied that he was not liable for taxes, because the assets belonged not to him personally, but were held in trust for the church. His attorney, Lawrence Tribe, failed to convince the first trial jury. Eventually the case worked its way up through appeals courts, but was denied a hearing by the Supreme Court. At stake was the money deposited in a New York bank allied with an import firm called Tong II Enterprises. The Unification Church argued this was under the direction of the church, and no personal profits were involved.

By the time the highest court refused to take it on appeal, the case had turned into a celebrated cause. Rev. Moon received support from the leaders and groups listed above. In general the following points were made. Rev. Moon had requested a bench trial (a trial before a judge) rather than a jury trial, but was refused. Second, a government agency (here, the IRS) should not be permitted to dictate the manner in which churches take care of their internal funding and use their own funds. The way such funds were spent was based on the specific content of the doctrines of the church. Thus, since every church enjoyed the freedom to pursue its own doctrine, it should have the attendant right to spend its funds as it sees fit. Third, many churches deposit church funds (obviously these are tax exempt) in the name of the local minister. Fourth, in the Roman Catholic church the property is often held in the name of the local bishop; the Unificationists were asking for the same right. Finally, as Tribe argued, the guaranteed constitutional right to the free exercise of religion was being threatened. By that he meant that when the courts are allowed to define the content of the doctrine, by dictating the manner in which funds are spent, they are assuming powers which are unconstitutional. Only the members of a church when acting in good faith should be allowed to define what they believe, and the courts must recognize that as a valid form of organized religion. Tribe summarized the matter; if church leaders follow the advice of their people and for such are sent to jail, "they will indeed be the first religious leaders since the ratification of the Constitution to be imprisoned because of the way they and their followers chose to organize their church's internal affairs."[18]

The federal government's case was less complicated, declaring that "to look at the quality of a taxpayer's proof hardly violates the First Amendment." While "a church is free to organize itself as it sees fit, religious leaders, no less than the average taxpayer, must assume the risk when they engage in undocumented transactions that the jury may not believe their account of the events."[19] In the eyes of the prosecution, religious bodies should not enjoy special protections not granted to other citizens engaged in business activities. The IRS is suspicious of those leaders who claim they have no personal interest at stake. American religious history has been replete° with examples of ministers who used their flock's funds for their personal benefit. The courts here accepted the government's contention that a significant difference existed between "the religious" on the one hand and "the economic" on the other.

That was, in essence, at the heart of the case: What did it mean to be religious? The government, the IRS, and the courts held for the separation of the religious from the economic sphere. A very large portion of the organized religious and legal communities held to another set of convictions. That is close to being a crisis.

## What Is at Stake?

How far are we willing to go to protect religious pluralism? How do we respond to the full extent of that diversity? Do we support the rights of everything and everyone from Arica Mind Control to Zen Buddhism? Do we celebrate being Amish, Baptist, Congregational, Disciples, and down to Zoroastians? Do we consider this diversity a sign of God's providence? Or would we feel better if they were members of our churches? Do we believe our hymns are better, our teachings more sound, our social outreach better balanced with our spirituality? In short, where do our judgments begin and end? On what basis do we justify criticizing others?

Are these new religions trends or fads? They do reflect clearly some of the     35
new momentum for religious living which came out of the 1960s. They are a form of "religious populism," a movement characterized by an emphasis on the promotion of faith for mass audiences. The new religions fit into that movement with their diversity and fluidity, holding high the needs of the individual seeker and ignoring the programs of the mainline bodies.[20]

*replete with:* Full.

Their presence also suggests how shortsighted those critics were who had predicted that our society was moving steadily towards total secularization. We were told that religious faith was soon to be replaced by more intelligence and mature morality. We were to celebrate "secular man" and the "secular city." Today the new religions help remind us of the innate religious dimension of our human spirits.

Commendable as those qualities are, we must look more concretely at the *kind* of religion the new groups promote. Three features stand out: (*a*) using their highly privatized authority leader, they emphasize more of a mystical union than a rational involvement in our society; (*b*) they concentrate on involvement with their immediate peer group rather than reaching boldly to meet the needs of victims of injustice and oppression; (*c*) they accept the reward system of individualistic capitalism; that is, their members live communally, while their money comes from the wealth amassed by a few persons.

To be concrete, is Lowell D. Streiker, a student of new religions, on the right track when he points to the Unificationists as an organization being in disarray, pouring "millions of dollars down the drain" and unable to hold on to recruits? Even though good public relations is as American as our favorite pie, isn't so much emphasis on public relations an unwise use of resources?

We are reluctant, however, to allow any person outside of a religious group to decide how it should spend its money. Dean M. Kelley answers: "How a religious body raises, invests and expands its funds cannot be divorced from its religious purposes, ministry and mission, and Government cannot intervene in the one without affecting the other."[21] That is a part of what is at stake.

40    What about the charges of deprogramming and brainwashing? What of the parents who tell of their children being lost to groups who use systematic forms of mind manipulation? At the same time, what of those seekers who tell the public they have been kidnapped by professional anticult ideologues,° treated to round-the-clock deprogramming, and forced to return to a society they had chosen to leave?

For several reasons, this controversy today lacks the intensity it generated a decade ago. First, the courts generally have ruled in favor of young adults, of legal age, who join and participate in the religious groups of their choices. Legislatures, by and large, have struck down pro-deprogramming proposals which would give preemptive° rights to parents over their recalcitrant° children. Second, at least the best-known new religions have softened or modified some of the earlier, more aggressive and objectionable recruiting and indoctrination practices. The Unificationists, for example, admit that their house in Oakland,

---

*ideologues:* Fervent supporters of a particular ideology (theory).    *preemptive:* Taking place in order to prevent something that is anticipated but hasn't happened yet.    *recalcitrant:* Defiant, resistant.

California, was carrying on some practices of mind-bending as charged by dropouts and parents; corrective practices were taken. At the mass wedding of over 2000 Unificationist couples in 1982 in Madison Square Garden, the officials made sure the parents of the newlyweds were in attendance and communicating with their children. Finally, several civil libertarian° groups and individual attorneys have made available their services to those who find they need legal counsel after they decide to leave a specific new religion.

## What Can We Do?

What can those of us in the pews do? It isn't enough to study about the new religions, or send letters to our lawmakers about appropriate legislation.

We can, first of all, do something often overlooked. We can witness for our faith to those among the new religions and to our friends. There are those who avoid such witnessing because of what Walter Martin has called the "disease of non rock-a-boatus ecclesiasticus—which disdains controversy."[22] Instead of promoting ease and nicety, churches would minister better by encouraging full discussion in major matters of faith.

Second, we can ask our public school officials to start or to improve the many curricular programs in world religions and religious literature. Very often, misunderstanding about the new religions comes from a lack of information. Schools can teach religious studies without these courses being turned into indoctrination.

Third, in both our schools and in congregational study programs, more attention can be given to exploring how related fields of learning can help us understand what it means to be religious. Cultural anthropology, sociology, and psychology offer rich insights into the issues we are exploring. . . .

Fourth, we can encourage our seminary° leaders to keep the curriculums of their respective schools in harmony with parishioners' needs and interests. Knowing that the role of the parish minister is becoming increasingly fragmented and complex, we want to send a message to religious educators for the need to maintain a balance between studying the foundations of the faith and the many ways in which our society uses that faith.

Fifth, as suggested by new religions specialists J. Gordon Melton and Robert L. Moore, congregations need to periodically assess their ministries to teens and young adults. Very often, it seems, churches accept as unchangeable the demographic° evidence that people within those age groups will stay away from church. The popularity of the new religions proves that to be wrong. Might there be an extensive broadening of social outreach programs such as

45

civil libertarian: One who opposes any limitations on individual rights.   *seminary:* Institution for the training of priests, ministers, or rabbis.   *demographic:* Relating to the statistical study of populations.

Lutheran Volunteers or the Mennonite volunteer program for young adults, which gives special attention to spiritual nurture and social activism?[23] Such programs exist, but are reaching only a few. Melton and Moore have stated, "If we in mainline Protestant churches do not help our young people by modeling a serious commitment to a life-affirming religion vision and praxis, then we should not be surprised that others step into the vacuum we in our smugness have created."[24] Not all young adults want to become Yuppies; some are ready for entering the world of sacrificial service. We need to find them.

Sixth, churches and families can concentrate more on helping older teens prepare themselves for the time they will leave the immediate family. That preparation will require more research and creative program-building than we have now to smooth the transition. The possibilities for planners here and in all the programs listed in this chapter are limited only by the imagination of the planners.

Seventh, we can face more fully the question: Can there be too much religious freedom? The courts have already established some clear boundary lines. Those who attempt in the name of faith to deny blood transfusions to their children have been overruled by the courts upholding the primary right of the state to protect life. Parents cannot let their young sons or daughters stand at dangerous street corners at night to distribute religious literature. The handing round of poisonous snakes in the name of proving God's protection is illegal. So too is polygamy° and the use of hallucinogens in organized religious worship. These are some examples of government regulation of religion.

50   The government has stepped in to protect citizens against fraud, embezzlement, kidnapping, and other such felonies whose perpetrators° have claimed religious freedom as their defense. But, acknowledging that, what would we say to a young adult who is considering joining the Salvation Army or a Trappist° monastery? Professor William J. Whalen has posed a compelling problem: What of the young man "who forsakes his family and friends to affiliate with a religious movement, sleeps five or six hours a day, denies himself sexual activity, lives on a diet largely bereft of meat or fish and turns over any income he receives to the head of his group?"[25] Is that any different from what today's new religions require?

Understanding the new pluralism can help us see what is involved when someone close to us looks favorably on a new religion. This religious exploration is filled with risk, some danger, and inevitable tension. Controversy and disappointment are bound to occur. By no means can the strains and stresses

---

*polygamy:* Marriage system that allows a spouse to have more than one mate at a time.    *perpetrators:* People who commit or execute an act.    *Trappist:* Related to a monastic order of the Roman Catholic church.

of this deepening crisis be eliminated or even sharply reduced. But when we see this exploration for what it is, we can view it as part of God's providential care.

## Discussion Questions

1. What limits would you place on religious pluralism in the United States? What should *not* be allowed?
2. Should church revenue be exempt from scrutiny by the Internal Revenue Service?
3. What would you do if your daughter or son started attending a program of one of the new religions?
4. Is being a Unificationist any different from being a Trappist monk or joining the Salvation Army?
5. Do you agree that the church lacks appeal for the highly idealistic young adult?
6. Should it change its programs to attract this group? How might it do that?

1. George J. Bryjak and Gary A. May, "The Fall of Sun Myung Moon and the Unification Church in America," *USA Today,* November 1985.
2. Ibid.; David G. Bromley, "Financing the Millennium: The Economic Structure of the Unificationist Movement," *Journal for the Scientific Study of Religion* 24 (September 1985): 253–74; at an SSSR conference in Savannah, Ga., on Oct. 26, 1985, Bromley mentioned the dollar figure used here.
3. Dick Anthony and Thomas Robbins, "Spiritual Innovation and the Crisis of American Civil Religion," as cited by Mary Douglas and Steven Tipton, eds., *Religion and America: Spirituality in a Secular Age* (Boston: Beacon Press, 1983), 234–39.
4. Herbert Richardson, ed., *Constitutional Issues in the Case of Rev. Moon* (New York: Edwin Mellen Press, 1984).
5. Ronald Enroth and J. Gordon Melton, "Why Cults Succeed," *Christianity Today,* March 16, 1984, pp. 15–17; Robert Bellah, et al., *Habits of the Heart* (Berkeley: University of California Press, 1985), pp. 235–37.
6. Enroth and Melton, "Why Cults Succeed," p. 15.
7. Thomas Robbins, "Marginal Movements," *Society,* May/June 1984, p. 48; an excellent discussion is in Rodney Stark and William S. Bainbridge, *The Future of Religion: Secularization, Revival and Cult Formation* (Berkeley: University of California Press, 1985), Chap. 2.
8. Enroth and Melton, "Why Cults Succeed," pp. 16–17.
9. Interview with Walter Martin in *The Arizona State Journal* (Tucson), September 1, 1984, pp. 1G, 3G.
10. Daniel Poling and George Gallup Jr., *The Search for America's Faith* (Nashville: Abingdon, 1980), pp. 17–19.

11. Enroth and Melton, "Why Cults Succeed" 16–17; based also on my conversations with Unificationists; see also Harriet S. Mosatche, *Searching; Practices and Beliefs of the Religious Cults* (New York: Stavron Educational Press, 1983), pp. 371–81.

12. *Minneapolis Star and Tribune,* April 8, 1985; figures are from the Rev. Chung Hwan Kwak of the Unification Church, given at a conference at the Chicago Marriott Hotel, June 29, 1985, which I attended.

13. Saul L. Levine, "Radical Departures," *Psychology Today,* August 1985, p. 23; a good bibliography is Brock Kilbourne and James T. Richardson, "Psychotherapy and New Religions in a Pluralistic Society," *American Psychologist* 39 (March 1984): 237–51.

14. Bromley, "Financing the Millennium," p. 253.

15. Richard Quebedeaux, *New Conversations,* Spring 1982, pp. 11–12; Commission on Faith and Order, National Council of Churches, "A Critique of the Theology of the Unification Church," 1977; news item, *Christian Century,* December 4, 1985, p. 1112.

16. Ibid.; see also the evidence in Herbert Richardson, *Constitutional Issues.*

17. Editorial, *New Yorker,* April 28, 1985, pp. 27–28; *Minneapolis Star and Tribune,* April 8, 1985; *Time,* April 22, 1985, p. 60; *Christianity Today,* April 19, 1985, pp. 50–51; September 7, 1984, pp. 56–62; *Christian Century,* June 5, 1985, p. 577; further documentation on the Unificationists in American politics is in Carolyn Weaver, "Unholy Alliance," *Mother Jones,* January 1986, pp. 14, 16, 17, 44, 46.

18. Tribe's quotation is in the General Baptist Committee on Public Affairs, *Report from the Capitol,* June 1984, p. 8; the most complete documentation is in the Richardson volume, see above, n. 4; *Christian Herald,* October 1984, p. 4; Leo Pfeffer, *Religion, State and the Burger Court* (Buffalo: Prometheus Books, 1984), pp. 214–15.

19. Baptist Joint Committee, *Report,* June 1984, p. 8; a helpful critical article of Moon is Michael Istkoff, "New Moon," *New Republic,* August 26, 1985, pp. 14–16.

20. Robert Wuthnow, *Experimentation in American Religion* (Princeton: Princeton University Press, 1978), pp. 189–201.

21. Dean M. Kelley, "What Does the Future Hold?" as quoted in Robert McNamara, ed., *Religion: North American Style* (Belmont: Wadsworth Publishing Co., 1984, 2nd ed.), p. 348; see also news story, *Time,* April 22, 1983, p. 60; Thomas Robbins, "Marginal Movements," *Society,* May/June 1984, p. 49.

22. Martin, *Arizona State Journal,* September 1, 1984, pp. 1G, 3G. See also the "anti-cult" books listed in Donna L'Aline, *The Anti-Cult Movement in America: A Bibliography* (New York: Garland Publishing Co., 1985); Martin E. Marty, "A Special Report," *Christian Century,* July 3–10, 1985, pp. 650–51; ibid., February 14, 1984, pp. 163–65; the definitive study is David G. Bromley and James T. Richardson, eds., *The Brainwashing-Deprogramming Controversy* (New York: Edwin Mellen Press, 1983); see also the best "anti-anticult" book, Thomas Robbins, et al., eds., *Cults, Culture, and the Law: Perspectives on New Religious Movements* (Chico, Calif.: Scholars, 1985).

23. A comprehensive guide to such organizations, "Voluntary-Service Opportunities" is in *The Other Side,* January/February 1986, pp. 21–28.

24. J. Gordon Melton and Robert Moore, *The Cult Experience* (New York: Pilgrim Press, 1982), p. 106 and Chap. 4.

25. William J. Whalen, "Christians Shouldn't Condemn Cults," *U.S. Catholic,* November 1984, pp. 13–18.

## QUESTIONS

1. Answer the questions posed by Jorstad at the end of this selection.
2. According to Jorstad, what is the difference between religious freedom and secularism?
3. Do you agree with Jorstad's assertion, "Mainline churches often fail to attract or hold adults because these churches do not teach that the joys and rewards of religious life require dedication and sacrifice— which many adults are willing to make"? If you disagree, why do *you* think many religions fail to appeal to more people?
4. List some characteristics that specialists mention when defining a "cult." Do you believe that cults and established religious denominations are very different? If so, in which ways?
5. How do you feel about people who seek out and/or join "new religions"?
6. Is this essay's introduction effective? What is Jorstad trying to accomplish in it?
7. Do you feel that Jorstad uses loaded language, or does he maintain an objective voice in this essay?

## CONNECTIONS

As the essays by Elizabeth Cady Stanton and Martin Luther King, Jr. noted earlier in this section, in our country's history religion has been used to justify both racism and sexism. Should religious beliefs be allowed to play *any* role in shaping public policy? Why or why not?

## ∼ The Unlimited Cosmos—A Personal Odyssey

*Alan Hale*

> Alan Hale was born in Japan but grew up in New Mexico. He attended the
> U.S. Naval Academy in Annapolis, Maryland; after receiving a bachelor's
> degree in physics in 1980, he remained in the Navy until 1983. In 1992 he
> earned his Ph.D. in astronomy from New Mexico State University. Since
> then, he has been actively involved in various efforts to enhance the scientific
> literacy of the general public, as well as in the promotion of space explo-
> ration and the development of commercial space operations. His scientific
> articles for the general public have appeared in such magazines as *Astron-
> omy, The Astronomical Calendar, Free Inquiry,* and *Space News.* In July 1995,
> Hale became a codiscoverer of the Hale-Bopp comet. The following article
> appeared in the Summer 1996 issue of *Free Inquiry.*

**WARM-UP:** What is atheism? Do you believe that many people in the
United States are atheists?

*When I heard the learn'd astronomer;*
*When the proofs, the figures, were ranged in columns before me;*
*When I was shown the charts and the diagrams, to add, divide, and measure them;*
*When I, sitting, heard the astronomer, where he lectured with much applause in the*
    *lecture-room,*
*How soon, unaccountable, I became tired and sick;*
*Till rising and gliding out, I wander'd off by myself,*
*In the mystical moist night-air, and from time to time,*
*Look'd up in perfect silence at the stars.*
                                    —WALT WHITMAN, from *Leaves of Grass* (1865)

1    With a Ph.D. in astronomy, I suppose I can be considered a "learn'd
    astronomer," and indeed I spend a lot of my time in front of a com-
puter terminal, poring over "the charts and the diagrams, to add, divide, and
measure them." But I am not one to forget what drew me to the field in the
first place; from my youngest days I have spent innumerable hours looking up
"in perfect silence at the stars," and I continue to do so to this day. In my view,
these two approaches to astronomy—indeed, to all sciences—are complementary; while I will always enjoy the spectacle of a star-studded night for its
own sake, it is the hours, years, and decades that I and other astronomers have
spent unraveling the secrets of the cosmos that give true meaning to that
spectacle.

It was natural, if perhaps slightly egotistical, for the earliest human beings to believe that the universe consisted of their own immediate surroundings, and that the various happenings in nature occurred at the whims of various supernatural entities; elaborate belief systems were constructed for the purpose of trying to convince these entities to produce one series of actions in lieu of others. Each scientific discovery, beginning with the fact that another tribe of humans lived on the other side of the mountains, has tended to remove this egocentrism° from our collective belief. As Carl Sagan so eloquently stated in his book *Pale Blue Dot* (Random House, 1994), "modern science has been a voyage into the unknown, with a lesson in humility waiting at every stop." While we've been engaged in removing ourselves from the center of the universe, we've also studied the processes of nature; and, while we're a long way from understanding everything that goes on around us, we've learned that there is no need to invoke supernatural forces as an explanation for the phenomena we see.

Although all the sciences have played a major role in this decentralization, it is perhaps astronomy more any other that has brought this "lesson in humility" down upon us. During the past two thousand years we've progressed from the idea that the Earth—as it was known at the time—was the center of all creation, to the realization that the Earth is only one of a set of nine planets, together with several smaller objects, orbiting a rather obscure star that is only one of several hundred billion similar stars contained within the Milky Way galaxy, itself only one of several hundred billion other galaxies scattered throughout the universe. With this view, the idea that we on the Earth hold some type of privileged position within the universe, or that one particular group of individuals on this planet holds a supernaturally ordained° privileged position over its other inhabitants, is recognized for the absurdity that it must be. However much we may not like it, our Earth, and we, its inhabitants, are trivially insignificant compared to the universe as a whole, and thus our personal interactions, our collective morality and, by consequence, our progress beyond where we are today, can only be derived from our own collective conscience. This view of the cosmos tells us that there is no universe-spanning entity that is going to take the trouble to visit this tiny remote dot in space and tell us how to live; we have to figure that out for ourselves.

Along these lines, then, I'd like to look at three recent astronomical discoveries that can and should play a significant role in how we view ourselves within the cosmos as a whole. The first two are major discoveries in their own right and only serve to increase the process of de-centralization that has been going on for the past several centuries. The third, while understandably

---

*egocentrism:* Egoism, excessive regard for one's self.     *ordained:* Established, consecrated.

important to me personally, cannot rank with the other two in terms of its overall importance; however, I believe it provides an important vehicle for those of us who understand our place within the cosmos to share this with our fellow human beings, and to introduce them to the wonders embodied by the "perfect silence" of the stars.

## Other Solar Systems

5      We've known of most of the planets within our own solar system for centuries, but all of these objects accompany and orbit around one specific star, our sun. But since the sun is only one of innumerable other stars throughout the universe, does it not stand to reason that many, if not most or even all, of those other stars also have planets orbiting around them? As likely and reasonable as such a scenario might seem, until fairly recently we did not possess the technology necessary to verify (or disprove) it.

All this, however, is starting to change, and we have now discovered that some of the other stars with which we share the cosmos are indeed accompanied by planets of their own. The first other solar system was discovered in what could probably be considered one of the most unlikeliest of places: around a pulsar, the shattered remnant of what was once a star far more massive than our sun. This discovery, made with the Arecibo radio telescope in Puerto Rico and announced by Alex Wolszczan in 1992—and verified with additional observations over the subsequent two years—tells us that planets can form under some of the most extreme and hostile environments imaginable, and implies that planetary formation should be a rather commonplace occurrence in the more benign environments that accompany stars more like the sun. (Since Wolszczan's announcement, potential planetary systems have been reported around one or two other pulsars, although none of these reports has been confirmed as of yet.)

Finally, during the past few months we've seen reports that some of the more normal stars in our own neighborhood are indeed accompanied by planets. Last October came the report from Michel Mayor and Didier Queloz of the Geneva Observatory that the ordinary sunlike star 51 Pegasi is accompanied by a Jupiter-sized planet orbiting fairly close in. Just this past January came the announcement by Geoff Marcy and Paul Butler (of San Francisco State University) that two more sunlike stars—70 Virginis and 47 Ursae Majoris—also are accompanied by planets that are not much larger than Jupiter. Since both these teams of astronomers—along with several others—are examining numerous other stars as part of their respective search programs, it is entirely possible that additional planets will be reported by the time this article reaches its readers.

These discoveries tell us several things. First, more or less as we expected, other solar systems do appear to be relatively common throughout the universe, and thus there is nothing particularly unique about our own system. At the same time, none of these other systems would be mistaken for a "carbon copy" of our system; all of them differ significantly from our system (and from each other) in some of the most basic characteristics. This implies, in turn, that there isn't even anything unique about the overall gross structure of our solar system; it would seem, once again, that there is nothing special about our system, but that solar systems can come in a variety of shapes and sizes, and that ours embodies only one particular kind of example.

As our science progresses and our techniques improve, it is reasonable to expect that at some point in the not-too-distant future we will find that, indeed, most of the stars around us have their own system of planets accompanying them. Although our experience with the recent discoveries suggests that this will not be true everywhere, it is certainly possible that around some of these stars we will find planets somewhat similar to our own Earth and, perhaps on these other "Earths" or perhaps even in what we might consider a less likely environment, we will find some indications that life has sprouted elsewhere. One thing seems almost certain: whatever we find will contain numerous surprises, and each discovery will serve to show that we are even less unique than we ever thought we were.

## Galaxies and Galaxies Galore

Seeing is believing; while we've been saying for some time that there are about as many galaxies throughout the universe as there are stars within our galaxy, it's nice to have real observational evidence to back this up. And now we have it; the so-called Hubble Deep Field (HDF), taken with the Hubble Space Telescope over a ten-day period in December 1995, shows galaxies upon galaxies upon galaxies stretching as far out in the universe, and as far back in time, as we can imagine. The HDF was exposed in a seemingly "blank" region of the sky slightly to the north of the Big Dipper's handle, and represents an area of sky smaller than can be resolved with the unaided human eye. At least 1,500 individual galaxies—many of which are far beyond the grasp of any Earthbound telescope—have been counted within this tiny slice of sky, and if we assume that this is representative of the universe as a whole—and we have every reason for believing so—then indeed the universe contains the unaccountable billions of galaxies that we have been postulating° all along.

*postulating:* Presuming, theorizing.

I urge readers to examine the HDF image and to pick out one of those tiny dim smudges for a closer look. That tiny, unremarkable patch of light is in actuality a galaxy, more or less the same size as our own, containing up to several hundred billion individual stars. It is far enough away that the light we see on this image took several billion years to get here. When we consider that this scene would be repeated almost *ad infinitum*° throughout the entire vault° of the heavens, we begin to realize just how large the universe really is, and how insignificant is our own little corner of it. If there is any recent discovery in astronomy that serves to give us our "lesson in humility," the Hubble Deep Field is it.

## Comet Hale-Bopp: Signs in the Night Sky

One night last July, while taking a break from one of my routine astronomical observational programs, I was fortunate enough to discover a new comet. While comet discoveries are normally not too big of a deal—up to a dozen or more are discovered every year—this comet has turned out to be a most interesting and unusual object. Comet Hale-Bopp—named after myself and an amateur astronomer in Arizona, Thomas Bopp, who discovered it at about the same time I did—appears to be intrinsically° one of the largest and brightest comets that has ever been seen. When it makes its closest approach to the sun in April 1997 it may well be one of the most spectacular comets that has appeared during this century, very possibly outshining even the brightest stars in our nighttime sky.

Throughout history, the appearance of a bright comet in the sky has often generated immense fear and trembling among many segments of Earthbound humanity, and on numerous occasions has been taken to be a sign of divine wrath and/or a portent° of future catastrophic events. Even in our supposedly more enlightened society of the late twentieth century, such beliefs continue to take hold, and I have already seen several bizarre predictions as to what Hale-Bopp portends for our planet. Some of these border on the ridiculous—e.g., the comet is an alien mothership, or is at least under the control of aliens, and will strike the Earth unless we agree to be their slaves from now on—but I have also seen some more "serious" statements as to what Hale-Bopp's appearance might mean. In particular, I have seen or heard of several claims that the comet's appearance was foretold in several prophecies—for example, within the writings of Nostradamus—and heralds some particular dire travails° our planet will experience within the forthcoming few years. I am also aware that several Christian fundamentalists have proclaimed that Comet

---

*ad infinitum:* Latin, meaning "to infinity". *vault:* Arch, dome. *intrinsically:* In itself. *portent:* Omen, sign. *dire travails:* Terrible agony, dreadful torment.

Hale-Bopp may be one of the "signs of the end times" that are foretold within the biblical book of *Revelation.*

The comet is none of this; it will be a temporary and—we hope—spectacular addition to our nighttime skies during the first few months of 1997, but that is *all* it will be. I believe, however, that Comet Hale-Bopp presents an unprecedented opportunity for the scientists and the scientifically literate in our society to share one of the natural—not supernatural—wonders of the night sky with the rest of the public. I have reason to believe that some segments of that public may in fact be ready for such a demonstration. For example, as I finish this article, the night sky is aglow with the light of another comet, Comet Hyakutake. This object, discovered by a Japanese amateur astronomer at the end of January, is currently in the process of making a close approach to the Earth, and for the time being is putting on a spectacular show in our northern sky. I'm somewhat gratified to see the public interest that is being directed toward this object, and the lack of mystical prognostications° concerning it—although this may well be due to the short lead time we had. If we can capitalize on this interest, then the potential for an increased appreciation for science among the public could be realized.

In the long run, if we can convince our fellow human beings that the    15
sights we see in the heavens—even something as wondrous as Comet Hale-Bopp will hopefully turn out to be—are purely natural phenomena, and that there is no need to invoke any supernatural or mystical elements as an explanation, then we will have taken a significant step toward preparing our society to deal responsibly with the technological and ethical issues with which it will be confronted during the twenty-first century. If, through the appearance of objects such as Comets Hyakutake and Hale-Bopp, we can bring our society closer to the true significance that is embodied within the first two discoveries I talked about above, then we and future generations will stand to reap enormous benefits from a more enlightened and scientifically literate public. This is an ambitious goal, to be sure, but one I believe we can't afford *not* to strive toward. The time is ripe for such an effort, and I urge all freethinkers and rationalists who are reading this to work together with me toward bringing this to pass.

**QUESTIONS**

1. What is the point made by the Walt Whitman poem that opens this essay?
2. Do you agree with Hale that, through our scientific discoveries, "we've learned that there is no need to invoke supernatural forces as

---

*prognostication:* Interpretation of "signs," foretelling.

an explanation for the phenomena we see"? What is the effect of his using the pronoun "we" in this statement?

3. What reasons does Hale offer to support his statement that "each [astronomical] discovery will serve to show that we are even less unique than we ever thought we were"? Do you think that he supports this claim effectively?

4. Throughout the essay, the author mentions the phrase "lesson in humility"—a lesson that, he claims, we learn from our discoveries about the universe. Could some people actually learn a "lesson in pride" from the same discoveries? Explain your answer.

5. Hale argues that if more people became convinced that "the sights we see in the heavens . . . are purely natural phenomena, . . . then we will have taken a significant step toward preparing our society to deal responsibly with the technological and ethical issues with which it will be confronted during the twenty-first century." Explain why the abandonment of our ideas about "supernatural powers" might allow us to deal better with our world.

6. Does Hale use any loaded words in this essay? If so, point some out, explaining what "load" they carry.

7. What kind of audience is Hale addressing? Is this essay directed at astronomers? Is it directed at religious people? Explain your answers.

8. What is your reaction to various discoveries about our universe that have been announced recently (like the ones discussed in this essay or the possibility of life on Mars)? Do these discoveries affect your life? Why or why not?

## CONNECTIONS

1. In the preceding selection, Erling Jorstad mentioned that young people in the United States seem to be moving away from traditional religious organizations. He offered some possible reasons for that trend as well as some possible responses to it. What reasons and responses might Alan Hale suggest for that trend?

2. Hale states that "Each scientific discovery, beginning with the fact that another tribe of humans lived on the other side of the mountains, has tended to remove . . . egocentrism from our collective belief." Based on Michael Dorris's essay "Discoveries," which introduces this section, do you think that Dorris would agree with this statement?

3. Hale suggests some conclusions that we might draw from the realization of our relative insignificance in this vast universe. Reread Winifred Gallagher's discussion of her visit to the Jimez hot springs and her own realization of the grandeur of the universe (included in her essay "The Science of Place," in Section 5), and compare her conclusions to Hale's.

# ∽ Planning Ahead

*Linda Robinson*

Linda Robinson was a freelance writer who lived in Belmont, California. The following article appeared in *The San Francisco Chronicle* on May 7, 1995. Robinson died in June of the same year.

**WARM-UP:** Describe some rituals associated with death and burials in America.

1    The first thing that hit me when I slid through the doors of the quiet little building was the smell of patchouli.° I carried that smell with me the rest of the day, and every time I turned my head and got a whiff of it from my sweater sleeve I'd think "Christ, I smell like a funeral home."

I've been to one funeral in my life—my mother's—but my stepfather made all the arrangements, so I've never set foot in a funeral home before. It's very clean, and tastefully furnished, like a model home. Soft blues and beiges. Silk flower arrangements. Big table lamps, glowing warmly on low tables.

A smiling young man with a most distressing tie collected me. After all the obvious effort at soothing that had gone into the decor, the violently purple and fuchsia° Jackson Pollock° tie was something of a mystery. Perhaps it was a deliberate focus for grief. It certainly aggrieved° me.

Joe, it turned out, was his name, and he had a nice firm handshake and a nice blond mustache and a ready smile. I was prepared for unctuous° or obsequious° or even false sorrow, but I was not prepared for matter-of-factness.

5    We sat on folding chairs at a conference table in the back, surrounded by bookshelves containing, I suddenly realized, samples of cremation urns. Joe brought me a surprisingly drinkable Styrofoam cup of coffee. I was there to make what, in the funeral biz, they call "pre-need arrangements."

The funeral we are arranging is for me.

I should have known the one person who could talk about death comfortably would be a funeral director. Even my doctor cries, but not Joe. He didn't offer condolences, he didn't sympathize, he didn't exclaim over how sad it is that I'll be leaving two small children behind.

---

*patchouli:* Oil or incense made from an East Indian plant.   *fuchsia:* A deep reddish purple.   *Jackson Pollock:* A 20th-century American painter, famous for creating abstract paintings by dripping or pouring paint in complex swirls and spatters.   *aggrieved:* Distressed.   *unctuous:* Here meaning "overly ingratiating".   *obsequious:* Servile, submissive.

I had come for practical information, and he was there to give it to me. I had expected a used-car salesman, but what I got was more like a session with my college adviser. Here are the options; tell me what you want. It was the most at ease I have ever felt talking about my own death.

I was filled with a vision of myself as the Sharp Shopper, the no-nonsense reader of Consumer Reports. I had heard stories about shady practices among morticians: overcharging grieving families, pushing expensive coffins and services and playing on guilt and sorrow.

I come from hard-bargaining practical Norse farming stock and no Music     10
Man was going to sell my family a trombone section. We'll get this "she would have wanted it this way" nonsense settled right here and now. I had attitude to spare.

Admittedly, we weren't talking about my dying, just about what was going to happen once I've left the party, so to speak. Joe showed me various combinations of options, from the Lenin-lying-in-state model on down to the shoebox-in-the-back-yard version. We discussed the scattering of ashes, but that involves a small boat three miles out in the Pacific, and it would take more than my mere demise° to get my seasick husband to cooperate with that.

While Joe went off to photocopy some figures, I wandered around, looking at the urns. Most were ceramic, but some were made of beautiful hardwoods, polished to a satiny sheen, with hinged lids.

I had a sudden overwhelming and vastly pleasing vision of being buried in my jewelry box. When he got back, I asked him if you could provide your own container for cremated remains, and he said yes, but you'd be surprised how many people neglect to bring a lid. I guess Saran Wrap would be really tacky, I said.

We went in to the other room to look at the coffins, too. I exclaimed over the rich dark woods, caressed a satin pillow, fogged up a bit of brass with my breath. Joe assured me that the coffin is also burned with the body during cremation. Not like burial at sea, where they yank that flag back as the body slips away. That always bugged me, that they didn't let the poor dead sailor keep the flag at least for company down there in the cold and dark.

Next we visited the chapel. It had an enormous plaster statue of Jesus in it.     15
I asked if it was permanent. Joe said no.

There was a little alcove° with padded chairs off to one side, where the immediate family could lurk and avoid all contact, if they wanted.

I rather suspect my husband, Steve, is an alcove kind of guy, but I'm having a hard time envisioning exactly who might show up to a do like this, and

---

*demise:* Death, passing.    *alcove:* Small recessed section of a room.

maybe he won't have much of anyone to avoid anyway. I find myself wanting to call people and get an RSVP, partly out of a need to massage my ego and partly because I am frankly curious about what it's going to be like.

What I really want is to be at this party myself. Almost two years ago, the surgeon went in to take out whatever he could of what the chemo had left, and found nothing to take out. (More has shown up since, unfortunately.) As soon as I got home from the hospital, we threw the biggest Lazarus° party you ever saw. There were people hanging out the windows, laughing and drinking and singing. My goal was to have the police show up. (We offered them a beer.) So whatever I plan for the funeral is going to be a real anticlimax, capped off by the fact that I don't get to go.

I'm trying to participate in everything I can think of *now* because I won't be here *then*. I really hate not knowing how things turn out. I will stick with a miserable murder mystery just to find out how it ends.

20        I pepper Steve with questions: What are you going to do with the insurance money? Will you sell one of the cars? Do you think you'll want to move to a different house? I try to think of everything that could possibly happen in the next 30 years, and figure out how it will turn out.

You should hear the road map for the boys' lives. Travis is 11, and just beginning to wonder if there isn't something about girls he hadn't quite noticed before now. James is 5 and has his first Tooth Fairy visit hanging by a thread. Planning a funeral is child's play.

It's not so much an issue of imposing my will on the future. Most of the impulse to arrange my own funeral is to relieve Steve of having to make expensive decisions at a difficult time. After all, I'm never going to know if they yank that coffin back at the last minute. The giant plaster Jesus won't be giving *me* fits.

In a way, I've got the easy part of this deal—I get to leave before the cleanup starts. But I want them to tell me how the story turns out. I need to know who marries the boys, and whether the runaway bunny turns up, and what color hair my granddaughter will have.

Somehow, I can defy time and participate in the future now. And somehow, if we've already talked about it, I'll be part of it when it happens.

**QUESTIONS**

1. What is the author's tone in this selection? Does it change as the essay progresses?

---

*Lazarus:* Someone who makes a comeback or is brought back to life; reference to the Gospel of John, where Jesus is described as bringing a man named Lazarus back to life.

2. Note the use of detail, of description, in this piece. What does it convey?
3. What practical explanation does the author offer for preparing her own funeral? What is the additional reason she eventually offers?
4. Is "pre-need arrangement" an example of jargon or euphemism?
5. Why had the author expected the funeral director to be like "a used-car salesman"? How does she find him to be instead? Why is he like this, according to her?
6. Have you ever been to a funeral parlor or participated in the planning of a funeral? Were your observations similar to Robinson's, or did you focus on other elements?
7. What were your feelings after you read this essay?
8. Why do you imagine Robinson wrote this essay? What might have been her purpose?

## CONNECTIONS

1. Using Jerry Muller's definition of the word, could Robinson be said to be acting "conservatively"? Explain your response.
2. Compare and contrast the image of death reflected in this essay with that presented in Anna Quindlen's piece, included in this section.

# ∾ Judgment Day

*Arturo Islas*

Arturo Islas was born in El Paso, Texas, in 1938 and grew up in the area
adjoining the Mexican border. He received his undergraduate and graduate
degrees at Stanford University; he stayed on as an English professor and
received several awards for his teaching. The following selection is the beginning of his first novel, *The Rain God,* which was published in 1984. His second novel, *Migrant Souls,* appeared in 1990. Islas was working on his third
novel when he died in 1991.

**WARM-UP:** Was there a person who acted as the matriarch or patriarch of your family? What did that person teach you? While growing up,
have you rejected any of that person's teachings?

1      A photograph of Mama Chona and her grandson Miguel Angel—Miguel
       Chico or Mickie to his family—hovers above his head on the study wall
beside the glass doors that open out into the garden. When Miguel Chico sits
at his desk, he glances up at it occasionally without noticing it, looking
through it rather than at it. It was taken in the early years of World War II by
an old Mexican photographer who wandered up and down the border town's
main street on the American side. No one knows how it found its way back to
them, for Miguel Chico's grandmother never spoke to strangers. She and the
child are walking hand in hand. Mama Chona is wearing a black ankle-length
dress with a white lace collar and he is in a short-sleeved light-colored summer suit with short pants. In the middle of the street life around them, they
are looking straight ahead, intensely preoccupied, almost worried. They seem
in a great hurry. Each has a foot off the ground, and Mama Chona's black hat
with the three white daisies, their yellow centers like eyes that always out-
stared him, is tilting backward just enough to be noticeable. Because of the
look on his face, the child seems as old as the woman. The camera has captured them in flight from this world to the next.
       Uncle Felix, Mama Chona's oldest surviving son, began calling the boy
"Mickie" to distinguish him from his father Miguel Grande, a big man whose
presence dominated all family gatherings even though he was Mama Chona's
youngest son. Her name was Encarnacion Olmeca de Angel and she
instructed everyone in the family to call her "Mama Grande" or "Mama
Chona" and never, ever to address her as *abuelita,* the Spanish equivalent to
granny. She was the only grandparent Miguel Chico knew. The others had

died many years before he was born on the north side of the river, a second generation American citizen.

Thirty years later and far from the place of his birth, on his own deathbed at the university hospital, Miguel Chico, who had been away from it for twelve years, thought about his family and especially its sinners. Felix, his great-aunt Cuca, his cousin Antony on his mother's side—all dead. Only his aunt Mema, the pariah° of the family after it initially refused to accept her illegitimate son, was still alive. And so was his father, Miguel Grande, whose sins the family chose to ignore because it relied on him during all crises.

Miguel Chico knew that Mama Chona's family held contradictory feelings toward him. Because he was still not married and seldom visited them in the desert, they suspected that he, too, belonged on the list of sinners. Still, they were proud of his academic achievements. He had been the first in his generation to leave home immediately following high school after being admitted to a private and prestigious university before it was fashionable or expedient to accept students from his background.

Mama Chona did not live to see him receive his doctorate and fulfill her                                5
dream that a member of the Angel family become a university professor. On her deathbed, surrounded by her family, she recognized Miguel Chico and said, *la familia,* in an attempt to bring him back into the fold. Her look and her words gave him that lost, uneasy feeling he had whenever any of his younger cousins asked him why he had not married. Self-consciously, he would say, "Well, I had this operation," stop there, and let them guess at the rest.

Miguel Chico, after he survived, decided that others believed the thoughts and feelings of the dying to be more melodramatic than they were. In his own case, he had been too drugged to be fully aware of his condition. In the three-month decline before the operation that would save his life, and as he grew thirstier every day, he longed to return to the desert of his childhood, not to the family but to the place. Without knowing it, he had been ill for a very long time. After suffering from a common bladder infection, he was treated with a medication that cured it but aggravated a deadly illness dormant since childhood though surfacing now and again in fits of fatigue and nausea.

"You didn't tell me you had a history of intestinal problems," the doctor said, leafing back through his chart.

"You didn't ask me," Miguel Chico replied. "And anyway, isn't it right there on the record?" He had lost ten pounds in two weeks and was beginning to throw up everything he ate.

"Well, I can't treat you for this now. I've cured your urinary infection. You'll have to go to a specialist at the clinic for the other. And stop taking the

---

*pariah:* Social outcast.

medication I prescribed for you." Later Mickie learned that no one with his history of intestinal illness ought to take the medication the doctor had prescribed. By then, it was too late.

He was allowed only spoonfuls of ice once every two hours and the desert was very much in his mouth, which was already parched by the drugs. Not at the time, but since, he has felt his godmother Nina's fear of being buried in the desert. Those chips of ice fed to him by his brother Raphael were grains of sand scratching down his throat. In the last weeks before surgery, as he lost control over his body, he floated in a perpetual dusk and, had it happened, would have died without knowing it, or would have thought it was happening to someone else.

There was one moment when he sensed he might not live. As the surgeon and anesthetist lifted him out of the gurney and onto the hard, cold table, each spoke quietly about what they were going to do. Mickie heard their voices, tender and kind, and was impressed by the way they touched him—as if he were a person in pain. He thought in those seconds that if theirs were the last voices he was to hear, that would be fine with him, for he longed to escape from the drugged and disembodied° state of twilight in which he had lived for weeks. His uncle Felix had been murdered in such a twilight.

The doctors set him down and uncovered him. He weighed ninety-eight pounds and looked pregnant.

"Your mother is waiting just outside," said the surgeon's voice at his right ear.

"I'm going to relax you a little bit so that this tube won't hurt your nose or throat," said the anesthetist at his left.

Someone began shaving his abdomen and loins. "God, is he hairy," said a nurse loudly.

Miguel Chico did not care whether or not he survived the operation they planned for him. When they described it to him and told him he would have to wear a plastic appliance at his side for the rest of his life—a life, they were quick to assure him, which would be perfectly "normal"—they grinned and added, "It's better than the alternative."

"How would you know?" he asked. "Let me die."

Thus, at first he was considered a difficult patient. Later on, the drugs seeped through, drop by drop, and conquered his rebelliousness. When the nurses came in to check on him every twenty minutes and to ask him how he felt, "Just fine," he would answer, even as he watched himself piss, shit, and throw up blood. Only later, when he survived ("It's a miracle," the surgeon told his mother, "his intestine was like tissue paper"), forever a slave to plastic

---

*disembodied:* Separated from the body or the physical world in general.

appliances, did he see how carefully he had been schooled by Mama Chona to suffer and, if necessary, to die.

Lying on a gurney in the recovery room, Miguel Chico came to life for the second time. Tubes protruded from every opening of his body except his ears, and before he was able to open his eyes, he heard a woman's voice calling his name over and over again in the way that made him wince: "Mee-gwell, Mee-gwell, wake up, Mee-gwell." Another voice from inside his head kept saying, "You cannot escape from your body, you cannot escape from your body."

He opened his eyes. In the gurney next to his there appeared a fat, straw-berry blonde on all fours screaming for something to kill the pain inside her head. "Nurse, give me something for my head" she yelled without stopping. The nurse, this time a delicate Polynesian dressed in bright green and wearing a mask, glided in and out of his vision.

"Now, now, sweetheart," she said to the fat woman in a lovely, lilting voice, "you're going to be all right, and I'll bring you something in just a minute." She disappeared with a lithe, dreamy motion.

The fat woman was not appeased and she screamed more loudly than before. He wondered why she was on all fours if she had just come from surgery. Only later did it occur to him that he might have imagined her. At the time, she awakened him to his own pain.

Looking down at himself, he saw that his body was being held together by a network of tubes and syringes. On his left side, by the groin, the head of a safety pin gleamed. He could not move his lips to ask for water, and from neck to crotch his body felt like dry ice, the desert on a cold, clear day after a snow-fall. If he had been able to move his arms, be would have pulled out the tubes in his nose and down his throat so that he, too, might shout out his horror and sense of violation. All of his needs were being taken care of by plastic devices and he was nothing but eyes and ears and a constant, vague pain that connected him to his flesh. Without this pain, he would have possessed for the first time in his life that consciousness his grandmother and the Catholic church he had renounced had taught him was the highest form of existence: pure, bodiless intellect. No shit, no piss, no blood—a perfect astronaut.

"I'm an angel," he said inside his mouth to Mama Chona, already dead and buried. "At last, I am what you taught us to be."

"Mee-gwell," sang the nurse, "wake up, Mee-gwell."

"It's Miguel," he wanted to tell her pointedly, angrily, "it's Miguel," but he was unable to speak. He was a child again.

They took him to the cemetery for three years before Miguel Chico understood what it was. At first, he was held closely by his nursemaid Maria or his uncle Felix. Later, he walked alongside his mother and godmother Nina or sometimes, when Miguel Grande was not working, with his father, holding

20

25

onto their hands or standing behind them as they knelt on the ground before the stones. No grass grew in the poor peoples' cemetery, and the trees were too far apart to give much shade. The desert wind tore the leaves from them and Miguel Chico asked if anyone ever watered these trees. His elders laughed and patted him on the head to be still.

Mama Chona never accompanied them to the cemetery. "Campo Santo" she called it, and for a long time Miguel Chico thought it was a place for the saints to go camping. His grandmother taught him and his cousins that they must respect the dead, especially on the Day of the Dead when they wandered about the earth until they were remembered by the living. Telling the family that the dead she cared about were buried too far away for her to visit their graves, Mama Chona shut herself up in her bedroom on the last day of October and the first day of November every year for as long as she lived. Alone, she said in that high-pitched tone of voice she used for all important statements, she would pray for their souls and for herself that she might soon escape from this world of brutes and fools and join them. In that time her favorite word was "brute," and in conversation, when she forgot the point she wanted to make, she would close her eyes, fold her hands in prayer, and say, "Oh, dear God, I am becoming like the brutes."

At the cemetery, Miguel Chico encountered no saints but saw only stones set in the sand with names and numbers on them. The grownups told him that people who loved him were there. He knew that many people loved him and that he was related to everyone, living and dead. When his parents Miguel Grande and Juanita were married, his godmother Nina told him, all the people in the Church, but especially her, became his mothers and fathers and would take care of him if his parents died. Miguel Chico did not want them to die if it meant they would become stones in the desert.

30    They bought flowers that smelled sour like Mama Chona and her sister, his great-aunt Cuca, to put in front of the stones. Sometimes they cried and he did not understand that they wept for the dead in the sand.

"Why are you crying?" he asked.

"Because she was my sister" or "because she was my mother" or "because he was my father," they answered. He looked at the stones and tried to see these people. He wanted to cry too, but was able to make only funny faces. His heart was not in it. He wanted to ask them what the people looked like but was afraid they would become angry with him. He was five years old.

There were other people walking and standing and kneeling and weeping quietly in front of the stones. Most of them were old like his parents, some of them were as old as Mama Chona, a few were his own age. They bought the yellow and white flowers from a dark, toothless old man who set them out in pails in front of a wagon. Miguel shied away when the ugly little man tried to give him some flowers.

"Take them Mickie," said his godmother, "the nice man is giving them to you."

"I don't want them." He felt like crying and running away, but his father had told him to be a man and protect his mother from the dead. They did not scare him as much as the flower man did.

A year later, he found out about the dead. His friend Leonardo, who was eight years old and lived in the corner house across the street, tied a belt around his neck. He put one end of the belt on a hook in the back porch, stood on a chair, and knocked it over. Nardo's sister thought he was playing one of his games on her and walked back into the house.

The next morning Miguel's mother asked if he wanted to go to the mortuary and see Leonardo. He knew his friend was dead because all the neighborhood was talking about it, about whether or not the boy had done it on purpose. But he did not know what a mortuary was and he wanted to find out.

When they arrived there, Miguel saw that everything was white, black, or brown. The flowers, like the kind they bought from the old man only much bigger and set up in pretty ways, were mostly white. The place was cold and all the people wore dark, heavy clothes. They were saying the rosary in a large room that was like the inside of the church but not so big. It was brightly lit and had no altar, but there were a few statues, which Miguel recognized. A long, shiny metal box stood at the end of the room. It was open, but Miguel was not able to see inside because it was too far away and he was too small to see over people's heads, even though they were kneeling.

Maria and his mother said that he must be quiet and pray like the others in the room. He became bored and sleepy and felt a great longing to look into the box. After the praying was over, they stood in line and moved slowly toward the box. At last he would be able to see. When the people in front of them got out of the way, he saw himself, his mother, and Maria reflected in the brightly polished metal. They told him it was all right to stand so that his head was level with theirs as they knelt. The three of them looked in.

Leonardo was sleeping, but he was a funny color and he was very still. "Touch him," his mother said, "it's all right. Don't be afraid." Maria took his hand and guided it to Nardo's face. It was cold and waxy. Miguel looked at the candles and flowers behind the box as he touched the face. He was not afraid. He felt something but did not know what it was.

"He looks just like he did when he was alive, doesn't he, Mickie?" his mother said solemnly.

"Yes," he nodded, but he did not mean it. The feeling was circling around his heart and it had to do with the stillness of the flowers and the color of Nardo's face.

"Look at him one more time before we go," Maria said to him in Spanish. "He's dead now and you will not see him again until Judgment Day."

That was very impressive and Miguel Chico looked very hard at his friend and wondered where he was going. As they drove home, he asked what they were going to do with Leonardo.

45    His mother, surprised, looked at Maria before she answered. "They are going to bury him in the cemetery. He's dead, Mickie. We'll visit him on the Day of the Dead. *Pobrecito, el inocente,*" she said, and Maria repeated the words after her. The feeling was now in his stomach and he felt that he wanted to be sick. He was very quiet.

"Are you sad, Mickie?" his mother asked before saying goodnight to him. "No."

"Is anything wrong? Don't you feel well?" She put her hand on his forehead. Miguelito thought of his hand on Nardo's face.

"I'm scared," he said, but that was not what he wanted to say.

50    "Don't be afraid of the dead," his mother said. "They can't hurt you.

"I'm not afraid of the dead." He saw the sand and stones for what they were now.

"What are you afraid of, then?"

The feeling and the words came in a rush like the wind tearing the leaves from the trees. "Of what's going to happen tomorrow," he said.

The next day, Miguel Chico watched Maria comb her long beautiful black and white hair in the sun. She had just washed it, and the two of them sat on the backstairs in the early morning light, his head in her lap. Her face was wide, with skin the color and texture of dark parchment, and her eyes, which he could not see because as he looked up her cheekbones were in the way, he knew were small and the color of blond raisins. When he was very young, Maria made him laugh by putting her eyes very close to his face and saying in her uneducated Spanish, "Do you want to eat my raisin eyes?" He pretended to take bites out of her eyelids. She drew back and said, "Now it's my turn. I like your chocolate eyes. They look very tasty and I'm going to eat them!" She licked the lashes of his deeply set eyes and Miguel Chico screamed with pleasure.

55    Maria was one of hundreds of Mexican women from across the border who worked illegally as servants and nursemaids for families on the American side. Of all ages, even as young as thirteen or fourteen, they supported their own families and helped to rear the children of strangers with the care and devotion they would have given their own relatives had they been able to live with them. One saw these women standing at the bus stops on Monday mornings and late Saturday nights. Sunday was their only day off and most of them returned to spend it on the other side of the river. In addition to giving her half of her weekly salary of twenty-five dollars, Juanita helped Maria pack leftover food, used clothing, old newspapers—anything Maria would not let her throw away—into paper bags that Maria would take to her own family. Years

later, wandering the streets of New York, his own bag glued to his side, Miguel Chico saw Maria in all the old bag ladies waiting on street corners in Chelsea or walking crookedly through the Village, stopping to pick through garbage, unable to bear the waste of the more privileged.

"Now, Maria," Juanita said, "if the immigration officials ask you where you got these things, tell them you went to bargain stores."

"Si, señora."

"And if they ask you where you have been staying during the week, tell them you've been visiting friends and relatives. Only in emergencies are you to use our name and we'll come to help you no matter what it is."

"Si, señora."

The conversation was a weekly ritual and unnecessary because Miguel Grande through his police duties was known by immigration officials, who, when it came to these domestics, looked the other way or forgot to stamp cards properly. Only during political campaigns on both sides of the river were immigration laws strictly enforced. Then Maria and all women like her took involuntary vacations without pay.

Mama Chona did not approve of any of the Mexican women her sons and daughters hired to care for her grandchildren. They were ill educated and she thought them very bad influences, particularly when they were allowed to spend much time with her favorites. Mama Chona wanted Miguel Chico to be brought up in the best traditions of the Angel family. Juanita scoffed at those traditions. "They've eaten beans all their lives. They're no better than anyone else," she said to her sister Nina. "I'm not going to let my kids grow up to be snobs. The Angels! If they're so great, why do I have to work to help take care of them?"

Miguel Chico could not remember a time when Maria was not part of his family and even though Mama Chona disapproved of the way she spoke Spanish, she was happy to know that Maria was a devout Roman Catholic. She remained so the first six years of his life, taking him to daily mass and holding him in her arms throughout the services until he was four. After mass during the week and before he was old enough to be instructed by Mama Chona, Maria took him to the five-and-ten stores downtown. If she had saved money from the allowance Juanita gave her, she would buy him paper doll books. He and Maria spent long afternoons cutting out dolls and dressing them. When he got home from the police station, Miguel Grande would scold Maria for allowing his son to play with dolls. "I don't want my son brought up like a girl," he said to Juanita in Maria's presence. He did not like to speak directly to the Mexican women Juanita and his sisters took on to help them with the household chores. Miguel Chico's aunts Jesus Maria and Eduviges left notes for the "domestics" (the Spanish word *criadas* is harsher) and spoke to them only when they had not done their chores properly. Mama Chona had taught

all her children that the Angels were better than the illiterate riffraff from
across the river.

"Maria does more good for people than all of them put together," Juanita
complained to her sister and to her favorite brother-in-law Felix, who shared
her opinion of his sisters. "They're so holier than thou. Just because they can
read and write doesn't make them saints. I'd like to see them do half the work
Maria does." Juanita knew that Jesus Maria and Eduviges considered Felix's
wife an illiterate and not worthy of their brother, who, after all, was an Angel.

"Apologize to your father for playing with dolls," Juanita said to Miguel
Chico. He did but did not understand why he needed to say he was sorry.
When his father was not there, his mother permitted him to play with them.
She even laughed when Maria made him a skirt and they watched him dance
to the jitterbug music on the radio. "Yitty-bog," Maria called it. Miguel
Grande had caught them at that once and made a terrible scene. Again, Miguel
Chico was asked to apologize and to promise that he would never do it again.
His father said nothing to him but looked at Juanita and accused her of turn-
ing their son into a *joto*. Miguel Chico did not find out until much later that
the word meant "queer." Maria remained silent throughout these scenes; she
knew enough not to interfere.

65    After Miguel Chico's birthday, several months after his friend Leonardo
"accidentally" hanged himself, Maria stopped taking him to mass. Instead, she
spent the afternoons when he got home from school talking to him about God
and reading to him from the Bible, always with the stipulation° that he not tell
his parents or Mama Chona. She especially liked to talk to him about Adam
and Eve and the loss of paradise. He loved hearing about Satan's pride and
rebelliousness and secretly admired him. Before he was expelled from the
heavenly kingdom, Maria told him, Satan was an angel, the most favored of
God's creatures, and his name was *Bella Luz*.

"Why did he turn bad, Maria?"

"Out of pride. He wanted to be God."

"Did God make pride?"

Miguel Chico learned that when he asked Maria a difficult question she
would remain silent, then choose a biblical passage that illustrated the terrible
power of God the Father's wrath. She loved to talk to him about the end of the
world.

70    Maria began braiding her hair and tying it up in a knot that lay flat on her
neck. It gave her a severe look he did not like, and he missed those mornings
when she let her hair hang loosely to her waist and brushed or dried it in the
sun, with his head on her lap. She did not allow him into her room any more

*stipulation:* Condition, requirement.

and asked him to leave if he opened the door and caught her with her hair still unbraided. The word "vice" occurred frequently now in her talks with him; everything, it seemed, was becoming a vice to Maria. She had become a Seventh Day Adventist.

His mother and Maria got involved in long, loud, and tearful arguments about the nature of God and about the Catholic church as opposed to Maria's new religion. They excluded him from these discussions and refused to let him into the kitchen where they wrangled with each other and reached no conclusions. Miguel Chico hid in his mother's closet in order not to hear their shouting.

"The Pope is the anti-Christ!" Maria said loudly, hoping he would hear. And before Juanita could object, Maria cited a passage from the Bible as irrefutable° proof.

"It's not true," Juanita said just as strongly, but she was not at ease with the holy book, and there was no priest at hand to back her up. She wept out of frustration and tried to remember what she had learned by rote in her first communion classes.

In the closet, Miguel Chico hugged his mother's clothes in terror. The familiar odors in the darkness kept him company and faintly reassured him. In the distance, the strident° voices arguing about God continued. What would happen if he told his mother and father that Maria was sneaking him off to the Seventh Day Adventist services while they were away at work or having a good time? His father had said to his mother that he would kill Maria if she did that.

The services—which were not so frightening as his father's threats and the arguments between his mother and Maria—were held in a place that did not seem like a church at all it was so brightly lit up, even in the middle of the day. There were no statues and the air did not smell of incense and burning candles. The singing was in Spanish, not Latin, and it was not the sort he enjoyed because it reminded him of the music played in the newsreels about the war. The people at these services were very friendly and looked at him as if they all shared a wonderful secret. "You are saved," they would say to him happily. He did not know what they meant, but he sensed that to be saved was to be special. The more he smiled, the more they smiled back; they spent most of the time smiling, though they talked about things that scared him a great deal, such as the end of the world and how sinful the flesh was. He could not rid himself of the guilt he felt for being there, as no matter how much they smiled, he knew he was betraying his mother and father and Mama Chona in some deep, incomprehensible way.

75

*irrefutable:* Undeniable, beyond doubt.    *strident:* Loud and harsh-sounding.

The voices of the women he loved were farther away now, which meant they were almost finished for the time being and would soon resume their household chores. His mother had just given birth to a second son and was staying home from work to nurse him. They named him Gabriel and Miguel Chico was extremely jealous of him.

Opening the closet door after the voices had stopped altogether, Miguelito stumbled over the clothes hamper and some of his mother's things spilled out into the light. He saw an undergarment with a bloody stain on it. Quickly, he threw the clothes back into the basket and shoved it into the closet. He was careful not to touch the garment. Its scent held him captive.

Maria swept him up from behind, forcing him to laugh out of surprise, and trotted him into the kitchen. Together they stood looking out into the backyard through the screen door. It was a hot day and the sun made the screen shimmer. Miguel saw his mother bending over the verbena and snapdragons that she and Maria took great pains to make grow out of the desert. The flowers were at their peak, and already he knew that the verbena, bright red, small, and close to the ground, would outlast the more exotic snapdragons he liked better. The canna lilies, which formed the border behind them, were colorful, but they had no fragrance and were interesting only when an occasional hummingbird dipped its beak into their red-orange cups. In the corner of that bed grew a small peach tree that he had planted at Maria's suggestion from a pit he had licked clean two summers earlier. It was now a foot high and had branched. His mother was approaching it. Leaning over him and with her hand on his face directing his gaze toward the tree, Maria whispered hypnotically, "Look at the little tree," she said very softly in Spanish so that his mother could not hear. "When it blooms and bears fruit that means that the end of the world is near. Now look at your mother. You must respect and love her because she is going to die." In front of him, in the gauzy brightness of the screen, the red of the flowers merged with the red stain he had seen a few moments before. He believed Maria. In that instant, smelling her hair and feeling her voice of truth moist on his ear, love and death came together for Miguel Chico and he was not from then on able to think of one apart from the other.

Two years later, in a fit of terror because he knew the world was going to end soon, he told his parents that Maria had been taking him to her church. His father threw her out of the house but allowed her to return a few weeks later on the condition that she say nothing about her religion to anyone while she lived in his house. The arguments stopped, and she no longer read to him from the Bible.

80    Maria treated him nicely, but she hardly spoke to him and spent more time caring for his brother. Once or twice Miguel Chico caught her looking at him sadly and shaking her head as if he were lost to her forever. One day after

school, when he was feeling bold, he said, "If God knew that Satan and Adam and Eve were going to commit a sin, why did He create them?"

"You must not ask me such things," she replied, "I'm not allowed to talk to you about them."

It was a lame answer and he knew that in some important way, he had defeated her. He hated her now and hoped that she would leave them soon and return to Mexico. When, several months later, she did go away, he stayed at Mama Chona's house all day and did not say goodbye to her. Juanita was upset with him when he got home.

"Maria wanted to tell you goodbye. Why didn't you come home before she left?"

"I don't like her any more," he said. "I'm glad she's gone." But later that night he felt an awful loneliness when he thought about her hair and eyes.


Long after Miguel Chico had completed his education and given up all forms of organized religion, a few years after his operation and his decision to live alone in San Francisco, his mother wrote him a long letter about Maria's visit to the desert. It was her first and only one, for she had moved to California and joined a congregation there. Except for her hair, which was now completely white, his mother said that she looked exactly the same. Miguel Chico reread the last paragraphs of the letter while sitting at his desk, occasionally looking out to the garden. The fog had not yet burned away and the ferns and lobelia were a neon green and blue. "She took me back to the years when I was young and you were a little boy," his mother wrote.

> She remembers all the things you did, even the long white dress she made for you and how you would dance and swirl around while she and I played your audience. She even got up and showed me how you danced! That surprised me because she still is very religious and I thought her church prohibited dancing.
>
> She eats raw cabbage "for her mind," she says, carrots for her eyes, and turnips for her arthritis. She looks healthy enough to me, but according to her she has diabetes, arthritis, varicose veins, and bad eyesight.
>
> One afternoon while I was resting, she cleaned all my flower beds. She still loves gardening. We took her across the river where she stayed a few days with a niece. Your father and I picked her up the following Tuesday on Seventh St. where she had called from a phone booth. She had walked through the worst parts of town completely unafraid, at least three miles.
>
> She left on Thursday because it snowed on Wednesday, and I didn't want to let her go. I was very sad to see her leave because I thought as I saw her get on the bus that I might never see her again.

I hope she comes back, Mickie, so that I can take her to visit all the family. She remembered every one of the Angels but only talked to some of them and to your godmother on the phone. I wasn't driving or getting out much. She told me it was all right because she had come to be with me anyway.

Your brother Gabriel came over several times during her visit when he was able to get away from his duties at the parish. Would you believe that the first time he came and even though she knows he is a priest, Maria asked him when he was going to get married. I thought this was rude but I didn't say anything. Gabriel replied quite strongly, though, "No, thanks. I've seen what marriage does to many people in my parish."

She promised to come and see us later in the year. I hope so.

Later, on his birthday, he received a letter from Maria herself. It was written in the kind of Spanish his grandmother deplored and was sent from Los Angeles.

My Dear Miguelito,

With all my love I write you this letter to greet you and offer my congratulations. I have wanted for a long time to find out your address so that I might write to you. Your little mother told me that you had been very ill with a terrible sickness but that you are now well. I'm very glad.

Your *mamita* is very beautiful still and I love her very much because she is very friendly and does not look down on anyone. Your father and brother were also very kind to me so that I must tell you that a week with them seemed like a day.

In three days, you will celebrate your birthday. I am going toward old age, 79, and I plan to walk into my eighties. I wish you long life and good health. May God bless you and keep you well, so that when the Father comes in the clouds of the sky, He will take you and me with Him to live in paradise and joy in the kingdom He is preparing for those who love Him, think in His name and keep His commandments.

I send you a hug.

Maria L. v. de Sanchez

Write me.

He meant to respond to her note right away, believing himself to be free of her influence and her distortions of religion and vice. He put it off, telling himself he would write as soon as his academic duties were finished for the year. She visited him in dreams, her hair loose and white and streaming to the floor, her immense jaw frozen in a perpetual smile that was alternately loving and terrifying.

A month later, Juanita phoned him from the desert to tell him that Maria was dead. She had been knocked down by a car as she was leaving her church service in Los Angeles. The driver was drunk. A child by her side had been killed outright. Maria survived a night and a day in the hospital, surrounded by members of her congregation, talking with them until she fell into a coma. She had died on the anniversary of his operation.

"Well, the end of the world finally came for her," he said.

"Oh, Mickie, don't be so heartless," his mother said quietly.                    90

"I'm not being heartless, Mother. She lived for the end of the world. Of course, it had to be some poor vice-ridden slob who caught up with her." In trying to joke about death with Juanita, he sensed that he was only making it worse for her.

"Well, anyway, I thought you would want to know," she said.

"Sure, Mom, and I'm sorry I sounded cold about it. I'm just tired of death and everything associated with it."

"Well, I'm going to have your brother celebrate a mass in her name. I know you don't believe in it, but I'm going to pray for her even if she did think we were all going to hell for being Catholics."

"You do what you need to, Mom. I'm going to look for peach trees in       95
Golden Gate Park for her."

"What are you talking about? Are you trying to be funny again?"

"No, Mom. I'm dead serious. I'll tell you that story sometime."

He did not go to the park that day and did not think very much about Maria or the family in general. He and his therapist had decided that Sundays made him even more melancholy than usual because they were "family" days and he knew that though the park would be filled with all kinds of people, he would find himself drawn to the family groups, especially if there were old people among them.

Instead, he did his laundry in the washeteria around the corner where he knew he would be in the company of those people who lived alone in the neighborhood. They would not disturb each other except to ask for change and would read their Sunday papers in peace and isolation like that of the islands in the Baltic he loved visiting every summer. When he got back, he put away his clothes and began to prepare supper for himself. He chopped mushrooms, onions, garlic, and tomatoes for the spaghetti sauce he had perfected over the years. His secret was to add sugar, marsala,° onion soup mix, and finally, one of the red chiles from the wreath his godmother gave him every Christmas and to let the concoction simmer off and on for two or three hours. Its flavor would improve throughout the week.

---

*marsala:* A type of wine.

100        While the sauce was bubbling, he put on his favorite records and went to the bathroom to change his appliance. It was a weekly ritual which took him an hour, or a little more if the skin around the piece of intestine sticking out from his right side was irritated. Without the appliance and the bags he attached to it and changed periodically throughout each day, he knew he could not live. He had forgotten what it was like to be able to hold someone, naked, without having a plastic device between them. He wanted to ask Maria if, on Judgment Day, his body would rise from the grave in its condition before or after the operation. He was still feeling bitterness toward her and all people who thought like her because they seemed so literal and simple-minded. This time, the skin around the stoma° looked all right and he finished the process before all the records had played out.

After supper, he tried to read in his study and found that he kept looking at the photograph in which he and Mama Chona are walking downtown. He had no photograph of Maria. In some vastly significant way, he felt he was still the child of these women, an extension of them, the way a seed continues to be a part of a plant after it has assumed its own form which does not at all resemble its origin, but which, nevertheless, is determined by it. He had survived severe pruning and wondered if human beings, unlike plants, can water themselves.

He was also beginning to see in his day-to-day life with the bag at his side that too many false notions surrounded people like him who have been given a reprieve. He did not automatically or necessarily see life more or less positively for almost having lost it. Nor did he come bearing insights from the other side of the grave to comfort and reassure those who have not yet been threatened.

He was still seeing people, including himself, as books. He wanted to edit them, correct them, make them behave differently. And so he continued to read them as if they were invented by someone else, and he failed to take into account their separate realities, their differences from himself. When people told him of their lives, or when he thought about his own in the way that is not thinking but a kind of reverie outside time, a part of him listened with care. Another part fidgeted, thought about something else or went blank, and wondered why once again he was being offered such secrets to examine. Later he found himself retelling what he had heard, arranging various facts, adding others, reordering time schemes, putting himself in situations and places he had never been in, removing himself from conversations or moments that didn't fit.

---

*stoma:* An artificial permanent opening created by a surgical procedure.

Most of the time his versions were happier than their "real" counterparts, and in making them so he was indulging in one of Mama Chona's traits that as a very young child—the child who was holding her hand forever in a snapshot—he loved most. Mama Chona was never able to talk about the ugly sides of life or people, even though she was surrounded by them. For her grandchildren she dressed up the unpleasant in sugary tales and convinced them that she believed what she was saying. Later, in his adolescence and while she still retained her wits, Miguel Chico hated her for this very trait, seeing it as part of the Spanish conquistador° snobbery that refused to associate itself with anything Mexican or Indian because it was somehow impure. What, Miguel Chico asked himself, did she see when she looked in the mirror? As much as she protected herself from it, the sun still darkened her complexion and no surgery could efface° the Indian cheekbones, those small very dark eyes and aquiline° nose. By then, his cousins and he smiled at each other when she began telling her tales of family incidents and relatives long since dead and buried. By then, in their young adulthood, they knew the "truth" and were too self-involved in their educations away from her and the family to give her credit for trying to spare them the knowledge that she, too, knew it. Slowly, she slipped into her fairy-tale world—at least outwardly, "Oh, my dear Miguelito," she said to him just after his first year at the University, "you are going to be the best-educated member of this family."

Sitting at his desk, gazing at the garden, fixing that old photograph forever outside of time and far from where it was taken, he knew she had not called him "dear." Mama Chona did not use endearments with anyone in the family. How silent she had been even when she talked—silent like those pyramids he had finally seen in Teotihuacan built to pay tribute to the sun and moon. He had felt the presence of the civilizations that had constructed them and, as he climbed the steep, stone steps so conceived as to give him the impression that he was indeed walking into the sky, he had seen why those people, his ancestors, thought themselves gods and had been willing to tear out the hearts of others to maintain that belief. The feeling horrified him still.

And Mama Chona was still very much a part of him. Perhaps, he told himself, watching the first wisps of fog drift in over his garden, perhaps he had survived—albeit in an altered form, like a plant onto which has been grafted an altogether different strain of which the smelly rose at his side, that tip of gut that would always require his care and attention, was only a symbol—perhaps he had survived to tell others about Mama Chona and people like Maria.

105

---

*conquistador:* A participant in the Spanish conquest of the Americas.   *efface:* Erase, wipe out.
*aquiline:* Resembling an eagle's beak.

He could then go on to shape himself, if not completely free of their influence and distortions, at least with some knowledge of them. He believed in the power of knowledge.

His need to give meaning to the accidents of life had become even more intense, and he had not yet begun to laugh at that need. Years earlier, he had started out to be a brain surgeon but had found his pre-med courses lifeless and impossible. Literature had given him another way to examine the mind. He knew he was no poet like his cousin JoEl, the most sensitive member of the family. He, Miguel Chico, was the family analyst, interested in the past for psychological, not historical, reasons. Like Mama Chona, he preferred to ignore facts in favor of motives, which were always and endlessly open to question and interpretation. Yet unlike his grandmother and Maria, Miguel Chico wanted to look at motives and at people from an earthly, rather than other-worldly, point of view. He sensed he had a long way to go.

He walked out into the garden. The fog was in and thicker than usual in his part of the City. He knew that during the early hours of the day it would moisten and freshen all he had planted there. In the morning, before going to teach his classes, he would get rid of the petunias. Their purple velvet color was fading and they were now rangy° and going to seed. Like a god, he would uproot them and discard them even after having loved and enjoyed them so much.

He felt Maria's hand on his face, her hair smelling of desert sage and lightly touching the back of his neck as she whispered in his ear. Every moment is Judgment Day and to those who live on earth, humility is a given and not a virtue that will buy one's way into heaven.

110    Miguel Chico left the garden, changed his bag, undressed and went to bed.


## QUESTIONS

1. What did Mama Chona teach Miguel Chico? Consider the lessons that the boy received from her.
2. Explain why Miguel is described as being "a child again" after his operation.
3. Why did Mama Chona and other members of the Angel family "look down" on the workers "from across the river"?
4. What did Maria, the nanny, teach Miguel Chico?
5. As an adult, does Miguel Chico value what Mama Chona and Maria taught him when he was young? Why or why not?

---

*rangy:* Tall and skinny, gangly.

6. Describe the narrator's attitude toward immigration, legal and illegal. If it is different from yours, explain the difference.
7. The story contains recurring mentions of plants—and gardening, planting, watering. Skimming through, in a second reading, look for some of these mentions. Who is doing the planting? Who is described as a plant? Is this recurring imagery symbolic? If so, what do you think it suggests?
8. Explain your understanding of the statement, "Every moment is Judgment Day and to those who live on earth, humility is a given and not a virtue that will buy one's way into heaven."
9. Identify the various cultural influences that shape Miguel Chico.
10. Is Islas making a statement about the way in which children from outside the cultural mainstream in the United States relate to their mixed cultural background? If so, what is his point?

## CONNECTIONS

1. Compare and contrast Miguel Chico's attitude toward death with the attitude expressed by Linda Robinson in "Planning Ahead."
2. Compare the order of events—the chronology—in Islas's story to that of any other short story from this text. What is the effect of Islas's technique?
3. The previous sections of this book focus on specific themes: growing up, gender, love, work, the environment. Discuss the way in which each of those themes is addressed in Islas's story, referring to specific elements from the text.

# Research: Writing from Increased Knowledge

· · · · · · · · · · · · · · · · · · · · · · · · · ·

When most college instructors use the word *research,* they don't have in mind the process that some students follow when they have to turn in a "research paper": go to the library, find a few books or journals that discuss the chosen topic, copy some of each source, mix the fragments, add some footnotes, and turn in the result as "their" project. First, let's be clear: In a research paper, the thesis statement about the subject should come from you, should be what *you* have to say about the topic—just as in any other essay. A research paper, however, demonstrates to a reader that what you are offering is a more informed opinion, shaped in part by the background fact-finding that you have done. Books and articles you've read, music you've listened to, movies and TV shows you've seen, and personal interviews you have conducted, if they are related to the topic, could be mentioned in your discussion of that topic. Of course, your sources should be credible, so that mentioning them will add to your essay's credibility.

As we explained in the previous section of this text, you can present your sources' views by quoting, paraphrasing, or summarizing them. You have to be very careful, however, not to plagiarize. (For a discussion of plagiarism, see p. 430.)

## *You Need to Write a Research Paper: What Now?*

You worry. You moan about the amount of work you'll have to do. You think about a subject you want to explore, or maybe you look at a list of possible topics but feel like it's written in a foreign language. Having done all of these things, you get to work.

*Choose a Topic*    First, you should choose a topic you're interested in—one you would like to read more about. If none of the topics suggested or assigned by your instructor fit in that category, come up with one of your own, but be sure to get it approved by your instructor before investing too much time. If your topic fits the general parameters of other topics, most instructors will be pleased to see you taking initiative, putting your own stamp on a project. They know that if you are personally interested in a topic, they will receive a more interesting paper from you.

Aside from being something you'd like to investigate more, your topic should also be something you have an opinion about. This is not to say that you should be close-minded and ignore any material that contradicts your views. However, having something to say about the research topic helps you prevent a problem many students run into: that while reading experts in the field, published authors, you will bow too easily to their views, and your paper will become merely a restatement of your sources. Sometimes students even end up sounding like distorted versions of the voices they have read—they abandon their own voice, their own writing style, in an attempt to sound more knowledgeable. Sometimes they copy sentences or phrases too closely, unintentionally committing plagiarism; many times, they simply sound awkward. To prevent this, you might want to prewrite before you launch into the search for sources; this early writing will allow you to discover what you know about a subject and what your opinion is, perhaps providing you with an idea for a thesis.

*Focus*  As in the case of any other essay, once you've decided on a research topic, you need to narrow it down so that you can fully address it. You also need to focus it enough to make a search for sources possible. "Love," for example, would load you with an overwhelming number of possible sources; "platonic love" begins to be more focused; "platonic love in the nineties" is even more specific. Keep in mind the length of the paper you need to write: Tackling an overly broad topic in a brief paper will force you to overgeneralize and barely skim the surface; a narrowed topic will allow you to explore your ideas in depth and bring them to life with examples, details, and powerful quotations from credible sources.

*Search*  Formal research papers, the kind you will most commonly encounter in college, require you to use the library. Plan on going there numerous times. The first step in the research process, therefore, is familiarizing yourself with the physical layout of the library you will use: Where are the computers you will use to search for information—both those listing books and those listing magazine articles? Where are the book stacks? the magazines? the bathrooms? You should also ask the research librarian whether the library offers any specialized databases and indexes that might help to focus your search on the particular discipline you are working in (some examples are the MLA database for English, the *Humanities Index,* and the *Business Periodicals Index*).

## Handling Outside Sources

*How Many?*  The number of sources you will want to incorporate into your essay depends on the writing situation, particularly if the paper has a certain length requirement. Many instructors include as part of an assignment a minimum number of sources they expect you to use. In any case, your paper should be more than just a collection of quotations and paraphrases: A five-page essay making reference to ten sources might seem like a raisin cookie made up primarily of raisins, with a thin coating of oatmeal holding them together. On the other hand, one raisin does not a raisin cookie make. So you need to find a balance. A balanced research paper will include several sources, yet your voice and ideas will still be dominant, weaving together a range of perspectives.

*Which Sources?*   There are a few criteria that you should consider when evaluating possible sources of information for your paper. Here are the main questions you need to ask:

- *Does the source discuss what you need?* You can often judge this by the title included in the index or database you are scanning; sometimes, however, you will need to skim through a book or essay's index or subheadings to determine whether it's a relevant source for your paper. You may also want to read the introduction, which probably will summarize the general ideas pursued in detail in the book.
- *Is the source available?* This is not a question for a professional scholar, but it's certainly an important question for a student pressed for time. Many libraries offer interlibrary loan services (they'll ask another library to lend them the material you need if it's not available on site), but this procedure can take several weeks. Still, it's not impossible; if the source you want is the most significant writing ever done about a subject, you should do all you can to locate it. If it's not a source you *must* have, you might want to look for others that are more easily accessible.
- *Is the source credible?* Whenever possible, you should look for scholarly books and journals—sources that clearly document their evidence and support their claims. Obviously, in many cases it's worth looking up the credentials of the people who are providing you with information and opinions. Finally, keep in mind that even experts might have a bias, a perspective influenced by their experience and by political, religious, and cultural beliefs that could affect their opinion(s) and writing. Sometimes the source of a publication makes its bias obvious, whereas sometimes the use of loaded language will give it away.

  An article in the *National Enquirer,* for example, is not credible: The magazine makes no secret about being a tabloid, and articles published in it rarely if ever document their sources. But what about sources such as *People* magazine, *Reader's Digest, The Nation, Forbes,* or *Time?* You should prefer sources that have a reputation for fairness and accuracy, that treat opposing views fairly, that are balanced rather than decidedly political or religious, and that are not associated with a special-interest group with a specific bias. It might be interesting to consult the National Rifle Association on the issue of gun control or Dr. Jack

Kevorkian on the issue of euthanasia, but you'd obviously have to find other sources as well. If you must use a source that is clearly biased, be sure to point out the bias when you discuss the source in your essay. Otherwise, your readers might note the omission and that you are attempting to cover up, insulting their intelligence.

Be especially cautious with online sources such as those from the Internet. The Internet includes a great deal of useful information, but it also includes a great deal of "information" that is biased or altogether bogus. Anyone can quite easily put a page on the World Wide Web. So be sure that you are quoting a reliable source.

- *Is the source current?* Unless you are using sources for historical perspective, in many fields you will need to look for the most current material you can find. Essays in journals, magazines, and newspapers tend to be more current than books or essays in anthologies; however, scholarly journals and books tend to be more thorough. Either way, never choose currentness over credibility.

*How?*   If possible, make photocopies of relevant pages from your sources so that you can scribble directly on those copies. Jot down notes—questions, disagreements with the text, personal experience that might support an author's perspective—and underline sentences or phrases worth quoting directly. If you can't make photocopies, take notes and copy down quotations in a notebook or on index cards of your own, remembering to note the page number(s) for the ideas you respond to. Always write down all the information you will need later for the "Works Cited" list: the complete name of the author or authors, the complete title of the selection (and, if necessary, the complete title of the book or magazine in which it appeared), the publisher's name and location, the day, month, and year of publication, the volume or issue number, and the page numbers for quotations and specific ideas you intend to paraphrase.

The information you will need to document a source will depend on two factors: the type of source to be documented and the style of documentation you are required to use. Most English courses prefer the Modern Language Association (MLA) style of documentation, which is presented in full in *The MLA Handbook for Writers of Research Papers,* 4th ed., by Joseph Gibaldi. Other styles include the APA, devised by the American Psychological Association and preferred in the social sciences, the Chicago Style, and the ACS (American Chemical Society) style, used for chemistry papers. Ask your instructor which style you should use for his or her course.

Through our earlier discussion of in-text attribution of credit to outside sources (in Section 5), as well as through our discussion of the list of works cited, which appears in this section, we provide an introductory discussion of

MLA style; however, for additional information about this and other documentation styles, you should consult the appropriate style guide. You'll find the guides in any college library, usually in the reference section. One additional word of caution: Although some of the selections included in this textbook are accompanied by lists of notes and citations, those lists follow a variety of formats (depending on the requirements of the publication in which they originally appeared). You should not use these uncritically as models for research paper format.

## Drafting the Research Paper

Writing a first draft of a research paper is not very different from drafting any other essay. You should prewrite to generate ideas. You should expect to write several drafts of the essay. And you should plan to revise a lot. But a research paper also requires you to integrate and document sources. As you prepare the rough draft, you may choose to write in the ideas and quotations that you want to include from your sources, or simply mark the points where these will eventually appear; for the sake of the flow of your ideas, you might skip them as you draft and incorporate them later.

In any case, insert quotations and paraphrases either where they will support your points or where you feel the need to refute another writer's arguments. Reread the segment in Section 5 that discusses the effective integration of source material: The MLA format requires you to include the name of the author(s) you are quoting, paraphrasing, or summarizing, as well as the number of the page(s) where you found the ideas. You can include the name either in a phrase introducing the information, or in the parenthesis that follows the material. For example, it's OK to write "human beings have long believed in the existence of only one god (Armstrong 247)"; however, it would be more effective to write, "In the essay 'In the Beginning,' Karen Armstrong states that human beings have long believed in the existence of only one god (247)."

Occasionally, you will need to cite a line or two that are already *quoted* in one of your sources. If you want to quote this material again in your writing, introduce it by giving credit to the person who originally said or wrote the words; then follow the quote with a parenthesis that states "qtd. in ____" ("qtd." is the abbreviation for "quoted"), filling in the blank with the last name of the author of the source in which you found the information.

## Preparing the "Works Cited" Page

A "Works Cited" list (or bibliography) is designed to allow your readers to easily find the original sources that you quoted or paraphrased in your essay. If you read a few sources but decided not to include anything from them in your paper, you should *not* include those in the list.

Following are some of the most common types of entries that appear on "Works Cited" lists, in MLA format. Consider both the examples and the explanations, because you must follow the format exactly.

For the reader's benefit, the "Works Cited" list must be arranged in alphabetical order by the last name of the primary author of each selection. If the author of a selection is not listed in your source, place the selection alphabetically by title. Note that the first line of each entry is aligned with the left margin and any additional lines in each entry are indented five spaces (or half an inch if you are using a word processor). Finally, the entries in the "Works Cited" list should be double-spaced, just like the rest of the essay. (For examples of "Works Cited" lists in correct MLA format, see those following the student essays by Darren Reese and Kevin O'Kelley, included in this section.)

### *Book*
**Islas, Arturo. *The Rain God.* New York: Avon, 1984.**

(The entry includes author, book title, city where the publisher is based, abbreviated name of the publishing company—words like "Books" and "Publishing Company" get dropped, and "University Press" becomes "UP"—and year of publication.)

If the book has more than one author, include the additional authors' names after the first author's name (last and first); don't reverse the order of the first and last names for the additional authors.

If you are including more than one book by the same author, follow the format presented here, but use three hyphens(---) instead of the author's name for each of the additional entries.

### *Selection in an Anthology*
**Rose, Phyllis. "Modernism: The Case of Willa Cather." *American Fiction: 1914 to 1945.* Ed. Harold Bloom. New York: Chelsea, 1986. 61–76.**

(The entry includes author, title of selection, title of book in which the selection appears, name of editor and/or translator when applicable, city where the publisher is based, name of publisher, year of publication, and page numbers for the specific selection quoted.)

### *Article in an Encyclopedia or Other Reference Book*
**"Antarctica." *Funk and Wagnalls Standard Reference Encyclopedia.* Ed. in chief Joseph Laffan Morse. New York: Standard Reference Works, 1966.**

Many articles in encyclopedias are not signed; however, if the author's name does appear, include it first—as you would in any other entry.

*Article in a Scholarly Journal*

Knapp, Terry J., and J. F. Raney. "Student-Athletes and Academic Course Work: A Ten Year Summary." *Perceptual and Motor Skills* 71 (1990): 793–95.

The number 71 in this example is the number of the magazine's volume; it is followed by the year of publication and the page numbers of the article (if the journal is paginated by year or volume). However, if the journal you are using is paginated by issue, add a period after the volume number and follow it with the number of the issue in which the article appears. For example:

Cristopher, Georgia B. "In Arcadia, Calvin: A Study of Nature in Henry Vaughan." *Studies in Philology* 70.4 (1973): 408–26.

*Popular Magazine Article*

Brownlee, Shannon. "The Myth of the Student-Athlete: College Sports Versus Education." *U.S. News and World Report* 8 Jan. 1990: 50–53.

In this case, the numbers following the magazine title simply represent the date when the article appeared, followed by the pages it covered.

*Newspaper Article*

Robinson, Phillip. "Joys of a New Joystick or Mouse." *San Jose Mercury News* 7 Apr. 1996: F1+.

If the name of the city in which the newspaper is published does not appear in the newspaper's title, include it in brackets after that title. The plus sign following the page number lets your readers know that the article continued on other pages.

*CD-ROMs*

"Japan." *Microsoft Encarta.* CD-ROM. Microsoft. 1992.

If the article in this entry had originally appeared in a printed source, you would have needed to provide all the publication information for that source just as you would for any other article, and only afterward add the title of the database, the word "CD-ROM," the name of the database publisher, and the copyright date of the database.

*Online Databases*

"Maundy Thursday in the Spains (La Colombia)." *American Record Guide* 57.2 (Mar.–Apr. 1994): 223. Online. CompuServe. Magazine Database Plus. 13 Apr. 1996.

For information gathered from online databases, enter the publication information as you would for any other article, followed by the word "online," the name of the computer service you used, the title of the database in which you found the article, and the date when you accessed the information.

*Personal Interview*
**Paley, Grace. Personal Interview. 1 Mar. 1995.**
To document a citation from an interview that you conducted, begin the entry with the name of the person you interviewed, followed by the words "Personal interview" and the date when the interview took place.

### Revising the Research Paper

In addition to the steps included in the checklist provided in Section 4, the revision of a research paper involves one more element: checking to see that you have clearly attributed to your sources any information that you found during the research. Even when you run across some information that appears in many different sources, err on the side of caution if you're not sure whether that information is common knowledge. If you believe your audience may not be familiar with a fact or idea that you want to mention in your paper, then, just to be safe, document it. This might prevent an accusation of plagiarism, and it will only make your essay appear more trustworthy.

## Topics for Writing about Issues in American Culture

· · · · · · · · · · · · · · · · · · · · · · · · · ·

1. Write an argumentative essay that defines what a good argumentative essay is and then argues whether or not a particular essay from this book meets the criteria established by your definition.
2. Using your own experiences with language as well as those described by Pei Kuan (Section 1), Ward Churchill, Gloria Naylor, Amy Tan, and Arturo Islas, write an essay about the positive and negative power of words.
3. Pretend that you are writing to a group of high school students: In an essay, offer an extensive definition of the term "college life."
4. In an argumentative essay, refute Kevin O'Kelley's thesis about the need for multicultural education.
5. Using Mark Crispin Miller's essay "Dow Recycles Reality" as a model, write an essay analyzing two or three magazine ads for different brands of the same product.
6. Using the essays by Neil Postman and Mark Crispin Miller as models, write an essay that summarizes and discusses subtle images and messages in a film or television series.
7. Write an argumentative essay about the impact of television on U.S. society today. Paraphrase or quote the views expressed on the subject

by various authors included in this text: Benjamin Barber (Section 1), Ellen Goodman (Section 2), and Neil Postman.

8. Write an argumentative essay that defines and describes what it means to be a person of your gender, race, or class. (Focus on only *one* of those aspects).

9. Write a researched argumentative essay that defines a term such as "conservative," "independent," "liberal," "moderate," "progressive," or "socialist" and describes the values, beliefs, attitudes, and goals of a person who fits that definition.

10. Write an argumentative research paper supporting or opposing affirmative action. Make sure to define your understanding of the term.

11. Write an argumentative research paper supporting or opposing a constitutional amendment to make English the official language of the United States.

12. Write an argumentative research paper supporting or opposing the legalization of prostitution.

13. Write an argumentative essay that either supports or opposes Anna Quindlen's views about "American anonymity." Draw on a variety of sources, including personal experience. Do you feel like a member of a community (or of several communities)? Do you feel anonymous?

14. Write an essay about the benefits and drawbacks of learning about many different religions. Do you feel that comparative religion should be taught in schools? Why or why not?

15. Write an essay comparing and contrasting death-related rituals in mainstream U.S. society with death-related rituals from other cultures. In the process, explain your understanding of some of the symbols involved in those rituals.

16. Write an argumentative research paper evaluating the impact of computer technology on our society.

17. In an argumentative essay, respond to Darron Reese's views regarding the image of student athletes on college campuses.

18. Write an essay arguing that Ursula K. LeGuin is wrong when she states that Americans reject fantasy and imagination.

19. Write an argumentative research paper that takes a position on whether or not our society should support genetic testing.

20. Write an essay exploring the state of race relations on U.S. college campuses today.

21. In an argumentative essay, argue against Ward Churchill's view that sports teams named after Native Americans should adopt different mascots and names.

22. Reread Louis Simpson's poem "American Classic"; then write a poem of your own, which, under the same title, describes what *you* see as the "classic" image of American society today.

## Acknowledgments

Paul Amarto and Sonia Partridge, "The Origins of Modern Vegetarianism" from THE NEW VEGETARIANS. Copyright © 1989 by Paul Amarto and Sonia Partridge. Reprinted by permission of Plenum Publishing Corp.

Yehuda Amichai, "Love is Finished Again" from THE SELECTED POETRY OF YEHUDA AMICHAI, edited and translated by Chana Block and Stephen Mitchell, Harper & Row, 1986. Copyright © 1986 by Chana Block and Stephen Mitchell. Reprinted by permission.

Benjamin R. Barber, "America Skips School." Copyright © 1993 by *Harper's Magazine*. All rights reserved. Reproduced from the November issue by special permission.

Dave Barry, "Taking the Manly Way Out" from DAVE BARRY TALKS BACK. Copyright © 1991 by Dave Barry. Reprinted by permission of Crown Publishers, Inc.

Becky Birtha, "In the Life" from LOVER'S CHOICE. Copyright © 1987 by Becky Birtha. Reprinted by permission of Seal Press, Seattle.

Barbara Brandt, "Less is More: A Call for Shorter Work Hours." Reprinted with permission of the author.

Michael Buenaflor, " It's Good to Know the Opposition" from NEWSWEEK, November 28. Copyright © 1994 Newsweek, Inc. All rights reserved. Reprinted by permission.

Rachel Carson, "The Obligation to Endure" from SILENT SPRING. Copyright © 1962 by Rachel L. Carson. Copyright © renewed 1990 by Roger Christie. Reprinted by permission of Houghton Mifflin Company. All rights reserved.

Willa Cather, "The Enchanted Bluff" from FIVE STORIES. Copyright © 1956. Published by Alfred A. Knopf, Inc.

Kate Chopin, "The Story of an Hour" from THE AWAKENING AND SELECTED STORIES. Published by Penguin Classics, 1986.

Ward Churchill, "Crimes Against Humanity" from *Z* Magazine, March 1993. Reprinted by permission of the author.

Sandra Cisneros, "Eleven" from WOMAN HOLLERING CREEK. Copyright © by Sandra Cisneros 1991. Published by Vintage Books, a division of Random House, Inc., New York, NY, and originally in hardcover by Random House, Inc. Reprinted by permission of Susan Bergholz Literary Services, New York. All rights reserved.

Tom Daly, "Dancing in the Cracks between Worlds" from WINGSPAN: Inside the Men's Movement by Christopher Harding, Ph.D. and Robert C. Frenier, published by St. Martin's Press, Inc., New York. Copyright © 1992 by Christopher Harding, Ph.D. and Robert C. Frenier.

Annie Dillard, "Living Like Weasels" from TEACHING A STONE TO TALK. Copyright © 1982 by Annie Dillard. Reprinted by permission of HarperCollins Publishers, Inc.

Michael Dorris, "Discoveries" from PAPER TRAIL by Michael Dorris. Copyright © 1994 by Michael Dorris. Reprinted by permission of HarperCollins Publishers, Inc.

Rosa Ehrenreich, "I Hate Trees" originally published in Ms. Magazine. Copyright © 1995 by Rosa Ehrenreich. Reprinted by permission of Rosa Ehrenreich and International Creative Management, Inc.

Martin Espada, "Federico's Ghost" from REBELLION IS THE CIRCLE OF A LOVER'S HANDS (Curbstone Press, 1990). Reprinted with permission of Curbstone Press, distributed by Consortiuum.

Warren Farrell, "Men as Success Objects" from THE FAMILY THERAPY NETWORKER, Nov./Dec. 1988. Warren Farrell is the San Diego-based author of WHY MEN ARE THE WAY THEY ARE and THE MYTH OF MALE POWER. He was formerly on the Board of N.O.W. in New York City.

Paolo Freire "The 'Banking' Conception of Education" from PEDAGOGY OF THE OPPRESSED. Copyright © 1970, 1993 by Paolo Freire. Reprinted by permission of the Continuum Publishing Company.

Winifred Gallagher, "The Science of Place" reprinted with the permission of Simon & Schuster from THE POWER OF PLACE by Winifred Gallagher. Copyright © 1993 by Winifred Gallagher.

Ellen Goodman, "It's Failure, Not Success." Copyright © 1977, The Boston Globe Newspaper Co./Washington Post Writers Group. Reprinted with permission. "Men Are From Earth, and So Are Women," Copyright © 1995, The Boston Globe Newspaper Co./Washington Post Writers Group. Reprinted with permission.

Christine Gorman, "Sizing Up the Sexes," Time, January 1, 1992. Copyright © 1992 Time, Inc. Reprinted by permission.

Francine du Plessix Gray, "On Friendship," reprinted with the permission of Simon & Schuster from ADAM AND EVE AND THE CITY by Francine du Plessix Gray. Copyright © 1987 by Francine du Plessix Grey.

Alan Hale, "The Unlimited Cosmos—A Personal Odyssey" from *Free Inquiry*, Summer 1996. Reprinted with permission.

Patricia Hampl, "Memory and Imagination" originally published in *The Dolphin Reader*. Copyright © 1985 by Patricia Hampl. Permission to reprint granted by The Rhoda Weyr Agency, New York.

Robert Hayden, "Those Winter Sundays" from ANGLE OF ASCENT: New and Selected Poems by Robert Hayden. Copyright © 1966 by Robert Hayden. Reprinted with the permission of Liveright Publishing Corporation.

Ruth Hubbard and Elijah Wald, "Genetic Labeling and the Old Eugenics" from EXPLODING THE GENE MYTH. Copyright © 1993 by Ruth Hubbard and Elijah Wald. Reprinted by permission of Beacon Press.

Artruro Islas, "Judgment Day" from THE RAIN GOD by Artruro Islas, published by Avon Books. Copyright © 1984 by Artruro Islas. Reprinted by permission of Artruro Islas and the Sandra Dijkstra Literary Agency.

Robert F. Jones, "A Modest Proposal: The Sequel" from SACRED TRUSTS: ESSAYS IN STEWARDSHIP AND RESPONSIBILITY, edited by Michael Katakis. Copyright © 1993. Published by Mercury House, San Francisco, CA. Reprinted by permission.

Erling Jorstad, "Pluralism: Finding the Boundaries for Religious Freedom" from BEING RELIGIOUS IN AMERICA. Copyright © 1986 Augsburg Publishing House. Used by permission of Augsburg Fortress.

Sam Keen, "The Rite of Work: The Economic Man" from FIRE IN THE BELLY. Copyright © 1991 by Sam Keen. Used by permission of Bantam Books, a division of Bantam Doubleday Dell Publishing Group, Inc.

# INDEX OF TERMS

# INDEX OF TITLES AND AUTHORS